W9-BWX-599

W. GLENN ROWE
The University of Western Ontario

CASES IN LEADERSHIP

SAGE Publications
Los Angeles • London • New Delhi • Singapore

For information:

SAGE Publications, Inc.
2455 Teller Road
Thousand Oaks, California 91320
E-mail: order@sagepub.com

SAGE Publications Ltd.
1 Oliver's Yard
55 City Road
London EC1Y 1SP
United Kingdom

SAGE Publications India Pvt. Ltd.
B 1/I 1 Mohan Cooperative Industrial Area
Mathura Road, New Delhi 110 044
India

SAGE Publications Asia-Pacific Pte. Ltd.
33 Pekin Street #02-01
Far East Square
Singapore 048763

Printed in the United States of America

Library of Congress Cataloging-in-Publication Data

Cases in leadership/edited by W. Glenn Rowe.
    p. cm.—(The Ivey casebook series)
Includes bibliographical references.
ISBN 978-1-4129-5017-6 (pbk.)
    1. Leadership—Case studies. 2. Management—Case studies. I. Rowe, W. Glenn.

HD57.7.C372 2007
658.4′092—dc22   2007002178

This book is printed on acid-free paper.

07 08 09 10 11   10 9 8 7 6 5 4 3 2 1

Acquisitions Editor:	Al Bruckner
Editorial Assistant:	MaryAnn Vail
Production Editor:	Diane S. Foster
Copy Editor:	Gillian Dickens
Typesetter:	C&M Digitals (P) Ltd.
Proofreader:	Caryne Brown
Cover Designer:	Edgar Abarca

THE IVEY CASEBOOK SERIES
A SAGE Publications Series

Series Editor
Paul W. Beamish
Richard Ivey School of Business
The University of Western Ontario

Books in This Series

CASES IN ALLIANCE MANAGEMENT
Building Successful Alliances
Edited by Jean-Louis Schaan and Micheál J. Kelly

CASES IN BUSINESS ETHICS
Edited by David J. Sharp

CASES IN ENTREPRENEURSHIP
The Venture Creation Process
Edited by Eric A. Morse and Ronald K. Mitchell

CASES IN GENDER AND DIVERSITY IN ORGANIZATIONS
Edited by Alison M. Konrad

CASES IN OPERATIONS MANAGEMENT
Building Customer Value Through World-Class Operations
Edited by Robert D. Klassen and Larry J. Menor

CASES IN ORGANIZATIONAL BEHAVIOR
Edited by Gerard H. Seijts

CASES IN THE ENVIRONMENT OF BUSINESS
International Perspectives
Edited by David W. Conklin

MERGERS AND ACQUISITIONS
Text and Cases
Edited by Kevin K. Boeh and Paul W. Beamish

CASES IN LEADERSHIP
Edited by W. Glenn Rowe

CASES IN LEADERSHIP

CONTENTS

Introduction to the Ivey Casebook Series

As the title of this series suggests, these books all draw from the Ivey Business School's case collection. Ivey has long had the world's second largest collection of decision-oriented field-based business cases. Well more than a million copies of Ivey cases are studied every year. There are more than 2,000 cases in Ivey's current collection, with more than 6,000 in the total collection. Each year approximately 200 new titles are registered at Ivey Publishing (www.ivey.uwo.ca/cases), and a similar number are retired. Nearly all Ivey cases have teaching notes available to qualified instructors. The cases included in this volume are all from the current collection.

The vision for the series was a result of conversations I had with Sage's Senior Editor, Al Bruckner, starting in September 2002. Over the subsequent months, we were able to shape a model for the books in the series that we felt would meet a market need.

Each volume in the series contains text and cases. "Some" text was deemed essential in order to provide a basic overview of the particular field and to place the selected cases in an appropriate context. We made a conscious decision to not include hundreds of pages of text material in each volume in recognition of the fact that many professors prefer to supplement basic text material with readings or lectures customized to their interests and to those of their students.

The editors of the books in this series are all highly qualified experts in their respective fields. I was delighted when each agreed to prepare a volume. We very much welcome your comments on this casebook.

—Paul W. Beamish
Series Editor

PREFACE

T he purpose of this leadership casebook is to expose MBA and undergraduate business students to cases that help them gain a better understanding of leadership. It is expected that this understanding will better enable them to be effective leader/managers and to more effectively lead their organizations given the opportunities and challenges they will face throughout their careers. This casebook may be used alone or serve as a supplement to a leadership textbook such as Northouse's (2007) *Leadership: Theory and Practice* (4th ed.). The cases selected for this casebook describe complex leadership issues that require the attention of the decision maker in the case.

In addition, the cases will generate much discussion in the classroom as students grapple with difficult real-world decisions that have grabbed the attention of real-world managers already. The casebook contains 30 cases from Ivey Publishing and 14 readings related to leadership issues from the *Ivey Business Journal*. Each chapter begins with a quote from a real-world CEO or recognized leadership expert with each quote selected to introduce the concepts and theories in each chapter.

For each chapter, I briefly summarize leadership concepts and theories and describe the relevance of the issues/problems in the case. As a whole, the cases provide students with the opportunity to practice and hone several skills. Some of these skills are the ability to analyze, to make decisions, to apply lessons learned, and to plan and engage in oral communication.

Kotter (1998) argued that business organizations are overmanaged and underled. Mintzberg (1998) suggested that as organizations become more diversified, those in leadership positions rely more on managerial skills and less on leadership skills. Rowe (2001) argued that large, overdiversified business organizations will lead to those with leadership skills only exercising managerial skills, using their leadership energy to fight the system or leaving the organization. All of which leaves many organizations without strategic or visionary leadership and only with managerial leadership. This casebook is designed to help students grapple with leadership issues so that they can more effectively exercise leadership as well as exercise effective managerial skills. Leading is different from managing (Kotter, 1998; Mintzberg, 1998; Rowe, 2001; Zaleznik, 1977), and most, if not all, business schools teach their undergraduate and graduate students to be effective managers. Few business schools do as well at giving their students the opportunity to develop leadership skills. This casebook is designed to help leadership professors facilitate a discussion on leadership concepts among business students and to engage students in that discussion.

The cases are selected for their integrative issues. These include globalization, diversity, ethical dilemmas, and motivation. These issues will surface in several cases and are not emphasized in only one case. There is opportunity for professors to refer to previous cases and to integrate learning from one case into another case. Of course, all of the cases have leadership implications—whether they concern leading within the organization, leading teams, and/or leading oneself.

REFERENCES

Kotter, J. P. (1998). What leaders really do. In *Harvard Business Review on leadership* (pp. 37–60). Boston: Harvard Business School Press.

Mintzberg, H. (1998). Retrospective commentary on the manager's job: Folklore and fact. In *Harvard Business Review on leadership* (pp. 29–32). Boston: Harvard Business School Press.

Northouse, P. G. (2007). *Leadership: Theory and practice* (4th ed.). Thousand Oaks, CA: Sage.

Rowe, W. G. (2001). Creating wealth in organizations: The role of strategic leadership. *Academy of Management Executive, 15,* 81–94.

Zaleznik, A. (1977). Managers and leaders: Are they different? *Harvard Business Review, 55,* 67–78.

ACKNOWLEDGMENTS

I want to acknowledge and thank all of those involved in the writing of this book. First, I want to thank the staff at Ivey Publishing, the case writers, and the *Ivey Business Journal* authors, without whom this casebook would not have been possible. Second, this project would not have happened without the initiative, encouragement, and support of Paul Beamish and Al Bruckner. Third, MaryAnn Vail displayed the nicest ability to encourage me to get done what needed to be done when it needed to be done. Fourth, Natalie Slawinski graciously took time from a very busy summer to write the brand-new strategic leadership chapter. Fifth, I want to thank Laura Guerrero for her consistently thoughtful work in helping me edit the book before sending it to Sage, for writing the chapters on culture and women, and for the great job she did in helping me select cases for inclusion in the casebook. Finally, Gillian Dickens did a wonderful job as my copy editor—thank you.

To the three most important people in my life: my wife, Fay;
my daughter, Gillian Fritzsche; and, my son-in-law, Ryan Fritzsche.

1

LEADERSHIP—WHAT IS IT?

CEOs tell us that their most pressing need is for more leaders in their organizations—not the consummate role-players who seem to surround them.

—Rob Goffee and Gareth Jones

Gary Yukl (2006) defines leadership as "the process of influencing others to understand and agree about what needs to be done and how to do it, and the process of facilitating individual and collective efforts to accomplish shared objectives" (p. 8). Peter Northouse (2007) defines leadership as "a process whereby an individual influences a group of individuals to achieve a common goal." These definitions suggest several components central to the phenomenon of leadership. Some of them are as follows: (a) Leadership is a process, (b) leadership involves influencing others, (c) leadership happens within the context of a group, (d) leadership involves goal attainment, and (e) these goals are shared by leaders and their followers. The very act of defining leadership as a process suggests that leadership is not a characteristic or trait with which only a few, certain people are endowed with at birth. Defining leadership as a process means that leadership is a transactional event that happens between leaders and their followers.

Viewing leadership as a process means that leaders affect and are affected by their followers either positively or negatively. It stresses that leadership is a two-way, interactive event between leaders and followers rather than a linear, one-way event in which the leader only affects the followers. Defining leadership as a process makes it available to everyone—not just a select few who *are born with it*. More important, it means that leadership is not restricted to just the one person in a group who has formal position power (i.e., the formally appointed leader).

Leadership is about influence—the ability to influence your subordinates, your peers, and your bosses in a work or organizational context. Without influence, it is impossible to be a leader. Of course, having influence means that there is a greater need on the part of leaders to exercise their influence ethically.

Leadership operates in groups. This means that leadership is about influencing a group of people who are engaged in a common goal or purpose. This can be a small Center for

Management Development in a business school with a staff of four, a naval ship with a ship's company of 300 (a destroyer) or 6,000 (an aircraft carrier), or a multinational enterprise such as Starbucks with more than 10,500 stores worldwide and in excess of 100,000 partners (employees). This definition of leadership precludes the inclusion of leadership training programs that teach people to lead themselves.

Leadership includes the achievement of goals. Therefore, leadership is about directing a group of people toward the accomplishment of a task or the reaching of an endpoint through various, ethically based means. Leaders direct their energies and the energies of their followers to the achievement of something together—for example, hockey coaches working with their players to win a championship, to win their conference, to have a winning (better than 0.500) season, or to have a better won-lost percentage than last season. Thus, leadership occurs, as well as affects, in contexts where people are moving in the direction of a goal.

Leaders and followers share objectives. Leadership means that leaders work with their followers to achieve objectives that they all share. Establishing shared objectives that leaders and followers can coalesce around is difficult but worth the effort. Leaders who are willing to expend time and effort in determining appropriate goals will find these goals achieved more effectively and easily if followers and leaders work together. Leader-imposed goals are generally harder and less effectively achieved than goals developed together.

In this casebook, those who exercise leadership will be referred to as leaders, while those toward whom leadership is exercised will be referred to as followers. Both are required for there to be a leadership process. Within this process, both leaders and followers have an ethical responsibility to attend to the needs and concerns of each other; however, because this casebook is about leadership, we will focus more on the ethical responsibility of leaders toward their followers. Finally, it needs to be said that leaders are not better than followers, nor are they above followers. On the contrary, leaders and followers are intertwined in a way that requires them to be understood in their relationship with each other and as a collective body of two or more people (Burns, 1978; Dubrin, 2007; Hollander, 1992).

In the previous paragraphs, leadership has been defined, and the definitional aspects of leadership have been discussed. In the next few paragraphs, several other issues related to the nature of leadership will be discussed: how trait leadership is different from leadership as a process, how emergent and appointed leadership are different, and how coercion, power, and management are different from leadership.

Trait Versus Process

Statements such as "She is a born leader" and "He was born to lead" imply a perspective toward leadership that is trait based. Yukl (2006) states that the trait approach "emphasizes leaders' attributes such as personality, motives, values, and skills. Underlying this approach was the assumption that some people are natural leaders, endowed with certain traits not possessed by other people" (p. 13). This is very different from describing leadership as a process. In essence, the trait viewpoint suggests that leadership is inherent in a few, select people and that leadership is restricted to only those few who have special talents with which they are born (Yukl, 2006). Some examples of traits are the ability to speak well, an extroverted personality, or unique physical characteristics such as height (Bryman, 1992). Viewing leadership as a process implies that leadership is a phenomenon that is contextual and suggests that everyone is capable of exercising leadership. This suggests

Leadership and Coercion

Related to power is a specific kind of power called coercion. Coercive leaders use force to cause change. These leaders influence others through the use of penalties, rewards, threats, punishment, and negative reward schedules (Daft, 2005). Coercion is different from leadership, and it is important to distinguish between the two. In this casebook, it is important for you to distinguish between those who are being coercive versus those who are influencing a group of people toward a common goal. Using coercion is counter to influencing others to achieve a shared goal and may have unintended, negative consequences (Dubrin, 2007; Yukl, 2006).

Leadership and Management

Leadership is similar to, and different from, management. They both involve influencing people. They both require working with people. Both are concerned with the achievement of common goals. However, leadership and management are different on more dimensions than they are similar.

Zaleznik (1977) believes that managers and leaders are very distinct, and being one precludes being the other. He argues that managers are reactive, and while they are willing to work with people to solve problems, they do so with minimal emotional involvement. On the other hand, leaders are emotionally involved and seek to shape ideas instead of reacting to others' ideas. Managers limit choice, while leaders work to expand the number of alternatives to problems that have plagued an organization for a long period of time. Leaders change people's attitudes, while managers only change their behavior.

Mintzberg (1998) contends that managers lead by using a cerebral face. This face stresses calculation, views an organization as components of a portfolio, and operates with words and numbers of rationality. He suggests that leaders lead by using an insightful face. This face stresses commitment, views organizations with an integrative perspective, and is rooted in the images and feel of integrity. He argues that managers need to be two-faced. They need to simultaneously be a manager and a leader.

Kotter (1998) argues that organizations are overmanaged and underled. However, strong leadership with weak management is no better and may be worse. He suggests that organizations need strong leadership and strong management. Managers are needed to handle complexity by instituting planning and budgeting, organizing and staffing, and controlling and problem solving. Leaders are needed to handle change through setting a direction, aligning people, and motivating and inspiring people. He argues that organizations need people who can do both—they need leader-managers.

Rowe (2001) contends that leaders and managers are different and suggests that one aspect of the difference may be philosophical. Managers believe that the decisions they make are determined for them by the organizations they work for and that the organizations they work for conduct themselves in a manner that is determined by the industry or environment in which they operate. In other words, managers are deterministic in their belief system. Leaders believe that the choices they make will affect their organizations and that their organizations will affect or shape the industries or environments in which they operate. In other words, the belief systems of leaders are more aligned with a philosophical perspective of free will.

Organizations with strong management but weak or no leadership will stifle creativity and innovation and be very bureaucratic. Conversely, an organization with strong leadership and weak or nonexistent management can become involved in change for the sake

that leadership can be learned and that leadership is observable through what lea
how they behave (Daft, 2005; Jago, 1982; Northouse, 2007).

Assigned Versus Emergent

Assigned leadership is the appointment of people to formal positions of authorit
an organization. Emergent leadership is the exercise of leadership by one group i
because of the manner in which other group members react to him or her. Exam
assigned leadership are general managers of sports teams, vice presidents of unive
plant managers, the CEOs of hospitals, and the executive directors of nonprofit org
tions. In some settings, it is possible that the person assigned to a formal leadership
tion may not be the person that others in the group look to for leadership.

Emergent leadership is exhibited when others perceive a person to be the most inf
tial member of their group or organization, regardless of the person's assigned fo
position. Emergent leadership is being exercised by a person when other people in
organization support, accept, and encourage that person's behavior. This way of lead
does not occur because a person is appointed to a formal position but emerges over t
through positive communication behaviors. Fisher (1974) suggested that some commu
cation behaviors that explain emergent leadership are verbal involvement, keeping w
informed, asking other group members for their opinions, being firm but not rigid, and t
initiation of new and compelling ideas (Fisher, 1974; Northouse, 2007).

The material in this casebook is designed to apply equally to emergent and assigne
leadership. This is appropriate since whether a person emerged as a leader or was assigne
to be a leader, that person is exercising leadership. Consequently, this casebook uses case:
that focus on the leader's "ability to inspire confidence and support among the people who
are needed to achieve organizational goals" (Dubrin, 2007, p. 2).

Leadership and Power

Power is related to but different from leadership. It is related to leadership because it is
an integral part of the ability to influence others. Power is defined as the potential or capacity to influence others to bring about desired outcomes. We have influence when we can
affect others' beliefs, attitudes, and behavior. While there are different kinds of power, in
organizations, we consider two kinds of power—position power and personal power.
Position power is that power that comes from holding a particular office, position, or rank
in an organization (Daft, 2005). A university president has more power than a dean of a
business school, but they both have formal power.

Personal power is the capacity to influence that comes from being viewed as knowledgeable and likable by followers. It is power that derives from the interpersonal relationships that leaders develop with followers (Yukl, 2006). I would argue that when leaders
have both position and personal power, they should use personal power a vast majority of
the time. Overuse of position power may erode the ability of a leader to influence people.
Of course, it is important to know when it is most appropriate to use position power and
to be able and willing to use it (Daft, 2005).

Power can be two-faced. One face is the use of power within an organization to achieve
one's personal goals to the detriment of others in the organization. The other face is that
power that works to achieve the collective goals of all members of the organization, sometimes even at the expense of the leader's personal goals.

of change—change that is misdirected or meaningless and has a negative effect on the organization. Bennis and Nanus (1985) expressed the differences between managers and leaders very clearly in their often quoted phrase: "Managers are people who do things right and leaders are people who do the right thing" (p. 221). Implicit in this statement is that organizations need people who do the right thing and who do the "right things right."

REFERENCES

Bennis, W. G., & Nanus, B. (1985). *Leaders: The strategies for taking charge.* New York: Harper & Row.

Bryman, A. (1992). *Charisma and leadership in organizations.* London: Sage.

Burns, J. M. (1978). *Leadership.* New York: Harper & Row.

Daft, R. L. (2005). *The leadership experience* (3rd ed.). Mason, OH: Thomson, South-Western.

Dubrin, A. (2007). *Leadership: Research findings, practice, and skills.* New York: Houghton Mifflin.

Fisher, B. A. (1974). *Small group decision-making: Communication and the group process.* New York: McGraw-Hill.

Goffee, R., & Jones, G. (2006). *Rob Goffee and Gareth Jones on what it takes to be an authentic leader.* (EMFD Thought Leadership Series). Accessed May 29, 2006, at http://www.efmd .org/html/.

Hollander, E. P. (1992). Leadership, followership, self, and others. *The Leadership Quarterly, 3*(1), 43–54.

Jago, A. G. (1982). Leadership: Perspectives in theory and research. *Management Science, 28*(3), 315–336.

Kotter, J. P. (1998). What leaders really do. In *Harvard Business Review on leadership* (pp. 37–60). Boston: Harvard Business School Press.

Mintzberg, H. (1998). Retrospective commentary on the manager's job: Folklore and fact. In *Harvard Business Review on leadership* (pp. 29–32). Boston: Harvard Business School Press.

Northouse, P. G. (2007). *Leadership: Theory and practice* (4th ed.). Thousand Oaks, CA: Sage.

Rowe, W. G. (2001). Creating wealth in organizations: The role of strategic leadership. *Academy of Management Executive, 15*(1), 81–94.

Yukl, G. (2006). *Leadership in organizations* (6th ed.). Upper Saddle River, NJ: Pearson-Prentice Hall.

Zaleznik, A. (1977). Managers and leaders: Are they different? *Harvard Business Review, 55,* 67–78.

THE CASES

Food Terminal (A)

In this case, a recently appointed store manager at a wholesale food company must make some decisions regarding management and leadership. The store is losing $10,000 per week, sales are spiraling downward, the key people in the company do not want him there, and employee morale is terrible.

AmeriChem, Inc.

An AmeriChem, Inc. plant was maligned at a corporate board meeting with accusations of general abuse of alcohol and drunkenness on the job. The health and safety manager knew that the groundless claims could completely destroy the plant's already doubtful reputation, and he had to decide whether to respond and how. The problems are analytically challenging and not clearly defined; they concern the difference between the interrelation of individual and collective interests.

THE READING

Are YOU a Leader-Breeder?

Will you be a leader-breeder or a leader-blocker? In this reading, one leadership expert describes the behaviors of a leader-breeder and briefly contrasts them with the behaviors of leader-blockers. This expert argues that leader-breeders hire and mentor high-potential individuals. In addition, they attract, retain, and develop talented people irrespective of their academic background. Leader-blockers hire easy-to-manage people and do not mentor or coach effectively.

THE FOOD TERMINAL (A)

Prepared by Leo J. Klus under the supervision of John F. Graham

Version: (A) 2001-08-10

In July 1991, three months after graduating from the Western Business School, 23-year-old Mike Bellafacia knew that he was in for a rough ride.

> When I arrived at the store, the staff morale was terrible. The previous manager had made a mess of things, the recession was hitting home, sales were spiralling downward quickly, and my store was losing $10,000 per week. To make matters worse, most of the key people in the company felt that I didn't deserve the store manager's position.

As the recently appointed store manager of the newest Foodco location in St. Catharines, Ontario, Mike knew that he had to turn the store around by improving its financial performance and the employee morale. He also knew that something had to be done immediately because the losses at this store were seriously affecting the entire company.

FOODCO LTD.

Foodco Ltd. (FC), with its head office located in St. Catharines, Ontario, was a large player in the Niagara Peninsula grocery retailing industry. FC, a retailer in this market since 1962, was currently made up of seven stores: three St. Catharines locations, one Welland location, one Port Colborne location, and two Lincoln locations. Most of the ownership and key management positions were held by Frank Bellafacia, Tony Bellafacia, and Rocco Bellafacia, as shown in Exhibit 1. Selected financial ratios for FC are shown in Exhibit 2.

FC had created a powerful presence in this industry by developing and refining a strategy that worked. Their product offering was that of any typical supermarket: groceries, meats, bakery and dairy items, packaged foods, and nonfood items. Each store carried eight to ten thousand

Personnel Organization

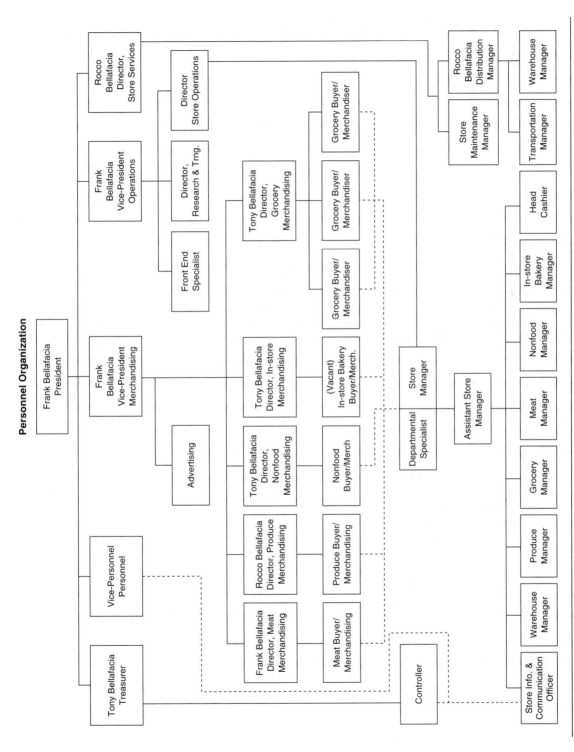

Exhibit 1   Personnel Organization Chart

	1986	1987	1988	1989	1990
PROFITABILITY					
Cost of goods sold	81.2%	80.2%	79.7%	78.7%	78.3%
Operating expenses	19.4%	18.7%	19.1%	19.6%	19.8%
Net income before tax	−1.1%	0.5%	0.3%	0.7%	0.7%
RETURN					
After-tax return on equity	0.0%	715.0%	n/a	725.0%	94.2%
STABILITY					
Interest coverage*	1.28x	1.36x	1.05x	1.19x	2.37x
LIQUIDITY					
Net working capital ($000)*	(1,447)	(2,051)	(13)	(316)	(243)
GROWTH					
Sales		26.0%	10.7%	14.1%	15.5%
Assets*		16.7%	3.8%	11.2%	9.6%
Equity*		−0.3%	1.2%	4.9%	19.5%

Exhibit 2   Selected Financial Ratios

*Denotes a ratio calculated from the statements of Bellafacia's Consolidated Holdings Inc.

different items. FC planned to widen the selection available by adding more lines and to follow a general trend in consumer preferences toward an increased percentage of nonfood items in the product mix. Central to FC's strategy was a well-managed marketing effort. Weekly flyers were distributed that highlighted five or six items. FC priced these items below cost to draw customers. The rest of the flyers' products were representative of all the product groups. FC's ability to differentiate itself from the other competitors centred on its corporate vision: low food prices and fast, friendly service. Central to the FC competitive strategy was the mandate to be the low-price leader among conventional supermarkets, during good and bad economic times. Mike Bellafacia stated: "This is a no frills and low price store for a no frills and low price clientele. Most markets are shifting in this direction." FC had developed aggressive expansion plans with six stores being considered for development.

THE RETAIL GROCERY INDUSTRY

The job of managing the store and the staff became crucial to the overall success of FC given the demanding challenges in the industry. The industry was shifting from a simple mass market to a spectrum of distinct, serviceable segments. A recent statistic stated that 30 percent of consumers switch stores every year. Moreover, a new Food Marketing Institute study found that consumers buy on the basis of the following criteria (ranked in decreasing priority): service, quality products, variety, and low prices. Thus, there was now more opportunity for competitive differentiation based on service and on quality than on price alone.

There were tremendous opportunities for niche players to enter the market, and such entrants had been observed. Health and organic food stores, fruit markets, and independent single-commodity stores (i.e., pet food stores)

Exhibit 3   Front Page of the Weekly Flyer

emerged and were servicing their target segments more effectively than the supermarkets were willing or able to do. Consumer demands varied from region to region, and many small independent retail grocers emerged to meet these demands both in the Niagara Peninsula and across all of Ontario. These independents managed not only to survive, but to take sizable portions of market share from the major chains. This shift toward niche marketing and catering to the local market outlined the need to employ store managers who understood how to please and retain the local customer.

THE ROLE OF THE STORE MANAGER

The success of FC depended upon each of the seven store managers operating his/her store consistently with the corporate strategy. Traditionally, the road to store manager (SM) began within one of the stores at a lower management position. The family culture within each Food Terminal location was very important to FC management. Thus, store managers were selected from within the company to ensure a leader who understood the FC vision and values. Five managers reported directly to the SM, as shown in Exhibit 4, and their development was an important job for the SM. The SM position became increasingly more important at FC. Many of the current SM functions that used to be handled by the head office were delegated downward to the store level to allow head office to focus on overall company strategy. The stores were now more attuned to the local market they serve. An SM was responsible for the following:

1. Ensuring that merchandising skills were strong among all department managers;

2. Monitoring local market information;

3. Focusing staff on organizational goals (such as sales, gross margin, and profit goals);

4. Organizing weekly staff meetings;

5. Developing all employees and encouraging staff training;

6. Generating and producing sales, gross margin, and profit objectives;

7. Meeting cost objectives (motivating the staff to be cost conscious);

8. Analyzing the performance of each inter-store department; and

9. Attending FC "Top Management Meetings" (TMMs).

MIKE BELLAFACIA'S BACKGROUND

Mike Bellafacia graduated from The University of Western Ontario with an Honors Business Administration degree (HBA). During his summers at university, he was assigned special projects from his father that focused on a variety of company problems. Mike would combine the analytical skills developed in the business school with his knowledge of the family business to address these issues. In his last year in the HBA program, Mike and a team of student consultants spent the year focusing on the long-term strategy and competitive advantage of FC. They examined every aspect of the company and developed many strategic recommendations for the top management at FC.

Upon graduation, Mike decided to work for FC. He planned to start off working in some of the various departments (i.e., the produce department) and at different stores within FC to work his way up in order to get the experience he needed to manage a store. This would have allowed him the opportunity to work under some of the most knowledgeable managers in the company. He didn't expect to be store manager so soon.

THE SCOTT & VINE LOCATION: THE FIRST MONTH

Mike's career at FC was supposed to begin in one of the departments in the company. Both Mike and FC management felt strongly about that. However, while Mike was on vacation in May, FC management made a chancy decision. As of June 1, 1991, Mike Bellafacia would take over the SM position at the Scott and Vine location from the existing SM. The store's performance was deteriorating, and Mike was expected to change things. Mike reflected on the first week at the three-month old location:

> When I first started I was extremely nervous. The district supervisor brought me to the store to have a meeting with the department managers, and I could see the look of disappointment in their eyes. Most of these managers had been forced to move to this new store from other locations. The staff morale was definitely low to begin with. Combined

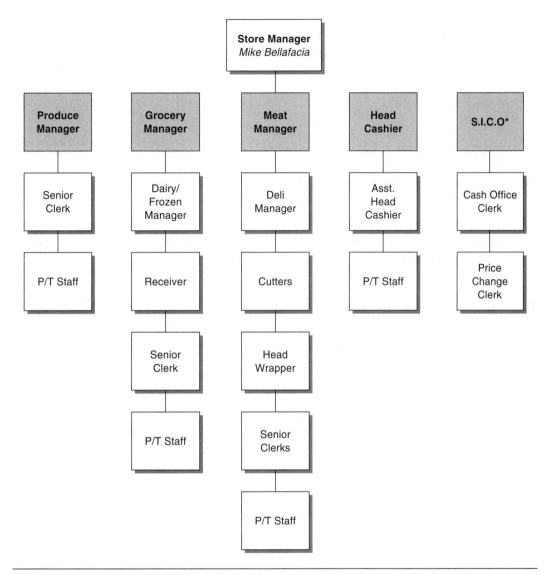

Exhibit 4   Scott & Vine Organizational Chart

*Store Information and Communications Officer. Responsible for maintaining the lines of communication between the store and head office.

with the fact that I am the boss's son, they probably assumed that I was sent to check on them.

After getting settled in, Mike began to realize that something was terribly wrong at the Scott and Vine food terminal. The store was not producing a bottom line, and many of the 95 employees were not performing well. Mike commented:

This building used to be a Food City that was on the verge of closing down. We acquired it and picked up where they left off. The task I had was to get above average performance from an average staff. They were just not driven to succeed, were poorly trained, and many of them, especially the managers, didn't want to be there.

The previous manager had performed poorly by FC standards. Although he had been an SM at other grocery stores, he was unable to create a productive atmosphere at this one. When this location opened, the sales level was $160,000 per week, but by Mike's first month it had dropped by 17 percent. FC management expected this location to be operating at over $200,000 per week. The other St. Catharines stores were operating at over $350,000 per week. They had a long way to go.

What took place at the Scott and Vine location was a symptom of a more serious problem: the performance of FC as a whole. Mike explained the situation:

> Some of what was happening here can be attributed to FC. They became fat cats and, in the process, they lost touch with the customers. Pricing had gone way out of line, cross-border shopping was cutting into our bottom line, and our marketing efforts were poor. The weekly ads that are developed by head office for all the stores were not drawing in customers like they used to. As a result, we had no word-of-mouth advertising which is so essential to a retail outlet. When our sales across the board went down, we had only ourselves to blame.

SORTING THROUGH THE DISORDER

The job of managing the Food Terminal was overwhelming, and the problems were endless. Some of the more prevalent problems are listed below:

1. Product rotation (a job monitored by department managers and very important for customer satisfaction) was handled improperly.

2. It was not uncommon to find empty counters and shelves.

3. The staff paid very little attention to cleanliness. (Customers complained about this.)

4. Customers were not treated with respect by those employees who had frequent contact with them.

5. Department managers were doing a poor job of managing and motivating the employees in their departments.

6. Department sales and gross profit results were poor. (See Exhibit 5 for a breakdown of departmental sales and gross profit figures.)

Difficulties arose within the staff that made the SM job even more strenuous. Mike described the situation:

> There were a lot of people problems that I had to face. The weekly staff meetings we had together were a joke. Instead of a time to interact and solve problems together, it was just a waste of time. As well, the entire staff was demoralized due to the continual failure to meet monthly performance goals since the store opened. We had the worst performance in the FC organization. The controller of the company told me that the Scott & Vine location was hurting the entire company. I felt as though head office was blaming me for the store's poor performance, and I knew that I had to set some goals that we could all rally behind.
>
> For the first month I was very autocratic. I had to be! I replaced all the cashiers that month, because of the numerous customer complaints about their attitude, but that was just the beginning of my problems. The part-time staff were continually standing around doing nothing. The receiver was not handling the deliveries very well. I found it tough to get along with the department managers. My worst employee problems came from the produce and meat managers. They just were not doing their jobs well. I tried going over the product orders with them, developing schedules, and assisting with their product display plans. I even brought in some of FC's department experts to go over things with them. They would not listen to any of my suggestions. Even though I had some problems with my grocery manager, I began to see that he had real potential for managing. There was some resentment toward me for being a family member and getting the SM position so young, and as a result, people would not open up to me. I also knew that some of the other SMs at other locations didn't want me to succeed, and I found myself conveniently left out of important SM meetings. To make

Departmental Performance

DEPARTMENT	SALES ($)	GROSS PROFIT ($)	% OF SALES
Produce	22,677	4,602	20.3
Grocery	77,363	12,467	16.1
Meat	32,963	7,629	23.1
Non-Food	4,784	1,228	25.7
IS-Bakery	2,337	934	40.0
TOTAL	140,124	28,860	19.2

Overall Store Performance (One Week)

WEEKLY INDICATORS	BUDGET ($)	ACTUAL ($)
SALES	155,000	140,124
GROSS PROFIT	33,683	26,860
EXPENSES:		
Wages	16,483	19,600
Supplies	1,895	1,410
Other Expenses	17,091	16,257
TOTAL EXPENSES	35,469	37,267
NET INCOME	(1,786)	(10,407)
# OF CUSTOMERS	7,723/WEEK	

Exhibit 5   Selected Financial Indicators – Scott & Vine Location

matters worse, after two months here, the general manager of FC made it known that I should be pulled out of this job.

FACING THE FUTURE

It was a tough season to compete in the retail grocery business. Mike Bellafacia found this out after only two months at the Food Terminal and the situation was now grave. The Scott and Vine location was losing over $10,000 per week and the sales level was stagnant. The staff morale had changed very little. Customers were not responding to advertisement efforts, and things looked as if they were going to worsen. Mike reflected on what had happened during these last two months and where things were going. He wondered if he was responsible for the mess the store was in—had he mismanaged his managers, thereby making the situation worse? Had FC made a big mistake putting him in the position of SM? Thinking back on his education, Mike commented:

> The business school helped me understand the decision-making process. I'm not afraid to make decisions, do analysis and pin-point problem areas. But it didn't teach me how to get the job done, the execution of a decision. More importantly, I was not prepared to deal with people who didn't have the training I did, or the desire to succeed as I did.

Although he was unsure about these issues, he focused on what he should do to get the Scott and Vine food terminal operating profitably, with good management and with a growing customer base. As he looked over the financial data, he wondered if he should lay off some employees to bring the wages expense down. Mike reflected on this: "We didn't have the sales to support the exorbitant number of employees we had at the store." He was concerned about how he would handle these layoffs. He also thought about the serious morale problem. Many of the employees were lazy and demotivated, and customers complained regularly about cleanliness and service. He wondered if there was a way to use the weekly meetings to his advantage. Things seemed just as complicated as they did in June.

AMERICHEM, INC.

Prepared by Professor Carol Tattersall

     Version: (A) 2000-09-12

On April 18, 2000, Ben Hartnet, Health and Safety (HS) manager with AmeriChem, Inc., a subsidiary of Barco, Inc., was clearly distracted as he walked through the plant. Tom Mann, the technical director, had just phoned to let him know that some very damaging and defamatory comments about the AmeriChem plant had been made by Cassandra Seare at a board meeting at Toronto head office earlier in the day. She claimed to have heard that there was an ongoing problem with drinking on the job at AmeriChem, and that this had been the cause of an accident that had occurred there two weeks ago. Hartnet knew that the comments were entirely insupportable, but that they could destroy the reputation of the plant; yet, he was at a loss as to how to deal with such slander. Nevertheless, he knew that he must respond immediately.

AMERICHEM COMPANY BACKGROUND

For more than a century, Barco, Inc., a large multinational company, had been manufacturing and marketing consumer products to the retail trade worldwide. In 1989, with a view to expanding their industrial and institutional operations and capturing a larger share of the North American market, the company acquired a plant in Windsor, Ontario, Canada, from an American competitor. The new subsidiary, CanChem, retained almost all of the plant personnel, including several in middle management, and became the head office for industrial and institutional business in North America. Over the next few years, due to some astute decisions in manufacturing, CanChem expanded and diversified.

In the mid-90s, Barco initiated various realignments within its North American business. This included three acquisitions over a period of four years. Each new acquisition necessitated a reorganization of management at every level, and a shift in corporate culture.

Barco first acquired an American company that operated a series of small plants in various locations in the southern United States. In this move, the existing president of CanChem was let go, the head office relocated to Tennessee and the president of the American concern became responsible for the new, merged company. The name CanChem, however, was retained.

MERGER OF CANCHEM AND AMERITOL

Barco's next move had greater repercussions. This time the company that Barco acquired, Ameritol, was much larger, and the merging of operations was further complicated by the fact that, because Ameritol's Canadian plant was just outside Toronto, the new company would now have two large plants in southwestern Ontario. After much deliberation, Barco decided to keep the CanChem plant in operation, close the Ameritol plant, but leave their Canadian head office in the Toronto location. The company name was also changed to AmeriChem.

While the fact that the original CanChem plant would remain open seemed encouraging, it soon became clear that management there would have little say in the actual running of operations. Over the first few months after the acquisition, almost all of the local management had been let go. Most positions disappeared, but those that remained were filled by Ameritol managers. The CanChem plant manager, who had also been vice-president of operations, was replaced by a manager from a smaller Ameritol plant in the midwestern United States, and the Canadian corporate offices were consolidated in the Toronto area.

In 1999, planning further to extend its market and manufacturing in the United States, Barco,

Inc. acquired yet another small company, Chemco. This move led to another consolidation of sales and marketing and to several changes in product lines. Corporate AmeriChem decided that profit margins for certain of the Windsor plant's products were too small to justify continuing to manufacture those lines, and informed the management that they must reduce their operations from three to two shifts, and lay off one-third of the workers. With termination of operations in a large part of the factory, the corporate group decided to relocate all warehousing for the area to the vacant space.

By mid-2000, the plant that had been head office for North America had employed 40 managers from corporate to junior level and 180 factory personnel. It had accommodated manufacturing, warehousing, and a development lab and had been reduced to five managers and 110 workers. In the last year, the plant manager had been replaced by a recruit from an outside company. After only four months, the new manager resigned, and while a search was conducted for yet another plant manager, the position was filled by the local human resources manager, who had come to AmeriChem shortly after the latest merger.

CONFLICTING CORPORATE CULTURES

After the buy-out of the small company in the southern United States, and the relocation of head office, middle management were discouraged by the loss of status, but they were still involved in, and enthusiastic about, the potential expansion into new areas. Little that affected the day-to-day running of the plant changed.

The merger with Ameritol was much more unsettling, especially for management. Under the new centralized system, decisions regarding all aspects of the plant's running were made at the corporate level. Changes were made rapidly, often suddenly, without any local input, and included all processes: reporting chains, financial operations and even computer systems. Although those managers from the original workforce who remained at the plant demonstrated co-operation and flexibility in adapting to the new methods, they found it more difficult to accept the dramatically different culture.

The CanChem factory had always fostered independence in its management, and in the years before the merger, had been developing strategies to move decision-making downward, offering more autonomy and responsibility to workers at all levels. The philosophy aimed to give all employees a sense of control of their own task area, and offered the extra motivation of profit sharing. Co-operation, information sharing and innovative thinking were encouraged, and good performance at any level would receive positive recognition.

The new AmeriChem management system was based on an entirely different model where decisions came from the top down, and involved little or no consultation with the parties involved. Independence was discouraged, and everything was done according to preset rules, and required documentation, usually on a predesignated form. Information, whether about budget, operations, personnel or any other issue was released only on a need-to-know basis, so that those at the plant had little sense of their role in the larger organization, or of future plans. Also, Rod Wall, the director of operations, would arrive, often without warning, and announce changes, cuts, etc. Clearly, the new AmeriChem management style and corporate culture clashed with the one that CanChem employees had come to expect, and a gap was developing between corporate and local management, who were uncomfortable about being expected simply to implement orders without explanation.

Wall, on the other hand, felt that the Windsor factory was inefficient, and that management needed to be more aggressive and make greater demands from the workers on the line. He had even reportedly referred to it as "The Windsor Country Club." While he had encountered no direct opposition, he sensed a resistance to his authority that he felt was undermining the attempts at corporate level to make this factory more productive. The Windsor management, on the other hand, were somewhat baffled and offended by Wall's apparent lack of respect for their experience and his refusal to offer explanations, or even to ask for their point of view. They strongly suspected that, for them, advancement in the new AmeriChem organization would be be difficult and very limited.

When the last acquisition took place, the workforce was reduced by one-third, and the management pared down to five, which included the various plant managers appointed by AmeriChem, the gap between the Windsor group and the corporate body became a definite rift. From the plant's point of view, the decisions made no sense: the cuts in manufacturing also undermined the infrastructure that supported all the other operations; the cuts to the workforce were too deep—those who were left were now having to work high-paid overtime hours. Eventually, several of the workers had to be called back, but they were given part-time contracts without benefits, causing even more insecurity and resentment among the line-workers.

From the perspective of the corporate management, and especially Wall, however, the Windsor plant was a thorn in the flesh. American head office had become convinced that both workers and management there were resistant to perfectly reasonable change, and were, consequently, unco-operative and unproductive. The remaining managers were viewed as, at best, recalcitrant and, at worst, subversive.

Meanwhile, the group in the Canadian head office, which had made all corporate decisions before the merger, was particularly disgruntled. They had stringently resisted the closing of the Ameritol plant outside Toronto, and took the "problems" at the Windsor plant as vindication of their view that Barco, Inc. had made a huge mistake in moving production to Windsor. Besides, they also resented that they were now responsible only for sales and marketing, and that the American head office seemed to be calling all the shots.

The Ameritol management had, however, fared somewhat better in the transition than the CanChem group: several had been moved to corporate positions and the previous plant manager, Tom Mann, was now the technical director. His approach to the management at Windsor was generally reasonable and respectful, and he was quite often willing to listen to their point of view. But while he was more approachable and positive than Wall, he unwittingly exasperated the Windsor group by frequently pointing out how much more efficient the Toronto area Ameritol factory had been than the Windsor plant.

BEN HARTNET, HEALTH AND SAFETY MANAGER

Ben Hartnet had joined Barco, Inc. straight from university and, for many years, had worked in various locations around Europe and Canada. He had come to CanChem from another division of the company. Although happy with his existing job and prospects, he felt that the move to head office of the new industrial division offered the possibility of a shift into the corporate sector. During the first four or five years he was involved in the negotiations and planning of expansion. He had been enjoying the challenge and rewards of his new position and was quite sure that he had made the right move.

With the first merger, although head office would no longer be in Windsor, he was still optimistic. He was very much involved in planning and strategy, and was travelling to the various sites in the United States to make recommendations about their viability for development or possible closure. Even in the massive disruption of the second merger, he was not entirely pessimistic; in several interviews with Wall he had been led to expect that prospects for advancement within the merged companies would be good.

Gradually, however, as the merger evolved and cuts were made at all levels, it became clear that it was extremely unlikely that anyone who had been part of the original CanChem team would be offered any real responsibility in the new organization. When the dust settled, only three of the original managers remained. In all of the

reshuffling, Hartnet had been moved through a variety of positions, and was now HS manager. It had become clear to Hartnet that his best prospect for the future was not at AmeriChem, and he had had some promising offers from outside contacts, but a decision to leave was complicated by other considerations. Because he had come to Barco while still very young, he was, at 51, less than four years from being able to retire with full pension.

Hartnet's present position was not without challenge, and it also took him to the various other AmeriChem locations, allowing him some opportunity to observe their operations and meet new people. Although the atmosphere at the plant was inevitably tense and unsettled, Hartnet had always got along well with his colleagues, and enjoyed the respect of his co-workers at all levels. Although Hartnet's management style was obviously very different from that of Wall, he felt quite at ease with Mann, the technical director to whom he reported. Mann seemed to have a fairly realistic sense of what was happening at the AmeriChem plant, and accepted that the workforce there was committed to making the factory profitable and successful. Hartnet believed there was no malice in Mann's comments about the superiority of the defunct factory where he had been plant manager. But, while Hartnet felt that Mann was fair and reasonable, he also knew that Mann firmly supported and would not question the overall corporate strategy.

Meanwhile, Hartnet immersed himself in developing his knowledge and skills in HS. He started working towards a diploma in the area, took night courses, went to residential workshops and met frequently with the HS managers from the other AmeriChem sites. He soon decided that he might even enjoy the next few years, and emerge with a whole new set of skills and experience. There was always, however, the threat that even his position might be cut. His ultimate survival, of course, was to a large extent outside of his own control. He knew that Wall, in particular, thought him far too unagressive. In effect, they simply had different management styles. Indeed, Hartnet was known to be very assertive when he felt the situation demanded it.

AN ACCIDENT IN THE WAREHOUSE

In the middle of the afternoon of April 4, 2000, Hartnet was walking through the warehouse when he heard a skidding sound followed by loud crash and a yell from a man obviously in some pain. Hartnet rushed to the aisle from which the commotion was emanating and found Don Page, a forklift driver, hopping on one foot, holding the other and cursing fiercely. The truck was partly buried, supporting a shelf whose main post had been knocked out by the vehicle's back end. Hartnet quickly cleared the area, ordered that the damaged racking be inspected and made safe until it could be repaired, and at the same time made Page sit out of harm's way with his damaged foot raised.

While waiting for the ambulance, which he had asked another worker to call, Hartnet asked Page what had happened. The driver claimed that his stand-up truck had gone out of control while he was maneuvering with two drums on the forks, and had careened backwards into the racks. When he saw that a collision was inevitable, Page had tried to jump off, but had caught his foot between the upright post and the truck.

Once the injured man had been removed to hospital, Hartnet set about finding some eye-witnesses so that he could prepare a full account of the incident. It was clear that this would be a "lost-time accident" and he would therefore have to notify not only the AmeriChem Occupational Health and Safety Committee, but also the Ministry of Labour. The nearest observer had been one of the mechanics, Bill Paquette, who claimed that he thought Page had been driving quite a lot faster than he should have in that area, but no one had actually seen the collision happen.

Next, Hartnet took photographs of the scene and the damage, and when he had finished, sent the truck for a full inspection. Knowing that this was one of the vehicles that had arrived in the last few days from one of the warehouses that was being absorbed into the AmeriChem space, he also inquired whether it had undergone safety checks before being put into service. Apparently it had not, and was now found to have some minor mechanical flaws, but the maintenance person who found the faults assured Hartnet that they would not have affected the vehicle's efficient operation.

Hartnet also instructed the shift supervisor to prepare a separate report. Next, he phoned the hospital to make sure that Page was comfortable, and to establish the seriousness of his injuries, but no definite information was yet available. Later that evening, Hartnet learned that Page had broken three small bones in his foot. Hartnet was relieved that the damage was relatively minor; it could have been much worse.

Hartnet spent the following day gathering more material for his reports, such as the maintenance records of the truck from its former location, and Page's work records. Hartnet was not entirely surprised, in light of Paquette's earlier remarks, that over the past six years, Page had received two disciplinary notices for driving incidents and, in April, had been given a general warning by his supervisor about the need to drive slowly. He had also, in accordance with company policy, received training each year both in groups and one-on-one.

NEW INFORMATION REGARDING THE INCIDENT

While Hartnet was beginning to do his write-up, the logistics manager, Dave Fisher, dropped by his office, looking a little uneasy. It seemed that one of the people who reported to Fisher had decided that, in everyone's best interests, he had to let him know that he had "smelled alcohol on Page's breath" when talking to him shortly before the accident. This was a new and very unwelcome twist, but Hartnet knew he must investigate further. He first decided to ask the warehouse workers about whether anyone had remarked on the possible inebriation. No one had, and one man who claimed to know Page well asserted "Page definitely had not been drinking. He was absolutely sober. I know what he's like even when he's only had a few."

Nevertheless, Page had to be asked directly and, fortunately, he was refreshingly honest. He had been out drinking until the early hours, but had been completely sober when he came to work on the afternoon shift—"not even hung-over." He had certainly not had a drink in the 12 hours before starting work. Hartnet believed Page, and was inclined to think that speeding was the most likely cause of the accident. By the end of the day, Hartnet felt he had enough information to write a basic report, but in the interests of future safety, he felt he needed to pursue the matter further.

On April 6, Hartnet completed his own inquiries and research, and filled in the report forms for the company (see Exhibit 1) and for the Ministry of Labour. Having collected all the necessary documentation, he also called a meeting for the next day, April 7, so that four members of the safety committee could conduct a full accident investigation. As HS manager, Hartnet felt the seriousness of the incident demanded a full inquiry, especially in its potential for having caused even more serious injury had the racking collapsed, or the truck run over Page or someone else. On April 13, they met again to try to determine the cause of the accident, but, perhaps more importantly, to establish some recommendations and guidelines to prevent any similar occurrence in the future.

Hartnet then wrote up the findings for the company records (see Exhibit 2). The incident had been unfortunate, but he felt that at least the accident response had been excellent: Page had received prompt attention, and further injury to others had been prevented. In the end, there were even some positive aspects: some weaknesses in the safety procedures had been revealed; new and more thorough processes had been implemented; the old regulations had been re-emphasized; and the workers had been made aware of the necessity of following all safety procedures at all times. AmeriChem's safety record was good, but even one accident was too many. Hartnet hoped everyone had learned from the experience, especially Page, about whom some decisions were still pending.

SOME UNEXPECTED REPERCUSSIONS

In the midst of the inquiries about Page's accident, Hartnet was to have gone to a Health and Safety Trade Show in Toronto, but had decided, since he was needed on site, to send three members of the Joint Health and Safety Committee (JHSC) in his place. On their return, they mentioned having met Cassandra Seare, the HS manager for sales and marketing at head office, and that she seemed very interested in the forklift incident. Hartnet smiled to himself. He had met Seare several times, at workshops and other venues, and had noted her predilection for melodrama; he hardly even dared acknowledge the thought, however, knowing that it invoked certain stereotypes of the female that he himself found offensive; he felt her histrionics were harmless.

But Hartnet was about to discover that Seare's tendency to overdramatize could be far from harmless. On April 18, he received a call from Mann, who seemed suddenly very tense about the forklift incident and needed to talk and find out more details. During the call, Mann revealed that another Barco, Inc. subsidiary in the Toronto area had also had a recent forklift accident and the Barco Canadian management would face some embarrassment as to why two subsidiaries had had similar incidents, yet the CanChem group had never been notified of the first accident. Hartnet wished he had known this earlier, but made no comment. He merely inquired why the matter was being raised yet again, since he thought it had all been settled to everyone's satisfaction.

"Well," Mann continued, "New details have come to light." He explained that at the board of management meeting at Canadian head office that day, the accident report was mentioned as part of the agenda, and Seare had dropped her bombshell. She said she'd met three of the Windsor people at a trade fair after the accident, and they had told her that the forklift driver was drunk. Also, she claimed that they had revealed that drinking on the job at the Windsor plant had been an ongoing problem, and with the stresses of job cuts, it had become much worse. Even more disturbing was the fact that the three had claimed they had reported the drunkenness to management, who simply indicated that nothing could be done. Persevering, they then raised it twice at the health and safety committee, to no avail.

Hartnet listened in disbelief. His first impulse was to roar with laughter at the sheer absurdity, but, clearly Mann was not amused. Instead Hartnet inquired, "Surely people there didn't give any credence to such ridiculous rumor-mongering?" Apparently, not only were they ready to believe the story, but others joined in the defamation, with comments such as "Well, we all know what Windsor's like." "The Toronto plant should never have been closed." "They don't even keep proper minutes." "Windsor's a disaster waiting to happen."

Hartnet was speechless. He took exception, particularly to the last two remarks. A representative from the Ministry of Labour, on a recent visit to the plant, had been so impressed with record keeping, communication, and the way business was conducted that he asked if they would be prepared to host a visit by the Minister of Labour. The Ministry wanted to use AmeriChem as an example of a plant with a good safety program. By this time, Hartnet had become used to the negative attitude of all parties towards the Windsor plant, and how impossible it seemed to dispel such perceptions, but this was almost surreal. The only response he was able to muster for Mann was to thank him for at least having the courtesy to let the Windsor group know what had happened.

As he walked out into the plant, Hartnet's mind was reeling as he contemplated the inevitable repercussions of Seare's histrionics, not only for him but for the whole plant. The integrity and what little credibility that AmeriChem, Windsor, still retained could be completely destroyed. What defence could there be against such charges, especially when Seare claimed they had been made by three of Hartnet's own committee members? Should he continue along the path of least resistance, and hope the whole thing would quickly fade, or should he respond, and if so, how? Normally a situation like this would call for a stiff drink, but clearly, in the circumstances, that would only help confirm the myths about the Windsor plant.

Raised by: Ben Hartnet		Date: 6th April 2000	
Location: Windsor	Country: Canada		Employee Group: Warehouse

Name of person(s) involved: Don Page

Full details of incident:

Don was operating a stand-up lift truck with two drums on a skid on the forks. He was travelling backwards and as he turned into an aisle he was unable to control the truck and the truck hit the upright post on the end rack, his foot was caught between the truck and the upright. He was transported to hospital by ambulance and has a broken bone in his foot.

A witness commented on the speed involved. Don had received recent fork truck training twice this year. An investigation is ongoing.

Nature of Incident Fork truck	Date/time of Incident: 4th April / 3:40 p.m.

Where treated (if applicable.)

At the location	Hospital: Grace Hospital

INCIDENT CLASSIFICATION	CODE		DESCRIPTION
AGENCY	AG	12	
TYPE OF INJURY	TI	06	
PART OF BODY	PB	09	
TYPE OF ACCIDENT	TA	06	

Generic Causes (please tick)

OCCUPATIONAL HEALTH		SAFETY	
Musculo-Skeletal		Cuts / Bruises	
Noise-Induced Hearing Loss		Manual Handling / Ergonomics	
Respiratory		Burns	
Skin		Eye Injuries	
Other (please state)		Driving	
		Slips, Trips and Falls	
		Other (please state) caught between	X

RECORDABLE			
F	LTA	RWA	MAA
	X		

Serious Potential   Incident

Exhibit 1   AmeriChem Inc. Occupational Health and Safety Incident Notification Form

Source: Company files.

Team members

- Ben Hartnet   Management Co-chair JHSC
- Susan Wong   Worker Co-chair JHSC
- Jim Sharp   Certified member (management) JHSC
- Mike Bentino   Certified member (worker) JHSC

The team members were all notified immediately following the accident and began their investigation. A follow up meeting was held on 7th April to review the documentation, interview witnesses and inspect the accident scene and the truck. A final meeting was held on 13th April.

Documentation

The following records and statements were available:

1. Employee Injury/Incident Investigation Form prepared by George Grant (Supervisor).
2. Occupational Health and Safety Incident Notification Form prepared by Ben Hartnet.
3. Notification of injury from Ben Hartnet to Mr. Smith (Ministry of Labour).
4. Statement given by Don Page to Ben Hartnet.
5. Statement from Joe Ouellette.
6. Eye witness report from Bill Paquette (mechanic).
7. Statement from Ben Hartnet.
8. Copies of maintenance reports on the truck involved from Truck Rite.
9. Photographs of the accident scene taken by Ben Hartnet.
10. Training records, forklift permit and driving infractions for Don Page.
11. Report from DT Lift on the condition of the truck after the accident.
12. Statement from John Ward (coworker).

Investigation

The team reviewed all the documentation, inspected the accident site, the damaged section of rack and the truck.

The team met with Bill Paquette who provided an eye witness account of the accident. He saw Don Page driving the truck backwards at a speed that Bill considered fast. Bill did not see Don slowing down and did not see the skid of lights that Don described; there was a bunk at the next aisle approx. 20 feet away. Bill knew that Don was going to hit the rack and did not think that the condition of the truck affected the outcome.

The inspection of the area and discussions with those present at the time of the accident indicate that conditions in the area were good. Lighting is excellent, the floor was dry and free of any debris. No skid of lights (as mentioned by Don Page) could be found and the nearest obstacle was the bunk (mentioned by Bill Paquette) which was some distance away, could easily be avoided and was clearly visible. The aisles are narrower than in the past but this section has been in use for several months by all drivers including Don Page and are sufficient for the trucks being used. The rack support hit by the truck had been bent through ninety degrees and indicated a high energy impact.

The report on the condition of the truck by DT Lift indicates that there were problems with both the plugging (forward/reverse) and the brakes. The mechanic clarified that the plugging fault would not have affected the ability to slow and reverse the truck. The mechanic's recommendation was that the truck be taken out of service. The maintenance records from Truck Rite show that the truck has been worked on six times in the past year; the most recent work was to the dead man pedal, linkage and micro-switches on 15th Feb. 2000. The day of the accident was the first day the truck had been on site and it had not been checked by the AmeriChem maintenance department prior to use, it had, however, been maintained by Truck Rite as indicated above.

Exhibit 2   Accident Investigation - Don Page 4th April 2000

Don Page's driving record shows that he had received training on 13th May 1999, one on one training on 28th March 2000 and a general warning from his supervisor on 1st April on the need to drive slowly. Over the past six years Don has received two disciplinary notices for driving incidents, the most recent was 11th Sept. 1997. 4th April was Don's ninth consecutive day at work and following the warehouse move the number of orders to be picked was high. Don states that he had not been drinking alcohol in the twelve hours prior to his shift commencing.

Conclusions

1. The team is unanimous that the primary cause of the accident was excessive speed.
2. Alcohol consumption on the day of the accident was probably not a factor.
3. The truck was in poor condition and should have been checked by AmeriChem prior to use.
4. The presence of an obstruction some distance away may not have directly caused the accident, but should have been removed.
5. Employee training had been frequent and adequate.
6. Other secondary factors which may have played a role include: new warehouse layout, narrower aisles than accustomed, different type of truck, hours of work, volume of work and different type of work.
7. Daily truck safety checks were being performed by the drivers but are not always documented.

Recommendations

1. Don Page not be allowed to drive a forklift until he has completed retraining and been successfully retested.
2. That Don Page undergo medical evaluation by the company doctor to confirm his fitness to return to work.
3. The possibility of fitting speed governors on all forklifts to be investigated.
4. No new or refurbished equipment to be put into service unless it has been checked and approved for use.
5. All forklift drivers to be reminded of the dangers of speed, to report and not use defective equipment, to stay inside their truck during an incident, and to complete the daily checklist for the truck safety systems.
6. The current practice of keeping aisles clear to be reinforced.

AmeriChem maintenance records for all forklifts to be reviewed to identify any potentially problematic trucks.

ARE YOU A LEADER-BREEDER?

Prepared by Jeffrey Gandz

One trait that makes a leader great is his or her ability to hire and mentor high-potential individuals. Enter the leader-breeder, who, unlike the leader-blocker, has the emotional intelligence and uncanny sense required to attract, develop and retain talent, regardless of their academic background. This Ivey professor and leadership expert describes who these leader-breeders are and how they contribute to high-performing organizations.

—Jeffrey Gandz

Increasing attention is being paid to how well executives develop tomorrow's leaders. Put simply, the executive who is a leader-breeder is much more valuable than one who is a leader-blocker. So, what is it that these "leader-breeders" actually do? This article will answer this important question.

RECRUIT HIGH POTENTIALS

Leader breeders recruit high potentials, even if they are hard to handle. They don't go for the safe, conventional hires. McKinsey & Co., for example, will hire people with first-class degrees from top universities, whether or not they have degrees in business. These people are unlikely to have the same thought processes as MBAs, something that will probably lead to longer meetings, greater difficulty in achieving consensus, and require more training and development. However, it will pay off in greater diversity of thought and higher quality solutions—which is the McKinsey product.

In order to recruit high potentials consistently, leaders must know the aptitudes—the inherent, natural characteristics of individuals—that correlate with high performance. These may be cognitive characteristics, dimensions of personality, or other natural talents that will become extraordinary ability with the right kind of developmental experiences. But they must also know the kinds of rewards that candidates are looking for and whether or not they can realistically provide them. Over time, good leaders will find out where to search for such people, how to attract them, how to sort out the true high potentials from those who have learned to deceive an interviewer or fake-out some simple paper-and-pencil test.

A leader-breeder is not put off by energetic, creative, talented people who don't look like everyone else or think along conventional lines or speak in conventionally polite forms. Naivety doesn't bother them, neither does lack of conformity, or even some arrogance. Naivety is often associated with clear thinking, non-conformity with creativity and arrogance with self-confidence. Each can be worked on if the leader is prepared to mentor and coach the acolyte.

COACH FOR COMPETENCIES

Leader-breeders know the essential competencies that high-potentials need to be effective in their roles and get ahead in the organization. There are many generic leadership competencies and even more that may be specific to an organization, role or corporate culture. They model those behaviors themselves or, if they lack them, are willing to 'fess up to their own deficiencies, emphasize the need for them, and either try to acquire them or build compensating mechanisms through the composition of their teams. The leader-breeder generally has some degree of humility and self-awareness and yet the confidence to coach others. They are more than willing to link high-potentials to other leaders who exhibit the required competencies. The coach does not have to dominate the relationship.

This coaching is ongoing, not just in formal performance-management sessions; also, it is true coaching not teaching or training. These coaches know what competencies are needed for success. They keenly observe their people, learn what turns them on and turns them off, look for their natural strengths and weaknesses, work on the former so that strengths lead to excellence and on weaknesses so that they become adequate, and encourage them to strive for personal bests.

Great coaches are great sensors. They understand what makes the person tick, what their natural aptitudes are and what needs to be taught. They understand that they must motivate people with high natural ability in order to get high performance and that such performance will not come without a clear sense of direction and the resources to enable it. They understand that the task of the coach is often to "round the edges" of assertive high-potentials, without dulling them.

MENTOR FOR CAREER DEVELOPMENT

Leader breeders are mentors. While competencies are critical to performance in a role, more is needed to help people advance in their careers. Most organizations have key values that they expect their leaders to exhibit and have a keen sense about what behaviors are appropriate under different circumstances.

There are taboos in organizations, and potential leaders must know what they are and when they are transgressing. There are highly political issues that must be handled very delicately, without appearing to be a political animal, just as there are unwritten rules and regulations that people need to know about. The fact that a chairman of a certain bank was the only one who used a red pencil, whereas the president used a green one, was not known to the young leader-wannabe who marked up a document for onward transmission in one of the reserved colours. The young executive who transgressed by telling off-colour stories at a management meeting, who was involved in a personal relationship with an assistant in an organization which frowned on such relationships, who used inappropriate language, who was not deferential to status-conscious colleagues . . . may sound like small potatoes. But the fact is that all of these behaviours impaired the effectiveness of these leadership neophytes. The mentor spots these missteps and brings them to the attention of the leader-to-be so that they can be addressed.

Mentors are people to whom the unsure, the inexperienced, the perplexed or the puzzled can turn for advice, interpretations and guidance. There may be an issue where someone needs to talk over some ethical concerns, the offer of a job positing or career move where someone is unsure whether it is right for them, or some uncertainty about the way ahead.

Mentoring can be initiated and requested by either someone requiring it or someone who offers it when she or he thinks that it is needed. But it can seldom be forced on either the giver or the receiver. Mentoring requires the establishment of a trusting relationship—the mentor will be seen as someone genuinely wanting to help the less experienced person while he or she, in turn, will be genuinely seeking advice and assistance.

GIVE CANDID FEEDBACK

Leader-breeders give candid feedback. They don't round corners or try to cushion critical feedback by wrapping it up in vague comments about how good the performance has been in the past or in dimensions other than the one that is being focused on. They don't follow some of the accepted wisdoms such as bracketing negative feedback with positive comments, using only positive reinforcement, and so on.

Those leaders who do this are not afraid that they will disable the performance of those to whom they give candid feedback; nor are they concerned that those to whom they give great feedback will somehow become less effective because of it. This is because this feedback is accompanied by coaching and mentoring and, as described below, sincere efforts to learn from failure. Swell-headedness can usually be controlled by reminding high potentials that the one sure way to fail to achieve the high potential is by behaving as if you are one!

Candid feedback does not have to be cruel feedback. Where it addresses basic aptitude deficiencies, people sometimes worry that it may be perceived as an attack on the person. As a result, they would rather not have this direct, difficult conversation. But, when the effort is accompanied by a genuine desire to see the person succeed at something which is more compatible with their basic inherent capabilities, giving the feedback can be constructive. I hold no rancor towards the professor who failed me out of medical school some 40 years ago, thereby doing a favor to the human race and redirecting me toward something for which I was better suited.

CREATE STRETCH ASSIGNMENTS

Good leaders encourage people to stretch themselves. You don't get the most from people by putting them on the rack and stretching them . . . you get more when they raise their own aspirations and use their own energy and frustration as drivers of increased performance.

Many organizations stretch people, sometimes to the point of breaking them. Even if they fall short of this, they may take some pleasure in forcing them to set unattainable targets in the belief that they will somehow do better if they chased the impossible dream. Many times this sort of pressure results in totally inappropriate behavior—the decision to book revenue when it is not certain, to postpone safety-related maintenance rather than incur a cost in a certain accounting period, to dump waste rather than have it recycled, or to put pressure on your people to the point where they start to disengage from the organization even while they appear to be pursuing stretch goals.

Good leaders just don't do this. They recognize that inexperienced high-potentials will tend toward establishing unrealistic targets and may lose perspective as they strive to achieve them. They are there—as coaches and mentors—to help them recognize these dangers and exercise the appropriate degree of self-control. This is the process whereby many high-potentials develop that critical dimension of executive performance . . . judgment.

This stretch may come at some risk to the leader who encourages it. I remember vividly the two product managers who were determined to develop and present their own product plans and, three days before the due date, did not have them done. I would have taken the responsibility for "mission not accomplished" and I admit, belatedly and a little shamefacedly, to having had a contingency plan in place in the form of my own draft plans to be used in the event that they did not perform. But they came through in the end . . per- haps not as well as I thought, rightly or wrongly, might have been done but sufficiently well that I was able to coach them to what I considered higher performance shortly after the due date.

REWARD AND REINFORCE SUCCESS

Leader-breeders reward and reinforce success. High potentials who are also high performers invariably have high needs for recognition and rewards, the latter because they are the tangible manifestation of recognition. Failure to reward people who achieve differentially from those who don't is simply unacceptable to high achievers.

This is true even if the task is "team effort." Those who see themselves as high achievers demand that the team leaders differentiate between the relative contributions of team members— sometimes a difficult thing to do.

Leader-breeders take the rewards that they have to offer and distribute them according to merit. If the average pay raise for a division is four percent, they don't give the best five percent and the worst three percent. They will give the best 10 percent . . . or more, the next best less, but still much more than the average. Of course this can only be done if some are paid very substantially below the average. Such leaders are prepared to do this.

But monetary rewards are only part of the reward picture. High performers are given many more opportunities than the average. They are given greater challenges, greater chances for development, interesting projects on which to work, and the opportunity for exposure to more senior levels of management.

More and more companies are recognizing this need for differentiation and are developing performance management and reward systems that demand it. Whether through forced ranking, bell-curving appraisals and rewards, top-grading or other mechanisms, distinctions are being made between top performers and those who are not. And once these distinctions have been made, managers are expected to act accordingly.

TREAT FAILURE AS LEARNING

Leader breeders hate to fail—but they also learn to treat failure as a learning experience. With greater challenge comes greater risk of failure. High potentials, setting stretch goals, are going to fail and it is how that failure is addressed that will make a difference in developing leaders.

Where failure is punished or blame is thrown around, little is learned. People get defensive, they avoid setting stretch goals, and play in their personal safety zones. Someone once described such an environment to me: "This place is like a marine boot camp. If you stick your head above the foxhole you get it shot off; if you keep it down you get it s—t on." Learning does not take place in such an environment and learners are not attracted to it.

Contrast this with the post-surgical conference that takes place when a patient passes away or to the product-withdrawal process that used to operate at the pharmaceutical firm I used to work for many years ago. Here we had to write a "reverse marketing plan" explaining why the product was being taken off the market. This often involved analyzing what went wrong with the plan that had been written to justify its launch. There was no blame thrown around; the assumptions leading to the marketing decision were identified and checked against actual events. The question was always "Why did we err?", rather than "Who erred?" And the outcome was learning and improvement. The founder of IBM, Thomas J. Watson, Jr., was famous for dissecting the errors made by his executives and then, rather than firing them—as they expected—moving them to new assignments, with some comment about the Company having made a considerable investment in their education.

There are, of course, some limits to "failure as learning." Smart people are not expected to make the same mistake twice; fatal errors tend to attract more blame than those that result in less drastic consequences; and failures that identify personally unacceptable behaviours such as laziness, carelessness, lack of integrity, or personally self-serving behaviours tend to be treated differently. This is acceptable within a leadership development culture.

LEADER-BREEDERS SURRENDER THEIR HIGH PERFORMERS FOR DEVELOPMENT

Leader breeders don't horde their talent, using them to deliver performance now at the expense of their development for the future. Hoarding talent is the most understandable of events—after all, the boss has often made a considerable investment in the development of a certain individual and wants to get some return on that investment. Also, the case can be made that having this individual operating at full capability benefits the organization and having people move on as soon as they become fully competent is detrimental to the organization.

Sound judgment must be exercised when planning the pace of change for individuals on developmental tracks. People need to have the experience of learning how to do something and then actually doing it—living with the consequences, good and bad. However, to stay beyond the point where the experience does not lead to further learning is a waste of potential talent.

The best leader-breeders are always conscious of this trade-off and stay in touch with their talent pools to ensure that development is continuing to take place. When it's not, they will aggressively intervene to ensure that the developmental opportunities keep coming their way. They will happily, if sometimes a little ruefully, carry the badge of being "talent exporters" to the rest of the organization. Many believe that this is more than off-set by the fact that those who do this attract other great talent to work for them, bringing fresh energy and perspective that leads to even better performance.

There are many challenges facing the organization that seeks to develop leadership bench strength. They must find out where great talent lives, attract, recruit, develop, deploy, and retain it. The leader-breeders in the organization make these things happen; the leader-blockers prevent them from developing. The leader-breeders have a multiplier-effect on leadership development . . . they are worth some multiple of their own leadership skills, with this multiple being reflected in the aggregate leadership strength in the organization. Increasingly, these leader breeders are being recognized in organizations and are being rewarded accordingly. Are you one of them?

Leader-Breeders	Leader-Blockers
• Recruit and select high potentials even if they're hard to handle • Coach for skills development • Mentor for career development • Give totally candid feedback on performance • Create stretch assignments • Reward and reinforce success • View failure as a learning opportunity and help their people learn from failure • Surrender their high performers for corporate challenges and personal development	• Recruit and select easy-to manage people • Don't coach or mentor effectively • Lack candor in their feedback • Fit people to jobs that are inside their comfort zones • Do not establish stretch goals • Do not reward differentially for success • Blame people for failures • Horde the people who get the job done

Exhibit 1   Developing Leadership Talent

2

LEADERSHIP TRAIT APPROACH

As Shakespeare said in Twelfth Night, *"Be not afraid of greatness . . . some men are born great, some achieve greatness and some have greatness thrust upon them." I believe that some leaders are born with the natural ability to lead, and some have to develop their leadership skills. When you have leadership responsibilities thrust upon you, you've got to somehow learn to manage—you either sink or swim. Most of us have leadership traits within us, but how these innate traits are nurtured and manifested depends very much on how we interact with other people. It often gets down to being in the right place at the right time as well as having the right circumstances.*

—Andrew Brandler[1]

Leadership trait research was developed to ascertain why certain people were great leaders. This research led to the development of the "great person" theory as it focused on the inherent characteristics and qualities of leaders who were considered to be great. This research also led to the nature argument, which said that only certain people were born with these traits and, consequently, only those certain people became great leaders. The research focused on finding those traits that discriminated between followers and leaders (Bass, 1990; Dubrin, 2007; Jago, 1982).

Eventually, researchers questioned the universality of leadership traits. It was argued that no one set of traits was appropriate in all situations. This led to the reconceptualization of leadership as relationships among individuals in social situations. Recently, researchers have returned to the trait approach. The nature of this research is different in that it now emphasizes the importance of traits in effective leadership.

Traits are attributes that include aspects such as values, needs, motives, and personality (Yukl, 2006). One very prominent leadership researcher (Stogdill, 1948, 1974) demonstrated that average leaders were different from average group members in several ways. In his first study (Stogdill, 1948), he identified the following traits: (1) intelligence, (2) alertness, (3) insight, (4) responsibility, (5) initiative, (6) persistence, (7) self-confidence, and (8) sociability. This study also identified that traits and situations intersected in the sense that some traits were more important in some situations if an individual was to be an effective leader (Yukl, 2006). Stogdill's (1974) second study reported on 10 traits associated with leadership in a positive way. These were (1) drive for responsibility and task completion, (2) vigor and persistence in pursuit of goals, (3) venturesomeness and originality in problem solving, (4) drive to exercise initiative in social situations, (5) self-confidence and sense of personal identity, (6) willingness to accept consequences of decisions and actions, (7) readiness to absorb personal stress, (8) willingness to tolerate frustration and delay, (9) ability to influence other people's behavior, and (10) the capacity to structure social interaction systems to the goal to be achieved (Northouse, 2007).

Mann (1959) determined that leaders were strong in traits such as (1) intelligence, (2) masculinity, (3) adjustment, (4) dominance, (5) extroversion, and (6) conservatism. He agreed that traits could help differentiate leaders from nonleaders. Lord, DeVader, and Alliger (1986) reviewed Mann's work and concluded that (1) intelligence, (2) masculinity, and (3) dominance are very important traits that people use to distinguish leaders. Kirkpatrick and Locke (1991) argued that leaders and nonleaders differ on six traits: (1) drive, (2) desire to lead, (3) honesty and integrity, (4) self-confidence, (5) cognitive ability, and (6) knowledge of the business. These writers argued for a nurture and nature perspective in that they believed that people can learn these traits, be born with them, or both. Summarizing the traits identified above suggests five that are mentioned most frequently: These are (1) intelligence, (2) self-confidence, (3) determination, (4) integrity, and (5) sociability. It is these five that we will focus on (Northouse, 2007).

Intelligence

Zaccaro, Kemp, and Bader (2004) found that leaders and nonleaders differ in their intellectual ability in that leaders have higher levels of intelligence than nonleaders. Their research suggests that having certain abilities helps one be a better leader—these are strong verbal, perceptual, and reasoning abilities. Conversely, their research also indicates that it may be counterproductive if a leader's intelligence is a lot higher than his or her followers' intelligence (Dubrin, 2007). This situation could lead to an inability to effectively communicate with followers as leaders may be too advanced in their thinking to be accepted and understood by their followers. Intelligence does allow leaders to more effectively develop social judgment and complex problem-solving skills. It also appears to be positively associated with effective leadership (Dubrin, 2007; Northouse, 2007).

Self-Confidence

Self-confidence means that you have a positive perspective on your ability to make judgments, to make decisions, and to develop ideas (Daft, 2005). Self-confidence aids people to develop as leaders (Yukl, 2006). It helps individuals to be assured of their skills, knowledge, abilities, and competencies. It encourages leaders to consider that influencing others is right and appropriate. It allows individuals to believe that their decisions will make a difference. In addition to being self-confident, it is important for a leader to be able to express that confidence to followers; one example of exhibiting self-confidence is being calm, cool, and collected in a crisis situation (Dubrin, 2007).

Determination

Determination is a trait that I like to call "stick-to-it-ive-ness." Others would describe it as having a task orientation—a desire to get the job done. Dubrin (2007) calls it tenacity. Daft (2005) calls it drive and says that it is related to having high energy. Many leaders have this sense of "stick-to-it-ive-ness"—this desire to finish the job and to do it well. Initiative, persistence, dominance, and drive go along with determination. Leaders with determination are willing to be assertive, to be proactive, and to persevere when the going gets tough. Determined leaders will demonstrate a sense of dominance, especially when followers need explicit direction and when there is little or no time to explain the reason for the direction being given.

Integrity

I like to think of integrity as consistency between what you believe, what you think, what you say, and what you do. Integrity is being trustworthy and honest. It is taking responsibility for one's actions and holding fast to strong principles. Followers trust and have confidence in leaders with integrity because these leaders do what they say they will do (Daft, 2005; Yukl, 2006). In the 1990s and 2000s, many political and business leaders abused the trust of their followers; consequently, trust of followers toward their leaders is absent in many organizations (Daft, 2005). This led to cynicism on the part of followers toward leaders in these arenas because many were disappointed in what was believed to be hypocritical behavior on the part of leaders. As those of you reading this casebook become leaders, you can be sure that your followers will demand that you demonstrate integrity in your beliefs, thoughts, words, and actions.

Sociability

Sociability is an important trait for leaders. Leaders who are sociable are more inclined to pursue enjoyable social relationships. They are empathetic to the concerns and needs of others and want the best for them. They exhibit friendliness, courtesy, tactfulness, diplomacy, and an outgoing personality. Their interpersonal skills are above average, and they develop a higher level of cooperation with, and among, their followers (Northouse, 2007).

These five traits are substantive contributors to effective leadership. However, the other traits listed earlier also contribute to effective leadership. Collins (2004) argues that two traits exemplify those with the highest level of leadership—a sense of humility and a steely resolve to get the job done. Their sense of humility means that they accept and take the blame when things go wrong but give others the credit when things go right. Their steely resolve means that they will find a way to go through, over, under, or around obstacles.

The Five-Factor Personality Model

Since the early 1980s, researchers have come to generally agree on five factors that determine an individual's personality. These factors are known as the Big Five and include neuroticism, extraversion, openness or intellect, agreeableness, and conscientiousness or dependability (Judge, Bono, Ilies, & Gerhardt, 2002; Yukl, 2006). Judge et al. (2002) found empirical support for personality traits being associated with effective leadership. In particular, extroversion, conscientiousness, and openness are positively associated with effective leadership, in that order of importance. Neuroticism is ranked third with openness but is negatively associated with effective leadership—in other words, less is better. Finally, agreeableness was only weakly, albeit positively, associated with effective leadership (Northouse, 2007).

Emotional Intelligence

Emotional intelligence combines our affective domain (emotions) with our cognitive domain (thinking) (Yukl, 2006). It is concerned with our understanding of emotions and applying this understanding to the tasks we engage in throughout our lives. Mayer, Salovey, and Caruso (2000) used four components to define emotional intelligence: being aware of one's ability to perceive and express emotions, having the ability to control our own emotions while behaving with integrity and honesty, being empathetic toward others and sensing organizational concerns, and effectively managing our own emotions and those involved in our relationships with other people (Dubrin, 2007). Another researcher (Goleman, 1995, 1998) suggests that emotional intelligence encompasses social and personal competencies, with social competence consisting of empathy, communication, and conflict management, while personal competence involves motivation, conscientiousness, self-regulation, confidence, and self-awareness (Northouse, 2007).

Emotional intelligence is a relatively new concept in leadership trait research. There is debate on how important it is in people's lives, with some arguing that it is very important in success at home, school, and work and others saying that it is somewhat important. It is reasonable to suggest that emotional intelligence is important to effective leadership as leaders with more sensitivity to their own emotions and the effect of their emotions on other individuals should be more effective (Yukl, 2006). Dubrin (2007) says that emotional intelligence is a supplement to cognitive ability and that leader effectiveness needs more than only emotional intelligence. More research is needed to give us a better understanding of the relationship between emotional intelligence and effective leadership.

How Does the Trait Approach Work?

The trait approach to leadership is not relational. It concentrates on leaders with no focus on followers or situations. The trait approach emphasizes that effective leadership is about having leaders with specific traits. Inherent in the trait approach is the suggestion that organizations will have better performance if they put people with specific leadership traits into particular leadership positions. In other words, selecting the right people will improve organizational performance (Northouse, 2007).

NOTE

1. Andrew Brandler is the Group Managing Director and CEO of CLP Group in Hong Kong.

REFERENCES

Bass, B. M. (1990). *Bass and Stogdill's handbook of leadership: A survey of theory and research.* New York: Free Press.

Brandler, A. (2006, March 28). Fear not greatness (Part 4 of 8, Ivey Leadership Series). *South China Morning Post,* Business Section.

Collins, J. (2004). Level 5 leadership: The triumph of humility and fierce resolve. In *Collection of articles—Best of HBR on leadership: Stealth leadership* (pp. 15–30). Boston: Harvard Business School Press.

Daft, R. L. (2005). *The leadership experience* (3rd ed.). Mason, OH: Thomson, South-Western.

Dubrin, A. (2007). *Leadership: Research findings, practice, and skills.* New York: Houghton Mifflin.

Goleman, D. (1995). *Emotional intelligence.* New York: Bantam.

Goleman, D. (1998). *Working with emotional intelligence.* New York: Bantam.

Jago, A. G. (1982). Leadership: Perspectives in theory and research. *Management Science, 28*(3), 315–336.

Judge, T. A., Bono, J. E., Ilies, R., & Gerhardt, M. V. (2002). Personality and leadership: A qualitative and quantitative review. *Journal of Applied Psychology, 87,* 765–780.

Kirkpatrick, S. A., & Locke, E. A. (1991). Leadership: Do traits matter? *The Executive, 5,* 48–60.

Lord, R. G., DeVader, C. L., & Alliger, G. M. (1986). A meta-analysis of the relation between personality traits and leadership perceptions: An application of validity generalization procedures. *Journal of Applied Psychology, 71,* 402–420.

Mann, R. D. (1959). A review of the relationship between personality and performance in small groups. *Psychological Bulletin, 56,* 241–270.

Mayer, J. D., Salovey, P., & Caruso, D. R. (2000). Models of emotional intelligence. In R. J. Sternberg (Ed.), *Handbook of intelligence* (pp. 396–420). Cambridge, UK: Cambridge University Press.

Northouse, P. G. (2007). *Leadership: Theory and practice* (4th ed.). Thousand Oaks, CA: Sage.

Stogdill, R. M. (1948). Personal factors associated with leadership: A survey of the literature. *Journal of Psychology, 25,* 35–71.

Stogdill, R. M. (1974). *Handbook of leadership: A survey of theory and research.* New York: Free Press.

Yukl, G. (2006). *Leadership in organizations* (6th ed.). Upper Saddle River, NJ: Pearson-Prentice Hall.

Zaccaro, S. J., Kemp, C., & Bader, P. (2004). Leader traits and attributes. In J. Antonakis, A. T. Cianciolo, & R. J. Sternberg (Eds.), *The nature of leadership* (pp. 101–124). Thousands Oaks, CA: Sage.

THE CASES

LG Group: Developing Tomorrow's Global Leaders

The firm's chairman has announced a corporate goal of increasing revenues from $38 billion to $380 billion between 1995 and 2005. Most of this increase is expected to come from new international sales. As a consequence, the firm must add an estimated 1,400 new global leaders to its management ranks. The chairman and his team must determine what these new global leaders should look like and how to develop them.

Vista-Sci Health Care, Inc.

The new senior vice president of marketing at Vista-Sci Health Care, Inc. must decide which of two very good candidates he should promote to the position from which he has just been promoted. Both of the candidates have demonstrated strengths and weaknesses in their current jobs; the question is whether these competencies and other personal characteristics will make them a good fit for their new roles.

THE READING

Immunity From Implosion: Building Smart Leadership

Smart leaders really are smart, and these coauthors outline eight qualities that smart leaders have—and need to have.

LG GROUP

Developing Tomorrow's Global Leaders

Prepared by Drs. J. Stewart Black and Allen J. Morrison
in collaboration with Dr. Young Chul Chang

Copyright © 1998, Ivey Management Services   Version: (A) 1999–01–22

On February 22, 1995, Bon Moo Koo, 51, took over the helm of the LG Group, one of the three largest Korean *chaebols*. Like a newly recommissioned ship, LG had recently undergone significant renovation and appeared to be in great sailing shape. The renovation and refurbishing had been directed by the former chairman, Mr. Cha-Kyung Koo, Mr. Bon Moo Koo's father. After steering through some stormy seas from 1985 to 1991, the clouds had cleared and LG's future looked sunny and bright. Group revenues had increased each year from 1991 through 1994, when they stood at a record US$38 billion.

Firmly established as the new captain, Chairman Koo was determined to build upon the legacy of his father and set a brave new course by transforming LG Group from a great Korean company into a world-class enterprise. To do this, he would need to lead the group into the uncharted waters of global competition. In 1995, Chairman Koo announced "LEAP 2005," his vision of the future. Of all the different elements of this vision,

the goal of increasing revenue to US$380 billion by 2005 with fifty percent coming from international sales was the most challenging. The emotion behind LEAP 2005 is conveyed in the following statement by Chairman Koo:

> If we do not compete on the world stage, we will have difficulty surviving. I announced this lofty target to prevent us from becoming complacent with our past successes.

In late 1997, nearly three years after Chairman Koo took office and just over seven years away from the magical date of 2005, Mr. Y. K. Kim faced a significant challenge in translating the Chairman's vision into reality. Mr. Kim was the head of the LG Human Resource (HR) team that was charged with the task of identifying and developing "HIPOs" (high potential individuals) and the global leaders that LG would need in the future. Mr. Kim, representing the Office of the Chairman, worked closely with Dr. Michael Lee,

Managing Director of LG Academy (LGA). LGA was the central training center for the entire LG Group with an annual budget of US$28 million and a professional staff of nearly 70 people.

Together Mr. Kim and Dr. Lee recognized that if LG achieved its revenue targets, it would likely be the largest private enterprise on earth. As such, the HR team estimated that LG would need approximately 1,400 new global leaders by 2005. About half would be Korean and half would be non-Korean. The central challenge for the HR team was to identify, hire, retain, and develop these needed global leaders.

Background

To understand what a quantum leap Chairman Koo's aspirations represented, it is necessary to understand some background on the country and businesses of Korea.

Korea's Economic Development

Korea's economic development over the last 50 years was nothing short of phenomenal. Prior to World War II, Korea's economy was primarily that of a third world, agrarian country. In the mid-1930s, about two-thirds of the working population were engaged in agriculture. Like many agrarian societies, the literacy rate in 1935 was only about 20 percent.

Although the country began to make some progress after the end of World War II, the Korean civil war reversed those gains and took a heavy toll on the country. Economically, the civil war devastated the country's industrial base. After the end of the war in 1953, virtually the entire industrial base of what is now South Korea had to be rebuilt. This base was rebuilt and thereafter developed with amazing success.

A few key statistics could provide a clear picture of the dramatic transformation of this country and its economy. In 1953, per capita GNP was just US$67. By 1963, it had risen to US$91. By 1973,

it stood at US$302. In 1983, per capita GNP had skyrocketed to US$2,014. By 1993, it had more than tripled to US$7,513. Nominal per capita GNP was projected to exceed US$30,000 by 2005, and by 2020 was expected to top US$77,000.

The transformation of the people was in many respects just as dramatic. From 1945 to 1995, the percentage of the working population in agriculture dropped from 67 percent to just under seven percent. As people moved from farms to factories, from villages to cities, literacy rates increased to 72 percent by 1962, and to 98 percent by 1996.

Korea's economic transformation took it from a third world country to a position on a par with many developed countries such as Italy and Spain in terms of per capita GNP. Many observers gave a significant portion of the credit to the various government officials and bureaucrats who guided Korea's industrial policy and to Korean business leaders who, during this period, built up some of the largest companies in the world.

Korean Chaebols

The primary economic engines for Korea's economic growth were the *chaebols*. Although Korean *chaebols* were often referred to as conglomerates, the term captured only part of the nature of *chaebols*. Like conglomerates, most Korean *chaebols* had a variety of companies operating in various industries. However, Korean *chaebols* were not legal entities because holding companies were not legally allowed in Korea. Consequently, the companies affiliated with each *chaebol* were a confederation held together by controlling families. Typically, the founding family controlled a majority of the stock in the related companies. The center of this web of companies was usually the "Office of the Chairman." In most cases, the chairman was a senior member of the controlling family. Nearly all of the large Korean *chaebols* started as small companies established by entrepreneurs.

Chaebols received their real boost in the 1960s. Devastated by the ravages of war, the government of South Korea was determined to rebuild the country. To ensure that the country's limited resources were used effectively and efficiently, the government targeted specific companies as engines of economic growth. The government used financial incentives in terms of taxes and protection from foreign competition to nurture and support these selected companies. *Chaebols* were given preferential access to loans and foreign exchange as well as subsidized interest rates. Government officials also used indirect influence to guide *chaebols* into new industries such as ship-building, automobiles, and steel.

Chaebols were the main drivers behind Korea's economic growth between 1960 and 1990. In 1996, the top 30 *chaebols* accounted for over 50 percent of Korea's GDP. The top four *chaebols* employed only three percent of the population, yet accounted for 60 percent of all exports and nearly a third of all company revenues within Korea.

Ironically, the phenomenal success of the country and the *chaebols* created new challenges and problems. As the country's wealth increased and the society became more democratized, organized labor movements proliferated. During the late 1980s, workers staged a number of strikes to demonstrate the sincerity of their demands for higher wages and better working conditions. Subsequently, wage rates increased dramatically. From 1985 to 1990, wages jumped 143 percent, not including the cost of new benefits that were also part of these new wage packages. By contrast, wages in Japan during this same period rose only 18 percent overall. People also began to worry about so much economic power in the hands of so few individuals and families. While *chaebols* contributed to the rapid industrialization and economic growth of the country, many Koreans became increasingly concerned about their economic power and resource misallocation.

In response to mounting public concerns and growing international pressure, the government began a series of reforms. The reforms were designed to "level the playing field" and provide medium and small-sized companies with greater opportunities to grow. The *chaebols* did not openly embrace every reform, and consequently, these reforms often moved slowly. Still the government was determined, and in some cases unilaterally changed a number of policies, such as removing the subsidized loans and restricted access to foreign exchange that the *chaebols* enjoyed.

LG GROUP HISTORY

LG began in 1947 as a small chemical company, called the Rakhee Chemical Works. The company was established by Mr. Bon Moo Koo's grandfather, Mr. In-Hwoi Koo, and initially manufactured household items such as hair combs, toothpaste, and soaps. From this base, the company expanded into more complex plastic products. As it expanded, LG created a tradition of pushing into new technological frontiers. For example, LG produced the first radio in Korea in 1958, as well as the country's first refrigerator. LG also led South Korea's push into greater energy self-sufficiency with the building of the Homan Oil Refinery in 1967.

Low Cost Strategy (1947–1987)

From its foundation and through most of its early history, LG focused on competing through low cost manufacturing. LG competed with other multinational corporations by leveraging Korea's low cost labor and government-subsidized cost of capital. LG also strongly emphasized high production volumes. As LG expanded into a variety of plastic products and consumer electronics, it continued its strategy of under-pricing competitors with products of acceptable, although not superior, quality. In the context of this strategy, it established the Lucky-GoldStar brand as a low-cost and acceptable quality products manufacturer.

As LG moved forward on its low cost strategy, it developed significant manufacturing capabilities. Some managers were concerned that this was achieved at the cost of under-emphasizing marketing competencies. Managers focused on producing high volumes and getting per unit costs as low as possible rather than on finding out what customers wanted, developing high quality products, or expanding marketing capabilities.

This general strategic orientation held for most of the businesses and industries into which LG expanded. By 1987, LG had businesses in chemicals, communications, energy, electronics, finance, insurance, machinery, metals, sports, and trade. While LG was strong in Korea, it was not an international technology or quality leader in any of its business segments, especially relative to world class foreign competitors.

Value Strategy (1987–1995)

By the mid-1980s, it was clear that the strategic thrust of LG needed to change. Several factors contributed to this recognition.

First, by the mid-1980s Korean consumers were more sophisticated than they had been during the 1960s and 1970s, and were increasingly aware of and demanding higher quality products. Also, the rising standard of living increased the ability of Koreans to afford higher quality products and services. Most Korean consumers were no longer happy with low quality, even if it did come at a low price.

Second, under international pressure, the Korean government began to relax trade barriers that made it easier for foreign companies to compete with LG in Korea. In many cases, these foreign companies had significantly higher product quality and features and, because of lower trade barriers, were increasingly price competitive with domestic Korean companies. This was extremely important given that a vast majority of LG revenues came from domestic sales (approximately 70 percent in 1980).

Third, the cost competitiveness of Korean companies began to slip. As wage rates increased in Korea, low cost labor began to erode as a source of comparative advantage. In addition, other countries, such as China, had significantly lower labor costs and were also coming up the technology curve. Consequently, competitors in developing Asian countries were quickly pushing LG out of its traditional low cost position. For example, Chinese companies were increasingly

able to produce consumer electronics (such as fans) that, while not technically sophisticated, were reasonably reliable and significantly cheaper, allowing them to under-price and out-position Korean competitors.

By the mid-to-late 1980s, these external changes started showing up in LG's financial performance. Between 1986 and 1987, sales dropped by US$1 billion (about a seven percent decline) and profits fell by 18 percent.

Refurbishing the Ship

Although the ship was not in any real danger of sinking, LG was listing badly and taking on water. It needed some serious refurbishing and restructuring. It was unthinkable for the aging Chairman, Cha-Kyung Koo, to hand over the helm until the ship was righted. To assist in turning LG around, Chairman Koo retained McKinsey & Co. as an advisor and undertook an extensive internal audit.

Given the environmental shifts, it was clear that LG had to become a value rather than a low cost player. This meant that customers, rather than low cost, had to become the dominant force in company decisions. But, what did customers really want? How did they use LG's products? What did they expect in terms of product reliability or service? These types of questions began to dominate LG and put customers at the center of its new strategic philosophy.

It was also clear that LG had to change its decision-making style. Like many Korean organizations, LG had a history of relatively centralized decision making and a top-down management process. This worked fine as long as the organization was small enough for top management to know everything that was going on and as long as the marketplace was fairly homogeneous. However, by the late-1980s LG had become a huge organization with revenues approaching US$20 billion and over 80,000 employees. Furthermore, whereas early in its history LG had been primarily focused on the domestic Korean market, increasingly it focused more on international markets. These markets and their customers often differed, not only from Korean markets and customers, but from each other as well. Consequently, it was impossible for top managers to know everything that was going on in such a large organization and across such diverse markets and customers. LG's management approach had to become more decentralized and more participative in nature. Decisions needed to be pushed down to where the action was.

The new management approach was implemented and was typically referred to in LG as "management by self-control." It allowed for much greater autonomy than had ever existed in the Group. Although most managers welcomed the opportunity for greater decision-making autonomy, many lacked experience with it. These managers had to change their mind-set from flawlessly executing orders to determining strategic direction.

To facilitate and reinforce this new approach, LG was restructured. In 1987, LG's various affiliated companies were divided into 21 "Cultural Units." The cultural units consisted of multiple Strategic Business Units (SBUs) grouped together by common "cultural" characteristics. SBU heads were given full profit and loss responsibility for their units, were expected to formulate specific competitive strategies, and were held accountable for results. Cultural Unit presidents focused on integration and coordination across SBUs.

Within SBUs, middle managers were charged with reviewing and reengineering business processes to ensure that they were efficient and effective. This reengineering was guided by the central strategic theme of providing value to the customer. This required managers to have a clear idea of customer needs, values, and preferences. In general, LG's top management wanted businesses structured and operated so that for a given amount of money spent, customers would get more of what they wanted in a product or service, and more than what they would get from a competitor's product or service.

Although managers kept a vigilant eye on costs, greater attention was also paid to quality than ever before. New and intense initiatives around "zero-defects" were undertaken and supported from the highest levels. Customer satisfaction became a key measure and important input into quality improvement programs.

By 1994, the results of all these efforts were beginning to show. Sales had increased each year from 1991 through 1994. The rate of return for the entire Group rose from a low in 1991 of just under one percent to nearly four percent in 1994. Net income was up nearly 800 percent, rising from US$128 million in 1991 to US$965 million in 1994.

New Face and Image

With the ship righted and ready to sail on a brighter course, it was time for a public recommissioning. This recommissioning occurred on January 1, 1995. On that date, Lucky-GoldStar Group officially changed its name to the LG Group. A new corporate identity program was launched, the center of which was a new Group logo—"The Face of the Future." The logo was designed to symbolize five key concepts which (translated directly from Korean) were:

- The World
- The Future
- Youth
- Humans
- Technology

These concepts were believed to be the keys to LG's future growth and prosperity.

LEAP 2005

When Mr. Bon Moo Koo took over as Chairman in 1995 (about one month after the public recommissioning), growth was the center of his new vision for the Group. He charted a course in his LEAP 2005 initiative that would take LG on a journey from being a leading company in Korea to being a leading company in the world. In the process, LG would become one of the largest and most admired enterprises in the world.

Basic Philosophy

To achieve the general objectives of Leap 2005, Chairman Koo articulated a basic philosophy. This philosophy was set forth with four key points:

1. Compete from a global perspective
   - Compete with world-class companies in the global market
   - Secure global management systems to be competitive on a world and regional basis
   - Secure and utilize people, finance, and technology from a global perspective to create world-class business systems

2. Create maximum value for customers, employees, and shareholders

3. Conduct business with integrity

4. Contribute to social development as a corporate citizen

This basic philosophy reaffirmed elements that had a long tradition in LG as well as adding new emphasis to other elements. The focus on valuing employees had been in LG from the beginning, as had the philosophy of contributing to social development through good corporate citizenship. The focus on creating customer value was relatively new, having been introduced with the restructuring efforts that started in 1987. However, the emphases on the global market and world class competitors were totally new, as was the greater emphasis on creating value for shareholders. Executives hoped that combining traditional philosophies with compatible new ones would provide employees with needed anchors so that they did not feel completely adrift while at the same time directing their attention toward new horizons.

Transitioning From the Old LG Culture

The new global orientation of LG required a new culture to support it. Although parts of the old culture did not fit the new environment, it did have valuable components. Consequently, the objective was to reaffirm what was still valid and add new cultural elements that were necessary for future success. The old culture was most often described by three words: stability, harmony, and respect.

Stability

In general, LG had a history of being a relatively stable company and culture. The company did not make radical shifts in strategy or practice. If LG entered a country, it tended to stay there. If it entered a new product or business segment, it tended to stick with it. Neither poor performing businesses nor managers were easily dropped from the Group.

Harmony

From its beginning, LG placed considerable emphasis on harmony. Some of that emphasis may have stemmed from its history. Mr. In-Hwoi Koo, the founding Chairman, believed strongly that harmony rather than conflict should dominate the atmosphere at work.

Respect

The emphasis on respect was reinforced both at the company and national level. Respect for authority and hierarchy have had a long cultural tradition in Korea. Much of this tradition tied back to Confucian philosophy that held: "Let the king be king. Let the subject be subject. Let the father be father. Let the son be son. In this there is order." As a consequence, respect for management authority and the roles of individual workers were strong values in LG.

The Chairman wanted the new culture to keep the tradition of harmony as well as respect for the individual. Stability, in contrast, could not be sustained. Technological innovations, mergers, acquisitions, divestitures, alliances, and so on, happened at such a rapid pace in the global environment that to accomplish the ambitions of Leap 2005, LG had no choice but to become more agile. Furthermore, unlike in the past, Korea would no longer be a protected market, but instead would become increasingly open to foreign competitors. Consequently, even stability at home could not be sustained. For LG to be a world leader, it would need to be as quick and nimble as the best global competitors.

The cultural value of respect would also need to play out differently in the future than it had in the past. In the past, respect had translated into a top down management style. However, beginning with the reorganization in 1987, it had become increasingly clear that while respect for others would always be important, top down management and strong emphasis on hierarchy would not allow LG to respond to the market as quickly as needed to stay competitive.

Establishing the New LG Culture

While retaining certain elements of the past culture, LG's top management tried to establish and reinforce four new cultural elements: challenge, speed, simplicity, boundarylessness.

Challenge

In many ways this new element was in direct contrast to the old value of stability. Going forward, LG needed to develop a culture that thrived on challenge rather than one that relied on stability. According to Chairman Koo, a business objective was challenging if the way to accomplish it was unknown. In other words, if you knew exactly how to accomplish an objective, then it was not challenging. On the other hand, an objective that you did not know how to reach would challenge you to think differently and to come up with "break-through" innovations.

Speed

The second new cultural element—speed—was critical to success in the fast-changing global environment. Managers had to develop a new perspective on time-based competition. Most managers were used to thinking about a year in terms of 365 days. But in fast-paced industries such as the Internet, "web years" lasted perhaps 90 days. In other words, as much changed on "the web" in 90 days as changed in

traditional industries in a year. Consequently, as LG pushed into new markets and higher technology industries, speed had to be a central value that permeated the Group's culture.

Simplicity

In a world as complex as the one LG was entering, keeping things as simple as possible was absolutely essential. For greater product reliability, fewer parts and simpler designs were necessary. Greater product simplicity would also help keep costs down. Quicker service time would require simpler products and business processes. Each additional step in a business process represented both increased costs and time delays, neither of which added value for the customer. If LG did not instill a cultural value around simplicity, the natural complexity of the global environment could cause the Group to respond with complex products and business processes that could turn into a tangled mess.

Boundarylessness

The rapid pace and sophisticated nature of the global environment made the past structure and practice of separated departments and sequentially "handing off" projects—from product research to product design to engineering to manufacturing to marketing to sales—unworkable. Functional, geographic, and even business boundaries of the past needed to become less like fortress walls and more like fuzzy lines. People from different disciplines and geographies increasingly needed to work together to analyze problems and figure out solutions.

STRATEGIC ORIENTATION OF LG

The growth objectives articulated by the Chairman in Leap 2005 were highly ambitious. LG was to grow from around US$38 billion in 1994 to US$380 billion by 2005. This objective represented a true challenge because no one knew exactly how to get there, even though by year-end 1996 Group revenues had increased to

US$73 billion. But growing revenues at any cost, such as profitability, was not acceptable. The Chairman made it clear that to be considered one of the best companies in the world, LG's financial performance also had to be among the best in the world.

Focus

New financial objectives meant that LG could no longer carry marginal businesses with poor performance. Either the managers heading those businesses had to fix them so that they were growing and making money or they would need to prepare them for divestiture. Although divestiture would need to happen in a way that honored LG's commitment to employees and retained remaining employees' loyalty to the Group, if a business could not be fixed to be a leader in its industry, it would be sold or shut down.

Focus would also be essential in terms of LG's geographic strategy. Although LG would compete across the globe, it would focus on *strategic markets.* Strategic markets were selected according to two primary criteria. The first was the expected economic growth and size of the market. The second was the extent of business opportunity in that market. Business opportunity was a function of how open the market would be to foreign firms, how intense the competition would be in that market, and what LG's capabilities were for competing there.

Based on expected economic growth and business opportunities, China and Southeast Asia were identified as strategic markets. These markets were expected to grow by eight to ten percent a year in real terms through 2005. In addition, these markets were increasingly open to foreign trade and investment, and LG had good capabilities for competing there.

Eastern Europe, Central and South America, the Middle East and Africa were all regions with potential economic growth, but were expected to grow more slowly than China and Southeast Asia. Furthermore, government restrictions and LG's relatively weak competitive positions made them less attractive. Still, LG did not intend to ignore these regions. In fact, LG had plans to establish regional headquarters in Europe, South America, Africa and the Middle East in the near future because of the market potential in these regions.

The developed markets of the United States, Japan, and Western Europe were expected to grow at much slower rates (one to three percent). Although these markets were relatively open, competition was quite intense, and LG generally had no particular competitive advantage in these markets. Thus, LG would continue to compete there because of the size of these markets, but would focus on China and Southeast Asia as areas of strategic growth.

Avenues of Growth

Simplified, LG could grow through existing and new products, and through existing and new geographies. The specific avenues of growth in each quadrant of this matrix are captured in Exhibit 1. Of the four cells in the matrix, managers anticipated that growth in the "existing products, existing markets" would be the most difficult. Significant revenue growth in this cell would require a product revolution in terms of new technologies or business models.

Technological revolution typically comes in two forms. The first is product technology innovation. This type of innovation provides products that do things that they never did before. As a consequence, customers of the previous product generation replace their old products with the new ones, and new customers are so enticed by the features and capabilities that they enter the market in significant numbers for the first time. The second technology revolution happens through process innovation. This type of innovation allows the product to be produced faster or more cost efficiently.

A business model revolution produces significant growth with existing products in existing markets because business process innovations provide significantly better value to customers. The significantly better value causes customers to purchase from the new "system" in significant

	Existing Products	New Products
Existing Markets	Product Revolution – New Technology – New Business Model	Product Extensions Product Startups Product Acquisitions Alliances with New Line of Business (NLOB) Partners
New Markets	Market Extensions Local Competitor Acquisitions Alliances with Local Enterprises	Product/Market Extensions Product/Market Startups NLOB Acquisitions Alliances with NLOB Enterprises

Exhibit 1   Avenues of Growth for FG

numbers. Wal-Mart did this in discount retailing and Microsoft did this with pre-installed operating system software.

Growth in the other three quadrants comes from extensions, startups, acquisitions, and various forms of alliances. While each of these activities shares some common managerial capabilities, each requires its own unique set of managerial capabilities for success. Each avenue of growth is difficult to manage successfully. Even if specific managers focused on just one of these avenues of growth, in order to grow ten-fold in ten years, LG would need hundreds of world-class managers in each of these cells and for each of these growth strategies.

Investment Decisions and Cash Flow

To reach growth objectives, top LG managers recognized that financial resources would need to be invested wisely for the greatest possible return. No longer would simple pay-back assessments be adequate. In the future, approved investments would not only need to pay back the original investment but would need to provide an attractive return on that investment based on a future cash

flow analysis. With these heightened investment requirements, LG would need a cadre of managers with more sophisticated knowledge of finance.

Customer Satisfaction

Chairman Koo believed that sustained revenue growth would only come through satisfying customers' needs. This orientation had already begun to be instilled throughout the Group by the restructuring his father had directed. Chairman Koo wanted to build on that. Customer satisfaction was established as a key measure of success in going forward. However, the Chairman did not want the organization to simply react to customer satisfaction and "fix things when customers were dissatisfied," but he wanted proactive management that would anticipate customer needs and satisfy them before the customer ever had a chance to voice dissatisfaction.

Quality

Increasingly sophisticated customers in Korea and around the world wanted products that were reliable and of high quality. To have the most satisfied customers, LG would need world-class quality in their products and services. Consequently, Leap 2005 continued the emphasis on high quality and zero defect initiatives.

Product Technology

Customers also wanted products with "the latest and greatest" features. Consequently, Leap 2005 stressed the role of technology and its acquisition. To have the most satisfied customers, LG would need leading-edge product technology and innovations to ensure that, compared to competitors, LG products had superior features and capabilities. In particular, Chairman Koo stressed the importance of acquiring differentiating technology.

Process Technology

Customers also wanted the greatest possible value, which meant that they wanted the best possible features in products and services for the lowest price. Therefore, acquisition of process technology was also important. Key managers believed that innovations enabling products to be made more cheaply, more reliably, or more quickly would enhance not only the value proposition made to customers, but LG's internal profit margins. Therefore, acquisition of process technology also became an important part of Leap 2005.

LEADER DEVELOPMENT CHALLENGE

Top management and the HR team were convinced that LG could not achieve the objectives of Leap 2005 without substantially more global leaders. Because LG had a domestic orientation in the past and because of the speed with which Leap 2005 required LG to change course to a global setting, leadership development emerged as one of the biggest challenges within the Group.

Working Environment

To be a leading global company, senior executives felt that LG would need to create a global working environment that included both Korean and non-Korean leaders. The Chairman articulated several aspirations that would demonstrate that LG was well on its way to creating a global working environment:

- Fill three to four business president positions with non-Koreans out of the nearly 50 positions (see Exhibits 2 and 3 for an overall review of LG's current size and structure).
- Fill 20 percent of executive positions at the office of the Chairman in Seoul with non-Koreans.
- Fill most top executive positions of foreign affiliates (approximately 129) with local national managers.

These were ambitious goals, but some executives were worried that if LG did not achieve these aspirations, it would encounter the same problem that Japanese multinational corporations had experienced. Several studies found that Japanese companies had significant difficulty attracting and then hanging on to top local executive talent in countries such as the U.S. This was primarily because local managers got frustrated by the "Bamboo Ceiling." The bamboo ceiling was the barrier non-Japanese executives ran into at a certain point in the hierarchy of the Japanese subsidiary. In the U.S., many American executives felt that they could rise only to a certain level within the Japanese foreign affiliates and no higher. American executives often felt that above that level only "Japanese expatriate managers need apply." Consequently, smart and capable managers would simply use their experience in a Japanese company as a springboard to better positions in other companies. This turnover of top local talent hurt the financial performance of Japanese companies throughout the world.

Some managers thought Korean companies, if they were not careful, would run into the same problem. Many felt that if LG could not attract and retain the best management and executive talent wherever in the world that talent existed, it would not be competitive with more culturally open-minded companies. But how could the Chairman's aspirations be achieved? What would

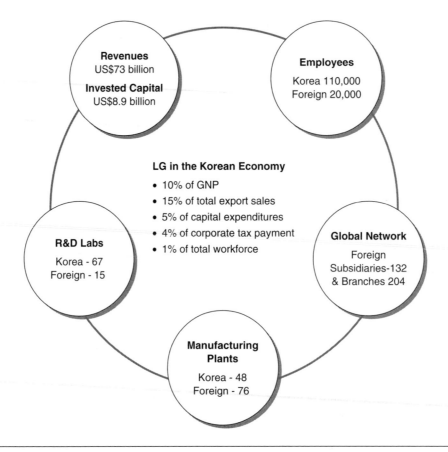

Exhibit 2   LG Group Overall Status, 1996

need to take place for this to be accomplished? How could numerous non-Koreans be effectively integrated into the head offices in Seoul? Where would they find three or four non-Koreans capable of being company presidents and effectively interacting with other Korean company presidents within the Group? These and other questions plagued the HR team.

Needed Competencies

Beyond these specific aspirations, LG had a much broader set of leadership needs. Mr. Kim estimated that LG needed 1,400 new capable global leaders to achieve the growth objectives of Leap 2005. What competencies would these

individuals need? Mr. Kim could generate a list of 20 or 30 needed competencies off the top of his head, but which ones were the truly important ones? With limited time and resources, LG could not afford to take a "shot gun" approach to global leader development. The HR team needed to identify a limited set of competencies on which they could focus assessment and development activities.

Development of Non-Korean Global Leaders

Since it was expected that 50 percent of revenues in 2005 would come from international sales, Mr. Kim expected that 50 percent of the

Trade and Services & Others (31.3% of Total Revenue)	Electric and Electronics (23.7% of Total Revenue)
• LG International Corp • LG Construction Co. Ltd. • LG Engineering Co. Ltd. • LG Energy Co. Ltd. • LG Mart Co. Ltd. • LG Department Store Co. Ltd. • LG Ad Inc. • LG EDS System • LG Investment Inc. • Han Moo Development Co. Ltd. • LG Homeshopping Inc. • LG Sports Ltd. • LG Leisure Co. Ltd. • LG Economic Research Institute	• LG Electronics Inc. • LG Electro-Components Ltd. • LG Semicon Co. Ltd. • LG Honeywell Co. Ltd. • LG Industrial System Co. Ltd. • LG Soft Ltd. • LG Information & Communication Ltd. • LG Telecom Ltd.
Chemicals and Energy (25% of Total Revenue)	**Finance (15% of Total Revenue)**
• LG Chemical Co. Ltd. • LG Petrochemical Co. Ltd. • LG MMA Corp. • LG Owens Corning Corp. • LG Siltron, Inc. • LG AlliedSignal Corp • LG Caltex Oil Corp. • LG Caltex Gas Corp • LG Oil Products Sales Co. Ltd. • Hoyu Tanker Co. Ltd. • Wonjeon Energy Co. Ltd.	• LG Securities Co. Ltd. • LG Investment Trust Management Co. • LG Insurance Co. Ltd. • LG Credit Card Co. Ltd. • LG Finance Co. Ltd. • LG Futures Co. Ltd. • LG Merchant Banking Corp. **Machinery and Metals (5% of Total Revenue)** • LG Cable & Machinery Ltd. • LG Metal Corp.

Exhibit 3   LG Business, 1996

1,400 new global leaders would need to be non-Korean. This meant that 700 non-Korean managers would need to be identified and brought up to world-class standards in short order (see Exhibit 4). Most senior LG executives believed that all company CEOs in LG would need to have a global orientation and global leadership capabilities. In general, the feeling was that as one went down the ranks of managers, the percentage of managers needing to be global leaders declined. This view was more or less true for both Korea and non-Korean future leaders.

But the 700 non-Korean global leaders only scratched the surface of the non-Korean leadership development challenge. Given that half of the targeted US$380 billion in revenues by 2005 was expected to come from international sales, it was estimated that LG would need approximately 340,000 foreign employees. (In 1996, LG had 110,000 Korean employees, 20,000 non-Korean employees). With a typical manager-to-employee ratio of 1-to-100, LG would need approximately 3,400 non-Korean managers, compared to the 200 it had in 1996.

LG's non-Korean leadership development needs were further complicated by the fact that LG's regional focus for growth was China and Southeast Asia. These were areas in which world-class managerial talent was in relatively short supply. Furthermore, LG was not the only

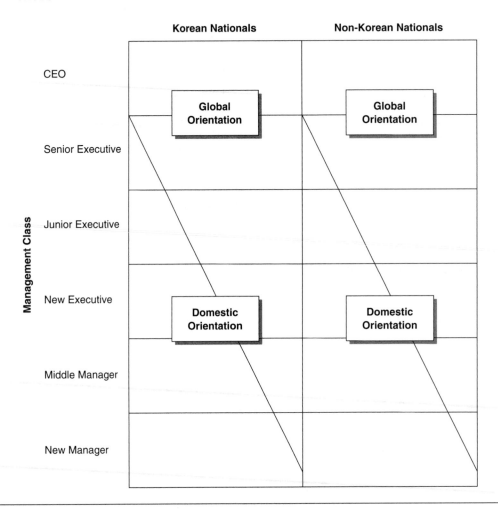

Exhibit 4   The Composition and Orientation of Future Global Leaders at LG

company that had targeted this region. Companies like General Motors, Coca-Cola, Exxon, Philips, Ericsson, Sony and other multinationals were equally committed to the region and had been aggressively acquiring and retaining the best local managerial talent.

How should LG identify high potential managerial talent in the region? What comparative advantage did LG have in acquiring and retaining this talent compared to global competitors such as General Motors or Philips? Furthermore, how should LG develop these high potential individuals

once they were hired? Also, was it even possible for a Korea-based team to effectively create and effectively implement a development plan for non-Korean managers? In other words, given that 700 future top LG leaders would be non-Korean, could a group composed of Koreans effectively hire, train, and retain this group? Would culture or other filters cause the HR team to look at information, interpret behavior, structure problems and solutions in ways that would be culturally bound and perhaps not be effective in meeting management development objectives?

Programs

Although Mr. Kim and Dr. Lee did not have the answers to all these questions, several programs were in place at the LG Academy to try to address these leadership development challenges. (See Exhibit 5 for a brief description of each program.) These programs spanned the entire range of employees, from non-managerial employees through company presidents.

The HR team recognized that younger employees and managers needed to be cultivated and developed early if LG were to have strong global leaders 20 years in the future, but these young managers would not be ready to assume significant global responsibilities by 2005. Even if they could be ready, would LG's culture allow a 35-year-old to run a significant business with international operations? Mr. Kim and Dr. Lee wondered if they should concentrate their energy on developing managers who were currently in their 40s.

Prioritization and Decision Time

In September 1997, the HR team met to decide how to proceed. Some members thought the issues needed more study. For example, clearly identifying the critical capabilities of future global leaders was a major challenge. Some argued that to make sure that the right capabilities were identified, more thought and data were needed. Other members of the team felt they knew enough to proceed without more research.

In addition to identifying leadership competencies, the HR team needed to determine how an agreed-upon set of leadership competencies should be developed. The team had identified a variety of approaches to assess the competencies of current LG managers—pencil and paper tests, supervisor evaluations, assessment centers, job performance, expert assessments, and so on. Would each of these be relevant for every career stage? While new managers would basically do whatever they were asked, Mr. Kim and Dr. Lee, in particular, wondered if senior managers would ever agree to participate in a pencil and paper test. They also wondered if current job performance would be a good indicator of potential in young managers. Also, would supervisor evaluations be valid for young managers who might very well have bosses that were not very high potential global leaders themselves?

Once high potential managers were identified and the gaps between existing versus desired leadership competencies were determined, the approach to develop these competencies had yet to be worked out. What role should job rotation and experience play in developing future leaders? What about international assignments? Should the nature of the assignment differ for young managers versus older managers? What about formal training and education programs? What sorts of programs would really be effective?

As members of the HR team grappled with these issues, the task ahead seemed daunting. In an effort to better structure the discussion, Mr. Kim and Dr. Lee agreed to focus the team on three key questions: (1) What were the key needed capabilities of future global leaders? (2) How should these capabilities be developed? (3) Could the team take the same approach to both these issues with Korean and non-Korean managers? With just over seven years remaining under Leap 2005, the HR team was under increasing pressure to not only find answers to these questions, but to put in place the infrastructure required to quickly develop the next generation of leaders at LG.

Non-Manager	Manager	Gen. Manager	Director	VP	President

Global Business Communication

Host Manager

Global Mind-set

Global MBA

Global Business Leader

Global Business Consortium

Global CEO Conference

Global Business Communication :	Short seminar designed to teach fundamental principles of cross-cultural communication.
Host Manager:	Program designed to help host country managers understand the strategy and structure of LG.
Global Mind-set:	Program intended to raise understanding of business globalization and the forces behind it.
Global MBA:	Two-Year MBA program. First half completed in Korea and the second half completed in the U.S.
Global Business Leader:	Six-Week program with modules in Korea, the U.S., and countries in Southeast Asia.
Global Business Consortium:	Focuses on strategic benchmarking among six member countries (ABB, BT, Lufthansa, SKF, SCB, and LG).
Global CEO Conference:	Designed to help senior executives address critical issues relative to LG competitive position.

Exhibit 5   Global Leadership Programs

Vista-Sci Health Care Inc.

Prepared by Professor Jeffrey Gandz

  Version: (A) 2006–03–31

For Allun Jones, this had been a good day. Senior vice-president, marketing and sales of Vista-Sci Health Care Inc.'s (Vista-Sci's) pharmaceutical division at 35—not bad for a university general arts graduate who had started at Vista-Sci as a medical representative, detailing its products to doctors and pharmacists, some 13 years ago. Now he would be responsible for the domestic marketing and sales functions of the pharmaceutical division of a multinational company that had some leading prescription and non-prescription brands ranging from antibiotics to skin creams.

Reporting to him, was a vice-president, product management who supervised a staff of eight product managers and assistant product managers, a vice-president, marketing research and her staff, a vice-president, marketing services and his staff, and a sales force of some 155 medical representatives, district managers and internal sales and sales training staff who reported to the vice-president, sales.

This promotion was a big one that would place him firmly on the next step in his career path, one that he believed could lead to the chief executive officer's (CEO's) job in seven-to-10 years. But he knew that it was an opportunity that required continued and indeed accelerated performance on his part; nothing came easily at Vista-Sci and performance was everything!

One rather urgent issue was his replacement as vice-president, product management. The role was a challenging one—he had been doing it for almost seven years, and those years had been difficult but exciting times. He had two candidates, both of whom had stellar records of performance as product managers but, as personalities and in their previous career paths, they were as different as any two people could be. Which one should he recommend? Or should he do the unexpected and look outside the domestic operation or even outside the company? This latter option would be an unusual one to take; Vista-Sci had an outstanding reputation as a developer of talent in the industry and tended to promote from within its own ranks.

The Vice-President-Product Management Role

Vista-Sci was a company that had embraced the marketing philosophy earlier and more completely than most pharmaceutical firms. Everything was focused on the customer, defined as the user of the company's products rather than the channels through which they were sold, prescribed or recommended. The firm spent millions of dollars on market research, believed that it was knowledgeable about customers' wants, needs and buying behaviors, and its research and development, marketing and sales efforts were driven by an intense commitment to customer satisfaction.

This marketing orientation pervaded the company. Packaging engineers were focused on making the products appealing and accessible to customers, researchers were searching for more appealing dosage regimens, leading to many products being reformulated into one-a-day, time-released formats; even accounts receivable staff were seeking ways in which the trades could spread their payments for seasonal products over a full year so that they would not run out of stock during "slow" periods, thereby inconveniencing customers.

But while this marketing orientation was intensely customer-focused, it also had a strong bottom-line orientation. Shareholders were to be delighted because the company was successful in satisfying customer needs. So every initiative, every new product, package, flavor, distribution drive was expected to pay off in bottom-line results.

Product managers were key players in executing this marketing orientation. Each of these men and women was expected to be a marketing professional. Many had formal business education—most had MBAs from well-recognized schools; some had started with the company as medical representatives (prescription products) or sales representatives (non-prescription products); many had science undergraduate degrees in disciplines such as pharmacy, pharmacology or biochemistry. Each was responsible for the performance of one or more products; its marketing, advertising, packaging, forecasting, line-extension development and the many other activities that went into product management.

These product managers shared many resources. When they wanted some market research, they would make the request of the vice-president, market research; their request might be competing with 10, 20 or more requests from other product managers. Sales force time was allocated to products, and product managers had to make their cases why their product, as opposed to some other product, should be allocated time by the sales force in, for example, the first quarter of next year.

There were formal mechanisms for planning priorities; for example, there was a "sales calendar" established annually, and product managers pitched for their allocation of sales time. There were systems development schedules and priorities, market research efforts were allocated to various products in a planned and budgeted way. But it was well known that the most "effective" product managers got the favored treatment from all those staffs that supported the marketing programs. It was one thing for product managers to get their products allocated for sales force attention. . . . and quite another to get the sales force motivated and excited about actually detailing or selling that product to doctors and pharmacists.

Product managers who made effective presentations, who related well to the sales force and who listened to the sales representatives' ideas about how to sell the products seemed to get more attention than others. Market researchers, packaging engineers, even credit analysts had their favorites among the company's eight product managers—usually the ones who took time to give them the "big picture," thanked them for their work, gave credit where credit was due and emphasized the team's efforts. There were other product managers who seemed to have more trouble getting the kind of involvement, participation and commitment from the marketing services, sales and other support functions. They were either too demanding or not demanding enough; too academic in their approach to marketing or not thoughtful enough, constantly promoting hare-brained schemes to support their products.

The product managers also maintained a number of external relationships. The company used three different advertising agencies among which it distributed its brands. Here, again, it was clear that some product managers seemed to get much better performance from agency personnel than others. Top copywriters and creative directors could make a huge difference in marketing a product and some of the product managers seemed to attract the very best agency personnel to work on their assignments. Others attracted lesser talent.

The vice-president product management was really the director of this marketing thrust, even though many of the key players did not report to this position. Packaging reported through production, accounting personnel through the controller, sales staff through the vice-president, sales. It was the responsibility of the vice-president product management to recruit, train and develop the product management staff and to ensure that while each was driving and promoting the interests of the assigned products, the whole unit worked as a team. It was the closest thing to corporate lion-taming that Allun Jones had ever experienced! Now he was moving onwards and upwards, and he needed to find a replacement.

Two candidates were apparent—both had strengths, and both had weaknesses.

JAMIE HERNANDEZ

When she joined Vista-Sci six years previously, Hernandez had just been terminated from her job with Ashridge Pharmaceuticals in England. She explained why to anyone who asked:

> One day the president was musing aloud about why sales were below plan. I told him: I'd just spent three days out with different members of the field sales force and we'd spent more time in coffee shops than in doctors' offices. I just thought that we weren't pushing hard enough. Ten minutes later, my boss, the vice-president marketing, was in my office telling me that I was being let go. No matter that I was absolutely right—he agreed with me . . . it was lack of sales effort. But I had managed to embarrass the vice-president of sales and he had insisted that my boss fire me, virtually as a condition for continued support by the sales department. So, despite being right, I was sacked—fired! Just shows, you can be right and wrong at the same time!

When he had interviewed Hernandez in the United Kingdom, Jones had been immediately attracted to her openness, her apparent willingness to learn from this incident, and her obvious enthusiasm for the industry and for the marketing role. Hernandez had been a pre-med student at a prestigious medical school in the United Kingdom but had not completed her program. "I was probably too young, had a great time at university, but my grades weren't that great! I just felt that being a doctor wasn't what I really wanted." So, without a degree but with some knowledge of pharmacology, physiology and anatomy, she had applied to a pharmaceutical company as a medical representative, calling on doctors in her assigned territory in London. She'd done that for three years:

> But there's just so many *Readers Digests* you can read while waiting for doctors to see you. After a

while, I was just bored stiff. The problem was, you couldn't get ahead in that company unless you have a university degree . . . I was stuck! It didn't matter how good I was at my job. In fact, I was working only three days a week—I could get all my assigned calls done in that time, my area manager didn't want me to do any more because it would show up other representatives and make it hard for him to explain why they weren't doing more. So I took up golf!

One day, coming back on a train from a meeting at head office, she'd started talking to a man who was the president of an engineering firm selling to the petro-chemical industry in Europe. He was drinking pretty heavily on the train and, by the time they reached London, he was semi-conscious. She helped him into a taxi and sent him on his way, not, however, before he'd given her a business card and said, "If you're ever looking for a job, give me a call."

The next day, she did. He couldn't remember the event at all! But, despite that—or maybe because of it—she ended up as the Redders Instrumentation and Valve sales manager for Europe.

> Great title, reasonable salary, a Jaguar as a company car, and lots of incentive pay for building the business. It was a great two years . . . but it came to an end when Redders was acquired by a larger company and my job was reduced in scope and opportunity. They wanted to keep me, but I just didn't see my future selling safety relief valves and instruments to petrochemical plants in Northeastern England.

While working as a medical representative at the pharmaceutical firm, Hernandez had enrolled in a continuing education program at a local polytechnic (community college) leading to a diploma in marketing. Armed with this accreditation, she applied for a job as a product manager at a very large U.S.-based multi-national pharmaceutical firm. She was successful in a series of full-day interviews, parted on good terms from Redders and joined Ashridge Pharmaceutical where she'd been completely happy until the day she was fired. This entire story had come out during her interview with Allun Jones:

It was one of the most refreshing and candid job interviews I think that I've ever conducted. That's the great thing with Jamie . . . what you see is what you get! She speaks her mind, tells it the way it is. Totally transparent. Passionate about what she wants to do, totally committed. And she's that way with everyone, from the CEO of the company to an accounts receivable clerk. And they all seem to respond well to her. They like working with her or for her; she never has any difficulty getting the best talent to work on her projects, new assistant product supervisors (freshly minted graduates, straight out of business school who are assigned to work for product managers) seem to want to work with her, despite the fact that she does not have the MBA-type education that others have.

True, her outspokenness does cause some ripples. Jamie does not suffer fools wisely and she sometimes is fast to judge people as fools. Her excitability is both an asset and a liability. There are few weeks that go by when I don't have someone in my office raising questions or complaints about how she's handled something. What I notice, however, is that they are not people who are directly involved in her projects. Rather, they are "observers" and they usually point out that Jamie is different from others, maybe just doesn't fit the usual Vista-Sci model. As far as I've been concerned, at least in the past, that's been a good thing. We need some more diversity around here . . . and Jamie's different. The outspokenness? Well she usually says "What do you expect, with a Scottish mother and a Mexican father . . . bland?

There was one incident that showed what a driving personality Hernandez was. One of her products was a specialized, bactericidal mouthwash that was positioned at dentists and dental hygienists to be recommended to their patients. It was very successful in this niche, with very high gross margins, limited advertising expenditures, but only seven percent share of the total mouthwash market. Hernandez wanted to reposition this brand into the broader consumer market.

She felt that with the professional endorsements, the highly appealing characteristics of the product and with the right kind of approach she could drive market share up to the 20 percent to 25 percent range.

The issue was that Vista-Sci already had a mouthwash brand with 35 percent share of market, positioned against this broader market. "No problem," said Hernandez; "Sure we'll cannibalize some of that market share but, overall, we'll boost our corporate market share by 10 or so share points." And she'd commissioned the research to support her point. In comparison tests and conjoint analysis studies, she had built the case for doing it. It convinced pretty well everyone . . . except the product manager of the other, consumer-oriented mouthwash brand. He was not, and never would be, convinced. Discussions had gotten pretty heated before Hernandez had been told to back off. Still, every chance she got, she made the point that they could be doing better in the mouthwash category if the company had accepted her approach.

There were other sources of friction. The company used a "full-costing" approach to making product "go/no-go" launch decisions; Hernandez—who, at that time had been studying for her MBA at a local university in the evenings[1]—had become convinced that they were making bad decisions by following this approach, that what they should really do was use a marginal-contribution approach. So, when making her proposal, that's how she did it. Routinely, the finance department sent back her analysis and told her to do it "the right way." She did . . . and it was "her" way! Of course, in the end, she did it their way because she wanted to get her projects approved. But she also wanted to make her point. "Eventually," she said, "they'll change. Sure I make a few waves, but if you don't, then people will keep on doing the same old things in the same old ways. I think I know how hard I can push and when to back off."

Unlike some of the product managers, Hernandez seemed to be liked and respected by all her peers. When there was hard work to be done and they needed help, she pitched in. When it was time to relax and party . . . Hernandez usually got the party organized, was the first to arrive and the last to leave. When others had ideas, she gave credit to them and she was reluctant to claim credit for her own initiatives. Had there been a vote for the "most popular product manager in the company" among both the product managers and sales force, she'd have won hands-down. To some extent, there was such a vote. Each year, all the product and assistant product managers in the company (not just the pharmaceutical division) held a "copy competition" where they presented their advertising strategies and creative work. Hernandez had won this competition in three of the last four years, partly due to the quality of the advertising she and her advertising agencies developed and partly because of the overall respect with which she was held by her peers.

Her official performance record was outstanding. Vista-Sci had a disciplined multi-factor scorecard approach to assessing performance and, on every measure, Hernandez had received top scores and maximum bonus. Sales of her products were booming, profit margins were on or above stretch targets, she got great scores from sales force reports on her effectiveness in working with them, her advertising agencies put their best creative people on her product assignments and the corporate marketing research manager reported that she framed her research issues better than anyone else in the company. It was, overall, a very positive picture.

Managers at Hernandez's level received a lot of unofficial feedback but also underwent an annual performance appraisal. Based on the competencies associated with the role, each product manager was given an overall rating that ranged from Unsatisfactory (1) through Needs Improvement (2), Satisfactory (3), Good (4), to Outstanding (5). These ratings determined the personal component of the annual bonus with Unsatisfactory receiving zero bonus and Outstanding receiving a bonus that was 50 percent of base salary. The difference between Good and Outstanding was 15 percent, a significant amount. More important, getting an Outstanding

rating was really considered the key to being considered for promotion at the next available opportunity.

Allun Jones could only remember one time during Hernandez's career at Vista-Sci when her performance had been an issue. About three years ago, Hernandez had come to see him one day, visibly distressed. Her mother had been diagnosed with Alzheimer's disease about a year ago—she had not mentioned this to Jones—and now appeared to be deteriorating fairly quickly.

Allun—I'm going to have to spend more time with her, especially until we can figure out what to do. You know, some of the weekend work and late nights will just have to be spent with my family— the other one, not the Vista-Sci one! And I think that I'll definitely use up my accumulated vacation this year and, maybe, even apply for a leave of absence for a couple of months.

They had discussed her workload and agreed that she could assign a couple of her minor brands to others and also put more responsibility on her product supervisors—she had two people whom she had trained really well and Jones felt that they could pick up any slack caused by Jamie backing off a little and even coping with a leave of absence for a couple of months.

There was one additional assignment that Jones needed completed during that year. For some time, he had been thinking of re-shuffling the brand allocations among the various product managers since he felt that some were relatively lightly loaded while others seemed overloaded. He also thought that they might be able to reduce the product management staff by at least one or two product managers (of the total of seven) and, perhaps, four or five of assistant product managers. There was some considerable pressure for him to do so; corporate was asking for a steady five percent annual increase in "people productivity" and the marketing department had been lagging this for several years.

Following several meetings, Jones had suggested to Hernandez that she interview the current product managers and their assistants, as well as others inside and outside the company with whom they worked, and then make her recommendations. After a month, he had met with her to review progress; she had not yet started the interviews but promised to do so "within the next few weeks." After another couple of months had gone by, Jones raised it in a regular monthly meeting. Hernandez reported that she had started interviews but had not yet formed any opinions about reorganization. Soon afterwards, Hernandez' mother's condition had deteriorated further and she took six weeks accumulated vacation time followed by a three-month leave of absence. At least that's what she was supposed to do. Actually, she called in fairly frequently and stayed in touch with her product supervisors on a pretty regular basis. Toward the end of this period she had made the difficult decision to place her mother in a nursing home.

On her return to work, full-time, Jones had spoken to her about the reorganization project:

> Jamie, the reorganization project is way, way behind schedule. And it forms 30 percent of your official goals for this year. . . . It could affect your bonus calculation this year. What's the problem?

Hernandez responded

> Well, I've spoken to several of the people—just informal discussions really—but I can't honestly say that I can see any areas where people seemed under worked or there seems to be any slack. We're doing real well in sales and I think that our advertising and research are better than ever. But I'll get some more focus on it and get back to you next month.

She didn't and, what's more, her annual performance rating had been due within the next couple of weeks. "What rating should I give her?" Jones had wondered. "If I downgrade her from Outstanding to Good, it would cost her quite a lot in bonus and might affect her prospects for promotion." Jones also knew that it would be hard to justify the downgrade to his boss, the CEO, who thought very highly of Hernandez. He had talked it over with the vice-president, human resources. "Be careful" he'd said. "Jamie is pretty

valuable to us and we'd hate to get her upset over this—after all, it was a different type of assignment . . . not her usual work. And there was her family problems . . . you'd expect some things to be done less than perfectly."

In the end, Jones had decided to ignore the unfinished project and had given Hernandez an "Outstanding" rating. He also decided, based in his own analysis, to downsize the product management department by five people. It was not a popular choice and certainly disrupted the "team" environment for a while but he felt that it needed to be done.

With Hernandez' mother settled into a good nursing home, things returned to normal in the Vista-Sci product management group. Hernandez was back to her normal self, doing her usual, outstanding job.

MICHAEL UPSHAW

"When it comes to personality," Jones observed, "you couldn't have a greater difference than between Jamie Hernandez and Michael Upshaw. Nor, for that matter, could you have people with different backgrounds."

Michael Upshaw had been brought up in the Midwestern United States, the son of a small-town college professor and a homemaker. He had been educated at a local high school where he'd been active in military cadets through the Reserve Officers Training Corps (ROTC), in both high school and college and, with the support of his local congressman, had won a place at West Point, the U.S. Army College. He'd ranked in the top third of his class, graduated as an army engineer, and then served three years in the army, two of them in Vietnam attached to a front-line infantry regiment where he had been slightly wounded and had eventually been honorably discharged.

Upshaw spoke little about his military service. In fact, he spoke little about himself at all. After the military, he had won a scholarship to a prestigious business school, graduating—again in the top third of his class—with an MBA and not a great deal of sense about what he wanted to do with the rest of his life.

He had been recruited by Vista-Sci while he was at business school and moved into the company in an assistant product manager role. Over the next three years Upshaw had worked for three different product managers as well as serving on a couple of special task forces, one working on a department-wide forecasting system and the other on a project for the chairman of Vista-Sci International, scoping out possibilities for site location of the international division's world headquarters. He had received good or outstanding appraisals after all of these assignments. Invariably these reviews singled out his thoughtful, disciplined approach to all the tasks he undertook. He took direction extremely well but, when he was left on his own, demonstrated reasonable initiative and resourcefulness. He blended in well with any team on which he was placed, pulled his weight on the team and was thought of as a good colleague by those who worked with him.

Promoted to product manager about five years ago, Upshaw had managed his products with disciplined thoroughness. Never an "ideas man" himself, he nevertheless was open to ideas from others, listened carefully to them and usually made good choices. His documentation of everything—from marketing plans to minutes of packaging meetings—was extensive and accurate.

Allun Jones made a point of discussing the performance and development needs of all of his staff with people with whom they frequently interacted. In reviewing his product managers' performance with John Middlestadt, the account supervisor at one of his advertising agencies, John had said:

> I'm always impressed with how well-prepared Mike (Upshaw) is. His creative briefs are first rate and, largely because of that, his projects run very smoothly. Come to think of it, I don't think that I can recall a single case where the budget ran over the forecasted amount or even when a project was delayed. No—Michael operates with military precision!

The other thing that helps him is his choice of people to work with. Some of your people attract the more way-out, unorthodox members of our creative staff. Jamie, for instance—now she's always pushing for unusual, breakthrough creative ideas for print and television advertising and even some creative media buy packages . . . she was one of the first into cable bundles . . . turned out to be a great buy. Michael, on the other hand. . . . well, he assembles a good team and then gets really good performance from them. It's a more "controlled" creative product . . . but it's good.

Allun had pushed the account supervisor: "I hear you. But tell me, honestly, if you had to assemble an absolutely first class creative team headed by a strong marketing person, would you go for Mike?" There was a long pause before John answered:

> I'm not sure. I know that I'd sleep well at night if I had Mike running the team. There would be no surprises and a pretty good product in the end. But I suspect that someone like Jamie would walk away with the awards for the best advertising campaign more often than Allun. Of course, you'd put a lot more work into the project as well . . . I mean, she'd need more supervision than Michael.

Jones had met several times with Michael Upshaw over the last two years to discuss his career aspirations. Unlike most other members of his Marketing staff, Michael had seldom asked about promotion or what it took to get ahead. He'd asked him about this once, suggesting almost that maybe Michael lacked some ambition. His response had been, characteristically cool:

> I suppose that I get that from having been in the military. You get used to having to put time in working on lower level jobs, some of which aren't all that exciting. I guess that you get used to just doing a good job and hoping and expecting that someone will notice and give you an opportunity to take on bigger challenges and responsibilities. I think that the same thing happens in business—not much point in putting myself forward if the job performance is not there. . . . I just let the performance speak for itself.

Allun Jones had also noticed that Michael did not seem to attract high potential junior staff the same way that others, including Jamie, did. While the people that he managed always spoke well of him, and believed that they had benefited from his teaching and coaching, he didn't seem to have the same magnetism as Jamie. When she went on campus recruiting trips and made presentations, there were crowds of students who came up to her asking questions and trying to impress her; when Michael did recruiting trips the responses were less enthusiastic—people listened politely but did not seem as eager to engage him in discussion.

People who worked for Michael found him to be a good boss—considerate, caring, willing to spend time with them. Sometimes Allun wondered if they had it a little too good—he remembered always feeling stretched and on the edge of having too much to do in too short a time when he had been a junior product manager or supervisor. Maybe Michael's superior organizing skills meant that his people had an easier time of it or maybe he just didn't stretch his people far enough.

Jones summarized:

He's good. Sometimes he's very good. But he's not, you know, exciting! He would be a good, safe appointment as vice-president, product management.

He'd make the routine decisions himself and probably come to me to talk through the tough ones. But I'm not convinced that we'd get any breakthroughs with Michael. At best, he'd do as good a job as I've been doing after he got some more experience.

THE DECISION

There were many thoughts on Allun Jones's mind as he drove home that night, not all of them making him feel comfortable.

Michael or Jamie? Which one would be best for the job; how would each react if the other got it . . . and did that really matter? How would the decision be viewed by the other product managers and assistant product managers at Vista-Sci, both in the pharmaceutical and other divisions?

He was also conscious of the fact that this was the first major "people" decision that he would be making in his new role. How this worked out may well determine his own future with Vista-Sci.

NOTE

1. She completed her MBA in three years of evening and weekend study.

IMMUNITY FROM IMPLOSION

Building Smart Leadership

Prepared by Sydney Finkelstein and Eric M. Jackson

At the top of every "smart organization" is "smart leadership," vital, open-minded leaders. Moreover, these leaders and their organizations have an early warning system that enables them to remain "smart," and ahead of their competitors. These authors, who have conducted extensive research on different types of "smart leaders," describe the eight key skill sets that all "smart leaders" have.

Have you taken the necessary steps to help maintain and grow your organization's preeminent market position? At some point, the officers and directors of Morgan Stanley, MassMutual, WorldCom, and Enron would have all answered "yes" to this question. All these firms had dominant market positions and were led by officers and directors with impeccable credentials. Over the last several years, our research has uncovered the key differences between these successful companies *that eventually failed in some manner and other very successful companies that have been able to retain and grow their market dominance.* We call the latter, "SMART Organizations," and they regularly track and improve in the Three Pillar areas of SMART Leadership, SMART Strategy, and SMART Process. In this article, we describe SMART Leadership and how to make it blossom in your organization.

INTRODUCTION

At the beginning of 2005, Morgan Stanley Lead Director Miles Marsh thought that the firm's performance was on-track. "Performance had turned up," he said, as earnings per share rose 18% in 2004 and the firm was #1 in stock underwriting. He and his fellow directors would no doubt have been surprised to learn that, just six months later, Chief Executive Philip Purcell would be ignominiously forced to resign his post, thus putting a cloud over the entire board.

It turned out that—despite several positive financial indicators—there were many warning signs that Morgan Stanley was headed for trouble. These signs went unheeded. The public and private battles, high-level executive turnover, and demoralized culture were not inevitable; it was through lack of attention that they became so.

In our research we have found that Morgan Stanley is not the first—nor likely will it be the last—highly successful organization that sowed the seeds of its own demise. Based on six years of research that went into the writing of *Why Smart Executives Fail*, as well as more recent research, we have identified the key organizational patterns that differentiate high-performance organizations like Morgan Stanley that fail in large part because of their success (what we call "Not-so-Smart Organizations") from other successful companies that have been able to maintain and grow their market dominance.

We call the latter, "SMART Organizations," and, in this article, we outline the key factors that can help you determine whether or not you are building an organization with "SMART Leadership."

THE "SMART ORGANIZATION" DEFINED

We have all seen successful organizations that have their day in the sun. Earnings are up, maybe there's a hot television show driving ad revenues, or there's a category-killer product that is generating a lot of buzz. The CEOs in these organizations are typically splashed across the covers of major business magazines, and ghost-written books often appear outlining the reasons why they have been successful. Alas, in many of these situations, the excitement does not endure. There are a couple of missed quarters or new competitors emerge with an even more interesting gizmo. Clothing retailer Mossimo and specialty footwear maker LA Gear come to mind. Where is the Second Act for these organizations?

For other one-time successful organizations, the Second Act is more of a slow bleed. They don't immediately head into bankruptcy. Rather these one-time giants quietly fade into market irrelevance, ceding market share and often profitability. Some of these firms are able to shake off the rust (look at Motorola's comeback under Ed Zander's leadership), while others must accept being acquired by competitors they used to dwarf in prestige and profits (think of Rubbermaid's acquisition by Newell). We call these organizations that struggle to maintain their market pre-eminence "Not-so-Smart Organizations," as their failures are almost always within their control. *Why Smart Executives Fail* outlines these major causes of corporate failure.

However, in our research leading up to and since the publication of the book, we noticed that there appeared to be other successful organizations that *were* able to keep churning out steady and consistent growth, quarter after quarter and year after year. Why? As we began to look closer at what was going on in these two types of organizations at the board level, at the top management team level, and across the entire organization, we noticed some compelling differences. For example, while the "Not-so-Smart Organizations" seemed almost consumed by their financial performance, other organizations paid close attention to their own financial indicators and remained carefully attuned to other key organizational factors as well. (Founder and CEO An Wang of Wang Labs, used to carry a note card displaying Wang Labs' stock performance versus IBM's.) Because these organizations all maintained and grew their market dominance we refer to them as "Smart Organizations."

Again and again, the same kinds of organizational factors appeared across these firms. There are three types of such firms, so we call them the Three Pillars of a "Smart Organization:" Smart Leadership, Smart Strategy, and Smart Process. Examples of "Smart Organizations" in our study included Four Seasons Hotels & Resorts under Isadore Sharp, Dell under Michael Dell and now Kevin Rollins, Gucci Group under new head Robert Polet, and the world's largest retailer, Wal-Mart Stores under Lee Scott. According to our research, it's only through paying attention to each of these "Three Pillars" that an organization can help ensure that it will continue to execute the necessary high-performance financial indicators that all boards, top management

team, investors, and analysts want to see. In the remainder of this article, we describe the role of the first of these pillars: Smart Leadership.

Smart Leadership

The first commonality that we found in Smart Organizations was their "Smart Leadership" at the Executive Team and Board levels. The "smart" label doesn't reflect their collective IQ (although all would have scored highly). Instead, what made their teams and boards "smart" was a combination of certain individual skill sets that each officer and director possessed. None of these organizations had "Imperial CEOs" with thousands of faceless followers. Instead, they had teams, boards, and leaders throughout the organization who were the stars of the show. These officers and directors had skill sets, knowledge, attitudes and behaviors that were in place in "Smart Organizations" but were conspicuously absent in successful companies that later headed towards failure.

Skill-Set #1: Breeding "Proactive Paranoia"

In "Smart Organizations," the executives and directors believed that their market leadership

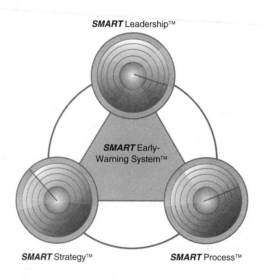

Exhibit 1   The Three Pillars of a "Smart Organization"

Not-So-Smart Organization Officer/Director Skill-Sets:	"SMART Organization" Officer/Director Skill-Sets:
Narcissistic Self-Image	Breeding "Proactive Paranoia"
Blurring Between Leader & Organizational Interests	Instilling "We Work for the Shareholders" Mentality Throughout Organization
Leader Has "All the Answers"	Executive Team & Board Has the Answers
Demanding 100% Support "Groupthink"	Ensuring There Isn't Top Team
Obsessed With Image	Projecting Authentic Leadership
Disregarding Major Obstacles	Facing Reality—No Matter if Good or Bad
Unwillingness to Learn	Desire to Learn From Mistakes
Deferring to Others for Decision Making Personal Accountability Bias	

was only a quarter away from slipping from their grasp. They maintained a healthy respect for all their competitors and never got too caught up in their success. Wal-Mart execs religiously track Target's and other retailers' moves, often visiting their stores at least once a month. By contrast, "Not-so-Smart Organizations" cavalierly disregarded the potential threat of competitors. Instead, they saw their market leadership as permanent and, perhaps because of this, often began spending lavishly on themselves and their corporate offices. Wal-Mart still requires all of its senior executives to share hotel rooms on corporate trips. And, if you have been to their Bentonville Home Office, you know that they don't waste an inch of space, stuffing cubicles together as tightly as they stuff product on Wal-Mart floor space. Sam Walton would be proud.

Skill-Set #2: "We Work for the Shareholders" Mentality

None of the "Smart Organization" officers and directors we studied breathed a whiff of entitlement—even when they founded the company. They didn't believe the company owed them anything. They saw it as a privilege to work for the organization and felt a deep responsibility to the shareholders (or stakeholders in the case of non-profits). They were very circumspect in spending company resources. By contrast, executives at "Not-so-Smart Organizations" often blurred the lines between their personal interests and the corporate interests. Robert J. O'Connell, CEO of MassMutual Financial Group, was recently dismissed after the board learned that the top female executive with whom he had had an office affair had overseen a $30MM padding of his supplemental retirement account and bought a Florida condominium from the company at a discounted price.

Skill-Set #3: The Executive Team and Board Have the Answers, Not Just the CEO

Instead of providing all the answers, CEOs at "Smart Organizations" consult frequently with members of their team and board. This is not to say that the CEOs still do not play a lead role in charting strategy. However, each officer and director is comfortable speaking up and in challenging the CEO's opinion. And, as important, the CEO knows that he/she doesn't have all the answers. Michael Dell puts it this way: "To assume that a CEO knows every single thing about every aspect of a company . . . I mean you take a guy like Jeff Immelt. Jeff's a great guy, a really smart guy. Can he know every single thing about all aspects of GE's business? Sorry. It ain't gonna happen. So, I think you got to have a system of processes and controls, and it's his responsibility, just as it is mine, to sit down with the teams on a regular basis and understand. 'Well, let's talk about your business, what are you doing, what's the control environment?' We rely on our teams to give us assurances." Together, the brainstorming and debate lead to better decisions. In "Not-so-Smart Organizations," you are much more likely to find the prototypical "Imperial CEO" providing the answers and believing that they are absolutely right.

Skill-Set #4: Preventing Groupthink

"Smart Organizations" are never cults, where people are too afraid to speak up. You never hear the phrase, "you're either with us or against us." And, you certainly do not find key dissenters forced out of the organization. "Smart Organizations" prevent "groupthink" from setting in at the Top Team or Board levels. Michael Dell is famous for asking at meetings, "What could go wrong? What are we not thinking of?" In "Not-so-Smart Organizations," CEOs "take out" those who are not being supportive. In the case of Philip Purcell at Morgan Stanley, he simply eliminated the jobs of two key Morgan executives (Vikram Pandit and John Havens) who he saw as not being on his side when outsiders started to complain about Purcell's performance.

Skill-Set #5: Projecting Authentic Leadership

We found that leaders at "Smart Organizations" weren't particularly fussed about how they or their organizations came across to others. It was much more important that they were clear on their own set of values and what their organizations

stood for. Whether others "got that" or not was inconsequential to them. As a result, they came across as authentic. Examples include Herb Kelleher at Southwest, Sam Walton at Wal-Mart, and—a more current case—Brian Roberts at Comcast. "Not-so-Smart organizations'" leaders were very conscious of their own and their organizations' image in the media. Great time, energy, and resources were spent crafting just the right media image. In some cases (think Carly Fiorina at HP), the effort probably ended up doing more harm than good.

Skill-Set #6: Facing Reality

The officers and directors from "Smart Organizations" had no trouble seeing themselves and their organizations for what they were at that moment. Even if they were already #1 in their market, they knew their weaknesses as well as their competitors' key strengths. An example of wanting to stay ahead of the curve is Robert Polet, new Chief Executive at Gucci Group. He recently took the unprecedented step of applying standard business practices (such as focus groups, hiring outside consultants, and using industry benchmarks to increase the rate of inventory turnover in their stores) to the formerly highly cloistered organization that structured itself around the vision of its former creative head, Tom Ford. And, although some longtime employees reacted to Polet's 'facing reality' tools "as if he'd used foul language," Gucci Group's sales are up 13% in the last quarter. By contrast, leaders at "Not-so-Smart Organizations" saw themselves as dominating their environments. One emerging leader who feared his organization had an over-inflated sense of how dominant they were in their market expressed his concerns this way, "we are a kitten, who looks in the mirror and sees a lion."

Skill-Set #7: Desire to Learn From Mistakes

Most organizations (and people) typically have a hard time admitting they have made mistakes. In fact, psychologists have demonstrated how cognitive biases often push people to persist in supporting bad decisions—even when we know logically that they do not make sense (throwing good money after bad). That's why most organizations' executives and directors don't want to hear about organizational mistakes. They want to hear success stories and see the financial indicators heading in the right direction. Sometimes, admitting a mistake is tantamount to an executive wearing the Scarlet Letter in front of the group. Yet, "Smart Organizations" don't run from mistakes; they embrace them. They understand that their future competitive advantage lies in their accurately understanding why a current venture or division or product has failed. And then taking corrective actions. In the case of Wal-Mart, although they were highly successful in the United States, some of their initial international forays were not as successful. Their mistake? Applying the U.S. store model, exactly as is, to these new markets. Their push into Argentina was especially painful. Yet, they learned from this experience in time to prepare for entering China, where Wal-Mart offers such local delicacies as barbecued pigeons, live frogs, and snakes of purported higher quality than that available outside the store at the local street market.

Skill-Set #8: Personal Accountability

Beyond the skill-sets listed above, there was one more which was found all too frequently among officers and directors in the "Smart Organizations" we examined: Personal Accountability. These men and women took their roles and responsibilities very seriously. They did not accept simple answers to complex questions.

They would push to further understand an organizational breakdown, or question an already successful process or division. Isadore Sharp, Chairman & CEO of Four Seasons Hotels and Resorts, has been responsible for driving this aspect of the firm's culture within its executives and employees for the last 35 years. One concept that epitomizes personal accountability has been etched into the culture as "The Golden Rule." Interviewed for this article, he explained the importance of this skill-set, and how it filters up to the Four Seasons' officers and directors: "The Golden Rule" is at the heart of our operating principles, and is part of every aspect of our business. Hotel staff are empowered to serve guests by making instant decisions, guided by the idea that one should treat others as one would be treated. Executives are similarly empowered, and made aware that with empowerment comes responsibility. In that way, we are all personally accountable for our role in the company's success.

CONCLUSION

To have Smart Leadership in your organization—and take the first steps towards Building a "Smart Organization"—you must first understand its components, which we have outlined in this article. The 8 key skill-sets must be assessed on a regular basis to make sure that leadership retains its vitality and open-mindedness that characterizes smart organizations and is so often the downfall of the not-so-smart organizations. It is only through careful attention to an early warning system that smart leaders and smart organizations can remain smart.

8 Skill-sets of "Not-so-Smart" Leaders:	How Morgan Stanley Fared:
Narcissistic Self-Image	Overdone executive offices on 39th floor
Blurring Between Leader & Organizational Interests	Purcell's pay had to match or exceed those at Morgan competitors—apart from Morgan's performance
Leader Has "All the Answers"	Purcell didn't consult with employees or clients
Demanding 100% Support	Those not onside with Purcell were forced out
Obsessed With Image	Purcell swept internal gripes under rug
Unwillingness to Learn	Two cultures of Morgan and Discover never were integrated even after 8 Years
Disregarding Major Obstacles	Purcell's response to criticism: "We just need to get out of the press"
Deferring to Others for Decision Making	Board calls internal complaints against Purcell "personal," based on "soft issues," and avoids discussion

Appendix A   Morgan Stanley vs. the 8 Skill-sets of "Not-so-Smart" Leaders[1]

3

LEADERSHIP SKILLS APPROACH

Some leaders are very charismatic, some are very quiet, but they always do three things very well. First, they have the ability to observe and speak what is on people's minds. Second, when they speak, others listen and say, "Yes, I believe that's the right thing to do" and the leader would align various constituencies without upsetting any of them. Third, people would feel that they are motivated, inspired, and doing things not because that is what the rule book says or because it has to be done. They're doing it because they want to do it.

—C. K. Chow[1]

In a manner similar to the trait approach, the skills approach to leadership is a leader-centered perspective. But the two approaches are different in that in the trait approach, we focused on personality traits that are considered inherent and relatively stable from birth, whereas in this chapter, we focus on a person's "skills and abilities that can be learned and developed" (Northouse, 2007). Skills suggest what leaders can achieve, whereas traits suggest who they are based on their intrinsic characteristics. The skills approach implies that skills, knowledge, and abilities are required for a leader to be effective. In this chapter, we focus on two studies that defined the skills approach: Katz (1974) and Mumford, Zaccaro, Harding, Jacobs, and Fleishman (2000).

Katz's Three-Skills Approach

Katz's (1974) seminal article on the skills approach to leadership suggested that leadership (i.e., effective administration) is based on three skills: technical, human, and conceptual.

Technical Skills

Technical skill is proficiency, based on specific knowledge, in a particular area of work. To have technical skills means that a person is competent and knowledgeable with respect to the activities specific to an organization, the organization's rules and standard operating procedures, and the organization's products and services (Katz, 1974; Yukl, 2006).

Technical skill is most important at supervisory levels of management, less important for middle managers, and least important for top managers such as CEOs and senior managers. Finally, technical skill is proficiency in working with *things*.

Interpersonal Skills

Contrary in contrast to technical skills, interpersonal skills are proficiency in working with *people* based on a person's knowledge about *people* and how they behave, how they operate in groups, how to communicate effectively with them, and their motives, attitudes, and feelings. They are the skills required to effectively influence superiors, peers, and subordinates in the achievement of organizational goals. These skills enable a leader to influence team or group members to work together to accomplish organizational goals and objectives. Human skill proficiency means that leaders know their thoughts on different issues and, simultaneously, become cognizant of the thoughts of others. Consequently, leaders with higher levels of interpersonal skills are better able to adapt their own ideas to other people's ideas, especially when this will aid in achieving organizational goals more quickly and efficiently. These leaders are more sensitive and empathetic to what motivates others, create an atmosphere of trust for their followers, and take others' needs and motivations into account when deciding what to do to achieve organizational goals. Interpersonal skills are required at all three levels of management: supervisory, middle management, and senior management (Katz, 1974; Yukl, 2006).

Conceptual Skills

Conceptual skills allow you to think through and work with ideas. Leaders with higher levels of conceptual skills are good at thinking through the ideas that form an organization and its vision for the future, expressing these ideas in verbal and written forms, and understanding and expressing the economic principles underlying their organization's effectiveness. These leaders are comfortable asking "what if" or hypothetical questions and working with abstract ideas. Conceptual skills allow leaders to give abstract ideas meaning and to make sense of abstract ideas for their superiors, peers, and subordinates. This skill is most important for top managers, less important for middle managers, and least important for supervisory managers (Northouse, 2007). I would offer one caveat. While conceptual skills are less important at lower levels of management, to be promoted to higher levels of management, it is important to develop and demonstrate this skill at all levels of management (Yukl, 2006). It is a skill than can be learned; consequently, I encourage you to take advantage of every opportunity to develop and the ability to learn conceptually.

Leadership Skills Model

This approach suggests that leadership is not just the purview of a few people born with traits that make them effective leaders. The skills approach implies that many people have leadership potential, and if they can learn from their experiences, they can become more effective leaders. This means involvement with activities and/or exposure to people and events leading to an increase in skills, knowledge, and abilities. This model is different from a "what leaders do" approach and focuses on capabilities that make leaders effective (Mumford, Zaccaro, Harding, et al., 2000; Northouse, 2007). The leadership skills approach by Mumford, Zaccaro, Harding, et al. (2000) has five elements: individual attributes, competencies, leadership outcomes, career experiences, and environmental influences.

Competencies are the most important element—the "kingpin"—in this model. Competencies lead to leadership outcomes but themselves are affected by a leader's individual attributes. In addition, the impact of leaders' attributes on leaders' competencies and leaders' competencies on outcomes is dependent on career experiences and environmental influences. In the next few paragraphs, I describe competencies, how attributes affect competencies, and how competencies affect leadership outcomes, and I briefly discuss the impact of career experiences on attributes and competencies and the impact of environmental influences on attributes, competencies, and outcomes.

Leader Competencies

Mumford, Zaccaro, Harding, et al. (2000) identified three competencies that result in effective leadership: problem solving, social judgment, and knowledge. These three work together and separately to affect outcomes.

Problem-Solving Skills. These are creative abilities that leaders bring to unique, vague, "hard to get a handle on" organizational problems. These skills include the following: defining problems and issues that are important, accumulating information related to the problem/issue, developing new ways to comprehend each problem/issue, and developing unique, first-of-its-kind alternatives for solving the problems/issues. Problem-solving skills operate in the context of an organization and its environment and require that leaders be aware of their own capacities and challenges relative to the problem/issue and the organizational context (Mumford, Zaccaro, Connelly, & Marks, 2000). The solutions or alternatives developed to solve problems and issues require that leaders be conscious of the time required to develop and execute solutions—whether the solutions are achieving short-term and/or long-term objectives, whether these objectives are organizational or personal, and the external context such as the industry, national, and international environments (Mumford, Zaccaro, Harding, et al., 2000).

Social Judgment Skills. These are skills that enable leaders to comprehend people and the social systems within which they work, play, and have a social life (e.g., friends and family) (Zaccaro, Mumford, Connelly, Marks, & Gilbert, 2000). Social judgment skills facilitate working with others to lead change, solve problems, and make sense of issues. Mumford and colleagues (Mumford, Zaccaro, Harding, et al., 2000) outlined four elements important to social judgment skills: perspective taking, social perceptiveness, behavioral flexibility, and social performance.

Perspective taking is sensitivity to others' objectives and perspective; it is an empathic perspective to solving problems, and it means that leaders actively seek out knowledge regarding people, their organization's social fabric, and how these two very important areas of knowledge intersect with each other.

Whereas perspective taking is associated with others' attitudes, *social perceptiveness* is about leaders knowing what people will do when confronted with proposed changes. *Behavioral flexibility* means being able to change what one does when confronted with others' attitudes and intended actions based on knowledge gained through perspective taking and social perceptiveness, respectively. Leaders with behavioral flexibility understand that there are many different paths to achieving change and the goals and objectives associated with change.

Social performance means being skilled in several leadership competencies. Some of these are abilities in persuading and communicating in order to convey one's own vision to others in the organization, abilities in mediation that enable the leader to mediate interpersonal conflict related to change and to lessen resistance to change, and abilities in coaching and mentoring by giving subordinates support and direction as they work to achieve organizational objectives and goals.

To summarize, Northouse (2007) stated that

> social judgment skills are about being sensitive to how your ideas fit in with others. Can you understand others and their unique needs and motivations? Are you flexible and can you adapt your own ideas to others? Last, can you work with others even when there are resistance and change? Social judgment skills are the people skills required to advance change in an organization.

Knowledge. Knowledge is the gathering of information and the development of mental structures to organize that information in a meaningful way. These mental structures are called schema, which means a diagrammatic representation or depiction. Knowledgeable leaders have more highly developed and complex schemata that they use to collect and organize data. Knowledge is linked to a leader's problem-solving skills. More knowledgeable leaders are able to consider complex organizational issues and to develop alternative and appropriate strategies for change. Knowledge allows leaders to use prior incidents to constructively plan for and change the future.

Individual Attributes

Mumford and his colleagues (e.g., Mumford, Zaccaro, Harding, et al., 2000) identified four attributes that affect the three leader competencies (problem-solving skills, social judgment skills, and knowledge) and, through these competencies, leader performance.

General Cognitive Ability. Think "perceptual processing, information processing, general reasoning skills, creative and divergent thinking capacities, and memory skills" (Northouse, 2007). This is a brief description of general cognitive ability. This type of intelligence grows as we age to early adulthood but declines as we grow older. General cognitive ability positively affects a leader's ability to acquire knowledge and complex problem-solving skills (Northouse, 2007).

Crystallized Cognitive Ability. Think "intelligence that develops because of experience." As we age and gain more experience, we acquire intelligence—this is crystallized cognitive ability. This type of intelligence remains relatively consistent and generally does not diminish as we age. As our crystallized cognitive ability increases, it positively affects our leadership potential by increasing our social judgment skills, conceptual ability, and problem-solving skills.

Motivation. Motivation affects leadership competencies in several ways. We discuss three ways in which motivation helps in the development of leadership competencies. First, a person must want to lead—there must be a willingness to engage in solving complex organizational issues and problems. Second, leaders must be willing to exert influence—to be willing to be dominant within a group of people. Finally, the leader must be willing to advance the "social good" of the organization (Northouse, 2007; Yukl, 2006).

Personality. This is the fourth attribute positively linked to leadership competencies. Northouse (2007) gives three examples of personality that affect how motivated leaders are to resolve organizational issues and problems. They are tolerance for ambiguity, openness, and curiosity. Leaders with confidence and adaptability may be helpful in situations of conflict. The skills model suggests that personality traits that aid in developing leader competencies lead to better leader performance (Mumford, Zaccaro, Harding, et al., 2000).

Leadership Outcomes

Individual attributes lead to leader competencies, which lead to leadership outcomes. It is noteworthy that without the development of leader competencies, individual attributes may have little effect on leadership outcomes. This reminds us that the leadership competencies element is the "kingpin" component of the leadership skills model. We discuss two leadership outcomes: effective problem solving and leader performance.

Effective Problem Solving. Mumford and his colleagues (e.g., Mumford, Zaccaro, Harding, et al., 2000) developed the skills model to explain variation in the ability of leaders to solve problems—this makes it a capability model. An effective problem solver develops unique, original, and high-quality solutions to issues and problems. Leaders with higher levels of competencies will be more effective problem solvers.

Performance. This outcome refers to the individual leader's job performance—how well he or she has performed. This is usually evaluated by objective external measures. Better performance leads to better evaluations. Leaders whose performance is better will receive better annual evaluations, larger merit pay increases, and recognition as better leaders. Effective problem solving and leader performance are linked, even though they are separate ways of measuring leadership outcomes.

Career Experiences

Career experiences affect both individual attributes and leadership competencies. We believe that some career assignments may develop a leader's motivation to be a better problem solver or be better at interacting with people. These career assignments may also help increase a leader's crystallized cognitive ability. Of course, this depends on being in assignments that have been progressively more difficult, with long-term problems and issues, and at increasingly higher levels in the organization's hierarchy. Arguing that leaders develop as a result of their career experiences suggests that leaders can learn leadership abilities and are not necessarily born with leadership abilities (Mumford, Zaccaro, Harding, et al., 2000; Northouse, 2007).

Environmental Influences

These are factors that are external to individual attributes, leader competencies, and career experiences and that affect leadership outcomes along with the effect of individual attributes through leadership competencies. We will not discuss particular external influences. However, we acknowledge that they exist and that they may affect a leader's ability to be an effective problem solver. They are factors that are considered beyond the control of the leader. Of course, leaders who use the environment as an excuse for their poor performance may not be allowed to continue in their leadership role/position if external factors are not the real cause of poor performance. Top-tier leaders use the environment with great caution and only when they are sure it is the real reason.

How Does the Leadership Skills Approach Work?

The leadership skills approach is mainly a descriptive model. This approach allows students of leadership to comprehend what it takes to be an effective leader rather than offering prescriptive ways to be an effective leader.

Katz's (1974) three-skills approach implies that where one is in an organization determines how important each skill is to a leader's effectiveness. The leadership skills approach (Mumford, Zaccaro, Harding, et al., 2000) is a much more complex model of leadership effectiveness that is based on rigorous research conducted on U.S. Army officers who ranged in rank from second lieutenant to colonel. This model suggests that leadership effectiveness as measured by outcomes is a direct result of leader competencies and the indirect result of individual attributes working through leader competencies. Finally, the model contends that career experiences work indirectly to affect leadership outcomes, while environmental influences work indirectly and directly to influence leadership outcomes.

NOTE

1. C. K. Chow is the CEO of MTR Corporation in Hong Kong.

REFERENCES

Chow, C. K. (2006, April 25). Invisible leadership (Part 8 of 8, Ivey Leadership Series). *South China Morning Post,* Business Section.

Katz, R. L. (1974, September/October). Skills of an effective administrator, *Harvard Business Review, 52*(5), 90–102.

Mumford, M. D., Zaccaro, S. J., Connelly, M. S., & Marks, M. A. (2000). Leadership skills: Conclusions and future directions. *The Leadership Quarterly, 11*(1), 155–170.

Mumford, M. D., Zaccaro, S. J., Harding, F. D., Jacobs, T., & Fleishman, E. A. (2000). Leadership skills for a changing world: Solving complex problems. *The Leadership Quarterly, 11*(1), 11–35.

Northouse, P. G. (2007). *Leadership: Theory and practice* (4th ed.). Thousand Oaks, CA: Sage.

Yukl, G. (2006). *Leadership in organizations* (6th ed.). Upper Saddle River, NJ: Pearson-Prentice Hall.

Zaccaro, S. J., Mumford, M. D., Connelly, M. S., Marks, M. A., & Gilbert, J. A. (2000). Assessment of leader problem-solving capabilities. *The Leadership Quarterly, 11*(1), 37–64.

THE CASES

Office Design Partners (Thailand) Ltd.

The managing director and the operations director of the manufacturing arm of a joint venture were experiencing severe difficulties. Transferred 3 years ago, they shared management responsibilities with other expatriates. The workforce was predominately locals. The performance of the company was not meeting expectations of either of the joint venture partners, a problem especially acute for the managing director, whose father was chairman of the partner's holding company. Problems included high turnover, changing roles with the recent departure of a firm originally in a three-way partnership, intercultural communications, and general confusions as to what to do.

Consulting for George Lancia

A young recent graduate has just been hired as a consultant by the tired owner of a small syndicate. His task is to solve the many problems existing within the various businesses, including restaurants, real estate, and a retirement home. The financial situation is severe, and there are several personnel conflicts. He must resolve these problems while effectively managing the owner.

THE READING

Building Leaders at Entry Level: A Leadership Pipeline

Developing managers to be effective at the next level is one of any company's most important tasks, and in this helpful article, the coauthors identify and describe the six steps in building a leadership pipeline to supply the next generation of effective leaders. As the authors write, "The six turns, or passages, in our pipeline are major events in the life of a leader. Grasping what each passage entails, and the challenges involved in making each transition, will help organizations build a leadership pipeline. It will also help build a leadership culture that will enable the organization to respond to changes and threats in the business environment."

OFFICE DESIGN PARTNERS (THAILAND) LTD.

*Prepared by Tom Gleave under the
supervision of Professor Joseph DiStefano*

Copyright © 1998, Ivey Management Services　　　　　　　　　　　　　Version: (A) 1999–02–08

In August 1996, Alex Chen and Robert Chang, the two most senior managers at Office Design (Thailand) Partners Ltd., needed to develop a strategy to ensure that the Thai joint venture company could proceed despite the recent defection of a principal participant. One month earlier, U.S.-based Executive Design Ltd., announced it was withdrawing from the joint venture, claiming that the relationship was impeding its progress in capturing market share in the rapidly emerging economies of Southeast Asia.

Chen and Chang recognized that there were several problems underlying the poor performance of the joint venture. At the top of the list of contributing factors were conflicts among the various people in the partnership. As Chang professed, "We were unsuccessful at localization because our management team was not united."

Given the significant cultural differences among the Thai, Taiwanese and North American managers and non-management employees, Chen and Chang needed to determine how they could best leverage the skills and capabilities of all the firm's people in a manner which would ensure greater harmony in the workplace.

COMPANY BEGINNINGS

Office Design Partners (Thailand) Ltd. (ODP) was an office furniture manufacturing, sales and distribution company that was established in Bangkok, Thailand in 1992. The partnership's roots could be traced to 1991 when three originating firms teamed up to build an office furniture manufacturing facility. These firms were Office Systems of Taiwan, and Metropolitan Finance and Thai Enterprise Group, both based in Thailand. Later in the year, Executive Design Limited, which had previously partnered with Office Systems in establishing joint sales offices in Hong Kong and Singapore, approached the three partners in an effort to secure participation in the manufacturing operation. Executive Design was accepted into the partnership in 1992 resulting in the following ownership arrangement:

Office Systems Ltd.

Office Systems Ltd. (OS) was a subsidiary of the Phoenix Group, a large, privately held, Taiwan-based multinational organization involved in several different lines of business including construction, trading, and the manufacture, sales and distribution of office furniture. The primary product lines offered by OS included steel office furniture, panel-based systems and office automation equipment. The company focused on manufacturing high quality products and prided itself on its ability to offer a wide range of products, while delivering superior customer service. All three of OS's Taiwanese manufacturing facilities were either ISO 9001 or 9002 certified. As well, comprehensive total quality management (TQM) programs were in place in virtually all of the company's programs and processes.

OS originally marketed office copier machines in Taiwan during the mid-1960s. However, in the mid-1970s, the company expanded its operations to include the manufacturing of steel office furniture by entering into a licensing agreement with the Japanese firm, Kyo-A Company Ltd. After firmly establishing itself in the Taiwanese market, a process which took 15 years, OS terminated its licensing arrangement with Kyo-A. OS was able to eventually develop into the largest office furniture manufacturer in Taiwan. By 1995, the company achieved more than 80 percent market share of the high end office furniture market, believed to be valued at approximately US$140 million.

Executive Design Ltd.

Executive Design Ltd. (ED), based out of Ann Arbor, Mich., was one of the world's largest manufacturers of office and institutional furniture. Founded in 1940s, the company had evolved into a full line manufacturer of office furniture with sales breaking the US$1.0 billion level in 1994. ED had over 7,000 employees worldwide involved in manufacturing operations, sales and distribution. The company specialized in manufacturing various office furniture systems, many of which were granted patent and trademark protection, as well as steel and wood desks,

Company Name	Home Base	Share %
Office Systems Ltd.	Taiwan	29.0
Executive Design Ltd.	USA	20.0
Metropolitan Finance	Thailand	25.5
Thai Enterprise Group	Thailand	25.5

credenzas and filing cabinets. It also enjoyed a very good reputation for producing high quality products. It was the first major office furniture manufacturer to become ISO 9001 certified and was also the first recipient of the Michigan Quality Leadership Award. In 1993, ED was included in the "100 Best Managed Companies" list published by *Fortune Magazine.*

The remaining partners of the ODP joint venture were the *Metropolitan Finance* and the *Thai Enterprise Group,* two of the most influential business empires in Thailand. These groups were family-dominated businesses of Overseas Chinese origin and were being run by second generation family members.[1] Each Group had extensive business interests both inside and outside of Thailand. Chatachai Suppapai was the head of the Metropolitan Finance and was considered by many to be Thailand's preeminent business tycoon. The family's 25 percent interest in Metropolitan Finance, Thailand's largest financial institution, was worth an estimated US$1.5 billion. The *Thai Enterprise Group* was involved primarily in shoe and textile production, as well as food-processing. The company held the distinction of being Thailand's No. 1 distributor of consumer goods based upon sales volume.

The inclusion of the Thai business groups served two purposes. Firstly, given Thailand's strong preference for majority local ownership of businesses, the Thai partners' 51 percent interest facilitated foreign investment into the country. Secondly, the broad influence of the two Thai families provided the joint venture company with immediate access to numerous business opportunities within the country. This was viewed as a particularly important factor for ODP since relationship building was an imperative for developing successful businesses in Thailand. Overall, however, there was very little daily involvement by the two Thai partners in the management of the joint venture.

Office Design Partners (Thailand) Ltd.

Office Design Partners (Thailand) Ltd. (ODP) was established in 1992 by the four partners. With an original capitalization valued at 400 million baht (US$16 million), the joint venture was able to direct significant resources towards the development of a 900,000-square foot state-of-the-art manufacturing facility, located in Chonburi province, about 150 kilometres east of the Thai capital. The plant focused on the production of both steel and wood office furniture systems and was expected to service the growing demand for these products in Thailand and its neighboring Southeast Asia nations. The facility became operational in 1992 and was followed by the opening of the company's showroom in May 1993. The 20,000-square foot showroom was the largest of its kind in Thailand and was located in one of the prime commercial districts in Bangkok. Upon its announcement to withdraw its involvement from the joint venture, ED was expected to sell its 20 percent stake to OS, thus raising the Taiwanese interest to 49 percent.

Prior to entering into their partnering relationship in Thailand, OS and ED had teamed up to open sales offices and furniture showrooms in both Hong Kong and Singapore. In 1990, ODP (Hong Kong) opened an office and a 1,100-square metre showroom in the heart of one of the territory's premiere shopping districts, Causeway Bay. The services offered by this office included furniture sales, computer-aided design of office layouts, project management and furniture installations for both the Hong Kong and mainland China markets. Also in 1990, ODP (Singapore) was established through the opening an office and 450-square metre showroom in the Central Business District of Singapore. Both of these offices were intended to pool the design and service strengths of the individual firms as well as provide customers with a wide range of high quality Taiwanese and American made office furniture products. Given ED's impending withdrawal from the joint venture, it was understood that ED would be discontinuing its activities in both the Hong Kong and Singapore sales offices.

COMPANY MANAGEMENT IN THAILAND

The Managing Director of ODP was Alex Chen, the son of the Phoenix Group's founding

Chairman, Ching Hua Chen. Like his father, the younger Chen was born and raised in Taiwan. While growing up he was able to gradually develop an understanding of his father's various businesses. He was educated in Taiwan, where he received his degree in economics, and over several years developed a functional fluency in both spoken and written English. As the son of the chairman, Chen felt significant pressure to ensure that ODP was successful or else risk a loss of face for the family. The second in charge at ODP was Robert Chang, who had also been born and raised in Taiwan. After completing high school in Taiwan, Chang completed his undergraduate business education in California. Chen and Chang, both in their mid-30s, had several years of experience working for OS in Taiwan before being transferred to Thailand in 1991 as part of the original start-up team.

The vast majority of the remaining staff of more than 130 employees at the Bangkok office were Thai. There were only two non-Asian "farang" (foreigners) working in the office. Ken Smith, a unilingual American, was a sales representative responsible for developing corporate accounts, particularly with offices of large multinationals which had recently moved to Thailand. Smith was perceived as being "a cultural bull in a china shop" by his fellow foreigner, Chris Phillips, a Canadian who was fluent in Thai and had lived in Bangkok for more than four years. Given Phillips' understanding of both the language and the culture, he was able to provide sales support to both local and multinational companies.

In the manufacturing facility, most of the managers were Taiwanese. However the majority of the supervisors, technicians and line employees were Thai. ODP went to considerable length to provide all 36 Thai manufacturing technicians with extensive training. This included six months of training on-site at OS production facilities in Taiwan. This way the Thai technicians were able to learn first hand the intricacies of OS's quality management programs and in turn disseminate these techniques to the line employees. ED's role during the start-up phase of the project in Thailand was advisory in nature. As such, ED

sent several site coordinators and project managers to Thailand on a temporary basis to provide initial assistance. No permanent ED personnel were assigned to the factory after the start-up phase was complete. Total employment at the factory eventually exceeded 300 people.

WHY THAILAND?

Thailand was an excellent location for a joint venture because of its strategic central position within Southeast Asia. It provided a natural supply point to Malaysia, Indonesia, Singapore and Brunei, all of which had been experiencing impressive economic growth rates over the past several years. Furthermore, the domestic economy had experienced such strong growth in recent years that the World Bank concluded that Thailand had been the fastest growing economy in the world over the previous decade.

The presence of high import tariffs in the region was an additional reason why both OS and ED decided to enter into a joint venture production facility in Thailand. In 1991, tariffs on imported office furniture were approximately 60 percent of the value of the goods, although this was expected to be reduced to 20 percent by 1996. While ODP recognized that these tariffs were to gradually decrease, the company felt that it could not afford to miss the growing opportunities that were currently available in the Thai marketplace, particularly since competition was only marginal in 1991. However, the longer the company waited, the less it would be able to take advantage of being a first mover in the market, especially with respect to the development of important business relationships.

A further incentive for participating directly in the Thai market was related to the high level of influence that local office designers exerted over their corporate customers. Most local office designers, who were commissioned to design layouts for both Thai and multinational firms, preferred to deal only with local office furniture manufacturers. The designers felt that only local producers could be truly responsive to the needs of the Thai market. Consistent with this view,

ED's motivation for entering into the Thai joint venture stemmed from its commitment to providing localized service on a global basis. For its part, OS was motivated by the access and organizational learning it would gain from partnering with one of the world's dominant office furniture manufacturers. Therefore, the joint venture would allow for the sale and distribution of high quality goods currently being produced by both manufacturing firms, as well as new furniture models considered suitable to the Thai market.

ODP's STRATEGY

The cornerstone of ODP's strategy for developing the Thai market was to place a great deal of focus and energy on offering high quality products coupled with superior customer service. It was ODP's intention to market and service all products that it manufactured using a direct selling approach, something that was relatively new to Thailand. The company expected that up to 70 percent of its sales efforts would be devoted to planning and advisory consultations with prospective clients. The aim was to ensure that clients were provided with solutions to their office operational requirements in the most cost-effective manner. The following extract from a recent ODP promotional package summarized the company's approach:

> New concepts in design and integrated planning will lead the Office Design Partners drive into the Thai market. Requirements for raw material and product quality, as well as new concepts of "service," are a unique benchmark in the Office Design Partners way of doing business. The promotion and elevation of product and service standards beyond the previously accepted Thai standards to higher, generally accepted international standards are considered to be very important by the company.

The company also demonstrated particular emphasis on the need for developing lasting relationships with both customers and business partners, as was evidenced by Chairman Chen's comments:

> Office Design Partners strongly believes that to be successful we must constantly build and maintain trust with our customers and our partners. We believe that such trust is attained through communication, mutual respect and cooperation, and that this relationship is the key to our ongoing success.

THE COMPETITION

The Thai office furniture market was highly concentrated, having only three main players. ODP was the newest entry into the market, which was previously being serviced by Rockworth Ltd. and Modern Form. Rockworth was a locally listed public company which had been in business for more than 15 years. It currently enjoyed an estimated 25 percent share of the market. The company's marketing strategy focused on the production and sales of paneling systems priced at a 30 percent discount relative to ODP. It dedicated modest sums to the promotion of its products by advertising occasionally in newspapers. It had a reputation in the industry as being a "copycat" company and was also known for having poor customer service and unreliable product availability. ODP suspected that Rockworth was suffering from attempts at producing too many different paneling systems simultaneously. This translated into manufacturing inefficiencies and, in turn, caused inventory stock-outs. Rockworth was believed to be targeting the same customer segments as ODP, using price as a key purchase decision criterion.

Modern Form was Thailand's oldest office furniture manufacturing and sales company, having been in operation for 25 years. It was a locally managed public company which had garnered 50 percent market share by 1996. The company focused on the production and sales of executive desks which were usually priced at a 10 to 15 percent discount below ODP's similar offerings. Modern Form was the heaviest promoter of the three major players and advertised extensively in both newspapers and trade magazines. The company had a strong local reputation for manufacturing good quality products. It was well known in the industry that it was also attempting to broaden its offerings to include products that met international standards. This was the primary reason for the company entering into a licensing agreement with Steelcase Office Systems in early 1996. Steelcase was an American-based office furniture manufacturing and marketing firm which enjoyed a globally recognized brand name as well as a reputation for state-of-the-art quality. The new licensing arrangement would allow Modern Form to leverage the Steelcase name and thus be able to target the high-end office furniture market with greater confidence.

PERFORMANCE ISSUES

By 1996, ODP had made considerable progress in terms of developing its revenue base. The size of the Thai office furniture market was estimated to be valued at about two billion baht (US$80 million) of which 25 percent was captured by ODP. Export sales for the company amounted to about 10 percent of total company sales with the primary destinations being Hong Kong, Singapore, Indonesia (via Singapore), Taiwan and the Philippines. Profitability was still elusive for the company, however. This was attributed to a variety of operational and managerial issues, most of which were rooted in the employee's inability to understand each other, which resulted in a failure to execute plans and procedures as they were intended.

Over the course of the company's evolution there were varying levels of participation by the partners in managing daily operations. For example, ED originally fielded several project managers during the start-up phase of the joint venture so as to provide advice and expertise. ED attempted to involve people in all areas of manufacturing operations, while the Taiwanese took an uncharacteristically passive stance. This was because the Taiwanese did not want to be seen as dominating the process. Furthermore, given ED's size and expertise, the Taiwanese felt that they had more to learn than they had to offer during the start-up. While ED viewed its role as one of

adviser, in contrast, the Taiwanese felt that the Americans were not hands-on enough. As for the two Thai partners, both Metropolitan Finance and Thai Enterprise Group offered little guidance to the joint venture over the years. However, when the Thai partners did offer occasional advice, such as in the area of personnel management, the Taiwanese managers were careful not to offend their counterparts, even if their instructions or suggestions were thought to be unrealistic.

According to Robert Chang, one of the main issues confronting the company was the inefficiency of simple daily communication and conversation between employees at all levels of the organization, particularly in the Bangkok office. English was often used as the common language but remained a highly imperfect vehicle for communication, particularly between the Thais and the Taiwanese. The Taiwanese believed that they were not as gifted in English or Thai as they would have liked and this had led to some serious communication problems over the years.

Another area concerning Chang was the inadequate development of the upper management team of Thai directors, particularly with respect to their competence for managing daily issues. He attributed this issue to the differences in working styles exhibited by the Thais and Taiwanese. For example, Chang claimed that the Taiwanese viewed their management style as hard working, flexible and adaptable. They were often apt to change their minds quickly in order to mitigate problems that had arisen or were predicted to surface. They believed strongly in the tenet that "if you make a mistake in the morning, you change things in the afternoon." On the other hand, Thais seemed to prefer seeing managerial directives written down. It was the Thai view that if something went wrong, it was the boss's fault because the Thai employees were not adequately informed. The Taiwanese view of Thais was that they were trained in obedience, preferred to listen and remained passive in the face of managerial problems or challenges. This was perceived as being indecisive as well as lacking in initiative.

The company was also quite concerned with the high turnover rate that it experienced in virtually all areas of its operations. For example, over the four-year period that the manufacturing facility had been operational, the retention rate for line employees was about 20 percent, and of the 36 technicians originally trained in Taiwan, only two remained. Similarly, turnover at the office in Bangkok was seen as "rampant." This was especially so in the finance and information systems departments, where personnel were typically turning over every six months to one year. Chang cited two major causes to explain the situation:

> It is very difficult to find people who possess both the technical and communication skills that we require. These types of people are in very high demand in Thailand and therefore job jumping has become a common practice due to the many opportunities that are available to them. The Japanese are especially good at luring workers away by offering higher wages. What people seem to forget is that there will be communication and cultural differences in the Japanese workplace as well.
>
> ODP has also been in the habit of trusting people during the interview stage. This is a source of concern because we have had instances where we were possibly not as rigorous in the recruitment process as we should have been. For example, when we were experiencing high turnover in the finance department we hired a new director of finance without thoroughly checking his background. As it turned out, he failed to close the company books for our fiscal year-end despite the fact that our annual audit was impending. When the auditors came to examine our accounts, they had nothing to audit. Needless to say, we fired the director.

A specific example of the consequences of miscommunication involved Ken Smith, the sales representative. Smith was eagerly waiting for supplies that were being imported from the U.S. and were to be passed on for immediate delivery to an important client. In this situation it was imperative for Smith to have a ready payment for the order so it could clear customs quickly and be shipped immediately to the local customer who had been patiently waiting for the order. In anticipation of the goods arrival, Alex Chen signed a cheque which was to cover all relevant importing costs for the order. When the time came to take the cheque to the customs clearing house, Smith could not find it and the accounting department claimed no knowledge of having ever issued the cheque. This caused Smith a great deal of frustration. He began by raising his voice to the point where everyone in the office could hear him. He then approached an accounting clerk and began peppering her with questions she was unable to answer. Smith then stormed into Chang's office demanding "action, action, action" on the issue at hand. This episode helped solidify Smith's reputation as being culturally insensitive.

Another incident involved a furniture installer who failed to show up at a client's office at the appointed time of 9:30 A.M. The installer had left work the previous day with the following morning's order already loaded onto the delivery van. After he did not show up at the customer's office the next day, it was discovered that he had traveled up country to help out his family with the annual harvest.

SIGNS OF LIFE

Despite the various problems that had plagued ODP's operation, there had been some obvious successes, the most notable being the completion of a US$4 million contract with Citibank in 1995. The contract called for ODP to supply and install office furniture and paneling systems for all 11 floors of Citibank's new office in Bangkok's financial district. Citibank was interested in dealing with ODP because of its access to the Race Paneling System developed by ED in the U.S.

In order to ensure that the contract was a success, ED and OS agreed to pool various out-of-country personnel to work in Thailand on the project. Firstly, three ED technicians, including the company's senior quality control manager, were dispatched to the Thai manufacturing facility to oversee employee training and the production of certain Race System components. These components included pads, partitions and beams. (The required components and furniture not produced in Thailand were imported from the U.S.) Although the factory was eventually able to produce components of suitable quality, the U.S. technicians commented that the Thai factory workers were somewhat slow in learning the production techniques, which in turn delayed the project slightly.

After the components were being satisfactorily produced, eight ED technicians and three project managers (two from the Hong Kong sales office, one from the U.S.) were sent to work at the Citibank site, along with one operations manager from ODP. The two project managers from Hong Kong were primarily responsible for training the team of Thai installers. The other project manager came from ED's U.S. operations and supervised the overall installation. The local operations manager was principally responsible for managing the team of Thai installers. The entire process of ordering the proper goods, designing the office layout and installing the furniture and paneling systems lasted five months, with the 12 key players remaining dedicated to the account for the duration of the project. The process progressed in a smooth manner with a few minor setbacks. Ultimately, Citibank was thought to have been impressed with the management of the operation. ODP further developed its goodwill with Citibank by offering extensive after-sales service support, including office layout adjustments and guarantees of spare parts inventories in Thailand.

DECISION

The withdrawal of ED from the joint-venture came at a time when the company was already experiencing difficulties on several fronts, particularly in the area of managing the cultural diversity of the people in the organization. However, Phoenix Group chairman Chen remained steadfast in his firm's efforts to penetrate the Thai market. He proclaimed that OS would redouble its efforts in order to ensure that the joint venture would be a success. To this end, he mandated that his son Alex remain totally committed and focused on the Thai operations, as this was a matter of family pride. Alex Chen and Robert Chang knew that they had a great deal of work ahead of them. The big questions were where should they begin to improve the company's operations and how should they go about doing it?

NOTE

1. See Appendix 1 for a discussion of the Overseas Chinese in Thailand.

Appendix 1

The Importance of the Overseas Chinese in Southeast Asia

Over the past several centuries, emigration from southern China into the neighboring countries of Asia has played a key role in the development of trade in the region. It is estimated that about 26 million overseas Chinese live in Taiwan, Hong Kong and Macao, while another 17.7 million live in the Southeast Asian nations of Indonesia, Thailand, Malaysia and Singapore, with a further 8.3 million dispersed throughout the rest of the world. The economic influence of the overseas Chinese remains as a very significant force when one considers their overall numbers and their relative level of wealth. It is estimated that the cumulative economic wealth of the 52 million overseas Chinese rivals the total GNP of China, whose population of more than one billion generates an economy valued at about $450 billion. Further evidence of this wealth can be seen with the economic impact that these groups have in both Indonesia and Thailand. For instance, while comprising only three to four percent of the Indonesian population, the overseas Chinese are believed to control approximately 75 percent of all privately held domestic assets within the country. Similarly, the overseas Chinese in Thailand constitute about 10 percent of the population while controlling an estimated 60 to 70 percent of the private wealth of the nation.

In should be noted that the use of the blanket term "Overseas Chinese," coupled with the tendency to view these peoples as a homogenous group, is inaccurate. The points of origin for the migrations to Southeast Asia came from several distinct regions within southern China, representing at least five separate social groupings, namely the Hakka, Hokkien, Chiu Chow, Hainanese and Cantonese. Each group has its own language and identity by clan and the sense of lineage remains very strong. Furthermore, the notion of the family within these groups remains especially strong. Therefore, the sense of loyalties within the overseas Chinese groups can be listed, in order of degree, as follows: family, lineage, village, company and nation. The concept of "networks" is also an important theme when discussing the overseas Chinese. The close ties forged by language, family, clan and village persist very strongly even though most emigration occurred several generations ago, and is reinforced by the fact that many of the émigrés were survivors of whatever crisis caused them to flee China. The result is that networks of those who could be trusted by reason of common descent become valuable assets to survivors.

The Chinese assimilation into Thailand was particularly effective, unlike in other countries in Southeast Asia where government policy was less receptive or where religious barriers made assimilation more difficult. As the Thai economy has prospered, most ethnic Chinese now consider themselves very much "Thai." They speak perfect Thai, eat Thai food, attend the best Thai universities. Therefore, in large part they tend to subscribe to many mainstream Thai values. However, whereas the Thai tradition tends to be strongly hierarchical, the Chinese tradition appears less so. The ethnic Chinese, much like their forebears, tend to place a high value on entrepreneurialism, flexibility, hard work and a respect for education and training with the males often demonstrating a strong desire to eventually be their own boss.

Source: Sea Change: Pacific Asia as the New World Industrial Center, James C. Abegglen. The Free Press, 1994.

Appendix 2

Thai Concepts of Relationships in the Workplace

Sam Ruam or "to travel the middle path" is a behavior where people exercise restraint and maintain composure during stressful situations. Thais strongly believe that it is necessary to avoid extreme displays of emotion, either positive or negative, while at work. If a senior manager were to lose control, Thais would lose respect for the manager. It is especially important to remember that exclamations directed at "the system" may be taken personally by Thai employees.

Kraeng jai is concerned with the restraint of one's own self-interest or desires in situations where there is a potential for discomfort or conflict. Examples of *kraeng jai* include the following:

- reluctance to disturb or interrupt others
- avoidance of asserting one's opinion or needs
- avoidance of demands for one's rights
- reluctance to pass on orders to a superior or peers of greater age and experience
- reluctance to ask questions when one does not understand certain situations

Hai Kiad means "to give respect" or "to show honor." This concept can be used as a means to motivate subordinates. This is often done by a senior person in charge who asks for a subordinate's advice on a particular problem or issue. The senior may also introduce the subordinate to others or he/she might praise the underling in front of others. It can also be demonstrated when a senior gently and respectfully corrects a subordinate employee for a faulty opinion or deed, thus demonstrating tact for a misdeed.

Nam Jai or "water from the heart" values genuine acts of kindness and is incorporated in the workplace by simply helping one's peers. This requires that the individual take the initiative in demonstrating a consideration for others. A very common form of *nam jai* is when someone brings some food into the office and offers it to everyone. The food is often brought back from a vacation or business trip to show one's colleagues that they were being remembered while the employee was away. Another form would be to reward employees with a night out on the town after they have been particularly busy and have worked overtime.

Source: Working With the Thais by Henry Holmes and Suchada Tangtongtavy. White Lotus Company Ltd., May 1996.

CONSULTING FOR GEORGE LANCIA

*Prepared by Michelle Linton under the
supervision of Elizabeth M.A. Grasby*

Version: (A) 2001-08-01

Cam Matthews shook his head as he looked over the financial statements in front of him. It was June 1993, and he had been hired as a consultant to bring George Lancia's organization under control. George, who wanted a break from the management of his various businesses, was concerned about the successes of his investments. Cam, a 24-year-old recent business graduate, knew upon reading the statements that the financial position was worse than George realized. Cam's foremost concern was how to manage and to relate to George. Cam believed significant changes would have to be made. He wondered what problems he should anticipate.

GEORGE LANCIA

George Lancia was the 45-year-old owner of the organization. He had worked on his own in order to support himself through high school. Upon graduation, he worked as a surveyor's assistant for two years, after which he sold securities for five years. At various times during these years he had owned a movie theatre, a drive-in theatre, and a restaurant. He had also begun to buy and sell real estate, including rental properties, and had created a substantial amount of wealth through these dealings.

In 1985, George was approached by Kevin Gibson with the idea of leading a syndicate to invest in several fast food restaurants in Eastern Ontario. George agreed to invest in this venture. By 1988, the restaurants' performances had failed to improve and George was forced to buy out the other investors.

Three years later, George was approached with another investment opportunity, a nursing home and retirement lodge in the small town of Sterling, Ontario. George responded with an offer that was accepted in principle; however, the actual agreement was still being completed by the lawyers.

George built a new house in 1991. By this time, all of his cash was tied up in six restaurants, the retirement home, the rental properties, and the new house.

MANAGEMENT STRUCTURE

George's investments were set up as individual, numbered corporations. In theory, this structure was intended to protect him from personal liability and to save the structure from problems in a single unit. However, two sources of exposure could not be avoided. Both George's reputation and his borrowing ability within this very small town would be hindered if any of the individual corporations were to go bankrupt. The banks and creditors had recently begun to ask for personal guarantees on any new debt requested by George.

In general, George made all decisions and approved all spending. His primary source of control was monthly financial statements, which he often viewed several months late and did not trust the accuracy of. He seldom had direct contact with his front-line employees.

George's secretary, Sharon, was 23 years old and had received a college diploma in bookkeeping. Sharon had been named the controller of the company. She prepared financial statements, managed the payroll, and handled supplier relationships. Her assistant, Caroline, who was 24 years old with a commerce degree from

Brock University, helped Sharon prepare the financial statements. Both women had a difficult time remaining productive during the day; statements were occasionally late or inaccurate. George was aware of this situation but wondered how the office computers would be run and the filing and banking handled without Sharon and Caroline. Because George wished to avoid any conflict, Sharon had an effective veto on the decisions in her area.

Restaurants

Kevin Gibson was the general manager of the restaurant operations. He was 22 years old when he started working for George. Kevin had no formal management education but had managed fast-food restaurants since the age of 18. George had given him full control over decisions at first, claiming that he "would totally step aside and let Kevin do his thing." When commenting on his own management approach, George said he "preferred to sell an idea rather than tell people what to do." George would review the monthly financial statements and then hold "grilling sessions" during which he would ask Kevin for explanations of any apparent poor results. Kevin would then be asked to project the next month's results. George would write down these projections and file them to be pulled out and pointed to during next month's "grilling session." George received other information informally from time to time, in the form of phone calls from banks, suppliers, employees, or the franchiser, whenever there were problems.

For various reasons, Kevin was unable to provide positive results over time, causing George to lose patience and to take back the formal authority. Currently, Kevin had no authority to make any decisions without George's approval; however, he did anyway. Most of the restaurant staff and suppliers had never heard of George and assumed Kevin was the owner. George wondered who would manage the restaurants if Kevin left and therefore did not want to create any friction between himself and Kevin. Additionally, George hoped Kevin would repay the money he

had loaned him on a handshake to finance Kevin's house.

Jeff Cranney, a 35-year-old with no management education or former management experience, managed the restaurant in Cobourg. He had invested a substantial amount of cash to build the store in 1991 and currently held 49 percent of the shares. However, this restaurant was not managed effectively and had significant operating problems. George was worried that he would be forced to buy Jeff out if these concerns were addressed.

John and Lucy Wilson approached George in September 1992 and asked him to sell them the restaurant in Peterborough. They provided two houses as a down payment and intended to pay the rest over time. From the perspectives of the bank, the employees, and the landlord, George remained responsible for the asset. John and Lucy were middle-aged with no management education or supervisory experience. John worked as a linesman for a power company; Lucy was a health care aide. George wanted to avoid any conflict here as well to prevent "being left with a real mess."

The Sterling Manor

The Sterling Manor was a nursing home and retirement lodge that housed 62 residents and employed close to 50 employees. The negotiations between George and the retirement home's initial owners, the Vaughans, were intense. The Vaughans, the Ministry of Health, and the bank had expressed considerable doubt about George's ability to run the home successfully. It was expected that any additional conflicts or problems would further hinder their perception of him.

At the same time, major changes in the industry were pending. The government had developed stricter regulations to increase the level of quality and service in the industry. These regulations stipulated how the funding should be allocated among nursing, food services, and housekeeping. These changes would reduce net profit considerably, and management would face a much greater challenge than before, when financing was plentiful and regulations minimal.

Linda Baxter was the administrator of the Sterling Manor. She had been a nursing assistant for 25 years and had a diploma in long-term care management. Linda was very personable and concerned about doing a good job. However, she lacked several important technical skills regarding computers, time management, and supervising. She had been hired by the Vaughans and continued to report to them on a regular basis. Whenever she and George disagreed, Linda stated that she still worked for the Vaughans and threatened to seek their decisions. The administration of the home was very disorganized. Phones went unanswered, and Linda's desk was piled with paperwork and mail dating back to 1989. Linda lacked focus or direction and felt that she was accomplishing very little. With the pending regulations, Linda was worried that others would question her competence; therefore, she reacted defensively when anyone attempted to get involved in her work.

Heather Irvin was the director of nursing at the Manor. She was a registered nurse with 30 years' experience. Heather found it difficult to organize and run a staff while dealing with all the conflict and confusion among George, Linda, and the Vaughans. She recognized the importance of management control in a nursing organization, where health and lives are at stake. It was her opinion that Linda did not understand how to operate a health business. So, in order to protect her own position, Heather refused to listen to Linda. Instead, she complained constantly to George about Linda. Because George knew very little about nursing, he could not effectively evaluate Heather's work. He worried about what would happen if she quit. He had not heard any negative comments from anyone else about her work, so he basically gave her complete freedom.

Real Estate

Margaret Dennett managed the apartment building in Belleville. She had been given authority to make decisions about the tenants and daily operations but continually called George about problems she encountered. George did not

have the time to find a replacement for her and therefore, to prevent upsetting Margaret, did not attempt to change the situation.

PERFORMANCE

Restaurants

The restaurant operation had performed poorly for the past three years. The stores had reached their overdraft limit several times, and George had been forced to inject $70,000 from his personal line of credit. Labor productivity was low, quality and service were substandard, current marketing activities were expensive and ineffective, and relations with banks, suppliers, and the franchisers were very poor. In the spring of 1993, Kevin had diverted $70,000 cash from the restaurants to secure equipment and working capital for an ice cream store, a venture that had lost $3,000 per month since its inception.

The Sterling Manor

The Sterling Manor had been barely breaking even for the past several months and was near its overdraft limit. The new union was in the midst of contract arbitration that, when completed in late 1993, would likely expose the home to a retroactive wage settlement of between $200,000 and $500,000. Whenever George accumulated money in the business, the Vaughans withdrew it as advance payment on the Manor's purchase price. George did not want to jeopardize the sale and was therefore reluctant to approach the Vaughans about this.

George did not understand the Ministry of Health's new funding model and did not know whether the home would be a good purchase, or even if it would survive, under the new system. George did not seem aware of the severity of the Manor's financial position.

George had almost reached the limit of his personal credit line and could not count on significant cash flows from his businesses in the short term. He had pledged to limit his withdrawals from the Manor; there were minimal funds coming from the restaurant operations; and recent vacancies had eliminated any positive cash flow from his rental properties.

GEORGE AND CAM

George and Cam had met several times during the spring of 1993. By this time, George was tired and wanted nothing more than to hand over the reins of his business to someone else and step back for a while. He wanted to remove himself from day-to-day management of all assets and to remain merely as a hands-off investor. In June, George hired Cam as a consultant, asking him to prepare a plan to bring the organization under control, specifically, to "find a way to clean up all the junk on my plate."

Cam had graduated in 1992 with a degree in business administration from Wilfrid Laurier University and had started working as a consultant to medium-sized businesses. His experience consisted of co-op positions[1] with large companies, part-time restaurant management during school, and research and consulting since his final year of school.

During their initial meetings together, George repeatedly said to Cam:

I've promoted myself to the level of my own incompetence. I know that now, and so from here on, I'm going to be like Henry Ford—I'm going to hire the expertise that I lack myself. That's where you come in—you have the education that I missed out on. I'll give you the benefit of my 25 years' experience in business, and you give me the benefit of your education.

Cam knew from the start that it would be a grave mistake to underestimate the value of George's "school of hard knocks" education, but felt that he, too, had several significant contributions to make. Cam wondered where to start. He wanted to make sure he had a good understanding of the organization and its problems before he made recommendations or attempted any changes. Cam also wondered if he should expect any problems in dealing with George.

NOTE

1. The university offered a business program that combined regular course work with work terms at various companies.

BUILDING LEADERS AT EVERY LEVEL

A Leadership Pipeline

Prepared By Stephen J. Drotter and Ram Charan

A CRISIS IN LEADERSHIP

Over the past several years, the swift, and most often forced, departures of CEOs have become commonplace at companies in North America, Europe and Japan. Among those affected are Xerox, Lucent, JC Penney, Gillette, Texaco and Nissan. Nor does the list end here.

Today, a new psychology grips the board of directors at companies like those mentioned above: If your CEO has failed, you should recruit from outside the company, where the pastures are always greener.

But those boards would be wise not to adopt that new psychology. For example, Rick Thoman at Xerox came from outside the company. Today,

Xerox is fighting for its life and some think it will not be able to survive. The crucial lesson is this: While recruiting from the outside and taking risks may seem like a solution, it is one for the short term. For the long term, management must build, develop and maintain a pipeline of skilled, prepared leaders from within the company.

Many companies have practised this lesson. Xerox was one, but it failed. It did so because it failed to develop managers who:

- Were prepared and had the necessary skills to be effective at the next level
- Could understand what is unique about their job, especially compared to the jobs held by their boss and direct reports
- Could hold their direct reports and themselves accountable for achieving the right results in the right way.

An important truth underlies these three important points: A crisis in leadership is the result of a company-wide breakdown rather than the actions or failure of one person. Moreover, finding the perfect CEO does not solve the crisis. Nor does going outside to fill senior leadership positions. In fact, going outside is an admission of failure and not very likely to succeed. Hiring an outsider masks the hard truth that a company has not developed a pipeline of leaders from among its ranks who can step in and manage the bigger challenges of the day.

Based on work originally done at General Electric in the 1970s as Critical Career Crossroads developed by Walter Mahler and later expanded to and tested in more than 80 companies, we developed a six-passage model for understanding the leadership requirements throughout an entire company. We call this model The Leadership Pipeline (*The Leadership Pipeline*, by Ram Charan, Stephen J. Drotter and Jim Noel, Jossey-Bass Inc., 2001).

The six turns, or passages, in our pipeline are major events in the life of a leader. Grasping what each passage entails, and the challenges involved in making each transition, will help organizations build a leadership pipeline. It will also help build a leadership culture that will enable the organization to respond to changes and threats in the business environment.

THE LEADERSHIP PIPELINE

PASSAGE 1: Managing Self to Managing Others

New, young employees usually spend their first few years in an organization as individual contributors. Whether in sales, accounting, engineering or marketing, their skill requirements are primarily technical or professional. They contribute by doing the assigned work within given time frames and in ways that meet objectives. By sharpening and broadening their individual skills, they make increased contributions and are then considered for promotions.

From a time-application standpoint, learning involves planning (so that work is completed on time), punctuality, content, quality and reliability. The work values to be developed include accepting the company's culture and adopting professional standards. When people become skilled individual contributors who produce good results, especially when they demonstrate an ability to collaborate, they usually receive additional responsibilities. When they demonstrate an ability to handle these responsibilities and adhere to the company's values, they are often promoted to first-line manager.

When this happens, these individuals are at Passage One. Though this might seem like an easy, natural leadership passage, it's often one where people trip. The highest-performing people, especially, are reluctant to change; they want to keep doing the activities that made them successful. As a result, many people make the transition from individual contributor to manager without actually making a behavioral or value-based transition. In effect, they become managers without realizing or accepting the requirements. Many consultants, for instance, have skipped this turn, having moved from transitory team leadership to business leader without absorbing much of the learning in between. When business leaders miss this passage, the result is frequently disaster.

First-time managers need to learn how to reallocate their time so that they not only complete their assigned work but also help others perform effectively. They must shift from doing work to getting work done through others. This is especially difficult for first-time managers. Part of the problem is that they still prefer to spend time on their old work, even as they take charge of a group. Yet the pressure to spend less time on individual work and more time on managing will increase at each passage. If people don't start making changes in how they allocate their time from the beginning, they're bound to become liabilities as they move up. It's a major reason why pipelines clog and leaders fail.

The most difficult change for managers to make at Passage One involves values. Specifically, they need to learn to value managerial work rather than just tolerate it. They must believe that making time for others—planning, coaching, and the like—is a necessary task and their responsibility. More than that, they must view this other-directed work as mission-critical to their success. For instance, first-line knowledge managers in the financial services industry find this transition extremely difficult. They value being producers, but they must learn to value making others productive. Given that these values had nothing to do with their success as individual contributors, it's difficult for them to make this dramatic shift.

While changes in skills and time application can be seen and measured, changes in values are more difficult to assess. Someone may appear to be making the changes demanded by this leadership turn. But, in fact, he or she is actually adhering to individual-contributor values. Value changes will take place only if upper management reinforces the need to shift beliefs, and if people find that they're successful at their new jobs after a value shift.

PASSAGE 2: Managing Others to Managing Managers

Few companies address this passage in their training, even though this is the level where a management foundation is constructed, and even though level-two managers select and develop the people who will eventually become a company's leaders.

Perhaps the biggest difference from the previous passage is that, at this level, managers must only manage. They need to divest themselves of individual tasks. The key skills they must master during this transition include selecting people to turn Passage One, assigning managerial and leadership work to them, measuring their progress as managers, and coaching them. At this point, managers must also see beyond their own job description and consider the broad strategic issues that affect the business overall.

Too often, people who have been promoted to manager-of-manager positions have skipped Passage One; they were promoted to first-line managers but didn't change skills, time application or work values. As a result, they clog the leadership pipeline because they hold first-line managers accountable for technical work rather than managerial work. They help maintain and even instill the wrong values in those individuals who report to them. They are essentially unable to differentiate between those who can do and those who can lead.

Managers at Passage Two need to be able to identify value-based resistance to managerial work, a common reaction among first-line managers. They need to recognize that the software designer who would rather design software than manage others cannot be allowed to move up to a leadership role. No matter how brilliant he or she might be at designing software, the individual will block the leadership pipeline if he or she does not derive satisfaction from managing and leading people. In fact, one of the tough responsibilities for managers of managers is to return people to individual contributor roles if they don't shift their behaviour and values.

Coaching is also essential at this level because first-line managers frequently don't receive formal training in how to be a manager; they're dependent on their bosses to instruct them on the job. Coaching requires managers to go through the instruction-performance-feedback cycle with their people; some managers aren't willing to reallocate their time in this way. In many organizations, coaching ability isn't rewarded (and the lack of it isn't penalized). It's no wonder that relatively few managers view coaching as mission-critical.

PASSAGE 3: Managing Managers to Managing a Function

Making this transition is tougher than it appears. While the difference between managing managers and managing a function might appear to be negligible, a number of significant challenges lurk below the surface. For example, communicating with the individual-contributor level now requires penetrating at least two layers of management, thus making the development of new communication skills mandatory. Functional heads must also manage some areas that are unfamiliar to them. They must not only endeavour to understand this foreign work but learn to value it as well.

At the same time, functional managers report to multi-functional general managers. They therefore have to become skilled in considering other functional needs and concerns. Team-play with other functional managers and competition for resources based on business needs are two major skills they must learn. At the same time, managers at this level should learn how to blend the strategy for their own unit with the business's overall strategy. This means participating in business-team meetings and working with other functional managers, and spending less time on purely functional responsibilities. This is why it is essential that functional managers delegate responsibility for overseeing many functional tasks.

Succeeding in this leadership passage also requires increased managerial maturity. In one

sense, maturity means thinking and acting like a functional leader rather than a functional member. But it also means that managers need to adopt a broad, long-term perspective. Long-term strategy, especially applied to their own function, is usually what gives most managers trouble at this stage. At this level, effective leadership entails creating a functional strategy that enables them to do something better than the competition. Whether it's coming up with a method to design more innovative products or reach new customer groups, these managers must push the functional envelope. They must also push it into the future for a sustainable competitive advantage rather than just for an immediate, but temporary, edge.

PASSAGE 4: Functional Manager to Business Manager

This leadership passage is often the most satisfying and challenging of a manager's career. For any organization, it's mission-critical: Business managers are responsible for the bottom line.

Business managers usually have significant autonomy, which people with leadership instincts find liberating. They also are able to see a clear link between their efforts and bottom-line results. At the same time, this passage also represents a sharp turn: A major shift in skills, time application and work values must take place. This is not simply a matter of thinking more strategically. Rather than consider the feasibility of an activity, a business manager must examine it from a short- and long-term profit perspective.

There are probably more new and unfamiliar responsibilities here than at other levels. For people who have only been in one function their entire careers, the position of business manager represents unexplored territory; they are suddenly responsible for many unfamiliar functions and outcomes. Not only do they have to learn to manage different functions, but they also need to become skilled at working with a wider variety of people than ever before; they need to become more sensitive to functional diversity issues and able to communicate clearly and effectively.

Even more difficult is the balancing act between future goals and present needs, and making trade-offs between the two. Business managers must meet quarterly profit, market share, product and people targets and, at the same time, plan three- to five-year goals. The trial of balancing short- and long-term thinking is one that bedevils many managers at this turn. It is why allocating time to think is a major requirement at this level: Managers need to stop doing something every second of the day and reserve time to reflect and analyze.

PASSAGE 5: Business Manager to Group Manager

This is another leadership passage that, at first glance, doesn't seem arduous. The assumption is that if you can run one business successfully, you can do the same with two or more businesses. The flaw in this reasoning begins with what is valued at each leadership level. A business manager values the success of his own business; a group manager values the success of other people's businesses. The distinction is critical because some people derive satisfaction only when they're the ones receiving the lion's share of the credit.

As you might imagine, a group manager who doesn't value the success of others will fail to inspire and support the business managers who report to him. Or, his or her actions might be governed by frustration; the individual is convinced he or she could operate the various businesses better than his or her manager. In either instance, the leadership pipeline becomes clogged with business managers who aren't operating at peak capacity because they're not being properly supported or their authority is being usurped.

Group managers must master four skills:

1. *Evaluate strategy in order to allocate and deploy capital.* This is a sophisticated skill that involves learning to ask the right questions, analyzing the right data, and applying the right

corporate perspective to understand which business strategy (prepared by business managers) has the greatest probability of success, and should therefore be funded.

2. *Develop business managers.* Group managers need to know which function-managers are ready to become business managers. Coaching new business managers is also important.

3. *Develop and implement a portfolio strategy.* This is quite different from a business strategy and demands a shift in how he or she perceives the business. This is the first time managers have to ask these questions: Do I have the right collection of businesses? What businesses should be added, subtracted or changed to position us properly and assure current and future earnings?

4. *Assess whether they have the right core capabilities to win.* This means avoiding wishful thinking, looking at resources objectively, and making a judgment based on analysis and experience.

A leader at this level must have a global perspective. People may master the required skills, but they won't perform at full leadership capacity if they don't think in broad terms, aren't able to factor in the complexities of running multiple businesses, and don't think in terms of community, industry, governmental and ceremonial activities. They must also prepare themselves for the bigger decisions, greater risks and uncertainties, and the longer time spans inherent to this leadership level. They must always be aware of what Wall Street wants.

PASSAGE 6: Group Manager to Enterprise Manager

When the leadership pipeline becomes clogged at the top, all leadership levels suffer. CEOs who have skipped one or more passages can diminish the performance of direct reports and individuals all the way down the line. They fail to develop other managers effectively, and don't fulfill the responsibilities that come with this position.

The transition during the sixth passage is much more focused on values than skills. To an even greater extent than at the previous level, people must reinvent themselves as enterprise managers. They must set direction and develop operating mechanisms to know and drive quarter-by-quarter performance that is in tune with longer-term strategy.

They must thoroughly understand how the organization executes and gets things done. The trade-offs involved can be mind-bending, and enterprise leaders learn to value these trade-offs. In addition, this new leadership role requires an ability to manage a long list of external constituencies proactively.

Enterprise leaders need to come to terms with the fact that their performance as a CEO will be based on three or four high-impact decisions each year. There's a subtle but fundamental shift in responsibility from strategic to visionary thinking, and from an operating to a global perspective. There's also a letting-go process that should take place during this passage, if it hasn't taken place already. Enterprise leaders must let go of the pieces, i.e., the individual products and customers, and focus on the whole, i.e., how well do we conceive, develop, produce and market all products to all customers.

Finally, at this level, a CEO must assemble a team of high-achieving, ambitious direct reports, knowing that some of them want his job, yet picking them for the team despite this knowledge. Also, this is the only leadership position that must shape the soft side of the enterprise.

Leadership pipeline problems occur at this level for two reasons:

1. *CEOs are often unaware that this passage requires a significant change in values.* Too many CEOs fail because they didn't recognize the requirement to make a full turn. They maintain the same skills, time applications and work values that served them well as group managers, and never adjust their self-concept to fit their new leadership role. They behave as though they are running a portfolio of businesses, not one entity. They must have the will and determination to change their work values.

2. *It is difficult to develop a CEO for this particular leadership transition.* Preparation for the position is the result of a series of diverse experiences over a long period of time. The best approach provides carefully selected job assignments that stretch people over time and allow them to learn and practise the necessary skills. Though coaching might be helpful, people usually need time, experience and the right assignments to develop into effective CEOs.

The Benefits of a Pipeline

Too often, organizations don't realize that their leaders aren't performing at full capacity because they aren't holding them accountable for the right things. Companies focus only on the economic requirements of a given job rather than the skills, time application and work values of a specific leadership level. As a result, a business manager is allowed to spend most of his or her time acquiring new customers rather than developing an effective business strategy. Or the business manager's boss, the group manager, never questions or explores what the business manager values about his or her work, and whether those values are appropriate for the leadership the company requires. But when this business manager's strategy is flawed and important goals aren't achieved, the group manager isn't held accountable (or held accountable for the right thing).

A well-defined leadership pipeline delivers important benefits

1. By establishing appropriate requirements for the six leadership levels, companies can greatly facilitate succession planning, and leadership development and selection processes in their organizations.

2. Individual managers can clearly see the gap between their current performance and the desired performance. They can also see gaps in their training and experience, and where they may have skipped a passage (or parts of a passage) and how that's hurting their performance.

3. HR can make development decisions based on where people fall short in skills, time application and work values, rather than rely on generalized training and development programs.

4. An individual's readiness for a move to the next leadership level can be evaluated objectively rather than tied to how well they performed in their previous position.

5. Leadership passages provide companies with a way to improve selection. Rather than basing their selection decisions on past performance alone, personal connections or preferences, managers can be held to a higher, more effective standard. Organizations can select someone to make a leadership turn when an individual is demonstrating some of the skills required at the next level.

6. A defined pipeline provides organizations with a diagnostic tool that helps them identify mismatches between individuals' capabilities and their leadership level. Therefore, remedying the situation or, if necessary, removing the mismatched person, which is more likely.

7. It helps organizations move people through leadership passages at the right speed. People who ticket-punch their way through jobs don't absorb the necessary work values and skills. The pipeline provides a system for identifying when someone is ready to move to the next leadership level.

8. It reduces the time needed to prepare an individual for the top leadership position in a large corporation. Because the pipeline clearly defines what is needed to move from one level to the next, there's little or no wasted time on jobs that merely duplicate skills.

From a pure talent perspective, however, the most significant benefit of a pipeline is that you don't need to bring in stars to prime the leadership pump and unclog the pipeline. You can create your own stars up and down the line, beginning at the first level when people make the transition from managing themselves to managing others. By moving people upward only when they have mastered the assigned level greatly increases their chances of success. Clearly defining the new requirements enables them to help themselves and help their direct reports. Everyone wins and so does the company. Recruiting outside for top positions will be greatly reduced.

A Small-Business Pipeline

In a company of less than 20 people, there is only one real leadership passage—from managing oneself (the owner) to managing others. The owner-founder usually has to move from being an individual contributor to a manager of other people. After designing a product or creating a service, he or she must hire more people. This marks the beginning of the leadership passage.

If the business is to survive, the owner must learn and value skills such as coaching, planning and rewarding employees. If not, people will either quit or, even worse, stay and perform poorly. A significant percentage of owner-founder enterprises fail to become large organizations. In many instances, they survive for one or two generations after the founder has left. In venture-capital-funded companies, founders are frequently replaced by more experienced managers from larger companies sooner rather than later. Given all this, a small company's leadership passages are limited by size and circumstance.

If the business evolves and more people and offices or stores are added, the owner must again go through a leadership passage. Because he or she can't be everywhere at once, the leader must appoint additional managers and hold them accountable for managerial work. He or she must ascertain that the work of the entire enterprise is integrated so that customers are properly served and resources used efficiently. Essentially, this business owner is going through Passage Two, from managing others to managing managers. In this role, he or she must make sure the total effort is profitable and sustainable. Setting goals based on what customers want and what the competition is doing is another new responsibility.

Small businesses often fail when a new level of leadership-management must be added. We worked closely with a financial service institution that did acquisitions lending to small business. The company asked us to help it determine, before the loan was made, whether the borrowing company could manage a larger company post-acquisition. We studied almost 50 loans and found that the companies that failed to manage the acquisition were headed by people who were reluctant to change their own work habits; they found it difficult to give up their hands-on involvement or trust a new layer of management. In other words, the leader-owner was unable or unwilling to make a crucial leadership passage.

A Small-Business Pipeline Model

As a business continues to grow, understanding the passages in this expanding organization is crucial. The group level (managers of several businesses) doesn't apply to the small-business model, and the work of the enterprise manager is done by the business manager (who runs the business for short-term and long-term results and deals with government agencies and key customers). Similarly, the functional manager's position in this small-business model is usually absorbed by the manager-of-managers layer.

With these differences in mind, smaller companies can reap the same leadership-development benefits as larger organizations.

Enterprise Manager

6

Group Manager

5

Business Manager

4

Function Manager

3

Managing Managers

2

Managing Others

1

Managing Self

4

LEADER STYLE APPROACH

There is no set formula to becoming a successful leader. While it takes all kinds of things, some of the common characteristics of a leader are charisma, edge, energy, an ability to execute and ethics. One has to build his/her own leadership style based on these basic principles. Of course, being hard working, having an ability to learn from anyone, having a willingness to listen and never giving up are some of the basic qualities that most leaders share.

—Simon Leung[1]

The leadership style approach is different from the trait approach and the skills approach. The trait approach emphasized the personality characteristics of leaders. The skills approach focused on the leader's competencies. The leadership style approach accentuates leader behaviors—in other words, what leaders do and how they act, particularly toward subordinates, in a multitude of situations to change subordinate performance and influence (Yukl, 2006).

These behaviors can be distilled into two broad types: initiating structure (task behavior) and consideration (relationship behavior). Task behavior makes it easier for group members (subordinates) to accomplish goals and objectives. Relationship behaviors make it easier for group members (subordinates) to feel at ease with the context in which they are operating, with other members of the group, and with whom they are themselves. The ultimate objective of the leadership style approach is to help in our understanding of how leaders integrate these two broad conceptualizations of behaviors to positively influence group members in efforts to achieve personal and organizational goals and objectives (Northouse, 2007).

Consequently, we describe three streams of research that focused on task and relationship behaviors and their intersection. The first stream was conducted at The Ohio State University (e.g., Stogdill, 1948) and pursued style research to demonstrate the need to account for more than leaders' traits (Dubrin, 2007). The second stream was conducted at the University of Michigan (e.g., Likert, 1961, 1967) and examined how leadership happened in small groups. The third stream (Blake & Mouton, 1964, 1978, 1985) researched how leaders used relationship and task behaviors in an organizational context (Yukl, 2006).

THE OHIO STATE STUDIES

As we see from Table 4.1, the Ohio State University studies found that leader behaviors clustered under two broad categories: initiating structure and consideration (Stogdill, 1974). Characteristics of both are included in Table 4.1.

These two behaviors were viewed as two separate and different continua. This means that an individual can be high on both, low on both, or high on one and low on the other (Daft, 2005). In addition, these behaviors need to be considered in context as in some situations, high consideration and low initiating structure may be appropriate, whereas in others, the opposite may be appropriate. Being high on both is the best form of leadership, but this is very difficult for many individuals (Daft, 2005; Northouse, 2007).

THE UNIVERSITY OF MICHIGAN STUDIES

As reported in Table 4.1, this body of research found results similar to the Ohio State studies. Their two broad categories were production orientation and employee orientation. Characteristics of both are included in Table 4.1.

Table 4.1   Task Behavior and Relationship Behavior

	Task Behavior	**Relationship Behavior**
Ohio State studies	*Initiating structure* Organizing work Giving work structure Defining role responsibilities Scheduling work activities	*Consideration* Building —respect —trust —liking —camaraderie between followers and leaders
University of Michigan studies	*Production orientation* Stress technical aspects Stress production aspects Workers —viewed as way to get work done	*Employee orientation* Workers —viewed with a strong human relations aspect Leaders —treat workers as human beings —value workers individuality —give attention to workers' needs
Blake & Mouton's grid	*Concern for production* Achieving tasks Making policy decisions Developing new products Process issues Workload Increasing sales volume	*Concern for people* Attending to people Build commitment and trust Promote worker personal worth Provide good work conditions Maintain fair salary/benefits Promote good social relations

Source: Adapted from Northouse (2007). Copyright © 2007, Sage Publications, Inc.

Contrary to the Ohio State studies, initially, these two types of leader behaviors were argued to be on opposite ends of one continuum (Daft, 2005), thus suggesting that leaders high on production orientation had to be low on employee orientation and vice versa. Later, the Michigan researchers came to agree with the Ohio State studies and view the two types of leader behavior as two separate continua. This meant that leaders could be viewed as being able to have high production and employee orientations. Some research viewed this as being valuable for employee satisfaction and employee performance, but most research was inconclusive (Northouse, 2007; Yukl, 2006).

THE BLAKE AND MOUTON GRID

Blake and Mouton (1964, 1978, 1985) developed their leadership grid to demonstrate that leaders helped organizations achieve their goals through two leader orientations: concern for production and concern for people. These two orientations resemble task behavior and relationship behavior, as shown in Table 4.1. Using the grid, the researchers developed five leadership styles.

The *authority-compliance* style describes leaders who are results driven, with little or no concern for people except to organize them in a way that keeps them from interfering with getting the job done. Communication with followers is limited and used only to give instructions regarding the task. These leaders are controlling, hard-driving, overpowering, and demanding—not nice people to work for. Some research suggests a higher turnover rate under this style of leadership (Yukl, 2006).

The *country club* style describes leaders with a high concern for people and a low concern for results or production. These leaders focus on meeting people's needs and creating a positive environment in which to work. Turnover rates seem to decrease under these leaders (Yukl, 2006).

Impoverished management describes leaders who have little or no concern for people or for production (Daft, 2005). They do enough to "not get fired," but mentally, they have probably already defected from the organization.

The *middle-of-the-road* style describes leaders who have a moderate concern for people and for production (Daft, 2005). These leaders are compromisers who do not push production hard or push to meet the needs of their followers to the maximum limit.

Team management style leaders emphasize getting results and interpersonal relationships. These leaders help employees focus on, and commit to, their work and promote teamwork and a high level of participation in work-related decisions by employees. Northouse (2007) suggests that the following phrases describe these leaders: "stimulates participation, acts determined, gets issues into the open, makes priorities clear, follows through, behaves open-mindedly, and enjoys working."

The team management style integrates high concerns for people and for production. It is possible to use a high concern for people and a high concern for production but not in an integrative manner. These leaders switch from the authority-compliance style to the country club style depending on the situation. An example would be the "benevolent dictator" who acts graciously to get the job done. This style is called *paternalistic/maternalistic,* and leaders who use this style do so because they consider that people are not associated with what it takes to achieve the organization's goals and purposes.

The final style based on the leadership grid is *opportunism.* This refers to a leader who opportunistically uses any combination of the five styles to advance his or her career.

Blake and Mouton (1985) argue that leaders usually have a style that is most dominant and one that is their "backup" style. Leaders revert to their backup style when the dominant style is not working and they are under a great deal of pressure (Northouse, 2007).

How Does the Leadership Style Work?

This style helps students, practitioners, and academics to assess leadership based on two broad dimensions: task behavior and relationship behavior. It does not tell leaders what to do but describes the major dimensions of what they do in their relationships with their job and their followers. This style suggests to leaders that how they affect followers "occurs through the tasks they perform as well as in the relationships they create" (Northouse, 2007). There may be a situation perspective to the leadership style approach in that some followers may need to be directed more while others may need to be nurtured and supported more (Yukl, 2006).

Note

1. Simon Leung is the Regional President, Motorola Asia/Pacific in Hong Kong.

References

Blake, R. R., & Mouton, J. S. (1964). *The managerial grid.* Houston, TX: Gulf.
Blake, R. R., & Mouton, J. S. (1978). *The new managerial grid.* Houston, TX: Gulf.
Blake, R. R., & Mouton, J. S. (1985). *The managerial grid III.* Houston, TX: Gulf.
Daft, R. L. (2005). *The leadership experience* (3rd ed.). Mason, OH: Thomson, South-Western.
Dubrin, A. (2007). *Leadership: Research findings, practice, and skills.* New York: Houghton Mifflin.
Leung, S. (2006, March 14). Ahead of his times (Part 2 of 8, Ivey Leadership Series). *South China Morning Post,* Business Section.
Likert, R. (1961). *New patterns of management.* New York: McGraw-Hill.
Likert, R. (1967). *The human organization: Its management and value.* New York: McGraw-Hill.
Northouse, P. G. (2007). *Leadership: Theory and practice* (4th ed.). Thousand Oaks, CA: Sage.
Stogdill, R. M. (1948). Personal factors associated with leadership: A survey of the literature. *Journal of Psychology, 25,* 35–71.
Stogdill, R. M. (1974). *Handbook of leadership: A survey of theory and research.* New York: Free Press.
Yukl, G. (2006). *Leadership in organizations* (6th ed.). Upper Saddle River, NJ: Pearson-Prentice Hall.

The Cases

Technosoft Russia

A supervisor at a telesales office has received very low ratings on an employee survey, and the marketing manager is concerned that this team leader is not performing well. The marketing manager must decide what actions are needed to improve the leadership skills of this supervisor.

Healthcare Equipment Corporation—Managing in Korea

The managing director of a health services company is becoming increasingly concerned about the state of leadership at the company's subsidiary. The source of the concern was the president of a wholly owned subsidiary who had been instrumental in ensuring the very successful launch of the operation during its start-up. Since then, however, the president's behavior has become increasingly problematic, to the point where he has become very disruptive to the operation. Therefore, it is necessary to craft a leadership development plan for him or else face the unpleasant task of having to terminate him.

THE READING

The New Infocracies: Implications for Leadership

The Information Age is creating a series of new organizational forms that are supplanting the bureaucracies of the Industrial Age. These so-called infocracies create new dilemmas for leaders and demand different decision-making structures and avenues of influence. Some leaders are holding on to their bureaucratic principles, which are no longer legitimate in the Information Age. In this article, the author defines infocracies and delineates the new principles for leadership in this new organizational form.

TECHNOSOFT RUSSIA

*Prepared by Fyodor Suzdalev under the supervision
of Professor James A. Erskine*

   Version: (A) 2004–06–30

On February 13, 2002, Ivan Chaikovsky, sales and marketing manager, finally received all responses from the Technosoft telesales team in Saint Petersburg regarding the performance of team leader Olga Peterson. Staff members had given Peterson a very low rating and Chaikovsky was not sure how best to proceed.

TECHNOSOFT

Technosoft, a global high-tech company with a corporate headquarters in the United States, opened a representative office in Saint Petersburg,

Russia, in 1993. At the time, Russia was only three years into the post communist era, and the business environment was not totally stable. Nevertheless, the Technosoft business had a very dynamic start and, by 2002, the representative office in Saint Petersburg had over 80 people on staff.

The Technosoft Saint Petersburg office was responsible for business development in Russia and ex-USSR countries like Ukraine, Byelorussia and Kazakhstan but excluding the Baltic countries (Latvia, Estonia, and Lithuania). Technosoft Saint Petersburg reported to the Eastern European Headquarters (EEHQ) located in Vienna. EEHQ was responsible for business development in Eastern European countries like Poland, Czech Republic and Hungary and, in turn, EEHQ reported to the European Headquarters (EHQ) located in Amsterdam. EHQ was responsible for Europe, the Middle East and Africa (EMEA). The last link in the chain was the link between EHQ and corporate headquarters in the United States. Each representative office and regional headquarters had a general manager (GM) who was responsible for territory revenues and all business development spending (see Exhibit 1).

Technosoft produced a wide range of software and hardware products for business and consumer markets. All products were developed in the United States, but operations like hardware production, compact disc recording, printing, packaging and shipping were performed in several production sites or operation centres. Physical units or stock keeping units (SKUs) like hardware items, software packages and licence agreements for corporate clients were shipped to distributors. Distributors then shipped SKUs to small and medium resellers, and resellers transferred them to customers (see Exhibit 2). In any particular country, Technosoft could have hundreds of small and medium resellers but relatively few distributors.

Technosoft small and medium resellers were the key part of the value chain. Most resellers added value to Technosoft products by working

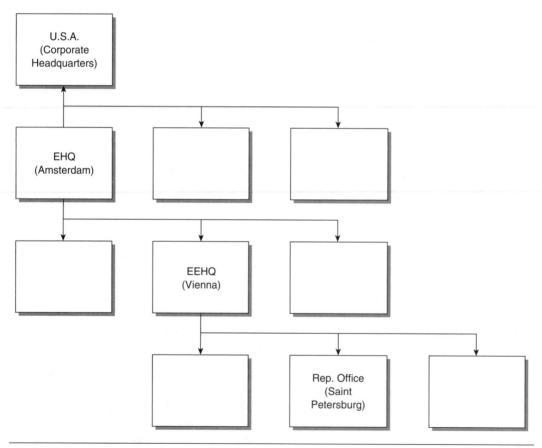

Exhibit 1   Technosoft Corporate Structure

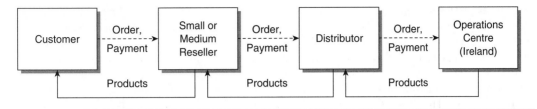

Exhibit 2   Value Chain

closely with a customer, understanding problems and providing a turn-key solution, often using third-party software and hardware. Some resellers specialized in training and support for Technosoft products, and some were developing their own products using Technosoft products for a component of their own solutions.

BUDGETING

A country budget consisted of revenues collected through the channel and expenses like payroll, premises and marketing expenses. Production and operating costs were excluded except for the costs incurred by creating localized versions of the products. This job was usually done by OC but the cost was transferred to the country budget. Marketing expenses included outsourcing and third-party orders.

Each GM was responsible for the budget of its own territory. The budget was formed on the subsidiary or representative office level, usually in June, and then revised in January every year. The budget procedure always included several day-long discussions with regional headquarters management concerning product forecasts, marketing plans and headcounts. Approved budgets were aggregated on regional levels and then passed to the next level (e.g., from EEHQ to EHQ) and the procedure repeated. During the year, business performance was closely monitored by headquarter management, and quarterly business review sessions were held in each Technosoft subsidiary or representative office.

Even though each Technosoft subsidiary or representative office had relative freedom in deciding what to do at the country level, each country management was supposed to apply corporate guidelines and regional marketing programs. Otherwise, the subsidiary had to explain why it had not applied them. Usually the price of explaining "why not" was much higher than that of simply implementing corporate guidelines and programs.

Each country allocated funds in the country budget for special programs/projects. At a country level, a program champion was typically assigned. In many cases, this program champion had other responsibilities within their department and had to form a "virtual" team across other departments to move projects along. This "horizontal" co-operation was an extremely important form of organizational design in Technosoft. For a program to be successful, its champion had to know key people in other units, their motives, relative power and their bosses. Usually this knowledge came after employees had spent six to 12 months in the organization.

Each special program was measured independently on the country level. If the program performed the best in comparison to other countries, its GM got additional bargaining power during budget approval process. Poor results in such a program could lessen the GM's credibility and, eventually, the country's reputation.

PERFORMANCE REVIEW

During the performance review process, managers assessed past performance of their subordinates and held discussions about future goals and actions. Performance review results affected employees' bonuses and potential promotion. The GM's performance was measured not only by budget and programs performance but also by his direct subordinates and the organizational health index (OHI). OHI was calculated annually based on results of performance review process, an integral part of which was the Technosoft poll.

There were two types of staff in Technosoft: full-time employees (FTEs) and temporary employees (TEs). FTEs had perpetual employment agreements and were on the Technosoft payroll. TEs had a limited period of employment in their contracts, usually three months, and in most cases were on some outsourcing company's payroll, though they had Technosoft e-mail addresses, access to Technosoft information resources and sat in a Technosoft office. Each month, Technosoft informed the payroll company about the TEs' monthly compensation and quarterly about renewing their contracts. TEs did not have many benefits, which FTEs had, such as stock option plans and health insurance. FTE headcount was kept small worldwide and increased very conservatively. On the other hand, the TE headcount varied widely.

The corporate performance review process involved the FTEs only. All collected data were stored in a corporate database, and every FTE's performance history was available from the start of their employment. Nevertheless, on the country level, some managers used some elements of the performance review program on their own initiative to manage and evaluate TEs. At the start of 2002, approximately 35 percent of the headcount in the Saint Petersburg representative office were TEs.

An important part of the performance review process, the Technosoft poll, was generated by only the FTEs. The poll was a long, Web-based questionnaire that was designed to measure the company's "internal climate." The questionnaire took more than 20 minutes to answer and included various sections about understanding company priorities and goals, customer satisfaction, job satisfaction, compensation, work environment and an evaluation of the manager's performance.

The poll was always conducted by an external, independent company. Every year, usually in May, all the FTEs received a link to the personal Web-page where the questionnaire was located. Each FTE had to follow their personal link and fill out the questionnaire. FTEs were supposed to complete this task within a 15-day timeframe. All data collected by the external company were passed to the corporate level, processed (OHI was calculated at this stage) and then distributed back to the country level. Apart from the aggregated results of a particular country, these data contained the regional average and the last year's results for comparison. The data were then discussed on the country level to identify areas for improvement and to create an action plan.

Each country assigned a "champ" to supervise the poll. This person was responsible for the response rate and the post discussion of results. The poll was a high priority program in Technosoft, and response rates of all countries were closely monitored by regional headquarters. Every GM wanted to keep the response rate at least as high as other countries (in many cases, greater than 90 percent). Program champs tried to stimulate colleagues to participate in the poll using incentives like a free computer mouse or other such gadgets.

The poll section in which each FTE evaluated their immediate manager was one of the most important parts of the poll. Managers who were responsible for lower-level supervisory staff used a specific section of the poll to evaluate the performance of these leaders. The results of this poll had a direct impact on each individual's performance review. Company standards required at least 75 percent positive answers ("strongly agree" and "agree" answers on the five-point scale for each question.) A low mark meant poor performance, a low bonus and, potentially, a demotion or dismissal.

TECHNOSOFT SAINT PETERSBURG

On the country level, each representative office comprised several business units. One of the business units in Technosoft Saint Petersburg was the small and medium business unit (SMB). The SMB director, Dubrovsky, had worked for Technosoft since 1995. The SMB unit brought in approximately 60 percent of Technosoft Saint Petersburg's revenue and was responsible for all channel activities, value chain monitoring and small and medium enterprise business development. Dubrovsky was a talented manager who had a great respect for Sergei Zolotov, the GM, since 1996, in Technosoft Saint Petersburg (see Exhibit 3).

Technosoft did not sell directly to customers and, before 1999, had almost no contact with small and medium enterprises. However, in 1999, Technosoft corporate headquarter's decided to push the idea of working with small and medium customers directly. Although the value chain was left unchanged, the Technosoft sales forces in the various SMB units were challenged to understand the market and organize direct marketing activities targeted on SMB customers. The marketing efforts produced leads which, in turn, had to be passed on to resellers. Technosoft

Saint Petersburg had neither the expertise nor the tools to use direct marketing methods or to handle generated leads. Dubrovsky hired Chaikovsky in August of 1999 as the SMB sales representative.

One of Chaikovsky's primary tasks was to decide which database to use for the sales and marketing activities to SMBs. He could either collect and maintain an inhouse database or use an agency list. The latter was usually less expensive than the former. Chaikovsky decided to build an inhouse database based on a key outsourced agency that provided support services for Technosoft customers and already maintained a purchases database. By the summer of 2000, a new customer database was created, and regular data updating routines were set up and controlled by Technosoft Saint Petersburg.

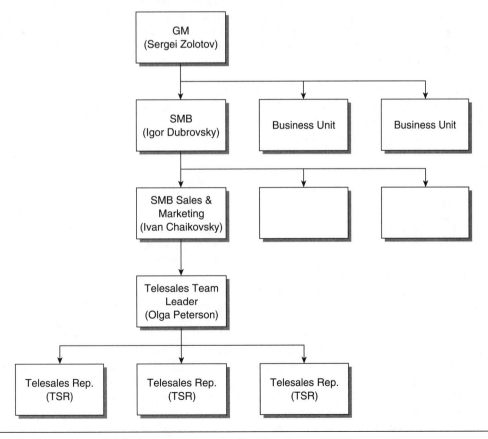

Exhibit 3   Technosoft Saint Petersburg Organization Chart

By this time, Chaikovsky had won the support and admiration of Dubrovsky. Chaikovsky kept all promises, was conservatively proactive and never let Dubrovsky down. Chaikovsky always asked for Dubrovsky's advice in order to test the water before going forward with some idea. Chaikovsky felt that Dubrovsky had an exceptional gift in determining the feasibility of new ideas. Usually this preliminary assessment helped everyone to understand the gaps in the business concept and to decide whether to collect additional data or drop the concept. However, in some situations Dubrovsky's position was imposed on Chaikovsky, despite his lack of agreement with it.

Even though Chaikovsky's SMB unit had a good database and was doing direct marketing work, he was worried about potential clients (leads) generated by his activities who were not being passed on to resellers and were eventually being lost. In response, Chaikovsky created a lead referral system where all generated leads could be captured and then distributed to resellers. The cost of developing the software was small, and Chaikovsky easily persuaded Dubrovsky to launch the project. Chaikovsky's system was developed and became one of the best practices in Eastern Europe. Eventually this system was replaced by a centralized corporate-wide sales and marketing support system (SMSS) and was implemented in every country.

TELESALES PROJECT

The lead referral system was a step in the right direction, but the system itself could not resolve the task of actively monitoring and following up on the leads. Moreover, Technosoft wanted to be sure that resellers did their best in order to maximize the Technosoft's part in any deal to satisfy its customers. Chaikovsky knew that, in some countries, telesales representatives were hired to follow-up on leads. These salespeople also made proactive calls to customers and hence became another source of leads.

Chaikovsky wanted to use telesales to generate and follow up leads in order to have full cycle

of working with SMBs. Chaikovsky knew that direct sales, even by phone, was an extremely powerful instrument. Other countries, like the United Kingdom, had successfully used a telesales force for generating leads. Most were using an outsourced telesales force with non-Technosoft management and the "many-to-many" telesales model where telesales representatives (TSRs) did not have an assigned sales territory and worked through assigned call lists. Hence, one customer could be assigned to different TSRs during different sales campaigns.

From the very beginning Chaikovsky knew that he wanted to fully utilize the relationship between the TSR and the customer when they got to know each other over a long period of time. Therefore he wanted to use the "one-to-many" telesales model where each TSR had an assigned sales territory and the opportunity to create a long-term relationship with customers. The one-to-many sales model was more complex and expensive, requiring well-trained TSRs and low staff turnover. It meant a long-term commitment but promised much higher returns than the many-to-many model. In the one-to-many model, TSRs used all marketing activities such as direct mailings, marketing programs and customer events as an additional lever or sometimes to occasionally call customers. Customers who were interested in buying Technosoft products or who had some issue that could be resolved only by a reseller, were transferred by the TSR to the reseller by SMSS (see Exhibit 4). TSRs were responsible for regularly monitoring the sales pipeline and contacting resellers when necessary.

Chaikovsky first approached Dubrovsky with his telesales idea in September 2000. Dubrovsky's first reaction was not encouraging. He had real concerns about the idea. He said: "Technosoft already has a channel and it is the resellers' job to sell. We don't want to confuse the customers. In addition, the telesales project is a long-term commitment, and I'm not sure that Russian customers are ready to buy over the phone." Chaikovsky tried to persuade Dubrovsky to test the concept. The factor that helped to change Dubrovsky's mind was that the U.S. subsidiary was also building a telesales force, and they were doing it using

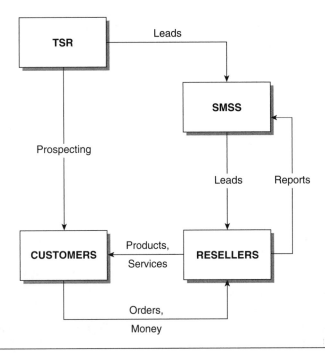

Exhibit 4   Telesale Process

the "one-to-many" model. In addition, EHQ had started to develop its own telesales concept. After two months, Dubrovsky finally agreed to support Chaikovsky's request to the GM for additional budget allocation.

Inspired by this small victory, Chaikovsky created a comprehensive description of future telesales business processes. He discussed these with colleagues in the SMB unit and with key people in other units (see Exhibit 5). Finally, Chaikovsky and Dubrovsky made a presentation to the GM in December and got his support. Additional budget would be allocated from January 2001 for one TSR to test the concept. Even though he had approved the telesales project, Dubrovsky remained reserved about its success.

Ironically, in December, EHQ launched an "SMB Telesales" program which was to be rolled out all over the EMEA. Suddenly telesales became a priority and appeared in many GM scorecards. Subsidiaries were encouraged to allocate funds for this project. The commitment for this project was so high that the EHQ program manager received additional funds to be distributed among countries that were implementing telesales projects. Technosoft Saint Petersburg was in a good position. Chaikovsky's budget was extended to include up to four TSRs over the next six months. Nevertheless, he followed Dubrovsky's strong advice and moved ahead with caution.

The project was started at an outsourcing vendor's location to provide customer support. The vendor was responsible for administration, service and all the necessary equipment like telephones, Internet connection and personal computers. Technosoft Saint Petersburg organized all the training activities and managed the work. The first TSR hired was a former vendor employee who had been working in customer support service and had a good knowledge of Technosoft products. January 2001 was spent polishing up all the procedures, signing agreements with resellers and training them, preparing the working environment and training the TSR. In February 2001, the first TSR started work and the project was launched.

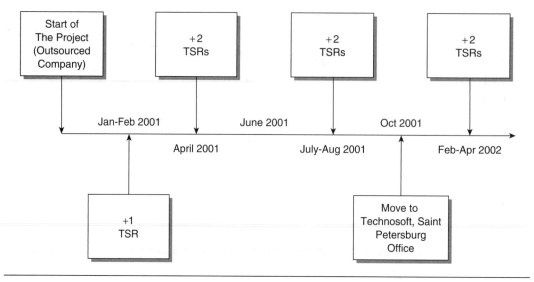

Exhibit 5   Telesales Project Timeline

February and March sales results showed that the concept was very well-accepted by customers and resellers. Surprisingly, customers were not put off by the TSR making "cold" calls. In April, Chaikovsky hired two more TSRs who had been recommended to him even though they did not have telesales experience. Chaikovsky had difficulty in finding adequate candidates and hired a recruitment agency. Unfortunately, the agency did not change the trend: good candidates were rare. Usually, successful people with telesales experience did not want to stay in telesales, and it was difficult to find a person who was smart, mobile and committed to spending at least one year in the telesales position. Chaikovsky did the primary selection of candidates, and then all selected candidates had to be approved by Dubrovsky.

TELESALES TEAM LEADER

Chaikovsky understood that he would not be able to manage a telesales team forever and still be responsible for his other projects as well, so he and Dubrovsky decided that the telesales project should eventually have its own team leader. In June 2001, Chaikovsky was about to hire a young woman, Olga Peterson, who had substantial sales experience. He felt other TSRs could obviously benefit from her experience, but she would require a higher salary than the current TSRs. Chaikovsky was unsure what to offer her when Dubrovsky suggested making her a team leader at the same salary as the TSRs. Chaikovsky preferred to wait at least three months before making such a decision since Peterson did not have any managerial experience. He finally agreed, especially as he could offer a lower salary to Peterson in return for the opportunity for her to become a manager. In addition, Chaikovsky thought it would be a good idea to make Peterson's compensation dependent on the performance of the group. Chaikovsky did not feel totally comfortable with this decision, but he reassured himself that everything would be fine. Peterson seemed to be a good person, and the other TSRs accepted her well at the beginning, admitting her superiority in sales skills.

By summer 2001, Chaikovsky, in co-operation with the Technosoft human resource manager, had developed formal job descriptions for the TSRs and the team leader. During July and August of 2001, two more TSRs were hired, making six members in the telesales team, including the team leader, Olga Peterson. At the same time, Chaikovsky and Dubrovsky made a decision to move the telesales team from the outsourcing vendor's site into the Technosoft office in Saint Petersburg in order to make the team more visible and manageable and to exploit the current facilities of Technosoft office, including Internet connections and phone lines. From the very beginning, the idea was to build the telesales project inhouse so there was no point in delaying relocation of the telesales force from the vendor site. All TSRs and the team leader stayed on as TEs and continued their employment contracts with the outsource vendor.

In February 2002, the telesales project at Technosoft Saint Petersburg added two more TSRs. With eight members on board, it was becoming highly visible, both on a country and a regional level. Following Dubrovsky's advice, Chaikovsky held several meetings with other business units to present the project and introduce the team and to explain how things worked and discuss possible synergies and ideas. Sergei Zolotov, Technosoft's GM, attended one of telesales team staff meetings held by Chaikovsky. Chaikovsky presented the team and all procedures and then asked each TSR to speak about their territory, customers, findings and sales results. Zolotov was delighted by the team performance, made several valuable comments and came up with even more ideas for future development.

A Technosoft EMEA internal conference was scheduled for April, and Chaikovsky had been asked to report on the successes in telesales project. The budgeting process for the next year was going to start soon, and Chaikovsky saw this as a good opportunity to request additional TSR positions. By summer 2002, he wanted the telesales group to have 14 members.

TELESALES POLL

Chaikovsky used the same procedures and processes to manage the telesales group as Technosoft managers used for the FTE group: staff meetings and personal reviews. Staff meetings were used to share information, discuss common issues, compliment and punish publicly. Personal reviews were used to assess individual performance, monitor goals, identify weak points and advise on courses of action. At the beginning, Chaikovsky held staff meetings and personal reviews every week, but when TSRs got used to their responsibilities and procedures, this habit converted into bi-weekly staff meetings and monthly personal reviews. Besides, Chaikovsky was a very approachable person, and the TSRs could ask him a question or have a chat anytime. Once a quarter Chaikovsky did "team building" activities devoted to the celebration of good quarter results.

Despite the fact that a comprehensive training program was developed for new TSRs, Chaikovsky spent a lot of time doing personal review sessions, trying to coach people to help them perform. He tried to understand personal problems and find unique strengths in each person. By December 2001, staff meetings were held once a month, and Chaikovsky stopped doing personal reviews, delegating the job to Peterson. He attended her first meeting with each TSR and gave her some feedback.

Before that, Chaikovsky and Peterson discussed how the staff meetings should be conducted, what the agenda could be, points to review in detail and how to behave. At the first meeting, Chaikovsky allowed Peterson to lead the discussion but steered the direction where necessary. After this meeting, Chaikovsky was basically satisfied with the way that Peterson controlled the discussion. His feedback was concerned with a specific part of the discussion. Peterson seemed to ask the right questions, but they sounded too formal and did not invite conversation; the goal of each performance review. Peterson promised to take this input into account.

In January, some rumors about conflicts between TSRs and Peterson came to Chaikovsky's attention. Chaikovsky spoke with some of the TSRs who complained about "stupid" call plans, unrealistic targets and constant push. Chaikovsky shared these concerns with Peterson, but she reassured him that the situation was under her control.

By February 2002, the one year anniversary of the project, Chaikovsky thought it would be a good idea to conduct a Technosoft poll among the telesales group even though the group were all TEs. He informed the Technosoft human resource manager about his idea and received full support. Chaikovsky created his own questionnaire, incorporating some questions and ideas from the corporate poll. Using a company internal tool, he put the Web-based questionnaire on the Technosoft intranet and asked the TSR team to fill it out. The questionnaire did not contain any personal information. The telesales poll contained sections about Chaikovsky's and Peterson's performances as managers.

The part concerning Peterson was filled out only by the five TSRs who had been working with Peterson at least six months. The two newest TSRs hired in February did not participate in the poll.

TELESALES POLL RESULTS

Poll results revealed some interesting information (see Exhibits 6, 7, and 8), but the part concerning Olga Peterson was discouraging. Peterson was not performing very well as a team leader. Chaikovsky was concerned and not sure what he should do.

Question	Strongly Disagree	Disagree	Neutral	Agree	Strongly Agree
1. I clearly understand Olga Peterson's mission.	1	1	2	1	
2. Olga Peterson's contribution to the group success is tangible.	1	2	2		
3. Olga Peterson's suggestions for SMB Telesales business improvement are relevant.		1	3	1	
4. Olga Peterson knows how to exploit various tools (SBL, Sprut, Technosoft Office, Technosoft Sales) for Telesales Business.		1	2	2	
5. Olga Peterson helps me to achieve my quota.	1	1	1	1	1
6. I ask Olga Peterson when I have a problem.	1	1	2	1	
7. Olga Peterson helps me to solve my problems.	1		3	1	
8. Olga Peterson helps me to determine priorities in my work.	2	2	1		
9. Olga Peterson is candid and honest when giving me feedback on my performance.			4	1	
10. Olga Peterson helps me to work with SBL smartly.		1	2	2	
11. Olga Peterson builds co-operation and teamwork within my work group.	1	1	2	1	

Exhibit 6   Olga Peterson's Telesales Poll Results

Source: Company files.

Question	Strongly Disagree	Disagree	Neutral	Agree	Strongly Agree
1. I have confidence in the effectiveness of Ivan Chaikovsky.					5
2. Ivan Chaikovsky helps me determine priorities for my work.			1	4	
3. Ivan Chaikovsky sets high but achievable standards of performance.			1	4	
4. Ivan Chaikovsky is candid and honest when giving me feedback on my performance.			2	2	1
5. Ivan Chaikovsky builds co-operation and teamwork within my work group.			2	2	1

Exhibit 7   Ivan Chaikovsky Telesales Poll Results

Source: Company files.

Question	Strongly Disagree	Disagree	Neutral	Agree	Strongly Agree
1. I work toward clear goals.					5
2. I have the authority to carry out the responsibilities assigned to me.			2	2	1
3. My work gives me a feeling of personal accomplishment.			1	1	3
4. When I do an excellent job, my accomplishments are recognized.		1	3	1	
5. I feel supported when I take risks in getting my work done.		1	2	1	1
6. I have received the training I need to do my job effectively.			2	2	1
7. I can see a clear link between my work and my work group's objectives.			1	1	3
8. My work group works toward clear goals.			3	1	1
9. The people in my work group co-operate to get the job done.		1	1	2	1
10. I would recommend my work group as a good place to work.			1	4	

Exhibit 8   Telesales Project's Poll Results   *(Continued)*

Question	Strongly Disagree	Disagree	Neutral	Agree	Strongly Agree
11. I am encouraged to work co-operatively with people in other groups.			3	1	1
12. My total compensation package (base pay, bonus, benefits) is fair.		1	4		
13. I believe Technosoft delivers best-in-class products.				1	4
14. I clearly understand Technosoft's vision.				2	3
15. I have confidence in the leadership of the GM of my subsidiary / region.					5
16. Even if I were offered a comparable position with similar pay and benefits at another company, I would stay at Technosoft.				3	2
17. I expect to work for Technosoft for _____. 18. (Neutral=Don't know, 19. Agree=2-4 years, 20. Strongly agree=4-10 years)			3	1	1
21. In my organization, senior management demonstrates through their actions that customer and partner satisfaction is a top priority.					5
22. How would you rate the satisfaction of your organization's customers? (Agree=Satisfied)			2	3	
23. I have the authority to make decisions in the best interest of customers.			3	2	
24. I have a clear understanding of customer needs and expectations.					5
25. The information I need to do my job is accessible and applicable.			3	1	1
26. People at Technosoft have a passion for the work they do.					5

Exhibit 8 (Continued)

Source: Company files.

HEALTHCARE EQUIPMENT CORPORATION—MANAGING IN KOREA

Prepared by Tom Gleave under the supervision of Professor John Eggers

In March 1996, Lynn Delaney, Managing Director of HealthCare Equipment Limited—Asia Pacific (HealthCare AP), was becoming increasingly concerned about the state of leadership at the company's Korean subsidiary. The source of her concern was S.Y. Lee, President of HealthCare AP's wholly owned Korean subsidiary. Lee had been instrumental in ensuring the very successful launch of the Korean operation during its start-up in 1993–94. Since then, however, his behavior had become increasingly problematic, to the point that he had become very disruptive to the operation. Therefore, Delaney needed to craft a leadership development plan for Lee, or else face the unpleasant task of having to terminate him.

COMPANY BACKGROUND

HealthCare Equipment Corporation, a wholly owned subsidiary of HealthCare Industries Inc., was an international leader in the research, development, manufacture and support of *in vitro diagnostics*—the testing of blood outside the body. The company provided public and private clinics and laboratories with various "automated immuno-assay test systems" (AITS) and consumable "reagents,"[1] as well as other tests and controls used for detecting and measuring a broad range of medical conditions. HealthCare Industries prided itself on remaining leading edge, having developed notable advances in the automation of laboratory procedures and pioneered the application of nucleic acid diagnostics as a means of quantifying different viruses. One of the company's key strategic aims was to seek out and establish close partnerships with other industry players in an effort to develop greater market opportunities. The company was based in Atlanta, Georgia, and had established subsidiaries in 20 countries while selling its products in over 70 others. By 1996, it had become the eighth largest diagnostic company in the world, with revenues projected to be US$675 to 690 million for the coming year, a six to ten percent increase over 1995.

The regional office for HealthCare Equipment Corporation—Asia Pacific (HealthCare AP) was in Singapore. The area managed by the office extended from China to the north, Korea to the east, Indonesia to the south and Pakistan to the west, in total covering 20 countries. A separate office was established in Japan because the Japanese market was large and mature enough to warrant its own operation. The Managing Director for HealthCare AP was Lynn Delaney, an Irish expatriate who had been working in Asia since 1982. Delaney first became involved in the immunodiagnostics[2] industry in 1979 when she became a sales representative in London, England, where she had completed her formal training in clinical technology. In 1982, she was dispatched to Australia with the mandate to establish an exclusive supply network with a major local distributor. Later, she became involved in marketing and sales, first in Hong Kong (1985) and then in Singapore (1986). She assumed the Managing Director's position of HealthCare AP in 1992. During the period under Delaney's leadership, sales for the Asia Pacific region had grown from about US$8 million (in 1992) to a projected $55–58 million in 1996. Despite the flat industry sales growth being experienced by most other diagnostics players in 1996, HealthCare AP was poised to achieve a 25 to 30 percent increase in its installed base of AITS, as well as 25 percent growth in reagents. HealthCare AP operated wholly owned subsidiaries in Singapore, Taiwan and Korea, while maintaining seven representative offices and ten exclusive country distributorships throughout the region.

HealthCare AP's key marketing strategy was to focus on the sales and installation of AITS along with the complementary reagents. The economics of the business demanded that a balance be struck between the sales of the two products. This was because a typical AITS installation yielded a one-time revenue of about US $70,000 per unit, with a profit margin of 45 percent if the unit was leased, or 60 percent if it was purchased. Meanwhile, the recurring annual consumption of reagent used in each installed AITS ranged from US$40,000 to $100,000 per year at a profit margin of about 50 percent. Therefore, a premium was placed upon the ability to sell AITS units to clients who were potentially heavy users of reagent.

DISTRIBUTION: A KEY SUCCESS FACTOR

One of the key factors for success in the immunodiagnostics industry was the establishment of secure and manageable distribution channels. In bringing its products to market, HealthCare AP relied upon exclusive distributorships throughout the various countries where it sold its products. These distributors were, in turn, managed by either an in-country representative office, a direct subsidiary company (as was the case in Korea), or by the regional office in Singapore. The criteria used by HealthCare AP to select its exclusive distributors included the following: sales volume in associated product lines; availability of credit for customers; market and product knowledge; and long-term market development strategy. Both the representative offices and subsidiary companies worked directly with the distributors to educate clients on the merits of the products, particularly AITS and reagents.

HealthCare AP's drive to establish a comprehensive distributor network in Asia evolved from a conflict between U.S. legislation and Asian business customs. As Lynn Delaney explained:

> In many Asian countries, whenever products are delivered, clients expect to receive about 10 percent of the invoice amount. However, doing so is contrary to U.S. law which prohibits U.S. businesses from paying "bribes" in order to secure contracts. Company officials who knowingly pay such bribes are subject to fines and prison terms, even if the transaction is completed outside the borders of the U.S. For me, it is highly debatable whether you can impose USA standards on Asian business practice. This is simply an Asian business custom—plain and simple. In any event, to comply with U.S. practice a network of distributors is used in most counties to avoid any possible trouble. That way, we can limit our concern to ensuring that the transactions we execute with our distributors are legally sound. There are also major cost-effective benefits to employing a distribution network when revenues are below a critical mass.

STARTING THE KOREAN OPERATION

HealthCare AP established its wholly owned subsidiary in Korea in 1993. Since then, annual sales had increased from an initial US$1.8 million to $9.0 million in 1995, although a downward trend was being experienced in 1996. Given HealthCare Industries Inc.'s strong belief in the need to localize management, Delaney hired S.Y. Lee as President of the new Korean subsidiary. While she recognized that hiring a local manager had obvious benefits, it also presented a unique set of management challenges. Delaney stated:

> We strongly believe in the localization of management; however, this raises some rather important issues for us. For instance, how much interference should our subsidiaries expect, or tolerate, from our regional office? At the same time, how much latitude should we allow in accommodating so-called "cultural differences" between the management teams of our subsidiaries and our regional operations? After all, our business has been built mostly on Western management ideas and practices, and we have been successful all over the world.

In rationalizing the selection of Lee, Delaney offered the following reasons:

I felt that Lee was suitable for a variety of reasons. First, he had attended the country's most prestigious learning institution, Seoul National University. This gave him immediate credibility in the marketplace, as well as access to well-placed alumni. These alumni could be used to develop client relationships, as well as provide the operation with access to the high calibre employees who were needed to fill the various finance, marketing, sales, service and administrative support roles in the office. Second, he had previously worked in the finance area and presumably understood the need for financial control. Third, he had also previously worked for a joint venture company involving Samsung and General Electric. This meant that he had likely been exposed to leading edge American business practices. What's more, his English was quite good and he also had quite a charismatic personality. I think part of the mystique came from the fact that he was a decorated Vietnam war hero, having undertaken some clandestine work for the Korean special forces. And since he was 54 years old, I thought that his age was ideal for our start-up operation. I anticipated that he could manage the subsidiary for five to eight years before being replaced by someone internally.

Delaney was very pleased with Lee's performance during the initial start-up phase of the Korean subsidiary. Sales growth was substantial over the first two years and he had been able to recruit very capable people to staff the steadily growing number of office and field marketing positions. HealthCare Equipment Corporation's head office was so impressed by the gains made in Korea that it congratulated Delaney and the Korean management team for making the subsidiary the most successful start-up operation in the company's history. In testimony to HealthCare—Korea's achievement, Delaney noted that "the method used in Korea during the start-up is still considered the model for HealthCare Equipment's entry into other undeveloped markets throughout the world."

UNDERCURRENTS

By fall 1995, Delaney began to detect that "a torrent of undercurrents was running through the Korean operation." The tensions in the office had become increasingly dysfunctional and manifested themselves in the formation of two opposing "cliques," with the sales and service departments at "loggerheads" with the marketing department, while the finance and administrative personnel remained neutral. As Delaney later discovered, this came about because there was a "disconnect" between the marketing department, which developed the sales forecasts and marketing programs for Korea, and the sales and service staff, who worked with the end-users. She noted that, under this arrangement, "the sales and service employees were the people in touch with the customer, yet they did not have ownership over the sales forecast to which they were held accountable." The problems soon became so severe that several people started to complain behind Lee's back, a behavior Delaney described as "very un-Korean."[3] This alarmed her because "Koreans were usually very deferential to authority and paid great attention to age and hierarchy."

After investigating the situation thoroughly, Delaney concluded that two main factors were contributing to the problems in Korea, both of which were directly related to Lee's management style. She commented:

> Lee is very much an adherent to the "old school" of Korean business. This means that he expects instant respect due to his age, position and background. He feels that, because of these factors, he warrants total control. I have learned that he has a very autocratic, "do as I say" attitude, and this leads him to have a sense of invulnerability. The other issue is Lee's perception of business priorities. I have discovered that he is very much a short-term planner. He remains very sales-driven, but has little understanding of the need for achieving a proper sales mix or the need for providing proper marketing support.

OTHER TROUBLING SIGNS

Delaney also cited several other indicators that suggested S.Y. Lee's leadership and management style was becoming more problematic. For example, like all other subsidiary and representative office leaders, Lee automatically assumed a position on both HealthCare AP's Executive Management and Strategic Planning Committees. However, whenever he attended these committee meetings, he refused to participate in any discussions. And, according to Delaney, "whenever he was called upon to present Korea's results, his presentations lacked professionalism." Furthermore, in terms of sales priorities, Lee emphasized the placement of AITS at the expense of providing adequate support towards the sale of the consumable reagents used in the AITS. Delaney recognized that "AITS placements were great, but our reagent sales were not." She surmised that Lee's rationale for emphasizing AITS sales was because he felt it was more important to meet revenue targets instead of profit targets. "He wanted to be seen as the 'hero of the day' based upon sales per period, but he failed to see the bigger picture."

Another issue that Delaney found particularly disconcerting about Lee's behavior was that his annual performance reviews were based largely upon areas he neglected. For instance, he was assessed according to his ability to meet profitability targets, his willingness to participate in Executive and Strategic Planning committee meetings, his team-building and people development initiatives and the overall team spirit he instilled in the office. At the same time, Delaney was becoming exasperated with Lee's failure to comply with her wishes. This caused her to employ an authoritarian management style with Lee with increasing frequency. She related:

> In trying to manage Lee, I would start by explaining the rationale for my request. Then I would give him the opportunity to respond accordingly. If he failed to do so, I would then lay down the law. For example, on one occasion, I concluded that he was deliberately trying to sabotage one of Korea's longest serving distributors, one that was established by me prior to the set up of the subsidiary company. This distributor was a high volume producer and provided us with one of our most profitable accounts. But all of a sudden Lee stopped giving the distributor proper organizational support

while starting to look for an alternative distributor. I suspect he was trying to establish his own legacy, but I tried to persuade him differently for obvious economic reasons. I figured he would understand what we should be trying to accomplish, but this did not appear to be the case. He continued to ignore my wishes until, finally, I simply said . . . "You will not interfere or negate any of the distributors' business activities whatsoever. It is as simple as that, and there will be no more discussion on the issue." I must say, I do not like using this management style. It lowers respect between a manager and myself and creates a duo of concern to method of implementation.

ASSESSING KOREA'S LEADERSHIP AND ORGANIZATIONAL CULTURE

In September 1995, Lynn Delaney attended a leadership and management program sponsored by the Singapore chapter of the Young Presidents Association. The program was conducted by Professor John Eggers (from the U.S.-based Center of Creative Leadership) and was designed to provide top-level executives with insights into the strengths and weaknesses of their leadership styles. Delaney found the experience so fruitful that she immediately hired Eggers to work with her in diagnosing both the leadership and organizational culture characteristics of her management team in Singapore. Once again inspired by the results, Delaney contracted Eggers to complete similar work on HealthCare—AP's operations in Malaysia, Taiwan and Korea.

The diagnosis and analysis of HealthCare—AP's management teams were done using a formal assessment tool—the *Organizational Culture Survey*.[4] The Organizational Culture Survey used 26 dimensions to evaluate the values, norms, behavior, structure and outcomes of an organization. The survey was developed to provide a systematic view of the organization by measuring dimensions related to systems, processes, total quality management, and diagnostic models. Research from the Center for Creative Leadership indicated that these organizational culture dimensions correlated highly with a company's financial success. By examining the output of the survey, it was hoped that links between a leader's behavior and organizational practices could be identified.

Eggers commenced the surveying of the Malaysian, Taiwanese and Korean operations in November 1995 and brought the initial results to Delaney's attention in February 1996. After an initial review of the results, she scheduled a meeting for the coming March in Singapore for all of the leaders recently surveyed, as well as HealthCare AP's senior management team, which had been previously surveyed. At the meeting, unbeknown to those surveyed, Eggers conducted the session by using Korea's results as the vehicle for discussion. The results were not labelled so that the graphs could not identify the operation surveyed. In gauging the reaction of the managers, Delaney suggested that "Lee was seemingly the only one who failed to recognize that the results were actually his." This episode crystallized her resolve that something drastic had to be done about Lee's management behavior, and caused her to state:

> I am very grateful for what Mr. Lee has accomplished in Korea. However, at this stage, I am not sure whether or not he can make the leap to the next level of development. Even if he can, I am not sure how to go about supporting him since we are so personally and culturally different. We have used

formal assessment tools to identify and quantify our problems in Korea, and hopefully these exercises will give us some insight about how to proceed. At the same time, I recognize that there is a need to accommodate the culture differences at play in Korea. But, at some point, I also have to be prepared to put a stake in the ground and say "culture differences or not, this is the culture and operating style of HealthCare." That said, the challenge remains to come up with a viable action plan that will remedy the situation because my preference is to work through this issue, instead of simply letting Mr. Lee go.

NOTES

1. AITS were sophisticated instruments which provided users with a range of immunoassays (tests), including tests for thyroid, fertility and cardiac diseases, as well as allergies and anemia. Reagents were the consumable quality control products used in the AITS during testing. Ms. Delaney likened the reagents to "the gasoline that drives the AITS, except that you can only use one specific (proprietary) gasoline for any given AITS."

2. Immunodiagnostics is the use of antibodies to find antigens.

3. See also Appendix 1—The Korean People

4. See Exhibit 1 for descriptions of the respective survey dimensions. See Exhibit 2 for the respective survey results in Korea.

Appendix 1

The Korean People

The Republic of Korea (South Korea) has a population of about 45.5 million which is growing annually at about one percent. Except for a small Chinese minority, the people are all ethnic Koreans, making Korea one of the most homogenous countries in the world. The country's Human Development Index, as established and assessed by the United Nations, ranks South Korea 32nd out of 146 nations. When adjusted for females, it ranks 35th, implying that Koreans generally have very good access to resources that allow them to pursue personal goals, but that women are less likely to earn a decent wage or attend college. Women are also underrepresented in government and business.

Confucianism permeates all aspects of Korean society. It encourages such practices as worshipping at shrines and ancestral tombs. In addition, Confucianism orders social behavior, stressing righteousness and filial piety (family relationships), especially between father and son. The Confucian ethic is evident in the general attitudes of Koreans. Many rituals of courtesy, behavioral formalities, and customs regulate social relations. Hard work and filial piety are highly regarded, although education is the most valued element of Korean culture because it is considered the key to success, respect and power. Koreans often use extreme modesty when speaking about themselves. They are reluctant to accept high honors and they graciously deny compliments. Success also depends greatly upon social contacts. Koreans are quick to make friends, whom they come to value highly. Friends expect to rely on each other for just about anything.

Confucian principles, although less important in modern Korean society than in the past, are still an integral part of social interactions, including greetings. How one is greeted depends on one's age and social standing relative to the greeter. In the case of new acquaintances, it is considered appropriate to ask about each other's age so that both parties will know how to behave towards each other. A bow is the traditional greeting, but is usually accompanied by a handshake between men. As a sign of respect, the left hand may support or rest under the right forearm during the handshake. Women shake hands less often than men do. Professionals who meet for the first time exchange business cards, presenting and accepting the card with both hands after a handshake. A common greeting is *Annyong haseyo?* (Are you at peace?)

Giving gifts as a means of obtaining favors is common, especially in the workplace, and accepting a gift carries the responsibility of reciprocity. Open criticism and public disagreement are considered inappropriate because they can damage another person's reputation. Out of respect for the feelings of others, Koreans may withhold bad news or adverse opinions, or express them in an indirect way.

Source: Culturgram '98, Publications Division, David M. Kennedy Center for International Studies, Brigham Young University, Provo, Utah.

Organizational Structure

1. Job Design — Jobs, reporting relationships, job support and work-flow are designed to meet organizational goals.

2. Work Group Processes — Work groups are organized effectively to reach company goals. Work and performance load is shared.

3. Organizational Integration — Work is well coordinated between groups. Each group's objectives are clear to all employees.

Human Relationships/Group Functioning

4. Conflict — Open discussion of differing views, ideas and suggestions is welcome. Constructive criticism is encouraged.

5. Job Pressure — Work load is positively challenging and can be completed in the hours allowed and with the tools provided.

6. Training and Development — People are trained and developed to increase their skills and advance within the company.

7. Selection — The selection process is effective in hiring the right people for each job. Employees are highly skilled.

8. Job Satisfaction — Employees are satisfied with their work and working relationships.

9. Commitment — Employees are committed to, and are proud to be at, the organization.

10. Trust — Rules and management decisions are seen as supporting the employees.

Leadership

11. Openness to Change — Leaders are quick to take advantage of improved ways of doing things. There is an openness to new ideas.

12. Planning — A visible, clearly stated planning process is used to direct the company's future.

13. Recognize Contributions — Employees are verbally recognized for a job well done.

14. Leadership Confidence Index — There is a trust and confidence in the organization's leaders to make competent decisions and plans for a successful future.

Vision

15. Vision Clarity — Company vision and goals are clear to all employees.

Communication

16. Openness and Vitality — The organization is quick to respond to changes, decisions are timely, and the pace is fast.

17. Challenge Up — Management is open to input from all employees.

Exhibit 1 Organizational Culture Survey Dimension Descriptions *(Continued)*

18. Downward Communication	All levels of the organization receive timely information and are well involved in change processes and decisions.
19. Across Groups Communication	Information from one group to another is quick and clear.
20. Performance Feedback	Employees receive constructive and timely feedback regarding their performance.

Decision Making

| 21. Getting Adequate Information | Decisions are based upon adequate information and employee input when needed. |
| 22. Delegating | When possible, decision making is carried out by employees or teams where the most accurate information is available. |

Motivation

| 23. Rewards/Social Justice | There is a clear connection between performance and pay. People who work hard are rewarded. |
| 24. Performance Facilitation | Policies, practices and work conditions encourage employees to perform well. |

Output

| 25. Product Quality | Products and service are of high quality. |
| 26. Customer Satisfaction | Customers are satisfied with the company's products and services. Future needs of customers are anticipated. |

Exhibit 1 (Continued)

Source: Entrepreneurial Performance Indicators Development Guide—Profiling the Potential for Entrepreneurial Growth. John H. Eggers & Kim T. Leahy (1996). Ewing Marion Kauffman Foundation, Center for Entrepreneurial Leadership Inc., Greensboro, NC.

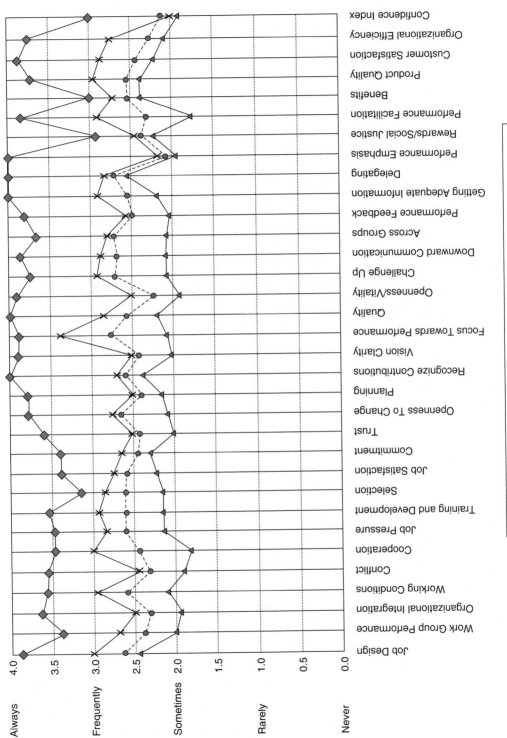

Exhibit 2   Organizational Culture Group Report

THE NEW INFOCRACIES

Implications for Leadership

Prepared by James G. Clawson

To understand the challenges of leading and managing in an infocracy today, just consider these common business scenarios: The account manager of a global company has to struggle to get peers in Sydney, Johannesburg, Kuala Lumpur and Paris to pay attention to his—and their—client. A rapidly growing financial services firm is built around an extraordinary database that allows it to segment its customer and employee base more than 6,000 different ways. A financial services firm grows by acquisition, using a sophisticated merger model based on a fast, accurate and detailed database. A huge insurance company relies heavily on an enormous database and computer network to direct its phone business. A Federal Reserve Bank realizes that it must reorganize its employees in order to utilize new, emerging technology. A global factory automation company struggles to eliminate bureaucracy.

In all of these situations, the leaders or managers are learning how to function in the new, emerging "infocracies." The Information Age is creating a series of new organizational forms that are supplanting the bureaucracies of the Industrial Age. These infocracies create new dilemmas for leaders and demand different decision-making structures and avenues of influence. Some leaders are lagging behind, holding on to the bureaucratic principles of leadership with which they grew up. Others are forging ahead because they have to and learning the new habits and means of leadership.

INFOCRACIES?

Prior to the Industrial Revolution, Eastern and Western societies were largely stratified according to an aristocratic model, which conferred leadership and power by birthright. Kings and noblemen (the leaders were almost always male) exercised extensive power over their subjects. While this male-dominated, lineage-based authority structure was codified around the 13th century with the formal adoption of primogeniture, it has actually been the dominant model for most of human history. Aristocrats were thought to be the primary possessors of the wisdom and the "right" to order and sustain society. The rights to govern and decide the fate of societies and their populaces ran, without fail, through the family line. Simply speaking, the underlying assumption that supported this arrangement could be summed up as "father knows best."

But the Industrial Revolution—as surely as, though less visibly than, the political revolutions in America and France—began to change all that. The advent of the steam engine during the late 18th century and the early 19th century, mass production techniques and petroleum spurred a change in the way societies viewed authority. People discovered that the dukes and the earls were ill prepared to administer the then new, emerging bureaucracies. Power gradually shifted to "offices" or in the French, "bureaus," which presumed a certain set of skills and abilities. This created a "succession" problem. Though it was relatively easy to identify the next king in an aristocracy, identifying the next person to hold the chief executive's office in the new Industrial Age required a wider-ranging search with a different set of criteria. As the new managerial system took hold, the underlying assumption shifted from "father knows best" to "the boss knows best."

In a world where few were educated enough to understand and deal with large-scale industrial problems, this assumption worked well enough. Large industrial organizations grew up during the 19th century with centralized decision-making structures and functionally specialized departments. Decisions that affected the organization as a whole filtered up to the chief executive. In an emerging industrial era, the titans of commerce were able to keep track of what was going on and, in general, to make decisions that grew their organizations. The personality and preferences of the Carnegies, Rockefellers, Fords, Sloans and Watsons of the world were stamped on their companies.

The transition from aristocracy to bureaucracy proceeded gradually. Indeed, it was nearly 100 years after the Industrial Revolution began that the German sociologist Max Weber codified the nature of bureaucracies in *The Theory of Social and Economic Organization*. His characterization of the tenets of bureaucracy, shown, is revealing. A comparison of Weber's summary with the tenets of aristocracies makes the differences clear.

THE EMERGENCE OF INFOCRACIES

In the 20th century, "bureaucracy" took on a negative connotation. The term came to be synonymous with poor service, slow decision making, thick interdepartmental boundaries, a lack of flexibility and the notion of perpetuating itself.

Being called a "bureaucrat" took on the quality of an epithet. Today's managers, unlike those of 150 years ago, would rather not be bureaucrats and instead aspire to being, entrepreneurs or leaders of high-performing organizations. The negative connotations of "bureaucrat" are only a few of the many signs that another global paradigm shift of similar scale to that of the Industrial Revolution is currently under way.

The Industrial Age is yielding to what most commentators have termed the Information Age, a turbulent business environment that places a premium on continuous learning, rapid communication, adaptability and at its centre—information. In such an environment, many of the former strengths of the bureaucratic model—a firmly established chain of command, rigidly uniform procedures, a "boss knows best" attitude—have become serious weaknesses. In industry after industry, companies have undertaken radical restructurings in search of a new organizational model to suit the demands of the Information Age. These new organizations have a number of groundbreaking features in common—features that attest to the widespread realization that the basis of power is no longer aristocratic lineage or office, but *information* (see "Principles of Infocracies"). The suffix "cracy" refers to power. Aristocracy, therefore, is power based on lineage. Bureaucracy is power based on office. Infocracy is power based on information (James Clawson, *Level Three Leadership,* chap. 1, Prentice Hall, 1999).

Weber's Bureaucratic Principles

1. Law supercedes personal judgment.

2. "Offices" have responsibility.

3. Incumbents of those offices have authority.

4. Obedience is to the office, not the person.

5. Offices are bound by a rational system of division of labor.

6. Offices fit into a hierarchy of authority; every office is subject to another office.

7. Incumbents should learn to fit into their offices.

The second figure is a diagram of the managerial paradigm shifts described above. The stimulants in the two shifts, the Industrial Revolution and the Information Revolution beginning with the advent of the computer in the 1950s, are shown at the top. Notice that the colour gradient indicates that the paradigm shifts were not instantaneous, but rather extended over long periods of time. In fact, we still have vestiges of the aristocratic system in place today in Japan, England and Thailand, for example. The slope on the Information Age transition is shown to be much steeper because it seems to be taking place more rapidly than the previous one. That said, there are many corporations and organizations today that slipping on that slope, reluctant as they are to embrace and learn the distinctive features of an infocracy and what the implications of those features are for leadership. Where is your organization?

In 1960, in IBM's *Think* magazine, Warren Bennis predicted that bureaucracies were dying. He predicted that the ponderous decision making and functional divisions of the Industrial Age bureaucracy would render them obsolete. He was right. I too remember sitting in a room with Jack Welch, who presided over the extraordinary growth and prosperity of the General Electric company for 20 years, and hearing him tell a story about visiting a room full of upper middle level GE managers and leaders. He said he gave a talk and then opened the session up for questions and answers. As he listened to their questions, he realized that he didn't have the answers, and what's more, he realized that he couldn't have the answers. At this point he realized that he needed to begin dismantling the bureaucracy that GE had become. His well-documented "Work-Out" effort that spanned the late 1980 and early 1990s—and that continues today—was the result. He hired four main consultants and 24 "lead" consultants to work with each of the major GE divisions to reduce or eliminate bureaucracy. As a participant in that effort, I began to see how the bureaucratic form, once the very foundation of economic growth, had become a significant inhibitor of that growth.

Infocracies share some characteristics with the bureaucracies they are replacing. They have not entirely abandoned hierarchy, and they have maintained certain internal policies, procedures and measurement systems in the interest of control and order. Leadership continues to be important. That said, Industrial Age bureaucracies were well represented by the pyramid-shaped organizational charts which have long been a fixture of the business world—the president at the top, the VPs in the next tier, and everyone aware of their place. Infocracies don't follow this blueprint. One very successful financial services company that a colleague and I visited recently has many characteristics of an infocracy. In fact an inquiry about the company's organization chart was met with "We don't have one. I guess we could sit down and I could explain it to you in a couple of hours, but it's not on paper and never has been." Information flow is the lifeblood of an infocracy, and in search of better circulation they have resorted to structures that have prompted a range of descriptive metaphors, from a network of neurons to a bowl of spaghetti.

Power in infocracies resides in no single person or office. Instead, it migrates to whoever is closest to the key personal challenges facing the organization at any given time and who has access to the relevant data for making the appropriate decision. Proximity to these challenges gives such people an information-based expertise that upper management often cannot match. As a result, management takes on a supporting rather than a directing role.

Much of this support consists of marshalling, from various functional divisions, the teams of people who will be best suited to each challenge. As teamwork and information exchange become more crucial, the flow of activity becomes less like a vertical chain and more like a decentralized, team-based network.

The key features of the new, emerging infocracies, as I see them, are shown on page 119. We have written these in part to show how they contrast with the principles of bureaucracy and also to add new features that seem to be emerging. We doubt that this is the "final" summary of the

Principles of Infocracies

1. Data supercedes policies and judgments.

2. Databases have responsibility.

3. Database interpreters have authority.

4. Obedience is to the data.

5. Interpreters are bound by converging interpretations of the data.

6. Interpreters link to other databases and their interpreters. Every interpreter is subject to these network nodes.

7. Interpreters should learn to understand their data.

8. Infocratic cultures tend to be non defensive and data-driven.

9. Hierachies tend to be flatter and more egalitarian.

10. Feedback flows in all directions.

11. Fear of arbitrariness declines as more decisions are based on data.

Paradigm Shifts in Management

Industrial Revolution		Information Revolution
PRIMOGENITURE **ARISTOCRACY** HISTORY THROUGHOUT 18TH CENTURY • power is distributed by gender and lineage • assumption is "Father knows best"	MAX WEBER **BUREAUCRACY** 19TH AND 20TH CENTURIES • power is distributed by gender and office • assumption is "Boss knows best"	BENNIS **INFOCRACY** INFORMATION AGE • power is redistributed to node interpreters • assumption is "Node interpreters know best"

Exhibit 1   Paradigm Shifts in Management

---

nature of infocracies and offer this definition as a starting point for the discussion about what infocracies are and how they are taking shape during this transitional period.

Faced with a business environment in which the rate of change continues to escalate, corporations in every industry have begun to adopt features of this revolutionary new model. Some of these changes are highly visible—such as the phasing-out of executive offices and other symbols of bureaucratic hierarchy and in companies with a half-hearted commitment to the new vision, reform may go no deeper than this. Other firms, though, not content to merely break down the walls between one level of management and another, are even blurring the boundaries between the organization and its surroundings. As information—and therefore power—flows more freely between vendors and customers, between stakeholders inside the company and those in the outside world, the very distinction between "inside" and "outside" begins to lose meaning.

The central feature of infocracies is that decision-making power emanates from databases. Peter Drucker and others have argued that it is not the information database that is the central feature, rather it is the "knowledge worker." While it is clear that data without interpretation is meaningless, it is also clear that intelligent organizational members are powerless without key information, regardless of their title or organizational authority. The history of bureaucracies over the last 30 years of the 20th century is nothing if not about how disconnected most senior managers became from their markets and the signals they were sending to them. The electronics, automobile, computer and public utility industries were all rife with examples of companies whose management missed the importance of the market signals they were receiving or had such poorly designed information systems that they never got the signals in the first place. Consequently, effective infocracies are emerging as organizations in which there is a general and effective marriage between access to relevant and current databases and the education and experience necessary to interpret them. In this model, the interpreters become the leaders and key decision makers rather than the nominal head of the organizational hierarchy. In many organizations, these interpreters are distributed widely throughout their networks so that the senior executives tend to get reports of decisions made rather than requests to make them. An examination of each of these characteristics is beyond the space allotted to this piece. Nevertheless, their implications for changes in leadership drive to the fore. The rest of this article will identify some implications of the infocratic

form for leadership, style and characteristics. This list will not include all of the implications of infocracies, but it may help us anticipate some directions.

INFOCRACIES AND THEIR IMPLICATIONS FOR LEADERSHIP

Because infocracies are based on power distributed by access to widely distributed information, they demand a different kind of leadership than bureaucracies. Power is gradually shifting from chief executives to node incumbents, people who operate at the confluence nodes of information networks and customer demands. Most of the management philosophies and techniques that business schools—and experience—have taught for the last 200 years have bureaucratic assumptions at their roots. In an infocracy, a bureaucratic-minded manager will face problems that the old tools simply will not fix. The leadership implications of infocracies are summarized in the sidebar. While space does not permit a detailed discussion of each of these evolving characteristics, it does allow us to at least introduce them.

Away From Command-and-Control Toward Data-Based Persuasion. Command-and-control leadership based on the bureaucratic model of POMC (planning, organizing, motivating, and controlling and its variants) becomes much less meaningful in a data-based power structure. When many have access to the data, the few are less able to decide unilaterally what should be done. Data-based persuasion becomes the dominant means of influence. With increasing data links to virtually every household, market research becomes more accurate. With links to suppliers and customers, production planning becomes more automatic. Leadership books that recognize this shift are already appearing. (Jay Conger, *Winning 'em Over: A New Model for Managing in the Age of Persuasion;* Simon and Schuster, 1998).

Leadership for Infocracies

1. Away from command-and-control toward data-based persuasion.

2 Non-defensive, high EQ, SQ and CQ.

3. Away from knowing toward need to know.

4. Away from information hoarding to information sharing.

5. Values based.

6. Higher emphasis on ethics.

7. Away from social Darwinian winners and toward transcenders.

8. Away from narcissism and toward joint recognition.

9. Away from high OH toward low OH.

10. Away from use and lose toward clean as you go.

Non-Defensive, High EQ, SQ and CQ. Infocratic leaders need to be relatively non-defensive. When information of all kinds, including performance evaluations, is flowing in all directions, the chief executive is no longer immune to bottom-up feedback. The explicit development of emotional intelligence that keeps leaders from being high-jacked by defensiveness will become increasingly important. IQ will be insufficient, as the ability to read emotions in others (SQ) and to recognize the need to change (CQ) will be essential in persuading others to change when the data implies they ought to. Where bureaucracies tolerate and even encourage power-based tirades by senior people, infocracies will require a more level, evidence-based set of leadership communications.

Away From Knowing Toward Need to Know. Mick McGill and John Slocum's article "Unlearning the Organization" points out a set of infocratic principles. Those who "know" how to run their businesses are becoming increasingly obsolete. Bureaucracies tend to promote people who know how to do a job; infocracies will promote people who have a thirst for learning and are willing to let go of yesterday's "knowledge"

in the face of today's data. Jack Welch put it succinctly: "Face reality as it is, not as it was or as you wish it were."

Away From Information Hoarding Toward Sharing Information. Functional bureaucracies with their competitive hierarchies tended to encourage comments like: "Sorry, that's on a need to know basis only." Infocracies encourage: "Yes, that's on a need to know basis, and you all need to know." Small and large information systems in infocracies will be designed to share data on all aspects of the organization with all its members so that those closest to the decisions will be supported immediately. The Chicago Park District worked extraordinarily hard in the mid-1990s under the leadership of Forrest Claypool and Carol Rubin (chief operating officer) to develop a data collection and distribution network that would describe the activities of the hundreds of facilities in its system. The challenge, as Claypool put it, was to "transform a moribund bureaucracy" into a vibrant organization that served the citizens of Chicago.

Values 4-Based. Subordinates in bureaucracies ultimately obey the authority of an office regardless of the incumbent. Members of infocracies respond to data that confirm a certain direction. The choice of directions is a value-based, strategic set of decisions. Employees no longer say: "Yes, sir" to the superior officer, rather they ask: "Do we agree on our goals and future vision?" and then, "What evidence do you have that we are going in that direction'?" This kind of persuasion presumes clarity of objective based on a set of values that have become increasingly more important. The first three leadership generations at the FMC Aberdeen plant in South Dakota established a set of values around which they designed and led the plant to extraordinary performance. These values were so central that it took nine days to train mature adults how to reconfigure their daily conversational patterns (to give accurate, descriptive feedback or data to each other). The new values also caused the company to hire people for interpersonal rather than technical qualifications (hiring a woman who had never welded, for example, to be a welder).

Higher Emphasis on Ethics. To the extent that bureaucracies encouraged members to think in terms of their own specialties (responding to others with the commonly heard, "That's not my department"), they also encouraged members to avoid general responsibility—whether it be for labour relations, diversity issues, pollution or other aspects of social responsibility. Infocracies share data rapidly and efficiently so that it is much easier for any member of the organization to learn what the company is doing on any front. Further, the impact of the Information Age on society generally means that no company can long expect to be hidden from public view—just as politicians now are faced with public scrutiny. In some cases, this lack of privacy in an infocratic age will demand and force leaders to adhere to higher standards of societally defined ethical standards. For example, *Fortune* magazine recently reported on the seemingly unethical practices of many new dot-com companies, with the clear intent of pressuring them to clean up their accounting acts. It was much harder to see and get this information in the Industrial Age; in the Information Age, public scrutiny will continue to sharpen and the information will be easier to access.

Away From Social Darwinism "Winners" Toward "Transcenders." It seems obvious that human civilization has far outstripped our genetic endowment. The "win/lose" contest resulting in the survival of the fittest has become increasingly dysfunctional economies and industries will have to learn to be interdependent rather than trying to kill off all competitors. In the Information Age, data will make that possible. Awareness of the dependencies of Information Age societies demands that infocratic leaders learn to consciously shape their development, rather than rely on genetic codes developed fighting, conquering and destroying neighbouring tribes. Increasingly, infocracies are intertwined with each other. Data links to suppliers, distributors, customers, point-of-sale inputs and related pieces of an interconnected global economy continue to "infect," in Mihalyi Csikszentmihalyi's terms, memes (like genes) powerful new ideas like viruses, take root and spread in what used to be relatively independent, stand-alone, win/lose-oriented companies. (Mihalyi Csikszentmihalyi, *The Evolving Self: A Psychology for the New Millennium,* Harper & Collins, 1993).

Away From Narcissism Toward Joint Recognition. Michael Maccoby recently described the pros and cons of the narcissistic leader (Michael Maccoby, "Narcissistic Leaders: The incredible pros, the inevitable cons," *Harvard Business Review,* Jan/Feb 2000, p. 69). Their weaknesses—sensitivity to criticism, inability to listen, lack of empathy, distaste for mentoring and intense competitiveness—are much better suited to a bureaucratic world than an infocratic one. Narcissists, for instance, like to build large edifices, a common feature of the bureaucratic age. Infocracies are much less impressed with large buildings that belie their underlying hierarchies than are bureaucracies. I once visited a potential client interested in reducing bureaucracy and became aware of the difficulties of the task driving into the parking lot that surrounded the huge, pyramid-shaped headquarters building. Some interpret the win/lose assumptions of most bureaucracies to be strong, and the assumptions of flatter, win/win organizations to be weak. Infocratic leaders will not be weak; it takes enormous mental toughness to listen to and deal with disconfirming data, and they will be required to be more honest in recognizing the contributions of the node interpreters throughout their organizations as essential to their joint success. In this kind of organization, narcissism increasingly becomes a liability.

Low Orientation to Hierarchy Away From High Orientation to Hierarchy. Infocracies are much flatter than bureaucracies. They are organized around networks and connections rather than hierarchies. ("Organigraphs: Drawing how companies really work," Henry Mintzberg and Ludo Van der Heyden, *Harvard Business Review,* Sept/Oct, 1999; reprint #99506). I am currently conducting research that suggests that "orientation toward hierarchy" may be a measurable difference in leaders and one that reflects a resistance to change in bureaucracies (high OH) or a willingness to work in an infocracy (low OH). Csikszentmihalyi's "transcenders," who consciously push against the genetic code that encourages domination and subjugation, come to mind; infocratic leaders will be transcenders who are able to push against and modify the assumptions of the bureaucracies in which they were trained.

Away From "Use and Lose" Toward "Clean as You Go." The Industrial Age coincided with the exploration and settling of the earth's land mass. As we have attained the farthest reaches of the "south forty" on our global ranch, we are learning that questions about the sustainability of the race are coming to the fore. With better data available to all, bureaucracies are no longer able to say to society that "sustainability is not my department." Leftovers of all kinds are now the target of recycling rather than disposal. One Swiss industrial filter manufacturer forced by

regulation to ship its waste to Spain for disposal retained Bill McDonough of the University of Virginia to help design a clean facility. In the end, some 4,900-plus chemicals used in the plant failed an environmental audit. The 20 some odd chemicals that "passed" were used in a design in which the company was later able to report that continuing its high quality of productivity, its effluence was cleaner than the water drawn into the system. This kind of social responsibility will become an increasing hallmark of the infocracy, where descriptive data on all aspects of operations will become available to insiders and outsiders alike.

There are a number of issues related to working and leading in infocracies that remain to be sorted out. For example, it remains to be seen how these issues will be experienced, designed and described: engagement, work/life balance, strategic thinking, relationship building, quality, sense making, innovation, organizational design and structure, learning and work addiction. These and other issues are being dealt with and created as infocracies gradually but inexorably replace the bureaucracies that preceded them.

The Information Age is spawning a new kind of organizational form, the infocracy, in which power is distributed by the size, strength and relevancy of its information networks and databases. As bureaucracies make this transition, some leading and some lagging, leaders who understand the different kinds of leadership demands that an infocracy implies will be better positioned to continue and expand their influence than those residual bureaucrats who dig in their heels and resist. Every person in a position of authority today would do well to reflect on the characteristics of infocracies, to define their own variant and, more importantly, to reflect on their own skills and leadership habits in that context. Even those who have accumulated significant power, particularly in an Industrial Age company, will someday have to acknowledge that in leadership, as Dylan once sang, "the times, they are a changin'"

Leadership for Inforcracies

1 Away from command-and-control toward data-based persuasion.
2 Non-Defensive, high EQ, SQ and CQ.
3 Away from knowing toward need to know.
4 Away from information hoarding to information sharing.
5 Values-based.
6 Higher emphasis on ethics.
7 Away from social Darwinian winners and toward transcenders.
8 Away from narcissicism toward joint recognition.
9 Away from high OH toward low OH.
10 Away from use and lose toward clean as you go.

Weber's Bureaucratic Principles

1 Law supercedes personal judgment.
2 "Offices" have responsibility.
3 Incumbents of those offices have authority.
4 Obedience is to the office, not the person.
5 Offices are bound by a rational system of division of labor.
6 Offices fit into a hierarchy of authority; every office is subject to another office.
7 Incumbents should learn to fit into their offices.

Principles of Infocracies

1 Data supercedes policies and personal judgments.
2 Databases have responsibility.
3 Database interpreters have authority.
4 Obedience is to the data.
5 Interpreters are bound by converging interpretations of the data.
6 Interpreters link to other databases and their interpreters. Every inerpreter is subject to these network nodes.
7 Interpreters should learn to understand their data.
8 Infocratic cultures tend to be non-defensive and data-driven.
9 Hierarchies tend to be flatter and more egalitarian.
10 Feedback flows in all directions.
11 Fear of arbitrariness declines as more and more decisions are based on data.

5

The Situational
Approach to Leadership

*A leader must be able to put a team together with the right people and struc-
ture the company in such a way that it will succeed. . . . It is good for leaders
to take a hands-on approach, but it is not possible for one person to do
everything. You need to delegate, which is not an easy task. If you do not
learn to let go, you will never be able to do everything that needs to get done.
But delegation and trust go hand in hand. You cannot empower someone to
make decisions and then interfere with their decisions at the same time. If
your staff is not sure about certain decisions, work with them and perhaps
make the decision with them jointly.*

—Cheng Yu Tung[1]

Contrary to other theories of leadership that are descriptive, the situational
approach to leadership is prescriptive. This leadership approach tells leaders
what to do in different situations and what not to do in other situations. This
approach is widely used in leadership development and training and has been refined and
revised several times (Blanchard, Zigarmi, & Nelson, 1993).

The situational leadership theory has two underlying assumptions. First, as situations
vary, so must a person's leadership. This means that leaders are able to adapt their styles to
different situations. Second, leadership is made up of a directive component and a supportive component, and these two components have to be exercised appropriately based on the
context. To assess the appropriate level of each component, it is critical that leaders evaluate
their subordinates and determine their level of competence and commitment to a given task
or job. Inherent in this latter assumption is that subordinates' levels of competence and commitment may change over time, requiring that leaders need to change their level of direction
and personal support to match these changing needs in their employees. The situational leadership approach suggests that leaders who are more capable of assessing what their subordinates need and changing their own style will be more effective as leaders (Dubrin, 2007).

This approach to leadership suggests that understanding situational leadership is best accomplished by discussing the two underlying principles: leadership style and subordinates' level of development (Northouse, 2007).

LEADERSHIP STYLES AND SUBORDINATE DEVELOPMENTAL LEVEL

As in Chapter 4, leadership style describes a leader's behavior when he or she tries to influence others. Thus, it includes directive or task behaviors and supportive or relationship behaviors.

These two groups of behaviors help subordinates to accomplish goals and to be positively encouraged in how they feel about their job, their coworkers, and themselves. Four styles based on being directive and supportive are suggested by the situational leadership approach. These are directing, coaching, supporting, and delegating. These are described along with brief descriptions as to when and why they should be used based on the developmental level exhibited by subordinates with respect to their competencies for, and their commitment to, getting the job done.

Directing Leadership Style

This style is directive and nonsupportive. Leader communications are focused on getting the job done with little or no communication effort focused on supportive behaviors. The communication effort is one-way and emphasizes instructions that give subordinates direction about what to do and how to do it. This style is associated with close and careful supervision (Northouse, 2007).

This style is most appropriate when subordinates are most committed but least competent in what to do and how to do it (low development level [D1]; see the Situational Leadership II model in Northouse [2007]). Because they are most committed, the level of leader support can be minimal, while the level of direction has to be high because subordinates

Table 5.1   Directive and Supportive Behaviors for Situational Leadership

Directive behaviors aid in goal achievement	Some supportive behaviors are
—by giving directions	—asking for input
—by establishing goals	—problem solving
—by establishing methods of evaluation	—praising
—by setting time lines	—sharing information regarding self
—by defining roles	—listening
—by showing how to achieve goals	—job related
In addition, directive behaviors	Supportive behaviors help subordinates to
—clarify what is to be accomplished	—feel comfortable with the situation
—clarify how it is to be accomplished	—feel comfortable with their coworkers
—clarify who will accomplish it	—feel comfortable with themselves
Often through one-way communication	*Often through two-way communication*

Source: Adapted from Northouse (2007). Copyright © 2007, Sage Publications, Inc.

are least competent. The reason for the lower level of competence is generally because subordinates are new to the job or task to be accomplished (Dubrin, 2007).

Coaching Leadership Style

This style is highly directive and highly supportive. Communications from the leader to followers focus on getting the job done and on employees' emotional and social needs. Communication is two-way in that leaders communicate to subordinates and encourage input from subordinates. Leaders still decide on what needs to be accomplished and how it will be accomplished (Northouse, 2007).

This style is most appropriate when subordinates have some competence but a lower level of commitment. They are learning their job but losing some of their commitment to and motivation for the job (moderate development level [D2]; see the Situational Leadership II model in Northouse [2007]). In this situation, the leader still needs to be directive but also needs to be supportive (Dubrin, 2007).

Supporting Leadership Style

This style is highly supportive but relatively low on direction. The leader focuses on supportive behaviors in his or her communications to subordinates to bring out the skills required to accomplish the task. Subordinates have control over day-to-day operations, but the leader is still available for problem solving if needed. These leaders give deserved recognition to subordinates in a timely manner and support subordinates socially when needed (Northouse, 2007).

This style is most appropriate when subordinates have the required job skills but lack the necessary commitment because they are uncertain as to whether they have the necessary skills (moderate developmental level [D3]; see the Situational Leadership II model in Northouse [2007]). Direction is not required in this situation, but a lot of encouraging support is needed to support subordinates in using their well-developed skill set (Dubrin, 2007).

Delegating Leadership Style

The delegating style is best described as low direction and low support. In this approach, employees have more confidence and motivation when leaders are less directive and less supportive. Leaders agree with subordinates on the end result but then back off and allow subordinates to be responsible for accomplishing the desired result. In essence, the leader gives the employees control and avoids any unnecessary social support (Northouse, 2007).

This approach is appropriate when subordinates are very skilled and highly committed (high developmental level [D4]; see the Situational Leadership II model in Northouse [2007]). In this situation, giving subordinates more control and less social support is best because of their seasoned skills and motivation to do their best for the organization. Being even a little directive or supportive may cause subordinates to work less skillfully and with less commitment as they sense a lack of trust on the part of their leaders (Dubrin, 2007).

How Does the Leadership Situational Approach Work?

The key to this approach is to understand that subordinates individually and as a group move along the developmental continuum. This movement could occur from day to day, week to week, or even over longer periods depending on the subordinates and the task to be accomplished. Effective leaders discern where subordinates are and adapt their style appropriately.

Questions that help leaders discern where subordinates are on the developmental continuum are as follows: What job needs to be accomplished? How difficult is the job? Do subordinates have the necessary skills to accomplish the job? Are subordinates sufficiently motivated to start and complete the job? In addition, understanding the directive and supportive behaviors available to leaders will enable them to use the appropriate behaviors depending on the answers to these questions (Northouse, 2007). The trait approach (Chapter 2) and the contingency approach (Chapter 6) suggest that leader style is fixed; the situational approach to leadership suggests that leaders need to behave in a manner that is adaptive and flexible (Yukl, 2006).

NOTE

1. Cheng Yu Tung is the Chairman of New World Development Co. Ltd. in Hong Kong.

REFERENCES

Blanchard, K., Zigami, D., & Nelson, R. (1993). Situational leadership after 25 years: A retrospective. *Journal of Leadership Studies, 1*(1), 22–36.

Dubrin, A. (2007). *Leadership: Research findings, practice, and skills.* New York: Houghton Mifflin.

Northouse, P. G. (2007). *Leadership: Theory and practice* (4th ed.). Thousand Oaks, CA: Sage.

Tung, C. Y. (2006, April 4). The school of hard knocks (Part 5 of 8, Ivey Leadership Series). *South China Morning Post,* Business Section.

Yukl, G. (2006). *Leadership in organizations* (6th ed.). Upper Saddle River, NJ: Pearson-Prentice Hall.

THE CASES

Brookfield Properties: Crisis Leadership Following September 11, 2001

Brookfield Properties is a publicly held North American commercial real estate company focused on the ownership, management, and development of premier office properties located in the downtown core of selected North American markets. Most of Brookfield's assets are in the United States, with headquarters in New York and an executive office in Toronto. Four of the properties that Brookfield owns are adjacent to the World Trade Center site, and on September 11, 2001, the terrorist attacks had an immediate impact on Brookfield employees, tenants, and physical property. With little reliable information and in the face of chaos and human tragedy, the president and chief executive officer must develop an action plan that will ensure the safety of all employees and tenants, deal with grief and suffering, assess the damage, enable the company to return to "business as usual," and reassure investors and the media of the company's commitment to restore Brookfield's position of market strength.

Elite, Inc. (A)

Elite, Inc. is a highly successful public relations firm. Elite's chief financial officer has been spending 18-hour days in an effort to get his work done. The newly appointed chief executive officer must determine the cause of the excessive workload and develop a strategy to deal with the chief financial officer's performance.

THE READING

Making Difficult Decisions in Turbulent Times

In turbulent times, some leaders make tough choices with courage and conviction. Others, however, remain indecisive. But most executives find ways to cope with uncertainty, ways that enable them to make sense of a confusing situation. In this article, the author describes seven strategies that leaders can use to cope with ambiguity and complexity when making decisions. He also points out their drawbacks, underlining the need to take great care when deploying these strategies.

BROOKFIELD PROPERTIES

Crisis Leadership Following September 11th, 2001

*Prepared by Elizabeth O'Neil under the
supervision of Professor Kathleen Slaughter*

Copyright © 2002, Ivey Management Services   Version: (A) 2003–01–13

It was 4 P.M. on September 11, 2001, and Bruce Flatt, president and chief executive officer (CEO) of Brookfield Properties Corporation, had just approved the press release that would be issued shortly from the Toronto, Canada, office. The World Trade Center (WTC) in New York City had been the target of terrorist bombings that morning and the city was in chaos. Brookfield's four properties adjacent to the WTC appeared to have sustained considerable damage, but no concrete information was available. It seemed that employees and tenants had been safely evacuated. Flatt had to quickly formulate an action plan to manage this crisis and then get some input from Ric Clark and John Zuccotti, who ran Brookfield's U.S. operations.

BROOKFIELD PROPERTIES CORPORATION

Brookfield Properties Corporation was a publicly held North American commercial real estate company whose origins were in sports facility management.

In 1924, Canadian Arena Corporation, the predecessor to Brookfield, built the Montreal Forum to provide facilities for hockey and other sporting and cultural events. Until 1972, Brookfield's earnings were derived principally from the ownership of the Montreal Forum and the Montreal Canadiens of the National Hockey League.

During the 1960s, Brookfield expanded into various facets of the real estate business and, in 1976, the company began to shift its focus to commercial real estate interests.

In 1990, a strategic decision was made to focus Brookfield's investments in premier office properties in select, high-growth, supply-constrained North American markets, including New York, Toronto, Boston, Calgary, Denver and Minneapolis. Over the next few years, the accumulation of these assets was completed through various purchases, including that of the former real estate assets of BCE Inc., Olympia & York, and Gentra Inc. (see Exhibit 1).

JUNE 30, 2002	Number of Properties	Leased	Office	Retail/ Other	Leasable Area	Effective Ownership Interest	Brookfield's Effective Interest
		%	000's Sq. Ft.	000's Sq. Ft.	000's Sq. Ft.	%	000's Sq. Ft.
NEW YORK							
World Financial Center							
Tower One	1	99.4%	1,520	108	1,628	100%	1,628
Tower Two	1	100.0%	2,455	36	2,491	100%	2,491
Tower Four	1	100.0%	1,711	89	1,800	51%	917
Retail		72.3%	—	287	287	100%	287
One Liberty Plaza	1	93.0%	2,194	20	2,214	100%	2,214
245 Park Avenue	1	99.9%	1,631	62	1,693	100%	1,693
Development sites							
CIBC World Markets Tower	1	—	1,200	—	1,200	100%	1,200
Penn Station	1	—	2,500	—	2,500	100%	2,500
	7	97.9%	13,211	602	13,813		12,930
TORONTO							
BCE Place							
Canada Trust Tower	1	99.6%	1,127	18	1,145	50%	573
Bay Wellington Tower	1	97.6%	1,295	42	1,337	100%	1,337
Retail, parking and office	2	98.3%	137	809	946	75%	705
Exchange Tower Block	2	98.4%	1,137	256	1,393	51%	708
HSBC Building	1	94.2%	188	37	225	100%	225
Queen's Ouay Terminal	1	97.6%	428	74	502	100%	502
Other	3	92.4%	1,198	137	1,335	28%	380
Development sites							
Bay-Adelaide Centre	1	—	1,000	800	1,800	50%	900
Hudson's Bay Centre	1	—	535	557	1,092	25%	273
BCE Place III	1	—	800	—	800	65%	520
	14	96.9%	7,845	2,730	10,575		6,123
BOSTON							
53 State Street	1	99.9%	1,091	70	1,161	51%	592
75 State Street	1	93.8%	742	260	1,002	51%	511
	2	97.4%	1,833	330	2,163		1,103
DENVER							
Republic Plaza							
Office	1	95.1%	1,247	—	1,247	100%	1,247
Development and other	1	—	400	548	948	100%	948
Trade Center	2	90.1%	767	43	810	100%	810
Colorado State Bank Building	1	97.5%	412	—	412	50%	206
	5	93.9%	2,826	591	3,417		3,211

Exhibit 1   Portfolio Listing—Commercial Properties by Region

JUNE 30, 2002	Number of Properties	Leased	Office	Retail/ Other	Leasable Area	Effective Ownership Interest	Brookfield's Effective Interest
		%	000's Sq. Ft.	000's Sq. Ft.	000's Sq. Ft.	%	000's Sq. Ft.
CALGARY							
Bankers Hall	3	91.4%	1,955	750	2,705	100%	2,705
Fifth Avenue Place	2	99.6%	1,427	254	1,681	50%	841
Petro-Canada Centre	2	98.0%	1,707	245	1,952	50%	976
Other	1	81.2%	—	108	108	100%	108
	8	95.5%	5,089	1,357	6,446		4,630
MINNEAPOLIS							
33 South Sixth Street (formerly City Center)	2	88.0%	1,082	695	1,777	100%	1,777
Dam Plaza	2	93.8%	593	638	1,231	100%	1,231
	4	90.4%	1,675	1,333	3,008		3,008
OTHER							
Royal Centre, Vancouver	1	92.4%	493	362	855	100%	855
Other	9	96.6%	2,920	884	3,804	100%	3,804
	10	95.3%	3,413	1,246	4,659		4,659
Total portfolio	50	96.1%	35,892	8,189	44,081		35,664
Less other shareholders' interests							1,212
Brookfield's net effective ownership interest							34,452

Source: Company files.

In September of 2001, Brookfield's market capitalization was approximately US$9 billion, with 80 percent of the assets held in the United States. Of the company's nearly 2,000 employees throughout North America, two-thirds were operating employees located in Brookfield's properties.

In addition to commercial property management, Brookfield operated an office management services business, which managed over 120 million square feet of real estate, and owned a master-planned residential development business, which accounted for approximately eight percent of Brookfield's asset value and constructed 3,000 single family homes annually (see Exhibit 2).

Brookfield was an inter-listed company whose shares traded on both the New York and Toronto stock exchanges under the symbol BPO.

COMPETITIVE STRENGTHS

Success at Brookfield was attributed to the strong teamwork demonstrated by employees, the customer service excellence that was a part of

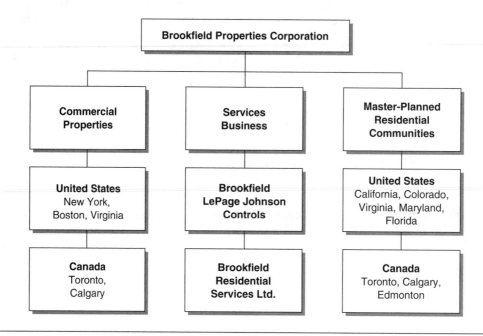

Exhibit 2   Brookfield at a Glance

Source: Company files.

the corporate culture, and the company's strategic portfolio management.

In addition, senior management believed the company was well positioned for continued growth based on the following factors.

Unique, High-Quality Portfolio

Brookfield's portfolio of landmark office properties, including the World Financial Center complex in Manhattan and BCE Place in Toronto, was recognized as unique in North America. The office properties were modern, averaged 1.4 million square feet in size and were focused in the central business districts of select, major North American cities. Eighty-five percent of Brookfield's portfolio was located in cities known for their ongoing high demand, such as New York, Boston and Toronto, ensuring stable, long-term growth.

Superior Quality Tenants

The quality and location of Brookfield's office properties, combined with a high commitment to service excellence, attracted highly successful organizations as tenants. Brookfield counted Merrill Lynch, JP Morgan Chase, Goldman Sachs, CIBC World Markets, RBC Financial Group, Petro-Canada, Lehman Brothers and TD Canada Trust among its clients. These clients possessed high credit quality and therefore ensured the long-term sustainability of rental revenues.

Financial Strength

A conservative debt structure, quality streams of cash flow and the ability to retain cash flow provided financial strength and flexibility to fuel strategic growth. Brookfield's financial performance was captured in its Fact Sheet (see Exhibit 3).

FACT SHEET
BROOKFIELD PROPERTIES CORPORATION

Brookfield Properties Corporation, with US$9 billion in assets, owns, develops and manages premier North American office properties. The Brookfield portfolio includes 50 commercial properties and development sites totaling 44 million square feet and 120 million square feet under management.

50
Premier Properties

The Brookfield Difference

Brookfield is an Investment in Quality. The company's strategic focus on investing in premier quality office assets in select markets is continuing to deliver solid financial performance, shareholder value and industry leadership.

From left to right:
Bankers Hall, Calgary
Republic Plaza, Denver
BCE Place, Toronto
World Financial Center, New York
53 State Street, Boston
CIBC World Markets Tower, New York

44
Million Square Feet

Premier Assets
- Brookfield's portfolio is distinguished by the size and quality of the assets, which attract and retain high credit quality tenants, resulting in a long-term high quality stream of cashflow for shareholders.

Brookfield's Properties Feature
- An average size of 1.4 million square feet
- A 15 year average age
- Technologically advanced infrastructure
- Locations proximate to major transportation hubs.

* Funds from operations

10
Year Average Lease Term

Track Record of Performance
- During 2001, we achieved 15% increase in FFO* growth per share, and 13% in Q1 2002.

Proactive Lease Management
- Leased over 9 million square feet in 2000 and 2001, over 4 times the amount of space contractually expiring and 450,000 square feet in Q1 2002.

Long-Term Lease Profile
- Brookfield's leases average 10 years with virtually no major leases expiring until 2005.

Internal Growth Built-In
- With in-place rents 30% below market and contractual step-ups built into leases, the company is delivering 6% operating income growth from currently owned office space.

Financial Flexibility
- Initiatives completed in 2001 generated over US$1 billion in cashflow with plans for $750 million in 2002.

FFO Growth Per Share

US Dollars
* FFO per share including actual termination and other gains as in 1999, 2000, 2001 and similar gains in 2002

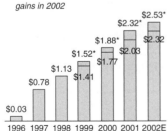

1996	$0.03
1997	$0.78
1998	$1.13
1999	$1.52* / $1.41
2000	$1.88* / $1.77
2001	$2.32* / $2.03
2002E	$2.53* / $2.32

Strong Financial Position

Nearly 100% of the commercial property debt is fixed rate and non-recourse. The average maturity is 11 years.

	March 2002
Debt to Total Capitalization	
– Market Value	53%
– Book Value	60%
Commercial Debt	
– Non-recourse	97%
Interest Coverage	
– Q1 2002 FFO	2.0x
– Mark-to-Market Rents	2.7x
Capital Base	US$2.7 billion

Stock Information

Symbol:	BPO
Exchanges:	New York, Toronto
Shares Outstanding:	161 million
Total Market Capitalization:	US$9.1 billion

BROOKFIELD

Exhibit 3   Fact Sheet

(Continued)

BROOKFIELD

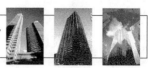

From left to right:
Petro-Canada Centre, Calgary
One Liberty Plaza, New York
Exchange Tower, Toronto

Strategic Priorities

- Maintain record of growth in FFO per share of greater than 15% and total cash return on equity of 20%
- Low-risk, high-return development of office properties on existing sites.
- Sale of partnership interests with institutional investors to surface value in mature assets.
- Acquisition of premier office assets in existing or new markets, consistent with current portfolio.

25 Major Properties Represent

80% Of the Portfolio

Portfolio Distribution by Square Feet

New York 36%
Toronto 24%
Boston 5%
Denver 7%
Calgary 14%
Minneapolis 7%
Other 7%

Geographic Distribution (By net operating income)

80% New York Toronto Boston

20% Denver Calgary Minneapolis

Value Per Share Comparison

Fully diluted shares outstanding:
165.5 million
(US Dollars)

$12.32 — Book Value
$20.00 — Market Value
$22.50 — NAV Analyst Consenus
$23.50 — NAV Brookfield

Average Lease Term (Years)

Brookfield's leasing profile is one of the strongest in the industry with one of the lowest rollover rates of any major North American office company.

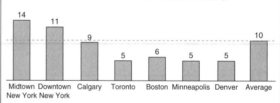

14 — Midtown New York
11 — Downtown New York
9 — Calgary
5 — Toronto
6 — Boston
5 — Minneapolis
5 — Denver
10 — Average

Brookfield's average lease term across the portfolio is 10 years.

In New York and Boston, virtually no leases expire until 2005.

Five Year Common Share Dividend History

(US dollars)	1998	1999	2000	2001	2002
Mar. 31	–	–	–	–	0.10
Jun. 30	0.07	0.10	0.12	0.13	–
Sept. 30	–	–	–	0.10	
Dec. 31	0.09	0.12	0.13	0.10	–

Effective September 2001, Brookfield initiated quarterly dividend payments replacing the semi-annual payment schedule. Record dates are set on the first business day of March, June, September and December.

Expected Earnings Release Dates

Quarter	Period Ending	Expected Release Dates
First	Mar. 31, 2002	Apr 22, 2002
Second	Jun. 30, 2002	July 31, 2002
Third	Sept. 30, 2002	Oct. 30, 2002
Fourth	Dec. 31, 2002	Feb. 2003

Investor Relations Contacts

Katherine C. Vyse,
Senior Vice President,
Investor Relations & Communications
Tel: (416) 369-8246
Fax : (416) 865-1288
E-mail: kvyse@brookfieldproperties.com

Melissa J. Coley, Vice President,
Investor Relations
Tel: (212) 417–7000
Fax : (212) 417–7194
Email: mcoley@brookfieldproperties.com

Exhibit 3 (Continued)

Source: Company files.

Market Leadership

The second largest office property company in North America by total market capitalization—over US$9 billion—Brookfield had established a leadership position in the key North American office markets with premier properties in prime downtown locations. In addition,

- Brookfield's master-planned community business was the largest Canadian-based residential development operation and among the largest home builders and land developers in the United States; and
- The services business was the largest provider of property management services in Canada.

Commitment to Customer Service Excellence

Brookfield was a leader in the real estate industry in providing innovative and timely customer service programs at the property level and for each individual tenant. This commitment was backed by extensive training and proactive recruitment practices that were embraced by the Brookfield team.

Brookfield's Management Team and Corporate Culture

Brookfield was a lean, fairly flat organization managed by a team of senior employees who worked hard to maintain the company's reputation for excellence (see Exhibits 4 and 5).

Roles tended to be fluid, with employees often taking on projects and responsibilities that were not formally a part of their job description. The pace was fast but disciplined, and after a long day it was not uncommon for the group to socialize together.

Within the tight-knit group, communication was not a problem. In describing the effectiveness of communications at Brookfield, Melissa Coley, director of arts and events marketing in New York, said, "It's easy to know what's going on around here. Our offices are close to each other, we eat lunch together, we just *know* what's going on. In fact, if Ric didn't stop by my office once a day to ask how things were going, I'd wonder what was up."

In Ric Clark's words:

This company was built around smart, dedicated, energetic, decent hard-working people. Since 90 percent of our New York employees have been with Brookfield for over 10 years, it makes sense that our corporate culture in New York is collegial. Our philosophy is "lead by example, share the credit, be a team player," and that's what we try to do around here. As part of that team, I try to make myself available to anyone who has an idea or an opinion to share—actually, more people than I'd care to admit have my personal cell phone number.

Outside hiring did happen when necessary, but whenever possible, employees were grown in-house. Clark's own career path was an excellent example of this progression. He began his career as a financial analyst, then became an analyst in the leasing department, and eventually worked his way up to become the director of leasing. He was then made chief operating officer (COO) for Brookfield's U.S. operations and eventually became president of the same.

Having been involved with new hires at all levels, Clark cared "more about what a person is all about than what his or her background is." This philosophy was well respected by his colleagues, one of whom remarked: "Ric's got a *great* gut. He sure knows how to pick 'em!"

Bruce Flatt's colleagues also exhibited a great deal of trust in and respect for his leadership. One of his senior vice-presidents (SVPs) said about his style:

Bruce is very, very good at recognizing the efforts of others in a genuine way. He always remembers to stop to say a simple "thank you" and lavishes praise publicly when things go well. And he is always calm and even-tempered, even when something goes wrong, which is a valuable talent when you are trying to encourage others to assume greater responsibilities, take risks and be creative. He is a true leader whom others gladly follow.

GORDON ARNELL
CHAIRMAN, BROOKFIELD
PROPERTIES CORPORATION

Gordon Arnell brings with him more than 25 years of real estate industry experience. Gordon joined Brookfield's predecessor company, Carena Developments Limited, in 1989 as President and CEO and was subsequently appointed Chairman and CEO of Brookfield. In April 2000, he assumed the role of Chairman.

Prior to joining Brookfield, Gordon was a senior executive at several major real estate companies, including Oxford Development Group Ltd. of Edmonton, Trizec Corporation Ltd. of Calgary, and Trilea Centres Inc. A lawyer by training, he also practiced litigation and commercial law in Calgary.

Gordon holds Bachelor of Arts and Bachelor of Law degrees from the University of Alberta and was called to the Bar of Alberta in 1958. He is a Director of Brookfield Properties Corporation, Brookfield Financial Properties Ltd. and BPO Properties Ltd.

RIC CLARK
PRESIDENT AND CEO, US
COMMERCIAL OPERATIONS

Ric is the President and Chief Executive of Brookfield's US commercial operations. Ric has been with Brookfield and its New York based affiliate, Brookfield Financial Properties (and its predecessor company, Olympia and York) since 1984 in various senior roles including Chief Operating Officer, Executive Vice President, and Director of Leasing.

Ric is a Certified Public Accountant and holds a business degree from the Indiana University of Pennsylvania. He is a member of the Brookfield Financial Properties' Board of Directors, a member of The Real Estate Board of New York's Board of Governors and a member of the Lincoln Centre Real Estate and Construction Council.

STEVEN DOUGLAS
EVP AND CFO, BROOKFIELD
PROPERTIES CORPORATION

Steve Douglas was appointed Executive Vice President and Chief Financial Officer in July 2001, following four years as Senior Vice President and Chief Financial Officer and three years in various senior management positions at Brookfield. In his current role, he is responsible for corporate finance, reporting, tax and treasury for Brookfield and its subsidiaries. Prior to joining the company, Steve was affiliated with Ernst and Young in Toronto.

Steve is a Chartered Accountant and holds a Bachelor of Commerce degree from Laurentian University in Sudbury, Ontario.

Exhibit 4   Management Team Bios

KATHERINE VYSE
SR. VP, INVESTOR RELATIONS
AND COMMUNICATIONS

Katherine Vyse joined Brookfield in early 2000. Her 14 year business career includes a similar role at a major North American real estate company and 10 years in the Financial Services industry. Katherine is currently responsible for expanding Brookfield's investor relations program and developing new investor relations and corporate communications vehicles and programs.

Katherine holds an MBA degree from the Ivey School of Business, a Bachelor of Arts degree from the University of Western Ontario in London, Ontario and a Retail Management Diploma from Sheridan College in Oakville. Katherine is a member of the Board of Directors of Canadian Investor Relations Institute (CIRI), Ontario Chapter.

MARK BROWN
SVP, FINANCE

Mark Brown was appointed Senior Vice President, Finance, in July 2001. Mark joined Brookfield in 2000 and has primary responsibility for managing the finance function for the U.S. commercial operations and contributing to the company's corporate financial strategies.

Prior to joining Brookfield, Mark spent 9 years with Salomon Smith Barney and Citicorp Real Estate, Inc. He holds a Masters of Business Administration from York University and a Bachelor of Commerce degree from Laurentian University.

JOHN ZUCCOTTI
DEPUTY CHAIRMAN,
BROOKFIELD PROPERTIES

John E. Zuccotti, Deputy Chairman of Brookfield Properties Corporation, has specialized throughout his career in planning, housing, real estate and municipal law. He has played a leading role in the development process of major residential and commercial projects in the New York metropolitan area, served as director or trustee of many planning and development boards and has lectured at numerous institutions, including Harvard, Columbia and Yale. John also served as the first Deputy Mayor of the city of New York from 1975 through 1977.

Prior to joining Brookfield, John served as President and Chief Executive Officer of Olympia and York Companies (U.S.A.) and as a Partner in the law firms of Brown & Wood and Tufo & Zuccotti.

John graduated from Princeton University in 1959 and received his law degree from Yale University Law School in 1963. He was an officer in the United States Army.

Exhibit 4 (Continued)

BRUCE FLATT
PRESIDENT AND CEO,
BROOKFIELD PROPERTIES

Bruce has been President and Chief Executive Officer since April 2000. Before joining Brookfield, he held a number of senior management positions at Hees International Bancorp Inc. from 1989 to 1992, and also worked for Arthur Young International, which is now part of Ernst & Young.

Bruce is a Chartered Accountant and holds a business degree from the University of Manitoba. Bruce is a director of Brookfield Properties Corporation, EdperPartners Limited, Noranda Inc. and Brascan Corporation.

DENNIS FRIEDRICH
EVP AND COO,
BROOKFIELD PROPERTIES

Dennis Friedrich was appointed Chief Operating Officer of Brookfield's US commercial operations in July 2001 following his role as head of Strategic Initiatives for the US property portfolio. In his current position, Dennis oversees Brookfield's commercial property operations comprising 18 million square feet of premier office space in New York, Boston, Denver and Minneapolis.

Prior to joining Brookfield, Dennis was co-head of Jones Lang LaSalle's Tenant Advisory practice in New York. He holds a business degree in finance from Baruch College and is a member of the Real Estate Board of New York.

David Arthur
President and CEO,
Canadian Operations

President and CEO of Brookfield's Canadian operations since February 1998, David is also Chairman of Brookfield LePage Johnson Controls. Through his 15 year career at Brookfield, David held the positions of President and Chief Executive Officer of Brookfield Commercial Properties Ltd., President and Chief Executive Officer of Brookfield Management Services Ltd. and a number of other management positions at related real estate companies. While at Brookfield, David has been involved in several major property acquisitions and new contracts, including the acquisition of the landmark Bankers Hall and Fifth Ave. Place complexes in Calgary.

David started his career with Cadillac Fairview and Cambridge Leaseholds. He holds a Master of Science in Urban Land Economics from the University of British Columbia and Bachelor of Urban and Regional Planning from the University of Waterloo. David is President of the Canadian Institute of Public and Private Real Estate Companies (CIPPREC) and is a member of the Young Presidents' Organization (YPO).

Exhibit 4 (Continued)

Source: Company files.

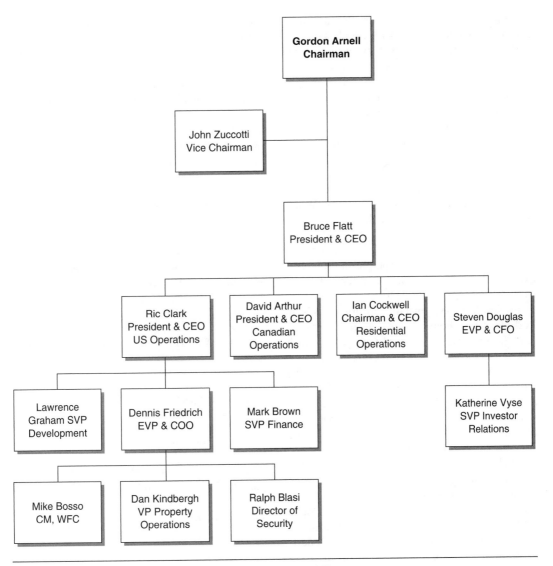

Exhibit 5   Commercial Property Operations Organizational Chart

It was generally agreed that this culture of hard work, camaraderie, respect and trust was consistent across all Brookfield's North American offices.

SEPTEMBER 11TH—WORLD TRADE CENTER ATTACKS

On September 11, 2001, the world watched in horror as the twin towers of New York City's World Trade Center (WTC) were destroyed by what appeared to be acts of terrorism.

At 8:48 A.M. on that fateful Tuesday, a hijacked passenger jet (American Airlines Flight 11 out of Boston) crashed into the North Tower of the World Trade Center, causing a massive fire through several stories of the building. Eighteen minutes later, at 9:03 A.M., a second hijacked jet (United Airlines Flight 175 out of Boston) crashed into the South Tower of the WTC and exploded, dispelling any thoughts that New Yorkers may have had about the crashes being accidental.

By 9:17 A.M., New York City airports were shut down by the Federal Aviation Association (FAA), and the Port Authority closed all bridges and tunnels in the New York area.

For the first time in U.S. history, at 9:40 that morning, the FAA halted all American flight operations across the country, and air traffic was diverted to the closest Canadian airports.

At 9:43 A.M., a third hijacked jet (American Airlines Flight 77) crashed into the Pentagon, which was then evacuated along with the White House. At 9:59 A.M. the South Tower of the World Trade Center collapsed. At 10:00 A.M., a fourth hijacked jet (United Airlines Flight 93) crashed just south of Pittsburgh in Somerset County, Pennsylvania. And at 10:28 A.M., the North Tower of the WTC fell.

In New York, Mayor Giuliani urged all New Yorkers to stay home if they had not yet come into the city. U.S. President George W. Bush reported that all security measures possible were being taken and asked for prayers from the public. Senior FBI sources reported that they assumed the four hijacked planes were part of a terrorist attack and that they suspected that Saudi militant Osama bin Laden was involved, based on "new and specific" information.

Media information coming out of Lower Manhattan was unreliable as the area had been declared a no-fly zone and the press could not access the WTC area, which had been cordoned off for several blocks. This led to much speculation as to the extent of the damage. Still, reports of death and critical injury made it to the forefront and, by mid-afternoon, 2,100 total injuries in New York were reported, with many more expected as rescue efforts progressed.

ADJACENT BUILDINGS

With the general state of chaos and confusion in Lower Manhattan, it was impossible to say with any certainty what the extent of the damage was to the buildings surrounding the World Trade Center. Building 7 of the WTC was reported to be on fire due to its proximity to the WTC attacks. With phone lines down and access to the immediate area blocked off, accurate information was unavailable, but it was assumed that buildings in the surrounding area had suffered severely. Speculation also arose regarding damage done to the World Trade Center slurry (or "bathtub") wall—the structure that protected the WTC from water leakage from the nearby Hudson River.

Four of Brookfield's properties, comprising approximately 30 percent of the company's total portfolio, were immediately adjacent to the WTC towers (see Exhibit 6) and had clearly sustained damage, but it was not known how much. In fact, three of these properties stood between the WTC and the Hudson River, and it was clear that other properties in the area were on fire or were severely damaged. The major tenants of these properties included:

- One World Financial Center (Lehman Brothers, Dow Jones, National Financial Services, and RBC Dain Rauscher);
- Two and Four World Financial Center (Merrill Lynch); and
- One Liberty Plaza (Goldman Sachs, Cleary Gottlieb, NASD, Bank of Nova Scotia, Zurich, and Royal Bank of Canada).

Lastly, it was reported in the media that One Liberty Plaza (a 2.2 million square foot property that was 100 percent owned by Brookfield) was on fire and in the process of collapsing.

BROOKFIELD RESPONDS

About that morning in New York, Clark said:

> I came into the office early that morning, around 7:00 A.M. I was working quietly in my office when I heard an explosion and felt the building shake. I ran to the other side of the floor [facing the World Trade Center] and saw a hole in about six floors of the building. It was a giant fireball.
>
> After calling home, I called Bruce and told him what had happened. He wanted to come to

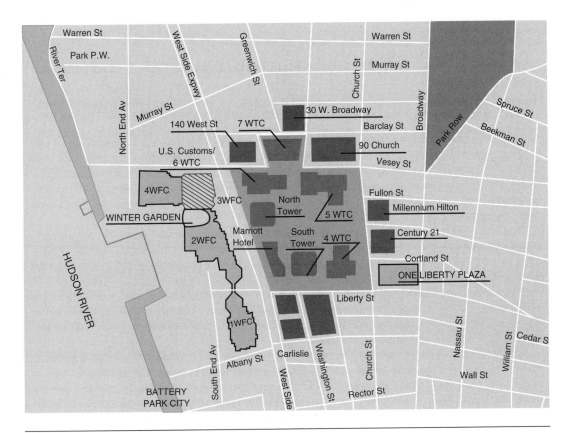

Exhibit 6   Lower Manhattan Properties

New York, but I told him not to come. I said "Bruce, don't do it. Don't come." It just wasn't safe. After the first plane hit, we evacuated all our employees and tenants—it was better to send them home than risk any potential harm.

Fortunately, Brookfield's corporate director of security, Ralph Blasi, had upgraded security procedures three years earlier when he assumed his position. He had hired a firm to develop emergency and disaster plans and manuals for all tenants, beginning with the New York properties, and all tenant evacuation plans had been revised. Prior to these changes, all 30,000 tenants had planned to evacuate into the Winter Garden area (a glassed-in atrium between the World Financial Center buildings) which had a capacity of approximately 2,500 people. Plans were changed to

ensure the safe and timely passage of all tenants in the event that an evacuation would be necessary (see Exhibit 7).

Flatt remembered his last conversation with Clark around 10:30 that morning, just before cellular phone connections went down. Clark told him:

Bruce—Ralph, Dan, and Mike are staying at the site. They're helping other buildings in the area evacuate. There are already cops on every street corner and they're trying to get everyone out of the area. I needed a security escort just to walk to the WFC buildings. I'm heading out of here now—I'll call you when I reach the Madison Avenue offices.

Flatt had seen the second WTC tower collapse on television shortly thereafter and had not had any contact with Clark since.

New York Times, July 10, 2002

COMMERCIAL REAL ESTATE; Disaster Planner Has Lessons From 9/11 to Offer, and Boston Listens

By MICHAEL BRICK

As Ralph A. Blasi remembers it, the man who was trying to enter the World Financial Center on Sept. 11 as buildings burned nearby claimed to be a Verizon employee. The man would not take no for an answer, says Mr. Blasi, the director of security for Brookfield Financial Properties, manager of the World Financial Center.

"Punch this guy in the face, as hard as you can," Mr. Blasi says he remembers telling one of his security guards, delivering an order that was effective in changing the man's mind before the punch itself needed to be delivered.

That is Mr. Blasi's favorite part of the story. He includes it every time he talks about the evacuation. It is funny, in a dark way, and it gets his audience's attention. But of far more importance to the property managers here in Boston who have asked Mr. Blasi to repeat his story is what he did in the years before the terrorist attacks in drawing up an evacuation plan.

"I was totally fascinated with the way he delivered it, the no-nonsense story," said Michael Quinn, a senior vice president of Meredith & Grew who manages the 24-story building at 160 Federal Street in Boston and who is president of the local Building Owners and Managers Association. "You could see him choking up. It was like he was reliving the whole thing."

Mr. Quinn heard the story with officials of the local fire, police and emergency management departments, and they have asked all the managers of this city's skyscrapers to come hear Mr. Blasi tell it again in July. The point of Mr. Blasi's story is that landlords must join together to make disaster and security plans. Such coordination is a hard sell, because these landlords are direct competitors who closely guard every aspect of their operations and services from one another, using the information to attract and retain the same tenants.

But now, in these times of rattled nerves, Mr. Quinn said, the landlords are changing their minds.

"It's not really going to cost any money to coordinate our evacuation plans with the city, but I think it's an effective marketing tool, something you can take back to your tenants," Mr. Quinn said. "The idea right now is to renew your tenants."

Mr. Blasi's story is particularly harrowing when he tells it in his own office at the World Financial Center in New York, where he sits before a picture window overlooking ground zero and, at its edge, the damaged shell of the Winter Garden. He did that for a visitor late last spring, before all the property managers in Boston became interested. The story begins with his background.

He was a 22-year veteran of the New York Police Department, including stints on patrol in Queens and Brooklyn and a job as a homicide detective. He retired in 1995, did a little bartending and private investigation and eventually took the job with Brookfield. In 1997, he started asking World Financial Center tenants, including Merrill Lynch, Lehman Brothers, Dow Jones and Fidelity Investments, about their evacuation plans. He checked with the Mercantile Exchange, too.

All told, by his count, about 30,000 people planned to gather in the Winter Garden, a 10-story atrium with glass ceiling panels that served as a public entryway to the World Financial Center and connection to the World Trade Center through the North Bridge. It was built to hold 2,500 people—a fact that greatly affected his disaster planning.

Exhibit 7   Disaster Planner Has Lessons From 9/11

When the first airplane hit the World Trade Center on Sept. 11, Mr. Blasi's staff cordoned off access to the North Bridge with ropes and posted a guard there, sending workers from the World Financial Center out into the streets. And turning away the man who claimed to be from Verizon.

That left room for people from the twin towers to evacuate across the North Bridge, which was eventually destroyed, and through the Winter Garden. Debris and bodies fell through the ceiling into the atrium, but many workers who might have been underneath were already trudging up the West Side Highway.

"The biggest thing now is showing there's a clear need to know what your neighbors are doing," Mr. Blasi said. "Everybody has their own plan, but nobody's talking."

He has not taken this story on the road as a public speaker espousing some new management trend. In fact, Mr. Blasi has traveled to tell his story only in Boston and Minneapolis, the two cities outside New York where Brookfield owns substantial amounts of office space in crowded downtown towers.

For Brookfield, the business purpose is not to promote Mr. Blasi but to enhance security for the company's tenants, said Richard B. Clark, the chief executive of the Brookfield Properties Corporation, which owns 95 percent of the company that employs Mr. Blasi.

"Security is only as good as the weakest link in the area," Mr. Clark said.

Here in Boston, the story has resonated.

"If you had all of these tenants evacuate out into this," Lt. James Hasson of the Boston Police Department said as he drove a cruiser down Congress Street, "it would clog the street up, and this is a major artery. This is the extent of the high rises in Boston, but it's a lot of workers, if you can imagine them pouring out."

Property managers have extensively discussed security since Sept. 11, obviously, but only now are they beginning to coordinate their efforts. Mr. Quinn said he was just now beginning to ask his competitors about their plans, but he fears that "most buildings are likely to go to Post Office Square," a 1.54-acre park in the Financial District.

Until these recent discussions, Mr. Quinn said, managers had focused on their own individual buildings, making decisions about what to spend on guards and cameras and electronic identification cards.

But now, as rents decline, they are pressed to find less expensive tactics without compromising safety. Rents in the best high-rises downtown here have fallen to around $45 a square foot, from $70 in 2000 and $59 a year ago. Various brokers and building managers here estimate that security costs have risen 10 to 20 percent since September, adding 50 cents to $1 a square foot to average annual asking rents, excluding any effects of the cost of terrorism insurance.

"You don't want to be too secure," said James E. Fox, an asset manager for CB Richard Ellis who handles 1 Beacon Street, a one-million-square-foot office tower downtown with 50 tenants who employ a total of 3,500 people. "You want to show your tenants that you're being cost-effective, but also safe."

That, in part, is why managers like Mr. Fox plan to go hear Mr. Blasi talk, as soon as Mr. Quinn can bring him back to Boston.

As property managers set budgets for 2003, said Stephen P. Lynch, executive managing director of the Boston office of the real estate services firm Cushman & Wakefield, they are looking for ways to market the notion of enhanced safety without spending a lot on added security. Coordinating their plans and communicating their intentions may be unusual, he said, but it is inexpensive.

"This is one topic area where landlords are in open dialogue," Mr. Lynch said.

Source: Reprinted with permission from the *New York Times.*

BROOKFIELD'S RELATIONSHIP WITH LOCAL OFFICIALS

Many official government agencies had arrived at the scene of the attacks to assist with rescue efforts and to maintain order. Flatt knew the main agencies that Brookfield would have to work with:

- At the federal level: FEMA—Federal Emergency Management Agency;
- At the state level: The National Guard; and
- At the local level: The New York City Department of Design & Construction (DDC), The New York City Office of Emergency Management (OEM), the Office of the Mayor of New York, and the New York City police and fire departments.

Brookfield had always maintained good relations with government authorities, which Flatt felt would ease their interactions over the coming days and weeks. He also knew that having John Zuccotti, former deputy mayor of New York, as Brookfield's co-chairman would be an advantage. Zuccotti was always well prepared to act as the statesman in government dealings.

CONCLUSION

It was 4 P.M. on September 11th, and Flatt sat at his desk, overwhelmed by the day's events and trying to decide what to do next. Brookfield had issued a press release (see Exhibit 8), but how would he make sure all employees and tenants were safe? How would they assess the damage and get beyond government barriers to start repairs, if that was even feasible? How would he deal with the grief and suffering being experienced by employees and tenants? Would offering reassurances of a plan to return to business as usual be insensitive with the degree of personal trauma being experienced? How could he reassure Brookfield's investors and the media of this commitment to restoring Brookfield's position of market strength? What was the best way to deploy his staff and structure communications to most effectively accomplish all this?

It was a critical time, filled with shock, horror, pain, suffering and potentially severe business losses. In the midst of chaos and uncertainty, Brookfield needed an action plan, quickly.

BROOKFIELD RESPONDS TO NEW YORK CITY TRAGEDY

New York, New York, September 11, 2001–(4:00 PM ETN) (BPO: NYSE/TSE)

Brookfield Properties Corporation, in response to the tragic events in the U.S., reported that its emergency plans were implemented, including the evacuation of tenants and employees from One Liberty Plaza and the World Financial Center, adjacent to the World Trade Center in downtown New York.

Bruce Flatt, President and CEO of Brookfield said: "We feel great empathy for the individuals and families involved in this tragedy and our hearts go out to them."

Brookfield has no ownership interest in the World Trade Center. Brookfield owns 100% of One Liberty Plaza, and 100% of Towers One and Two and 50% of Tower Four of the World Financial Center. From all accounts to date, Brookfield's properties sustained no structural damage. Glass replacement and clean-up programs will commence at the earliest opportunity.

Brookfield is co-operating with government and security authorities.

Mr. Flatt concluded "Our prayers go out to all of the victims of this great tragedy and their families."

* * * * * * * * * * * *

Exhibit 8   September 11th Press Release

Brookfield Properties Corporation, with over US$8 billion in assets, owns, develops and manages premier North American office properties. Brookfield also operates real estate service businesses and develops residential master-planned communities. The Brookfield portfolio spans 60 commercial properties and development sites totaling 46 million square feet. Brookfield is inter-listed on the New York and Toronto Stock Exchanges under the symbol BPO. For more information, visit the Brookfield Properties Web site at *www.brookfieldproperties.com.*

Contact Information
Katherine C. Vyse
Senior Vice President, Investor Relations and Communications
Brookfield Properties Corporation
Tel: (416) 369–8246
Fax: (416) 865 - 1288
Email: kvyse@brookfieldproperties.com

ELITE INC. (A)

*Prepared by Jessica Frisch under the supervision
of Professors Ann Frost and Lyn Purdy*

Copyright © 2003, Ivey Management Services — Version: (A) 2003–10–06

It was April 1, 2000, and Fran Benson, chief executive officer (CEO) of Elite Inc., had just entered her office for the day. As usual, Benson went directly to her computer to check her e-mail. To her dismay, she had received another late-night message from Greg Jakes, the company's chief financial officer (CFO). Recently, Jakes had been spending 18-hour days at the office trying to get his work done. Jakes spent inordinate amounts of time checking over his daily tasks and projects and, even with the long hours at work, he could not meet his deadlines. With increasing pressure from the board of directors, Benson knew something had to be done about Jakes.

COMPANY BACKGROUND

Elite Incorporated, a highly successful public relations firm, was founded in Toronto, Ontario, in 1960. The company's founders, Carl and Frank MacNeil, studied business at the University of Toronto, and the brothers had always had a keen business sense. Upon Frank's graduation in 1958, he took a job as a financial analyst with a large Canadian bank in order to gain business experience and learn more about the Canadian marketplace. When Carl graduated two years later, the brothers started up their own public relations firm using capital from their family and a substantial loan. Frank assumed the role of president and CEO while Carl assumed the role of vice-president, operations.

Elite became an incorporated business in 1972. For the next two decades, the company experienced great success with growing profits and healthy financial stability. The early 1990s, however, were troublesome for Elite. In 1991, Frank and Carl decided to purchase a new head office building in downtown Toronto. The combination of the large financial investment and the overall recession put the company into extreme financial difficulties. Nonetheless, with strong commitment from the management team, the company was profitable again by the first quarter of 1993. In 2000, Elite had 400 employees, offices in Toronto, Montreal and Winnipeg, and the brothers had received numerous awards for entrepreneurial excellence.

COMPANY CULTURE

From its beginnings in the early 1960s, a distinct corporate culture could be observed at Elite. The small work force of 50 employees was flexible and co-operative, creating a relaxed and enjoyable atmosphere. Management and employees had a close relationship with open lines of communication. Daily meetings between executives and middle management and weekly meetings between middle management and employees helped keep information flowing throughout the organization. Employees reported a high level of job satisfaction. Frank and Carl, excited about their new business, would often take employees out for drinks on Fridays after work.

As the company continued to grow in the 1970s, the culture began to change. The co-operative nature of Elite had turned far more competitive; employees competed against one another for bonuses and pay increases. Also, Frank and Carl were less involved in the business than they had been in the company's formative years. As the work force grew to over 200 people, a gap formed between management and employees; there seemed to be no goal congruence between employee goals and corporate objectives. New employees did not take the same pride in the company's success as those who helped start the business from scratch.

One noticeable aspect of the company culture in the late 1970s concerned the employee demographics. With the exception of the clerical and administrative staff, 95 percent of Elite's managers were male. This trend continued into the

1990s. Frank and Carl became concerned with the corporate culture at Elite, and their concerns were validated when employees chose to unionize in 1980.

Many factors led Elite employees to form a union. First, the flow of communication within the company had broken down. Although daily and weekly meetings were once a core part of Elite's culture, by the late 1970s, meetings were often skipped or cancelled altogether. Senior executives worked on the top floor of head office; management completely isolated themselves from the teams they were responsible for leading. Employees felt that management did not have respect for them, their needs or their ideas. Second, an "us" versus "them" culture had evolved in the company. All the power and decision making was in the hands of a few senior managers. Elite employees were not empowered to make decisions regarding their work; employees always had to ask for senior management approval, even when making minor changes to their projects. The third major factor that contributed to unionization was the punitive method of leadership at the company. Employees reported incidents of being screamed at for doing something "wrong."

The Service Employees International Union (SEIU) local formed in 1980, and it took years for Elite's management to adapt to its presence. Although management's relationship with the union had been somewhat amicable throughout the 1980s and 1990s, tension could be felt between management and the union. Frank and Carl often reminisced about the way things used to be at Elite.

A CHANGE IN LEADERSHIP

During the financial troubles of the early 1990s, employees and management worked together to revive the company. However, the 1990s presented many corporate challenges that required long hours at the office; Frank and Carl were working very hard and were becoming tired.

Frank MacNeil, CEO of Elite, decided to retire in 1999. Carl, VP Operations, also decided that he wanted to leave the company to pursue another business opportunity. Elite would need a new CEO. Frank was a perceptive individual and a realistic manager; he realized Elite's culture had deteriorated. Before leaving the company, he thought it was essential to obtain some guidance. Frank wanted suggestions about improving internal relations, and most importantly, he wanted recommendations regarding what he should look for in a new CEO.

Frank sought the advice of Rob Packard, a well-respected management consultant in the Toronto area. Packard agreed that many areas of the company needed improvement. Regarding the search for a new CEO, Packard looked Frank in the eye and said, "You need something fresh in here to shake things up."

A New CEO in 1999

Frank and Carl received several applications for the CEO position. They spent weeks going through résumés and interviewing candidates until they found Fran Benson. Benson was the vice-president of operations at a rival public relations firm in the Toronto area. She was admired by her employees and praised by the executive team. Benson had an undergraduate degree in mathematics and an MBA degree from a renowned Canadian business school. Frank felt that she was exactly what the company needed. Benson accepted the position on November 8, 1999, and she knew that she had a big job ahead of her. She spent hours in meetings with Frank and Carl, and she obtained advice, suggestions and records from Packard.

Benson started the transition by introducing herself to the employees. She met with each department individually; she set up coffee and doughnuts and spent time exchanging ideas and objectives regarding the company's direction. Benson knew it would be critical to create a strong bond with both her employees and, in particular, with her senior management team.

One senior manager remaining with Elite was Greg Jakes, the company's CFO. Jakes was an essential member of Benson's team, but unfortunately, Benson had already received some mixed reviews regarding his performance.

Greg Jakes

Jakes, a 50-year-old husband and father of five, was a loyal member of the Elite team. He had a business degree from McMaster University and was a certified management accountant (CMA). Prior to joining Elite, Jakes had held a management position at a multinational accounting firm for eight years. His recommendations from his former employer were positive; however, Elite was warned that as the organization grew, "Jakes would only be able to take the company so far."

Jakes was hired in the early 1980s as the CFO. He led the finance team at head office, consisting originally of five employees and growing to 13 employees by 2000. Jakes was responsible for compiling Elite's financial statements, conducting risk management analysis and investing the organization's funds. Jakes also worked with the information technology (IT) department on occasional projects. During the early 1990s, Jakes helped Elite overcome its financial troubles. He showed a high level of commitment and had in-depth knowledge of Elite's financial systems and general ledger.

Jakes had been the CFO of Elite for his entire career with the company, and when the CEO position became available, he eagerly applied. However, unknown to Jakes, there was no chance of his getting the promotion. The board of directors felt that he lacked the necessary leadership skills to advance and, furthermore, they did not consider him to be highly effective as the chief financial officer.

Jakes certainly had some positive attributes. He was known in Elite as a very nice man with a great sense of humor. He was liked by his co-workers, was known as a pleasant boss, and he was respected for being a good husband and father. Unfortunately, Jakes also presented some serious problems.

Throughout the years, Jakes had not been able to keep pace with the increasing level of complexity in the organization and within his role. In fact, it had become evident that Jakes had difficulty getting his work done and, for whatever reason, this situation was allowed to persist. Jakes spent far too much time paying attention to the details of his work. He was afraid of making a mistake and therefore spent inordinate amounts of time checking over his daily tasks and projects. It was not uncommon for Jakes to spend 18-hour days at the office to get things done. Even then, he could not meet the deadlines; the company's monthly financial statements often came out four weeks late. Jakes's behavior rubbed off on his team as well; the finance department repeatedly handed in late assignments or did not get assignments done at all. Jakes had so many projects going at once that he could rarely meet people's requests; he would start a task and would forget about it as he moved on to the next one. He did not know how to delegate, and it sometimes seemed as though he did not have a firm understanding of his work. Often, Jakes would be unable to answer questions about the material he was working on.

Furthermore, Jakes was not proactively managing the cash of the company. Frank and Carl had continuously asked him to research the diversification of Elite's investments, but Jakes never followed up on the requests. Every day that Jakes waited was costing the company significantly.

BENSON'S TASK

Benson had been warned about Jakes when she took the position of CEO. There were so many challenges for Benson that, five months into the job, she had not yet addressed the situation. Despite the fact that Jakes had been turned down for the position of CEO, he had been very receptive to Benson. He helped her adapt to the company by sharing information and knowledge.

In the first few months of Benson's time with Elite, she had recognized many of Jakes's traits about which she had been forewarned. She had given him three new projects, and two were already past deadline. Also, she had received many late-night e-mails from Jakes regarding work that should have easily been completed during regular office hours.

Benson wanted to make a good impression with the board of directors at Elite, and she realized that she needed her entire executive to be motivated, competent and reliable. Furthermore, the company's board of directors, consisting of 12 major shareholders, had noticed Jakes's inefficiencies, and they were demanding that the situation be resolved. The board members were empathetic to his historical importance to the company; however, they were demanding changes in his behavior.

Benson needed Jakes to improve in three key areas: she needed him to re-engineer the company's financial systems, to be proactive about the company's financial issues and, at the very least, she needed him get his work done on time. Jakes was a pivotal figure in Elite, and Benson wondered how she could help him improve his performance.

MAKING DIFFICULT DECISIONS IN TURBULENT TIMES

Prepared by Michael A. Roberto

In their own way, complexity and ambiguity tyrannize decision making. What managers need are strategies for making clear, accurate judgments under stressful conditions.

Napoleon Bonaparte once said that, "Nothing is more difficult, and therefore more precious, than to be able to decide." He recognized that a few critical decisions put leaders to the test. In turbulent times, some leaders make tough choices with courage and conviction. Others cannot cope with the complexity and uncertainty. They remain indecisive, and their rivals gain the upper hand.

Like Napoleon, today's business leaders must cope with a great deal of ambiguity as they make important choices about the future. They face uncertainty with regard to world politics, macro-economic growth and stability, technology and changing consumer tastes. Many worry that an unknown event will transform their entire industry in a matter of a few weeks or months.

Most executives find ways to cope with this uncertainty. They adopt strategies for simplifying complex situations so that they can make decisions quickly and effectively. These strategies enable managers to make sense of a confusing situation. In this article, I describe seven strategies that leaders can employ to cope with ambiguity and complexity as they make critical decisions. The strategies are reasoning by analogy, imitation, rules of thumb, reformulation, deference to experts, rigorous debate, and experimentation. These strategies often prove very effective because they enable leaders to make accurate judgments under stressful conditions. Unfortunately, each of these strategies has serious drawbacks as well. When employing these techniques, many leaders draw the wrong conclusions, make biased estimates, pursue flawed policies, or impede the development of commitment within their management teams. Thus, leaders must use these strategies with great care.

1. REASONING BY ANALOGY

Business leaders often draw analogies with past experiences when faced with a complex problem. They draw comparisons to similar situations or circumstances from their past or the history of other organizations, and deduce certain lessons from those experiences. John Rau, a former CEO and business school dean, argues that analogies provide a wealth of information: "The fundamental laws of economics, production, financial processes and human behaviour and interaction do not change from company to company or industry to industry. Reading about other companies makes me a better decision maker because it provides a store of analogies" (J. Rau, "Two Stages of Decision Making," *Management Review,* December 1999). Indeed, researchers have shown that people in a variety of fields, from foreign policy to firefighting, reason by analogy as a means of coping with complexity and ambiguity. Analogies prove especially useful when decision makers do not have access to complete information and do not have the time or ability to conduct a comprehensive analysis of alternatives. They enable people to diagnose a complex situation very quickly and to identify a manageable set of options for serious consideration.

Unfortunately, most analogies are imperfect. No two situations are identical. Many decision makers spot the similarities between situations very quickly, but they often ignore critical differences. In foreign policy, officials often refer to

the "Munich analogy" when making decisions. When confronted with international aggression, many world leaders argue against appeasement by drawing comparisons to Hitler's belligerence during the 1930s. They argue that British Prime Minister Chamberlain's decision to appease Hitler in 1938 actually encouraged him to pursue further expansion. Political scientists Richard Neustadt and Ernest May point out, however, that not every situation parallels the circumstances in Europe in the late 1930s. For example, they argue that President Truman would have been well served to identify the differences, as well as the similarities, between Korea in 1950 and Czechoslovakia in 1938. Ignoring these distinctions may have impaired the United States' strategy during the Korean conflict.

Business leaders often draw imperfect analogies as well. Take the recent dot-com boom, for example. Several market research firms projected the growth of on-line advertising by drawing analogies between the Internet and other forms of media. They examined the historical growth in advertising in other media industries and projected Internet growth by selecting the analogy that they deemed most appropriate. In doing so, they failed to recognize the critical differences between the Web and other media such as television and radio. Similarly, many research firms project the demand for new technologies by drawing analogies to the adoption rates for VCRs, personal computers and cell phones. Again, the differences among these technologies are often rather striking, yet they receive scant attention.

> *"Analogies prove especially useful when decision-makers do not have access to complete information and do not have the time or ability to conduct a comprehensive analysis of alternatives."*

2. IMITATION

When faced with uncertainty and environmental turbulence, some business leaders emulate the strategies and practices of other highly successful firms. After all, why reinvent the wheel; one way to simplify a complex problem is to find someone who has already solved it. Learning from others can pay huge dividends. At General Electric, former CEO Jack Welch launched a major best practice initiative in 1988. He credits this initiative with fundamentally changing the way that GE does business and produces substantial productivity gains. Welch and his management team identified approximately 20 organizations that had long track records of more rapid productivity growth than GE. For more than a year, GE managers studied a few of these firms very closely. They borrowed ideas liberally from these organizations and adapted others' strategies and processes to fit GE's businesses. For instance, they learned "Quick Market Intelligence" from Wal-Mart and new product development methods from Hewlett-Packard and Chrysler. Over time, imitating others became a way of life at GE, and it produced amazing results.

All of this learning sounds wonderful, but imitation has its drawbacks. In many industries, firms engage in "herd behaviour." They begin to adopt similar business strategies, rather than develop and preserve unique sources of competitive advantage. Take, for example, the credit card industry. Many firms have tried to emulate the highly successful business model developed by Capital One. Over time, company marketing and distribution policies have begun to look alike, rivalry has intensified, and industry profitability has eroded. Consider too the many instances in which a leading firm decides to merge with a rival, touching off a wave of copycat acquisitions throughout an industry.

In times of great turbulence and ambiguity, executives may feel safe imitating their rivals rather than going out on a limb with a novel business strategy. However, the essence of good strategy is to develop a unique system of activities that enables the organization to differentiate itself from the competition or to deliver products and services at a lower cost than its rivals. Simply copying the strategies and practices of rival firms will not produce a unique and defensible strategic position. It takes great courage to stand alone when rivals engage in herd behaviour, but it can pay huge dividends. Being different does not mean that a firm refuses to learn from others. For instance, General Dynamics studied its rivals very closely during the turmoil in the defence industry in the early 1990s, and observed that many firms had decided to pursue commercial diversification to compensate for diminishing military spending. The company's historical analysis indicated that aerospace firms had not fared well during past diversification efforts. Therefore, it chose to focus on defence despite the precipitous decline in industry demand. Many rivals ridiculed this strategy at the time. Yet for the past decade, General Dynamics has generated shareholder returns well in excess of those of most large competitors.

3. RULES OF THUMB

In many situations, managers cope with ambiguity and complexity by adopting a rule of thumb, or heuristic, to simplify a complicated decision. These shortcuts reduce the amount of information that decision makers need to process, and shorten the time required to analyze a complex problem. Often, an entire industry or profession adopts a common rule of thumb. For example, mortgage lenders assume that consumers should spend no more than 28 percent of their gross monthly income on mortgage payments and other home-related expenses. This provides a simple method for weeding out consumers with high default risk. Computer hardware engineers and software programmers have adopted many rules of thumb to simplify their work. Many of us are familiar with one such rule, Moore's Law, which predicts that the processing power of computer chips will double approximately every 18 months. Finally, the conventional wisdom in the venture capital industry used to suggest that firms should demonstrate four consecutive quarters of profits before launching an initial public offering. Alas, many venture capitalists regret abandoning this rule during the dot-com frenzy of the late 1990s.

Many executives also develop heuristics for their own firms.

In most cases, heuristics enable managers to cope with ambiguity and to make sound judgments in an efficient manner. Rules of thumb can be dangerous, though. They do not apply equally well to all situations—there are always exceptions to the rule. While industries and firms employ many idiosyncratic rules of thumb, researchers also have identified several, more general heuristics that can lead to systematic biases in judgment. Let's consider two prominent shortcuts: availability and anchoring. Individuals typically do not conduct a thorough statistical analysis to assess the likelihood that a particular event will take place in the future. Instead, they tend to rely on information that is readily available to them in order to estimate probabilities. Vivid experiences and recent events usually come to mind very quickly and have undue influence on people's decision making. This availability heuristic usually serves people well. However, in some cases, easily recalled information does not always prove relevant to the current situation and may distort our predictions.

When making estimates, many people also begin with an initial number drawn from some information accessible to them at the time, and they adjust their estimate up or down from that starting point. Unfortunately, the initial number often serves as an overly powerful anchor, and restrains individuals from making a sufficient adjustment. Researchers have shown that this "anchoring bias" affects decision-making even if people know that the initial starting point is a random number drawn from the spin of a roulette wheel! In sum, many different rules of thumb provide a powerful means of coping with uncertainty and complexity. But they also impair managerial judgment when people fail to recognize their drawbacks and limitations.

4. REFORMULATION

Social psychologist Karl Weick has noted that decision-makers can gain traction on complex problems by reframing them as "mere problems." Complicated issues can overwhelm people because they cannot cope cognitively and emotionally with the uncertainty, complexity and stress associated with trying to solve the problem. Redefining a serious challenge as a series of smaller problems enables people to make decisions more manageable. They can adopt a strategy of "small wins" in order to build momentum and make steady progress toward achieving the overall objective.

Business leaders employ this strategy all the time. For example, when Bill Anders took over General Dynamics in 1991, the company stood at the brink of bankruptcy. He framed the immediate problem as the need to generate the cash required to pay down the enormous amount of debt carried on the company's balance sheet. To address this issue, the firm divested several businesses and sold a number of assets. Then, Anders and his team set out to tackle a series of other problems that had contributed to the firm's poor performance. Another example occurred when Julie Morath became the Chief Operating Officer at Minnesota Children's Hospital and set out to tackle the complicated and highly sensitive problem of medical errors. To make early progress, she broke down the challenge into a series of smaller initiatives, and gradually shifted the organization's entire approach to patient safety.

The risk associated with a "small wins" strategy is that leaders might choose to make incremental adjustments in a firm's strategy, while missing the opportunity and the necessity for more radical changes. My colleague, Clayton Christensen, has written extensively about how firms can become fixated on making incremental improvements while failing to recognize disruptive changes in technology. Effective managers utilize a "small wins" approach but recognize its limitations. For instance, when Kevin Dougherty and his team crafted an e-commerce strategy for Sun Life's group insurance business, they focused first on the opportunity to create value by transferring existing business processes to the Web. After experiencing some success, they recognized the incremental nature of many of the

changes that they had made. Dougherty and his team worried that a competitor might use the Internet to create a completely different business model. They did not want to be "Amazoned" by such a rival. Therefore, the team began intense discussions about the possibility of more radical changes in the business unit's strategy. Dougherty's team coped effectively with uncertainty by keeping their eye on the big picture while pursuing a series of small wins.

5. DEFERENCE TO EXPERTS

Most executives rely heavily on experts in a pertinent domain to inform their decision making in complicated situations. Occasionally, top teams bring in outsiders who can offer knowledge and experience that are unavailable within the firm. On many senior teams, managers defer to other members who have relevant expertise on a particular issue. These experts have credibility, and command respect from others inside as well as outside the organization. For example, I have observed a top team in which one member exerted a great deal of influence on acquisition decisions because he had negotiated many merger deals throughout his career.

When making complex, unstructured decisions, experts can play an important role because they bring to bear a rich accumulation of experiences from which they can draw inferences, develop hypotheses and pose challenging questions. Their experience enables them to recognize patterns over time and across situations. They can use this pattern recognition ability to simplify complex situations very quickly and effectively.

Some teams, however, do not make good decisions when they defer to experts. Experienced members of a group can dominate a discussion and discourage constructive dissent. As a result, teams may converge prematurely on a suboptimal alternative. The Kennedy administration's infamous decision to support an invasion of the Bay of Pigs provides a vivid example of this phenomenon. In that decision process, experts from the Central Intelligence Agency exerted undue influence during the decision-making process. During those early days of the Kennedy administration, less experienced advisers deferred to the CIA officials, and even engaged in self-censorship when they held opposing views. Consequently, the Kennedy team failed to test critical assumptions embedded in the CIA plans and considered a very narrow range of options. By all accounts, the input and advocacy of a few highly credible experts proved to be a burden rather than a blessing.

Deference to experts may also diminish a team's commitment to a decision, and thereby impede implementation. Consider the case of a division president who typically assigned a small subgroup of his management team to analyze decisions in detail. For each situation, the division president selected individuals with relevant expertise. The subgroup developed and evaluated alternatives, and then shared their recommendation with the entire team. Naturally, others viewed these recommendations as a fait accompli and did not feel comfortable expressing dissent during the team meetings. If they had objections, they waited to raise them at some future date, often derailing the implementation process. In short, deference to experts may diminish commitment if other team members feel that they have not had an adequate opportunity to express their views and to influence the final decision.

6. RIGOROUS DEBATE

Rather than relying on expert judgments, some management teams may wish to grapple with ill-structured decisions by stimulating a rigorous debate among all members. In situations of great uncertainty, a lively debate can clarify and refine people's ideas, and enhance shared understanding of complex problems. In his book, *Only the Paranoid Survive* (Currency/Doubleday, 1996), Intel chairman Andy Grove explained that "debates are like the process through which a photographer sharpens the contrast when developing a print. The clearer images that result permit management to make a more informed—and more likely correct—call." Indeed, constructive conflict

encourages the generation of multiple alternatives and ensures that teams will critically evaluate each option. Healthy "debate also enables managers to separate facts from assumptions, and to surface and evaluate the latter very carefully.

"Many successful business leaders employ constructive conflict as a means of clarifying and sharpening their ideas during uncertain times."

Many successful business leaders employ constructive conflict as a means of clarifying and sharpening their ideas during uncertain times. For instance, Chuck Knight, the former CEO of Emerson Electric, always sparked heated debates during his firm's strategic planning meetings. He asked tough questions and forced his managers to examine all sides of an issue. Knight believed that debate provided a clearer assessment of the threats and uncertainties in the competitive landscape. Similarly, Jack Welch often explained that constructive conflict was an essential feature of strategic planning at General Electric. As one of his colleagues once said, "Jack will chase you around the room, throwing arguments and objections at you. Then you fight back . . . if you win, you never know if you've convinced him or if he agreed with you all along and was just making you strut your stuff" (J.L. Bower, "Jack Welch: General Electric's Revolutionary," Harvard Business School Case Study 0–394–065).

Conflict and dissent can prove to be very productive if managed appropriately. However, many debates result in a stalemate between opposing camps within management teams. Subgroups retrench into rigid opposing positions and cannot resolve their differences. Often, these stalemates lead to interpersonal conflict, ranging from personality clashes to emotional outbursts and personal attacks. This dysfunctional form of conflict makes it difficult to build commitment, and diminishes the likelihood that team members will want to cooperate with one another during implementation. For these reasons, leaders must adopt a variety of techniques for managing conflict effectively. These include discouraging the use of inflammatory language, asking people to argue several different sides of an issue, shifting people out of their traditional roles, and requiring teams to revisit key facts and assumptions when an impasse is reached.

7. EXPERIMENTATION

The final technique that executives employ to cope with ambiguity in strategic decisio making is experimentation. In this mode, managers avoid making a big bet under murky conditions. Instead, they stage a small test, gather feedback and adjust their strategy based upon what they have learned. They may run a second experiment at that point, or managers could decide to make a much bolder move. Alternatively, they could decide to abandon the project. This type of learning process enables managers to gradually reduce uncertainty and gather new information about customers and markets. For instance, throughout Home Depot's history, managers have tested new retailing concepts that they were not certain would become popular with customers. During the test, they gathered customer feedback and evaluated various measures of performance. Then, they made a decision regarding how to proceed. Many of these concepts evolved over time based upon the learning from these experiments.

When managers engage in experimentation, they need to be aware of the sunk-cost effect—the tendency for people to escalate commitment to a course of action in which they have made substantial prior investments of time, money or other resources. If people behaved rationally, they would make choices based on the marginal costs and benefits of their actions. The amount of any previous unrecoverable investment in that activity should not affect the current decision. Unrecoverable investments represent sunk costs that should not be relevant to current choices. However, research demonstrates that people often do consider past investment decisions when choosing future courses of action. In particular, individuals tend to pursue activities in which they have made prior investments. Often, they become overly committed to certain activities despite consistently poor results. As a result, individuals often escalate their commitment to failing courses of action. The sunk-cost effect can make it particularly difficult for decision makers to abandon unsuccessful experiments. Because managers do not want to "waste" their prior investment of time, energy and money, they may persist with future tests or scale up projects despite signs of poor performance during the initial experiment.

Process Evaluation

There is no magic bullet when it comes to making complex decisions in a turbulent environment. Managers must develop a repertoire of strategies that they can employ under these conditions. Moreover, they need to develop their management team's capability to utilize these practices and techniques. At the same time, leaders must be keenly aware of the risks associated with each strategy, and they need to raise the awareness of those around them.

Leaders should not stop there. They also must audit their decision-making processes, preferably in real time. As their management teams discuss complicated problems, leaders need to step back and assess the quality of the decision-making process. They must identify the strategies that managers are using to cope with uncertainty and complexity, and try to spot any dysfunctional behaviour.

To audit their decision process, leaders can ask some simple questions: What shortcuts are we employing? Is the team converging prematurely on a single alternative? Are experts exerting undue influence? Have we drawn the appropriate analogy? Are we engaging in herd behaviour? Have we discouraged dissent? Leaders ought to encourage their entire management team to ask these kinds of questions. They should strive to raise everyone's awareness about process issues. By doing so, leaders will enhance their team's ability to make tough choices under stressful and uncertain conditions, and hopefully, avoid the dismal fate of the Emperor Napoleon.

6

THE CONTINGENCY THEORY OF LEADERSHIP

Getting strategy right means matching people with jobs—a match that often depends on where a business is on the commodity continuum.

It goes without saying that you cannot pigeonhole. Good people are too multifaceted. That said, I would still make the case that due to their skills and personalities, some people work more effectively in commodities and others are better in highly differentiated products or services. . . . The right people for [a commodity] business are hard-driving, meticulous and detail oriented. They are not dreamers, they're hand-to-hand combat fighters. . . . At the other end of the spectrum, it's generally a different kind of person who thrives, not better or worse, just different.

—Jack Welch

In Chapter 5, we described the situational approach to leadership as an approach that suggested to the leader what to do in different situations. This requires a great deal of flexibility on the part of the leader (Yukl, 2006). In the contingency theory of leadership, it is assumed that the leader's style is relatively stable and needs to be matched with the most appropriate situation for the leader's style (Daft, 2005). Fiedler and Chemers (1974) call contingency theory a leader-match theory. The closer the match between leader style and a particular situation, the more effective the leader will be.

LEADERSHIP STYLES

As with the theories in Chapters 4 and 5, in contingency theory leadership, styles are broadly described as falling into two categories: task motivated and relationship motivated (Dubrin, 2007). Fiedler (1967) placed these two styles on opposite ends of a continuum and developed a scale he called the Least Preferred Coworker (LPC) scale. When a leader scores high on the LPC, it means that the leader is relationship oriented, whereas being low on the LPC means that the leader is task oriented (Daft, 2005). Task-oriented leaders want to achieve goals. Relationship-oriented leaders want to develop close relationships with their followers (Yukl, 2006).

SITUATIONAL VARIABLES

The contingency model helps leaders evaluate three variables using a dichotomous measure. In essence, leaders ask three questions: Are the leader-member relations good or poor? Is the task structure high or low? Is the leader's position power strong or weak? Answering these three questions allows leaders to determine what situation they are in and whether their style is a good match for that situation (see Figure 6.1).

Criteria for assessing these three variables are shown in Table 6.1. The variables need to be assessed in the order they are presented in Figure 6.1 and Table 6.1. As these are fairly self-explanatory, we will discuss the intersection of leadership styles with the situations defined by these three variables.

As mentioned, the order of these three variables is important. Leaders should examine leader-member relations, then task structure, and, finally, position power (Yukl, 2006). Good leader-member relations combined with high task structure and strong leader position power (Position 1 in Figure 6.1) is a very favorable situation for leaders. Poor leader-member relations combined with low task structure and weak leader position power (Position 8 in Figure 6.1) is the most unfavorable situation for leaders.

Contingency theory suggests that leaders with a low LPC score (those who are very task motivated) will be most effective in these two situations. In addition, leaders with middle LPC scores will be effective in Position 1 as well as being effective when the situation is assessed as being somewhat less favorable (Positions 2 to 3 in Figure 6.1). Furthermore, leaders with low LPC scores are effective in Positions 2 to 3. Finally, in situations that are moderately favorable to somewhat less favorable (Positions 4 to 7 in Figure 6.1), leaders with a high LPC score (very relationship oriented) will be most effective (Dubrin, 2007).

Leader-Member Relations	Good				Poor			
Task Structure	High Structure		Low Structure		High Structure		Low Structure	
Position power	Strong Power	Weak Power	Strong Power	Weak Power	Strong Power	Weak Power	Strong Power	Weak Power
Preferred Leadership Style	1	2	3	4	5	6	7	8
	Low LPCs Middle LPCs				High LPCs			Low LPC

Figure 6.1   Contingency Model

Source: Adapted from Fiedler (1967). Used by permission.

Table 6.1   Three Variables in the Contingency Model

Leader-member relations	*Good*	*Poor*
	Subordinates —like leader —trust leader —get along with leader	Atmosphere —unfriendly —friction between leader/followers Followers —no confidence in leader —no loyalty to leader —not attracted to leader
Task structure	*High*	*Low*
	Task accomplishment —requirements clear —few paths to achieving task —end to task clear —solutions limited	Task accomplishment —requirements vague and unclear —many paths to achieving task —end to task vague —many correct solutions
Leader's position power	*Strong*	*Weak*
	Leader has authority to —hire subordinates —fire subordinates —promote —give pay raises	Leader has no authority to —hire subordinates —fire subordinates —promote —give pay raises

Source: Adapted from Northouse (2007). Copyright © 2007, Sage Publications, Inc.

How Does the Contingency Theory of Leadership Work?

The answer to this question is not entirely clear. Why are leaders with low LPC scores best in very favorable and most unfavorable situations? And why are leaders with high LPC scores most effective in situations that are moderately favorable? These are two questions that are still unanswered. Fiedler (1995) has suggested why a mismatch between situation and style may not work. A mismatch leads to anxiety and stress, more stress leads to coping mechanisms developed earlier in a leader's career, and these less developed coping mechanisms lead to bad leader decisions and, consequently, negative task outcomes (Northouse, 2007).

However, while we may not be able to explain why a mismatch between style and situation does not work and a match does work, we can predict whether a leader will be effective in certain situations and not in others. Consequently, assess several work-related situations based on the three variables in the contingency model, assess your own leadership style (are you mostly task oriented, relationship oriented, or somewhere in the middle?), and choose the best situation for your leadership style (Daft, 2005).

REFERENCES

Daft, R. L. (2005). *The leadership experience* (3rd ed.). Mason, OH: Thomson, South-Western.

Dubrin, A. (2007). *Leadership: Research findings, practice, and skills.* New York: Houghton Mifflin.

Fiedler, F. E. (1967). *A theory of leadership effectiveness.* New York: McGraw-Hill.

Fiedler, F. E. (1995). Reflections by an accidental theorist. *The Leadership Quarterly, 6*(4), 453–461.

Fiedler, F. E., & Chemers, M. M. (1974). *Leadership and effective management.* Glenview, IL: Scott, Foresman.

Northouse, P. G. (2007). *Leadership: Theory and practice* (4th ed.). Thousand Oaks, CA: Sage.

Welch, J., & Welch, S. (2005). *Winning.* New York: Harper Business.

Yukl, G. (2006). *Leadership in organizations* (6th ed.). Upper Saddle River, NJ: Pearson-Prentice Hall.

THE CASES

A Difficult Hiring Decision at Central Bank

The case is designed to encourage readers to select among three highly qualified candidates for an important managerial position. In doing so, readers are required to establish the set of criteria that they believe should be taken into account when making an important hiring decision for the bank. Through the process of considering and prioritizing potential criteria with respect to the three potential candidates, readers are led to evaluate and reflect on the vision, mission, and core value of the bank.

Christina Gold Leading Change at Western Union

The chief executive officer of Western Union had just begun implementing a new organization structure. Changing the structure set out a clear message of Gold's desire to change the company's mind-set to a new more global culture. Already the CEO was finding that leaders in the United States were reluctant to give up control of product lines. At the regional level, she had keen leaders in place who wanted to push out the responsibility within their own regions and move toward a decentralized plan. While the CEO supported this notion in principle, she wanted to ensure that the right leaders could be placed in decentralized offices in order to execute on the six strategic pillars that she had laid out for the organization. One thing was certain—the CEO had made it clear that no revenue decreases would be forgiven amid the change. Many considerations had arisen: What pace of change should she take? How would she deal with resistance to change? How could she ensure that the new structure would support Western Union's global expansion?

THE READING

What Engages Employees the Most, or the Ten Cs of Employee Engagement

In selecting this reading, I looked for one that suggested leaders need to be high on relationship behaviors. I believe that most businesses will be in that middle portion (Positions 4 to 7) on the contingency model, and this is where the model suggests that we need relationship-oriented leaders.

Practitioners and academics have argued that an engaged workforce can create competitive advantage. These authors say that it is imperative for leaders to identify the level of engagement in their organization and implement behavioral strategies that will facilitate full engagement. In clear terms, they describe how leaders can do that.

A Difficult Hiring Decision at Central Bank

Prepared by Mark S. Schwartz and Hazel Copp

Version: (A) 2006–01–24

The Challenge

Martin Smith, vice-president (VP), Regional Sales at Central Bank, had recently been let go, and the search for his replacement was taking place. As part of the recruitment process, several candidates for the position needed to be ranked, while taking into account Central Bank's recently established vision, mission and values (see Exhibit 1).

Background

The position would require managing a number of employees in a region just outside of Toronto (see Exhibit 2).

Through conversations with Smith's former supervisor, Central Bank's Executive Resources established the background that led to Smith's dismissal:

- "Values driven" and well liked by his staff
- Strong community ties/profile
- Lowest turnover rate in segment
- Employee satisfaction scores in middle of pack
- Region in last place; results poor/growth stalled
- Integration of new segment incomplete
- Critical new processes/procedures not bought into or implemented
- Dismissed the previous week, decision unpopular in Region
- Three years away from early retirement, 30 years with Central Bank

Smith's former supervisor also provided a summary of "what went wrong":

- Need to be liked got in the way of critical changes
- Thought there was a trade-off between performance and values
- Couldn't make the tough people calls

Vision

- To be the leader in client relationships.

Mission (Employees)

- To create an environment where all employees can excel.

Mission (Clients)

- To help them achieve what matters to them.

Mission (Community)

- To make a real difference in our communities.

Mission (Shareholders)

- To build the highest total return for shareholders.

Core Values: Trust

- Act with integrity, honesty, and transparency, open and candid, treat others with dignity and fairness, behave according to ethical principles, operate with integrity and support our colleagues.

Core Values: Teamwork

- Work collaboratively with others; share info; respect opinions of others, listen attentively, ask for input and feedback.

Core Values: Accountability

- Live up to commitments, accept overall responsibility for behavior, admit mistakes and learn from them, seek clarity on roles.

Exhibit 1   Central Bank's Vision, Mission and Values

BUSINESS UNIT DESCRIPTION

With over 1,200 locations in the Canadian marketplace, our premiere Retail Banking segment represents the soul of the Central Bank brand and is the key to our long-term success. Our in-branch retail professionals provide a range of financial services to clients, from savings and chequing accounts, mortgages and loans, small business credit solutions and investment products, to complete financial planning.

PURPOSE OF POSITION

To lead effective and profitable sales execution of multiple customer offers in the Region and to maximize the contribution generated by its retail customers. Lead the advancement of the Region's market share and profitability through delivery of an excellent customer and employee experience.

Work closely and cooperatively with internal service and operations providers and other regional colleagues to better position Central Bank as the pre-eminent financial services provider in Canada. To improve Central Bank's reputation with customers, regulators and government and create an environment where employees can excel.

Provide leadership to the design and execution of segment-wide and cross-segment initiatives.

Exhibit 2   Job Posting - Vice President, Sales

ACCOUNTABILITIES OF POSITION (KEY OUTCOMES AND ACTIVITIES)

Establish a vision and clear purpose for the region; inspire commitment to the vision in employees and colleagues in a manner that puts the best interests of Central Bank and its customers first.

Develop, communicate and manage an aggressive regional sales plan aligned to national strategies and based on a deep understanding of regional market conditions, customer segments and resource requirements; drive the sales, business development and sales management processes for the region.

Build a customer-focused, high-performing sales team in the region that focuses on maximizing profitability, growth and customer loyalty; employ rigorous hiring practices/policies to ensure newly hired and current sales staff subscribe to all of Central Bank's values and professional standards.

Ensure all delegated roles, responsibilities and accountabilities are well defined and understood; apply metrics to measure and manage performance and foster continuous improvement.

Lead employees through periods of organizational change and maintain high levels of motivation during transition period; coach and mentor staff; actively support staff in their professional growth and personal development.

Deliver customer offers in accordance with core Central Bank business strategies, risk management requirements and Brand standards; build keen awareness of governance and regulatory requirements and closely manage process to monitor adherence.

Develop close partnerships with local leaders of all customer segments; build integrated sales plans where possible to maximize customer coverage.

Model the values of the organization internally and in the community; encourage staff to actively participate in their communities and publicly acknowledge their efforts.

COMPETENCIES (SKILLS AND KNOWLEDGE)

Highly developed leadership skills; experience turning around a business or managing significant business change is highly desirable.

Proven ability to develop and manage a world-class sales force in a highly competitive business environment. Candidates must have:

- a track record for delivering aggressive financial and business growth targets;
- a staffing model and experience recruiting high performing sales staff;
- a well-honed and highly successful coaching methodology;
- demonstrated sales prospecting and sales tracking capabilities.

Expert knowledge of business and financial planning processes is required; demonstrated financial discipline and cost management capabilities.

Ability to manage relationships between various customer offers, delivery channels and support/supplier groups; demonstrated ability to work collaboratively across Central Bank to achieve collective business goals and satisfy customer needs.

Ability to instill respect for risk management and compliance requirements and deliver effective processes/ systems to manage all aspects of operational, regulatory, market, credit and reputational risk.

Ability to translate strategic intent into action, communicate action/direction openly and effectively up, down and across the region.

Able to represent Central Bank in various external communities of interest.

ATTRIBUTES REQUIRED

Trustworthy (e.g., Integrity); Relationship builder; Team Player/Builder; Accountability (i.e., Results orientation); Customer focus; Adaptability

- Said he bought into sales process/disciplines but didn't enforce the process
- Hadn't built appropriate relationships with colleagues in other strategic business units; no previous goodwill to help smooth integration of new segment
- Business continually left on table due to poor teamwork between segments
- Would blame others (often Head Office) for lack of success
- Should have moved on Smith earlier, *but* he'd been around for so long

Smith's former supervisor provided an indication of what he believed was needed:

- Major turnaround
- Build new team; exit players who can't deliver
- Hire well; recruit people who can deliver and have required values
- Get buy-in into new sales processes/value of a more disciplined approach
- Employ a person who can build trust/relationships with other segments to grow business
- Hire a candidate who could ultimately prove to be a good "succession" candidate.

The Candidates

Following an initial screening and interview process (see Exhibit 3) conducted by Central

---

1. **Describe the culture in which you do your best work.**

Charlotte Webb:

I'm the sort of person who likes a work environment that provides some challenges professionally. So far, Central Bank has provided that for me. What's most important to me now is the ability to grow career-wise. I like working with bright people, in an organization that is willing to take some risks. I'm not talking about recklessness, but I like working for an organization that wants to operate at the "cutting edge" with respect to conducting business, one that is attuned to the market, uses technology and analytics to the fullest, and knows where it wants to play. It's also important to me how organizations treat their people, that people are rewarded not only for achieving goals, but for how they are achieved as well.

Scott Warren:

I guess I can speak best about the Royal, which puts a heavy focus on being number one. That's the sort of place where I do my best work. I like everything to be fast paced, with clear deadlines to meet. As well, when the firm allows its managers and employees to take reasonable risks, and be rewarded for results, that's best for me, that's when I'm most motivated. I also like "hands-off" managers, I really don't like being micromanaged.

James Skinner:

The First Northern bank culture works for me, it's critical to me that employees and customers are treated with respect and dignity, where people can work as a team. I don't subscribe to the "star" system, where only the top performers receive all of the rewards. I like to think through the short- and long-term implications of what we do, and I appreciate a culture that supports that. I really dislike the "churn" that results from poor planning and last minute changes. Those sorts of twists and turns are really tough on people.

2. **What's the toughest call you have had to make?**

Charlotte Webb:

While working at a Central Bank branch as a summer student, a friend of my dad's came in, and asked me for some personal information on his ex-wife's bank accounts. They were going through an ugly divorce, and

---

Exhibit 3   Interview Questions/Responses of the Three Candidates

it was very awkward for me given my family's connection to say no, and my desire to please an important customer. I knew that I shouldn't give him the information, and I politely refused, but he became very vocal and threatened to pull out his accounts. I knew I was doing the right thing but it was pretty tough, I was so junior at the time.

Scott Warren:

I can't say anything I've ever had to do was really that "tough" or "difficult." I guess I'm just the sort of person who does what has to be done, and tries not to think too much about it afterwards. But if I had to pick something, it would be when I was working as an executive director in corporate finance in Australia, and there was pressure coming from Head Office to close off our loan book, since we were beginning to close down Australia. One of our clients was in trouble could easily have been put on the watch list. He had a seasonal business and was desperate to buy more time. It was still within my discretion in terms of what to do, but it was somewhat of a tough call to let his account ride since I could have had some difficulties with Toronto, but I did think the guy deserved a chance, and in the end everything worked out and we got our money back.

James Skinner:

Well, it probably was last year when my wife got sick, and I had to give up an opportunity to become a senior VP in the Calgary office. It was an opportunity that I had been waiting for, for years. In the end you make the right decision for your family, but it wasn't easy, letting the opportunity that I had worked for slip through my fingers.

3. What would you be afraid to find if you got this job?

Charlotte Webb:

I wouldn't exactly say "afraid" is the right word, but if you're asking me what I think the biggest challenges would be, I would say winning over the staff, who will know I don't have a lot of line experience, and introducing sales discipline to the group, but it's a challenge I'm happy to accept. It's not the first time I've gone in without all the required skills, but I think my record shows I've not only met the desired targets, but exceeded them as well.

Scott Warren:

I'm concerned that it would take forever for me to get ahead, and that people don't really get rewarded for producing results. I'm willing to do whatever it takes, to deliver, but my expectation would be that I would be rewarded accordingly.

James Skinner:

This is a very important question for me, so I'm very glad you asked it. I am concerned whether Central Bank is more focused on the "numbers," than on people. I know this is perhaps the wrong perception, but I'm also concerned about teamwork issues at Central Bank; too many "silos" and "revolving doors." It's certainly perceived to be a very different culture here, but despite my concerns, I believe I'm up for the challenge.

4. How do you feel about the recent emphasis being placed on corporate governance?

Charlotte Webb:

It certainly has been a lot of work for managers throughout the organization. I used to spend 5 percent of my time on what I would loosely call governance, but in the last year that has shot up to 45 percent. No one could argue that this isn't critical, or necessary, but I certainly would hope that once we have installed the governance engine,

Exhibit 3 (Continued)

that the time requirements will be reduced. It's not just about enforcing rules and regulations and policies, it's also about making sure you've hired the right people.

Scott Warren:

I guess you're referring to *Sarbanes-Oxley* and the Basel Accord stuff. I'm really not sure whether it will make a difference at the end of the day in terms of discouraging the "bad apples"—I think all of those CEOs and CFOs involved in the recent scandals knew what they were doing was wrong, but did it anyways. People always seem to find a way around laws and regulations. But at the end of the day, it's important for the banks to comply with what the regulators want, because none of us can afford to lose the trust of our customers. But hopefully as the checks and balances are built into the system, it won't continue to be as cumbersome as it has been at the front end.

James Skinner:

I'm very happy to see the renewed emphasis being placed on corporate governance. It's been needed for a while to remind everyone of the importance of having rules and regulations. I think that people have forgotten that firms have responsibilities to their shareholders and the public. I believe that unfortunately sometimes very ethical people can be placed into an organization with certain pressures to perform that can make them do some very bad things. We need to renew the public's faith in the corporate world, and this seems to be the best way of doing it.

5. Describe an ethical dilemma you have faced in the workplace and how it was resolved.

Charlotte Webb:

I was in an awkward situation a few years ago. The department was required to dramatically reduce its expenditures. What this meant was that we could no longer sponsor things like department lunches, or have prizes for reaching certain goals. At first the managers accepted it, but then a number of people started to become upset when they saw how the VP, who enforced the rules with all of us, was continuing to spend on lavish dinners, staying at upscale hotels, and continuing to use limos. None of these expenses seemed to lead to a return on business, everyone could see the VP taking people out, he wasn't even discreet about it. When people started complaining to me, I decided to see the VP. I suggested to him that he might be setting a poor example for everyone, and that he might want to cut down on the expenses before someone decided to raise the issue with his supervisor. He became very annoyed, said he wasn't really prepared to discuss it with me further, that there was an agenda that I wasn't fully aware of. Although it appeared afterwards that he did in fact cut down on some of the excesses, unfortunately our working relationship was strained from then on, in fact sometimes he was quite verbally abusive to me, and on one occasion he even pushed me to tears in front of a group of colleagues. After that, I just took the first opportunity I could to move out of that division.

Scott Warren:

I'm not sure if I've every really faced a true ethical dilemma, but I did have an issue once that related to Royal's Code of Conduct. In about half my branches, I have responsibility for wealth management, we were courting some high net worth individuals, and I wanted to plan a day that they would really enjoy and differentiate us from the other banks. But that meant taking me over my approved entertainment budget. I knew Royal's code spoke about "moderate" business entertainment, but these were some pretty important potential clients. I wanted to take them golfing and for dinner at Glen Abbey, since I certainly couldn't take them to the local municipal course. I debated whether I needed to get my supervisor's approval since I suspected my supervisor would probably stick to the code, and wouldn't be able to see the bigger picture. As it happened, my supervisor was away on vacation, and I was able to get it approved by Head Office. When my supervisor returned he was very upset at first that I had gone over his head to get approval, until he found out that I managed to bring in about $30 million dollars in new assets, which he agreed justified the few thousand spent.

Exhibit 3 (Continued)

> James Skinner:
>
> I think I've probably faced many ethical dilemmas over my career. It's hard to pick just one, but if I had to it would probably be the story of how I met my wife at First Northern bank. She was my administrative assistant at the time, and I struggled with whether to disclose the relationship, particularly when it became more serious, knowing that it was "taboo," that it was frowned upon. The way we resolved it though was to hide the relationship, to the point where no one had any idea we were together. In the end the dilemma resolved itself, we ended up getting married, my wife ended up leaving the bank, and no one knew any differently.

Exhibit 3 (Continued)

Bank's Executive Resources, the number of final candidates had been reduced to three. The following provides a summary of each of the final candidate's profiles.

1. Candidate: Charlotte Webb (Internal Candidate)

Current Position: Senior Director, Customer Experience, Marketing Division (Toronto)

Status: First round interview with VP, Executive Resources completed

Background

Webb was the only internal candidate to be short-listed. She worked at Central Bank during summers while in university, initially as a teller, and then in the marketing division and for one year between her undergraduate and postgraduate degrees. Webb was recruited to the World Bank from the London School of Economics, and assigned to the World Bank offices in Geneva and Washington, DC, for a total of four years.

A desire to return to Canada prompted her to reconnect with Central Bank. Initially hired as a senior analyst in January of 1998 by the Corporate Strategy unit, she had exposure to many of Central Bank's businesses and, while in that role, led a number of strategically critical and enterprise-wide projects. In 2001, Webb was seconded into Central Bank's Small Business Division to help implement a new go-to-market strategy she had crafted. The role was made permanent, and she was appointed general manager (GM), Small Business Sales and Operations in early 2002. In January of 2004, Webb applied for and secured her current role in the Marketing Division (see attached résumé, Exhibit 4, for greater detail).

People were eager to work for Webb because of the emphasis she put on personal development. Many of her "graduates" had gone on to bigger and better roles because of the challenges/ exposure she provided and her willingness to hire on potential and coach/mentor for missing skills.

Webb was currently viewed as one of Central Bank's highest potential level 10s. She sustained high performance ratings over the last six years and had been the recipient of numerous internal awards based on her superior contributions to the organization. While this new position would constitute Webb's first front-line role, this experience would fill an important development gap for her.

At her most recent performance review, Webb requested just such an opportunity to round out her experience and wondered aloud how many more years she was destined to spend at the same level. She also voiced disappointment that Central Bank had gone outside the organization repeatedly for VP hires, overlooking talented insiders. Retaining Webb was a priority for Central Bank.

Education

Havergal alumna. Has undergraduate degree in Mathematics and Statistics from the University of Waterloo. Graduate of the London School of Economics.

Charlotte M. Webb
177 Roxborough Drive, Toronto, Ontario M8T 2C7
Phone: 416-376-8827
E-mail: charlotte.webb@cibc.ca

CAREER SUMMARY

Seasoned author and executor of far reaching corporate strategies that deliver tangible business results. Demonstrated thought, people and values leadership capabilities. Award winning corporate and community citizen.

EDUCATION

1994   Masters in Economics, London School of Economics, London, England
1991   Bachelor of Science, Applied Mathematics & Statistics, University of Waterloo (Ontario Scholar - full scholarship to university)

PROFESSIONAL EXPERIENCE

Central Bank: 1998—Present

February 2003—Present
Senior Director, Customer Experience & Communication, Marketing Division

- Led initiative to transform customer experience at Central Bank in all delivery channels. Worked across SBU lines to engage all relevant participants in cultural and operational changes required to position Central Bank as the premiere Canadian Bank.
- Diagnosed root causes of customer dissatisfaction and defection; segmented issues into employee and operations related challenges and recommended solutions. Received approval for 80% of suggestions, achieving buy-in from all business units and infrastructure groups. (Cost reduction delaying implementation of remaining 20%).
- Developed innovative training programs for front line staff that minimized time away from customers, provided a standard Central Bank customer interface across Central Bank, improving both customer and employee satisfaction ratings.
- Worked with product groups and front line management to reduce product "fatigue"; reduced number and complexity of products available, producing just-in-time interactive training modules that significantly increased sales volumes.
- With process re-engineering specialists, explored solutions to common customer irritants related to lengthy or unreliable processes/procedures; liaised with Technology & Operations Division to resolve existing challenges and gain support for new initiatives.

August 2000—January 2003
General Manager, Small Business Sales & Operations

- Led Small Business executives through design of new go-to-market strategy for segment; assessed lifetime value of small business client by conducting statistical and segmentation analysis; analysed competitive environment and best practices.
- Provided strategic options and led deliberations to validate and choose optimal direction; worked with VP, Strategic Initiatives to translate strategy into operational plan for deployment across Canada.

Exhibit 4   Résumé: Charlotte E. Webb

- Implemented new sales and resourcing model for segment which included new client team configuration, revised roles and accountabilities and new sales discipline. Provided tools to assess sales versus service capabilities and introduced new compensation plan to incent sales force.
- Worked with central operations group to achieve better efficiencies and improve client service; liaised with Branch Banking group to facilitate improved in-branch service of Small Business clients and to increase cross selling opportunities.
- Achieved: 24% revenue growth, versus corporate target of 12%; ten point increase in client satisfaction ratings, grew market share by 5%.

May 1998—August 2000
Senior Analyst, Corporate Strategy, Office of the Chairman

Responsibilities included leading projects, analyzing/developing new business opportunities; providing analytical support for key business decisions.

Projects included:

- Customer Strategy Project for Business Segment: Led customer preference/conjoint statistical analysis, resulting in the divesture of unprofitable unit and increased investment in profitable business.
- Growth Strategy for E-Business venture: Worked with McKinsey to explore feasibility of moving successful banking venture into US and European markets. Helped develop detailed go forward plan, emphasizing regulatory challenges and recommending alliance partners.

August 1994—November 1997
The World Bank, Washington, D.C.; Geneva

- Supporting teams comprised of World Bank, Eastern European Development Commission and the United Nations in the financial restructuring of the Balkan States.
- Conducted preliminary needs assessment for economic reconstruction of the Ukraine. Supported commission examining banking needs/functions in various developing countries.

Scholarships and Awards

1999	Present: Rated "exceeds expectation" on all performance evaluations
2004, 2002, 2001	Quarterly Achiever Award Recipient
1991	Big Sister of the Year Award
1992	Young Woman of Distinction, Toronto YWCA
1987	Ontario Scholar
1987	University of Waterloo Entrance Scholarship

Affiliations:

- United Way Coordinator and Spokesperson
- Run for the Cure Campaign Manager for GTA
- Board of Directors, Centre for Family Literacy
- Chair of Fund Raising, Bayview Centre for Abused Women

Strengths Relative to This Role

- Highly intelligent, superior analytic and strategic skills
- Very eager to learn, had taken every opportunity to acquire new skills/perspectives
- Big-picture thinker, had long-term perspective
- Very high energy level, expected a lot of herself and others
- Positive, can-do attitude, engaging, gets things done
- Quick study, had grasped complex and diverse business equations with relative ease
- Superior knowledge of financial needs and delivery preferences of this segment's customers (currently leading initiative to enhance the quality of customer experience in all delivery channels)
- Had successfully developed strategies, objectives and sales programs for several business segments, key contributor to the sales measurement and tracking systems currently in use
- Had operationalized and executed a sales program for Small Business that resulted in aggressive growth, successfully led a roll-out of sales process across Canada
- Respected and well liked by her team, Employee Commitment Index (ECI) scores among highest in Bank
- Very principled, good examples of doing the right, rather than the expedient, thing
- Good influencing skills, successfully delivered initiatives across SBU lines despite competing agendas

For Consideration

- Minimal front-line interaction, had "knowing" rather than "doing" perspective of sales
- Had hired several professional staff, but never exited anyone
- While her roles had clearly influenced the direction of the business, most of her interactions had been with Head Office types
- Had led "thought" turnaround, rather than "people/business" turnaround
- Could personalize issues, on occasion, cared too much and got emotional
- Thinks very quickly, question whether she could bring others (slower staff) along
- Suspect she will always do "the right thing" but occasionally came across a bit pedantic/righteous

- Once raised concerns over supervisor's seemingly improper use of his expense account, matter later resolved as a "misunderstanding"

Of Interest

- This candidate had been very active in both Central Bank's Run for the Cure and United Way efforts. Several years ago, Webb was named "Young Woman of Distinction" by the Toronto YWCA for her work with the Big Sisters' group. Albeit junior, she was a popular member of Central Bank's informal women's network
- Webb is the niece of a Central Bank Board member. The Director commented on "Webb's great interest in this role" when he bumped into the hiring manager at a recent social gathering

Webb was five months pregnant, and it was not clear how long a maternity leave she would require.

2. Candidate: Scott Warren

Current Position: VP, Retail Bank, Toronto West & Hamilton, Regional Bank

Status: Interviewed by executive search firm and VP, Executive Resources, Central Bank

Background

Warren originally planned to pursue a career in the foreign service or international law but a stint with Nesbitt Burns (between his undergraduate and law degrees) sharpened his interest in financial services. Recruited to McKinsey's Montreal office after articling with a prominent Ottawa law firm. Recruited by Regional Bank (former client) two years later to work on a high-profile new venture in Australia; Warren returned to Toronto after the venture was terminated and was put on an accelerated management program. Served 12-month stints in both Audit and Risk and was then selected from bank's high-potential pool to work as executive assistant to Regional Bank's chairman. Warren moved out of the chairman's office into his first executive posting and his first line role. He had been in this post, the smallest territory nationally, since December 2001 (see Exhibit 5).

Warren was chaffing against Regional Bank's long-term and disciplined approach to development and felt that he should have been moved to a bigger, more complex mandate or promoted to senior vice-president (SVP). He believed that he could move up the ladder more quickly here, given (in his view) Central Bank's penchant for hiring externally and promoting on perceived potential rather than experience. Warren was told by Regional Bank in March that a move was imminent but this promise seemed to have been lost in the noise around the massive restructuring of Regional Bank's senior ranks. Most troubling was the fact that Warren's sponsor had been exited.

Education

Toronto French School Alumnius; BA, Government, Harvard; LLB, Osgoode Hall Law School, York University

Strengths Relative to This Role

- Extremely bright, versatile player; voracious learner
- Driven, results oriented, huge capacity for work
- Executed turnaround of small but lucrative territory, moved area from last to first place in 18 months
- Exited 35 percent of sales staff and redeployed additional 15 percent more
- Designed hiring profile/recruitment process for sales staff now adopted by the rest of the bank
- Increased sales volumes by 60 percent for the last two years, significantly exceeding profitability and cost management targets
- Worked closely with customer relationship management (CRM) area and Risk Management to hone prospecting skills and reduce losses
- Contributed to and piloted new sales training program for Regional Bank, led national initiative to "measure and manage" more effectively
- Key contributor to bank initiatives within his division and across the bank
- Moved to west end of the city to better participate in community activities

For Consideration

- Hinted of intellectual arrogance, a bit condescending around Regional Bank's "superiority"
- Difficult to get handle on what Warren personally accomplished in Australia; became vague when pressed for details, alluded to Regional Bank strategic gaffe
- Believe Warren cares about people but suspect he doesn't always show it
- Intense, could be overpowering for more reticent team members
- May not always give credit to others; seemed to be a one-man show on occasion
- Activity level on the job and elsewhere was awesome, but how much is too much?
- Enthusiasm engaging but candidate interrupted, wanted to speak rather than listen

Warren's tenure in any position had not exceeded two years—not sure how much success candidate can claim for projects initiated before his arrival or executed after his departure.

Of Interest

- Warren was working on his MBA (Richard Ivey School of Business, University of Western Ontario) and was actively campaigning to be the next and youngest president of the National Club, which he hoped to revitalize. He was also an avid runner (finishing both the Boston and New York marathons in the middle of the pack) and longtime skier (visited his family's chalet at Mount Tremblant in Quebec as often as possible).

A preliminary and very discreet reference was obtained from a former peer (now a SVP at Central Bank) of Warren's at Regional Bank. The individual confirmed Warren's long-term potential, superior results and high-potential status at Regional Bank but described him as "overly ambitious" and "political."

3. Candidate: James (Jim) Skinner

Current Position: District Vice-President, First Northern Bank

T. Scott Warren
28 Bayview Crescent, Oakville, ON M3P 1B9
Telephone: 905-846-3321 (Home); 416-307-2215 (Business); 416-537-9856 (Cell)
Confidential e-mail address: melissaandscott@rogers.com

PROFILE

A seasoned financial services professional with broad managerial experience. Motivated by challenging environment, aggressive goals, teamwork and the opportunity to make a tangible contribution to an organization's performance.

PROFESSIONAL EXPERIENCE

Royal Bank of Canada

December 2002—Present
Regional Vice President, Toronto West & Hamilton

Led all aspects of Regional Bank's retail business in Toronto West & Hamilton area; executed dramatic turn around of region (last to first place) within first 18 months. Sales volumes increased by 60%; significantly exceeding profitability and cost management targets. Steps to achievements:

- Assessed existing branch location and resource deployment; closed branches in four unprofitable locations, piloted two new state of the art branches with enhanced physical design and front-end technology.
- Significantly upgraded Regional talent pool, exiting 35% and redeploying 15% of workforce; designed and implemented comprehensive assessment process (now adopted by Regional Bank overall) for sales ability; seeded region with top talent identified in recruitment blitz.
- Used available Customer Relationship Management (CRM) tools and Risk Management expertise to mine more affluent pockets in region, greatly increasing the number in profitable customers and reducing credit losses.
- Helped design and pilot training program for front line staff; content included advanced use of CRM tools, prospecting techniques and selling "the Regional Bank way".
- Re-segmented customer population along "share of wallet" and potential to cross-sell lines; focused efforts on high yield sales activities resulting in increased sales volume of most profitable products.
- Negotiated successful referral program with Regional Bank colleagues to grow customer base.
- Led measure and manage project for Regional Bank Branch Banking, redesigning sales metrics and rewards.

October 2001—October 2002
Acting Vice President, Office of the President & CEO

- Chosen from the high potential pool for assignment. Responsible for ensuring the smooth operation of the President & CEO's business day by anticipating needs, organizing events, undertaking strategic analysis and preparing presentations. Work with departments throughout the organization to deliver pertinent and timely information to the President and CEO's office.
- Operate as a conduit for information from the bank's various divisions to the President & CEO's office.

June 2000—October 2001
Accelerated Management Program, Toronto, Canada

- Audit Division: Participated in audits of Wealth Management and Retail Banking units in Canada, West Indies and Guernsey. Co-led project to define new Audit philosophy for Regional Bank and to enhance the effectiveness of the function.
- Risk Management: Assigned to Credit Adjudication for Commercial Bank Group; participated in initiative to re-engineer end-to-end credit processes relating to Commercial and Corporate Banking.

Exhibit 5   Résumé: T. Scott Warren

February 1998—March 2000
Executive Director, Regional Bank, Australia

- Crafted strategy, provided legal expertise for Regional Bank entry into Australian corporate finance market; led integration efforts with newly acquired firm.
- Originated, negotiated and executed senior debt, mezzanine and equity financings for acquisitions, leveraged buy-outs, and other structured corporate finance transactions.
- Developed valuation models and negotiated to sell Regional Bank's corporate finance business in Australia.

January 1996—February 1998
Management Consultant, McKinsey & Co., Montreal, Canada

- Created customer profitability strategy for Travel and Hospitality client. Helped reposition brand, did service profit chain analysis and recommended product and service innovations which resulted in brand turnaround.
- Helped Canadian Oil & Gas company launch new venture for European exploration and production, significantly broadening their operating base and increasing profitability.
- Performed business unit, product/channel and customer profitability studies for retail wealth management business unit, resulting in product bundling and pricing policy changes.
- Developed acquisition and integration strategy for Corporate banking arm of leading Canadian bank. Developed detailed integration plan and managed "first 100 days" project teams, including contractual negotiations, regulatory requirements and infrastructure build.

May 1994—May 1995
Articling Student, Wise, Strong & Kessler,
Barristers and Solicitors, Ottawa, Ontario

- Provided corporate, commercial, securities, tax, insolvency, and litigation legal services.

EDUCATION

1994   LLB (Bachelor of Laws), Osgoode Hall Law School, York University
1991   BA (with Honors), Government, Harvard University

ACHIEVEMENTS AND INTERESTS

Fluent in French
Currently working on MBA (Richard Ivey School of Business, The University of Western Ontario)
Qualified for and completed the Boston and NYC marathons in 2003 and 2004
Competitive skier—competed with Team Canada in 1994 Winter Games
Member of the National Club (nominated to run in Presidential election 2005)

Status: Interviewed by executive search firm and VP, Executive Resources, Central Bank

Background

Skinner grew up in Toronto's East end where his father owned a printing business. He ran the office for his father for two years after his graduation from Ryerson University. At the suggestion of the manager, Skinner joined the local First Northern Bank branch where his family banked. He progressed through the ranks to Bank Manager (including a two-year stint in the West Indies) and was moved through increasingly senior roles in Human Resources, Commercial Bank and Risk Management, returning to retail banking as a District Vice-President in 2000 (see attached resume, Exhibit 6, for more detail).

Beginning in 1996, First Northern Bank agreed to sponsor Skinner's executive MBA (EMBA)

program in recognition of his strong leadership capabilities and to supplement his rather weak academic background.

Skinner was in the process of moving to Calgary to a larger and more senior District VP role (with a promise to re-evaluate the role for possible upgrading to SVP) when his wife became seriously ill. Skinner elected to remain in Toronto where family support and better treatment is available to his wife. His old role was backfilled quickly with a rising star, and Skinner has spent the last 10 months without portfolio, working on special assignments and getting progressively frustrated. He was open to talking to headhunters for the first time in his career.

Education

High School; Business Administration Diploma, Ryerson University; Fellow, Institute of Canadian Bankers; Canadian Securities Course; EMBA, University of Toronto

Strengths Relative to This Role

- People management/motivation was a key strength
- Able to build trust, trusted advisor to senior management and staff alike
- Clearly saw the correlation between employee satisfaction and customer satisfaction

---

James (Jim) Skinner
11 Moorecroft Road, Ajax, Ont, M4N 2S5
Home: 905-777-0456; Business: 416-437-8813
E-mail: jamess@rogers.ca

PROFESSIONAL EXPERIENCE

Bank of First Northern
1979 to present

February 2004—Present

On interim assignment with EVP, Retail Branch Banking.

Projects include:

- Initiative examining correlation between employee and customer satisfaction.
- Macro planning for replacement of segment's aging executive population.
- Roll out of new technology/CRM tools to branch network.

March 2000—December 2003
District Vice President, Toronto East

- Assumed responsibility for troubled Toronto East Region during restructuring of GTA regional territories. Merged two smaller districts into largest mandate in Ontario, reduced FTE and rolled out new sales process concurrently.
- Formed Employee Association to ensure employee voice heard during major transition, to augment communication strategy and garner input/insight into regional dynamics and build marketing strategies.

Exhibit 6   Résumé: James (Jim) Skinner

- Assessed staff for sales versus servicing skills, finding jobs for all employees displaced in process; introduced disciplined sales process to Region, traveling to all branches at least bi-monthly to personally coach branch managers and communicate expectations to all levels.
- Initiated annual "Customer First Award" for District employee who best exemplifies customer service and monthly award (extra vacation days or gift certificates) for "Best Assist" given for teamwork resulting in new or expanded business.
- Built strong alliances with segment peers to increase business flow and provide broader market and community coverage.
- Recognized as most improved district in 2001. Received Best District Award (Ontario) 2003 and 2004 for highest sales volumes, top quartile Employee Commitment and lowest NIX ratio.

October 1998—March 2000
General Manager, Credit, Ontario Region

- Co-led initiative to re-engineer credit approving/adjudication and compliance reporting process for Small Business and Agriculture portfolios.
- Engaged line staff in streamlining front end credit approval processes, using behavioural scoring and technology assisted decisioning tools.
- Introduced base line accreditation requirements for Risk Managers and credit training for all front line originators.
- Dramatically reduced credit losses and significantly improved credit approval time.

August 1996—October 1998
General Manager, Small Business Banking, Central Toronto

- Implemented Small Business strategy in Central Toronto, the largest market in Canada; led the change management effort to reposition the Small Business offer, adding wealth management products to traditional credit focus.
- Chaired the GTA Risk Committee, significantly improving the region's risk profile through the development and implementation of sound risk and governance practices and policies.
- Achieved highest improvement award in Employee Index in 1997.
- Publicly recognized for strong contribution to operations and infrastructure groups.
- Partnered with external groups to develop added value programs for Small Business clients.
- Delivered on cost containment and client retention targets, exceeding sales targets by 31%.

June 1995—August 1996
General Manager, Service Effectiveness, Western Canada, Calgary

Seconded to Regional Head Office to deploy successful sales & services strategies developed for Main Branch, Calgary across the Western Division.

- Developed and implemented a business retention and development plan for the Division;
- Expanded the Regional Call Centre's mandate to augment customer support;
- Aligned service response to segments, providing differentiated service to high value customers;
- Developed and implemented Local Market Management in the Division;
- Met retention objectives and exceeded sales targets by 120MM by year end.

Exhibit 6 (Continued)

August 1992—May 1995
Director, Retail and Private Banking Services, Main Branch, Calgary

Responsible for managing Retail and Private Banking, Main Branch, Calgary

- Designed and launched a customer-centric sales and service model; differentiated high net worth customer experience from standard service
- Restructured Main Branch to better implement new customer strategy, make productivity gains and increase profitability.
- Increased individual sales capacity by 95%, increased branch customer satisfaction ratings (in top 10 branches nationally). Won national Customer Service Excellence Award.

June 1990—July 1992
Human Resources Officer, Head Office, Toronto

Seconded to Human Resources to help implement a major restructuring of Retail Banking; provided field perspective for organization design, training and recruitment specialists:

- Conducted span of control and capacity planning for realigned districts;
- Helped design and facilitate new training and orientation programs;
- Revamped roles and responsibilities for newly crafted line positions;
- Established selection criteria for senior District leaders and conducted first line interviews.

1985—1990
Branch Manager

- Managed increasingly larger and more complex branches in Ontario, Western Canada and Atlantic Canada. Key achievements: (1) The effective leadership and development of staff; (2) Continually exceeding sales and profitability goals.

1979—1985

- Progressed through a number of line roles to Branch Manager

EDUCATION

1996   EMBA, University of Toronto
1991   Fellow, Institute of Canadian Bankers
1981   Canadian Securities Course
1975   Business Administration Diploma, Ryerson

AFFILIATIONS

Director, Canadian Parkinson Society
Treasurer, Pickering Lions Club
Trustee, Separate School Board, Durham Region
Coach, Boys Intermediate Soccer

Exhibit 6 (Continued)

- Track record for turning around under-performing units grounded in First Northern Bank way: doing more with less, employees for life, if humanly possible
- Didn't shoot from the hip, down to earth, honest and open
- Achieved results through people and teamwork
- Results focused, takes time to understand the variables
- Strong on process, cutting time and money where possible
- Mature, strong communicator

For Consideration

- While capable of meeting immediate business and "values" needs, Skinner may be a less viable succession candidate
- Not clear if Skinner could take necessary tough stand without usual First Northern Bank safety net for employees
- Whether Skinner was committed to leaving First Northern Bank was unclear; Skinner's

ability to adjust to/change Central Bank's culture was also questionable
- Significant front-line experience, but candidate lacked analytical/strategic depth

Of Interest

- Skinner, a First Northern Bank lifer, was reluctant to leave but felt he needed to find a "real job" soon. He was concerned about the adverse publicity Central Bank had generated over the last few years and his perception that it "chews up and spits out executives," "eating its young," to quote Skinner
- During the interview (his first, in 26 years) Skinner confessed he was very nervous about starting over again at 50 and was worried about adjusting to a new corporate culture
- His wife required periodic visits to the Mayo Clinic and First Northern Bank had been very supportive with time off and professional support for him and his three teenagers. He wondered if Central Bank would be as helpful and compassionate

---

CHRISTINA GOLD LEADING CHANGE AT WESTERN UNION

Prepared by Jordan Mitchell under the supervision of Professor Alison Konrad

Version: (A) 2005–12–13

Introduction

In early 2003, Christina Gold, chief executive officer (CEO) of Western Union, had just begun implementing a new organization structure. Gold had joined Western Union in May 2002 with a key focus of unifying the company's U.S. operations with its international division. In guiding the company to act as one entity, Gold proposed a change from a U.S. centric product line focus to a regional structure with three main divisions: the Americas; Europe, Africa, the Middle East and South Asia; and Asia-Pacific.

Changing the structure sent out a clear message of Gold's desired change in mind-set to a new type of global culture. Already, Gold was finding that leaders in the United States were reluctant to give up control of product lines. At the regional level, she had keen leaders who wanted to push out the responsibility within their own regions and move towards a decentralized plan. While Gold supported this notion in principle, she wanted to ensure that the right leaders could be placed in decentralized offices in order to execute on the six strategic pillars that she had laid out for the organization. As well, she wanted to match responsibility with authority by giving the regional heads profit and loss responsibility. With this responsibility at the regional level, she wondered how new products would develop under a regional structure. Gold was also aware of the need to consider recruiting, training and development of new leaders as the company was growing most rapidly in emerging markets, such as India, China, Eastern Europe and Africa.

One thing was certain—Gold had made it clear that no revenue decreases would be forgiven amidst the change. Many considerations had arisen: What pace of change should she take? How would she deal with the resistance to change? How could she ensure that the new structure would support Western Union's global expansion?

Christina Gold

Born in 1947 in the Netherlands, Gold moved to Canada at age five. She attended Carleton University in Ottawa where she earned a degree in geography in 1969, and upon graduating, secured a job at a coupon-centre clearinghouse. A year later in 1970, she joined Avon Canada as an entry-level inventory control clerk. Gold worked her way up through more than 20 positions before being promoted to president of the entire Canadian Avon division in 1989. Gold became well known for training sales representatives on selling techniques and time management. Dedicating time to joining representatives on sales calls, Gold explained her rationale; "I'd go out with the sales reps who were doing well and with the ones who were doing badly, and I'd pass what the successful ones were doing on to the others." [1]

In November 1993, Gold was selected from a number of candidates to run the entire North American Avon organization in New York. For several months, she and her husband maintained a commuting marriage between New York and Montreal before he was able to relocate to New York. Within six months at Avon, she was credited with rejuvenating the energy level among sales representatives, with one sales representative sending her flowers with a note saying, "Thanks for bringing springtime back to

Avon." [2] In a show of appreciation to the sales force, Gold asked that all salaried Avon employees hand-write 100 thank-you notes to representatives. But Gold clarified an important aspect of communication, "Motivation isn't all prizes and things. It's listening." [3]

In 1996, Gold was promoted to lead the development of global direct selling in an executive vice-president role, and in the same year was named one of the top 25 U.S. managers. During the same time, Gold was one of the three women insiders predicted to be promoted to the CEO post of Avon; however, all three of the internal candidates were passed over for Charles Perrin, former CEO of Duracell International Inc. [4] Gold left Avon in early 1998 after a 28-year career and established The Beaconsfield Group, a consultancy focused on global direct selling and marketing/distribution strategies. [5] In September 1999, Gold was selected as the CEO of Excel Communications, a $1.3 billion Dallas-based firm, to lead the company's rollout of direct telecommunications selling. With the changing infrastructure in the telecommunications landscape within the next three years, Gold successfully launched a direct-selling strategy. In May 2002, Gold transitioned after Bell Canada Enterprises (BCE) sold the company. Gold became president of First Data Corporation's largest division—Western Union.

First Data Corporation in Brief

First Data Corporation was established in 1992, when American Express spun off the division through an initial public offering. [6] Three years later in 1995, First Data merged with First Financial Management Corporation, which owned Western Union.

First Data's focus was facilitating the purchase of goods and services through almost any form of payment. In carrying out its business aim, First Data provided electronic commerce and payment services solutions to three million merchants, 1,400 card issuers and millions of individuals by the end of 2002. As First Data stated on its Web site, "You may not realize it, but First Data touches your life every day.

Whether writing a check at the supermarket, buying dinner with your credit card or ordering a book online, we're connecting with you to make those transactions happen—safely and securely."[7] It had four central business segments: payment services, merchant services, card issuing services and emerging payments.

First Data had realized steady growth and had experienced a compound annual growth rate of 7.5 percent in revenues and 21.6 percent in net income from 1998 to 2002.[8] As of the end of 2002, First Data had revenues of $7.6 billion and net income of $1.2 billion.[9] First Data's strategy to grow hinged on expanding the reach of its core businesses, developing long-term contractual agreements with customers for steady and predictable revenue flows and responding to new e-commerce initiatives.

Western Union In Brief

Western Union was founded in Rochester, New York, as The New York and Mississippi Valley Printing Telegraph Company in 1851. When the name changed to Western Union, the intent was to integrate acquired companies and unite the United States from east to west. Western Union had a number of firsts, such as the invention of the stock ticker in 1866, the electronic money transfer in 1871, the credit card in 1914, the singing telegram in 1933 and intercity facsimile service in 1935.[10]

Western Union posted sales of $3.2 billion in 2002, an 18 percent increase from the prior year.[11] Eighty percent of Western Union's revenues came from consumer-to-consumer (C2C) money transfers.[12] The number of consumer money transfers grew from 55.8 million in 2001 to 67.8 in 2002 with predictions that the number of these transfers would rise to more than 80 million in 2003. The remaining 20 percent of revenues was derived from consumer-to-business (C2B) transactions.

By early 2003, Western Union had approximately 4,500 employees of which 40 percent were based in the United States. Most of the workforce was non-unionized except for 1,200 call centre employees located in the Missouri, U.S. branch office. Western Union operated in 182,000 locations in 195 countries. More than 59,000 of the locations were located in North America (United States, Canada and Mexico), while the remaining 123,000 were made up of international agent locations. Agreements with international agents were typically made with banks and national post offices.

Agent Network

All of Western Union's international agents entered information into a common data processing system, where the payment was processed and made available to the receiving location. A consumer sending money paid a transfer fee on the amount sent to the receiver. Both the "sending" and "receiving" agents received a commission as did Western Union's corporate operation. Western Union also benefited from the differences in exchange rate spreads, which it recorded as additional revenue.

Robin Heller, Western Union's soon-to-be vice-president, operations talked about how the company maintained consistency across its expansive agent network:

> We have to ensure the same brand promise whether someone is at a retail brick-and-mortar location, online or by telephone. We do that by asking for the same pieces of information in the same order and we make it very easy to execute. From that, we look at what we need to do to add to our training, the forms we use or the screens that agents use. We use the same system across the entire world.

Christina Gold shared her view of what it took to lead a geographically separated operation:

> You have to be sensitive to other cultures and other people, and that's true in New York City as well as in Bangkok. Each person's needs are different, and the leader has to be aware and flexible enough to work with each person effectively. One thing that does get in the way is language and communication issues. Using abbreviations and acronyms in Japan, for example, can make people feel ostracized. It's

not inclusive. People feel left out or misunderstood. Another thing that can happen is that people do not understand what you are asking of them—they don't see it as a directive, but rather as a general comment. So to be effective in a global team requires more patience, more focus, you need to repeat things and get feedback to ensure people understand each other. Everything takes more thought and more patience. It's important not to jump to conclusions and to really listen.

Western Union's Consumer

Western Union's major consumer segment was the migrant worker who earned money in one country and used money transfer services to send funds to family and loved ones in another country. This target consumer typically did not have a bank account. Hikmet Ersek, senior vice-president, EMEA (Europe/Middle East/Africa and South Asia), Western Union stated, "We're dealing with a lot of immigrants who may experience problems in their host countries and where they work. The idea is that they will be served well and with a smile."

Heller spoke about the importance of customizing the Western Union experience to significantly different audiences:

> Our agents will try to localize the look and feel and the location of the office. They do the marketing at a local level. Take Africa for instance: in Africa there's a big festival culture so, we do skits or little plays at the festival to advertise our services.

See Exhibit 1 for an example of Western Union's advertising from around the world.

Western Union's Strategy

By late 2002, Gold and her executive team had developed six core strategies for Western Union:

1. Develop a global brand

2. Enhance global network distribution

3. Expand adjacent markets such as WesternUnion.com and Prepaid services

4. Develop future business leaders within the organization

5. Increase productivity

6. Execute on service excellence

Gold talked about the driver of Western Union's growth and the challenges going forward:

> [The driver is] obviously the core business, which is the money transfer business. The consumer-to-consumer business is the growth engine. We're looking to grow our commercial business, our bill-payment business in the United States. And we're now extending that globally. We are starting to develop (our prepaid business) around the globe. Our challenge and our opportunity is to keep that growth in the double digits. I think part of it's really looking at building the right brand for Western Union. The fact we're growing so quickly and growing around the globe are key things as we develop our business and our brand in India and China.

Reorganization

In order to align the company's organizational structure to the six core strategic focuses, Gold began a reorganizing program in early 2003. Prior to the reorganization effort, the structure mirrored Western Union's parent company, First Data, in that it had a U.S. business and an international business.

The executive team was made up of Christina Gold as president and six other senior executives. Four senior vice-presidents were in charge of the following product lines: Consumer Money Transfer, Mexican Money Transfer, Bill Payments and Corporate Services. One executive commented on the individuals responsible for the worldwide development of products: "The four executives run those products for the entire world, but they are very U.S.-centric."

The other two executive positions were Western Union's chief financial officer (CFO) and the senior vice-president of Western Union International. Annmarie Neal, senior vice-president, Talent, First Data and co-acting senior vice-president of human resources for Western Union, was one of the first to draw out a rough

Colombia, Ecuador and Peru

United States and Canada

Multilingual — European

Ukraine

Senegal

Congo

Mali

Exhibit 1   Examples of Global Western Union Advertising

Source: Company files.

version of the new structure on a white board. She talked about the goals in making a change to the structure:

> The main impetus is to allow Western Union to bring their services to market more effectively. The second major reason is to manage redundancy. We have a head of marketing for both the U.S. and international businesses. So one of the biggest thrusts is to have brand consistency across the globe. We also want to build the financial infrastructure and really place the financial decisioning in the right areas. With information technology, the aim is to have common platforms. For human resources, the idea is to have the ability to move talent around the globe. Whether that be from South East Asia or to the Americas. Western Union is very domestic in resources, but we see all the growth coming from other areas.

Alternatives Considered

In developing the new proposed structure, Gold and her executive team first established the core strategic focuses and looked at each region and considered structures that would be effective. Alternatives included making minor changes to the product line—focused structure, rolling out a structure organized by functional area such as sales, marketing, operations, finance and IT or considering a structure based on geography. The team chose to reorganize the company into a decentralized structure covering three main regions: the Americas; Europe, the Middle East and Africa; and Asia/Pacific. Annmarie Neal described the process for choosing a regional structure:

> We really wanted to reflect the global business and cut down on the idea of a domestic and international business. So, it became pretty obvious that we would choose a regional structure, but our organizational structure is constantly evolving. When we looked at a product organization structure, we realized pretty quickly that it wasn't going to work, simply because we had a number of products in the domestic business. But we really had only one business in the international market, which was money transfers. So we discarded that option pretty quickly. One of the big debates was the corporate

role of marketing and what should be done at the regional level. We decided that strategy for loyalty and brand would reside at the corporate level whereas the execution of such strategies would be done in the regions.

Gold gave her view:

> Currently, we have a domestic business and an international division. It doesn't make sense for a global business the way it is now; whatever country you're in is "domestic." So, [the idea is to] have a regional structure. [My hope is that] we will have common goals and share a lot more ideas. There will be a lot more communication and sharing of resources. For example, the plan is to have a global marketing plan whereas currently we have separate marketing for domestic and each international area. It'll be much better from a customer perspective because the global services allow each region to spend their time focusing on specific customer needs.

Challenges With Reorganizing

In making the change, Gold had to first convince the First Data management team and then the First Data board of directors. The total cost of the restructuring was estimated at US$4 million and included provisions for relocation and recruitment in a few key positions. Gold's one central mandate for the organization was that revenues could not be negatively affected. In facilitating the change, Gold used her executive team, as well as the services of human resources, to define the key processes, design the structure of the new organization and define responsibility within the structure.

Defining Responsibility

In defining responsibility, two main issues had arisen: Who would lead the development of new products? and Who would have profit and loss accountability in the organization?

Development of New Products

The company had been promoting three new business areas: commercial services, the Web site,

WesternUnion.com and the prepaid card. Prepaid cards included a gamut of products ranging from prepaid wireless and telephone cards to prepaid debit cards.

Company executives needed to decide whether there should be a product leader or whether regional leaders could take on the responsibility. Some executives argued that sufficient time could not be devoted to developing them at a regional level. Ersek stated:

> Something like the prepaid card is led by a product manager. I think that until it becomes big enough, it should stay under the product manager and then it is handed over to the regional heads. See, prepaid cards for me makes up about $200,000 in revenues, out of over $1.5 billion in revenues. My priority will be the larger numbers. But a product manager can put the marketing effort into this, build the product and then hand it off.

Profit and Loss (P&L) Responsibility

Another central challenge was deciding on whether profit and loss responsibility should rest with the regional heads or whether it should be based on corridors. Western Union defined corridors as, "country-to-country money-transfer pairs"[13] such as the U.S.-Mexico, UAE-India and Spain-Morocco. The company's worldwide operations had approximately 15,000 corridors[14] with approximately 500 of the top corridors making up 80 percent of money transfer activity. Changes in the corridors were heavily influenced by immigration patterns, country regulations and geo-economic conditions.[15]

While it was common that many corridors would be based within one region, such as the United States to Mexico under the Americas canopy, it was also common that corridors crossed international frontiers. Ersek explained:

> We have the unique challenge of sending and receiving. If I send money from Spain to Brazil, I need someone in Brazil. One of the big discussions is whether to have region or corridor heads. Some people feel that we needed to give the P&L responsibility to corridor heads. I am against this.

Part of the reason, is that there have been big dynamic changes in corridor traffic.

Some managers felt that changes to corridor traffic were heavily linked to external factors outside of the control of Western Union making it too difficult to hold leaders responsible for top-line revenue results. Other executives believed that responsibility would be clearer if it mirrored the transaction flow between countries.

Decentralization at the Regional Level

While decentralization was not a prerequisite in the new regional design, some executives felt that decentralization would enable the regions to get closer to the company's customers.

In the Europe, Middle East, Africa and South Asia division, the recently appointed Vice-President, Hikmet Ersek, wanted to decentralize the region by opening up a number of smaller offices in each country. Ersek believed the plan would put Western Union closer to its customers and agents allowing faster response times and enhanced service. Ersek stated, "I want to move from having five offices to having 35 or more different offices—like small agile teams. Obviously, there are some things that need to be central, like creating the brand and network development."

However, moving to the decentralized plan had its challenges. Ersek indicated:

> In order to decentralize, there are lots of questions from the legal and finance departments at the headquarters in Denver. Eventually, I want to put an office in Tashkent. However for many people Tashkent is an unknown quantity and they have some concerns. Finding the right people is a challenge. In a place like Tashkent, in Uzbekistan, we would have to find people who understood the code of conduct. We have to have people that we can trust. They need to accept and understand what it means to be part of a U.S. and a global company. Also, many of the local agents think that we are opening up branches. So, we have to assure them that we are opening up offices to support the agents.

Other executives felt that decentralization had its limits due to cost and human resource constraints. Neal balanced Ersek's view:

I want to listen to all of the ideas around the globe. But, decentralizing regions could add to a significant increase in infrastructure cost. There's colonization in spirit and I think with some adaptation it could work. Where it gets tricky, is making a change without thinking through implications for the rest of the organization. We need to think about leveraging opportunities around the globe.

Recruiting for New Positions

Proposed changes in leadership included moving the head of Western Union International in Paris, France, to the company's headquarters in Colorado to assume the position of president of Western Union Americas, including all countries on both continents.

Formerly the senior Vice-President for Eastern Europe, Hikmet Ersek, had taken the role as the senior vice president responsible for Europe, the Middle East, Africa and South Asia. A role was still required to be filled for the Asia-Pacific division as the former president of the Asian division had left the company. Two new corporate roles were set to be created: senior vice-president of business development to be filled by Mike Yerington, a 30-year Western Union veteran, and senior vice-president, operations to be filled by Robin Heller. Scott Schierman would continue as chief financial officer with greater day-to-day operational duties.

Overall, Western Union recruited approximately 500 individuals a year—some of the roles were to fill the four percent attrition rate, while others were to fill positions created by internal growth. One of the major challenges was recruiting individuals who possessed an understanding of operating in China and India. While growth was through adding agents in both countries, Western Union did not have to recruit staff in each location. However, the company needed to place people at the corporate level to manage the marketing, operations and information technological consistency. As Neal explained: "A lot of folks confuse being global with being from a different country. It doesn't mean that you're global if you have a different colored passport. We're looking for people that have a global mind-set."

Executive Development Programs

As of early 2003, First Data was making changes to the company's development program. Previously, the program was called First Leaders, which contained 12 modules whereby participants could learn about aspects of leadership such as enhancing communication, risk-taking, conflict resolution and motivating employees. Jana Johnson, vice-president, executive development, First Data, commented on the old program:

What you had was a director sitting in a room with administrative assistants and attendance was not mandatory. So, a lot of times people wouldn't come or people would attend a call on their cell phone and the types of issues that were coming up weren't necessarily helpful for everyone.

With the effectiveness of the old program dwindling, First Data executives planned a new leadership series, "First Executives," that was more in line with developing a pipeline of leaders for top management positions. Johnson explained the burning need at the First Data level, "At the First Data level, one of the critical things was succession planning and we identified 134 top critical positions. Specifically the goal was to have three high-confidence candidates per critical role by 2007."

The new program—First Executives—had 30 participants at an original cost of $7,500 per person in First Data of which 15 were Western Union executives. The plan was to add another 30 participants by the end of 2003. Each participant was given an executive coach who helped develop managerial and leadership abilities. In addition, they were all given mentors and given the opportunity to shadow a senior executive.

The Culture Change

The words "culture change" were frequently talked about within both First Data and Western

Union. First Data had the reputation of being a conservative culture steeped in the financial industry. Some observers felt that the Western Union had a stronger identity due to its history and product focus. Ersek talked about the difference in the culture between Western Union and its parent:

> A company like First Data is driven by statistics, this has to be the case if you are listed on America's "Most Admired" list and if you are a major employer. With Western Union outside of America we still have the pioneering spirit that made Western Union famous in America. For Western Union International, the sky is the limit. We are still growing in double digits.

Johnson talked about change in both organizations:

> It's a culture of change and we need leadership change. We're big and we know we're big. We know we need to change but we're just not sure what we need to change into. You can't control change, but you have to learn how to manage it and how to lead it. It's the messiness of change. And, it is messy.

Heller offered her view of changing Western Union:

> The biggest issue is probably the fear of the unknown and the fear of change. It's very important that we have the talent in place first and then we can look at the restructuring. You can always do any amount of restructuring or managing change that you need to do if you have the right people.

Gold as the Leader of the Change

"She was masterful at reading the organization's readiness," commented Neal on Gold's leadership in initiating the organizational design change. Executives credited Gold with instilling a deep understanding of branding and marketing at Western Union while managing disparate personalities and cultures. Heller explained how Gold fostered leadership among Western Union executives and how she was leading the change:

> She doesn't bring rank into the situation. She always has time for us—she has a high level of accessibility and with her grinding schedule it's amazing. She's very much about inquiring and asking instead of telling. She gives feedback and ideas and listens openly to other ideas. Everyone has a voice. But don't take that the wrong way. She can make decisions. She can definitely make decisions! She takes it all in and then makes the call.

Ersek talked about his relationship with Gold:

> She gives autonomy, but she also keeps a hand on things. She is tough and has high standards and expects all her managers to adhere to these standards. This is something I admire very much about her, because she doesn't expect anything of anybody she cannot deliver herself. And, sometimes, I say, "Christina, that's not doable," and she says, "I'll help you do it." After she understood my region, her leadership has basically been, "What's your decision, Hikmet?" And through that, she is sending signs to others that the responsibility is being pushed into the regions.

Neal observed Gold:

> Christina's a very tough executive. And by tough, I mean that she sets very high objectives. She is constantly stretching her executives. Christina is masterful in managing the globe and I don't mean just the employees. I'm talking about developing strong relationships with our agents and with government officials. I think a major thing about her leadership is how she empowers her revenue-generator executives. It's hard to keep track with some being several hours away and in a different time zones. But, she seems to manage this exceptionally well.

Considerations Moving Forward

Gold was eager to lead Western Union through a major structural change from a company organized by product line to a geographically aligned organization. Gold wanted to ensure that the structure would support the company's strategic aims and give strength to Western Union's global expansion. She had a number of considerations: the pace of change, how to assuage resistance to the change and how to ensure that the new structure would help to follow the new strategic direction.

NOTES

1. Claudia Deutsch, "Avon's Montreal recruit has Gold touch with reps," *New York Times,* April 5, 1994, p. B10.

2. Ibid.

3. Ibid.

4. "Avon chooses outsider as heir apparent," *The Record,* December 12, 1997, p. B03.

5. "New CEO at Excel Communications . . .," PR Newswire, September 15, 1999.

6. First Data Fact Sheet, Company Documents.

7. First Data Corporate Web site, www.firstdata corp.com, accessed December 23, 2004.

8. *First Data Annual Report,* www.sec.gov, accessed December 31, 2002, p.17.

9. Ibid.

10. Western Union Fact Sheet, Company Documents.

11. *First Data Annual Report,* www.sec.gov, December 31, 2002, p.33.

12. Ibid.

13. *First Data Annual Report,* www.sec.gov, December 31, 2002, p.34.

14. Ibid.

15. Ibid.

WHAT ENGAGES EMPLOYEES THE MOST OR, THE TEN C'S OF EMPLOYEE ENGAGEMENT

Prepared by Gerard H. Seijts and Dan Crim

Practitioners and academics have argued that an engaged workforce can create competitive advantage. These authors say that it is imperative for leaders to identify the level of engagement in their organization and implement behavioural strategies that will facilitate full engagement. In clear terms, they describe how leaders can do that.

A professor in a recent executive education program on leadership elicited a lot of laughs by telling the following joke: "A CEO was asked how many people work in his company: 'About half of them,' he responded." After the session, several participants put a more serious face on the problem when, while chatting, they bemoaned the fact that, in their organization, a significant number of people had mentally "checked out."

Quite clearly, CEOs and managers should be very concerned about a waste of time, effort and resources in their organizations. The reason is simple: If people are not engaged, how can these same leaders attain those business objectives that are critical to improving organizational performance?

What do we mean by employee engagement? How much does a lack of employee engagement cost an organization? What steps can leaders take to make employees want to give it their best? These and other questions are the focus of this article.

WHAT IS EMPLOYEE ENGAGEMENT?

An engaged employee is a person who is fully involved in, and enthusiastic about, his or her work. In his book, *Getting Engaged: The New Workplace Loyalty,* author Tim Rutledge explains that truly engaged employees are attracted to, and inspired by, their work ("I want to do this"), committed ("I am dedicated to the success of what I am doing"), and fascinated ("I love what I am doing"). Engaged employees care about the future of the company and are willing to invest the discretionary effort—exceeding duty's call— to see that the organization succeeds. In his book, Rutledge urged managers to implement retention plans so that they could keep their top talent. The need to do so is supported by a 1998 McKinsey & Co. study entitled *The War for Talent* that reported that a shortage of skilled employees was an emerging trend. Today, there is widespread agreement among academics and practitioners that engaged employees are those who are emotionally connected to the organization and cognitively vigilant.

Is There a Crisis in Employee Engagement?

We believe that executives must be concerned about the level of engagement in the workplace. For example, the *Gallup Management Journal* publishes a semi-annual Employment Engagement Index. The most recent U.S. results indicate that:

- Only 29 percent of employees are actively engaged in their jobs. These employees work with passion and feel a profound connection to their company. People that are actively engaged help move the organization forward.
- Fifty-four percent of employees are not engaged. These employees have essentially "checked out," sleepwalking through their workday and putting time—but not passion—into their work. These people embody what Jack Welch said several years ago. To paraphrase him: "Never mistake activity for accomplishment."
- Seventeen percent of employees are actively disengaged. These employees are busy acting out their unhappiness, undermining what their engaged co-workers are trying to accomplish.

A Towers Perrin 2005 *Global Workforce Survey* involving about 85,000 people working full-time for large and mid-sized firms found similarly disturbing findings. Only 14 percent of all employees worldwide were highly engaged in their job. The number of Canadians that reported being highly engaged was 17 percent. Sixty-two percent of the employees surveyed indicated they were moderately engaged at best; 66 percent of employees in Canada were moderately engaged. And 24 percent reported that they are actively disengaged; the corresponding number in Canada was 17 percent.

The survey also indicated that on a country-by-country basis, the percentages of highly engaged, moderately engaged, and actively disengaged employees varied considerably. And the results showed some interesting, perhaps counter-intuitive, results. For example, Mexico and Brazil have the highest percentages of engaged employees, while Japan and Italy have the largest percentages of disengaged employees. In their report, the authors interpreted these and other findings as an indication that employee engagement has relatively little to do with macro-economic conditions. Instead, it is the unique elements of the work experience that are most likely to influence engagement.

Does Engagement Really Make a Difference?

Should executives be concerned about these findings? Perhaps a more interesting question to executives is: "Is there a strong relationship between, say, high scores on employee engagement indices and organizational performance?" It seems obvious that engaged employees are more productive than their disengaged counterparts. For example, a recent meta-analysis published in the *Journal of Applied Psychology* concluded that, " . . . employee satisfaction and engagement are related to meaningful business outcomes at a magnitude that is important to many organizations." A compelling question is this: How much more productive is an engaged workforce compared to a non-engaged workforce?

Several case studies shine some light on the practical significance of an engaged workforce. For example, New Century Financial Corporation, a U.S. specialty mortgage banking company, found that account executives in the wholesale division who were actively disengaged produced 28 percent less revenue than their colleagues who were engaged. Furthermore, those not engaged generated 23 percent less revenue than their engaged counterparts. Engaged employees also outperformed the not engaged and actively disengaged employees in other divisions. New Century Financial Corporation statistics also showed that employee engagement does not merely correlate with bottom line results—it **drives** results.

Employee engagement also affects the mindset of people. Engaged employees believe that they can make a difference in the organizations they work for. Confidence in the knowledge, skills, and abilities that people possess—in both themselves and others—is a powerful predictor of behavior and subsequent performance. Thus, consider some of the results of the Towers Perrin survey cited earlier:

- Eighty-four percent of highly engaged employees believe they can positively impact the quality of their organization's products, compared with only 31 percent of the disengaged.
- Seventy-two percent of highly engaged employees believe they can positively affect customer service, versus 27 percent of the disengaged.
- Sixty-eight percent of highly engaged employees believe they can positively impact costs in their job or unit, compared with just 19 percent of the disengaged.

Given these data, it is not difficult to understand that companies that do a better job of engaging their employees do outperform their competition. Employee engagement can not only make a real difference, it can set the great organizations apart from the merely good ones.

Leading the Turnaround

Consider the words of Ralph Stayer, CEO of Johnsonville Sausage. In the book, *Flight of the Buffalo: Soaring to Excellence, Learning to Let Employees Lead,* he writes:

> I learned what I had to in order to succeed, but I never thought that learning was all that important. My willingness to do whatever it takes to succeed is what fueled Johnsonville's growth. In 1980 I hit the wall. I realized that if I kept doing what I had always done, I was going to keep getting what I was getting. And I didn't like what I was getting. I would never achieve my dream. I could see the rest of my business life being a never-ending stream of crises, problems, and dropped balls. We could keep growing and have decent profits, but it wasn't the success I was looking for.

The CEO observed that his employees were disinterested in their work. They were careless—dropping equipment, wasting materials, and often not accepting any responsibility for their work. They showed up for work, did what they were told to do, and, at the end of their shift, went home; the same routine would be repeated the next day. An employee-attitude survey showed average results. To Stayer, it appeared that the only person who was excited about Johnsonville was himself. He began to feel like a babysitter for his executives and staff. Stayer also realized that he could not inspire Johnsonville to greatness and as a result, the business he was running was becoming vulnerable.

Stayer found solutions to these problems in a meeting with Lee Thayer, a communications professor. Thayer explained to Stayer that a critical task for a leader is to create a climate that enables employees to unleash their potential. It is not the job of a CEO to **make** employees listen to what you have to say; it is about setting up the system so that people **want** to listen. The combination of the right environment and a culture that creates wants instead of requirements places few limits on what employees can achieve. Thayer's message resonated with Stayer, as it should among business executives.

Stayer began to recognize the difference between compliance and commitment, and that an engaged workforce was what he needed to help improve organizational performance. He also learned that he needed to change his own leadership behaviour first. Leaders cannot "demand" more engagement and stronger performance; they can't stand on the sideline and speak only "when the play goes wrong" if an engaged workforce and great performance are what they desire. But what should leaders do, or consider doing, to increase the level of engagement among employees?

The Ten C's of Employee Engagement

How can leaders engage employees' heads, hearts, and hands? The literature offers several avenues for action; we summarize these as the Ten C's of employee engagement.

1. Connect: Leaders must show that they value employees. In *First, Break All the Rules,* Marcus Buckingham and Curt Coffman argue that managers trump companies. Employee-focused initiatives such as profit sharing and implementing work-life balance initiatives are important. However, if employees' relationship with their managers is fractured, then no amount of perks will persuade employees to perform at top levels. Employee engagement is a direct reflection of how employees feel about their relationship with the boss. Employees look at whether organizations and their leader walk the talk when they proclaim that, "Our employees are our most valuable asset."

One anecdote illustrates the *Connect* dimension well. In November 2003, the CEO of WestJet Airlines, Clive Beddoe, was invited to give a presentation to the Canadian Club of London. Beddoe showed up late, a few minutes before he was to deliver his speech. He had met with WestJet employees at the London Airport and had taken a few minutes to explain the corporate strategy and some new initiatives to them. He also answered employees' questions. To paraphrase Beddoe, "We had a great discussion that took a bit longer than I had anticipated." Beddoe's actions showed that he cares about the employees. The employees, sensing that he is sincere, care about Beddoe and the organization; they "reward" his behavior with engagement.

2. Career: Leaders should provide challenging and meaningful work with opportunities for career advancement. Most people want to do new things in their job. For example, do organizations provide job rotation for their top talent? Are people assigned stretch goals? Do leaders hold people accountable for progress? Are jobs enriched in duties and responsibilities? Good leaders challenge employees; but at the same time, they must instill the confidence that the challenges can be met. Not giving people the knowledge and tools to be successful is unethical and demotivating; it is also likely to lead to stress, frustration, and, ultimately, lack of engagement. In her book *Confidence: How Winning Streaks and Losing Streaks Begin and End,* Rosabeth Moss Kanter explains that confidence is based on three cornerstones: accountability, collaboration, and initiative.

3. Clarity: Leaders must communicate a clear vision. People want to understand the vision that senior leadership has for the organization, and the goals that leaders or departmental heads have for the division, unit, or team. Success in life and organizations is, to a great extent, determined by how clear individuals are about their goals and what they really want to achieve. In sum, employees need to understand what the organization's goals are, why they are important, and how the goals can best be attained. Clarity about what the organization stands for, what it wants to achieve, and how people can contribute to the organization's success is not always evident. Consider, for example, what Jack Stack, CEO of SRC Holdings Corp., wrote about the importance of teaching the basics of business:

> The most crippling problem in American business is sheer ignorance about how business works. What we see is a whole mess of people going to a baseball game and nobody is telling them what the rules are. That baseball game is business. People try to steal from first base to second base, but they don't even know how that fits into the big picture. What we try to do is break down business in such a way that employees realize that in order to win the World Series, you've got to steal x number of bases, hit y number of RBIs and have the pitchers pitch z number of innings. And if you put all these variables together, you can really attain your hopes and dreams . . . don't use information to intimidate, control or manipulate people. Use it to teach people how to work together to achieve common goals and thereby gain control over their lives.

4. Convey: Leaders clarify their expectations about employees and provide feedback on their functioning in the organization. Good leaders establish processes and procedures that help people master important tasks and facilitate goal achievement. There is a great anecdote about the legendary UCLA basketball coach, John

Wooden. He showed how important feedback—positive *and* constructive—is in the pursuit of greatness. Among the secrets of his phenomenal success was that he kept detailed diaries on each of his players. He kept track of small improvements he felt the players could make and did make. At the end of each practice, he would share his thoughts with the players. The lesson here is that good leaders work daily to improve the skills of their people and create small wins that help the team, unit, or organization perform at its best.

5. Congratulate: Business leaders can learn a great deal from Wooden's approach. Surveys show that, over and over, employees feel that they receive immediate feedback when their performance is poor, or below expectations. These same employees also report that praise and recognition for strong performance is much less common. Exceptional leaders give recognition, and they do so a lot; they coach and convey.

6. Contribute: People want to know that their input matters and that they are contributing to the organization's success in a meaningful way. This might be easy to articulate in settings such as hospitals and educational institutions. But what about, say, the retail industry? Sears Roebuck & Co. started a turnaround in 1992. Part of the turnaround plan was the development of a set of measures—known as Total Performance Indicators—which gauged how well Sears was doing with its employees, customers, and investors. The implementation of the measurement system led to three startling conclusions. First, an employee's understanding of the connection between her work—as operationalized by specific job-relevant behaviors—and the strategic objectives of the company had a positive impact on job performance. Second, an employee's attitude towards the job and the company had the greatest impact on loyalty and customer service than all the other employee factors combined. Third, improvements in employee attitude led to improvements in job-relevant behavior; this, in turn, increased customer satisfaction and an improvement in revenue

growth. In sum, good leaders help people see and feel how they are contributing to the organization's success and future.

7. Control: Employees value control over the flow and pace of their jobs and leaders can create opportunities for employees to exercise this control. Do leaders consult with their employees with regard to their needs? For example, is it possible to accommodate the needs of a mother or an employee infected with HIV so that they can attend to childcare concerns or a medical appointment? Are leaders flexible and attuned to the needs of the employees as well as the organization? Do leaders involve employees in decision making, particularly when employees will be directly affected by the decision? Do employees have a say in setting goals or milestones that are deemed important? Are employees able to voice their ideas, and does leadership show that contributions are valued? H. Norman Schwarzkopf, retired U.S. Army General, once remarked:

> I have seen competent leaders who stood in front of a platoon and all they saw was a platoon. But great leaders stand in front of a platoon and see it as 44 individuals, each of whom has aspirations, each of whom wants to live, each of whom wants to do good.

A feeling of "being in on things," and of being given opportunities to participate in decision making often reduces stress; it also creates trust and a culture where people want to take ownership of problems and their solutions. There are numerous examples of organizations whose implementation of an open-book management style and creating room for employees to contribute to making decisions had a positive effect on engagement and organizational performance. The success of Microsoft, for example, stems in part from Bill Gates' belief that smart people anywhere in the company should have the power to drive an initiative. Initiatives such as Six Sigma are dependent, in part, on the active participation of employees on the shop floor.

8. Collaborate: Studies show that, when employees work in teams and have the trust and cooperation of their team members, they outperform individuals and teams which lack good relationships. Great leaders are team builders; they create an environment that fosters trust and collaboration. Surveys indicate that being cared about by colleagues is a strong predictor of employee engagement. Thus, a continuous challenge for leaders is to rally individuals to collaborate on organizational, departmental, and group goals, while excluding individuals pursuing their self-interest.

9. Credibility: Leaders should strive to maintain a company's reputation and demonstrate high ethical standards. People want to be proud of their jobs, their performance, and their organization. WestJet Airlines is among the most admired organizations in Canada. The company has achieved numerous awards. For example, in 2005, it earned the number one spot for best corporate culture in Canada. On September 26, 2005, WestJet launched the "Because We're Owners!" campaign. Why do WestJet employees care so much about their organization? Why do over 85 percent of them own shares in the company? Employees believe so strongly in what WestJet is trying to do and are so excited about its strong performance record that they commit their own money into shares.

10. Confidence: Good leaders help create confidence in a company by being exemplars of high ethical and performance standards. To illustrate, consider what happened to Harry Stonecipher, the former CEO of Boeing. He made the restoration of corporate ethics in the organization a top priority but was soon after embarrassed by the disclosure of an extramarital affair with a female employee. His poor judgment impaired his ability to lead and he lost a key ingredient for success—credibility. Thus the board asked him to resign. Employees working at Qwest and Continental Airlines were so embarrassed about working for their organizations that they would not wear their company's uniform on their way to and from work. At WorldCom, most employees were shocked, horrified, and embarrassed when the accounting scandal broke at the company. New leadership was faced with the major challenges of regaining public trust and fostering employee engagement.

Practitioners and academics have argued that competitive advantage can be gained by creating an engaged workforce. The data and argument that we present above are a compelling case for why leaders need to make employee engagement one of their priorities. Leaders should actively try to identify the level of engagement in their organization, find the reasons behind the lack of full engagement, strive to eliminate those reasons, and implement behavioral strategies that will facilitate full engagement. These efforts should be ongoing. Employee engagement is hard to achieve and if not sustained by leaders it can wither with relative ease.

7

THE PATH-GOAL
THEORY OF LEADERSHIP

Leaders should build organizational capabilities to allow everyone to excel in everything they do or have to do. . . . So my emphasis is on creating a process in which people can personally build upon those capabilities and then collectively as an organization develop organizational capabilities. Leaders should help to de-complicate processes and to make them transparent so that people can succeed in what they have to do and what they want to do.

—Jacques Kemp[1]

The path-goal theory of leadership is similar to the situational and contingency theories of leadership in that it prescribes appropriate leadership styles for interacting with subordinates. It is different from the situational and contingency theoryies in that path-goal theory adds more variables to what leaders need to consider in their relationships with employees. In essence, the path-goal theory of leadership "is about how leaders motivate subordinates to accomplish designated goals" (Northouse, 2007).

Based on expectancy theory, path-goal theory suggests that employees will be motivated if three conditions are met. These are the following: Employees believe in their ability to perform their assigned work-related tasks, they believe that their work-related efforts will lead to appropriate outcomes, and they believe that these work-related outcomes will be meaningful.

The key to understanding the path-goal theory of leadership is to think about the path that subordinates must follow to achieve goals assigned. They Subordinates are motivated by their leader to achieve these goals when leaders clearly define the goals, clarify the path to completing the goals, remove obstacles to completing the goals, and provide support to help achieve the assigned goals (Northouse, 2007). This is illustrated in Figure 7.1.

Path-goal theory has several components that leaders need to assess if they are to create a positive association between subordinate motivation and goal achievement. Different leadership behaviors will differentially affect subordinate motivation, and this impact will depend on subordinate and task characteristics (Northouse, 2007). These four components of path-goal theory are shown in Figure 7.2.

Figure 7.1   The Basic Idea Behind Path-Goal Theory

Source: From Northouse (2007). Copyright © 2007, Sage Publications, Inc. Reprinted with permission.

Figure 7.2   Major Components of Path-Goal Theory

Source: From Northouse (2007). Copyright © 2007, Sage Publications, Inc. Reprinted with permission.

LEADER BEHAVIORS

Initially, four leader behaviors were assessed but with the understanding that others would be examined as research continued. These were directive, supportive, participative, and achievement oriented (House & Mitchell, 1974; Yukl, 2006).

Directive Leadership

This leadership style emphasizes giving direction to subordinates regarding their tasks (Daft, 2005). These directions include the end result expected, how the task will be accomplished, and the schedule for task completion. In addition, the leader clarifies performance expectations and explicitly outlines the required standard operating procedures, rules, and regulations (Yukl, 2006). This style increases subordinate morale when there is task ambiguity (Dubrin, 2007) and is similar to the task-oriented or initiating structure style (Daft, 2005).

Supportive Leadership

These leaders are approachable (i.e., open-door policy), friendly, and empathetic to their subordinates' needs and well-being (Yukl, 2006). They expend extra effort to ensure the workplace has an enjoyable environment, and they create an atmosphere of honor, respect, and equality for their subordinates in the workplace. This style is most appropriate for improving morale when tasks are boring, frustrating, repetitive, stressful, and dissatisfying. Subordinates who are uncertain of their capabilities, situation, and future appreciate this style more (Dubrin, 2007). In addition, this style is similar to the people-oriented or consideration style (Daft, 2005).

Participative Leadership

These leaders encourage employees to actively participate in the decision-making process that determines how the group will achieve its goals. They do this through consultation, solicitation of employee suggestions, and using employee ideas in the decision-making process (Daft, 2005). This style is most likely to enhance the morale of subordinates who are well motivated and engaged in tasks that are nonrepetitive (Dubrin, 2007).

Achievement-Oriented Leadership

This leadership style challenges employees to work at a performance level that is the best possible. The leader sets a very high standard and continuously seeks to improve performance above that initial standard (Daft, 2005). Achievement-oriented leaders also express a great deal of confidence in the abilities of employees to set and achieve very demanding goals (Yukl, 2006). This style is most appropriate for improving morale when subordinates have a high need to achieve and are working on tasks that are characterized by variety and ambiguity (Dubrin, 2007).

The path-goal theory is different from trait theory in that leaders are not constrained to a leadership style that depends on their personality. It is also different from contingency theory in that leaders do not have to be matched to particular situations or the situation changed to match leader style. House and Mitchell (1974) argue that leaders may be flexible (similar to situational leadership in Chapter 5) and exercise all or any of the four styles described above. They suggest that it will depend on the subordinate and task characteristics. In addition, leaders may integrate styles should the situation require a blending of two or more styles (Dubrin, 2007). In the next two sections, I describe the subordinate and task characteristics on which the impact of leader behavior on subordinate motivation depends.

Subordinate Characteristics

Several characteristics determine how much satisfaction (present or future) subordinates will obtain from a leader's behavior. Four have been studied intensely. These are "subordinates' needs for affiliation, preferences for structure, desires for control, and self-perceived level of task ability" (Northouse, 2007).

Subordinates with a higher need for affiliation should prefer supportive leadership as friendly, concerned leadership will give these subordinates greater satisfaction. On the other hand, subordinates who work in uncertain situations and have a tendency to be dogmatic and authoritarian should prefer directive leadership as this type of leadership gives "psychological structure and task clarity" (Northouse, 2007).

Whether subordinates have an internal or external locus of control determines which leader behaviors give more satisfaction. Internal locus of control suggests that subordinates believe that the decisions they make affect what happens in their lives, while external locus of control suggests that subordinates believe that what happens in their lives is beyond their control. Subordinates with an internal locus of control should find participative leadership more satisfying as it gives a greater feeling of being in charge and of being an important part of the decision-making process. On the other hand, subordinates with an external locus of control should prefer directive leadership as it parallels their belief that external forces control what happens to them (Northouse, 2007).

Finally, self-perceived level of task ability is important in determining how leader behaviors affect subordinates' satisfaction and motivation. Subordinates with a higher perception of their own competence at performing specific tasks should prefer less directive leaders. As subordinates assess that they are becoming more competent, directive leadership may become superfluous and seem more controlling than necessary (Northouse, 2007).

Task Characteristics

Task characteristics also have a major effect on how leader behaviors affect subordinates' satisfaction and motivation. These characteristics include the subordinates' task design, the organization's formal authority system, and subordinates' primary work group (Northouse, 2007). For example, when there is task clarity and structure, well-established norms and customs, and a clear formal authority system, subordinates will not need leaders to provide goal clarity or coaching in how to achieve these goals. Subordinates will consider that their work is of value and that they can accomplish their tasks. Leaders in this situation may be viewed as more controlling than necessary, having little or no empathy and, therefore, unnecessary.

Other situations may need leaders to be more involved. In a context where there is goal ambiguity, leaders can provide structure. Repetitive tasks may require supportive leadership given the mechanical nature of these tasks. When there is a weak authority system, leadership may be required to provide clarity regarding rules and what is needed to accomplish assigned work. Finally, leaders may be required to encourage teamwork and acceptance of role responsibility when group norms and customs are weak.

Path-goal theory has a special focus on assisting subordinates to get around, over, under, or through obstacles that are keeping them from achieving their tasks. Obstacles may be responsible for subordinates having feelings of frustration, uncertainty, and being threatened. Path-goal theory implies that leaders should assist subordinates in getting around these obstacles or removing the obstacles from the path to task completion.

Helping subordinates in this way will increase their perceived level of task ability and their level of satisfaction and motivation.

House (1996) has reformulated path-goal theory by adding four new leader behaviors. These are facilitating subordinates' work, decision-making processes that are more group oriented, allowing work groups to network and represent themselves, and providing leader behavior that is based on values that are not focused solely on the bottom line. The essence of the reformulated theory is no different from the original—subordinates need leaders who will provide what is needed, and only what is needed in the subordinates' environment and what is needed to make up for deficient skills, knowledge, and abilities (Northouse, 2007).

HOW DOES PATH-GOAL LEADERSHIP THEORY WORK?

Table 7.1 suggests several possibilities as to how the path-goal theory of leadership integrates leader behavior with subordinate and task characteristics. While the theory is conceptually complex, it is also very pragmatic and gives direction to leaders with respect to assisting subordinates in accomplishing their work in a manner that provides them with satisfaction and motivation. The theory assumes flexibility on the part of leaders and suggests that leaders should choose leader behaviors that best suit subordinate needs and work situations. I provide some examples in the next paragraph.

First, if you as a leader see that the path is ambiguous, rules are unclear, and there is complexity and that subordinates are authoritarian and dogmatic, then you should be a directive leader to provide guidance and psychological structure. Second, if the work is repetitive, not very challenging, mundane, and mechanical and if subordinates are unsatisfied, need a human touch, and have a higher need for affiliation, then you should be a

Table 7.1   Path-Goal Theory: How It Works

LEADER BEHAVIOR	GROUP MEMBERS	TASK CHARACTERISTICS
DIRECTIVE LEADERSHIP *"Provides guidance and psychological structure"*	Dogmatic Authoritarian	Ambiguous Unclear rules Complex
SUPPORTIVE LEADERSHIP *"Provides nurturance"*	Unsatisfied Need affiliation Need human touch	Repetitive Unchallenging Mundane and mechanical
PARTICIPATIVE *"Provides involvement"*	Autonomous Need for control Need for clarity	Ambiguous Unclear Unstructured
ACHIEVEMENT ORIENTED *"Provides challenges"*	High expectations Need to excel	Ambiguous Challenging Complex

supportive leader to develop and provide a nurturing atmosphere. Third, when you see that the path is ambiguous, the way is unclear, the task is unstructured, and subordinates have a need for autonomy, control, and clarity, then you need to be a participative leader who invites subordinates into the decision-making process. Finally, if the path is ambiguous, the task is challenging and complex, and subordinates have high expectations for what they can achieve and a higher need to excel, then you need to be an achievement-oriented leader who challenges subordinates.

Of course, as I mentioned earlier, leaders may find it appropriate to exercise two leader behaviors simultaneously. It may be that the situation and subordinate characteristics call for you as a leader to be achievement oriented and supportive (Dubrin, 2007). I find that in my teaching, I set a high standard for students to challenge them to achieve, and I offer as much support as possible (without doing the work for them) to help and encourage them to achieve to the best of their ability. There is an ethical component to this leader behavior. You have to know your students well enough to have expectations for achievement on their part that are achievable.

Leaders who are effective meet subordinates' needs. They help subordinates set goals and the path to take in achieving these goals. Effective leaders assist subordinates in getting around, through, or in removing obstacles. Finally, leaders are effective when they assist subordinates in the achievement of their goals by guiding, directing, and coaching them along the right path.

NOTE

1. Jacques Kemp is the Chief Executive Officer, ING Insurance Asia/Pacific in Hong Kong.

REFERENCES

Daft, R. L. (2005). *The leadership experience* (3rd ed.). Mason, OH: Thomson, South-Western.

Dubrin, A. (2007). *Leadership: Research findings, practice, and skills.* New York: Houghton Mifflin.

House, R. J. (1996). Path-goal theory of leadership: Lessons, legacy, and a reformulated theory. *The Leadership Quarterly, 7*(3), 323–352.

House, R. J., & Mitchell, R. R. (1974). Path-goal theory of leadership. *Journal of Contemporary Business, 3,* 81–97.

Kemp, J. (2006, April 18). Creating organizational capabilities (Part 7 of 8, Ivey Leadership Series). *South China Morning Post,* Business Section.

Northouse, P. G. (2007). *Leadership: Theory and practice* (4th ed.). Thousand Oaks, CA: Sage.

Yukl, G. (2006). *Leadership in organizations* (6th ed.). Upper Saddle River, NJ: Pearson-Prentice Hall.

THE CASES

The Bay Kitchener

The human resources/operations manager must design an action plan to implement the mission statement he has developed: The store will offer the best in customer satisfaction. The challenge lies in translating this goal into specific actions for the three groups of employees involved in sales: sales supervisors, department heads, and sales associates.

Each of these groups will play a different role in attaining the goal, and therefore each group will require training and motivation.

Blinds To Go: Staffing a Retail Expansion

Blinds To Go is a manufacturer and retailer of customized window coverings. The company has been steadily expanding the number of stores across North America. The vice chairman is concerned with the lack of staff in some of these newly expanded stores. With plans for an initial public offering within the next 2 years, senior management must determine what changes need to be made to the recruitment strategy and how to develop staff that will help them achieve the company's growth objectives.

THE READING

Setting Goals: When Performance Doesn't Matter

Performance-based goals are commonly used to evaluate an employee, but in certain situations, goals based on performance may not be appropriate. Those situations occur when an employee is faced with new or complex tasks, and in this case, says the author, it may be better to set goals that are based on an employee's progress in learning a task than on his or her actual performance in completing it. This article explains why setting short-term goals in conjunction with long-term goals is sometimes the best way to achieve success.

THE BAY KITCHENER

Prepared by Krista Wylie under the supervision of Elizabeth M.A. Grasby

 Version: (A) 2000–12–20

On Monday, May 8, 1995, Emree Siaroff, the new Human Resources/Operations Manager at the Bay store in Kitchener, Ontario, Canada, was thinking about the mission statement he had just finished typing:

> The Bay Kitchener will offer the best in customer satisfaction that can be offered by any retailer in the Kitchener-Waterloo area or by any Bay store in the Ontario Region.

After two weeks in his new position, Emree had decided this statement would constitute his personal objective for the upcoming year. During the next week, Emree wanted to ascertain what this goal would mean to the Bay Kitchener and how this goal could be met.

The Retail Industry

Retailers in Canada faced increasing competition as American retailers continued to enter the Canadian market. This competition ultimately resulted in consumers who expected lower retail prices and higher levels of customer service. Consequently, many Canadian retailers were forced to restructure their organizations in order to remain competitive. Some retailers declared bankruptcy because they could not adapt quickly enough to the changes in their competitive environment. Other retailers thrived in this environment.

Overall, the retail industry in Canada achieved relatively strong sales growth in 1994. A key measure of this performance, Department Store Sales (DSS), rebounded from a 1.7 percent decrease in 1993 to a 3.8 percent increase in 1994. This increase was attributed to strong sales in junior department stores while, on average, major department stores continued to experience decreased sales. Junior department stores, such as Zellers, K-Mart and Bi-Way, sold a more limited selection of merchandise than major department stores; for example, junior department stores did not sell appliances or furniture.

The Hudson's Bay Company

The Hudson's Bay Company (HBC) was Canada's oldest corporation and largest retail department store. It had two major operating divisions: Zellers and the Bay. Since 1994, Zellers' strategies included combatting the impact of new competitors, such as Wal-Mart, from the United States. Simultaneously, the Bay continued its strategic plan to be Canada's best fashion department store.

Through these two divisions, HBC covered the Canadian retail market from British Columbia to Nova Scotia and targeted consumers at all price levels. In 1994, HBC's sales and revenues increased by 7.1 percent to $5.8 billion, and operating profits increased by 1.5 percent to $369 million over 1993. As well, HBC increased its market share of DSS from 39.5 percent in 1993 to 40.6 percent in 1994. HBC planned to continue this substantial growth in the future.

On January 1, 1995, there were 103 Bay stores all across Canada. In support of the Bay's objective to be Canada's leading fashion department store, renovations were completed in 17 locations in 1994, with plans to renovate additional stores in 1995. Contrary to the general trend of decreased sales in major department stores that was observed in DSS calculations, the Bay's sales and revenues increased by 7.8 percent to $2.2 billion in 1994, and operating profits increased by 32.5 percent to $161 million over 1993. The large increase in operating profits was attributed to several factors including increased sales, a higher gross profit and the controlling of expenses.

The Bay Kitchener

The Tri-City area of Kitchener, Waterloo and Cambridge was located in South-western Ontario and had a population of 379,900 people as of June 1, 1994. The area had been growing at an average rate of 2.5 percent since 1986. The average income per capita in Kitchener was $18,800, five percent above the national average income in Canada. While 79 percent of the citizens spoke English as their first language, historically there were many German people that settled in Kitchener as well. Four percent of Kitchener's population spoke German as their first language.

Located in Fairview Park Mall, off Ontario Highway 8, the Bay Kitchener was a larger than average-sized suburban store, covering 185,000 square feet over three floors. It served customers in and around Kitchener, Waterloo, Cambridge, Guelph and Woodstock. This market was likely going to be affected by a new Bay store opening in Waterloo, 15 kilometres away from the Bay Kitchener. Located in the Conestoga Mall, the new store was 110,000 square feet covering a single floor and was scheduled to open in August 1995.

The Bay Kitchener operated with a total staff of 232 people, including a team of four executives. The majority of staff were in sales. Of those, there were 172 sales associates, 20 department heads and seven sales supervisors (see Exhibit 1). The remaining employees provided retail support such as loss prevention, receiving, in-store marketing, visual presentation, and various clerical duties including sales audit, cash office, switchboard, and inventory management.

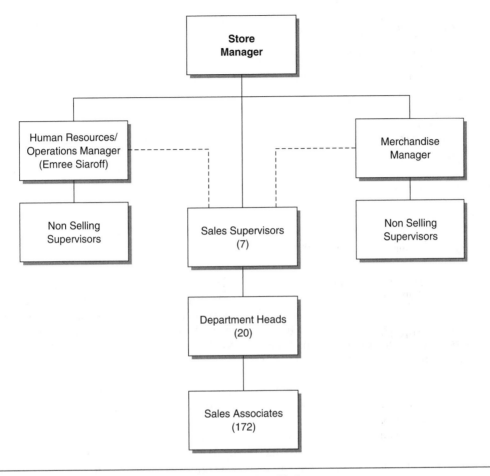

Exhibit 1   Abbreviated Organizational Chart for the Bay Kitchener

Sales Associates

According to the job description, a sales associate's role was to be courteous, to maintain customer service standards and to continually improve his or her selling skills. The Bay had developed specific customer service standards (Exhibit 2) that sales associates were expected to follow. These standards served to increase sales and profitability in a variety of ways. For instance, prompt customer acknowledgement not only increased sales by turning browsers into buyers but also increased profitability by discouraging thefts since customers in the presence of an attentive sales associate were unlikely to steal merchandise. As well, since customers generally spent three times more money if they made a purchase using a credit card instead of cash, a sales associate who regularly asked customers if they would like to make their purchase on their Bay card helped to increase sales.

Sales associates were evaluated after being employed at the Bay for 30, 60, and 90 days, and then annually, by their supervisors. These evaluations were based on each sales associate's customer service skills, sales support behaviour,

---

CUSTOMER SERVICE STANDARDS

1. Acknowledge every customer within 20 seconds.

2. Make the customer feel welcome or encourage them to wait.

3. Ask "Is that on your Bay card?"

4. Offer an "add-on item" or service.

5. Ensure the sales transaction is efficient.

6. Thank the customer by name.

7. Invite them to return.

8. Be friendly and courteous.

Exhibit 2   Customer Service Standards

---

attendance, appearance and professionalism (see Exhibit 3). Although evaluations were not used to determine wage increases, they were used when considering people for promotions. To help supervisors evaluate the customer skills behaviour of each sales associate, two tools were used: mystery shops and mini-shops.

Mystery shops involved people employed by a company that was contracted by the Bay. These people made purchases, like actual customers, observing, and, therefore, evaluating, whether the sales associate had complied with customer service standards. Mystery shopping could occur any time and provided a snapshot of both appropriate and inappropriate employee behaviours. During mini-shops, supervisors observed a sales associate throughout a customer transaction and evaluated the associate's performance against the same customer service standards that a mystery shopper used (see Exhibit 4).

Between the formal mystery shops and informal mini-shops, an employee's customer skills behaviour was thoroughly evaluated. As well, these tools provided an opportunity for interim feedback to employees. In addition to the supervisors' immediate feedback regarding how the employee handled the transaction during a mini-shop, the human resources/operations manager or store manager tried to speak to each employee within 48 hours of their having been "mystery shopped." Since they received frequent feedback, employees knew continually how they were performing. If necessary, they could make improvements to their customer skills behaviour.

Mystery shop results provided the only quantifiable data for comparison of the Bay Kitchener's performance to other Bay stores. These results were calculated by adding up the number of "yes" responses on the evaluation form and dividing by the total number of criteria for which "yes" could have been achieved. As of May 1995, the Bay Kitchener had been scoring mystery shop results averaging 79 percent. One of the 28 stores in the Ontario region had been averaging 97 percent. In order for the Bay Kitchener to be able to offer the best in customer satisfaction, sales associates would need to improve their mystery shop results significantly.

The company also believed that these front-line employees should be empowered to handle more of the customers' needs. For example, if a customer would not buy a shirt that had a small stain on it unless they received a 10 percent discount, the sales associates should be able to meet the customer's request immediately rather than having to approach their supervisor for approval. It was believed this empowerment would help sales associates gain a better understanding of the rationale behind the Bay's customer service standards and that if they truly understood these standards they would be better equipped to follow through on them. It would, however, be difficult to quantify how this empowerment would improve customer satisfaction.

Sales Associate Performance Review:

Part A:

Name:	Unit/Location:
Position:	Date:
Department:	Review Period: From To

Part B: Customer Skills Behaviour:
{enter the appropriate level of performance from the expert system, Distinguished, commendable, competent, Adequate, Provisional}

	Selling Skill	Rating	Comment
1.	Acknowledgment		
2.	Friendliness		
3.	Offer Help/Determine needs		
4.	Product Knowledge		
5.	Add-on Selling		
6.	Multiple Customers		
7.	Listening Skills		
8.	Clientele/full service selling		

Overall Summary of Customer Skills Behaviour:

Sales Support Behaviour Rating:
Housekeeping, stock, paperwork, systems, policy, cooperation, derendability

SUMMARY RATING: Total Performance:

Part C: Standards Review:

Attendance:

Commendable	Meets Standard	Area of Concern	Improve/Alternative

Dress Code (business dress attire):

Commendable	Meets Standard	Area of Concern	Improve/Alternative

Exhibit 3   Sales Associate Performance Review   *(Continued)*

Professionalism (suitable conduct for customer satisfaction):

Commendable	Meets Standard	Area of Concern	Improve/Alternative

Part D: Overall Summary of Previous Performance:

After discussion with the associate, complete this area:

Part E: Major Challenges/Objectives on the job:

Description	Target Date

Part F: Personal Skills/Knowledge Development Objectives:

Description	Target Date

Part G:

	Signature:	Date:
Sales Associate:		
Supervisor:		
Human Resources Manager:		

Exhibit 3 (Continued)

CUSTOMER SATISFACTION SHOPPING REPORT

Shopper's Letter	Store		Department	Month	Week
Sales Associate Name				Clerk Number	

1. Acknowledgment/Greeting

	Yes	No
a) When you came into view of an associate were you acknowledged within 20 seconds?		
b) Did the acknowledgement make you feel welcome, and/or encourage you to wait? (eg. "Hi, how are you today? Thanks for waiting.")		
Comment:		

2. One-on-One Service

	N/A	Yes	No
a) Were you approached and offered help promptly?			
b) Did the associate display curiosity and genuine interest in determining your needs?			
c) Did the associate offer/demonstrate product knowledge?			
d) Did the associate add on related merchandise to build a multiple sale?			
e) Were you invited to fill out a clientele card (if applicable)?			
f) Did the associate display enthusiasm and desire to make the sale?			
Comment:			

3. The Sales Transaction

	N/A	Yes	No
a) Were you asked to use your Bay card or if not, were you offered an application?			
b) Did the associate offer an extra ITEM (add-on) or SERVICE?			
c) Was the transaction efficient?			
d) Were you THANKED by NAME?			
e) Were you INVITED to RETURN?			
Comment:			

Exhibit 4   Customer Satisfaction Shopping Report   *(Continued)*

4. Overall Impression

	Yes	No
a) Did the associate favourably impact your shopping experience? (Extra care given and/or extra polite)		
Comment:		

5. General Comments

6. Regional Focus Question

	Yes	No
Reviewed With Sales Associate By	Date M D Y	

Part 1 - Employee's File   Part 2 - Store Manager   Part 3 - Training Dept.

Exhibit 4 (Continued)

Department Heads

Department heads were expected to perform the same tasks as sales associates and, additionally, to be involved in the display of merchandise, to have superior knowledge of stock levels and products, to be aware of upcoming sales plans, to help sales associates meet customer needs and to act as coaches to sales associates. Department heads were evaluated in the same way as sales associates, using the same criteria outlined in Exhibit 3. Their additional duties were also evaluated. Due to their additional responsibilities, department heads earned a higher wage than sales associates.

The department heads at the Bay Kitchener needed to be supported more in their role as coaches to the sales associates. The department heads were in an ideal position to act as coaches since they spent more time on the sales floor working with sales associates than sales supervisors. Management wanted to ensure that department heads took full advantage of the opportunities they had to assist sales associates in becoming better salespeople. Specifically, they wanted to see department heads guide sales associates through the process of meeting the customer service standards. For instance, if a department head heard a sales associate close a sale without suggesting additional appropriate merchandise, they wanted the department head to discuss the transaction with the sales associate, providing assistance on how a sales associate might have gone about suggesting additional merchandise.

Furthermore, it was felt that department heads could be more involved in sharing information with sales associates than they were currently. Department heads were generally full-time employees and were, therefore, present for most meetings where information was passed on to employees. Many sales associates, however, worked on a part-time basis and were often unable to attend these meetings. Given this, department heads were in the best position to consistently and accurately relay information from these meetings. With this information exchange in place, the Bay Kitchener would be in a better position to meet its objective of offering the best in customer service.

Sales Supervisors

Based on their job description, sales supervisors were responsible for all customer service activities and presentation of merchandise. As well, they were responsible for supervising sales associates and department heads in order to ensure that the Bay provided superior customer service while achieving maximum profitability. Specifically, sales supervisors were responsible for their area's discipline, training and development, scheduling, payroll and sales. Supervisors were also responsible for their own hiring.

In order for supervisors to be effective in their positions, they needed to spend the majority of their time managing and coaching the people working in their area. Because supervisors chose the people who worked in their area, they were more likely to do a better job of coaching and managing their team. However, supervisors were currently not completely involved in the hiring process. In the future, the Bay Kitchener wanted to provide both the opportunity and the training necessary to allow supervisors to do all of their own hiring.

Meeting the Goal

After analyzing their roles in the store, it was apparent that each of the aforementioned groups would play a unique role in meeting the goal that he had set. In order for the Bay Kitchener sales team to be ready to meet the challenge, some specific training and development had to be provided to each group of employees. As well, each group had to be motivated to work towards achieving the goal.

Training and Development

Computer Based Training (CBT) modules were one resource available to provide interactive training in specific areas to any Bay employee. There were numerous courses (see Exhibit 5); however, not all courses were appropriate for all employees. Therefore, before anyone took a CBT course, it was important to ensure that the course would be beneficial to the employee in the role that he or she would play in achieving the goal.

Another common training practice used by the Bay was sales clinics. These clinics were 15 to 20 minute training sessions which focused on meeting a specific customer service standard. They included an introduction, a brief lecture, a role play or some other activity, and a conclusion. Generally, sales clinics were run by sales supervisors but could, theoretically, be run just as effectively by department heads.

Motivation

Management often walked around the store talking to employees on a regular basis. This practice was valuable in building good working relationships with the staff so that they felt comfortable relaying ideas, feedback or concerns. These interactions could be used to motivate employees to work towards the main objective of improved customer satisfaction.

Regarding other motivational tools, management was willing to explore any possibility if they felt that it would increase the employees' desire to offer superior customer service. They knew that empowering employees was often an effective motivator. As well, a staff room that was frequented by almost all employees and morning meetings which were attended by everyone in the store at the time seemed like opportune times to somehow motivate the employees.

The Next Step

Based on his two and a half years of experience in the same position at a different Bay store, Emree was aware that setting a goal was the first, and perhaps the easiest, step in effecting change. Some points that required consideration included:

ORIENTATION COURSES

- Corporate Perspectives (corper)
- Designing Your Career (career)
- Keyboard Skills (keycbt)
- Workplace Hazardous Material Information System (whmis)

MERCHANDISE EDUCATION

- Retail Marketing in the Future (rtlmrk)
- Retail Method of Inventory (retail)
- Sales Leadership (leader)
- Merchandise Information Management. (cmim)
- Support Departments (supdep)
- Human Resources (human)
- Professional Selling (sell)
- Advanced Professional Selling (sell2)
- Employee Development (empdev)
- Merchandise Strategy (merch)
- Merchandise Perspectives (merper)
- Customer Satisfaction (custom)
- Customer Satisfaction for Auxilliary Staff (auxcus)
- Bay Card Dollars (baydol)
- Customer Refunds (refund)
- Buyer Negotiations (negol)
- Stock Shortage (short)
- Purchase Journal Checker (pjchec)
- Sales Promotion (promo)
- Cheque Authorization (cheque)
- Sales Associate Commission System (sacs)

SELF-DEVELOPMENT COURSES

- Time Management (gstimx)
- Decision Making Skills (gsdecx)
- Effective English for Business Writing (gsengx)
- Letter, Memo and Report Writing (gslmrx)
- Strategies for Business Writing (gsbusx)
- Management Performance (gsmgtx)
- Financial Skills (gsfinx)
- Dealing With Stress (stress)
- Controlling Your Time (time)

SUPERVISORY COURSES

- Corporate Ethics (ethics)
- Supervisory Practices Program (sppl)
- Interviewing Skills (inview)
- Presentation Skills (pres)
- Negotiation Skills (snegot)
- How to Answer Employee Questions (bquest)
- How to Coach (coach)
- How to Delegate (deleg)
- How to do Perf. Appraisals (parcbt)
- Managing Employee Safeguards (bguard)
- How to Motivate (motiv)

OPERATIONAL COURSES

- Health, Safety and the Law (hslaw)
- Health and Safety Representative (hsrep)
- Accident Investigation (hsacc)

PRODUCT KNOWLEDGE COURSES

- Service Insurance (insur)
- Jewellery (jewel)
- China (china)
- Communication Technology (comtec)
- Toys (toys)
- Sporting Goods (sports)
- Nursery Accessories (baby)
- Shoes (shoes)
- Linens (linens)
- Small Appliances (small)
- Cameras/Small Electronics (camera)
- Women's Fashions (wfash)
- Men's Fashions (shirt)
- Women's Fashion Accessories (wfacc)
- Electronics (elect)

SYSTEMS COURSES

- Electronic Mail (email)
- Big Ticket Inventory Sales Floor Procedure (btis)
- Basic Automated Stock Inventory Control System (basics)
- Purchase Order Inquiry (poms)
- Purchase Order Entry System (poes)
- National Vendor System (msonvs)
- National Stock Assortment List (nsal)
- Line Budget (line)
- Gift Registry (regis)
- Price Management (price)
- Managing Unit Food Cost (food)

1. Communicating the objective so that everyone supported and felt committed to the goal.

2. Determining a way to measure the employees' efforts to achieve the goal and to provide feedback to employees.

3. Devising a training and development plan that would be effective for each of the sales associates, department heads, and supervisors in meeting the goal.

4. Motivating each of these groups within the sales team to attain the goal.

The next step required a concrete action plan that would enable the Bay Kitchener to offer the best in customer satisfaction. Although Emree recognized that his plan would take months to implement, he wanted to complete an outline before the end of the week.

BLINDS TO GO: STAFFING A RETAIL EXPANSION

Prepared by Ken Mark under the supervision of Professors Fernando Olivera and Ann Frost

Version: (A) 2001–10–09

INTRODUCTION

"Staffing stores is our most challenging issue as we plan our expansion across North America," exclaimed Nkere Udofia, vice-chairman of Montreal-based Blinds To Go (BTG). "There are locations now where we've got physical store buildings built that are sitting unstaffed. How are we going to recruit and develop enough people to meet our growth objectives? What changes should our company make?" It was August 2, 2000 and Udofia knew that if Blinds To Go was to continue to grow 50 percent in sales and add 50 stores per year, the issue of staffing would be front and centre.

THE DEVELOPMENT OF THE BLINDS TO GO RETAIL CONCEPT

This retail fabricator of window dressings began as a one-man operation. Growing up in the Côtedes-Neiges district in Montreal, Canada, David Shiller, the patriarch of the Shiller family, started in business in 1954. Stephen Shiller, his son, joined the business in the mid-1970s, convincing his father to focus on selling blinds. Called "Au

Bon Marché," as it was known in Quebec, the Shillers began to create the production system that allowed them to cut the normal six- to eight-week delivery time frame for custom blinds to 48 hours. The customer response was overwhelming and the business took off.

Stephen Shiller exclaimed:

We gave them food, kept them busy while they waited for their blinds to be ready. The factory was literally next to the store and we offered our one-hour delivery guarantee, which kept our customers happy. Our St. Leonard store, the prototype for the current Blinds To Go stores, opened in 1991. Prior to that, people used to drive for up to 100 miles to come to our stores.

At that point, in early 1994, we realized what a hot concept we had on our hands—our sales were higher for each consecutive store opened, and none of our competitors could replicate our model. They were either manufacturers or retailers: none were both. None could hope to deliver the 48-hour turnaround we promised, had our unique sales model, which is 100 percent commission-based, or had our attention to customer needs.

By June 2000, Blinds To Go operated 120 corporate-owned stores across North America

(80 U.S. stores, 40 Canadian stores), generating in excess of US$1.0 million in sales per store (having a staff of between six to 20 people per store). Blinds To Go expected to add an average of 50 new stores per year for the next five years, 80 percent of which was targeted to be U.S. expansion stores.

RETAIL OPERATIONS

It was senior management's belief that quality of staff was even more important than store location, the surrounding customer demographics or advertising. Stephen Shiller, president, tested this belief with the East Mississauga, Ontario store.

In 1999, the East Mississauga store had experienced declining sales and high employee turnover. Analysing the demographic data surrounding the store left management with the impression that the store was a victim of poor location and cannibalization from another BTG store 10 miles away. However, Stephen Shiller suspected that the real problem was in the quality of the store's staff. Stephen Shiller commented:

> We let the store continue on its downward sales trend as we trained a management team for this store. Although I was quite sure that the quality of people was at fault, I was determined to use this as a lesson to show the rest of the company how important it was to have first-class talent. After six months of waiting, we put in an 'A' management team and trained staff. In one week, we doubled our sales and we tripled our sales in one month. That was a lesson we must never forget.

There were four staff roles in the stores—the sales associate, the selling supervisor, the assistant store manager and the store manager. The sales associates were the most junior employees and their job was to follow a set plan to help walk-in customers purchase a set of blinds. If they proved to be consistent sales performers, they would be promoted to selling supervisors or assistant store managers. Selling supervisors were assistant managers in training and usually had been one of the best sales associates. Assistant managers were in charge of the store when the store manager was not scheduled to work. The store manager was directly responsible for overall store operations, including closing sales, motivating and developing staff, and handling customer service issues such as repairs and returns.

Generally, a very good sales associate was promoted to selling supervisor six to nine months after hiring date. To become a store manager generally took another six to 18 months. However, because of the enormous variation in personal potential, these progression targets were by no means fixed.

The BTG selling process involved a very high level of interaction with the customer, which set a very high level of service expectation. At the retail stores, the emphasis on customer satisfaction and sale closure led to a higher volume of orders relative to their retail competition. Outlined in the Blinds To Go University Manual (training program for new sales staff) were the following four operating guidelines:

- Service and Satisfy Every Customer
- Never Lose a Sale
- Make the Customer Feel Special
- Bring the Manager into Every Sale to Give the Customer "Old Fashion Service"

Salespeople were expected to bond with a customer through a personal greeting, then ask open-ended questions about their product needs. The purpose of the next few minutes of interchange between associate and customer was to understand the customer's primary concerns and work towards a sale by resolving those issues. Next, associates emphasized to the customer the quality of the product, large selection and warranties. At this point, the associate would listen to any customer objections, and try to address them. The associate would price the product(s), then introduce the customer to the store manager. After walking the store manager through the order, the associate would deduct any relevant coupons, then attempt to close the sale.

All employees of BTG, even up to the president, prided themselves on being able to sell blinds to customers. During store visits, it was not uncommon to see senior management helping out the staff in dealing with an overflow of customers.

COMPENSATION OF RETAIL STAFF

The commission-based structure fostered a high-energy, sales hungry culture at Blinds To Go. Todd Martin, the director of retail planning and operations explained:

> We know people come to us because they need blinds. An example of our culture in action is a manager who is unhappy with closing eight of 10 sales, because with the tools at his disposal, he should be able to close all 10. Even if the customer is just looking because they want to buy a house in six months, we can take their worries away from them. He should be able to sell to 10 out of 10 customers.

Todd Martin also believed there was a healthy competitive environment among sales associates. He offered:

> In the store, there are no rules on grabbing customers—in my two years here, I've never seen a problem with staff fighting for customers.

As BTG grew from a one-store operation, the Shillers kept a commission pay structure for its salesforce, believing that it best motivated performance. From experience, they knew that a suitable salesperson could, with the commission structure, make more money at BTG than at a comparable retail outlet. The focus had been on hiring energetic, personable people who loved the thrill of a sale.

A CHANGE IN COMPENSATION RESULTS IN SALES DECLINE

In 1996, the Shillers decided to change the compensation system from full commission to salary. This change was the result of a recommendation from a newly hired vice-president of store operation who had been the vice-president of a major U.S. clothing retailer. Her intention was to attract more recruits for Blinds To Go's expansion phase by standardizing store operations and compensation. At that time, there were already 15 stores and expansion was underway. Based on her prior experience at the U.S. retailer, she led the change from full commission to paying sales associates a wage of Cdn$8 per hour. This was intended to make sales associates less entrepreneurial and more customer-service focused. Store manager compensation was also revised to reflect a higher base salary component relative to commissions. A more casual uniform was mandated in place of the business casual attire that was being worn at stores. In an attempt to differentiate the roles of sales associates and store management, it was decided that the store manager would no longer be involved in the sale. Though skeptical of this recommendation, the Shillers reluctantly agreed to proceed as suggested, rolling out these changes in 1996.

Sales declined between 10 percent to 30 percent in both new and existing stores from 1996 to 1997. Overall staff turnover increased to more than 40 percent from a pre-1995 figure of 15 percent. This problem was further exacerbated by the fact that rapid store expansion into Toronto, Philadelphia and Detroit had required the deployment of skilled store staff, thinning the ranks of existing stores. The Shillers attributed this decline in performance primarily to the change in the compensation structure.

BTG REVERTS TO COMMISSION-BASED COMPENSATION

Unsatisfied with this turn of events, a change was made in the leadership of the stores' team. A variation of the commission-based compensation plan was brought back in May 1998 (see Exhibit 1). Udofia explained why he believed that commission was key to the sales culture of Blinds To Go:

> When we made the 1996 change, the base salary of $8/hour made it much easier to staff the store, but we were attracting a lower caliber of people—our best commission-based people did not like it and left. Having learned our lesson, we went back to

our roots, brought back the old culture and experienced a sales turnaround. But, we've never 100 percent recovered from it and are still playing catch-up today.

Since the return to commission-based compensation in 1998, store sales improved across the board, and within a few months, stores were posting between 10 percent to 30 percent increases in sales from the previous year (see Exhibit 2).

This dramatic turnaround was accomplished with the aid of several other initiatives. First, all U.S. district sales managers (DSMs) were brought to Toronto to see top-performing stores, thus establishing a performance benchmark. Next, a BTG employee stock option plan for store employees (all full-time sales associates were made partners and given shares in the company) was implemented along with a sales award and recognition program. Also, weekly development conference calls between senior management and the district sales managers and training managers were set up for the purpose of constant updates and to facilitate group learning. Finally, a manager/assistant training program was tested in the U.S. in early 1998.[1]

The 1998 shift back to commission caused another huge turnover in BTG stores. This was unfortunate, because, from a staffing perspective, BTG had still not fully recovered from the previous compensation change. The need for additional staff was further aggravated due to BTG's continued push for growth and the tight U.S. and Canadian labor markets (four percent unemployment) in which it operated.

Another concern was that a commission-based compensation structure would not work in the U.S. Martin explained:

> The U.S. folks seemed uncomfortable with 100 percent commission. They seem to prefer a straight wage or salary. Thus, we have not figured out our compensation system, but for now, it's largely commission based. We know that for the people who are good, they will figure out what they need and go get it. Commission for us is like an insurance policy on our hires—the better you are the more you make. If you don't like servicing the customers, you leave.

Along with the reversion to the proven BTG compensation structure, Blinds To Go emphasized the practice of promoting their managers from within. Senior management believed that sales managers had to be properly motivated and provided them with a combination of store sales commission and opportunities for rapid advancement in the growing organization. However, being a top salesperson did not necessarily guarantee promotion, as Blinds To Go also looked at a matrix of sales, drive, presence, and people skills. Martin explained: "So even with the top salespeople, they have to be solid in their other attributes to be chosen for management. If the person is driven, he or she will ask for what it takes to be promoted."

ATTRACTING QUALITY RETAIL SALES CANDIDATES

BTG was looking for people who possessed certain sales-driven qualities. Martin explained:

> We look for people who have the "gift of the gab," no ego, are honest, like sales, are driven and hungry for an opportunity, and have good leadership and good people skills. People have to possess these core values. We're partners—we want other people who want to be our partners. We pay for performance. You bet on yourself. You get rewarded because you're performing. Entry-level sales associates get 1,000 stock options after 90 days. At another successful retailer start-up that has since gone public, their people only received 500 options each.

Having recognized that quality of staff was paramount, BTG devoted resources to ensure that it hired the right people as it was estimated that 80 percent of their expansion needs would be for new U.S. stores. BTG store staff was very diverse. In terms of gender, it was a 50/50 split between men and women. Among associates, high school was the most common education level, followed by college students, then college graduates. In Ontario, Canada, 20 percent of the associates were recent immigrants who had college or professional qualifications. The average

Corporate Formula	Original	1995 to 1996	Current
Sales Associate	$3 to $5/hr + 3% sales	$8/hr	$6 to $8/hr minimum, OR 6% sales (whichever was higher)
Managers/Assistants	$10,000 to $20,000/yr + 1.5% – 3% of overall store sales	$25,000 to $40,000/yr + 0.25% – 0.5% of overall store sales	$10,000 to $20,000/yr + 1.5% – 2.5% of overall store sales

Actual Results	Original	1995 to 1996	Current
Sales Associate Top 20% of class ($14,000/sales/week)	$620/wk	$320/wk	$840/wk
Sales Associate Average Success ($10,000/sales/week)	$500/wk	$320/wk	$600/wk
Sales Associate Marginal Performer ($6,000/sales/week)	$380/wk	$320/wk	$360/wk
Sales Associate Poor Performer ($3,000/sales/week)	$290/wk	$320/wk	$240/wk

Manager Top 20% (2.5% of store sales)	$75,000/yr	$52,500/yr	$67,500/yr
Manager Average Success (1.2% of stores sales)	$50,000/yr	$40,000/yr	$50,000/yr
Manager Poor Performer	$35,000/yr	$35,000/yr	$40,000/yr

Exhibit 1   BTG Pay Structure History

	Pre-1994	1995 to 1996	1997 to 2000
New stores/year	N/A	25	20
New store average sales	$1 million	$0.7 million	$1.2 million
Versus comparable store sales year ago	3%	–20%	+15%

Exhibit 2   Sales Turnaround

age of associates was distributed over a typical bell curve between the ages of 18 to 50.

Over the last few years, BTG had tried several recruiting methods to varying degrees of success. There were several formal and informal programs that worked to entice qualified personnel to apply to BTG.

Employee Referral

Having current staff refer friends and family to BTG seemed to be the most effective way to attract a candidate already briefed on the BTG concept. A recent addition to create an incentive to refer was the "BMW" contest where staff could win the use of a BMW car for a year if they referred 10 eventual hires that stayed for at least three months. Employee referrals alone did not currently satisfy BTG's hiring needs.

Internet Sourcing

BTG used the Internet in two ways: BTG solicited résumés at its blindstogo.com site; DSMs and recruiters actively searched online job sites like Monster.com and other job sites to contact potential candidates.

DSM Compensation Readjustment

To put more emphasis on staffing in early 2000, DSMs' incentive bonus was changed from a sales target to new staff quota target. Historically, district sales managers had received an incentive bonus based on sales. Thus, a large part of the DSM's role had evolved to include recruiting responsibilities—the DSM now had to hire 10 new sales associates a month.

BTG Retail Recruiters

Professional recruiters were hired in early February 1998 and had been paid annual salaries ranging from $30,000 to $60,000. Recruiters generate leads through cold calls (in-person and via telephone), networking referrals, colleges, job fairs, the Internet, and employment centres. Even though they were given some training and recruiting objectives, the initial recruiters had averaged around four hires per month (against the company objective of four hires a week). "Overall, the performance was sub-optimal," lamented Martin. "By paying them a base salary, we divorced performance from pay and they became administrators." For recruiters, a switch was made in early 2000 to a mix of salary and commission. "They will still need to average four hires a week—but we've increased our training and the 'per hire' commission will focus them on results," Martin concluded.

Newspaper Advertising

BTG used weekly newspaper advertising for nine months starting in mid-1998. Although this method generated a sufficient number of candidate leads, senior management believed that this medium did not generate the quality of candidates that it needed—newspaper advertising attracted people who did not possess the skills and core values that BTG was looking for.

Store Generated Leads

Each BTG had a "help wanted" sign on its window, and walk-in traffic, along with customer referrals, resulted in some sales associates becoming hired. Overall, this was very successful only in stores located in densely populated areas with foot traffic.

The Hiring Process at Blinds To Go

Once potential candidates were persuaded to apply, a store visit was arranged. The purpose of this visit was to acquaint the potential candidates with the BTG environment and for them to get an overview of the job of a sales associate. Subsequently, the DSM administered a telephone interview. If the candidates were selected to proceed beyond this screen, two additional face-to-face interviews awaited them—one with the DSM and another with the store manager. BTG hired associates against these six criteria:

1. "Gift for Gab"

2. Outgoing personality

3. Energetic and motivated

4. Honest

5. Likes sales or dealing with people

6. Positive

If the candidate was selected to be a sales associate, then references were checked and offers extended.

THE RESULTS OF HIRING PROCEDURES

Before collecting data, it was the impression of senior management at BTG that the most effective method of attracting quality candidates was employee referral, followed by Internet sourcing, and then DSM recruitment. To confirm their suspicions, BTG tracked the yield of different hiring methods for June and July 2000 and as of the end of July, had these results to show:

Recruiting Method	June	July	Total (2 mth)
Cold Call (Recruiters)	9	0	9
Walk-ins	31	16	47
Internet	9	3	12
Employee Referral	39	20	59
DSM hires (Direct/ Rehires/ College)	8	8	16
Total	96	47	143

Martin explained that the highest ratio of leads to hire was in the employee referrals. This was partially attributed to the fact that referrals generally pursued employment with BTG, excited by the opportunity that a friend or family member who was a BTG employee had recounted. Cold calling was thought to have the lowest close rate because the recruiter had to first educate, then convince potential recruits. But cold calling was thought to be time-efficient if the recruiter was good. Recruiters were focused on non-store sources (cold calling, Internet, schools, etc), store sources (store walk-ins and employee referrals) were handled by the DSM. Recruiters were now paid $20,000 a year with a bonus of $150 to $500 for each successful hire, defined as a hire who stayed at least three months.

STAFF TURNOVER

BTG also began tracking staff turnover and had created a turnover list from existing data. A large percentage of staff voluntary turnover occurred in their first four months. The higher turnover after eight months was partly due to termination because of sales underperformance. Also, sales associates who were not progressing as fast as their peers would inevitably be dissatisfied, leaving for other jobs.

Number of Staff Leaving and Length of Stay (Numbers From June and July 2000)

Length of Stay	1 to 4 months	5 to 8 months	8+ months
Total	29	12	13

BLINDS TO GO FUTURE NEEDS

BTG needed these additional staff to proceed with its expansion plan of 50 stores per year and to fill current store requirements.

Position	Current complement	Extra personnel needed for expansion (per year)
Sales Associate	1,000	500
Selling Supervisor	150	50
Asst. Store Manager	150	50
Store Manager	150	50

Udofia had one more pressing concern on his mind:

We're planning an initial public offering in the next one to two years. The key to our success is our ability to recruit and develop enough people to meet our growth objectives.

He wondered what strategy he should follow to meet the staffing challenge ahead.

NOTE

1. This program eventually evolved into the Legends Training Program, where the best training managers at BTG were relocated to new regions to motivate, train and coach new store employees.

SETTING GOALS

When Performance Doesn't Matter

Prepared by Gerald H. Seijts

When it comes to assessing an employee today, it is very tempting to set goals based on performance. But while there is not necessarily anything wrong with setting goals, there is at least one situation where goals based on performance may not be appropriate. That situation exists when an employee is facing a task that is either new or complex. I believe that, in such a case, it may be better to set goals that are based on an employee's progress in learning a task, than on his or her actual performance in achieving or completing it. And as I will describe in detail below, only after the employee has mastered or learned how to do a particular task, should performance goals be assigned.

BACKGROUND

Edwin Locke and Gary Latham's goal-setting theory is considered to be one of the most effective motivational theories. (Gary Latham is Secretary of State Professor of Organizational Effectiveness at the Rotman School of Management, University of Toronto; Edwin Locke holds the Dean's Chair in Motivation and Leadership at the Robert H. Smith School of Business, University of Maryland at College Park.) Locke and Latham's goal-setting theory can be summarized as follows:

1. Setting specific, challenging goals leads to higher performance than setting no goals or abstract goals such as doing one's best. This is because specific goals (e.g., generate $1 million in new business for the year, and reduce industrial accidents by 20 percent in our London plant) define what constitutes an acceptable level of performance. Abstract goals, in contrast, allow individuals to give themselves the benefit of the doubt in evaluating their performance as a success. In the absence of a specific, challenging goal, individuals have a strong tendency to assume that their performance is better than it actually is. Therefore, individuals do not typically give their maximum effort when they are instructed to merely do their best. Specific goals are best attained when quantitative terms are set and a deadline for attaining the goal is added.

2. There is a linear relationship between the difficulty level of the goal and performance: The

higher the goal, the higher the performance. Only when individuals reach the limits of their abilities will that linear relationship level off. General Electric, for example, encourages its workforce to set extremely ambitious goals, since they have the potential to get employees to perform in ways they never imagined possible. Goal setting does not work, however, if the goal is totally beyond one's reach. For example, a goal stating that 25 percent of annual sales must come from new product development could be seen as unrealistic if individuals do not have the appropriate knowledge, tools and means to meet the goal. Goals thus need to be realistic or believable to have a positive effect on performance. Commitment becomes harder to obtain with increased goal levels. It is virtually axiomatic that if individuals are not really trying to reach a goal, then the goal will not lead to improved performance.

3. Feedback is necessary, but by itself it is not sufficient to cause goals are to affect performance. For example, individuals who are progressing at a slower rate than required to meet a goal must know this in order to be able to adjust their effort level, or to look for more effective strategies for attaining the goal. The most effective feedback is that which allows individuals to make adjustments so that they can grow and develop their skills and effectiveness. At the same time, however, providing feedback in cases where individuals are not committed to a specific, challenging goal has little effect on performance. It has been well documented that it is important to set goals and obtain feedback to increase performance. Providing employees with accurate feedback, however, can be a challenging exercise.

4. Employee participation and incentives affect performance only to the extent to which they lead to the setting of, and commitment to, specific, challenging goals. For example, in contrast to what some individuals believe, participation in goal setting is more valuable as an information exchange (e.g., to discuss potential task strategies and agree on what a realistic goal involves) than as a method of gaining commitment to goals.

MOTIVATIONAL AND COGNITIVE MECHANISMS

Goals affect performance through three motivational mechanisms: choice, effort and persistence. A specific goal facilitates choice by encouraging activities that are relevant to achieving a goal and by discouraging those that are not goal-relevant. This means that if an individual's goal is to increase his or her teaching ratings from a 6 to a 6.5 on a 7-point scale, he or she will not spend much time on activities that are unrelated to attaining that goal. Setting a specific, challenging goal produces the appropriate effort because having a difficult goal requires people to adjust their effort to the level of the goal. When individuals set a specific goal, they tend to persist in their efforts until they reach their goal. Committed individuals persist in their efforts even when they encounter setbacks and obstacles to achieving their goal.

In addition to affecting motivation, goal setting also influences cognitive processing in that having a goal stimulates the development of specific strategies to attain it. On a novel task, or one that is perceived as being complex, it is not always obvious how individuals should complete or master it. Hence, formal planning, creative thinking and problem solving may be necessary in order to discover how the assigned or self-set goal can best be attained. For example, Latham and his colleagues investigated the effects of goal setting on the performance of loggers. In one of these studies, truck drivers were assigned a specific goal in terms of an average number of trips from the logging sites to the mill. Following the goal-setting program, truck drivers used their radios to co-ordinate their efforts so that there would always be a truck at the logging site when timber was ready to be loaded. Performance improved as a result of the goal setting and employees' subsequent search for strategies to attain the goal.

Individuals can be forced to think outside the box in order to meet ambitious goals. For example, how can we cut costs by 40 percent or reduce product-development time from years to months? Employees are forced to create new ways of attaining challenging goals because the old, routine ways of getting things done is no longer appropriate, and they have to start thinking of better ways of organizing work and doing their job.

PERPLEXING FINDINGS

A fundamental tenet of Locke and Latham's goal-setting theory is that setting a specific, challenging goal results in higher performance than merely urging individuals to do their best. A series of studies recently conducted by Ruth Kanfer and Phillip Ackerman, Professors of Psychology at the Georgia Institute of Technology, attracted a lot of attention from goal-setting researchers and practitioners. In part, this was because the results of their studies contradicted one of the basic tenets of goal setting: air cadets, performing a complex air traffic control task, performed worse when they were assigned a specific, challenging goal compared to when they were instructed to do their best.

Kanfer and Ackerman concluded that when a task is novel or complex, that is, when an individual is in the process of learning how to perform a task, performance decreases when a specific, difficult goal is set rather than a "do best" goal. This is because, on complex tasks, a specific, difficult goal demands greater concentration and attention relative to what is required when individuals are urged to do their best. Thus, a specific, difficult goal distracts attention from the development and evaluation of task-relevant strategies on a task where the appropriate strategies have yet to be developed. In other words, Kanfer and Ackerman argued that when people have not yet learned the appropriate strategies for performing a task in an effective manner, and hence are in a learning mode, the direct-goal mechanisms of choice, effort and persistence are no longer sufficient to ensure high performance. Instead, individuals should focus on identifying and implementing task-relevant strategies. Kanfer and Ackerman's finding that specific, challenging goals can have a

negative effect on performance has been replicated in several other studies.

These research findings suggest that a task's complexity compromises the normally positive effects that specific, challenging goals have on performance. The results also suggest that there may be a flaw in Locke and Latham's goal-setting theory, and that hence we should exercise caution regarding the setting of ambitious goals in organizational settings.

SOLVING THE INCONSISTENCIES

I came to Canada in 1993 to pursue my strong interest in motivation and performance, and did my doctoral work under the guidance of Gary Latham. Gary and I assumed the role of detectives, or critical evaluators, in reviewing the literature on motivation. In doing so, we discovered the work of Albert Bandura on proximal (short-term or sub-goals) and distal (long-term or end-goals) goals. (Albert Bandura, a Canadian, is the David Starr Jordan Professor of Social Science in Psychology at Stanford University.) Bandura argues that an individual's performance on a complex task is optimal when explicit, proximal goals that are instrumental in achieving a distal goal are set. Proximal goals provide clear markers of progress and reduce the risk of self-demoralization that can occur when current accomplishments are gauged against a distal goal. Proximal goals provide individuals with additional, specific information about performance that is not revealed when a distal goal alone is set. That is, inherent in proximal goals is an increase in the frequency of feedback that can be crucial for altering strategies, while persisting in attaining the distal goal.

Support for the wisdom of setting proximal goals in conjunction with a distal goal can be found in several clinical and health intervention studies. For example, Bandura's research on weight-loss programs has shown that dieters who set proximal goals lost more weight than individuals who set a distal goal alone. The rationale for this finding is that when feedback on progress in relation to a particular goal is frequent, dieters are able to evaluate their ongoing goal-directed behaviour accurately. Remedial action can be taken when there is a discrepancy between the goal that has been set and the actual performance. Thus, it appeared to us that, for a complex task, a distal goal unaccompanied by a series of proximal goals is too distant to suggest strategic behaviours to attain it.

Setting proximal goals in conjunction with a distal goal can enhance an individual's confidence in his or her abilities to handle challenging situations and attain ambitious goals. Proximal goals facilitate the identification of a series of controllable opportunities of modest size that produce visible results or "small wins." When a solution is put in place, the next solvable problem that allows a proximal goal to be attained becomes visible, eventually leading to the attainment of the distal goal.

A compelling example of how proximal goals can affect one's self-confidence, motivation and subsequent performance is the case of the swimmer John Naber. Naber captured four gold medals and one silver medal at the 1976 Olympics in Montreal, breaking four world records along the way. He is considered among the best swimmers the U.S. has ever known, and now serves as a noted sports commentator and one of that country's premier motivational speakers. Naber states that his success can be attributed, in part, to his approach to goal setting, which consisted of trying to gain a few hundredths of a second each day and/or each week over a span of several years in preparation for Montreal. His distal goal, or terminal product, was to win the gold. Thus, he set himself a specific goal in terms of finishing time, a time that, he believed, would all but guarantee him the gold medal. For each year, month, week, day, and even training session, Naber then set proximal goals that appeared attainable.

In a business simulation, Latham and I replicated the finding obtained by Kanfer and Ackerman. We used an assessment-centre exercise in which participants operated a toy-manufacturing enterprise. Participants who were assigned a distal or end-goal alone earned profits that were not as good as participants who had been urged to do their best. However, assigning proximal goals in addition to a distal goal led to higher profits than did encouraging participants to do their best. Our results also indicated that those participants who had proximal goals and a distal goal had the highest confidence in achieving their goals. The results of our research thus suggest that Kanfer and Ackerman, as well as Bandura, were right. The findings that we obtained are also consistent with Locke and Latham's goal-setting theory: Proximal goals serve an important role in the acquisition of knowledge and skill as well as fostering self-confidence in goal achievement.

PROXIMAL GOALS: IMPLICATIONS

These findings have some interesting implications for human resource management in the areas of mentoring and the transfer of training to a job. For example, mentors should be encouraged to set proximal goals in addition to a distal or end goal to increase work satisfaction and decrease turnover among their proteges. Examples of proximal goals include providing opportunities for proteges to improve their decision-making skills, to expand their social network, and to foster their understanding of current health-care management leadership challenges. If management is concerned about a particular individual's level of absenteeism, the distal goal should be to increase attendance within a specific time frame. The distal goal can be broken down into measurable, manageable steps. Proximal goals are specific behaviours that the individual has to engage in to attain the distal goal. Examples include dealing with job stress and implementing behavioural strategies to solve conflict with colleagues. Setting proximal goals in addition to a distal goal during training interventions can facilitate the transfer of training to the workplace. Proximal goals should be set for knowledge and skill acquisition during the training program. Distal goals should be set to maintain and enhance the acquired knowledge and skills when the trainee returns to the workplace.

LEARNING GOALS

One explanation why specific, challenging goals can have a detrimental effect on the performance of a complex task is a lack of proximal goals. A second explanation is that individuals were assigned the wrong goal—an outcome rather than a learning goal. Outcome goals focus attention on a specific quantity or quality of something to be achieved (e.g., obtain certification within two years to win customer trust, and cut and delimb three trees per hour). If appropriate task strategies are known (based on either previous experience or the result of training), having specific, challenging outcome goals increases the likelihood that these strategies will be used, and hence, performance enhanced. A learning goal is one that is specific and difficult in terms of the number of strategies an individual needs to discover in order to learn how best to perform a task. For a task that requires learning, that is, where individuals have yet to identify the requisite strategies to perform it in an effective manner, a specific, difficult learning goal should be set because it shifts attention to the development and implementation of task-relevant strategies, and away from task-outcome achievement.

Frequently, in organizational settings, suitable task strategies are not known and must be discovered through problem solving and trial and error. For example, how can start-up companies establish long-term success as opposed to flash-in-the pan gains? How can organizations restore earnings and shareholder value in a complex, intensely competitive marketplace? What strategies are available to work groups when some members discover that others are reluctant to commit to the group goal and instead pursue their own self-interest? New organizational members face challenging and often competing demands. What should these newcomers do to make better use of their time and resources? Learning goals can be assigned to salespeople

spending more time thinking about specific ways to approach a customer and make a sale.

Few researchers have looked at the differential effects of specific, challenging outcome versus learning goals on tasks that are perceived as complex. Together with Gary Latham, I examined the effects of outcome and learning goals on a complex scheduling task. The findings were unambiguous: The assignment of learning goals led to higher goal commitment, higher confidence in mastering the task, and higher performance than the assignment of outcome goals. Research in educational settings has found that setting outcome goals on complex tasks such as solving math problems can trigger apprehensions of failure that, in turn, lower self-confidence in mastering the task. Learning goals have been shown to have a positive influence, and outcome goals a negative influence, on problem-solving strategies and requests for assistance.

Management researchers have also begun to address an issue related to outcome and learning goal assignment—goal orientation. Goal orientation refers to dispositions or traits in developing or demonstrating one abilities. A learning goal orientation suggests that individuals are more interested in mastering the procedure or process (e.g., putting in golf, using the driver) than they are with the outcome (e.g., their golf score). When tasks are approached from a learning-goal orientation, individuals attempt to understand something new or increase their level of competence. A performance- or outcome-goal orientation, in contrast, implies that individuals are less interested in mastering the knowledge or skill, procedure or process than they are with the outcome. Individuals with a performance-goal orientation are predisposed to showing others that they can perform the task well. These individuals strive either to demonstrate their competence via task performance or to avoid negative judgments of their competence.

Goal orientation explains different response patterns. For example, employees differ in their reactions to obstacles and setbacks in their work efforts. Individuals with a learning goal orientation view obstacles and setbacks as a challenge that can be mastered with additional effort and problem-solving strategies. A learning-goal orientation is associated with openness to new experiences. In contrast, individuals with a performance-goal orientation view setbacks as an indication of low abilities and are pessimistic about their potential for improvement. These individuals tend to avoid challenges.

There is also evidence that individuals with a learning-goal orientation differ in their reaction to feedback from individuals with an outcome-goal orientation. The former views feedback as a useful learning exercise and important information for self-assessment and personal development, whereas the latter tends to interpret feedback as a personal attack.

The issue of learning- versus performance-goal orientation is a fascinating one. Though viewed as a stable trait, goal orientation can also be considered—a state of mind that can be influenced through goal instructions.

LEARNING GOALS: IMPLICATIONS

Goal setting has a positive effect on both motivation and learning. Research indicates that outcome goals should be set when motivation is the issue, that is, when individuals have the abilities and knowledge needed to perform the task. Learning rather than outcome goals should be set when individuals initially lack the requisite knowledge to perform the task. Learning goals are similar to outcome goals in that both should be specific and challenging, so that they will have an effect on task performance.

Learning goals can be tied to career development strategies such as action-learning programs that include the use of mentors and peers, along with 360-degree feedback to maximize learning from work assignments and projects. Learning goals also have implications for pretenured faculty. Rather than emphasizing outcome goals to pretenured faculty during their first few years on the job, deans, department chairs, and area group coordinators should emphasize learning goals. Such goals stress discovering ways (e.g., auditing classes of faculty who are excellent in the classroom, sending manuscripts to respected scholars requesting critical comments, and inviting scholars to collaborate who complement one's strengths) to achieve the desired outcome: tenure and promotion. In the end, whether in an academic institution or a public company, this exercise will demonstrate the considerable value of learning goals.

8

THE LEADER-MEMBER EXCHANGE THEORY OF LEADERSHIP

"It's the intangibles that are the hardest for your competitor to imitate," he [Herb Kelleher] notes. "You can buy an airplane and a terminal, but you can't buy the spirit of the people." That "spirit of the people" is a big part of what management experts mean when they talk about corporate culture. The beliefs and values that guide employee behavior can improve performance by motivating workers toward a common goal and instilling in them a sense of purpose. They become loyal not to the CEO or their immediate boss, but to the company's vision.

—Pandya and Shell[1]

The family analogy was quintessential Mary Kay Ash, who set up a corporate culture that emphasized, among other things, the importance of relationships and a sense of inclusion.

—Pandya and Shell[2]

As the quotes above suggest, the leader-member exchange (LMX) theory of leadership is concerned with the interactions between leaders and followers (Daft, 2005). The trait, skills, and style approaches to leadership emphasized leadership from the leader's perspective. Situational, contingency, and path-goal theories of leadership are centered on the follower and the context in which the leader and follower interact with each other. In essence, these theories are about what leaders do to each of their followers (Northouse, 2007). The focal point in LMX theory is the dyadic relationship between a leader and each of his or her followers. In other words, LMX theory is concerned with the differential nature of the relationships between leaders and each of their followers (Daft, 2005; Dubrin, 2007; Yukl, 2006). I will describe two waves of studies that have examined the LMX theory of leadership.

THE EARLY STUDIES

Graen and his colleagues (Dansereau, Graen, & Haga, 1975; Graen, 1976; Graen & Cashman, 1975) were the forerunners in the early studies related to LMX theory. They emphasized the vertical dyadic linkages that leaders developed with each subordinate. The relationship that a leader developed with his or her workgroup was the combination of all of these vertically dyadic relationships. This led to two broad types of relationships: those considered in-group relationships and those considered out-group relationships.

In-group relationships develop when leaders and followers negotiate that followers would do more than required by their job description, and leaders would provide more than that required by the formal hierarchy. Out-group relationships form when leaders and followers stick to the defined roles that are based on the formal hierarchy. In-group members are given more responsibility, more participation in decision making, more interesting job assignments, more tangible rewards, and more support for career advancement (Daft, 2005; Dubrin, 2007; Yukl, 2006) by their leaders. In addition, in-group members communicate more, are more involved, and are more dependable than out-group members (Dansereau et al., 1975). Out-group members do what is required and no more (Yukl, 2006). They may be physically present but will only do what is necessary to retain their jobs. Mentally, they may have defected from their jobs, even though they still come to work, do enough to keep their jobs, and then go home. They will not go the extra mile that is often required to achieve higher levels of effectiveness.

THE LATER STUDIES

Where as early studies focused on the differential nature of in-groups and out-groups, the later studies focused on enhancing organizational effectiveness. Essentially, empirically based studies have found that where there are higher quality leader-member exchanges, there are lower employee turnover, better employee evaluations, more frequent promotions, better work assignments, more participation by employees in decision making, enhanced commitment to the organization, more favorable attitudes toward the job, and greater support and interest from the leader (Graen & Uhl-Bien, 1995; Liden, Wayne, & Stilwell, 1993; Northouse, 2007).

In essence, these studies demonstrated that leader-member exchange quality was positively related to results for leaders, their followers, the groups in which leaders and followers interacted with each other, and the organization as a whole (Graen & Uhl-Bien, 1995). This suggests that organizations where leaders develop good working relationships with each individual subordinate will outperform those organizations where the leader-member exchange reflects mostly out-group member relationships (Yukl, 2006).

LEADERSHIP MAKING

The later studies led to a prescriptive approach to leadership that has come to be called *leadership making*. Leadership making suggests that leaders need to form high-quality, or in-group, exchanges with mostly all of their subordinates, not just a small minority. Leadership making is also about the development of partnership networks beyond the workgroup throughout the rest of the organization. Developing these networks should lead to better organizational performance and greater career progress for those leaders who engage in this practice (Graen & Uhl-Bien, 1995; Northouse, 2007).

There are three phases to leadership making (Graen & Uhl-Bien, 1991). They are the stranger phase, the acquaintance phase, and the partnership phase (Daft, 2005). In the stranger phase, the leader-member exchanges resemble those described earlier as out-group exchanges. In this phase, members are more concerned with their own self-interest than with what is best for the group.

In the acquaintance phase, the leader or member makes an offer to do more for each other. This is a testing period during which the leader and the subordinate are checking each other out to see if they trust each other enough to shift to in-group status or the partnership phase. During this phase, member self-interest lessens, and there is more of a focus on the group's goals and objectives.

In the mature partnership phase, leader-member exchanges are similar in quality to in-group exchanges described earlier. Leader-members who are in this stage with each other have developed a high level of "mutual trust, respect and obligation toward each other" (Northouse, 2007). Each leader-member relationship has been tested, and there is a confidence that the leader and member can count on each other. In this stage, leaders positively affect each member and are positively affected by each member. These leader-member exchanges go much farther than those previously defined as out-group exchanges in that there is a transformational nature to these exchanges that allows leaders and followers to pursue what is better for the team and the organization rather than their own self-interests (Northouse, 2007).

First Impressions

Some research (Liden et al., 1993) suggests that the leaders and members need to be aware that first impressions matter. Their results suggest that the initial expectations of leaders toward members and initial member expectations of leaders were positively associated with the leader-member exchanges 2 and 6 weeks later. In addition, initial expectations of the members toward their leader were good predictors of leader-member exchange quality 6 months into the relationship. This means that the leader-member exchange may be formed in the first days and that the old adage—You have only one chance to make a good impression—may be true (Dubrin, 2007).

How Does the LMX Theory of Leadership Work?

The LMX theory of leadership is both descriptive and prescriptive. In both cases, the heart of the LMX theory is the vertical dyadic relationship developed between a leader and each of her or his subordinates.

From a descriptive sense, LMX theory implies that we need to understand that in-groups and out-groups exist in groups and organizations and that as leaders, we participate in their development. Goal accomplishment with in-groups is substantively different than with out-groups. In-group members willingly work harder than required and are more innovative in accomplishing goals. Consequently, leaders give in-group members more opportunities, more responsibilities, more support, and more time.

Out-group members work differently than in-group members with their leaders. They work strictly within the guidelines governing organizational roles and only do the minimum necessary. Leaders are fair to these group members in that they respond to them by strictly adhering to any contractual obligations. However, they are not given any special treatment by their leaders. These out-group members receive the benefits that they are due and required based on their contract but nothing more.

From a prescriptive sense, Graen and Uhl-Bien's (1991) leadership-making model allows us to comprehend LMX theory the most. Their prescription is to develop relationships with all subordinates who are similar to those described earlier for in-group members. In other words, give all subordinates the chance to accept new responsibilities, nurture better quality relationships with each subordinate, develop relationships based on trust and respect with all subordinates, and make the whole workgroup an in-group (Daft, 2005). Finally, leaders should form high-quality partnerships with people throughout the organization (Daft, 2005; Northouse, 2007).

Whether we view the LMX theory of leadership as descriptive or prescriptive, it works by emphasizing the dyadic relationship that both leaders and followers see as special and unique. Northouse (2007) suggests that "when these relationships are of high quality, the goals of the leader, the followers, and the organization are all advanced." Implied in this statement is that these goals are clearly defined and understood, as well as shared among all leaders and followers—this may be one of the prime responsibilities of leaders: to ensure the development of high-quality relationships between leaders and each follower. I encourage each of you to be willing to lead others but to also understand the responsibility you take on for developing special, unique relationships with each of your subordinates.

NOTES

1. Herb Kelleher is the chairman of Southwest Airlines. He served as the CEO from 1982 to 2001.
2. Mary Kay Ash founded Mary Kay Cosmetics (later called Mary Kay, Inc.) in 1963 and served as chairman until she became chairman emeritus in 1987.

REFERENCES

Dansereau, F., Graen, G. B., & Haga, W. (1975). A vertical dyad linkage to leadership in formal organizations. *Organizational Behavior and Human Performance, 13,* 46–78.

Daft, R. L. (2005). *The leadership experience* (3rd ed.). Mason, OH: Thomson, South-Western.

Dubrin, A. (2007). *Leadership: Research findings, practice, and skills.* New York: Houghton Mifflin.

Graen, G. B. (1976). Role-making processes within complex organizations. In M. D. Dunnette (Ed.), *Handbook of industrial and organizational psychology* (pp. 1202–1245). Chicago: Rand McNally.

Graen, G. B., & Cashman, J. (1975). A role-making model of leadership in formal organizations: A developmental approach. In J. G. Hunt & L. L. Larson (Eds.), *Leadership frontiers* (pp. 143–166). Kent, OH: Kent State University Press.

Graen, G. B., & Uhl-Bien, M. (1991). The transformation of professionals into self-managing and partially self-designing contributions: Toward a theory of leadership-making. *Journal of Management Systems, 3*(3), 25–39.

Graen, G. B., & Uhl-Bien, M. (1995). Relationship-based approach to leadership: Development of leader-member exchange (LMX) theory of leadership over 25 years: Applying a multi-level, multi-domain perspective. *The Leadership Quarterly, 6*(2), 219–247.

Liden, R. C., Wayne, S. J., & Stilwell, D. (1993). A longitudinal study on the early development of leader-member exchange. *Journal of Applied Psychology, 78,* 662–674.

Northouse, P. G. (2007). *Leadership: Theory and practice* (4th ed.). Thousand Oaks, CA: Sage.

Pandya, M., & Shell, R. (2006). *Lasting leadership.* Upper Saddle River, NJ: Wharton School Publishing.

Yukl, G. (2006). *Leadership in organizations* (6th ed.). Upper Saddle River, NJ: Pearson-Prentice Hall.

The Cases

Caribbean Foods Limited, Trinidad (Revised)

The newly hired group product manager of Caribbean Foods Limited (a wholly owned subsidiary of Intasco Ltd. USA, and importer of Intasco's food, bakery, and pet food products) was frustrated after just 6 weeks in his position. His creativity was being stifled, there was no pleasing his boss, and he was beginning to doubt himself. He began to consider his alternatives: Should he try to work things out? Should he change his style and just work with the system to fit into the culture of the company? Should he resign?

Moez Kassam: Consulting Intern

A summer assignment is turning into a nightmare for an intern at a large consulting firm. He has just received his third reprimand from his boss and is concerned how this relationship is distracting him from the project he needs to complete and how it could hurt his chances of obtaining full-time employment. He must decide how he can salvage the relationship with his boss and whether this organization is the best fit for him.

The Reading

Leadership Ltd: White Elephant to Wheelwright

The leader who recognizes his or her limitations is also the leader who recognizes the contribution of followers. Business history tells us that leaders do not have to be perfect. But they must recognize that their imperfections and their limitations will doom them to failure unless they rely on their subordinates and followers to fill in the gaps. As this British academic explains and illustrates, leadership is the property and consequence of a community, rather than the property and consequence of an individual leader.

CARIBBEAN FOODS LIMITED, TRINIDAD (REVISED)

*Prepared by Fabian Marks under the
supervision of Professor James A. Erskine*

Version: (A) 2000–07–06

I have absolutely no confidence in you. . . . Get out of my office!!

Mark Davis left John Donovan's office on August 21, 2000, completely humiliated. It was not the first time he had been humiliated by the general manager. The past six weeks as group product manager of Caribbean Foods Limited, Trinidad, were the most frustrating of his young career.

Mark returned to his office, locked his door, stared into space and thought to himself:

> A few weeks ago, I was on a fast track to a brilliant career. At Dovan West Indies Limited, I was creating, developing and contributing to growth. Now, I feel like a machine returning to work every day. I am certainly not being paid to think! From the first day, there has been tension between John and myself. The six weeks now seem like six months with all the frustrations. I am having enough problems adjusting to John's hands-on style of management. But to compound this with the unnecessary humiliations, I'm not sure I can go on any longer. I just can't seem to please my boss and I feel like a complete failure. I have thought of resigning before, but there are few marketing manager opportunities available in a small country like Trinidad and Tobago. I also have my reputation and my responsibilities towards my new wife.

CARIBBEAN FOODS LIMITED

Caribbean Foods Limited (CFL) was a well-established, wholly owned subsidiary of Intasco, USA. Intasco was one of the largest food and beverage companies in the world with consolidated sales over US$17.0 billion. CFL was established as Intasco's Trinidad subsidiary in 1928 to import and market Intasco's brands of products. Products included assorted nuts, cereals, snack foods, bakery products, dessert products and pet foods. All Intasco's products enjoyed high market shares with brand names, such as Bakers, Delico, and Krispic, being regular household names throughout the islands.

In 1978, Intasco expanded its facilities in Trinidad in the southern Caribbean, nine miles from Venezuela and began manufacturing operations. CFL's main product groups included cheese-coated corn snacks in various flavors, two brands of baking powder, powdered gelatins in various flavors, powdered soft drink mixes in various flavors, baking soda and imported nuts and cereals. Manufactured products increased to 84 percent of sales; sales were TT$26 million and net profit before tax was 28 percent of sales.

CFL had relatively low overhead levels compared to the rest of the industry. Highly automated machinery and established systems and procedures allowed CFL to operate with 80 factory employees working three shifts and 25 sales and office staff (see Exhibit 1). CFL's exports were a significant percentage of total sales, enabling the company to be classified as a net foreign exchange earner by the Central Bank of Trinidad and Tobago. This classification provided the company with access to foreign exchange, as required, to import raw materials and packaging. CFL sourced cheaper, but high quality, packaging materials from Venezuela and Brazil versus the traditional, more expensive North American and European supplies.

John Donovan, 33 years old, became CFL's youngest general manager in 1992. He had joined the company two years earlier as

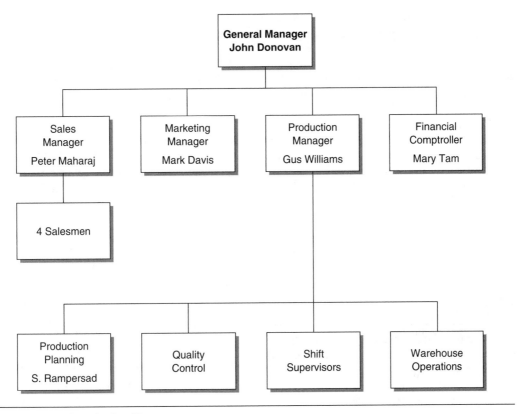

Exhibit 1   Organization Chart

Marketing Manager. Much of CFL's current culture and market position had been developed under John Donovan's high performance, high pressure style of management. He was once quoted as saying, "If you don't keep them (staff) on their toes now, when things get rough, you won't be able to get anything done."

Mark Davis

Mark Davis graduated from The Richard Ivey School of Business in 1999 with an Honors Degree in Business Administration. In May 1999, he took a product manager position with Dovan West Indies Limited (DWI), a Trinidad-based subsidiary of Dovan International, one of the largest consumer product companies in the world. Dovan International held dominant market shares for detergents, personal care products, food and beverages in most developing countries. Mark was responsible for the marketing of over 15 personal care products throughout Trinidad and Tobago. His products included leading brands of soaps, deodorants and toothpaste. Mark enjoyed a high level of independence and decision-making freedom that enhanced his abilities at DWI. Mark reflected on his experiences at DWI:

My personality in the DWI marketing environment fit very well. The marketing director, Greg Alleyne, gave me a lot of latitude to exercise my creativity and my initiative in promotions, advertising and marketing plans for the personal care product group. Greg joked with all the product managers, calling us "babies" because we were so inexperienced, but at the same time, he brought out the best in us by encouraging "crazy" ideas, brainstorming sessions, and respecting our opinions.

Mark performed well under this environment and enjoyed working with the marketing team. Besides executing advertising and promotion strategies in collaboration with the advertising agency, he was also very involved in the development and launching of new products. When Dovan International acquired Quest Brands Limited, Greg assigned Mark the responsibility for incorporating the additional nine brands of lotions, face creams, petroleum jelly and perfumes into his personal care portfolio. Mark's suggestions were well-received by Greg and his contributions facilitated the smooth incorporation of Quest products into Dovan's personal care group. After one year, the personal care products maintained their market leadership positions and Mark received the highest evaluation of the four product managers.

The Offer

In June 2000, Mark received a call from a human resources consultant who asked him if he was interested in talking about a position in another company. Mark accepted an appointment out of curiosity. At the interview, the consultant outlined the marketing manager's position available at CFL. CFL was looking for an experienced marketing manager to take charge of developing CFL's advertising, promotion, distribution and new product development for the local market. The position required regular communication with the sales manager, the sales staff, and CFL's advertising agency. Since the current marketing manager would be emigrating to the United States on July 17, 2000, the incoming marketing manager would have to be an independent self-starter. Mark was intrigued with the opportunity, and an interview was scheduled for Mark to meet with John Donovan and Jeffrey Chang, the current marketing manager, at CFL's office two days after meeting with the consultant.

At the interview, the general manager noted that the size of the company was significantly smaller than DWI in terms of sales and staff, but also highlighted the significant opportunities for growth through the introduction of new products.

John tested Mark's knowledge of advertising and product development and found that Mark understood the process from his experience at DWI. DWI and CFL did not carry any competing products. Mark left the interview one hour later excited by the possibility of a new challenge at a higher position and salary in a rapidly growing company.

Two days later, Mark sent a letter to John expressing some of his ideas that had developed from the discussion (see Exhibit 2). When Mark did not receive a reply the following week, he forwarded another letter to John (see Exhibit 3). Two days after sending the second letter, Mark received a phone call from the consultant:

Consultant: What the hell you doing, man! You trying to blow it?

Mark: What do you mean?

Consultant: CFL was seriously considering your application until you sent that second letter. What the hell got into you to do that?

Mark: I was just trying to show a little initiative. Besides, I hadn't heard from them and its been 10 days now.

Consultant: It's one thing to show initiative, and the first letter was fine, but TWO letters? Look, if you don't want to blow it, just have a little patience. Don't write any more letters, and I'll get back to you.

The next week, on July 4, 2000, Mark received a call from the consultant with the offer he received from the general manager to start work at CFL on July 10, 2000. Mark promised to call back the consultant in 10 minutes after he spoke with his wife.

The opportunity to be marketing manager of Caribbean Foods Limited at 25 years of age was difficult for Mark to turn down, especially as the salary offered was in fact 20 percent higher than what he was currently earning at DWI. Being one-sixth the size of DWI in terms of sales and staff, Mark thought there would be even more management flexibility at CFL. He looked

June 15, 2000

The General Manager
Caribbean Foods Limited
Trinidad

Attention: Mr. John Donovan

Dear Mr. Donovan:

First of all, I would like to thank you for considering me for the Marketing Manager's position at Caribbean Foods Limited (CFL). It was a pleasure meeting both yourself and Jeffrey, and I thoroughly enjoyed our discussion.

During the interview, you enquired about my experience in advertising and product development. One key product I have been working on at Dovan West Indies Limited (DWI) is the toothpaste line. Please find enclosed two copies of Dovan's toothpaste cartons, one being the traditional carton, and the other being the revised version that I have developed in collaboration with DWI's advertising agency. Besides the packaging facelift, the relaunch also included a change from metal to plastic tubes, and from screw caps to fliptop caps. I also worked with the advertising agency in developing the advertisement and promotional material. The entire relaunch has seen DWI's toothpaste market share increase from 18 percent to 29 percent over the past three (3) months alone. The toothpaste line is just one of thirty products I have been managing at DWI.

As you outlined in the interview, however, marketing CFL's food and beverage products is distinctly different from marketing detergents and personal care products. With some exposure, however, I believe that I can effectively fulfil the Marketing Manager's role within your organization.

I look forward to hearing from you soon.

Sincerely,

Mark Davis

Encl.

Exhibit 2   First Follow-Up Letter

Source: Company records

THE FIRST WEEK

On July 10, 2000, Mark showed up for work on time. He visited Jeffrey who introduced him to his secretary. Jeffrey also introduced Mark to the general manager's secretary, who informed him that John would normally be in by 9:30 A.M. and was expecting to see him. At 9:30 A.M., Mark went to see John in his office. Mark did not receive the welcome he was expecting. He recalled the first meeting:

John seemed very preoccupied at the meeting, a lot more serious than the person I met at the interview. I was surprised when he told me that my position was group product manager and not marketing manager. John assured me, however, that I would be performing all of the marketing

forward to running the marketing and sales departments and contributing to the rapid growth of the company. With the support of his new wife, be called back the consultant and accepted the offer to join CFL.

June 26, 2000

The General Manager
Caribbean Foods Limited
Trinidad

Attention: Mr. John Donovan

Dear Mr. Donovan:

Since our interview almost two weeks ago, I have been thinking of the key opportunities for new product developments and expansion within Caribbean Foods Limited (CFL).

I was surprised to learn about the significant opportunities for introducing new Intasco products for the Trinidad market. I believe that the potato chips market represents a key opportunity for growth for CFL. The snacks market is currently dominated by corn snacks. Our familiarity with North American culture leads me to believe that high quality potato chips sold under the popular Krispic brand would outsell the lower quality corn snacks once the price is right.

The biscuits market is also another area that is serviced by low quality local manufacturers. Given Intasco's strengths in the biscuit industry and their dominance in the North American biscuit market, CFL has significant resources available for growth. Again, given our familiarity with North American branded products and the market's assumptions for the superior quality of Intasco's brands, CFL can also be a major player in the local biscuit market.

Moreover, there is tremendous potential to service the broader Caribbean market with these products and increase CFL's export earnings since these markets are also serviced by the same low quality local suppliers.

While I do not have any figures pertaining to the cost of the equipment or the required breakeven for these two projects, I would be anxious to pursue these opportunities if I were given the opportunity to do so.

Sincerely,

Mark Davis

Exhibit 3   Second Follow-Up Letter

Source: Company records

manager's functions and with one or two years' experience, my position as marketing manager would be confirmed. John suggested that I learn as much as I could from Jeffrey while he was around, because once he was gone John wasn't sure how much time he could spend with me. The welcome lasted five minutes. I left the meeting feeling either that John had mixed feelings about hiring me, or that he was disappointed at losing Jeffrey Chang.

Mark returned to his office to learn as much as he could from Jeffrey Chang about the job, and

about John Donovan. Jeffrey spent as much time as he could with Mark going over the products, the key competitors, the respective marketing strategies outlined for each product group, product development plans for the next six months, new product launches planned, advertising under development and the reporting requirements for internal management and for CFL's Regional Head Office in Puerto Rico.

Multinational subsidiaries were normally required to submit annual operating plans to their head offices and CFL followed this practice. The 2001 operating plan was recently prepared by CFL management and it described in detail:

1. The local economy and markets;

2. Individual product strategies;

3. Advertising developments and planned promotions;

4. Product launches and deletions;

5. Target market shares;

6. Projected sales volumes;

7. Projected profits;

8. Capital expenditures;

9. Cash flows.

Jeffrey advised Mark to carefully study CFL's 2001 Annual Operating Plan and Mark used every free moment he had to review the plan in Jeffrey's office. As this was a confidential document, no one was allowed to remove it from the office. John Donovan would occasionally stop by the marketing manager's office for casual discussions with Jeffrey. During one of these visits, Mark remembered being well-directed by John that Mark's role within CFL over the next year or so was clearly laid out in the plan. Mark was required to implement strategies rather than develop them until he gained enough experience to develop his own plan.

Mark was bothered that the general manager seemed to keep him out of the conversations whenever he dropped into the marketing manager's office for a talk. During brief exchanges, Mark felt as if John Donovan was deliberately trying to let him know that he was inexperienced.

John seemed to have a lot of respect for Jeffrey's opinions. Mark also recognized that Jeffrey, at just 27 years of age, was extremely knowledgeable about the industry. Jeffrey had previously worked for a large Swiss multinational subsidiary in Trinidad for seven years. He had worked through the ranks of the company to eventually become product manager for many of their food and beverage lines before he was

recruited to join CFL. Mark realized that Jeffrey not only had a lot of experience, but had also developed a natural marketing talent and was well respected.

The friendly relationship between Jeffrey Chang and John Donovan that had developed over the years was quite apparent. Their relationship made Mark feel uncomfortable, because the general manager seemed to be distancing himself from Mark. It seemed to Mark, however, that the general manager was not as close to the other managers in the company. Mark was becoming more concerned as to whether he could effectively replace Jeffrey Chang.

Mark met the key managers and supervisors in the organization with whom he would be communicating frequently. Foremost among these was CFL's 29-year-old sales manager, Peter Maharaj, who was in charge of the four salesmen as well as the company's fleet of vehicles. Peter had been with the company for two years and had developed a good rapport with the retailers during this time. Peter and his sales force were well-respected throughout the organization. Jeffrey suggested that Mark work closely with the sales manager for feedback on sales, customers and promotions.

Jeffrey also introduced Mark to Stephen Rampersad, CFL's 30-year-old inventory control supervisor for the past five years. Because Stephen was in charge of ordering raw and packaging materials, he interacted with the marketing manager to schedule production and plan inventories whenever promotions were being considered. He also played a crucial role in sourcing packaging materials for all product developments.

THE SECOND WEEK

After Jeffrey Chang left the job, Mark spent the second week on the road familiarizing himself with customers, distribution channels and the salesmen. Peter Maharaj prepared a schedule for Mark to travel different routes with the salesmen to meet some of CFL's key retailers. He found the trips to be quite useful and thought he had developed a good understanding of CFL's key customers based on the sales data and other information supplied by the salesmen.

THE THIRD WEEK

The third week, Mark began to focus on the job at hand. The group product manager's job required that several tasks be coordinated at the same time: the advertising agency would be working on several advertisements; Stephen Rampersad would be sourcing packaging for new products; new tubs for baking powder and custard powder needed to be sourced locally to replace imported packaging that utilized scarce foreign exchange; promotions in the trade needed to be evaluated; new promotions were being developed with various suppliers of stickers, packaging and giveaways; inventories needed to be monitored; sales reports and trends had to be analyzed; and marketing reports and sales projections needed to be prepared weekly and monthly.

Mark began following up on the progress of several tasks through conversations with Stephen and Peter and telephone calls to suppliers and the advertising agency. He remembered Jeffrey's advice, however, to ensure that reports were prepared on time as a priority. Based on the report schedule supplied by Jeffrey, Mark needed to send off a few reports to Intasco's Regional Head Office in Puerto Rico. He informed John of his intentions, who advised him:

John: Just give them what they need to know. Don't add any more than necessary. You give them too much information and they start asking questions. Make sure you copy me on all information going to Puerto Rico.

John Donovan stopped making his casual visits to the marketing manager's office once Jeffrey Chang had left. John did not have an open-door policy and based on the "cold vibes" Mark was getting, he thought it best to figure things out for himself and try to get things done independently. If he had any questions or problems, he thought it best to ask either Stephen Rampersad or Peter Maharaj before bothering the general manager.

The Krispic Promotion

One of Mark's urgent assignments left over by Jeffrey Chang was to implement a promotion for a six-pack of Krispic Corn Snacks. A large local competitor, Funtime Snacks, recently reduced the pack size on their cheese snacks and priced their product to be more competitive than CFL's Krispic corn snacks. Jeffrey decided to defend his market share by countering with a promotion which featured six packs of Krispic Corn Snacks in different flavors packaged in one pre-printed plastic bag sold at a discount.

The promotion could either be run as a co-op whereby individual retailers participated by sharing the cost of the discount and promoting the item in their media advertising, or as a national promotion open to all retailers who wanted to purchase the six-pack. In the case of the latter, CFL would normally advertise the promotion and assume the costs. Since the distribution decision had not been made, Mark discussed the promotion with the sales manager, and subsequently decided to structure the promotion as a co-op. Mark sold the promotion to about eight key, large retailers he had met during his customer familiarization program.

Two days later, John spotted the promotion notices in Peter Maharaj's office and stormed into Mark's office:

John: Was this how I told you to run this?!!

Mark: You didn't tell me how you wanted it run. I just thought that since the decision hadn't been made, I would go with a co-op.

John: Before you do anything in future, you better pass it through me first!

With this brief exchange, John just shook his head and walked out.

At this point, Mark started asking around if this was typical of John's style. He confronted both Peter and Stephen with the incident and soon found out that everyone just conformed to the general manager's demands.

THE FOURTH WEEK

During the fourth week, Mark and John visited CFL's advertising agency to discuss some of the advertising and promotions under development. Before the meeting, John mentioned to Mark that he was quite surprised that the new television advertisement for the Krispic corn snack was completed so quickly since the filming took place just two days ago. He suspected that the agency was giving CFL a "rush" job because he thought the editing was to be done in the United States or Venezuela. After viewing the ad, it was quite obvious to all that the editing was poorly done.

> John criticized the agency on at least 10 counts. Areas for improvement were pointed out after about every three seconds of tape. I agreed with John on most of the errors, but his tone of voice left the account executives and the creative director of the agency almost speechless. John stormed out of the meeting leaving instructions to re-shoot most of the ad and re-edit the entire ad by the following

week. I had been to several advertisement evaluation sessions where suggestions were made and discussed, but I had never seen a client criticize an agency like that before. I just naturally followed John out of the office.

The Sales Report Suggestion

The next day, Mark pulled a copy of CFL's daily sales report from his IN-tray (see Exhibit 4). Mark had come across this document daily but placed it in the OUT-tray for filing because he did not think that the information provided was useful. Mark thought that the report should at least provide a sales breakdown by product or size. While this was supplied monthly, he felt a need for a more timely breakdown to see the results of the promotions and to compare actual weekly and year-to-date sales with budget and with last year's results. Mark approached John in the office corridor with his idea for improving the information system. John's response surprised him.

John: You don't have enough experience to be suggesting anything. I worked with the system and the previous managers worked with the system. Why can't you work with it?!!

Date: August 2, 2000		
		Sales
Salesman #1:	Martin Joseph	$25,967
Salesman #2:	Anand Rampersad	$29,426
Salesman #3:	Suzanne Chow	$22,165
Salesman #4:	Pedro Pierre	$18,906
TOTAL SALES		$96,154
Peter Maharaj	Date: August 31, 2000	
Sales Manager		

Exhibit 4   Sample of Daily Sales Report

Source: Company Records

Mark felt as if his creativity was being stifled and wondered how he could please his new boss.

THE FIFTH WEEK

The Price Restructuring Meeting

Last week the Government of Trinidad and Tobago announced a major financial restructuring program to satisfy the International Monetary Fund. John Donovan knew that such a move would immediately affect raw material imports. He notified all managers of an emergency meeting to adjust CFL's prices. As a lot of costing and pricing information needed to be available, he gave all managers two days to prepare for the meeting. John especially asked Mark to develop a current list of retail prices for competitive products as well as CFL's products. Mark prepared a form for the salesmen to record prices for competitors' and CFL's products while they were in the stores. He passed this list on to Peter who administered the process to his sales staff. The next day, Mark collected all the forms, compared the salesmen's prices to those from some of his own research, and summarized the data for presentation at the meeting.

At the meeting, John asked for current competitive retail prices of baking powder at supermarket chains.

Mark: I don't have average prices for all the supermarket chains but I have the prices at various supermarkets and independents.

John: Mark, you should know that supermarket chains normally have a 30 percent markup on manufacturer's prices while independent retailers normally carry a 20 percent markup. What is really important here is the breakdown to set prices and volume discounts to be competitive at both retailing levels.

Mark: I understand that, but you did not make it clear to me that you wanted the competitive retail prices broken down in any particular structure.

John: That's because you don't listen!!

John's admonishment ended the conversation. Mark handed over the list he had prepared to John and the meeting went ahead using the prices that were available. Mark felt embarrassed among the other managers and did not say another word for the rest of the meeting.

THE LAST EXCHANGE

After five weeks, Mark was disappointed and disillusioned. He did not know where he stood with the general manager or with CFL. Mark decided that he would just do what he was told to do as well as he possibly could. He was beginning to lose confidence in his own abilities and decided not to suggest anything until John had the confidence in him to listen to him.

John interrupted Mark's thoughts.

John: You! Come into my office! Right now!!

Mark had never sat in John's office, but he felt as if this was not going to be a friendly meeting. Mark followed the general manager to his office.

John: How the hell could you go talking to your friends at Dovan about our operations? Those were some of our closely guarded secrets!

Mark knew he was guilty. He had no idea how John found out, but said nothing.

John: I have absolutely no confidence in you . . . Get out of my office!!!

Mark returned to his office, shocked and lost. He knew the conversation John had referred to. A few days earlier, Mark ran into one of DWI's product managers in a shopping mall and a casual conversation tripped over into some confidential issues. It did not matter any more how John found out about the conversation. Mark felt his credibility was as good as destroyed. He reflected on his feelings as he sank back in his chair:

> I don't know why John didn't fire me there and then in his office. He had every reason to. Why was he keeping me on when we seemed to be just frustrating each other? Why did he hire me in the

first place? My creativity and initiative are being stifled. John may intend to continue operating like this, but I'm not sure I can.

Several alternatives raced through his mind. Should he go back to the general manager's office and try to work things out? Should he change his style and just work with the system to fit into the culture of the organization? Should he resign? As he considered his alternatives, he began thinking of his family.

MOEZ KASSAM: CONSULTING INTERN

Prepared by Ebrahim El Kalza under the supervision of Professor James A. Erskine

Version: (A) 2006–06–07

> That's not at the Matthews standard! You're going to have to perform at a higher level if you want to work here!

Summer Associate Moez Kassam slowly rubbed his temples as his senior manager, Sherif Mahfouz, at Matthews Management Consulting stormed out of the client office they shared. It was early August 2003, and Kassam had been in Abu Dhabi for only two weeks. Already his dream assignment was becoming a nightmare. He felt he could do no right, and was beginning to lose confidence in his abilities. This was the third time he had been scolded, and he felt his chance of leveraging the internship into a full-time offer with Matthews was in serious jeopardy.

THE CONSULTING INDUSTRY

Since the burst of the dot-com bubble in 2000, many articles, in business magazines, had

characterized the industry's decline and even forecasted its demise. With the consulting industry's role in scandals such as Enron, the glut of MBA graduates available and their lack of accountability, some of the shine had certainly rubbed off the industry.

Strategy consultants offered wisdom in exchange for money; they helped a client's top executives navigate the strategic challenges in leading companies. The fortunes of consultants depended on the future prospects of large corporations. Although, in theory, poor economic conditions could create work for consultants, the reality was that a corporation's budget for consultants was typically the first to go in tough times.

During the dot-com boom, strategy consulting companies had been faced with two serious threats: their "general" approach was being outflanked by smaller, more specialized e-commerce experts, and the Internet start-up frenzy created a serious war for talent. Many consulting companies had been forced to offer ludicrous pay packages and hire a large number of employees to handle the high volume of business. When the dot-com bubble burst, losses mounted, clients disappeared and growth came to a halt. Heavy layoffs were necessary to recoup the lost investment in e-commerce, and many international offices were closed. This left many firms with an uncertain future, and those who remained suffered from low employee morale.

In the wake of these hard times, consulting companies began to restructure to deal with the changing business environment. The migration of former consultants into the industry allowed large corporations to build in-house consulting units, decreasing the demand for professional strategic advice. The increased competition for clients resulted in increased hours and shrinking case lengths for consultants, as well as a bias towards "over-selling" cases by partners in order to attract business.

MATTHEWS MANAGEMENT CONSULTING

The Firm

Matthews was a top-tier global strategy consulting firm, with a reputation for producing implementable, data-driven solutions for its clients. In exchange for large fees, Fortune 500 clients were supplied a high-powered team of bright and capable consultants to tackle their most difficult business problems.

The firm consistently ranked among the top-three consulting firms in the world, and employed more than 2,000 people in 20 countries. Consulting at this level was considered a prestigious business, and the lucrative compensation packages, early exposure to senior executives and key decision makers, and the numerous opportunities available upon leaving the firm attracted the best and brightest from top-ranked business, engineering and liberal arts programs. The average stint at a consulting firm ranged from two to four years, and alumni were typically lured by their clients into high-paying executive positions in large multinationals or used the

network and skills they accumulated to launch a new company.

As coveted as they were, internships and full-time placements at Matthews were not easy to come by. Since the firm's competitive advantage was based on providing clients with "the best and the brightest," hiring procedures were strenuous and highly competitive. A want-to-be consultant was required to pass two or three rounds of case and fit interviews, meeting with several senior consultants at each stage. Even so, only half of summer interns were offered full-time positions.

The rewards of a career in consulting came at a price. Consultants typically worked between 60 and 90 hours per week, maintained an unpredictable and onerous travel schedule and often spent up to four days a week at the client site. If a client happened to be overseas, a consultant could be asked to relocate for the duration of the engagement, which could last up to six months or more. The intense commitment and uncertainty resulted in family and social pressure, stress and often burnout.

Structure

Matthews employed a "one firm" or global model: all professionals were paid out of a consolidated bonus pool. Although each office had its own identity and core clients, this system made it in everyone's interest to share resources, such as people and expertise, across all offices to best meet client needs. Occasionally, consultants were staffed on two cases at once in order to maximize their utility and expedite their development. This was widely known as the "50/50" staffing model, but consultants often joked about how it was really "80/80" due to competing demands and heavy workloads.

Teams were composed of the best available mixture of industry experience and expertise. A partner with knowledge of a particular industry would sell the firm's services in what was referred to as a "bake-off"; a company looking for advice invited a number of consulting firms to propose a preliminary solution, approach, plan and fee structure. The company would then select from among the proposals. Once a case was sold, the partner would bring in a manager, who subsequently staffed the team with the appropriate mix of consultants and associates (see Exhibit 1).

Culture

Matthews Worldwide

Matthews's employees often said how astounded they were by the high similarity of different offices; no doubt due to a very strong and discriminating culture. Many related it to an old law firm, where you had to earn your stripes and the right to speak, and more importantly, the right to be heard.

The firm prided itself on offering clients data-driven, profit-focused results, and offering employees world-class training and access to the best clients. It also provided several unique opportunities to employees, including stints in foreign offices, postings to a not-for-profit subsidiary and invitations to world-wide social events.

Matthews Toronto

The Toronto office staffed about 40 consultants at various levels and had been hit especially hard by layoffs due to the tough economic climate. Despite being merged with a nearby U.S. office, Matthews Toronto worked hard to maintain a distinct Canadian identity, becoming known for expertise in pulp and paper, mining, forestry and

---

Partner

A partner, or principal, extensive industry has expertise and 10 years of consulting experience. A partner's duties include selling the engagement, appointing a manager to head the tactical team, providing guidance, working closely with the client's CEO (or equivalent) and delivering the final presentation.

Manager

The manager is the tactical leader of the team and is responsible for assembling the team, working with the partner to prepare a hypothesis (or "answer first"), defining the analysis required to verify the hypothesis, identifying the different work streams and assembling the right team to complete them. Managers typically work the most hours and are under the greatest strain.

Case Team Leader

A senior consultant with two to three years of experience is referred to as a Case Team Leader, or CTL. CTLs support the manager by taking on one or two work streams, and are expected to help develop some of the more junior members of the team.

Consultant

The consultant position is either a promotion for star associates, or an entry level positive for MBA hires. Consultants are expected to take ownership of a work stream and are given direct client interaction.

Associate Consultant

Associate consultants are undergraduate hires. They typically have little previous work experience, and are given intensive training in their early months. Associate work is usually quite analytical, and there is very limited, if any, client exposure. Parts of work streams are carved out for and owned by an associate. Ideally, responsibility is increased as the associates demonstrate their ability. After two years, successful associates will be promoted to senior associates and have their MBA sponsored by the firm, contingent on a promise to return for at least two years upon its completion.

Exhibit 1   Typical Team Structure and Roles

financial services, as well as its reputation for hard work and a sociable climate. Matthews Toronto hired its associates from the top business and engineering programs in Canada.

MOEZ KASSAM

Moez Kassam knew from a young age that he wanted to be in business, and from his first job at 14 washing dishes, he knew he wanted to be the boss. Graduating at the top of his high school class with acceptance letters from Canada's top business schools in hand and an offer to work for a top consumer packaged goods company, he knew he was off to the right start. By the summer of 2002, Kassam had worked for three top-tier corporations, had started two businesses and had launched the first youth-initiated international trade mission in Canadian history. Still, he felt like he was not getting the most out of his business education. Upon reviewing his options and consulting with many mentors and friends, Kassam applied and was accepted into the honors program at the Richard Ivey School of Business at The University of Western Ontario with the hopes of becoming a strategy consultant.

With four years of business schooling, including the first year of his MBA and three years at another institution, some corporate experience under his belt and a knack for speaking his mind, Kassam felt confident that he was well positioned for success and a career in consulting.

> My value proposition is different from most want-to-be consultants. I've had some great and unique experiences for someone my age and learned a lot of useful skills along the way. I also love thinking up creative ideas to tough business problems. Consulting is the best way for me to solidify and test out these skills and ideas. It'll be great training for when I'm ready to run my own business.

By working extremely hard, Kassam focused and achieved an A average during the first semester of his sophomore year. He spent the winter break learning about the various firms and preparing for the strenuous interviews. In early March, he received a phone call from Matthews Consulting offering him the summer internship he desired most. He accepted on the spot.

THE ABU DHABI ENGAGEMENT

Kassam started his internship at Matthews on May 26, 2003, and spent the first week training and meeting the Toronto staff. He was well rested from his month-long trip to Egypt and was eager to get to work. Two other fellow students from a different section were also hired as interns, as well as an MBA graduate. Matthews's human resources staff had hinted during training that the Toronto office did not have enough analysts to meet demand, and that they would hope to extend offers for full-time positions to all the interns, provided they met performance standards.

After completing his first assignment—a diagnostic on the operations of a large U.S. paper mill—with a satisfactory performance review, Kassam waited to be staffed on his next project. When word went around the office of an opportunity in Abu Dhabi, Kassam sent an e-mail to the manager on the project, Sunjay Singh, detailing his desire to participate. Kassam cited how his ability to speak Arabic would be helpful in communicating with the client, as well as his past international work experience in Malaysia and Mexico. He took a measured risk by copying the partner heading the project on the e-mail, since associates, let alone interns, rarely communicated directly with partners. Singh seemed to be impressed by Kassam's keenness and commended him on his initiative.

Kassam was disappointed to learn that he would not be staffed on the case, but continued to send the manager research papers that he deemed relevant to the Abu Dhabi project. On a Thursday afternoon in mid-July, already one week into the case, he received a call from the partner asking if he could be ready to leave for Abu Dhabi the next day. They would need his help, the partner said, to complete some customer interviews in Arabic. Kassam was ecstatic about the opportunity and went home to pack his suitcase.

The Client

The client was one of the largest private equity firms in the Middle East and the largest consumer user of consultants in the region. Many of the client's top managers were former consultants themselves and, as such, were shrewd project managers and quite business-savvy. This was the first time Matthews had worked with this client, and the project was viewed as a vital foothold in establishing a Middle Eastern presence.

The client was looking to invest hundreds of millions of dollars in a novel and risky manufacturing technology that utilized some of the country's natural resources. Matthews had been asked to determine the economic feasibility of such an investment, and to render a "go" or "no-go" decision in one month's time. The client selected Matthews based on demonstrated experience in the industry and the promise of a data-driven solution.

The Matthews Team

Matthews staffed a five-person team on the project: an experienced manager, two case team leaders who were mere months away from promotion to manager and two very junior associates. The senior staff all had experience in the client's industry, and one of the junior associates had only worked on private equity cases. The team was drawn from four Matthews's offices: Toronto, London, Paris and the fledgling Middle Eastern practice based in Beirut, Lebanon (see Exhibit 2).

Working in Abu Dhabi

Abu Dhabi, an island off the coast of Saudi Arabia in the Arabian Sea, was the conservative capital of the United Arab Emirates (UAE) (see Exhibit 3). The UAE was an oil-rich country of 2.5 million people, one-quarter of which were descendants of the nation's founding tribes. These "Nationals," as they were called, enjoyed special privileges, including access to the benefits of designated petrol trusts that provided them with subsidized housing, health care, education, full employment and many other incentives. The rest of the population was largely composed of Arab, Indian and South-East Asian immigrants and Western expatriates working for large multinational subsidiaries. The intense heat, which often surpassed 50°C, made summer a time for vacations to more palatable climates. This left the city desolate and hot, with not much to do.

As soon as he arrived, Kassam was quickly introduced to the team and the client managers, and put to work. Since the engagement was already in progress, he was handed a series of binders and reports to review in order to ramp up and was given several assignments and deadlines. He was to source, book and complete 50 customer interviews across five Middle Eastern countries in his first two weeks. No further direction was given, and Kassam began to think of ways to tackle the problem. He drafted a list of questions for his direct supervisor, Mahfouz, who was to monitor his performance and provide guidance when necessary.

When provided with the questions, Mahfouz made it clear that he was quite busy and that Kassam would have to learn to be a source of solutions rather than questions. Mahfouz took Kassam through his first three interviews, and then left him to complete the rest. Kassam was instructed to thoroughly complete a pre-written questionnaire for each interview, enter it into a word processor and e-mail it to Mahfouz for review.

Although he knew that consulting was a demanding profession, Kassam was not prepared for the intensity of this project. He found himself working 16 hours a day, seven days a week, without pause for the four weeks he was there. He had worked overseas before, but never for this long under such strenuous circumstances or without access to friends or family. The number of complex political challenges he faced within the team and with the client only added to the pressure and made it difficult to dedicate himself to his work.

CHRIS MCKIBBIN, PARTNER

Education:	MBA (Insead)
Expertise:	Pulp & Paper, Financial Services, Insurance
Experience:	Investment banking (2 years), Matthews Consulting (9 years)
Languages:	English, French, Spanish
Home office:	Toronto, Canada

SUNJAY SINGH, MANAGER

Education:	B. Eng., MBA (MIT)
Expertise:	Airline, Insurance, M&A, Private Equity
Experience:	Manufacturing (2 years), Matthews Consulting (7 years)
Language:	English, Urdu
Home office:	Toronto, Canada

SHERIF MAHFOUZ, CTL/MANAGER

Education:	B. Eng., Masters in Government & Policy (Harvard)
Expertise:	Middle East, Private Equity
Experience:	Civil engineer (3 years), Consulting (7 years), Matthews Consulting (2 years)
Languages:	English, French, Arabic
Home office:	Paris, France (Middle East practice reports to Paris under the current structure)

SHENNY MORSTERN, SENIOR CONSULTANT

Education:	MBA (Insead)
Expertise:	Retail, Airline, Insurance, Financial Services
Experience:	Matthews Consulting (6 years)
Languages:	English, French
Home office:	London, UK

JEAN BRISEBOIS, ASSOCIATE CONSULTANT

Education:	B. Com. (HEC Paris)
Expertise:	Private Equity
Experience:	Matthews Consulting (2 years)
Languages:	English, French
Home office:	Paris, France

MIKE BROWN, ASSOCIATE CONSULTANT

Education:	B. Com. (Queens)
Expertise:	Retail
Experience:	Matthews Consulting (1 year)
Languages:	English
Home office:	Toronto, Canada

MOEZ KASSAM, ASSOCIATE CONSULTANT INTERN[1]

Education:	HBA Candidate (Ivey)
Expertise:	Pulp & Paper
Experience:	Venture Capital (internship), Marketing (internship), Various international assignments
Languages:	English, French, Arabic
Home office:	Toronto, Canada

Exhibit 2   Team Member Profile

1. A late appointment to the team.

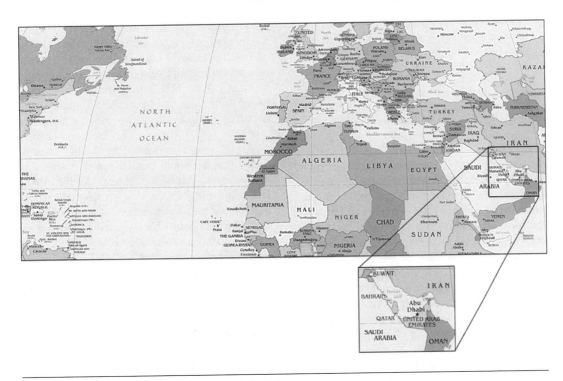

Exhibit 3   Map of North Africa and the Middle East

SHERIF MAHFOUZ

Mahfouz was in his early 40s and had been with Matthews for just over one year but had more than seven years of consulting experience in the Middle East with a competing firm, an engineering degree, a Harvard graduate degree in public policy, experience in the industry and spoke three languages including Arabic. He had been hired in order to help build Matthews's Middle Eastern business. Through informal conversation, Mahfouz's goals became clear to Kassam: to establish Matthews's presence in the Middle East and leverage that into a partnership in the firm. Mahfouz even mentioned that there may be opportunities in the new office, assuming Kassam performed well. Mahfouz worked especially hard, juggling several engagements at once, and often appeared tired and stressed. He had just built a new house in Beirut and would

often speak of it fondly and wonder out loud when he would finally have time to enjoy it.

THE FIRST INCIDENT

In the first week, Kassam worked hard to complete 15 interviews and scheduled 10 more for the following week. He spent every spare minute reading up on the company and industry and discussing the progress of the other work streams. While on the phone with a customer, Mahfouz walked into the client office, customer surveys in hand, and cast Kassam a sideways glance. Kassam finished the interview, updated Mahfouz on his progress so far and asked him what he thought of the work he had already completed.

I'm glad you're getting the hang of it, but we're behind schedule here. The client needs 50 interviews done, and done well. I'm under a lot of pressure to get this done, and I can't do that while you're submitting this kind of trash to me. There are spelling mistakes and errors in the documents. Some questions are incomplete. I can't put my name on this. I want them fixed, and I want to have a schedule for the interviews in my hand ASAP. This is not some school project. This is serious business.

Mahfouz went on to correct him on an Arabic word he had heard Kassam mispronounce in his last interview, handed him a stack of completed interviews covered in red ink and walked out of the room. Kassam began to browse through the stack and noticed that although there were a few typos, thought that many of the edits were subjective and frivolous. He was angry at himself for making so many careless errors, and felt that he was off to a rocky start with his new boss.

At nearly 10 P.M., Mahfouz walked back into the room, silently packed his laptop computer, folded away the schedule Kassam had left for him on his desk and, without looking directly at him, told Kassam he would require an update at breakfast the next morning, 7:30 A.M. sharp. Frustrated because his first interview was at 9 A.M. and he knew he would once again get very little sleep, and embarrassed by the way he was being treated, Kassam finished the edits and quickly summarized the week's findings. As he made back for the hotel, he checked his watch. It was 12:30 A.M.

The Second Incident

Kassam showed up at breakfast 10 minutes late, and found that Mahfouz had finished his breakfast and was impatiently reading the paper. As he sat down, Mahfouz said nothing. Feeling awkward, Kassam got up to get his breakfast from the buffet. As he came back to the table, Mahfouz was checking his watch, and glanced up at Kassam, who started to apologize for being late. It was 7:45. Kassam pulled out his notes for the update and began reading. Mahfouz raised his hand and told him to finish his breakfast. There was no longer time to go through the update. Ten minutes later, Mahfouz asked for the bill, put on his suit jacket and walked to the door. Kassam left his half-finished breakfast and followed him out. Mahfouz walked three paces ahead of Kassam the entire way to the client office.

As soon as they settled in, Mahfouz mentioned that he would be in a senior meeting all morning, and that he would leave for the city of Doha, in nearby Qatar, that evening. He would debrief with Kassam before leaving. Kassam spent the hour before his interview improving his weekly update and e-mailing it to Mahfouz. Five minutes before his first scheduled interview, a senior member of the client's team, Laurent, knocked and entered the office. After asking where Mahfouz was, he began to question Kassam first on his progress and then on his background and experience. Kassam gave very general answers and assured Laurent that everything was going well. As soon as Laurent left, Kassam let out a sigh of relief.

At lunch, Kassam mentioned what had happened to one of the other associates. The associate explained that this was not surprising, since the client's management team, comprising former consultants, was disgruntled because it did not receive the team of people that it was promised. The management team claimed that Matthews had "pulled a bait-and-switch" and had replaced the industry experts they promised at the point of sale with a team of younger, less-experienced (and consequently less expensive) consultants. Kassam felt that his young age and lack of experience were likely to exacerbate the issue.

During their debrief meeting, Mahfouz asked Kassam how the morning had gone. He thanked him for the update and commended him on a job well done. Soon after, he asked if Kassam had spoken to Laurent. Kassam reiterated the conversation and mentioned that he had felt uncomfortable during Laurent's probing. Mahfouz grimaced and said that he would speak to Laurent and Singh on the issue.

The next morning, Singh called Kassam into an empty office, and began to chastise him on speaking with the client.

Sherif told me about your conversation with Laurent. The client is already weary about the age of the team. The last thing we need right now is more problems. I don't want you speaking to him again. Any questions on the progress of your work should be directed to Sherif or me. Is that clear?

Before Kassam could respond, Singh checked his watch, told him he was late for a client update and walked out of the room.

THE THIRD INCIDENT

The team continued to work throughout another weekend in one room, while Kassam worked through his interviews in another. He had undertaken the habit of e-mailing an update to Mahfouz at the end of each day, and was receiving positive feedback on his progress. Halfway through the following week, Mahfouz appeared at the office for the first time in five days. Kassam asked him about his trip, and was told that he would hear all about it at lunch. Mahfouz seemed in high spirits, and Kassam felt that perhaps their relationship was improving. Mahfouz asked Kassam for a written update on the status and findings of the interviews for the morning's client meeting. With two scheduled interviews, Kassam knew he would be pressed to complete the report on time. Scared of jeopardizing Mahfouz's good mood, he promised it would be completed by the required time.

With only 45 minutes to complete the necessary document, Kassam amalgamated the daily updates he had sent Mahfouz over the past two weeks and formatted them for clarity and coherence. Since Mahfouz had commended him on his updates, Kassam felt confident that it would be satisfactory.

Mahfouz rushed in minutes before his meeting, picked up the document, thanked Kassam and rushed out.

Just before their scheduled lunch, Mahfouz came back into the office, with a foul look on his face. He proceeded to yell at Kassam for the lack of care he took in putting together the document.

That's not at the Matthews standard! You're going to have to perform at a higher level if you want to work here! I trust you to help me prepare for a client meeting, and you give me this? You had better get your act together. I want a proper summary and updated plan by the time I get back from lunch with Sunjay!

Tired, frustrated and angry, with no family, friends or mentor to turn to, Kassam sat alone at his desk and contemplated his options. He knew how critical team work was to the position, and did not want to appear incapable in front of the team's manager. Kassam wondered if consulting was the right career for him. More important, he felt that not receiving an offer would be detriment to finding an alternative full-time position in the fall. All of his hard work seemed to be going to waste over what he felt were small and avoidable errors. He counted the days until his return to Canada and marked the date on his calendar. He wondered what he could do to salvage something positive during his remaining days in Abu Dhabi.

LEADERSHIP LTD: WHITE ELEPHANT TO WHEELWRIGHT

Prepared by Keith Grint

January/February 2005

Complaints about leaders and calls for more or better leadership occur on such a regular basis that one would be forgiven for assuming there was a time when good leaders were the norm. But a trawl through the leadership archives reveals no such golden past—there never was a time when heroic leaders were plentiful and solved all our problems. Sadly, this myth of past greatness has set up a model of leadership that few individuals, if any, can ever match. Today's candidates for greatness are shuffled in and out of the top jobs, never quite measuring up to the "great ones" that came before.

The traditional solution to this perceived weakness in contemporary leadership candidates is to demand better recruitment criteria that separate the "weak" from the "strong." However, this only reproduces the problem, rather than solving it. An alternative approach is to start from where we are, instead of where we would like to be. In other words, we need to accept that all leaders are necessarily flawed, and they are not the embodiments of perfection that we would like them to be.

The traditional approach resembles a "white elephant," defined as both a mythical beast that is itself a deity and an expensive, foolhardy endeavour. In ancient Thailand, the king gave a white elephant to unfavoured nobles because the animal's special dietary and religious requirements would ruin the men.

The white elephant approach to leadership is also reminiscent of Plato's philosophy. In answer to the question "Who should lead us?" Plato said, the wisest among us—the individual with the greatest knowledge, skill, power and resources of all kinds. Plato's leadership criteria have a lot in common with our own, current search for omniscient leaders who are charismatic and larger than

life, and who will displace all the bland, miserable failures whom we previously recruited to that same position, using precisely the same selection criteria.

An alternative approach is to work to inhibit and restrain the inherent weakness of leaders. Karl Popper provides a foundation for this approach: Just as we can only disprove rather than prove scientific theories, so we should adopt mechanisms that inhibit leaders rather than surrender ourselves to them. For Popper, democracy was an institutional mechanism for deselecting leaders, rather than a benefit in and of itself. While democratic systems within non-political organizations are a rare find, similar processes ought to be replicable elsewhere. Otherwise, subordinates who question their leader's direction or skill will continue to be replaced by those who are "more aligned with the current strategic thinking"—otherwise known as Yes People. In turn, such subordinates become transformed into Irresponsible Followers whose advice to their leader is often limited to Destructive Consent: They may know that their leader is wrong, but there are all kinds of reasons not to say as much; hence, they consent to the destruction of their own leader and possibly their own organization.

Popper's warnings about leaders, however, suggest that it is the responsibility of followers to remain as Constructive Dissenters. Followers should help to inhibit leaders' errors that might undermine the ability of the organization to achieve its goals. Constructive Dissenters attribute the assumptions of Socratic Ignorance to their leaders, rather than Platonic Knowledge. They know that nobody is omniscient, and they act accordingly.

Of course, for this to work, subordinates need to remain committed to the goals of the organization while retaining their spirit of independence from the whims of their leaders. It is this paradoxical combination of commitment and independence that provides the most fertile ground for Responsible Followers. Four possible ways of linking the issues of commitment and independence are reproduced below:

The emperor: The hierarchy probably contains the most typical form of relationship between leaders and followers. In a conventional hierarchy, a leader is deemed to be superior to his or her followers by dint of superior personal qualities of intelligence, vision, charisma and so on, and is therefore responsible for solving all the problems of the organization. Such imperial ambitions resonate with the label for this form of leader: the emperor. In turn, this arrangement generates followers who are only marginally committed to the organization's goals—often because these are reduced to the personal goals of the leader. The followers remain literally "irresponsible" because of the Destructive Consent associated with the absence of responsibility.

The cat herder is rooted in a similar level of disinterest in the community. But, combined with an increase in the level of independence from the leader, the consequence is a formal

"anarchy," without leadership and without the community that supporters of anarchism suggest would automatically flow from the absence of individual leaders. The result is a leader that resembles a herder of cats—an impossible task.

The white elephant generates community spirit in buckets, but only because the leader is deemed to be a deity, a divine leader whose disciples are compelled to obey through religious requirement. Followers' consent remains constructive if—and only if—the leader is indeed divine. Although many charismatics generate cults that would ostensibly sit within this category, the consent is destructive because the leader is in fact a false god, misleading rather than leading his or her disciples.

The wheelwright denotes an organization where the leaders recognize their own limitations, in the fashion of Socrates. Leadership is distributed according to the perceived requirements of space and time (a rowing squad in which the leadership switches between the cox, the captain, the stroke and the coach, depending on the situation; the English rugby team that won the World Cup in 2003 operated on the same basis, with a formal captain, plus "captains" of the forwards, the backs, the line out and the scrum). That recognition of the limits of any

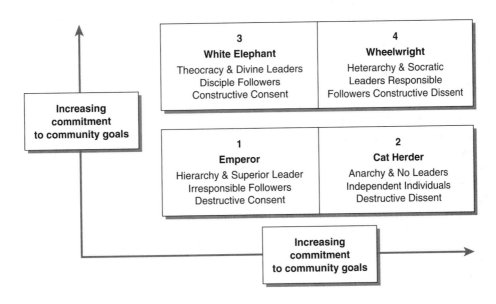

individual leader generates a requirement for Responsible Followers to compensate for these limits, and is best served through Constructive Dissent. Followers are willing to dissent from their leader if the latter is deemed to be acting against the interests of the community.

The recognition that Wheelwrights are reliant upon the knowledge of their subordinates also holds true for the relationship rooted in power. While Plato's White Elephants rest on Mount Olympus like mythical Greek gods, holding irresistible power and manipulating the lives of mortals at will, Popper's Wheelwrights should be resisted for precisely this reason. Yet it should also be self-evident that an individual can have virtually no control over anything or anybody—as an individual. Indeed, we have known for a long time that leaders spend most of their time talking, and not actually "doing" anything.

THE REAL POWER OF LEADERS

In effect, leaders might pretend to be omnipotent, to have the future of their organizations and its members in their hands, but this can only ever be a symbolic control, because leaders only get things done through others. In short, the power of leaders is a consequence of the actions of followers rather than a cause of it. Otherwise, no parents would ever be resisted by their children, no CEO would ever face a defeat by the board of directors, no general would suffer a mutiny, and no strikes would ever occur. That they do should lead us to conclude that no leader is omnipotent, and that the kind of leadership is a consequence of the kind of followership, rather than a cause of it.

Emperors might construct formal hierarchies in the hope that subordinates will execute their (im)perfect orders, but Cat Herders seldom even entertain that hope. Popper's Wheelwrights work through networks and relationships because that's where power is actually generated—it is essentially distributed like a wheel, not concentrated in an Emperor, not irresistibly embodied in a White Elephant, and not before a Cat Herder.

None of this is new: Helmuth von Moltke, chief of the Prussian General Staff from 1857–1888, understood Clausewitz's dictum that the local concentration of force was critical for military success. He also recognized that the nascent system of decentralized leadership already present in the Prussian army was crucial to achieving this. After all, a central commander in Berlin, or even a few kilometres behind the battle, had no way of understanding, let alone controlling, what was happening in each and every sector of the battle. The result was a system of leadership rooted in general directives, not specific orders; strategic aims, not operational requirements. This enabled a decentralized control that facilitated distributed leadership and the ability of local ground commanders to seize the initiative rather than await orders.

Perhaps an ancient Chinese story, retold by Phil Jackson, coach of the phenomenally successful Chicago Bulls basketball team, makes this point rather more emphatically. In the 3rd century BC, the Chinese emperor Liu Bang celebrated his consolidation of China with a banquet, where he sat surrounded by his nobles and military and political experts. Since Liu Bang was neither noble by birth nor an expert in military or political affairs, some of the guests asked one of the military experts, Chen Cen, why Liu Bang was the emperor. In a contemporary setting, the question would probably have been: "What added value does Liu Bang bring to the party?" Chen Cen's response was to ask the questioner a question in return: "What determines the strength of a wheel?" One guest suggested that the strength of the wheel was in its spokes, but Chen Cen countered that two sets of spokes of identical strength did not necessarily make wheels of identical strength. On the contrary, the strength was also affected by the spaces between the spokes, and determining the spaces was the true art of the wheelwright. Thus, while the spokes represent the collective resources necessary to an organization's success—and the resources that the leader lacks—the spaces represent the autonomy for followers to grow into leaders themselves.

In sum, holding together the diversity of talents necessary for organizational success is what distinguishes a successful leader from an unsuccessful one: Leaders don't need to be perfect, but they do have to recognize that their own limitations will ultimately doom them to failure unless they rely upon their subordinate leaders and followers to fill in the gaps. So find a good wheelwright and start the organizational wheel moving. In effect, leadership is the property and consequence of a community, rather than the property and consequence of an individual leader.

9

Transformational Leadership

Anyone can be a leader—no matter what their background is—as long as they have a clear vision of what the organization's goal should be and can lead or inspire people toward this goal. Business, communication, and interpersonal skills can all be learned, but at the end of the day, it is the drive that you possess that counts. You can learn all of the technical skills, but you have to have the will to succeed. You have to have the fire in your belly. Personal motivation is the key.

—Vincent H. C. Cheng[1]

Transformational leadership is an involved, complex process that binds leaders and followers together in the transformation or changing of followers, organizations, or even whole nations. It involves leaders interacting with followers with respect to their "emotions, values, ethics, standards, and long-term goals, and includes assessing followers' motives, satisfying their needs, and treating them as full human beings" (Northouse, 2007). While all theories of leadership involve influence, transformational leadership is about an extraordinary ability to influence that encourages followers to achieve something well above what was expected by themselves or their leaders.

Early researchers in the area of transformational leadership coined the term (Downton, 1973) and tried to integrate the responsibilities of leaders and followers (Burns, 1978). In particular, Burns (1978) described leaders as people who could understand the motives of followers and, therefore, be able to achieve the goals of followers and leaders. As I discussed in Chapter 1, he considered leadership different from power as leadership is a concept that cannot be separated from the needs of followers.

Burns (1978) differentiated between transactional and transformational leadership. He described transactional leadership as that which emphasizes exchanges between followers and leaders. This idea of exchange is easily seen at most levels in many different types of organizations.

He described transformational leadership as that process through which leaders engage with followers and develop a connection (one that did not previously exist) that increases the morals and motivation of the follower and the leader. Because of this process, leaders assist followers in achieving their potential to the fullest (Yukl, 2006).

Bass and colleagues (Bass, 1998; Bass & Riggio, 2006; Bass & Steidlmeier, 1999) differentiated between leadership that raised the morals of followers and that which transformed people, organizations, and nations in a negative manner. They called this pseudo-transformational leadership to describe leaders who are power hungry, have perverted moral values, and are exploitative. In particular, this form of leadership emphasizes the leader's self-interest in a manner that is self-aggrandizement and contrary to the interests of his or her followers (Northouse, 2007). Kenneth Lay and Jeff Skilling might be examples of this form of leadership in their roles as chair and CEO of Enron, respectively. Authentic transformational leaders put the interests of followers above their own interests and, in so doing, emphasize the collective good for leaders and followers (Howell & Avolio, 1992).

CHARISMATIC LEADERSHIP

"Charisma is a special quality of leaders whose purposes, powers, and extraordinary determination differentiate them from others" (Dubrin, 2007, p. 68). Weber (1947) emphasized the extraordinary nature of this personality trait but also argued that followers were important in that they confirmed that their leaders had charisma (Bryman, 1992; House, 1976). The influence exercised by charismatic leaders comes from their personal power, not their position power. Their personal qualities help their personal power to transcend the influence they have from position power (Daft, 2005).

House (1976) provided a theory of charismatic leadership that linked personality characteristics to leader behaviors and, through leader behaviors, effects on followers. Weber (1947) and House (1976) both argued that these effects would be more likely to happen when followers were in stressful situations because this is when followers want deliverance from their problems. A major revision to House's conceptualization has been offered by Shamir, House, and Arthur (1993). They argue that charismatic leadership transforms how followers view themselves and strives to tie each follower's identity to the organization's collective identity (Northouse, 2007). In other words, charismatic leadership is effective because each follower's sense of identity is linked to the identity of his or her organization.

A TRANSFORMATIONAL LEADERSHIP MODEL

Bass and his colleagues (Avolio, 1999; Bass, 1985, 1990; Bass & Avolio, 1993, 1994) refined and expanded the models suggested by Burns (1978) and House (1976). Bass (1985) added to Burns's model by focusing more on the needs of followers than on the needs of leaders, by focusing on situations where the outcomes could be negative, and by placing transformational and transactional leadership on a single continuum as opposed to considering them independent continua. He extended House's model by emphasizing the emotional components of charisma and by arguing that while charisma may be a necessary condition for transformational leadership, it is not a sufficient condition—more than charisma is needed.

Transformational leadership inspires subordinates to achieve more than expected because (a) it increases individuals' awareness regarding the significance of task outcomes, (b) it encourages subordinates to go beyond their own self-interest to the interests of others in their team and organization, and (c) it motivates subordinates to take care of needs that operate at a higher level (Bass, 1985; Yukl, 2006).

There are eight factors in the transformational and transactional leadership model. These are separated into three types of factors: transformational factors consisting of idealized influence, individualized consideration, inspirational motivation, and intellectual stimulation; transactional factors consisting of contingent reward, management by exception–active, and management by exception–passive; and one nontransformational/nontransactional factor, that being laissez-faire (Yukl, 2006).

Transformational Leadership Factors

This form of leadership is about improving each follower's performance and helping followers develop to their highest potential (Avolio, 1999; Bass & Avolio, 1990). In addition, transformational leaders move subordinates to work for the interests of others over and above their own interests and, in so doing, cause significant, positive changes to happen for the good of the team and organization (Dubrin, 2007; Kuhnert, 1994).

Idealized Influence or Charisma. Leaders with this factor are strong role models with whom followers want to identify and emulate. They generally exhibit very high moral and ethical standards of conduct and usually do the right thing when confronted with ethical and moral choices. Followers develop a deep respect for these leaders and generally have a high level of trust in them. These leaders give followers a shared vision and a strong sense of mission with which followers identify (Northouse, 2007).

Inspirational Motivation. Leaders with this factor share high expectations with followers and motivate them to share in the organization's vision with a high degree of commitment. These leaders encourage followers to achieve more in the interests of the group than they would if they tried to achieve their own self-interests. These leaders increase team spirit through coaching, encouraging, and supporting followers (Yukl, 2006).

Intellectual Stimulation. Leaders with this factor encourage subordinates to be innovative and creative. These leaders support followers as they challenge the deeply held beliefs and values of their leaders, their organizations, and themselves. This encourages followers to innovatively handle organizational problems (Yukl, 2006).

Individualized Consideration. Leaders with this factor are very supportive and take great care to listen to and understand their followers' needs. They appropriately coach and give advice to their followers and help them to achieve self-actualization. These leaders delegate to assist followers in developing through work-related challenges and care for employees in a way appropriate for each employee. If employees need nurturance, the leader will nurture; if employees need task structure, the leader will provide structure (Northouse, 2007).

Transformational leadership achieves different and more positive outcomes than transactional leadership. The latter achieves expected results, while the former achieves much more than expected. The reason is that under transformational leaders, followers are inspired to work for the good of the organization and suborn their own self-interests to those of the organization.

Transactional Leadership Factors

As suggested above, transactional leadership is different from transformational leadership in expected outcomes. The reason is that under transactional leaders, there is no individualization of followers' needs and no emphasis on followers' personal development—these leaders treat their followers as members of a homogeneous group. These leaders develop a relationship with their followers based on the exchange of something valuable to followers for the achievement of the leader's goals and the goals of the followers. These leaders are influential because their subordinates' interests are connected to the interests of each leader (Kuhnert, 1994; Kuhnert & Lewis, 1987).

Contingent Reward. This factor describes a process whereby leaders and followers exchange effort by followers for specific rewards from leaders. This process implies agreement between leaders and followers on what needs to be accomplished and what each person in the process will receive. This agreement is usually done prior to the exchange of effort and reward.

Management by Exception (MBE). This factor has two forms—active and passive. The former involves corrective criticism, while the latter involves negative feedback and negative reinforcement. Leaders who use MBE (active) closely monitor their subordinates to see if they are violating the rules or making mistakes. When rules are violated and/or mistakes made, these leaders take corrective action by discussing with their subordinates what they did wrong and how to do things right. Contrary to the MBE (active) way of leading, leaders who use MBE (passive) *do not closely monitor subordinates* but wait until problems occur and/or standards are violated. Based on their poor performance, these leaders give subordinates low evaluations without discussing their performance and how to improve. Both forms of MBE use a reinforcement pattern that is more negative than the more positive pattern used by leaders using contingent reward.

The Nonleadership Factor

As leaders move further from transformational leadership through transactional leadership, they come to laissez-faire leadership. Individuals in leadership positions who exercise this type of leadership actually abdicate their leadership responsibilities. This is absentee leadership (Northouse, 2007). These leaders try to not make decisions or to delay making decisions longer them they should, provide subordinates with little or no performance feedback, and ignore the needs of subordinates. These leaders have a "what will be, will be" or "hands-off, let-things-ride" approach with no effort to even exchange rewards for effort by subordinates. Leaders who do not communicate with their subordinates or have any plans for their organization exemplify this type of leadership.

OTHER PERSPECTIVES OF TRANSFORMATIONAL LEADERSHIP

Two other streams of research contribute to our comprehension of transformational leadership: These streams are research conducted by Bennis and Nanus (1985) and Kouzes and Posner (1987, 2002). Bennis and Nanus interviewed 90 leaders and, from these leaders' answers to several questions, developed strategies that enable organizations to be transformed.

Kouzes and Posner interviewed 1,300 middle- to senior-level leaders in private and public organizations. They asked each leader to tell about his or her "personal best" leader experiences. From the answers these leaders provided, Kouzes and Posner developed their version of a transformational leadership model.

The Bennis and Nanus (1985) Transformational Leadership Model

Bennis and Nanus (1985) asked questions such as the following: "What are your strengths and weaknesses? What past events most influenced your leadership approach? What were the critical points in your career?" (Northouse, 2007). The answers to these questions provided four strategies that transcend leaders or organizations in their usefulness for transforming organizations.

First, leaders need to have a clear, compelling, believable, and attractive *vision* of their organization's future. Second, they need to be *social architects* who shape the shared meanings maintained by individuals in organizations. These leaders set a direction that allows subordinates to follow new organizational values and share a new organizational identity. Third, leaders need to develop within followers a *trust* based on setting and consistently implementing a direction, even though there may be a high degree of uncertainty surrounding the vision. Fourth, leaders need to use *creative deployment of self through positive self-regard*. This means that leaders know their strengths and weaknesses and focus on their strengths, not their weaknesses. This creates feelings of confidence and positive expectations in their followers and builds a learning philosophy throughout their organizations.

The Kouzes and Posner (1987, 2002) Transformational Leadership Model

On the basis of their interviews with middle- to senior-level managers, Kouzes and Posner (1987, 2002) found five strategies through content analyzing the answers to their "personal best" leadership experiences questions.

First, leaders need to *model the way* by knowing their own voice and expressing it to their followers, peers, and superiors through verbal communication and their own behaviors. Second, leaders need to develop and *inspire a shared vision* that compels individuals to act or behave in accordance with the vision. These inspired and shared visions challenge followers, peers, and others to achieve something that goes beyond the status quo. Third, leaders need to *challenge the process*. This means a willingness to step out into unfamiliar areas, to experiment, to innovate, and to take risks to improve their organizations. These leaders take risks "one step at a time" and learn as they make mistakes.

Fourth, leaders need to *enable others to act*. They collaborate and develop trust with others; they treat others with respect and dignity; they willingly listen to others' viewpoints, even if they are different from the norm; they support others in their decisions; they emphasize teamwork and cooperation; and, finally, they enable others to give to their organizations because these others feel good about their leaders, their job, their organizations, and themselves. Fifth, leaders need to *encourage the heart*. This suggests that leaders should recognize the need inherent in people for support and recognition. This means praising people for work done well and celebrating to demonstrate appreciation when others do good work.

This model focuses on leader behaviors and is prescriptive. It describes what needs to be done to effectively lead others to embrace and willingly support organizational transformations. The model is not about people with special abilities. Kouzes and Posner (1987, 2002) argue that these five principles are available to all who willingly practice them as they lead others.

How Does the Transformational Leadership Approach Work?

This approach to leadership is a broad-based perspective that describes what leaders need to do to formulate and implement major organizational change (Daft, 2005). These transformational leaders pursue some or most of the following steps. First, they develop an organizational culture open to change by empowering subordinates to change, encouraging transparency in conversations related to change, and supporting them in trying innovative and different ways of achieving organizational goals. Second, they provide a strong example of moral values and ethical behavior that followers want to imitate because they have developed a trust and belief in these leaders and what they stand for.

Third, they help a vision to emerge that sets a direction for the organization. This vision transcends the various interests of individuals and different groups within the organization while clearly determining the organization's identity. Fourth, they become social architects who clarify the beliefs, values, and norms that are required to accomplish organizational change. Finally, they encourage people to work together, to build trust in their leaders and each other, and to rejoice when others accomplish goals related to the vision for change (Northouse, 2007).

Note

1. Vincent H. C. Cheng is the chairman of the Hong Kong and Shanghai Banking Corporation (HSBC) in Hong Kong. He made history when he was appointed as chairman because he was the first ethnic Chinese to hold this position since the establishment of HSBC in 1865.

References

Avolio, B. J. (1999). *Leadership in organizations* (6th ed.). Upper Saddle River, NJ: Pearson-Prentice Hall.

Bass, B. M. (1985). *Leadership and performance beyond expectations.* New York: Free Press.

Bass, B. M. (1990). From transactional to transformational leadership: Learning to share the vision, *Organizational Dynamics, 18,* 19–31.

Bass, B. M. (1998). The ethics of transformational leadership. In J. Ciulla (Ed.), *Ethics: The heart of leadership* (pp. 169–192). Westport, CT: Praeger.

Bass, B. M., & Avolio, B. J. (1990). The implications of transactional and transformational leadership for individual, team, and organizational development. *Research in Organizational Change and Development, 4,* 231–272.

Bass, B. M., & Avolio, B. J. (1993). Transformational leadership: A response to critiques. In M. M. Chemers & R. Ayman (Eds.), *Leadership theory and research: Perspectives and directions* (pp. 49–80). San Diego: Academic Press.

Bass, B. M., & Avolio, B. J. (1994). *Improving organizational effectiveness through transformational leadership.* Thousand Oaks, CA: Sage.

Bass, B. M., & Riggio, R. E. (2006). *Transformational leadership* (2nd ed.). Mahwah, NJ: Lawrence Erlbaum.

Bass, B. M., & Steidlmeier, P. (1999). Ethics, character, and authentic transformational leadership. *The Leadership Quarterly, 10,* 81–227.

Bennis, W. G., & Nanus, B. (1985). *Leaders: The strategies for taking charge.* New York: Harper & Row.

Burns, J. M. (1978). *Leadership.* New York: Harper & Row.

Bryman, A. (1992). *Charisma and leadership in organizations.* London: Sage.

Cheng, V. H. C. (2006, March 7). Passion from within (Part 1 of 8, Ivey Leadership Series). *South China Morning Post,* Business Section.

Daft, R. L. (2005). *The leadership experience* (3rd ed.). Mason, OH: Thomson, South-Western.

Downton, J. V. (1973). *Rebel leadership: Commitment and charisma in a revolutionary process.* New York: Free Press.

Dubrin, A. (2007). *Leadership: Research findings, practice, and skills.* New York: Houghton Mifflin.

House, R. J. (1976). A 1976 theory of charismatic leadership. In J. G. Hunt & L. L. Larson (Eds.), *Leadership: The cutting edge* (pp. 189–207). Carbondale: Southern Illinois University Press.

Howell, J. M., & Avolio, B. J. (1992). The ethics of charismatic leadership: Submission or liberation? *Academy of Management Executive, 6*(2), 43–54.

Kouzes, J. M., & Posner, B. Z. (1987). *The leadership challenge: How to get extraordinary things done in organizations.* San Francisco: Jossey-Bass.

Kouzes, J. M., & Posner, B. Z. (2002). *The leadership challenge* (3rd ed.). San Francisco: Jossey-Bass.

Kuhnert, K. W. (1994). Transforming leadership: Developing people through delegation. In B. M. Bass & B. J. Avolio (Eds.), *Improving organizational effectiveness through transformational leadership* (pp. 10–25). Thousand Oaks, CA: Sage.

Kuhnert, K. W., & Lewis, P. (1987). Transactional and transformational leadership: A constructive/developmental analysis. *Academy of Management Review, 12*(4), 648–657.

Northouse, P. G. (2007). *Leadership: Theory and practice* (4th ed.) Thousand Oaks, CA: Sage.

Shamir, B., House, R. J., & Arthur, M. B. (1993). The motivational effects of charismatic leadership: A self-concept based theory. *Organization Science, 4*(4), 577–594.

Weber, M. (1947). *The theory of social and economic organizations* (T. Parsons, Trans.). New York: Free Press.

Yukl, G. (2006). *Leadership in organizations* (6th ed.). Upper Saddle River, NJ: Pearson-Prentice Hall.

The Cases

Mayor Rudolph Giuliani, Knight of the British Empire

Rudolph Giuliani was the mayor of New York City during the events of September 11, 2001, and became world renowned for his leadership. Outlined is a description of his background, his first few years in office, the troubles he faced in his last year in office, and the sudden shift in his popularity post–September 11, 2001.

Red Cross Children's Home: Building Capabilities in Guyana (C)

An orphanage and foster care home for young children was located in Guyana. It was staffed by women who were paid a small monthly stipend. The facility was in a poor physical state, the 54-hour workweek was exhausting, and absenteeism was rampant. The new director tried to turn the facility around by repairing the building, improving the working conditions, and seeking staff input. On the country's national holiday, however, none of the staff reported for work. The director decided to implement new rules and a system of accountability. When the local public hospital staff went on strike, the director of the children's home was asked to run the hospital with its volunteers. After 8 weeks, she returned to the children's home to discover that it was thriving, despite her absence. She decided that her work was completed and returned to Canada. Nearly 2 years later, the former director visited the children's home and reflected on her management efforts.

The Reading

Drucker's Challenge: Communication and the Emotional Glass Ceiling

The supreme challenge for a leader is to change human behavior, a formidable, if not impossible, task. But the leader who is emotionally intelligent (who is aware of and comfortable with his or her own self) will have a far greater chance of changing the behavior of others than a leader who is not aware of himself or herself. Using theories from esteemed management thinker Peter Drucker, the author points out that leaders who inspire are those who have resolved their own identity crisis. But that is much easier said than done, and the daunting nature of the task is encapsulated in Drucker's Challenge, which states that every human being has an emotional glass ceiling, a natural "resistance to changing" identity. This ceiling is broken only when communication is so compelling that it overcomes that resistance. How leaders can accomplish this goal is the subject of this article.

Mayor Rudolph Giuliani, Knight of the British Empire[1]

*Prepared by Ken Mark under the supervision
of Professor Christina A. Cavanagh*

Version: (A) 2003-02-12

Introduction

Rudolph Giuliani, the mayor of New York City, was going to receive a honorary knighthood from Britain, announced the *National Post* on October 15, 2001. The award, reported in the British press on Saturday and confirmed by official sources on October 14, 2001, followed Giuliani's widely praised leadership in the wake of the September 11 terrorist attacks on New York that killed thousands of people and destroyed the twin towers of the World Trade Center. The award, "Knight of the British Empire," was the highest honor the Queen could bestow on a foreign citizen.

Britain's *Sunday Telegraph* newspaper quoted a Buckingham Palace official saying:

The Queen believes that Rudolph Giuliani was an inspiration to political leaders around the world, as well as to his city. She was grateful for his support for Britons bereaved by the tragedy and feels that this will also be a gesture of solidarity between America and Britain. Her regard for Mayor Giuliani is reflected in her desire to present the honour in person at Buckingham Palace.

RUDY GIULIANI, MAYOR OF NEW YORK CITY

Giuliani had spent his adult life searching for missions impossible enough to suit his extravagant sense of self. A child of Brooklyn who was raised in a family of fire fighters, cops and criminals, he chose the path of righteousness and turned his life into a war against evil as he defined it. As a U.S. attorney in New York during the 1980s, Giuliani was perhaps the most effective prosecutor in the country, locking up Mafia bosses, crooked politicians and Wall Street inside traders.

When Giuliani was elected mayor of New York City in 1993, more than a million New Yorkers were on welfare, violent crime and crack cocaine had ravaged whole neighborhoods, and taxes and unemployment were sky-high. It was fashionable to dismiss the place as ungovernable. Mayor Giuliani made good on his promise, doing away with New York's traditional politics of soft and ineffectual symbolism. The public was shocked and delighted to find that the streets were safer and cleaner. And the public did not care how he did it. If Giuliani picked fights big and small, if he purged government of those he deemed insufficiently loyal, so be it. "People didn't elect me to be a conciliator," Giuliani said.

He governed by hammering everyone else into submission, but in areas where that strategy was ineffective, such as the reform of the city schools, he failed to make improvements. Although by 1997 he had cut crime by two-thirds, his job-approval rating had declined to 32 percent. New York City was getting better, but the mayor seemed to be getting worse. Black minority leaders complained that his aggressive cops were practising racial profiling, stopping and frisking people because of their race. Giuliani launched campaigns against jaywalkers, street vendors, noisy car alarms, and a crusade against publicly funded art that offended his moral sensibilities. But the pose seemed hypocritical at best when Giuliani, whose wife had not been seen at City Hall in years, began courting another woman, Judi Nathan.

In typical New York fashion, he was a dichotomous mix of public sentiment and disdain. *Time* magazine reported, on May 28, 2001, that Giuliani was poised to leave his office on a wave of goodwill, with opportunities for future office. Despite announcing the end of his marriage to the press corps before he told his wife, he had garnered a level of public sympathy not usually available to adulterers, thought to be due to his unfortunate bout of prostate cancer overriding the simultaneous appearance of his new girlfriend.

As a public figure, his life was more than just an open book. It was a constant and daily analysis of every aspect of his colorful life. Perhaps not since the Princess of Wales had a public figure become so newsworthy even if only on a local scale. There were hundreds of stories written about him and just as many colorful headlines announcing the firing of his estranged wife's staff and rumors of him leaving the New York City mayor's mansion due to the ongoing divorce drama.

THE TRANSFORMATION BEGINS

Through circumstances both inexplicable and extraordinary, a controversial mayor who was set to leave office in 2002 took the reigns of a crisis on what became known as the twenty-first century's "Day of Infamy"—September 11, 2001. Countless newspapers published stories of Giuliani mobilizing the city's emergency services, running through smoke-filled basements wearing a gas mask and urging survivors to head north. As *Newsweek* reported, September 24, 2001:

> Giuliani, wearing a gas mask, was led running through a smoke-filled basement maze and out the other side of the Merrill Lynch building on Barclay Street, where the soot they're now calling "gray snow" was a foot deep. Stripping off the gas mask, Giuliani and a small group set off on foot for a mile hike up Church Street, urging the ghostly, ash-caked survivors to "Go north! Go north!" A distraught African American woman approached, and the mayor touched her face, telling her "It's going

to be OK." Farther up, a young rowdy got the mayoral "Shhhhhh!" he deserved. That set the tone. He was sensitive and tough and totally on top of everything. Even his press criticism was, for once, on target. And even his harshest critics offered nothing but sincere praise.

In recent years, Rudy Giuliani has been a cranky and not terribly effective mayor, too distracted by marital and health problems to work on the city's surging murder rate. But in this cataclysm, which he rightly called "the most difficult week in the history of New York," the city and the country have found that the most elusive of all democratic treasures—real leadership.[2]

A *Barron's* report, on September 24, 2001, was even more on point:

It is no secret that disaster has yielded a remarkable change in the public persona of Rudy Giuliani. Vanished is the mean mayor who badgered hot-dog vendors, threatened museums, sought to bludgeon dissent and indulged in an open and nasty row with his estranged wife. And in his place is, well, the essential Rudy: generous, sympathetic, indefatigable, levelheaded, unfailingly reassuring, a man for all crises.

The real Rudy, in other words. We say that because we've known Rudy for something close to a quarter of a century; indeed, for a spell between government jobs he represented Dow Jones, the parent company of Barron's, and, we can personally attest, was one hell of a lawyer. More to the point, he was also that rare combination of tough when he had to be and tender when he should have been, funny, bright and argumentative (natch), a great guy to knock off a bottle or two of vino with. Rudy has done a lot of silly things as mayor, but it doesn't surprise us one whit that when the unimaginable happened, he did everything right and with incomparable style.[3]

As his popularity soared, Giuliani played with thoughts of returning to serve a third term. *Time* magazine reported on October 8, 2001 that Giuliani had received 15 percent of the primary vote, all from write-in ballots. This result underlined Giuliani's undiminished popularity in the eyes of the public:

On a typical day last week, he found simple words to console the two children of Inspector Anthony Infante at St. Theresa's in the morning, then managed the ego of the Rev. Jesse Jackson as he took advantage of Giuliani's media entourage to nominate himself negotiator-in-chief. In the evening, Giuliani called on a stricken crowd at Temple Emanu-El to stand and applaud Neil Levin, the head of the Port Authority, who died helping his employees escape. Reverting to tireless cheerleader, he ended his day at Yankee Stadium watching Roger Clemens pitch against Tampa Bay.[4]

Bolstered by this show of support from the public, Giuliani summoned the three leading mayoral candidates to his office at Pier 92 and demanded to be allowed stay in office for another three months—or else he would enter the mayoral race against them and win. Al Sharpton, a supporter for Fernando Ferrer in the 2002 New York mayoral election, was unimpressed with this move. Unmoved by Giuliani's achievements, he referred to reports of Giuliani's heroics on September 11, 2001, arguing that on that day, "We would have come together (as a city) if Bozo was the mayor."

NOTES

1. This case has been written on the basis of published sources only. Consequently, the interpretation and perspectives presented in this case are not necessarily those of Rudolph Giuliani or any of his employees.

2. Jonathan Alter, "Grit, Guts and Rudy Giuliani," Newsweek, September 24, 2001.

3. Alan Abelson, "Up & Down Wall Street: Weighing Consequences," Barron's, September 24, 2001.

4. Margaret Carlson, "Patriotic Splurging," Time, October 15, 2001.

Red Cross Children's Home: Building Capabilities in Guyana (C)

*Prepared by Michelle Goffin and Alan Marr under
the supervision of Professor Joerg Dietz*

Version: (A) 2002-09-18

THE STAFF

In February 2002, Goffin returned to Guyana for the first time since June 2000. She was excited to see what had happened to her initiatives at the Guyana Red Cross Society's (GRSC) Children's Convalescent Home (CCH) and to visit with her former staff. She noted:

> I was surprised after I left the country that the people I missed the most were my staff. I suppose I didn't miss the kids individually because they were always leaving us. However, some of my employees were with me for the whole three years. We went through so much together, and ended up feeling more like a family than a boss and her employees.

Goffin also had many questions about her employees' motivations and why they did what they did. She commented:

> I never fully understood why these young women ever worked at the CCH before I was there. The former director and the matron demeaned and belittled them constantly. For many of them, the pay was lower than their cost of transportation for getting to work. The physical conditions were deplorable, and just watching the children was depressing. I learned, however, that several factors made the staff come to work regardless of the conditions. First, many of the Guyanese managers that I observed managed their employees through fear, dominance and punishment. One employee told me that she simply did not expect fair and respectful treatment at work. Second, these young women had literally nothing else to do. Work, as miserable

as it was, made them feel more important and useful. They did not have money, did not go to school and did not have any other distractions from total boredom and apathy. They looked for any escape—no matter how bad it seemed. This became obvious after the CCH had become a happy environment. At that time, the staff, more often than not, would show up on their days off to play with the children. Over half the girls would take children home on their days off or for overnight visits.

> The other thing to remember about my staff was the lack of formal training before I got there. Without formal training the girls would treat the children as they did at home. Children in Guyana were to be seen and not heard, and they were not treated with respect. There was not a lot of playfulness or stimulus and the word childcare didn't really exist in anybody's vocabulary. I said that I wanted happy children and took for granted that they knew what I meant by happy children. It seemed that their parents had not played with them, and the staff, in turn, did not understand how playing with and respecting a child fostered healthy behaviors and self-esteem.

> It took me almost three years to understand what had originally motivated the actions of my staff in the first few months. I could not figure out why some of the Guyanese women made choices without thinking about the future repercussions of these choices—choices that consistently made their lives harder and more unpleasant. An extreme example of these choices was the behavior of the mothers who had children placed in the CCH. Not only did they have children they could not care for, but also they would become pregnant again within months of leaving their children at the CCH. It didn't make sense to me: Why would they do things that were so obviously self-defeating?

I finally recognized many of these women felt that they had no control over their life and no hope for their future. They had been raised as poor people in a poor country with a sense of inevitable defeat. Often, their parents or others around them had lived the same desperate lives, providing (in my opinion) negative role models. Hopelessness, and a lack of positive role models made them live completely in the present with no thought of what might impact their future. While my staff were not this extreme, their lack of caring for the quality of their work and their neglect for the children before I got there seemed to be a result of their lack of positive role models or appreciation for life.

Management Style

Goffin was also able to gain some insight into the staff's initial opinion of her, and why her change efforts did not initially succeed. She said:

I learned that my staff had certain expectations of foreigners who came to help. Typically, foreigners would come in, announce dramatic changes that were determined without involving the staff, and then leave after a few months. My employees figured that they could wait me out, and no matter how much I tried to improve the situation at the CCH, it would return to its former state when I left. They didn't doubt that I worked very hard and supported them, but they didn't believe that I could last even four months. It took them a while to recognize that I was going to stick around for a long time, to understand that I tried very hard to be open and transparent with them, and that they could trust me.

When I started docking pay and firing people, I really got the employees' attention. They could no longer ignore me or try to wait me out, because if they did, they risked losing money or their jobs. The pay increases also worked but not in the way that you might expect. Sure, they enjoyed the pay increase, but the increased expectations that I placed on them with the pay raise were just as important. The fact that they felt needed was likely the single most important thing I could have done to improve their self-esteem.

I cannot say that there was a single incident that allowed the staff to start trusting me, but there were definitely a series of events that built this trust. Trust is a two-way street and I made the leap before they did, several times. I also went to bat for

them at the GRSC headquarters, and at the CCH, and no other previous directors ever did that.

Culture Shock

Goffin also noted that change was difficult to implement due to language and cultural issues:

In 1998, when I became the director of the CCH, I soon realized that my staff and I spoke two different languages—figuratively and literally. I could barely understand most of the girls because their accent was so thick. They spoke Creolese, which at best can be considered a very broken English dialect. By the same token, I really think that a majority of my staff did not understand me. My children certainly didn't. I assumed that they understood what it was that I tried to do. In hindsight, they had no idea. When you can't communicate properly, you can't expect anything to work properly.

Another language barrier was written communications. The large majority of my staff could read and write, if at all, only at a basic level. What I failed to understand for a long time was that there is a very distinct difference between the ability to read and the ability to comprehend what you are reading. These girls had learned by rote and most of them, while they could read something out loud could not follow actions or understand anything beyond a single sentence. For a long time, I thought my staff either ignored my written instructions to spite me or were just lazy. I knew they could read, as I would often have them read out to me written instructions that I left, but I never realized that they could not comprehend and follow my instructions. Once I understood this, I would verbally pass messages along with written instructions, or simplify my messages and double-check for understanding.

The communication gap went beyond language though. I remember one incident that made me realize just how different the culture and the basics of everyday life were. I had to have the staff toilets repaired because they would break down almost weekly. The toilet seats would break off and they would continually clog because the staff flushed newspapers, diapers, and other garbage down them. I would leave signs and told the girls not to flush anything down the toilets, but to no avail. Finally, one of the staff took me aside and explained to me that the majority of the girls did not know how to use a toilet because they did not have them at home. Away from the CCH, they used a hole in their backyards where they would squat. Because the holes were not connected to plumbing, they could drop anything down the hole without any repercussions. Not being told otherwise, they used the toilets at work like they used their holes at home. At work, the girls would stand on the toilet seats to squat—thus breaking them regularly—and they would throw debris into the toilet, not understanding that the debris would not fit down the plumbing. I had to give them all a lesson on how to use a toilet. After this, I did not assume anything and did not take anything for granted.

POSTSCRIPT

Finally, Goffin noted:

> The new director of the CCH could not maintain the CCH as I had left it, confirming my concerns about bringing in a Guyanese director. I was heartened, however, to discover that several of my staff had decided to take control of their lives. Two of them had been admitted into the nursing program at the public hospital. One of them was an instructor for the Red Cross Youth Program and the head caregiver had left in January 2002 to open her own daycare.

DRUCKER'S CHALLENGE: COMMUNICATION AND THE EMOTIONAL GLASS CEILING

Prepared by Paul Wieand

Building social capital is imperative for a leader today. But to meet that challenge, a leader must do nothing less than change human behaviour, a formidable, if not impossible, task.

During the past two decades, no psychological concept has had a greater influence on leadership development than emotional intelligence. On the other hand, no other concept in the past 20 years is so tied to ancient wisdom: 2,000 years ago Socrates declared that the attainment of self-knowledge is humanity's greatest challenge; Aristotle added that this challenge was about managing our emotional life with intelligence. This is at the heart of leadership development in today's complex, dynamic business environment.

This article will describe the relationship between psychological complexity, human potential and communications, and how they relate to emotional intelligence and, ultimately, build social capital.

THE IMPORTANCE OF PETER DRUCKER

The current popularity of emotional intelligence can be seen as a discontinuous extension of the psychological revolution during the '60s and early '70s, when the human potential movement, popularized by Abraham Maslow, dominated business literature.

In the history of business, Peter Drucker stands alone as a bridge between that earlier era and today. Drucker is both an intellectual and a pragmatist, and at 92, he has observed the major changes in both epochs and been a force of change himself. In his work he consistently points out that while the context of organizations and leadership has changed, human nature has not.

Drucker also understands the need for complexity. He says, "We can't learn anything by simplifying difficult issues. We have got to complexify them." Ultimately, Drucker values simplicity, but he realizes that "getting there" means making connections to the past and to related fields. His work is a tool for making these connections. Before discussing Drucker further, it is necessary to identify what is, and what is not, truly new about the concept of emotional intelligence.

EMOTIONAL INTELLIGENCE

By themselves, the discoveries in emotional intelligence are not new. What is new is that for the first time we can scientifically validate, through brain scanning technology, the fact that our emotions play a central role in moulding thinking and logic. New discoveries in neurophysiology have also advanced our understanding of the critical relationship between emotions and values.

With respect to human development, two significant issues have emerged which have an immediate impact on, and practical application for, leadership development. One is that the emotional component of the brain, the limbic system, is capable of hijacking both our intellect and our values. What is not new is that this hijacking occurs without our awareness. This is simply not good, for when the thinking and the processing of values are controlled by emotions outside of awareness, humans have a strong tendency to develop attitudes and behaviours that destroy trust and relationships. Values can be determined on an ad hoc basis, leading to inconsistency in relationships and decision-making.

A second significant fact is that the emotional system is changed neither easily nor quickly. Making significant changes to the limbic system usually requires approximately one year; making those changes enduring ones is highly dependent on social interaction. This scientific discovery sounded the death knell for the idea that significant, enduring change can take place quickly,

by insight alone, or in isolation, outside of a relationship. Reading about or studying emotional intelligence is as likely to have an impact on its development as reading a book on playing golf. Emotional intelligence is acquired through experience, in relationships.

IDENTITY AND THE EMOTIONAL GLASS CEILING

Thirty years before the discovery of emotional intelligence, Drucker noted that deep and fundamental human change takes place at the level of identity. He observed that such change is most likely to occur as a result of communication in the form of social interaction around shared values. To paraphrase Drucker, the most effective communication requires altering the emotions of others. The most powerful communication may be nothing more, but nothing less than, shared experience, without any logic whatever.

If Drucker is right, emotional intelligence becomes a powerful tool for moving an individual toward realizing his or her potential only when the change is grounded in his or her identity. In other words, increasing emotional intelligence requires altering identity. At the same time, science has shown us that identity's emotional component is the most difficult and complex to alter. Drucker observed that altering emotions is, for the most part, a communications challenge that succeeds only when it breaks through a person's "emotional glass ceiling." Psychologists often refer to this event as a boundary experience.

The basic psychological forces of "every" human being are strongly organized against achieving higher emotional intelligence.

DRUCKER'S CHALLENGE

In 1969, Drucker wrote one of his few theoretical and psychological papers and presented it to the Fellows of the International Academy of Management, in Tokyo. One of the most insightful statements in this paper brings together psychological complexity, human potential and communication in a way that can shed light on the practical application of emotional intelligence. We call this statement "Drucker's Challenge," and it states: "At its most powerful, communication brings about conversion, that is, a change of personality, values, beliefs, aspirations. But this is a rare existential event, and one against which the basic psychological forces of every human being are strongly organized."

Drucker's Challenge recognizes that every human being has an emotional glass ceiling, a natural resistance to changing identity. Moreover, this ceiling is broken only when communication is so compelling that it overcomes that resistance.

While this is not a revelation for a psychologist, it presents a unique and profound challenge for most executive coaches, the individuals who are usually responsible for significantly increasing another person's emotional intelligence. It is a challenge because the basic psychological forces of "every" human being are strongly organized against achieving higher emotional intelligence.

There is a myth about the difficulty and complexity of human development, and to understand it we must first understand the relationship between identity and emotional intelligence.

The Identity System: Reconceptualizing Emotional Intelligence

Emotional intelligence is an evolving concept, one that lacks even a standard definition. More important, it is not grounded in an integrated existential context. Understanding the existential component of Drucker's Challenge is a necessary first step in effectively using emotional intelligence as a vehicle for human development. An appreciation of the identity system can greatly facilitate that understanding.

The foundation of identity rests on three major, interrelated psychological and existential factors.

1. The relationship between emotional intelligence and identity. Much of the current literature would lead you to believe that emotional intelligence is an independent system that subsumes identity. In fact, it is the other way around. Identity is the whole system and emotional intelligence is just one component of that identity. When Drucker refers to a "rare existential event," he refers to what is required to alter the identity system. Any perceived change in emotional intelligence will be short lived if it is not accompanied by a change in identity. Moreover, this is not only a rare event. It is an existential one that alters personality, values, beliefs and aspirations.

2. The core components of the identity system. Here, again, psychology and neuroscience have come together and, in a way, reached a consensus. Identity is composed of three primary components that can be viewed as the brain's core subsystems—emotions, values and intellect. Neuroscience has revealed that all three subsystems are processed in different parts of the brain. What makes emotional intelligence such a powerful concept is that the emotions play a unique and powerful role in altering identity.

Leaders function at their best—when they are consistent in their values, actions and words, and therefore, trust is high—when they are aware of their emotions and maintain a balance between emotions, values and the intellect, and when values are the leading subsystem in identity. When emotions remain outside of awareness, they—along with intellect—tend to drive the identity system. Behaviours that are inconsistent because they are emotionally driven are often rationalized, and it becomes difficult to have values that remain consistent. The result is that words and action tend to be inconsistent and serve only the individual, who has little empathy or regard for others. The primary by-product is a decrease in open, honest communication, which over time, tends to lead to distrust.

When values are the driver—overriding both emotional reactivity and intellectual rationalization—words and actions become consistent, creating attitudes and behaviours that foster open, honest communication. This consistent communication in turn creates trusting relationships.

3. The dynamics of identity. If it is to adapt and survive, every system, including human identity, needs an "organizing principle." The task of the organizing principle is to help the system reach its potential. One way to isolate the most powerful organizing principle in human identity is to examine the characteristics of people who survive and adapt at the extreme boundaries of human existence. In other words, what are the personality traits that actually grow under the most adverse circumstances? The question is all the more interesting since Drucker's Challenge states that the basic psychological forces of every human being are strongly organized against change.

THE SURVIVOR PERSONALITY

Extensive research has been done on two groups of people who meet these criteria, wartime paratrooper survivors and concentration camp survivors. The research reveals that these "survivor personalities" have two characteristics in common, both of which involve very adaptive emotional capabilities.

First, values are the driver of the survivor personality. While the intellect can change at the speed of thought and emotions can change at the speed of impulse, values are relatively constant and tend to change at the speed of trust. Values, because they transcend the individual, can infuse an individual with the need for continuity and stability, both of which are necessary to survive under extreme conditions. Victor Frankl, the Viennese psychiatrist and concentration camp survivor, and author of *Man's Search for Meaning*, observed that extreme, tortuous conditions actually strengthened certain identities because the conditions forced people to clarify their values.

A second characteristic these survivors have in common is that they are able to use a broader range of emotions than other personality types. This makes them better able to adapt to complex social situations and enables them to develop social support systems. Al Seibert, a psychologist, former paratrooper and the originator of the "survivor personality," found that the survivor personality is predominantly paradoxical; it is made up of combinations of opposites. Survivor personalities have an ability to be humble and fierce, strong and vulnerable, logical and intuitive, self-confident and self-critical, serious and playful. They use their emotions in a way that makes them both strong and flexible, and they use them to get the best out of others. But to have core values that are consistent yet flexible requires that an individual have an extremely adaptive emotional capacity. Researchers often describe individuals with these capabilities as genuine and authentic.

AUTHENTICITY AND EXCEPTIONAL LEADERSHIP

The connection between authenticity and exceptional leadership is very significant. Authenticity can be viewed as the most advanced form of identity and the ideal condition for increasing the effectiveness of emotional intelligence. It is characterized by an emotional capacity that continuously strives to reach its potential in a way that maximizes trusting relationships. Increasing emotional intelligence is a complex challenge, one that involves breaking through one's own emotional glass ceiling as a necessary first step, and then using this capacity to help others do the same in a way that transcends individual differences.

The authentic person communicates trust by being genuine and non-defensive, and by allowing consistent access to his or her value system. Values, particularly empathy, are clearly developed and communicated, so that authentic people are true to both themselves and others.

Being true to humanity gives authenticity a transcendent quality by elevating dignity and respecting differences in people and cultures.

Increasing authenticity requires courage—the courage to be oneself—without sacrificing the values that bond leaders with others. When authenticity is viewed in this way, empathy becomes an act of courage and trust becomes the foundation of communication. Words are the least powerful form of communication, an artifact of the failed theory that logic and rational thought alone are the supreme elements of effective communication. Drucker is correct when he says that, "the whole person comes with the words." Identity, who you are, speaks louder than words.

Human potential, especially for leaders, cannot be a derivative of IQ alone. In an age in which IQ, in the form of intellectual capital, has become a commodity, EQ has become the driver of competitive advantage. Most organizations will continue to fail to build high-performance cultures if they do not require leaders at every level of the organization to have a high degree of emotional intelligence.

Authenticity and the Post-Modern Leader

Estimates suggest that 70–80 percent of major reorganizations and re-engineering efforts fail over the long term. The primary reason for failure is the destruction of social capital. From the beginning of the Industrial Revolution until the last few decades, physical capital was the most valued form of capital. As the technological revolution evolved and then exploded during the '80s and '90s, a premium was placed on intellectual capital. We did not realize that this shift occurred, to a great extent, at the expense of social capital, and until its demise came to be seen as a crisis.

Very few companies have historically factored in, in any meaningful way, the social and relational consequence of major organizational change. Most reorganizations, even today, emphasize changes in strategy, structure and cost reductions; they do not give equal weight to the human issues and the reorganization's negative impact on social capital. When most organizations make major changes, they fail to manage the emotional component intelligently, something that requires "authentic" leadership. In our experience, however, senior management in general, and CEOs in particular, too often resist breaking through their own emotional glass ceiling. They are not authentic leaders.

Many executives that were trained as leaders, especially during the '60s, have failed to realize that the demands of building social capital, the "people" component in the business world, have changed. Maximizing human potential has become one of the most important and enduring competitive advantages, primarily in its ability to retain and attract talent. Without doubt, today's post-technological revolution has changed the requirements for leadership.

Margaret Mead was perhaps the first anthropologist to see the new challenges facing organizations in the industrialized world. In her 1970 book, *Culture and Commitment*, she writes, "We are the first generation to develop our identity during a time when the forces of change are greater than the forces of non-change." Winston Churchill, a contemporary of Mead, wrote, "We are shaping the world faster than we can change ourselves, and we are applying to the present the habits of the past." The existential psychologist E. Van Deurzen-Smith states that, "The cultural component of identity has never before been so unstable, and this instability is anxiety-producing."

In today's world, leaders must not only be able to help people in the organization realize their human potential. They must also be able to lead during a time of instability, uncertainty and continuous change. To do so, leaders must be emotionally flexible, paradoxical, non-defensive, empathic and values-driven. In short, leaders must model authenticity.

Executive coach Peter Koestenbaum claims that leaders today must address "existential quandaries" similar to those found in Drucker's Challenge. He writes, "Nothing is more practical [today] than for people to deepen themselves. The more you understand the human condition, the more effective you are as a businessperson. Human depth makes business sense." His primary solution is to help executives become more authentic and to deepen their understanding of human nature.

Technical competence is still a necessity today, but leaders who can role model authenticity at every level of the organization are equally important. This new reality is reflected in the current emphasis by some of the world's most admired companies on developing the emotional intelligence of leaders. Leaders who are both technically competent and authentic have the greatest ability to attract and retain talent and build social capital. Building social capital begins with deepening the capacity of leaders to model authenticity. This requires changes at the level of identity. An authentic leader then has the emotional flexibility and strength to deal with the discontinuity of change, and to create a reasonable sense of stability during tremendous upheaval.

Once an organization understands that who a leader is as a person speaks more powerfully than what he or she says, the connection between identity and communications becomes clear. Authenticity and effective communications are mutually inclusive, and no organization in today's world runs well in the long run without effective communications.

Authentic leaders are able to manage their own emotional lives with intelligence and leverage, by evoking higher levels of emotional intelligence in others in the organization. Howard Gardner, a Harvard psychologist and author of *Leading Minds: An Anatomy of Leadership*, offers valuable insight into the human and emotional process that takes place when leaders can leverage their own development to help others develop those same qualities. At the risk of oversimplifying his work, Gardner views authentic leaders as those who have the ability to create a sense of group identity. They serve as role models with whom the group identifies and which it can emulate. With a sense of

trust at the core of these relationships, open, honest, candid and empathic communication leads to strong relationships that create stability amidst uncertainty and change. The leader's stability is experienced as a part of the group's stability. Gardner adds a powerful insight into the emotional process that enables this to take place: "It is the particular burden of the leader to help other individuals determine their personal, social and moral identities; more often than not, leaders inspire, in part, because of how they have resolved their own identity issues."

Breaking Through

When leaders find the courage and humility to identify and break through their own emotional glass ceiling, they can begin to do the same for others. As leaders develop a better understanding of the nature of human change and its connection to effective communication, they become more realistic about the time frame and the knowledge required for successful leadership development and cultural change. They recognize that the short-term cost of building social capital far outweighs its long-term benefits, both financial and human.

More often than not, leaders inspire, in part, because of how they have resolved their own identity issues.

Drucker's Challenge reflects the magnitude of the effort required to increase emotional intelligence in leaders. There are no quick or easy ways to accomplish these changes in identity. Change begins with a realistic appraisal of the self, a process of reflection that increases self-knowledge and leads to a humble acceptance of one's real limitations and recognition of one's strengths. When leaders develop a more accurate self-concept, they can utilize those around them to compensate for their natural limitations and leverage their strengths. Clarification of values is paramount so that leadership, work life, and values are more closely aligned, over time, creating stability and a passion and commitment to work.

However, one must realize that a deeper awareness of the complexity of emotions and how they influence decision making and reacting to others is critical.

These are the difficult and rewarding challenges of leadership development in today's complex and rapidly changing world. Leadership development, at its best, is human development. You simply cannot be a world-class leader if you are first of all, not a world-class person, and you cannot be a world-class person if you are not authentic. This is why authenticity is the most advanced form of emotional intelligence.

10

TEAM LEADERSHIP

A leader is someone who has a vision and is able to assemble a team to make that vision come true. A leader must also be very quick thinking and able to solve daily problems as they happen. Every business will experience bumps along the way and leadership will help to steer the company through them. Companies can prosper only if leaders clearly know where they want to take them, and if staff respect and believe in their leaders.

—Allan Zeman[1]

Being an effective leader means understanding the nature of leadership as it applies to leading teams. Some researchers (Zaccaro, Rittman, & Marks, 2001) suggest that leadership may be the most important element in whether teams succeed or fail. Contrary to previous leadership theories, where I focused on a leader and followers, in this chapter, the leadership function can be exercised by the leader in charge of the team, shared by members of the team, or both (Daft, 2005). Some researchers refer to this shared leadership model as team leadership capacity (Day, Gronn, & Salas, 2004).

THE TEAM LEADERSHIP MODEL

The team leadership model described in this chapter gives central importance to team leadership capacity in achieving team effectiveness. When the word *leadership* is used, it refers to team leadership capacity. The model itself offers a way of thinking for leaders sharing the team leadership role and should be used to determine team issues and problems as well as several alternatives to resolve these issues and problems while being cognizant of the team's resources and capabilities and the external challenges and opportunities. The word *external* could mean the organization external to the team and/or the environment external to the organization of which the team is a part. Figure 10.1 summarizes the team leadership model used in this chapter.

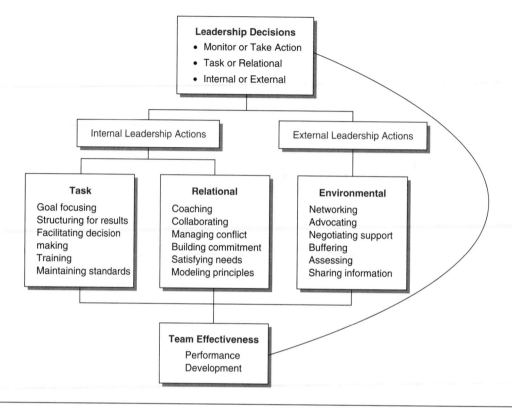

Figure 10.1   Hill's Model for Team Leadership

Source: From Northouse (2007). Copyright © 2007, Sage Publications, Inc. Reprinted with permission.

Effective leadership in teams assumes behavioral flexibility, problem-solving skills applicable to teams, and using discretion when determining if leader intervention is necessary. In the model in Figure 10.1, the first box suggests that leadership decisions affect team effectiveness directly and through internal and external actions that leaders can decide to take or not take.

Leadership Decisions

These decisions are as follows: (1) Should I continue to monitor, or do I need to take action? (2) If I need to take action, is it task or relationship focused or both? (3) If I need to take action, do I need to intervene inside the team or in the team's external environment (the organization or the environment external to the organization)?

Should I Continue Monitoring or Take Action Now? Knowing when to take action this is a very important leadership skill to develop. Intervening too soon could be more damaging to team effectiveness than waiting. However, waiting could sometimes cause more damage than intervening now. This skill develops through experience (similar to most leadership skills), and leaders need to understand that sometimes they will intervene too soon or too late, but sometimes they will get it right. The ability to get it right generally increases as leaders develop more experience in a team setting. The important thing to remember is to learn from intervening too soon or too late.

To determine when to intervene, leaders need information. This requires the ability to scan and monitor the internal team dynamics and the external environment in which the team operates. In addition, formal leaders need to let informal team leaders share this task and be open to informal team leaders coming to them with internal team problems and external environmental issues that could help or hinder the team (Barge, 1996; Fleishman et al., 1991; Kogler-Hill, 2007).

Should I Intervene to Take Care of Relational and/or Task Needs? If team leaders decide they need to intervene, then they must determine whether intervention is necessary to improve problems and issues related to task/structure and/or whether to help improve interpersonal relations among team members, including the team leaders. Effective team leadership focuses on both task and relational issues/problems as a high level of task productivity, combined with superior intrateam relationships, leads to best team performance and development. For virtual teams, it may be necessary to focus on intrateam relationships and then work on fixing issues/problems related to getting the job or task done (Kinlaw, 1998; Pauleen, 2004). Trying to fix task related problems first may exacerbate the intrateam relationship problems to such a degree that it may make fixing both types of problems much more difficult.

Should I Intervene Within the Team or External to the Team? This decision is also very important. In the previous paragraph, I suggested that team leaders need to focus on task and intrateam relations. It is also important for team leaders to know when and if they need to intervene between the team and its external environment—be it within the larger organization or even external to the organization. Effective team leaders are able to balance the internal and external demands placed on their teams and to know if and when to intervene in one or in both.

Leadership Actions

The leadership decisions described above affect team performance and development through the actions team leaders take internally and externally. These actions are listed in Figure 10.1 and are based on research that discusses team performance. It is important for team leaders to assess the problem and select the right action or set of actions. The model in Figure 10.1 is a good guide for inexperienced team leaders and will become more useful as leaders gain experience that allows them to internalize the model to the point where it becomes almost tacit—that is, leaders respond to situations without even thinking about the model.

The actions listed in the model are not all-inclusive, and astute team leaders will add others and maybe delete some as they gain leadership experience in a team environment. What is most important is developing the ability to discern when an intervention is needed and the appropriate action to take during the intervention.

Internal task leadership actions are used to improve a team's ability to get the job done. They include the following:

- Being focused on appropriate goals
- Having the right structure to achieve the team's goals

- Having a process that makes decision making easier
- Training team members through developmental/educational seminars
- Setting and maintaining appropriate standards for individual and team performance

Internal relational actions are those required to improve team members' interpersonal skills and intrateam relationships. They include the following:

- Coaching to improve interpersonal skills
- Encouraging collaboration among team members
- Managing conflict to allow intellectual conflict but not personal conflict
- Enhancing team commitment
- Satisfying the trust and support needs of team members
- Being fair and consistent in exercising principled behavior

External leadership actions are those required to keep the team protected from the external environment but, at the same time, to keep the team connected to the external environment. These include the following:

- Networking to form alliances and gain access to information
- Advocating for the team with those who affect its environment
- Negotiating with senior management for recognition, support, and resources
- Protecting team members from environmental diversions
- Examining external indicants of effectiveness (e.g., customer satisfaction surveys)
- Providing team members with appropriate external information

One practice that worked for me was having my boss's boss speak to my team at the start of a difficult project. This was much appreciated by the team members and showed the team members that senior management supported the project.

The critical point is that team member needs, in support of the goals agreed upon, are met either by the team leader or other team members. Of course, the better this is done, no matter by whom, the better will be team effectiveness (Kogler-Hill, 2007).

Team Effectiveness

Team effectiveness consists of two overarching dimensions: team performance and team development. Team performance refers to whether and how well team tasks were accomplished, and team development refers to how well the team was maintained in accomplishing the team's tasks. Several researchers have suggested criteria for assessing team effectiveness. In this casebook, we will use the Larson and LaFasto's (1989) criteria.

I will present these criteria in the form of questions to help in assessing team effectiveness. The better a team is assessed to be on these criteria, the better the team is performing:

- Does the team have specific, realizable, clearly articulated goals?
- Does the team have a results-oriented structure?
- Are team members capable?
- Is there unity with respect to commitment to the team's goals?
- Is there a collaborative climate among team members?
- Are there standards of excellence to guide the team?

- Is there external support and recognition for the team?
- Is team leadership effective?

These criteria are important in assessing team effectiveness. Effective team leaders will find formal and informal ways of examining themselves and their team against these criteria. Finally, team leaders must be willing to take action to correct weaknesses on any of these criteria (Kogler-Hill, 2007).

How Does the Team Leadership Model Work?

The model in this chapter is a mental map for helping team leaders constantly assess their team's effectiveness, as well as when and where the team's leaders need to intervene. If an intervention is needed, is it internal task, internal relational, or external? This constant analysis is necessary for continuous team improvement. Just as hockey general managers need to continuously assess their team coaches and players, whether winning or losing, team leaders in nonsports organizations need to continuously push for improvement and, for example, must know when it is appropriate to change the coach and/or team members. The team leadership model assists in this push for continuous improvement and helps determine weaknesses that might need an intervention on the part of a member of the team's shared leadership structure.

To continue with the sports analogy, it may be necessary for the team captain to hold a players-only meeting, it may be appropriate for the coach to change team strategy when playing different teams, and/or it might be appropriate for the general manager to change the coach and/or team players. Lou Lamoriello, the general manager of the New Jersey Devils National Hockey League team, changed his team's coach with eight games to play at the end of the 2000 season and ended up winning the Stanley Cup. Since he became the general manager in 1987, the Devils have won three Stanley Cups (the most by any general manager since 1987), and Lamoriello has done this with a different coach each time.

Note

1. Allan Zeman is Chairman of Lan Kwai Fong Holdings Ltd. in Hong Kong.

References

Barge, J. K. (1996). Leadership skills and the dialectic of leadership in group decision making. In R. Y. Hirokawa & M. S. Poole (Eds.), *Communication and group decision making* (2nd ed.), (pp. 301–342). Thousand Oaks, CA: Sage.

Daft, R. L. (2005). *The leadership experience* (3rd ed.). Mason, OH: Thomson, South-Western.

Day, D. V., Gronn, P., & Salas, E. (2004). Leadership capacity in teams. *The Leadership Quarterly, 15,* 857–880.

Fleishman, E. A., Mumford, M. D., Zaccaro, S. J., Levin, K. Y., Korotkin, A. L., & Hein, M. B. (1991). Taxonomic efforts in the description of leader behavior: A synthesis and functional interpretation. *The Leadership Quarterly, 2*(4), 245–287.

Kinlaw, D. C. (1998). *Superior teams: What they are and how to develop them.* Hampshire, UK: Grove.

Kogler Hill, S. E. (2007). Team leadership. In P. G. Northouse (Ed.), *Leadership: Theory and practice* (4th ed.), (pp. 207–236). Thousand Oaks, CA: Sage.

Larson, C. E., & LaFasto, F. M. J. (1989). *Teamwork: What must go right/what can go wrong.* Newbury Park, CA: Sage.

Northouse, P. G. (2007). *Leadership: Theory and practice* (4th ed.). Thousand Oaks, CA: Sage.

Pauleen, D. J. (2004). An inductively derived model of leader-initiated relationship building with virtual team members. *Journal of Management Information Systems, 20*(3), 227–256.

Zaccaro, S. J., Rittman, A. L., & Marks, M. A. (2001). Team leadership. *The Leadership Quarterly, 12,* 451–483.

Zeman, A. (2006, March 21). Mr. Lan Kwai Fong (Part 3 of 8, Ivey Leadership Series). *South China Morning Post,* Business Section.

The Cases

The 1996 Everest Tragedy

In May 1996, two world-renowned climbers, along with some of their clients and guides, perished on Mount Everest in the mountain's deadliest tragedy to date. The accounts of survivors imply that biased decision making contributed to the tragedy. Did a decision lead to this tragedy, or was it an unfortunate mountaineering accident? The case provides the opportunity to explore decision biases such as framing, escalation of commitment, anchoring, and overconfidence and the issues of leadership style, group behavior, team management, and communication.

Century Park Sheraton Singapore

A hotel's personnel director wonders if he should attempt to get even greater employee involvement after setting up Work Excellence Committees. The committees are composed of union and management representatives at sectional, departmental, and top management levels, and they provide the coordinating mechanism for the hotel's many productivity activities. The positive end result was progress in labor-management relations.

The Reading

Why Innovation Happens When Happy People Fight

If it's not if you win but how you play the game, then playing—or working—with humor and an upbeat positive attitude are surely the right way to play. Besides, these are the teams that usually win.

THE 1996 EVEREST TRAGEDY

Prepared by Khushwant Pittenger

Version: (A) 2004-03-30

In May 1996, two world renowned climbers, along with some of their clients and guides, perished on Mount Everest (Everest) in the mountain's deadliest tragedy to date. Were these deaths unfortunate mountaineering accidents, or did some poor decisions significantly contribute to the dangers leading to the deaths?

INTRODUCTION

According to Jon Krakauer, "attempting to climb Everest is an intrinsically irrational act—a triumph of desire over sensibility. Any person who would seriously consider it is almost by definition beyond the sway of reasoned argument."[1] Yet, Krakauer was one of 150 climbers and their 300 Sherpa guides and porters who were in the process of climbing Mount Everest on the weekend of May 10, 1996, the deadliest in the mountain's history.[2] That season, a record number of 98 climbers had reached the summit, yet 15 climbers had died on the mountain, 11 during the weekend of May 10.[3] The deaths might have been written off as a natural element of the sport and the increasing commercialization of the mountain, had it not involved two of the most experienced and famous climbers in the world and some of their clients of questionable abilities, who had paid approximately $70,000 each to set foot on top of the world. Krakauer was one of the fortunate clients who lived to tell the story. Other survivors have published their accounts as well.[4]

INTERNATIONAL COMPETITION AND THE MOUNTAIN WITHOUT MERCY

Rob Hall's expedition group, Adventure Consultants Guided Expedition (Adventure Consultants), had boasted in an American mountaineering journal 100 percent success in reaching the Mount Everest summit.[5] Hall perhaps had reason to be boastful: he had climbed Mount Everest four times. In six years, he had guided 39 clients to the summit, more than the total number of people who had reached the summit in the 20 years following Sir Edmund Hillary's first climb in May 1953.[6] On this particular weekend, the accomplished New Zealander, Rob Hall, was guiding a party of eight—his largest client team ever. He was, however, not the only famous climber with clients on the mountain. Scott Fischer of Seattle was the leader of Mountain Madness Guided Expedition (Mountain Madness). He also had eight clients, and his company was a direct competitor of Adventure Consultants Guided Expedition, Rob Hall's company. Actually, Hall had "stolen" Jon Krakauer from Fischer's expedition by offering *Outside* magazine, which sponsored Krakauer, a sweeter deal in exchange for publicity. In addition, 14 other expeditions from around the world, including a team sponsored by IMAX, were on the mountain in the spring 1996 with lofty ambition.[7] No doubt, this was a remarkable story in the making.

Everest's summit is the highest in the world with a height of 29,028 feet. It is a place where the difference between life and death may be only one small step. One wrong step can plunge a climber to death either in Nepal or China. More than 150 climbers have died on their way up to the summit or on their way down from the summit.[8] "Going to the summit is entirely optional but returning is mandatory."[9] A significant number of climbers die on their return from the summit when they run out of energy, oxygen, thinking ability and daylight. It is a place where the most minor ailments turn deadly, people lose their desire to eat and the thinking level becomes that of a child. Minor wounds do not heal, a dry cough cracks ribs, exposure of limbs to the elements can instantly make them as fragile as glass and the body starts to eat into its own muscle to stay alive. It is a place where severe storms develop quickly and unpredictably and often rob climbers of their most precious resource—sight. On the average, only one in seven climbers actually reaches the summit, and yet approximately 700 people have reached the summit.[10] One can only wonder why anyone would want to climb Mount Everest. The answer can be found in the British mountaineer George Mallory's classic 1924 response, "Because, it's there." George Mallory is speculated to have died on his way down from the summit.

Obviously, death on Mount Everest is neither unexpected nor unusual. Yet, the world was in shock when 11 climbers perished on the mountain during the weekend of May 10, 1996. Particularly newsworthy were the deaths of Rob Hall and Scott Fischer, two of the most experienced climbers in the world. Fischer had gained world-wide notoriety in 1994 for climbing Everest without supplemental oxygen and removing 5,000 pounds of trash from the mountain as part of the Sagarmatha Environmental Expedition.[11] The experience and the fame seemed to have made Fischer confident— perhaps overconfident. When asked about the risks, he was noted to tell a reporter shortly before the 1996 climb, "I believe 100 percent I am coming back. . . . My wife believes 100 percent I'm coming back."[12] Fischer cajoled Krakauer into joining his expedition to write an article for *Outside* magazine with statements like, "Hey, experience is overrated. It's not the altitude that is important, it's your attitude. You'll do fine. . . . These days, I'm telling you, we've built a yellow brick road to the summit."[13] Fischer made these claims even though he had never guided a commercial expedition to the summit, he suffered from a chronic clinical illness related to gastrointestinal parasites and he had reached the summit only after three previous unsuccessful attempts. Fischer died on his

return from the summit only 1,000 feet from the safety of Camp Four.

Fischer's attitude seemed to match that of his rival commercial operator, Rob Hall, of Adventure Consultants. Hall failed to guide any of his clients to the summit in 1995, and his co-founder, Gary Ball, had died of altitude sickness in the Himalayas in 1993. Yet, Hall's company placed ads in American mountaineering magazines claiming "100 percent Everest success."[14] Rob Hall's cockiness could be attributed to his ability to successfully guide 39 climbers of various abilities to the top in the past and his ability to save all his clients' lives under the worst of circumstances in 1995. His extraordinary success in the past seemed to have led him to believe, "there was little he couldn't handle on the mountain."[15] Yet, on May 10, 1996, Hall died on the mountain, along with two of his clients and one of his guides.

The Deadly Decisions

Were the deaths of Fischer, Hall and others just natural events due to unpredictable weather and bad luck, or did other human factors play a role? Ironically, it was Fischer who told a reporter before his 1996 expedition, "I am going to make all the right choices. When accidents happen, I think it's always human error. . . . You come up with lots of reasons, but ultimately it's human error."[16] One accomplished guide put it rather bluntly: "The events of May 10 were not an accident, nor an act of God. They were the end result of people who were making decisions about how and whether to proceed."[17] Coburn concluded that, "lives were lost as a result of compounding factors."[18] However, even he pre-qualified his statement, "But if one or two decisions, out of many hadn't been made . . . the outcome may have been very different."[19] Can we learn anything from this extreme case for climbing our own mountains in the workplace and guiding/leading others to the desired peaks of performance?

Everest is considered the toughest mountain to climb because the altitude makes even simple mountaineering exceptionally difficult. It took 101 years since its discovery before Hillary and Tenzing successfully reached the summit and returned alive to tell the story in May 1953. However, Mount Everest's popularity has been steadily increasing. With its popularity has come its commercialization. In 1996, 16 expeditions paid $70,000 a team plus an additional $10,000 a member if the expedition had more than seven members. Another 14 expeditions paid $15,000 a team to China to climb the mountain from the Tibetan side. There were five Web sites posting daily dispatches from the base camp, including NOVA's Web site, which received as many as 10,000 visits a day following the news of disaster on the mountain. A number of reporters were part of these expeditions to write stories for their respective publishers, including Jon Krakauer, who was to write about the commercialization of the mountain for *Outside* magazine. The IMAX team spent 5.5 million dollars to film the climb of Everest. Guided climbs to the summit became a subject of controversy world-wide. There were commercial expedition leaders who themselves had never climbed Everest. Krakauer quotes Rob Hall, "With so many incompetent people on the mountain, I think it is pretty unlikely that we will get through the season without something bad happening up high."[20] Obviously, Hall was not thinking of anything bad happening to him or his clients.

Hall had the reputation of being a very methodical, organized and caring person. He was known to pay close attention to all the details, including the health and well-being of team members and their equipment. He paid his staff well and even had a paid doctor on staff. He was the epitome of an efficient operator, and his clients felt they were with the best commercial guide on the mountain. No wonder he had little trouble finding clients for the last seven years, even if he charged $65,000 a person. He was well-respected by his guides, clients, Sherpas and even other teams. He mediated labor disputes, co-ordinated equipment sharing responsibilities among expeditions and even tried to establish agreements on summit climbing dates

to avoid crowding on the treacherous route at the top. He used the traditional five-week acclimatization process to get his clients accustomed to the thin air of the mountain, as the Everest summit has only one-third the oxygen of air at sea level. If climbers were dropped off on the summit from sea level, they would die within minutes from altitude-related illnesses. Like most other guides, Hall gathered his team in Nepal in March and took them to the base camp, at a height of 17,600 feet, in the beginning of April. From there, over a period of a month, the teams made grueling climbs back and forth to a series of four camps established higher up on the mountain at different heights in order to steadily acclimate their bodies to increasingly low levels of oxygen. Unlike many other commercial guides, Hall personally escorted his entire team up and down those climbs. He was always there when any of his clients suffered altitude illnesses or injuries related to mountaineering. His tactics might have been efficient, but they created and reinforced the clients' dependence on him.

Scott Fischer had a different strategy for his team. He had given his clients free rein in going up and down the mountain for acclimatization. His main guide, who was from Russia, had a different philosophy about client service. He did not share Fischer's western perspective of meeting all the needs of his clients. One of Fischer's clients said, "I doubted that I'll be able to count on him when it really mattered."[21] The Russian guide believed in the survival of the fittest, and many of these clients were not fit for such a demanding environment. Many of Hall's and Fischer's clients were well-to-do professionals with busy careers who had little time for real mountaineering on a regular basis. They used gym equipment to get ready for the climb. This is not to say they did not have any previous mountain climbing experience. Actually, their previous mountain successes might have given them a dangerous sense of confidence. Fischer personally had to do a lot of hurried and unscheduled running back and forth between the camps to help his clients in trouble. His team doctor was inexperienced and was there only on a voluntary basis. His most experienced Sherpa, who had climbed Everest three times previously without bottled oxygen, was poorly acclimatized for the summit this year and probably would not be there to support Fischer during the acclimatization of the team. Almost the entire month of April, the Sherpa was busy with the rescue of another Sherpa on the Mountain Madness team who had to be brought down to the base camp and later evacuated to Kathmandu before he died in late April. Fischer, an energetic and charismatic person by nature, was described as being "extremely wasted" during his ascent to the summit.

Mountain Madness, Scott Fischer's company, had been a fiscally marginal enterprise since its launch in 1984. In 1995, Fischer's income was $12,000. His family had been supported mostly by his wife's income as a pilot for Alaska Airlines. During the past year, however, she had been involved in a sexual harassment lawsuit with her employer. This was Fischer's chance to enter the Everest market and emulate Rob Hall. The competition between Fischer's Mountain Madness and Hall's Adventure Consultants for the high end of the market was obvious. Hall had failed to take any clients to the summit in 1995. If he failed again this year, Fischer was likely to become a formidable threat. He already had the strategic advantage of being based in the United States as more than 80 percent of clients came from the United States. The need for market advantage was the reason Rob Hall had significantly undercut Fischer in his negotiations with *Outside* magazine to get Jon Krakauer on his team. He bartered for magazine space, in exchange for $55,000. Scott Fischer's cash-strapped enterprise probably was unable to match the deal. Fischer, however, did manage to have Sandy Pittman, a New York socialite and freelance reporter for multiple national papers magazines and television networks, on his team.

The Pressure to Perform

The presence of reporters among the teams was a double-edged sword. They provided visibility and notoriety world-wide through their reporting, much of which was posted on the Internet on a daily basis. Their presence also, however, created pressure for performance among the team members and leaders. One of the clients on Rob Hall's team, Beck Weathers, commented on the presence of reporters among the teams, "I was concerned that it might drive people further than they wanted to go. And it might even for the guides . . . they want to get people on top of the mountain because . . . they're going to be written about, and they're going to be judged."[22] This thinking bears credence in light of Scott Fischer's comments, "If I can get Sandy to the summit, I'll bet she'll be on TV talk shows. Do you think she will include me in her fame and fanfare?"[23] The pressure to push beyond the limits was not all external. After investing a significant amount of money and an inordinate amount of time and effort in the ordeal, few would have had the courage to turn their back on the summit less than two vertical miles and a few days away. Jon Krakauer reported, "Doug was hell bent on joining the summit push even though . . . his strength seemed to be at a low ebb. 'I have put too much of myself into this mountain to quit now, without giving it everything I've got.'"[24] Doug Hansen was a 46-year-old postal worker from Seattle who had paid for this trip by working the night shift and doing construction work during the day. This was his second attempt to reach the summit with Rob Hall. In 1995, he had been turned around by Hall only 300 feet away from the summit because of their late arrival at the peak. Hansen died on his way down from the summit on May 10, 1996.

Hansen's sentiments were shared by others regardless of their physical condition. Beck Weathers, a pathologist from Dallas, insisted on attempting the summit on May 8 and 9, even though he was suffering from near blindness because of the impact of altitude on his vision correction eye surgery and his feet had been badly wounded by his brand new boots. He survived miraculously after he had been left for dead on the mountain and his family had been notified of his demise.

The expedition leaders were not blind to these dangers; they were very cognizant of them. Hall had expressed concerns about his clients' inability to turn around on their own by impressing upon them how important it was for them to unconditionally obey him and his guides on the mountain during their final push to the summit. On their ascent on May 6, Hall had drawn their attention to another climber whom they encountered on his way down. The climber had turned around at 2 p.m. only 300 feet and an hour away from the summit. Hall said, "To turn around *that* close to the summit . . . *that* showed incredibly good judgment . . . I am impressed—considerably more impressed, actually, than if he'd continued climbing and made the top."[25] In the month of April, Hall repeatedly underscored the importance of having a predetermined turn-around time, either 1 p.m. or 2 p.m., and abiding by it no matter how close people were to the top. Unfortunately, he did not establish a specific time on the day they reached the summit and did not himself abide by the generally understood principle of turning around no later than 2 p.m.

Who Is the Leader of the Team?

The need for clear instructions and leadership was critical for these teams. In comparison to traditional mountain climbing teams, these teams were large and consisted of strangers with a wide range of abilities and experiences. This created a worrisome situation because the actions of a single member—bad knots, improper hooking-up or a fall—can jeopardize the safety of the entire team. No wonder Jon Krakauer "hoped fervently that Hall had been careful to weed out clients of dubious ability." He was not reassured by the actions of his teammates who brought unbroken, new boots or were seen not knowing how to hook the crampons on their boots for climbing the glacier. Under such circumstances, no wonder Hall and Fischer felt the need to establish their authority over their team members, including the guides, as unquestionable. Immediately prior to the departure for the summit from the base camp, Hall was reported to say, "I will tolerate no dissension up there. . . . My word will be absolute law beyond appeal."[26] The clients were obedient because dependence upon leaders, guides, Sherpas and passivity had been encouraged from the beginning.[27] Even the guides knew their place in the pecking order. One guide in Fischer's team later reported, "I was definitely considered the third guide. . . . So I didn't always speak up."[28] There were pay differences. Senior guides were paid twice as much as the junior guides. In addition, they were the only ones with radios for two-way communication on the day of summit—an error that is considered to have contributed to the tragedy.

For the summit push, Hall had instructed the team to "climb in close proximity . . . within a hundred metres of each other." The result was that on May 10, the team performed at the level of the slowest member of the team on the final summit day when they were to climb from Camp Four to the summit and return in a grueling race against time and elements. The stronger members of the team had to stop and wait periodically for the slower members to catch up for periods that added up to more than four hours just on their way up. In addition, these waits created crowding on narrow, treacherous pathways and bottlenecks, which added at least another four hours of delays for the stronger members. The result was that no one reached the summit before 1 p.m. on May 10. In the absence of a clear directive from Fischer or Hall about when to turn around, the members kept ascending. Only six members from the two teams (three guides and three clients from the two teams) reached the top by 2 p.m. Doug Hansen and Rob Hall were the last ones to arrive at 4 p.m.—fully two hours behind the generally understood turn-around time of 2 p.m. Not every member of the team, however, succumbed to the temptation. Four members of Hall's team did turn around when they were caught in a bottleneck and realized they would not reach the top by 1 or even 2 p.m. Hall seemed disappointed in their decision, perhaps because Fischer's clients were continuing to push forward at that time and the weather still looked good.

Communication in Times of Crisis

The weather turned deadly very quickly in the evening during the teams' descent on May 10. The availability of only two radios on each team made communication scarce, chaotic and unreliable, right when precise communication and leadership mattered most to the members who were socialized to be passive and dependent. The 3,000-foot climb (less than one vertical mile) to the summit from Camp Four is a 16- to 18-hour race under the best of circumstances. These were not the best of circumstances. Even the strongest members had taken 14 hours on their way up because of wasted time waiting for the slower members and the bottlenecks. Most of the climbers on the two teams, as a result, were running out of canned oxygen. During their acclimatization, many were seen using oxygen at altitudes lower than where it is considered essential. Almost no one was coping well with wind chill factors near 100 degrees below zero, white-out conditions, little canned oxygen to support their bodies or brains, and no leaders for moral support or physical guidance. Only two clients, Krakauer and Adams, barely managed to make it down to Camp Four before the conditions became utterly hopeless. Twenty-seven individuals were lost on the mountain that night.[29] The climbers were disoriented and suffering from hallucinations and exhaustion. Some of them huddled only 200 feet away from Camp Four for hours waiting to be rescued. Through combined heroic acts of some Sherpas, guides and the clients in Camp Four, most of them eventually were brought down to the sparse safety of Camp Four. Scott Fischer and Rob Hall were not among them. They were caught in the storm too high up, and were beyond help. Scott Fischer's poor physical health and possible illness had slowed down his descent to a crawl. His image of invincibility led others to ignore his condition. They focused their energies on saving themselves or the other "weaker" climbers. Doug Hansen had used all he had to reach the summit. Rob Hall took 10 hours to negotiate a descent with Hansen that others would negotiate in a half-hour. Even when his friends at the lower levels urged him to save himself, Hall refused to abandon Hansen. Some have suggested that Hall was in an impossible situation. Leaving a live client on the mountain certain to die in order to save himself would have ruined his credibility as a guide. At the same time, staying with the client under deadly conditions was certainly going to kill him.[30] Also, Hansen told teammates Hall had called him a dozen times urging him to give the summit a second chance and offering him a reduced rate to come back. Neither Hansen nor Hall made it down. By the time the storm cleared, 11 climbers had died, and one died later from his injuries. Of the dead, four were from Adventure Consultants and three from Mountain Madness.

NOTES

1. Jon Krakauer, Into Thin Air: A Personal Account of the Mt. Everest Disaster, Anchor Books, New York, 1997, p. xvii.

2. J. Adler and R. Nordland, "High Risk," Newsweek, Society Section, May 27, 1996, p. 50.

3. B. Coburn, Everest: Mountain Without Mercy, National Geographic Society, New York, 1997.

4. A. Boukreev, and G.W. DeWalt, The Climb, St. Martin's Press, New York, 1997; D. Breashears, High Exposure: An Enduring Passion for Everest and Unforgiving Places, Simon & Schuster, New York, 1999; B. Weathers, Left for Dead: My Journey Home from Everest, Villard Books, New York, 2000.

5. J. Adler and R. Nordland, "High Risk," Newsweek, Society Section, May 27, 1996, p. 50.

6. B. Coburn, Everest: Mountain Without Mercy, National Geographic Society, New York, 1997.

7. Jon Krakauer, Into Thin Air: A Personal Account of the Mt. Everest Disaster, Anchor Books, New York, 1997.

8. B. Coburn, Everest: Mountain Without Mercy, National Geographic Society, New York, 1997.

9. B. Weathers, Left for Dead: My Journey Home from Everest, Villard Books, New York, 2000.

10. B. Coburn, Everest: Mountain Without Mercy, National Geographic Society, New York, 1997.

11. Jon Krakauer, Into Thin Air: A Personal Account of the Mt. Everest Disaster, Anchor Books, New York, 1997.

12. Ibid

13. Ibid, p. 263.

14. J. Adler, and R. Nordland, "High Risk," Newsweek, Society Section, May 27, 1996, p. 50.

15. Jon Krakauer, *Into Thin Air: A Personal Account of the Mt. Everest Disaster*, Anchor Books, New York 1997, p. 84.

16. Ibid, p. 84.

17. B. Coburn, *Everest: Mountain Without Mercy*, National Geographic Society, New York, 1997, p 192.

18. Ibid, p. 193.

19. Ibid, p. 193.

20. Jon Krakauer, *Into Thin Air: A Personal Account of the Mt. Everest Disaster*, Anchor Books, New York 1997, p. 182.

21. Ibid, p. 193.

22. Ibid, pp. 177-178.

23. Ibid, p. 221.

24. Ibid, p. 191.

25. Ibid, p. 190.

26. Ibid, p. 216.

27. Ibid.

28. Ibid, p. 260.

29. G. Rummler, "Everest Strikes Back", *Milwaukee Journal Sentinel*, Lifestyle Section, Sunday, June 23, 1996, p. 1.

30. B. Coburn, *Everest: Mountain Without Mercy*, National Geographic Society, New York, 1997.

CENTURY PARK SHERATON SINGAPORE

Prepared by Sing Chee Ling under the supervision of Professor Joseph J. DiStefano

Version: (A) 2003-04-28

Chua Soon Lye, Personnel Director at Singapore's Century Park Sheraton, had played a central role in the hotel's program to build greater employee commitment. Though Mr. Chua was pleased with the smooth implementation of the work excellence committees in the hotel, he wondered if the base of employee involvement was firm enough to move to even greater employee responsibility in decision making in the future. Over drinks in the hotel's lounge, Mr. Chua elaborated upon his concerns.

> The work excellence committee was formed within this organization to achieve the goals of increased organizational effectiveness and improved employee welfare through a process of union-management joint consultation on work-related issues. While we have made significant progress in reaching our goals through improved labour-management relations, we have yet to reach our final objective of an equal sharing of the responsibility in decision making in all aspects of the hotel's operations. Could these aspirations be too demanding of our people? Had the pace of our program for employee participation been too rapid?
>
> On the other hand, I believe that the success of activities like work excellence committees is built upon a momentum. Thus, I feel the need to press forward to the next level. This "dilemma" is a happy one in fact, because it arose as a consequence of our success.

THE HOTEL

Century Park Sheraton Singapore (CPSS), a 464-room, luxury hotel, decorated in classical English 19th century style, was officially opened in January 1979. It is a 14-storey hotel situated on Nassim Hill, off Tanglin Road, on one end of the Orchard Road tourist belt. It was the first ANA-managed hotel[1] in Singapore.

The hotel, situated on 11,500 square metres, offers the following facilities: Hubertus Grill, a western-style grill room; Unkai, a Japanese restaurant; a 250-seat coffee house and café terrace; a cocktail lounge; discotheque; a 180-seat function room; and a swimming pool.

Under the general manager and the resident manager are the departments of sales, purchasing, front office, accounts, food and beverage, personnel, engineering, housekeeping and security. (See Exhibit 1.) The maximum number of

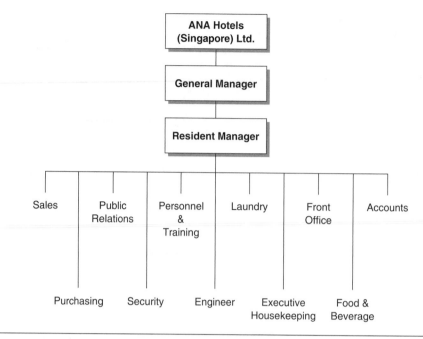

Exhibit 1   Simplified Organization Chart Showing Reporting Relationships

employees had been around 640, but by August 1985 the level had dropped to 504.

The Chinese constituted the majority in the hotel's workforce; Indians, Malays, and Eurasians made up the balance. A small number of expatriate personnel were also employed for their expertise. The General Manager and some chefs were German, while the Resident Manager, the Director of Food and Beverage, and the Executive Chef were Swiss.

The CPSS, like the other hotels within the industry, provides on-the-job training in various functions. This was because the Singapore population had little experience in the hotel industry. While it was quite common for management personnel to have university or other professional qualifications, rank-and-file personnel were likely to have some secondary education or hold trade certificates. Because the education system offered instruction in the four official languages of the country, some hotel employees were more literate in Chinese, Malay or Tamil than in English. English, however, is the language used for official communication.

A great number of CPSS's employees subscribe to the Food and Drinks Allied Workers' Union, the union for the hotel industry. This union is affiliated with to the national federation of unions. But the union's role has to be seen in the context of a country which prides itself on favourable labour-management relations and boasts a record of not having had a strike since 1977.

EARLY EFFORTS

Mr. Chua, who had worked in the personnel function in both the shipbuilding and aircraft servicing industries, had joined the CPSS Hotel in 1979. Over the years, he witnessed the change in labour-management relations. Mr. Chua traced the sequence of events.

> We got off to a slow start. Before 1981, the labour-management characteristics in the hotel were more typical of traditional confrontational attitudes between labour and management. This impeded efforts at bringing about change to raise productivity.

We wanted to increase productivity through restructuring jobs. This led to the formation of a nine-person joint union and management committee called the Job Enlargement and Enrichment Committee in May 1982. The original implementation of these changes was to have been around October of that year. Job restructuring, in effect, would mean a recombination of duties, or more shifts, e.g., the pool attendant, groundsmen and housemen, originally three jobs, were to become one. Cashiers were expected to manage the till at more than one location in the hotel. Despite reassurances that training would be provided and that there were to be no retrenchments, there was more talk than progress.

I am proud of the fact that we began on the productivity effort through human resources management even before the government launched its productivity movement. This is a nationally promoted effort to increase productivity consciousness in the Singapore workforce. By 1982, we had started both the quality circle and the work excellence programs. But I felt that we were making progress only after the labour contract was negotiated, and new union leaders were elected in that year. In retrospect, 1982 was a turning point.

THE WORK EXCELLENCE PROGRAM

The concept underlying the work excellence committee was first introduced to Singapore in 1981. It was believed that improved labour-management cooperation would result from regular consultation on work-related issues by committees comprised of labour and management representatives. This concept was the theme of the May Day seminar organized by the National Trade Union Congress (NTUC). The Shangri-la Hotel, which was the first hotel to embark on this program of labour-management cooperation, was heralded as the model for work excellence committees in the hotel industry. It was also at this seminar that the acronym WE committee (WE standing as much for "us" as for work excellence) was established.

The adoption of WE committees in CPSS took place through a series of steps. Separate meetings at top management, departmental, and union levels were held through the months of July and August 1982 to discuss the feasibility of WE committees. When union and management met jointly, the meetings were conducted with the aid of an official from the National Productivity Board (NPB).[2] The consultant from NPB emphasized that his role would lessen progressively as improvements in labour-management cooperation were made. It was only after the preliminary groundwork was laid that a joint formal application was extended to the NPB to organize WE committees in the hotel.

An important part of installing WE activities was the training session organized for 27 persons from both union and management over a period of three days. Activities of the program included games in small group sessions to learn different methods of conflict resolution. One session resulted in both management and union recording two unflattering lists outlining their perceptions of each other. Union members perceived the management to be, among other things, sarcastic, high in flattery, autocratic, and making empty promises. On the other hand, management perceived the union leaders to be revengeful, insincere, and giving lip service. The discrepancy between the desired and actual state of affairs was the starting point for future improvements.

Monthly WE meetings were to follow. Minutes for these meetings were recorded. The early meetings were concerned with the setting up of steering WE committees, and the drawing up of a "code of conduct." (See Exhibits 2 and 3.) Training of key personnel was completed by April 1983. Those leading in forming sectional WE committees were the security, accounting, housekeeping and laundry departments. Other departments seemed to Mr. Chua to be dragging their feet.

SOME RESULTS

By July 1983, the stalemated job enlargement exercise was brought under the umbrella of the WE program. Revised job descriptions, made

J. CONSTITUTION FOR WORK EXCELLENCE COMMITTEES

   1. Work Excellence Committee

      1.1 It is a committee within an organisation, made up of management and employee representatives for joint consultation. Joint consultation, in its simplest form, is an arrangement to enable management and employee representatives to come together to discuss work-related issues to improve the overall effectiveness of the organisation as well as the well-being of the workforce at the enterprise level.

   2. Purpose of the Work Excellence Committee

      2.1 The primary purpose of WE Committee is to build a harmonious labour-management climate within an organisation to achieve the organisational goals.

   3. Objectives of the Work Excellence Committee

      3.1 To create a congenial climate throughout the hotel.
      3.2 To encourage labour and management to discuss and co-operate on work-related issues.
      3.3 To foster trust among all employees.
      3.4 To instill a sense of pride, dedication and commitment to work.
      3.5 To promote mutual respect, understanding and team spirit.
      3.6 To involve employees in planning, problem solving and information sharing.
      3.7 To promote teamwork and advise on small group activities, e.g., QC Circles in the hotel.
      3.8 To provide employees with social, cultural and recreational programs.

   4. Functions of Steering Committee

      4.1 To advise other WE Committees and sub-committees.
      4.2 To give guidelines and direction for other WE Committees to operate and function.
      4.3 To have consultation between management and union employee representatives at the highest level.
      4.4 To initiate the setting up of WE Committees in the whole organisation and co-ordinate their activities.
      4.5 To monitor the progress of WE Committees and sub-committees.
      4.6 To deal with whatever problems that may arise affecting the whole organisation.
      4.7 To initiate programmes that affect the whole organisation.
      4.8 To monitor the industrial relations climate in the whole organisation.
      4.9 To explain to employees the rationale of policies and activities to the companies.

   5. Composition of WE Steering Committee

      5.1 The committee is comprised of representatives from the management and labour, preferably with equal number from each side.
      5.2 The management representatives are appointed by the General Manager while the Union representatives are appointed by the Union.
      5.3 The Chairman shall be selected by the WEC. The Chairman will appoint a designate who will chair in his absence.
      5.4 The term of office of the Committee members shall be three full years.

   6. Secretariat

   7. Meetings

   8. Duties and Responsibilities

   9. Attendance by other persons

   10. Code of Behaviour

   11. Publicity

   12. Amendments to Constitution

Exhibit 2   An Abridged Version of the Constitution for Work Excellence Committees

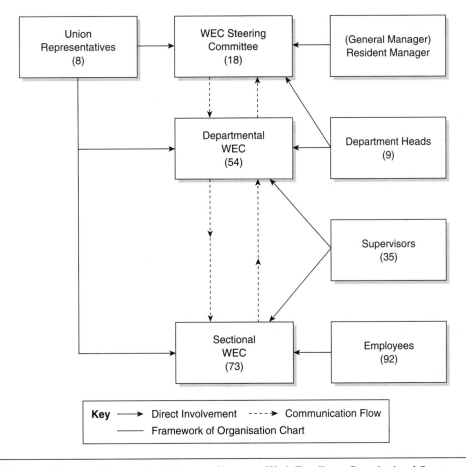

Exhibit 3   Diagram 1: Century Park Sheraton Singapore Work Excellence Organisational Structure

possible by employees taking on a wider range of job duties, were submitted by departments.

Progress was also seen in the widening range of topics discussed by the WE steering committee. By October 1983, the meeting agenda had moved beyond the problem of setting up WE committees to issues including incentive schemes, operational hours of the café, job training, time cards for middle management, salary adjustments and second-tier wage adjustments (a merit scheme operating in Singapore). Because the NPB consultant felt that the meetings were proceeding well, he no longer attended meetings.

CPSS's early efforts did not go unrecognized—it was one of the six recipients of the first Productivity Award given by NPB. (See Exhibit 4

for criteria.) This recognition was to foreshadow other improvements at the hotel.

Dahak Ibrahim, chairman of the branch union at the hotel, noted at a national work excellence convention in mid-1984:

Improvements in efficiency have not been confined to the hotel operation. Labour-management cooperation has also resulted in improved benefit and welfare schemes. Less time is spent on grievances—we used to have monthly grievance meetings. I have found our colleagues also more open and accepting of changes.

At this same convention, it was reported that there were seven department WE committees,

The National Productivity Council will once again be considering nominations for the National Productivity Awards this year. The Awards, introduced in 1983, are presented annually to organisations in recognition of their good productivity practices.

The following guidelines are used in the selection of companies for the Award:

- A company's training tradition or efforts to train and develop staff.
- The state of labour-management relations in the company and the existence of cooperation mechanisms such as Work Excellence Committees.
- A company's management philosophy which draws out the best in their people and includes respect for individual excellence within the context of teamwork as well as respect for work discipline.
- The efforts put in by the company to enhance employees' loyalty and identification with the company through various measures, e.g., company welfarism, promotion programmes such as 3Ps, in-house newsletters, etc.
- Worker participation activities of the company, e.g., small group activities like QC Circles.
- Good occupational safety and health record and work environment.
- A company's efforts in quality and in mechanisation, automation, computerisation and other improvements in technology.

Organisations interested in the Awards can write to or call Miss Judith Choo of the National Productivity Awards Secretariat, National Productivity Board, 55 Cuppage Road #08-16, Cuppage Centre, Singapore 0922, tel. 7345534 ext. 293.

Published by NPB
Singapore Productivity News
June 1985

Exhibit 4   National Productivity Awards 1985

21 sectional committees and 197 WE committee members in the Sheraton.

Employee numbers had been decreasing even in years when the occupancy rates were increasing. In August 1985, the staff complement was down to 504 persons. Despite Mr. Chua's attempts to maintain a low profile on CPSS's productivity efforts, there was pressure to share their experiences through talks and conferences. As the word of their successes spread, CPSS also increasingly received visitors anxious to learn about the productivity movement.

QUALITY CIRCLE ACTIVITIES

The QC program was started in February 1982, at the suggestion of Mr. Zimmer, then Sheraton's Resident Manager, upon his return from a seminar on quality circles organized by the Singapore National Employers Federation. Workshops were organized for QC facilitators and leaders. By August, Sheraton's pilot circle, "The Searcher," was in operation in the Laundry department. After two months of activities, it made its first presentation to management as part of the activities for "Productivity Month." After this presentation, enthusiasm was high. Other circles formed were "The Adventurer" in Security, "Homemaker" in Housekeeping and "Improve the QCC" in the kitchen. However, by July 1983, Mr. Chua noted that attendance at QC steering committee meetings was falling off.

By then the WE program was also in operation. CPSS also participated in other activities to support government-promoted programs. Among them was the "Use Your Hand Exercise" (see Exhibit 5), organized on a fortnightly basis from November 1983. Sheraton also took an active part in the "Courtesy Month," the "Productivity Month," and the "Save Water Campaign."

There were other activities more specific to the hotel—the "Ken Fixit" program (a preventative maintenance program specifically for guest rooms), the Preventative Maintenance Program (with a more general focus on all equipment) and the Training and Rewriting Procedures Program (aimed at simplifying procedures and reducing the volume of paper work).

Interest in QC activities continued to fall. One QC leaders' meeting which was to have been held had to be cancelled due to poor response. The problem of low enthusiasm with QCs was discussed at WE meetings and the decision to continue activating interest in QCs was adopted. More QC leaders were trained in April 1984, and a QC workshop was organized to keep the QC effort alive.

Meanwhile, Mr. Alex Kuenzli, a Swiss hotelier whose last posting was in Mauritius, had succeeded Mr. Zimmer as the Resident Manager. He commented in hindsight about QC activities.

It would have been better if we had the organization structure first to support small group participation activities like quality circles. We started the QCs first, which was then followed by the work excellence committees. If we had proceeded the other way around, it is likely that we could have sustained interest in QCs longer.

Helping Hands

Recently, a burst steam pipe in the laundry department created a mini crisis because it started to flood the basement. The situation called for quick, decisive action and flood fighters.

Laundry Manager, Richard Kooi, receiving helping hands and brooms from colleagues when all pulled up sleeves and cuffs to help curb the flood.

The water was bailed out in a little over 30 minutes. □

Personnel Director Chua Soon Lye; Laundry Manager, Richard Kooi and Front Office Manager, Sam Tay up to their knees in work.

Exhibit 5   Helping Hands

COME CONCERNS

The Changing Hotel Industry

While the late 1970s and the early 1980s saw an increasing number of tourist arrivals and optimistic predictions which led to the overbuilding of new hotels, the tide was beginning to turn by 1984. A sense that the growth momentum was coming to a halt and that harder times were ahead was already prompting the management at CPSS, more experienced than other newcomers in the industry, to take steps to plan for the change. By mid-1985, their fears were becoming fact. Room occupancy at CPSS fell to an all-time low of 63 percent, a drop from 80 percent in 1984, and 75 percent in 1983, and even poorer occupancy rates were forecast for the industry.

In spite of the current uncertain economic situation and competition (which Mr. Kuenzli described as "like a jellyfish"), he had confidence that CPSS had a better chance than many others of surviving the recession. His hotel had adopted the policy of reducing manpower by attrition and of increasing productivity through the programs managed by Mr. Chua.

The improved labour-management relations had enabled the hotel to function with less staff, but with no apparent drop in performance. Mr. Kuenzli noted with pride that the staff managed the increased occupancy in 1984 well, even though there were 100 fewer people to do more work. Mr. Kuenzli explained:

> The WE committees are now part of the solution to the current situation. We are hoping that the improved understanding of the employees achieved through our efforts in the last few years will help us meet the competition in further lowering costs and providing better service.
>
> No, I am not impatient at what appears to be long discussions over issues in these committees. I can sit through them as well as anybody else.
>
> The difference I see between Singapore and German labour-management cooperative efforts is probably one of degree of commitment. Issues discussed here in Singapore tend not to be as petty. And there is just that much more enthusiasm.

We also try to keep employees informed about the hotel's economic performance. This is done through briefing sessions which I personally conduct, and which are specially scheduled for staff of different departments. All hotel employees are invited to attend. Sometimes members of the audience, not so fluent in English, may not exactly follow all I am saying, but they appreciate the trouble I am taking. Afterwards, they may get an explanation from the others about what I have said.

At the session for the general administrative staff held on July 18, 1985, Kuenzli started off the meeting by expressing his confidence that the CPSS would continue to succeed despite heavy competition (which he admitted was reaching a stage where even he was beginning to be somewhat apprehensive). He informed members present about a 14 to 15 percent drop in occupancy rates for gazetted hotels,[3] due to the decline in tourist arrivals.

Charts of the hotel's economic performance were presented, as were figures of the planned versus actual gross operating profits. Mr. Kuenzli emphasized that despite the cost savings of S$800,000[4] as a result of declining staff strength, there was a shortfall from loss in the budgeted gross operating profit. He also mentioned the loss leaders in the hotel. Members at the meeting were briefed on the hotel's latest efforts at boosting sales, and given an update on the opening of the new Sheraton Towers and its possible impact on the Century Park Sheraton. Though Sheraton Towers was positioned at the top end of the exclusive range in hotels, its room rates quoted during the opening period were competitive with Century Park Sheraton's rates.

Demands on Middle Management

Mr. Chua, an unassuming man with an infectious enthusiasm, described the pressures on the management of the hotel in the implementation of a participative philosophy.

> We try to manage by example. It means that we are tough on keeping manpower costs down within our own departments. For example, the personnel

department runs on a staff of three, including myself. We encourage our managers to pitch in whenever necessary. Mr. Moser, our Food and Beverage manager, will help to clear tables; Mr. Kuenzli set an example by even washing toilets—we have that on video! I am glad to see our management staff pitching in spontaneously.

Ironically, an indirect measure of our success is perhaps reflected in the fact that it is becoming increasingly difficult to recruit management people from outside this hotel who can meet the demands of the job. People from within the ranks of this hotel seem better suited for management positions. We have tried quite recently to employ a few management personnel from other hotels, but found that these newcomers experienced some difficulties in adjusting to our organization. Our high expectations of management personnel make even our own employees feel somewhat apprehensive about accepting management positions within the hotel.

Mr. Kuenzli echoed this view:

I do not mind admitting that I am rather demanding of my managers, more so than of the rank-and-file. I expect each manager to work at labour-management cooperative efforts even if he meets with little enthusiasm from his department and feels discouraged about his attempts.

FUTURE DIRECTIONS FOR LABOUR-MANAGEMENT RELATIONS

Reflecting on the past few years, Mr. Chua wondered what steps he could take to ensure the continuing success of the programs and to move to a new level of commitment and involvement.

There are increasing challenges ahead. I am a little apprehensive that some among us feel that we have "arrived" at labour-management efforts for the hotel. Winning the productivity award and having many people interested in studying our success may have lulled us into thinking that all is well. We have to push forward in order not to fall behind. Besides, we must plan now to be ahead of the competition in labour-management cooperation, which means that we should be pressing towards getting our employees involved in making decisions in the hotel. Are we ready for this next challenge?

I also think our promotion of the WE committees detracted from the quality circle movement, when actually these activities should be complementary. Ideas for improvements can be generated by these circles, and then channelled through the WE committees. I would like to see a revival of interest in quality circles.

While I appreciate the top management's acknowledgements of my efforts, I think it is not quite right that I should be needed to keep enthusiasm high for the program. I noticed upon my return after having been away for a few weeks last year that there was a slight falling off of activities in my absence. This should not be so. A truly successful program should be independent of particular individuals . . . and that should also be part of our next objectives.

NOTES

1. This is a chain of hotels owned or managed by All Nippon Airways.

2. The National Productivity Board (NPB) is a statutory body charged with the responsibility of the implementation of productivity efforts. Among its activities were the conducting of extensive training courses for management and supervisors. It also promotes specific productivity programs like Quality Control Circles and joint labour-management consultation schemes like the work excellence committees.

3. Hotels which met the evaluation scheme for luxury.

4. Cdn$480,000.

WHY INNOVATION HAPPENS WHEN HAPPY PEOPLE FIGHT

Prepared by Robert I. Sutton

If it's not if you win but how you play the game, then playing—or working—with humour and an upbeat, positive attitude is surely the right way to play. Besides, these are the teams that usually win.

When people agree with me I always feel I must be wrong.

> Ambrose Bierce,
> playwright and satirist

Multiple disciplines in the same studio, fights over what radio station to listen to, divergent perceptions over appropriate work hours, modes of dress, codes of behaviour, even what was perceived as quality of work . . . all of this I saw as rich and yeasty opportunity for the kinds of friction I wanted to turn into light rather than heat. The uneasiness in my stomach and the fireworks in my brain told me there was some vital connection between the abrasiveness itself and original thinking.

> Jerry Hirshberg,
> founder and president,
> Nissan Design International

If you agreed with me all the time, there wouldn't be any need for one of us. Guess which one?

> Musician Neil Young,
> explaining to producer David Briggs
> why their constant arguments were
> crucial to his creativity

If you want innovation, you need happy warriors, upbeat people who know the right way to fight.

A growing body of research suggests that conflict over ideas is good, especially for groups and organizations that do creative work. Constant argument can mean that there is a competition to develop and test as many good ideas as possible, that there is wide variation in knowledge and perspectives.

When everyone in a group always agrees, it may mean they don't have many ideas, or it may mean that avoiding conflict is more important to them than generating and evaluating new ideas. It may even mean that people who express new ideas are ridiculed, ostracized and driven out of the group. Regardless of the reasons, lack of conflict and dissent means that the group is unlikely to express and develop many valuable new ideas. Groups—and societies—that stifle people with new, untested ideas undermine both imagination and personal freedom. As Robert F. Kennedy said, "It is not enough to allow dissent. We must demand it." This is sound advice for any leader who wants a constant supply of new ideas. Or to paraphrase chewing-gum magnate William Wrigley Jr., "When two people in business always agree, one of them is unnecessary."

CONFLICT—THE GOOD AND THE BAD

When an idea has moved beyond infancy, but is still unproven, constructive conflict is crucial for developing and testing its value. Conflict is a sign that there is a contest for ideas in the organization, that people are developing and assessing many possibilities. Even at this stage, however, not all conflict is constructive. Arguments are crucial to creativity, but people need to learn how and when to fight. In the very earliest stages of idea generation, conflict (and the criticism it entails) is damaging when it causes ideas to be rejected before they can be developed well enough to be evaluated. Worse yet, when conflict rages, fear of ridicule or humiliation causes people to censor themselves before proposing silly or strange, but possibly useful, ideas. This is why idea generation techniques, like brainstorming, require participants to "withhold judgment" or "avoid criticism."

Peter Skillman is a product designer and master brainstorming leader who works for Handspring, the maker of personal digital assistants. Skillman trains people not to attack others' ideas in brainstorming groups: "If somebody says that an idea sucks, when somebody says something nasty, I ring a little bell. I make a joke out of it, but it stops them from ripping apart ideas we need to build on and think about more."

Conflict is also destructive once the creative process has run its course, and it is time to implement an idea. Agreement is important once an idea has been developed, tested and the right path has been chosen; agreement helps assure that everyone will use the same methods, in the same way, and is working toward the same ends. If you were having a simple and proven operation like an appendectomy, you wouldn't want an argument in the operating room about how it should be done.

Research on group effectiveness distinguishes between two types of conflict: destructive and constructive. The destructive kind is "emotional," "interpersonal" or "relationship-based"—participants are not fighting over which ideas are best, but because they dislike each other or feel threatened by one another. Destructive conflict upsets and demoralizes people, and groups that fight this way are less effective in both creative and routine tasks (Jehn, K. A., "A Multi-method Examination of the Benefits and Detriments of Intragroup Conflicts," *Administrative Science Quarterly,* 40, 1995).

Constructive conflict—also referred to as "task," or "intellectual" conflict—happens when people argue over ideas rather than personality or relationship issues. This kind of conflict occurs when people "base discussion on current factual information" and "develop multiple alternatives to enrich the debate" (Eisenhardt, K., J. L. Kahwajy, and L. Bourgeois III, "How Management Teams Can Have a Good Fight," *Harvard Business Review,* July-August, 1997). These are fights about ideas, which ones are best, and why, in an atmosphere of mutual respect.

Some of the most creative groups and organizations in history were made up of people who respected each other, but fought mightily over ideas. Bob Taylor, a psychologist turned research administrator, encouraged exactly this kind of conflict, first among computer scientists at the U.S. Defense Department's Advanced Research Projects Agency in Washington state, and later at Xerox PARC in the 1970s (Hiltzik, M., *Dealers of Lightning,* Harper Business, New York, 1999). These scientists and engineers, more than any others, are responsible for the technologies that made the computer revolution possible-including the personal computer, the Internet and the laser printer.

Here is how Taylor managed meetings when these researchers met. "Each participant got an hour or so to describe his work. Then he would be thrown to the mercy of the assembled court like a flank steak to a pack of ravenous wolves. I got them to argue with each other," Taylor recalled with unashamed glee. "These were people who cared about their work . . . If there were technical weak spots, they would almost always surface under these conditions . . . it was very, very healthy." It was not to be personal. Impugning a man's thinking was acceptable, but never his character. Taylor strived to create a democracy where everyone's ideas were impartially subject to the group's learned demolition, regardless of the proponents' credentials or rank" (see Hiltzik above).

Intel, the leading semiconductor company, takes this idea more seriously that any company I know. All full-time employees are required to take a home-grown, half-day class on "constructive confrontation," where people learn about and practise how to fight about ideas in an atmosphere of mutual respect.

It Pays to Be Happy

There is much evidence that being upbeat rather than unhappy, or optimistic rather than pessimistic, is a personality characteristic that is stable throughout one's life. One study that followed people over a 50-year period, for example, showed that having an upbeat personality as an adolescent was a strong predictor of job satisfaction decades later (Staw, B.M., N.E. Bell, and J.A. Clausen, "The Dispositional Approach to Job Attitudes: A Lifetime Longitudinal Test," *Administrative Science Quarterly,* 31, 1986). Hiring such upbeat people is one of the best ways to limit destructive personal attacks, and has many other benefits as well.

Humour, joking and laughter are among the main tools that effective groups use to keep people focused on facts, rather than have the situation degenerate into personal conflict. Anthropologists, psychologists and sociologists have shown that humour can help group dynamics in many ways—the irony in many jokes and funny comments helps people remember not to take life too seriously, the laughter it promotes releases tension. I once watched a bankruptcy attorney defuse tension about charging high fees to creditors (who were already owed millions of dollars by the bankrupt firm he represented) by using a stream of tasteful lawyer jokes. Humour can be damaging when it is used against people who are different, but can be constructive when used to raise sensitive issues and deliver serious messages in less threatening ways, which is especially important for promoting a contest between opposing ideas or choices.

A study of conflict in top-management teams at high-technology firms found that the most effective groups consistently used humour, telling lots of jokes during meetings and pulling pranks like decorating the office with plastic flamingos. As the researchers put it: "Speakers can say in jest things that might otherwise give offence, because the message is simultaneously serious and not serious. The recipient is allowed to save face by receiving the serious message while appearing not to do so. The result is communication of difficult information in a more tactful and less personally threatening way." (Eisenhardt et al., 1997, *Harvard Business Review*).

Humour is one of many ways to make people happy. The list is endless: Give them interesting work, treat them with respect, pay them a lot, give them free food, and so on.

Regardless of how you make your company a happy place, there is a huge amount of literature on the advantages of positive emotion, especially for creative tasks. These studies have examined the differences between happy and unhappy, optimistic and pessimistic people; people who have a positive effect versus a negative one; happiness versus sadness, and so on. No matter what you call it, there is strong evidence that travelling through life in a good mood is a good thing, especially if you want to be creative.

Many experiments show that when people are put into a good mood, say, by giving them candy or showing them a funny movie, they will be more creative. For example, they are better at inventing diverse and unusual ways for getting a candle to burn without dripping, or at finding more obscure and remote associations between words and ideas. People in good moods are "more cognitively flexible—more able to make associations, to see dimensions, and to see potential relationships among stimuli—than are persons in a neutral state." In other words, they generate more varied ideas and combinations of those ideas, which are crucial aspects of creative work.

And Optimistic

Research on the link between optimism and pessimism is even more pertinent to how creative work unfolds in real organizations. Martin Seligman, a professor at the University of Pennsylvania, has shown that optimists tend to view setbacks as temporary, as not their fault, and as something that won't pervade every aspect of life. In contrast, pessimists have a terrible time with failure, blaming themselves, believing that a single failure means they will fail from then on, that it will pervade every aspect of their lives.

Innovative companies generate many unsuccessful ideas. Consider the example of Skyline, a group of toy designers at IDEO Product Development in Palo Alto, California. Skyline keeps close tabs on its ideas because it sells and licenses concepts for toys that are made and marketed by big companies like Mattel. Brendan Boyle, founder and head of Skyline, said that in 1998, the group (which had fewer than 10 employees) generated about 4,000 ideas for new toys. Of these 4,000 ideas, 230 were thought to be promising enough to develop into a nice drawing or working prototype. Of these 230, 12 were ultimately sold. This "yield" rate is only about one-third of one percent of total ideas, and five percent of ideas that were thought to have potential. As Boyle says, "You can't get any good new ideas without having a lot of dumb, lousy and crazy ones. Nobody in my business is very good at guessing which are a waste of time and which will be the next Furby."

Using Happy Warriors to Spark Innovation

- Avoid conflict of any kind during the earliest stages of the creative process, but encourage people to fight over ideas in the intermediate stages.
- Encourage—and teach—people to use tasteful jokes to release tension when arguments over ideas start becoming too tense and personal.
- Teach people how to recognize the differences between interpersonal conflict and intellectual conflict. Use classes and mentoring, and your own actions, to teach them the right (and wrong) way to fight.
- Find examples of how fighting the right way led to more innovation in your company, and tell stories about these successes.
- Senior managers need to set the right example, by openly arguing about ideas and avoiding nasty interpersonal conflict
- If people, including senior managers, continue to engage in nasty personal conflict despite efforts to teach them not to, punish them. If all else fails, fire them.
- Hire upbeat people and do everything possible to keep them that way. Emotions are contagious, so make sure upbeat people interact a lot with others in the company.
- Teach people—through classes, mentoring and setting a good example—to build resistance to rejection and failure.
- Hire a few grumpy people, but keep them away from other people in the company most of the time because emotions are so contagious. When you need their expertise, bring them out briefly and then send them back into isolation.
- If people are upbeat and optimistic, but can't learn how to fight over ideas, they might be better off doing routine rather than creative work.

People who do such work need to be optimistic, for it inoculates them against the loss of energy and effort that follows each failure. People in innovative companies can't view dead ends, errors and failures as reasons to give up, or they will never develop the few successful ideas that ultimately result from this potentially disheartening process. People who are successful in creative work, and are involved in other kinds of tasks with high failure rates, might need to be more than just optimistic. To keep moving forward, and to maintain their mental health, they might benefit by deluding themselves about the probability of success. They might be—and perhaps ought to be—prone to overestimating their chances of success, to deluding themselves into believing that things are and will be better than the evidence suggests at the time.

A study that compared how managers in large organizations and entrepreneurs made decisions found that the entrepreneurs were much more likely to be overconfident in their decisions. Overconfidence may cause problems if it means that firms continue pursuing ideas long after they have proven to be failures. But having more confidence than is warranted by the objective evidence has compensating virtues. Entrepreneurs—and people who do other innovative work—who overestimate their odds of success may work harder and be better at convincing others to help them succeed, which may increase the—albeit low—chances that any single new idea or company will succeed. An added benefit of such "self-enhancing illusions" is that people who consistently fool themselves into believing that things are wonderful enjoy superior physical and mental health compared with their more realistic and morose colleagues (Taylor, S.E., Positive Illusions, Basic Books, New York, 1989).

EMOTIONS ARE CONTAGIOUS

I don't want to leave you with the impression that negative, grumpy or nasty people have no role to play in companies. You might hire a few grumpy people because there is evidence that they are less likely to take risks than upbeat people, and better at finding things wrong with ideas. One study—a simulated decision about whether or not to race a car given a substantial risk that the engine would fail—found that MBAs and engineers with less upbeat personalities were better at unearthing negative information and took fewer risks (Roberts, D. R. "The Influence of Emotional State on Decision Making Under Risk," Unpublished Doctoral Dissertation, Graduate School of Business, Stanford University, 1993). This decision had elements of realism because the students used actual data about the link between outside temperature and engine failure that NASA administrators used in their ill-fated decision to launch the *Challenger* space shuttle. So, in high-risk situations, a few negative people can be especially valuable.

Yet you must be careful before hiring grouchy people. Much research suggests that emotions are contagious, that negative feelings can spread like a disease in a company (Hatfield, E., J. T. Cacioppo, and R. L. Rapson, Emotional Contagion, Cambridge University Press, Cambridge, England). One solution to this dilemma is to hire a few grumpy people, but keep them away from everyone else in the company most of the time. I got this idea from a company that had a grumpy engineer who was sometimes nasty and insensitive, but renowned for his ability to uncover errors and problems that others overlooked. Even though everyone else in his building worked in cubicles, they gave him a private office with a door, and brought him out mostly when errors and mistakes needed to be detected. Then, he went back in isolation! Other executives have told me about at least another half-dozen or so "local grumps" and "resident critics" who are given—or elect to take—a work area that is isolated from others in their company.

So, there you have it. If you want to have a creative workplace, find some happy people and teach them how to fight!

11

STRATEGIC LEADERSHIP

NATALIE SLAWINSKI

The University of Western Ontario

There are three categories of people—the person who goes into his office, puts his feet up on his desk, and dreams for twelve hours; the person who arrives at 5:00 am and works for sixteen hours, never once stopping to dream; and the one who puts his feet up, dreams for one hour, then does something about those dreams.

—Steven J. Ross[1]

In the past 20 years, researchers have begun to pay more attention to the study of strategic leadership, which has come to be viewed by many as a critical aspect of firm success (Daft, 2005). Broadly speaking, strategic leadership refers to the study of executives who have overall responsibility for the firm and how their decisions affect organizational outcomes (Finkelstein & Hambrick, 1996). The focus is on top managers because they usually have decision-making responsibilities that affect the whole organization—including the other organizational members—and its overall performance (Daft, 2005).

Strategic leaders create a sense of purpose and direction, which guides strategy formulation and implementation within the firm (Daft, 2005; Hosmer, 1982; Shrivastava & Nachman, 1989). They also interact with key stakeholders, such as customers, government agencies, and unions, especially when these relationships are critical to firm performance (House & Aditya, 1997). Organizations and the environments in which they operate are increasingly complex and ambiguous. Therefore, strategic leaders must navigate through these complexities and develop strategies that will allow their organizations to be successful, whether they are for-profit or nonprofit.

Another perspective of strategic leadership focuses on the specific activities and behaviors of strategic leaders that can improve the success of the firm (Ireland & Hitt, 1999; Rowe, 2001). This perspective argues that in an ever-changing complex business environment, strategic leaders may be a source of competitive advantage. Ireland and Hitt (1999) define strategic leadership as the "ability to anticipate, envision, maintain flexibility, think strategically, and work with others to initiate changes that will create a viable future for the organization" (p. 43). Given the challenges that firms face in an often turbulent and unpredictable global environment, Ireland and Hitt have identified six components of strategic leadership that will lead to enhanced organizational performance: determining the firm's purpose or vision, exploiting and maintaining core competencies, developing human capital, sustaining an effective organizational culture, emphasizing ethical practices, and establishing balanced organizational controls.

DETERMINING THE FIRM'S PURPOSE OR VISION

The first component of strategic leadership consists of determining the firm's purpose or vision. This means that strategic leaders must articulate a clear and realistic statement about why the firm exists and what is distinctive about it. This statement will then empower members of the organization to develop and execute strategies that are in line with the vision of the firm.

EXPLOITING AND MAINTAINING CORE COMPETENCIES

Strategic leaders exploit and maintain core competencies. Core competencies are resources and capabilities that give firms an edge over their rivals. Strategic leaders need to understand which combinations of resources and capabilities are valuable, rare, costly to imitate, and difficult to substitute for, as these will allow the firm to gain a competitive advantage.

DEVELOPING HUMAN CAPITAL

Strategic leaders are effective at developing human capital. Human capital refers to the knowledge, skills, and abilities of the firm's employees. Because these employees are critical to the success of the organization, strategic leaders invest in them through training and mentoring.

SUSTAINING AN EFFECTIVE ORGANIZATIONAL CULTURE

Strategic leaders sustain an effective organizational culture. An organization's culture is a complex combination of ideologies, symbols, and values that are shared by employees of the firm. Strategic leaders learn how to shape a firm's shared values and symbols in ways that allow the firm to be more competitive.

EMPHASIZING ETHICAL PRACTICES

Strategic leadership involves the emphasis of ethical practices. Top managers who use honesty, trust, and integrity in their decision making are able to inspire their employees and create an organizational culture that encourages the use of ethical practices in day-to-day organizational activities.

Establishing Balanced Organizational Controls

Organizational controls refer to the formal procedures that are used in organizations to influence and guide work. These controls act as limits on what employees can and cannot do. There are two types of internal controls: strategic and financial. Strategic controls are accomplished through information exchanges that help to develop strategies, whereas financial controls are accomplished through setting objective criteria such as performance targets. Strategic controls emphasize actions, whereas financial controls emphasize outcomes. Financial controls can be especially constraining and can stifle creativity in organizations. Strategic leaders must establish balanced organizational controls by incorporating the two types in order to allow employees to remain flexible and innovative.

In addition to accomplishing the above activities, strategic leaders must balance the short-term needs of their organizations while ensuring a future competitive position. Rowe (2001) defines strategic leadership as "the ability to influence others to voluntarily make day-to-day decisions that enhance the long-term viability of the organization, while at the same time maintaining its short-term financial stability" (pp. 82–83). This type of leadership is a synergistic combination of visionary leadership, which emphasizes investing in the future, and managerial leadership, which emphasizes preserving the existing order. Strategic leaders focus on both the day-to-day operations and the long-term strategic orientation of the firm, recognizing that neither can be ignored if a firm is to be successful.

Importantly, strategic leaders have strong positive expectations of the performance they expect from their superiors, peers, subordinates, and themselves (Rowe, 2001). These expectations encourage organizational members to voluntarily make decisions that contribute to short-term stability and long-term viability of the organization. As such, strategic leaders do not have to expend as much effort on monitoring and controlling employees. It is also important that those leaders who already exhibit strategic leadership abilities encourage their development in other organizational members. In this way, strategic leadership can exist at all levels of the organization. Strategic leaders also select the next generation of leaders to ensure that the organization will continue to have strategic leadership in the long term (Boal & Hooijberg, 2000).

Strategic Leadership Versus Leadership

In Chapter 1 of this casebook, leadership was defined as the process of influencing others in order to accomplish a goal. The focus was on the relationship between the leader and follower in a group context and on the process of leading in order to achieve a goal. So how is strategic leadership different from leadership? The main difference is that leadership can be accomplished at any level of the organization and can have an impact on different types of organizational goals, such as increasing the sales of a particular product line or reducing the turnover of employees.

Strategic leadership, on the other hand, is mainly concerned with, but not necessarily restricted to, the higher levels of the organization, given that executives are in a unique position to influence the direction and vision of the organization (Finkelstein & Hambrick, 1996). Strategic leadership has an impact on organization-wide outcomes, such as the financial performance of a small manufacturing company or the strategic change of a large multinational company. The difference can also be thought of as leadership "in" organizations versus leadership "of" organizations (Boal & Hooijberg, 2001). The leadership approaches discussed throughout this book are mainly concerned with how leaders affect followers "in" the organization, whereas strategic leadership is primarily concerned with the leadership "of" organization by top managers. But as we saw earlier, leaders at all levels of the organization can have an impact on organizational performance. The focus of strategic leadership is often on top-level executives such as CEOs because they tend to have more power and are given responsibility for the overall performance of the firm. They are also held accountable by shareholders for the success of the firm, and poor performance can lead to their dismissal.

POSITIONAL VERSUS BEHAVIORAL

In contrast to some of the other theories within the realm of leadership, such as the trait approach and the skills approach, the strategic leadership perspective is not as well developed. Furthermore, there is a lack of agreement regarding what strategic leadership is. As we have seen, strategic leadership has come to have several different, but often complementary, meanings. Some (e.g., Finkerstein & Hambrick, 1996) view it as having to do with one's position in a company, while others (e.g., Ireland & Hitt, 1999) view it as a set of behaviors that lead to superior performance.

The positional view argues that anyone holding the position of CEO or another top executive position is a strategic leader because of his or her decision-making power and level of responsibility. This perspective looks at the differences in psychological characteristics of strategic leaders to examine how these differences affect their organizations (Finkelstein & Hambrick, 1996). Others view strategic leadership as a set of activities that leaders must perform if they are to enhance organizational performance. For example, strategic leaders are those who sustain an effective corporate culture (Ireland & Hitt, 1999). A related perspective (Rowe, 2001) on strategic leadership views it as a leadership style that individuals may possess at any level of the organization. Rowe (2001) argues that organizations that have CEOs who are strategic leaders will create more value than those who have visionary or managerial leaders.

As we saw in the definitions above, there is no consensus on exactly what strategic leadership is, but certain themes do emerge. For instance, most of the definitions or conceptualizations of strategic leadership mention the importance of studying CEOs and other top managers to better understand why some firms outperform others. Whether it is viewed as a style of leadership, a set of activities, or a broad area of study, strategic leadership is viewed by many as critical to firm success, especially given our complex, global business environment.

Several themes emerge in the literature concerning what strategic leaders do to increase firm performance. They look after both the short-term operational side of their organization and the long-term directional aspects, such as defining the firm's purpose (Phillips & Hunt, 1992; Rowe, 2001). Strategic leaders select and develop other organizational members to ensure that these successful strategic leader abilities will exist throughout the organization, not just at the top. They influence others by behaving ethically and transparently. Strategic leaders who have overall responsibility for the firm (such as a CEO) articulate a vision that will provide the organization's members with meaning and guidance. They are also in a position to influence external constituents, such as suppliers, unions, and government agencies. Strategic leaders who incorporate these important activities can help ensure the future competitiveness of the firm.

NOTE

1. Steven J. Ross is the former chairman and co-CEO of Time Warner.

REFERENCES

Boal, K. B., & Hooijberg, R. (2001). Strategic leadership research: Moving on. *The Leadership Quarterly, 11,* 515–549.

Daft, R. L. (2005). *The leadership experience* (3rd ed.). Mason, OH: Thomson, South-Western.

Finkelstein, S., & Hambrick, D. C. (1996). *Strategic leadership: Top executives and their effects on organizations.* St. Paul, MN: West.

Hosmer, L. T. (1982). The importance of strategic leadership. *Journal of Business Strategy, 3,* 47–57.

House, R. J., & Aditya, R. N. (1997). The social scientific study of leadership: Quo vadis? *Journal of Management, 2*(23), 409–473.

Ireland, R. D., & Hitt, M. A. (1999). Achieving and maintaining strategic competitiveness in the 21st century: The role of strategic leadership. *Academy of Management Executive, 13,* 43–57.

Loeb, M. (1993, January 24). Steven J. Ross, 1927–1992. *Fortune,* p. 4.

Phillips, R. L., & Hunt, J. G. (1992). *Strategic leadership: A multi-organizational-level perspective.* London: Quorum Books.

Rowe, W. G. (2001). Creating wealth in organizations: The role of strategic leadership. *Academy of Management Executive, 15,* 81–94.

Shrivastava, P., & Nachman, S. A. (1989). Strategic leadership patterns. *Strategic Management Journal, 10,* 51–66.

THE CASES

Vic Young and Fishery Products International (A)

Fishery Products International Ltd. is one of the largest seafood companies in North America. In January 2000, Vic Young marked his 15th anniversary as the only chief executive officer of the company. Under his leadership, the company overcame the collapse of the North Atlantic fishery to become an international seafood company and an important contributor to the Newfoundland and Labrador economy. However, its share price has languished, and the company was recently the target of a hostile takeover bid. The bid was unsuccessful, due partly to government regulation on the company's stock ownership, but Young realizes another attempt is possible and wonders how to maintain shareholder confidence in Fishery Products' current board and management team.

Compassion Canada

Compassion Canada is a nonprofit ministry focusing on the holistic development of poor children in developing countries. Over the past 10 years, the organization has only doubled its sponsorships. The chief executive officer must analyze the organization's performance and develop a strategic plan that will enable Compassion Canada to reach its goal of fivefold growth over the next 10 years.

THE READING

You're an Entrepreneur: But Do You Exercise Strategic Leadership?

This brief article describes the differences among the concepts of strategic leadership, visionary leadership, and managerial leadership. In addition, it defines strategic leadership. It describes two entrepreneurs who developed large organizations that created wealth for their owners.

VIC YOUNG AND FISHERY PRODUCTS INTERNATIONAL (A)[1]

Prepared by John Melnyk, Tami L. Hynes and W. Glenn Rowe

Version: (A) 2004–02–03

In January 2000, Vic Young marked his 15th anniversary as the chief executive officer (CEO) of Fishery Products International Ltd. (FPI).

As the only CEO of FPI since its inception in December 1984, Young had led the company through a host of challenges—labor unrest, the loss of a crucial source of supply, international expansion, economic recession and a recent hostile takeover bid by competitors.

In the process, FPI had grown to become one of the largest seafood companies in North America, producing and selling a wide range of seafood products around the world. Its important role in its home province's economy was recognized with a Newfoundland and Labrador Export Award in 1998. Young was named *Financial Times* CEO of the Year in 1994, and made an Officer of the Order of Canada in 1996 as "a model of corporate responsibility for industry leaders."[2]

FPI's earnings per share (EPS) from operations for 1999 were $0.72,[3] up from $0.55 in 1998, a fourth consecutive annual increase. Despite this, the company's stock had languished in thin trading on the Toronto Stock Exchange

(TSE), and the company had been the target of an unsolicited takeover bid in November 1999. Although that bid had been unsuccessful, Young realized that another attempt was very possible and wondered how he could convince shareholders to remain confident in FPI's current board of directors and management team.

HISTORY

The North Atlantic fishery had a long history. Early explorers returned from voyages to the New World with stories of fish so numerous "they impeded the progress of the ships" and "could be scooped up from the side of the boat in a basket."

This seemingly inexhaustible resource drew European settlers to the region as early as the 1500s. They built a fishery based on hard work and simple technology—small wooden boats, nets handled by hand and family operations—that continued almost unchanged for hundreds of years, becoming the basis for a regional economy and way of life. However fish stocks migrated away from the coastline during winter, so it was a seasonal industry, and thus supported only a meager living for most.

The advent of large steam-powered fishing vessels in the mid-1900s held promise to break the cycle of seasonal employment and government support that had become prevalent in the region that by then had become "Atlantic Canada."[4] These large trawlers could follow the fish out to sea in winter and use huge mechanized nets to harvest year-round, storing catches at sea for up to 10 days at a time. This mass-production fishery carried on by company-owned trawlers far out at sea became known as the "offshore" fishery, and the smaller closer-to-shore operations of independent fisherman as the "inshore" fishery.

The prospect of large catches on a year-round basis led to significant investment in new processing capacity throughout the region, often generously encouraged by government in the hope of generating permanent employment; the number of fish processing plants jumped from 89 in 1971 to 249 in 1982. These developments led to widespread economic optimism that drowned out concerns of some fishermen and scientists who had begun to notice that the fish were not as plentiful as in the past.

By the early 1980s, declining catches, high interest rates and changing consumer tastes towards higher quality products caused several fishing companies to fail, despite escalating government loan guarantees and direct subsidies intended to preserve employment in the region.

In response to this situation, the government of Canada and the affected provincial governments stepped in to restructure the Atlantic fishery. Two of the largest independent companies, National Sea Products (based in Nova Scotia) and Fishery Products Ltd. (based in Newfoundland), were chosen as the vehicles to create an economically viable and competitive industry.

Fishery Products International—A Fresh Start

In December 1984, Fishery Products Ltd., two other corporate entities and assets from several other seafood companies were amalgamated to form Fishery Products International Ltd. Through a $150-million package of cash and conversion of debt to equity, the federal government ended up holding 63 percent of the new company; the Newfoundland and Labrador government, 26 percent and the Bank of Nova Scotia, 11 percent.

Vic Young, then chairman and CEO of Newfoundland Hydro Group, a provincial Crown corporation,[5] was jointly appointed by the provincial and federal governments to lead the newly formed company. Young had started his career with the provincial government in 1968 and had risen to deputy minister of the Treasury Board at age 27, from which position he later served as special advisor to the Premier of Newfoundland and Labrador.

At the time of Young's appointment, FPI was still operating under bankruptcy protection and embroiled in a major strike. Young was able to resolve these issues and under his leadership, the company quickly embarked on a modernization program, closing or selling marginal assets and investing in the 19 processing plants, 58 fishing vessels and eight port facilities it continued to operate.

FPI operated as a Crown corporation for its first three years, suffering losses in 1984 and 1985, but achieving profitability by 1986. As had been planned at the time of the government intervention, FPI was then returned to the private sector, albeit with some conditions.

An Act Respecting the Return of the Business of Fishery Products International Limited to Private Investors (the FPI Act), passed by the Newfoundland government to privatize FPI, stipulated that no single shareholder could own more than 15 percent of FPI's common voting shares; that shareholders could not act in concert to circumvent this provision; that a majority of the members of the board of directors be residents of Newfoundland; that the company could not apply to continue under another jurisdiction; that the company could not exit the business of harvesting, processing and marketing seafood; and that only one member of management could be a member of the board of directors. The limit of

* tonnes (1 tonne = 2,205 pounds)	1999	1998	1997	1996	1995	1994	1993	1992	1991	1990	1989	1988	1987
Landings[1]*													
Groundfish	21,400	16,400	7,800	9,900	5,200	10,800	45,000	69,000	111,100	123,400	139,300	164,000	172,700
Shellfish	10,200	8,500	6,600	5,400	3,600	4,000	Shellfish included in Other until 1994						
Shrimp	16,100	16,300	9,400	6,400	6,400	5,100	Shrimp included in Other until 1994						
Other	1,500	2,800	3,300	3,300	300	300	11,400	9,800	11,800	12,400	12,000	13,600	8,900
Total	49,200	44,000	27,100	25,000	15,500	20,200	56,400	78,800	122,900	135,800	151,300	177,600	181,600
Procurement[2]													
Groundfish fillets	15,500	15,300	15,700	14,500	16,100	14,900	11,900	8,200	4,500	4,200	4,100	2,100	1,900
Semi-processed groundfish	3,000	6,300	8,900	7,400	7,900	10,500	4,900	2,300	—	—	—	—	—
Raw shrimp	2,300	2,700	2,800	1,800	1,600	1,400	n/a	—	—	—	—	—	—
Total	20,800	24,300	27,400	23,700	25,600	26,800	16,800	10,500	4,500	4,200	4,100	2,100	1,900
Value-added production *	29,300	28,700	29,300	25,100	24,400	25,700	21,500	18,900	19,300	20,800	16,300	17,200	16,300
Active vessels (during year)[3]	18	15	13	14	12	13	31	47	51	51	61	66	66
Active plants (during year)[3]	11	11	10	10	9	9	10	17	19	19	19	19	19
Total employees (during year)[3]	3,400	3,400	3,200	3,000	2,600	2,600	3,900	7,200	8,400	8,400	8,600	8,600	8,600

Exhibit 1 Selected Operating Statistics

Source: FPI Annual Reports. Where figures have been restated in later reports, the most recent figure has been used.

1. Landings were harvested by FPI itself or purchased from independent Newfoundland fishermen.
2. Procurement quantities were obtained other than by "landing," primarily from international sources.
3. Some of the vessels, plants and employees shown as active during the year may not necessarily have been active by year end.

15 percent ownership per shareholder was also enshrined in the FPI bylaws.[6]

Despite these conditions, FPI's initial public offering (IPO), April 15, 1987, was successful, raising $177 million that was used to buy out the governments' positions. Pension funds and financial institutions took the bulk of the stock, but 560,000 shares were granted to eligible employees, not including executives.

On its first trading day FPI stock closed up $3 from its issue price of $12.50, and within a few months had risen to $21.25. The shares paid dividends at an annual rate of $0.48, raised to $0.56 in December 1987. That year FPI also distributed $6.6 million in profit-sharing to its employees, plus a special $1 million "Award for Excellence" for their contribution to the company's turnaround; it also paid a bonus to its inshore fishery suppliers for their "demonstration of loyalty." The company's achievements were recognized with a Gold Medal for Productivity at the 1987 Canada Awards for Business Excellence, and a Canada Export Award.

Even before privatization, Young had set about to make the company more market-driven and diversified, investing heavily in technology and its workforce, in order to be able to meet consumer demands for higher quality products.

In June 1987, FPI completed the conversion of an old primary-processing[7] plant in Burin, Newfoundland, into a world-class secondary-processing[7] facility, tripling its capacity to 7,000 tonnes per year, well above demand at the time. That same month, FPI entered into a joint-venture agreement to market FPI secondary-processed products in Japan with with Nichiro Gyogyo Kaisha (Nichiro), the third largest Japanese seafood trading company.

FPI had been exporting raw materials to Japan for years, but the Japanese consumer market posed very different challenges, including a maze of government regulations, culturally specific business customs and exacting demands for unusual quality and packaging standards.

Nevertheless, FPI persisted, and with the help of three quality control specialists from Nichiro working in the Burin plant alongside FPI employees for a time, eventually achieved the capability to produce to rigorous Japanese specifications. A successful launch in February 1988, made FPI the first North American seafood company to have its value-added products on Japanese retail shelves.

Crises and Changes

In January 1989, the Government of Canada announced the first of what was to become a series of reductions in fishing quotas for the Atlantic Canada fishery, in response to mounting concerns about the state of the fish stock. Each of these reductions was a hotly debated compromise between environmental pressure to protect the dwindling fish stocks and political pressure to maintain employment in Atlantic Canada by keeping the fishery open. Before long, the room for compromise, like the fish stock itself, was exhausted, and a complete moratorium on harvesting several groundfish species,[8] including cod, was imposed on September 6, 1993.

Groundfish, of which cod was the most common and valuable, had been the basis for 85 percent of FPI sales in the late 1980s—in 1987, FP had "landed" (either harvested itself or purchased from independent Newfoundland fishermen) 172,700 metric tonnes of groundfish, primarily cod; in 1995, it would land just 5,200 tonnes, none of which was cod. As a result, 6,000 FPI employees eventually lost their jobs, as trawlers were deactivated and plants were closed (see Exhibit 1); even then, capacity utilization in the remaining plants was only 65 percent. Surplus assets were sold or leased to the extent possible, but often for only nominal amounts. Newfoundland-based assets had to be written down by $85 million, and the company suffered losses in the early 1990s (see Exhibits 2 and 3).

During this period, the company did its best to cushion the blow for its employees and their communities by spreading what work there was among its plants to allow as many workers as possible to qualify for Employment Insurance[9] (EI) payments from the federal government. Nevertheless, labor unrest and angry public demonstrations were widespread.

All figures '000s	1999	1998	1997	1996	1995	1994	1993	1992	1991	1990	1989	1988	1987
Assets													
Current Assets													
Cash	$916	933	5,609	4,981	5,460	1,659	7,256	3,595	3,776	6,190	5,828	34,102	36,048
Accounts Receivable	80,644	90,424	84,155	78,178	71,747	67,521	58,379	69,517	61,905	67,945	57,245	42,305	38,992
Inventories	119,471	123,866	150,012	111,374	122,002	124,151	112,126	130,449	97,360	87,588	87,909	68,632	65,448
Pre-paid Expenses	5,637	4,429	3,896	3,024	2,874	1,832	1,967	2,475	2,781	2,825	2,520	2,210	2,084
Total Current Assets	206,668	219,652	243,672	197,557	202,083	195,163	179,728	206,036	165,822	164,548	153,502	147,249	142,572
Property, Plant and Equipment (P,P&E)	93,677	89,318	71,165	67,501	66,140	74,585	76,694	95,907	152,403	158,522	159,334	154,123	134,610
Other Assets	14,057	16,782	11,681	10,353	14,839	12,985	11,508	10,829	6,954	6,348	16,396	7,777	1,074
Total Assets	$314,402	325,752	326,518	275,411	283,062	282,733	267,930	312,772	325,179	329,418	329,232	309,149	278,256
Liabilities and Shareholders' Equity													
Current Liabilities													
Bank Indebtedness	$43,124	70,373	65,880	42,101	68,430	51,410	49,264	56,928	21,974	19,171	13,818	—	—
Accounts Payable & Accrued Liabilities	37,252	31,739	41,654	38,211	35,084	45,488	49,073	64,045	48,615	47,782	56,782	41,853	45,363
Current Portion of Long-term Liabilities	8,351	8,262	6,488	8,546	6,077	6,357	5,671	7,363	6,398	7,557	7,856	5,929	3,174
Total Current Liabilities	88,727	110,374	114,022	88,858	109,591	103,255	104,008	128,336	76,987	74,510	78,456	47,782	48,537
Long-term Liabilities	62,323	57,471	58,351	37,042	30,314	32,244	32,415	37,414	34,230	40,615	47,785	38,593	17,487
Total Liabilities	151,050	167,845	172,373	125,900	139,905	135,499	136,423	165,750	111,217	115,125	126,241	86,375	66,024
Share Capital	48,044	48,439	49,148	52,117	52,023	51,973	51,942	51,926	160,558	160,524	161,099	158,621	158,430
Contributed Surplus	75,083	75,383	75,836	79,413	79,413	79,413	79,413	108,645	Contributed Surplus included in Share Capital above				
Retained Earnings*	41,535	33,331	24,905	16,712	10,602	13,881	—	(13,865)	53,434	53,722	41,951	64,153	53,802
Foreign Currency Translation Adjustment	(1,310)	754	4,256	1,269	1,119	1,967	152	316	(30)	47	(59)		
Total Shareholders' Equity	163,352	157,907	154,145	149,511	143,157	147,234	131,507	147,022	213,962	214,293	202,991	222,774	212,232
Total Liabilities and Shareholders' Equity	$314,402	325,752	326,518	275,411	283,062	282,733	267,930	312,772	325,179	329,418	329,232	309,149	278,256

Exhibit 2   Consolidated Balance Sheets for Years Ending December 31

* Accumulated Deficit cancelled by a transfer from Contributed Surplus in 1993.

Source: FPI Annual Reports. Where figures have been restated in later reports, the most recent figure has been used.

All figures $000's except per share	1999	1998	1997	1996	1995	1994	1993	1992	1991	1990	1989	1988	1987
Sales	$ 708,911	681,563	675,945	664,598	643,009	665,596	601,179	590,351	542,937	535,044	349,791	366,611	395,705
Cost of Goods Sold	633,124	614,467	613,617	606,473	593,096	598,250	549,844	536,373	483,046	468,924	314,347	302,808	285,671
Gross Profit	75,787	67,096	62,328	58,125	49,913	67,346	51,335	53,978	59,891	66,120	35,444	63,803	110,034
Commission Income	3,327	2,382	2,968	3,665	3,394	4,645	2,789	6,502	7,281	8,437	1,156		
Gross Profit plus Commission	79,114	69,478	65,296	61,790	53,307	71,991	54,124	60,480	67,172	74,557	36,600	63,803	110,034
Administration and Marketing	45,456	42,152	39,963	39,865	39,711	40,718	32,975	44,945	44,988	47,335	33,687	29,444	27,966
Depreciation and Amortization	9,883	8,967	8,656	7,872	8,484	8,380	10,040	12,441	15,005	16,694	14,849	13,360	13,763
Profit Sharing	1,541	1,088	1,063	840	—	1,684	—	—	110	586	—	1,837	7,599
Interest	7,146	7,467	5,890	5,669	8,242	6,786	6,667	6,210	5,074	4,566	665	159	46
Operating Expenses	64,026	59,674	55,572	54,246	56,437	57,568	49,682	63,596	65,177	69,181	49,201	44,800	49,374
Operating Income	15,088	9,804	9,724	7,544	(3,130)	14,423	4,442	(3,116)	1,995	5,376	(12,601)	19,003	60,660
Gain (loss) on Foreign Exchange						715	1,005	3,202	(998)	(104)	(1,334)	(1,808)	(2,270)
Gain (loss) on Disposal of PP&E				21	438	182	959	203					
Share in gain (loss) of joint venture							(1,027)	(1,675)					
Extraordinary Item(s)	(965)						(20,000)	(65,000)	(185)	7,962	(7,500)		26,959
Income before Income Taxes	14,123	9,804	9,724	7,565	(2,692)	15,320	(14,621)	(66,386)	812	13,234	(21,435)	17,195	85,349
Income Taxes	4,097	1,378	1,531	1,455	587	1,439	746	913	1,100	1,463	767	440	27,386
Net Income	10,026	8,426	8,193	6,110	(3,279)	13,881	(15,367)	(67,299)	(288)	11,771	(22,202)	16,755	57,963
Net Income per share	$ 0.66	0.55	0.51	0.37	(0.20)	0.85	(0.94)	(4.10)	(0.02)	0.72	(1.38)	1.05	3.62

Exhibit 3   Consolidated Statements of Income for Years Ending December 31

Source: FPI Annual Reports. Where figures have been restated in later reports, the most recent figure has been used..

307

Over time, FPI was able to compensate somewhat by developing an international procurement network to source cod and other groundfish (from Alaska, Iceland, Norway and Russia) for processing in Newfoundland and by developing uses for other groundfish species for which the stock in Canadian waters was more plentiful. However, even by 1999, the company's groundfish processing was still limited to three plants operating on a seasonal basis.

The effect on FPI's revenue was mitigated by the October 1989 acquisition—FPI's first—of Clouston Foods of Montreal, an international seafood trading, marketing and brokerage operation with a substantial presence in the Canadian market. The acquisition operated as a separate division for a time, buying and selling seafood, primarily shrimp, throughout the world. These new activities added $202 million to FPI 1990 sales (see Exhibit 4), albeit at a lower margin than the production activities. The Clouston division also came to act as FPI's marketing arm in Canada and Europe, as FPI placed new emphasis on producing and marketing secondary-processed products.

In September 1992, FPI acquired the U.S. foodservice business of National Sea Products. This strengthened the company's position in the American market and brought the established value-added shrimp brand "Treasure Isle" to its product portfolio. At first, FPI had to contract out production for this new line, but soon brought it in-house at its Boston plant, as shrimp and other shellfish[10] became an important new product category for the company.

Shrimp was the largest species component of per capita seafood consumption in North America on a dollar basis, and demand was growing. In 1990, FPI commissioned a new shrimp freezer trawler to take fuller advantage of the cold-water shrimp resources off Newfoundland and Labrador that were still in a healthy state. In the following years, it twice upgraded its shrimp processing facility in Port au Choix and also converted an idle groundfish plant at Port Union to shrimp. By the late 1990s, the company had become dominant in the

Newfoundland cold-water shrimp industry, even introducing a new branding strategy, "FPI Ice Shrimp, from the Icy Cold Waters of Newfoundland."

By 1995, these adjustments in progress had stabilized the company's situation, but there was a significant downturn in the seafood market that year. In response, FPI consolidated its two U.S. processing plants into one (realizing $5 million from sale of the redundant plant), and subsequently consolidated U.S. warehousing operations around the remaining plant in Danvers, Massachusetts. These changes resulted in annual operating savings of $2.5 million and superior distribution capabilities for the U.S. market.

Seafood trading continued to make up a significant portion of FPI sales. However, towards the end of the decade, the company chose to focus on core product lines and eliminate any categories in which FPI could not differentiate.

THE SEAFOOD INDUSTRY

Seafood was a global commodity, sourced, processed, sold and consumed worldwide. The Food and Agriculture Organization of the United Nations (FAO) estimated that 30 million people worldwide derived a living from the fishing industry in 1997, and that 95 percent of fishers were from developing countries.

After increasing steadily for more than 30 years, annual world harvest of fish from natural habitat had dropped sharply in 1990, stabilizing between 90 million and 95 million tonnes through the mid-1990s. The FAO estimated that 70 percent of marine species were then being harvested at, or beyond, sustainable levels. As a result, aquaculture (fish farming) was becoming more important, producing 28 million tonnes worldwide in 1997, more than double the 1990 quantity.

Human consumption of seafood grew steadily throughout the 1990s, but growth was slowing due to supply constraints. Seafood was generally well regarded as a healthy and nutritious food, but had to compete with other protein sources

All figures $000's	1999	1998	1997	1996	1995	1994	1993	1992	1991	1990	1989	1988	1987
Sales by Business Segment													
Primary Processing	217,056	176,144	139,454	144,200	117,700	133,900	140,782	171,490	198,028	227,300	221,933		
Secondary Processing	224,463	218,506	204,812	183,700	183,700	183,900	186,618	140,310	121,372	105,700	95,568		
Total FPI Division				327,900	301,400	317,800	327,400	311,800	319,400	333,000	317,500	366,611	395,705
Seafood Trading	267,392	286,913	331,679	327,900	313,800								
Clouston Division				342,700	341,600	347,800	273,800	278,600	223,500	202,000	32,300		
				Difference between Clouston Division and Seafood Trading in 1995 and 1994 is non-seafood products									
Gross Profit by Business Segment													
Primary Processing	32,144	28,762	16,390	22,400									
Secondary Processing	27,451	26,306	30,414	19,600									
Total FPI Division					37,000	48,200	35,800	_Not separately reported_					
Seafood Trading	16,192	12,028	15,524	16,100	12,900	19,100	15,500	_Not separately reported_					
Clouston Division													
Profit by Business Segment													
FPI Division[1]				3,500	500	9,900	1,800	_Not separately reported_					
Clouston Division				2,600	(3,800)	4,000	2,800	_Not separately reported_					
Sales by Subsidiary[2]													
Canada	230,021	205,677	175,812	190,857	185,254	190,626	156,024	157,609	154,149	151,801	79,240	65,765	49,996
United States	413,406	409,966	445,953	422,844	401,497	418,122	398,284	377,789	331,728	324,346	233,298	264,263	314,342
Europe	65,484	65,920	54,180	50,857	56,258	56,848	46,871	54,953	57,060	58,897	37,253	36,583	31,367
Profit (loss) by Subsidiary (before income taxes and profit sharing; includes commission income)													
Canada[1]	7,858	7,253	4,331	3,828	2,397	10,112	(10,397)	(3,637)	1,588	11,027	(23,542)	17,635	58,951
United States	8,537	3,942	6,945	4,847	(5,833)	5,713	(3,434)	2,893	1,460	3,155	2,367	1,097	7,001
Europe	234	(303)	(489)	(270)	744	1,179	237	1,033	(2,126)	(362)	(260)	300	37

Exhibit 4   Selected Results by Business Segment and by Subsidiary

Source: FPI Annual Reports. Where figures have been restated in later reports, the most recent figure has been used.

1. Years 1992 and 1993 exclude the effect of major writedowns of Newfoundland-based assets.
2. A small portion of sales by Canadian subsidiary is international, primary to Asia. Otherwise, sales by subsidiary are a valid proxy for sales by geographic region.

such as poultry, pork and beef, as well as pasta, all of which were very cost-competitive.

Japan and the United States were traditionally the top seafood importers by a wide margin. Canada ranked 11th in seafood imports and sixth in seafood exports in 1997. Most of Canada's fish products were exported to the United States (see Exhibit 5) where American consumers spent almost $50 billion per year on seafood products. Japan and the United Kingdom were Canada's second and third most important export markets respectively.

In most countries, raw material was purchased through free market, auction and/or direct sales mechanisms. Prices were thus driven by global supply and demand, reflecting a variety of factors: seasonal variations in yields, supply interruptions due to natural disasters, changes in the cost of fishing inputs such as fuel oil, trade restrictions such as tariffs and foreign exchange rate fluctuations.

The market for seafood products was highly competitive, with buyers at all levels demanding high-quality product and service at competitive prices. Processors purchased raw material (fish) from seafood harvesters and developed basic or value-added packaged seafood products to be marketed through wholesale and/or retail channels around the world. Generally, margins were highest for the fish harvesters at the beginning of the supply chain, and for retailers and restaurants selling to end-consumers.

Fishery Management

The sustainability of global fish stocks was a critical issue for the industry. Significant overfishing in many parts of the world had seriously depleted stocks of certain species, threatening the viability of both harvesters and fish processors.

Industry and government had joined efforts in many countries to try to ensure a sustainable resource base, and the Northwest Atlantic Fishing Organization (NAFO) attempted to promote international consultation and co-operation for "the optimum utilization, rational management and conservation of the northwest Atlantic fishery resources."[11] In Canada, the federal Department of Fisheries and Oceans (DFO) worked with provinces and territories to manage fishery resources and balance quotas with processing capacity.

Under the Law of the Sea, Canada had economic jurisdiction over the 200-mile zone off the coast of Atlantic Canada. This area was divided into three divisions and 16 zones. The DFO established "total allowable catch" (TAC) quotas for each of these zones to limit how many fish could be harvested each year; this allocation also, in effect, divided the resource among the four Atlantic Canada provinces.

The TAC for each zone was split between the inshore and offshore fisheries, and the offshore

Origin/Destination	Jan-98	Jan-99	Jan-00
Canada to United States	649	807	1,106
Canada to All Countries	1,480	1,603	2,052
Canada to All Countries — shrimp, scallops, crab, groundfish only	909	964	1,215

Exhibit 5   Canadian Fish Exports (Cdn$ millions)

Source: Industry Canada (2000).

quotas were then allocated to individual companies by means of licences, giving them the right to harvest certain amounts of specific fish. FPI regularly received the largest TAC allocation of any company.

Fish processors also required licences for each species; these were issued by provincial and territorial governments. Only Canadian-controlled companies were eligible for these licences.

These regulations strictly limited foreign access to fish stocks off the Canadian coast, and as a consequence, many European nations imposed high tariffs on Canadian seafood imports. However, neither Canadian regulations nor the voluntary NAFO guidelines could prevent foreign vessels from fishing just outside the edge of Canada's 200-mile economic zone. This was a source of constant concern to the Canadian fishing industry.

Competition

Besides FPI, major publicly held competitors in the international seafood industry included Sanford Limited, Icelandic Freezing Plants Corporation Plc. and High Liner Foods Inc. (see Exhibit 6). There were also a number of significant privately held competitors. These included Clearwater Fine Foods Inc. and The Barry Group of Companies.

Icelandic Freezing Plants Corporation Plc. (IFPC) employed nearly 1,400 people of whom 1,300 were based outside of Iceland in subsidiaries

Firm	FPI Ltd.	High Liner Foods Inc.	Sanford Limited	IFPC Plc.
Headquartered	Canada	Canada	New Zealand	Iceland
Revenue	$ 708,911	$ 302,392	$ 265,555	$ 760,125
Net Income	$ 10,026	$ (4,067)	$ 40,740	$ (3,731)
Total Assets	$ 314,412	$ 219,901	$ 297,979	$ 381,425
Current Ratio	3.32	1.68	1.25	1.14
Cost of Goods Sold %	89%	74%	Not Published	87%
ROE (After Taxes)	6.14%	–0.06%	18.40%	–6.28%
ROE (Before Taxes)	9.00%	–0.05%	22.00%	N/A
Earnings per Share	$ 0.66	$ (0.56)	$ 0.41	$ (0.12)
Number of Employees	3,000	1,500	13,005	1,300
Subsidiaries & Associates	4	3	18	6
Ownership/ Shareholders	Maximum 15% per shareholder	No Restrictions; (two shareholders own in aggregate over 50%)	2,547 shareholders; one shareholder holds 37%; no maximum evident	Information not available

Exhibit 6   Significant Publicly Held Competitors in the Seafood Industry

Note: All figures on consolidated basis for 1999, converted if necessary to Canadian dollars using nominal rate of January 1, 2000.

Source: Corporate Web sites and Annual Reports.

located in Europe, Russia, Norway, the United Kingdom and the United States. IFPC offered over 40 species, primarily harvested near Iceland, and sold in over 30 countries including the Far East. Its customers included large supermarkets, distributors, wholesalers, as well as restaurants and food processors for its product line of whole frozen fish, fillets and fillet portions, shellfish and a wide variety of convenience products.

Sanford Limited (Sanford) was New Zealand's largest seafood company with 18 subsidiaries, associate companies in four countries and 1,500 employees. Sanford produced a wide range of seafood products, primarily for export to Europe (31 percent of sales) and to North and South America (23 percent). Sanford was one of the oldest publicly listed companies in New Zealand. One shareholder owned 37 percent of the company.

There were approximately 1,000 seafood companies operating in the United States, and 150 in Canada. These varied widely in size and product line. Like IFPC and Sanford, many of these firms (including FPI) were vertically integrated, fishing from company-owned vessels, processing in company-owned plants, and distributing and marketing through in-house representatives.

Canadian-based High Liner Foods Ltd. (High Liner), formerly National Sea Products, was the largest Atlantic Canada-based supplier of fresh groundfish to the U.S. market. It processed and marketed seafood under High Liner and other brands and had a strong position in the retail frozen seafood market. The company operated in Nova Scotia, Ontario and the United States and employed 1,500 people. High Liner procured most of its raw material internationally, although it also harvested approximately 11,000 tonnes of seafood each year from Nova Scotia to Labrador. Even so, the company's advanced processing facilities operated at just over 40 percent capacity. High Liner had recently diversified into non-seafood products by acquiring Italian Village, a pasta products operation. Two corporate investors owned more than 50 percent of High Liner's shares.

The Barry Group of Companies (The Barry Group), based in Corner Brook, Newfoundland,

was a fourth-generation family business established in 1910. It owned and operated 17 plants in Atlantic Canada employing more than 3,000 people, and marketed its products under the Ocean Leader and Seafreeze brands.

Clearwater Fine Foods Inc., (Clearwater) based in Halifax, Nova Scotia, specialized in lobster, sea scallops, surf clams and shrimp. The company owned and operated eight shore-based processing plants in Atlantic Canada as well as 23 vessels with capacity to harvest more than 20,000 tonnes of fish per year. Clearwater employed more than 2,000 people, 1,100 of whom had been added since the cod moratorium had been announced.

FISHERY PRODUCTS INTERNATIONAL LTD. IN 2000

FPI was headquartered in St. John's, Newfoundland and Labrador, Canada, and had subsidiaries in the United States and Europe.

Company advertisements proclaimed "the FPI flag flies proudly in 42 countries." FPI maintained sales offices in Canada (St. John's, Montreal, Toronto, Calgary and Vancouver), the United States (Danvers, Massachusetts and Seattle, Washington), Reading, England, and Cuxhavin, Germany, as well as a brokerage and distribution network throughout North America and Europe. The Canadian operation handled exports to Asia.

The company also had co-packing arrangements in shrimp-processing plants in Thailand, Ecuador, Indonesia and Mexico; at fish-processing facilities in Norway and Chile; and at aquaculture farms and secondary-processing plants in China. Integrated information systems kept employees around the world connected to suppliers, customers and each other in real time.

Products and Marketing

FPI produced and marketed primary- and secondary-processed seafood products including cold-water shrimp, snow crab, sea scallops, cod, flounder, sole, redfish, pollock, Greenland halibut, haddock and capelin.

FPI was a leading marketer of primary-processed cold-water shrimp and snow crab in Europe, North America and Asia. Three-quarters of FPI's value-added sales were to the foodservice market (restaurant and hotel chains, airline caterers, hospitals, etc.) and wholesale club stores in the United States. Most of the remaining 25 percent went to restaurant and retail markets in Canada, where FPI was the leading supplier to the private label market. Some went to overseas markets, primarily Switzerland, which was the only tariff-free European country for Canadian seafood exports in 2000.

The company conducted product development through a full-time staff of food scientists and food technologists. FPI's development staff often worked closely with customer menu-development departments, to generate new process concepts and value-added products. New product launches annually generated more than 15 percent of FPI sales.

FPI had developed a strong brand and a reputation for quality. Buyers frequently requested FPI products by brand name, and the company was regularly recognized for its sales and marketing excellence by industry associations and independent trade organizations. In 1999, FPI received "outstanding supplier" awards from North America's largest independent foodservice distributor, largest retail chain, and several national restaurant chains.

These customers tended to be somewhat flexible regarding price if they were assured of a stable and high-quality supply. However, large customers such as McDonald's, Price Club and Red Lobster posed a special challenge for FPI and all seafood companies because of their price sensitivity. These customers demanded top quality and excellent service, but were quite prepared to switch suppliers or even change to substitute foodstuffs at a certain price point.

The company's seafood trading business earned commission income by brokering internationally sourced seafood products such as black tiger and warm water shrimp (which made up 60 percent of trading sales), king crab, farmed scallops, North Atlantic lobster, salmon and sea bass. These products, many originating from aquaculture, were sourced from other producers in North America, Southeast Asia, South America and Europe.

Operations

FPI reported its operations in three categories: primary processing, secondary processing and seafood trading (see Exhibit 4).

Primary processing turned fresh-caught fish into ready-to-market basic products (such as loose fillets or shrimp) or into inputs for further value-added processing. All primary processing was done in Atlantic Canada through nine processing plants, many of which had been upgraded to state-of-the-art technology.

Secondary processing increased the value of primary-processed products by adding non-seafood ingredients such as batter, stuffings and sauces to create finished products ready for consumers' plates. FPI's two secondary processing plants (Burin, Newfoundland, for the Canadian market and Danvers, Massachusetts, for the U.S. market) had recently been upgraded with new technologies such as automated weighing, packaging and freezing capabilities and now had a combined annual capacity of 43,000 tonnes of value-added products.

All FPI plants were treated as cost centres. As a result, plant management tended to be very cost-conscious and operated relatively independently of the marketing side of the company.

Raw material for the plants was partially sourced by FPI's own fleet of 18 fishing vessels—12 outfitted for catching groundfish, five for sea scallops and one for shrimp—that operated off Newfoundland and Nova Scotia and were serviced from the company's refit centre in Burin. This backward integration reduced volatility in raw material costs and secured a certain volume of supply. However, natural conditions and government quotas limited its total catch, so FPI also purchased raw material from more than 3,000 independent Newfoundland fishers, and sourced 25 seafood species from over 30 countries. FPI technical personnel worked with suppliers at source around the world to ensure quality and to build long-term supplier relationships.

Quality Assurance and Environmental Awareness

All seafood companies were required to adhere to strict quality assurance standards. FPI's quality assurance practices and processing facilities continually met or exceeded the Canadian Food Inspection Agency's (CFIA) regulatory requirements. FPI was periodically audited by the CFIA, the U.S. Food and Drug Administration, the U.S. Department of Commerce and customers.

FPI's quality management programs were based on the principles of Hazard Analysis Critical Control Point (HACCP), originally developed by the Pillsbury Company to provide safe food for American astronauts. An HACCP system involved inspection at different points of the production process, rather than simply inspecting the end product. Many importers, including all U.S. companies, accepted seafood products only from foreign suppliers using an HACCP system.

FPI was committed to maintaining a sustainable fishery and regularly stated its support for the DFO's conservation measures, difficult as those had been for the company. Management structure included a standing committee that monitored operations to ensure regulatory compliance and sound environmental policies. The company continually improved its fishing practices to avoid catching undersized fish or restricted species and fully supported independent-observer monitoring of its harvesting operations.

FPI vessels and crew had participated in 25 directed research surveys in co-operation with the DFO to gather scientific data on which TAC quotas were based. FPI also supported two research chairs in oceanography and fish conservation at Memorial University in St. John's with more than $800,000 in grants.

Human Resources

Teamwork and innovation have been the heart and soul of our success. . . . While seafood is our business, people are our strength.

—Vic Young, FPI 1999 Annual Report

Of FPI's 3,400 employees worldwide, 3,000 worked in Atlantic Canada. The company's annual reports consistently attributed its success to the commitment of its employees. Turnover was low among staff and executive management.

Trawler workers, plant workers and fishers were unionized through the Fish, Food and Allied Workers (FFAW) affiliated with the Canadian Auto Workers (CAW). The company's relationships with its employees and their unions, as well as with the communities in which it operated, were positive. Many people attributed this to Young, whose negotiating abilities were recognized beyond the company; as a special mediator for a 1994 labor dispute between Newfoundland and Labrador teachers and the provincial government, Young was credited with preventing a bitter strike.

Collective agreements had provided for wage increases for FPI's Newfoundland-based employees in eight of the last nine years, and the company considered the wages it paid to be "industry-leading." As well, the company had a defined benefit pension plan and a profit-sharing plan that distributed 10 percent of pre-tax profit before extraordinary items to employees. FPI also reserved over 200,000 shares issuable at market value for its employee share purchase plan.

In 1997, FPI appointed its first female plant manager, Angela Bugden, at its Riverport, Nova Scotia, scallop-harvesting operation. Bugden was also responsible for the five scallop trawlers and the refit yard for those vessels.

As part of its long-standing commitment to the professional development of its employees, FPI had invested in teamwork training for the management teams at its two shrimp plants. Team building posed some special challenges in the small, closely knit Newfoundland communities, in which a single extended family might include a member of plant management, a union representative, as well as independent fishermen and plant employees. As a result, information about cost structure was closely held.

Leadership and Governance

CEO Young had led FPI for all of its 15-year existence to date, becoming a prominent figure in the process. During that period, he was named *Financial Times'* 1994 CEO of the Year, inducted into the Order of Canada in 1996 and, that same year, awarded an honorary doctorate by his alma mater, Memorial University.

Young was very active in the business community, as a director of four other prominent Canadian corporations and a member of a number of fishing industry associations and advisory committees. He also regularly lent his support and stature to a variety of worthy causes.

As chairman, CEO and president, Young was the only member of management on FPI's 12-member board of directors (see Exhibit 7). The 11 other members were all unrelated, as defined by TSE guidelines. Seven members were from the province of Newfoundland and Labrador, three from Ontario and one from New Brunswick. One position on the Board was reserved for FFAW, a legacy of the agreement ending the 1984 strike at FPI. In 1999, the board of directors, as a group, owned less than one percent of FPI's outstanding stock.

The chairperson of the board's human resources committee was designated the role of dealing with matters of governance, including overseeing the relationship between the board and senior management. It was not unusual for senior management other than Young to attend board meetings to present business information. However, at each meeting the board held some discussions without the CEO or other management in attendance.

Finance

In the early 1990s, the company struggled with severe industry supply shortages, and recorded losses from 1991 through 1993 (see Exhibit 3). Since then, with the exception of a loss in 1995, due to lower quotas and poor market conditions in the United States and Mexico, EPS had improved every year. In 1999, FPI paid a dividend ($0.12 per share) on its common stock for the first time in 11 years.

FPI practised conservative fiscal management, maintaining high liquidity and low debt, because "Fish and debt don't mix," as Young was fond of saying. Like other local seafood companies, FPI financed some independent harvesters through mortgages secured against their vessels; it had helped some inshore fishers convert their boats to shrimp fishing in this way. Accounts receivable credit risk was minimal as FPI's 10 largest customers made up less than 30 percent of sales and no single customer represented more than six percent.

FPI stock traded on the TSE. Since 1987, its share price had declined to a range between $5 to $7 on comparatively low trading volume (see Exhibits 8 and 9). FPI had taken advantage of this situation to buy back one million common shares at an average price of $6.75 during 1997, and continued to buy back shares in 1998 (250,300) and 1999 (164,400). Nevertheless, a $100 investment in FPI's IPO, including reinvestment of all dividends, was worth only $59.50 at the beginning of November 1999. The same investment over that period in the TSE index would have been worth $192. However, if placed in High Liner Foods (the successor company to National Sea Products), $100 would have declined to less than $6!

During the summer of 1999, FPI initiated discussions with the government of Newfoundland and Labrador about dropping the 15 percent ownership limit per shareholder on FPI stock, arguing that it restricted the company in its ability to raise capital and enter into mergers or strategic alliances. These discussions resulted in the understanding that if FPI were to propose a major initiative requiring large amounts of capital, the government would consider removing the share ownership restriction, although the onus would be on FPI to convince shareholders, employees and the communities affected of the wisdom of doing so.

	Member since	
James C. Ballie	1992	Partner, Tory, Tory, DesLauriers and Binnington Toronto, Ontario
R. William Blake, PhD	1999	Dean, Faculty of Business Administration, Memorial University
Bruce C. Galloway	1999	Company Director Oakville, Ontario
Janet C. Gardiner	1987	Treasurer, Chester Dawe, Ltd. St. John's, Newfoundland and Labrador
Michael F. Harrington	1998	Senior Partner, Stewart McKelvey Stirling Scales St. John's, Newfoundland and Labrador
Albert F. Hickman	1984	President, Hickman Motors Ltd. St. John's, Newfoundland and Labrador
Thomas E. Kierans	1990	Chairman & CEO, Canadian Institute for Advanced Research Toronto, Ontario
Rev. Desmond T. McGrath	1987	Education Officer, Fish, Food and Allied Workers, St. John's, Newfoundland and Labrador
Frances M. Nichols, FCA	1991	Chartered Accountant Grand Falls-Windsor, Newfoundland and Labrador
Elizabeth Parr-Johnston, PhD	1994	President & Vice-Chancellor, University of New Brunswick Fredericton, New Brunswick
Vincent G. Withers	1995	Company Director St. John's, Newfoundland and Labrador
Victor L. Young	1984	Chairman and CEO, Fishery Products International Ltd. St. John's, Newfoundland and Labrador

Committees of the Board of Directors		
Audit	**Growth & Diversification**	**Human Resources**
Vincent G. Withers (Chair)	James C. Baillie (Chair)	Albert F. Hickman (Chair)
Janet C. Gardiner	R. William Blake, PhD	James C. Baillie
Michael F. Harrington	Bruce C. Galloway	R. William Blake, PhD
Alfred F. Hickman	Thomas E. Kierans	Bruce C. Galloway
Rev. Desmond T. McGrath	Elizabeth Parr-Johnston, PhD	Michael F. Harrington
Frances M. Nichols, FCA	Vincent G. Withers	Thomas E. Kierans

Exhibit 7   1999 Board of Directors

Source: FPI Annual Reports

THE TAKEOVER BID

We want FPI to become leaders in the global fishing industry. . . . We intend to accomplish this by bringing knowledgeable and experienced fishing-industry investors into the ownership group and by making a substantial infusion of new capital and management support into FPI's operations.

—Bill Barry, speaking for NEOS Seafoods Inc.

On November 5, 1999, FPI announced that it was the target of an unsolicited takeover bid.

Year	High	Low	Close	Trading Volume '000s	Shares outstanding '000s	Dividends Paid	
						Per Share	Total '000s
1999	$ 9.00	$ 4.90	$ 7.75	5,301	15,108	$ 0.12	$ 1,822
1998	$ 7.70	$ 4.30	$ 5.00	3,865	15,252	$ —	$ —
1997	$ 7.70	$ 5.35	$ 6.80	5,189	15,487	$ —	$ —
1996	$ 6.45	$ 4.30	$ 5.50	6,336	16,451	$ —	$ —
1995	$ 9.00	$ 4.40	$ 5.25	12,138	16,431	$ —	$ —
1994	$ 7.75	$ 4.60	$ 7.25	5,291	16,421	$ —	$ —
1993	$ 4.40	$ 3.05	$ 3.50	4,838	16,415	$ —	$ —
1992	$ 7.38	$ 2.65	$ 3.10	3,305	16,411	$ —	$ —
1991	$ 8.63	$ 4.85	$ 6.38	3,420	16,407	$ —	$ —
1990	$ 7.00	$ 4.00	$ 4.80	2,852	16,402	$ —	$ —
1989	$ 11.25	$ 5.63	$ 5.75	7,262	16,392	$ —	$ —
1988	$ 17.25	$ 8.00	$ 10.00	13,440	16,019	$ 0.40	$ 6404
1987	$ 21.25	$ 12.25	$ 17.13	21,491	16,004	$ 0.38	$ 4161

Exhibit 8 Common Share History

Note: FPI shares were first issued to the public at $12.50 on April 15, 1987. The stock closed at $15.50 that day, on volume of 200,350 shares traded between $15.75 and $15.38.

Source: FPI Annual Reports and Yahoo.ca Finance, January 27, 2003.

	1994	1995	1996	1997	1998	1999
TSE 300 Composite Index	100	115	147	169	166	219
TSE Food Processing Index	100	109	139	235	164	133
Fishery Products International	100	72	76	94	69	109
High Liner Foods	100	60	79	113	138	44

Exhibit 9 Comparative Total Return Indices

Source: BMO Investorline 2000b, bmoinvestorline.com/QuotesCharts, June 5, 2000; Yahoo.ca Finance, January 27, 2003.

NEOS Seafoods Inc., a newly formed consortium (40 percent owned by Clearwater, 40 percent by The Barry Group and 20 percent by IFPC) offered $9 per share to acquire 100 percent of FPI's outstanding stock. FPI shares closed up $1.35 to $8.50 that day, on volume of 113,730.

Young promptly responded that the offer was below book value per share of $10.75 and "extremely low." He further pointed out that any successful bid on FPI would have to persuade both the shareholders and the Newfoundland and Labrador government to lift the 15 percent ownership cap in FPI bylaws and provincial legislation respectively, although he also stated that, "We're not going to hide behind that restriction in respect to this bid."

Newfoundland and Labrador Premier Brian Tobin described FPI as a "vital institution" but indicated that the government would consider lifting the ownership restriction, given a "deal specific" acquisition or merger opportunity that was deemed to be in the best interest of the province. *The Telegram* (the St. John's daily newspaper) quoted Tobin as saying:

> Our interest is not a commercial one and our interest is not a shareholder interest. Our interest is a public policy interest. Our analysis will have nothing to do with shareholder value. . . . our analysis will have to do with how many jobs in how many locations, how many species, how much technology, how much technology transfer and what new opportunities.

Both FPI and NEOS moved quickly to make their respective cases to shareholders, the public and other stakeholders. NEOS took out full-page ads in newspapers throughout the province, explaining its intentions for the company, highlighting its principals' track records and claiming that FPI needed more entrepreneurial management to capitalize on "An Ocean of Opportunity." Bill Barry, who acted as its primary spokesperson, promised NEOS would invest in new and existing processing plants, leading to more jobs and longer periods of work, as well as guarantee a fixed percentage share of FPI's TAC to existing plants and their communities.

FPI ran its own full-page ads highlighting its achievements over the past decade and praising its 3,000 Newfoundland-based employees as the "heart and soul" of the company. Over the next few weeks, Young also issued 10 internal bulletins to keep employees informed and invited them to contact him directly with any questions or concerns, even providing his residence phone number.

Both parties also met with representatives of the communities in which FPI operated and of the unions that represented the majority of FPI employees.

Critics of the deal, including FFAW, argued that The Barry Group, which already had partnerships with other fish companies in the province, would control the entire shrimp fishery and much of the crab and cod fisheries if the bid went through. Concerns were also raised about NEOS's ability to live up to its promises, especially given its announced intention to replace $150 million of FPI equity with debt. FFAW also cited the positive labor relations climate at FPI and noted that only five of the 17 plants in The Barry Group were unionized.

By mid-November, FFAW's 30,000 membership had voted "resoundingly" against the deal, and all but two of the municipalities in which FPI operated plants had stated their opposition to the takeover and urged the government to leave the ownership cap in place. Buzz Hargrove, president of the CAW, with which FFAW was affiliated, called on the provincial government to make a quick decision to keep the legislative restrictions in place, and thus end the uncertainty for the communities involved.

By contrast, the Fisheries Association of Newfoundland and Labrador, which represented producers, was in favor of removing the ownership cap. And NEOS contended that shareholders together holding over 50 percent of FPI's shares had formally asked FPI to hold a shareholder meeting on or before December 28 to evaluate NEOS's proposal. (FPI later acknowledged such a request from shareholders holding more than *five* percent.) It was rumored that some of these investors were also lobbying the government to remove ownership restrictions on FPI.

On November 28, Young and the special committee of the FPI board of directors struck to deal with this matter issued a circular formally recommending that shareholders reject the NEOS offer and calling a special meeting of shareholders for January 17, 2000, to consider removal of the ownership cap from the company bylaws. It was considered inappropriate to hold such a meeting during the Christmas season, because some shareholders might have to travel a long distance to attend.

The provincial Progressive Conservative party, then in opposition, publicly came out against the deal on November 29 and suggested that there should be further restrictions on FPI, such as requiring legislative approval to transfer harvesting, processing or marketing units within the company or to make any changes in the operating status of FPI plants.

The special committee of the FPI board of directors subsequently met with NEOS principals on December 6 to discuss their proposal. According to FPI, this meeting resulted in no new information and no change of opinion on the offer.

Shortly thereafter, the provincial government announced it would not consider the issue of removing the ownership restriction before the NEOS offer was due to expire at the end of the month, and NEOS withdrew its offer on December 8. That same day, Young announced that FPI would be reactivating three of its south coast processing plants for more than 20 weeks each in the coming year—something that had not happened for the last seven years.

FPI shares closed down $1.20 to $7.55 on December 9 on volume of 35,000. When all was said and done, contesting the NEOS bid had cost FPI close to $1 million, lowering overall earnings per share to $0.66 for the year.

OTHER DEVELOPMENTS

FPI stock had traded much more actively than usual during the final quarter of 1999, and among the transactions were significant purchases by Sanford, the New Zealand fishing company. Sanford CEO Eric Barratt indicated that this position in FPI was a long-term investment, not a short-term play due to the takeover bid.

By January 2000, Sanford had accumulated a 15 percent ownership position in FPI, making it equal to FPI's other two other major shareholders, MacKenzie Financial Corporation (a Canadian

mutual fund company) and Hamblin Watsa Investment Counsel (a Toronto investment management firm). The next two largest shareholders were another family of Canadian mutual funds and a municipal employees' pension fund, each owning 11 percent.

In this context, Vic Young pondered the upcoming special meeting of shareholders and the many challenges that no doubt lay ahead for him and for FPI in the year 2000 and beyond.

NOTES

1. This case has been written on the basis of published sources only. Consequently, the interpretation and perspectives presented in this case are not necessarily those of Fishery Products International Ltd. or any of its employees.

2. Governor General of Canada Web site: http://www.gg.ca/Search/honours_descript_e.asp?type=2&id=3624 (January 27, 2003).

3. All currency figures in Canadian dollars, unless otherwise noted.

4. Atlantic Canada is a collective name for the four Canadian provinces located on the east coast of Canada bordering the Atlantic Ocean: Newfoundland and Labrador, Nova Scotia, New Brunswick and Prince Edward Island. The province of Newfoundland and Labrador comprises the island of Newfoundland and the mainland region of Labrador.

5. "Crown corporation" is a Canadian term for a business entity owned by government.

6. A limit on ownership per shareholder was not unprecedented in Canada. Similar conditions had been or were still in place for Air Canada (10%), Petro-Canada (15%), Canadian National (15%) and Canadian banks (10%).

7. Primary processing turned fresh-caught fish into ready-to-market basic products such as loose fillets or into inputs for further processing. Secondary processing, also known as value-added processing, increased the value of fresh-caught fish or primary-processed inputs by adding non-seafood ingredients such as batter, stuffings and sauces to create finished products ready for consumers' plates.

8. Groundfish, so named as a category because they swim close to the ocean bottom, include cod, flounder, pollock, flounder, redfish, turbot, sole, perch, haddock, greysole, sea bass and yellowtail.

9. Employment Insurance was a program oper-ated by the Government of Canada as a financial safety net to protect Canadians from hardship when they lost their jobs and while they were looking for work. Workers in the fishing industry could qualify for payments under special terms—in some cases, as little as 10-weeks' work.

10. Shellfish, so named as a category because they have shells, include shrimp, lobster, crab and scampi.

11. NAFO Web site, www.nafo.ca (January 27, 2003).

COMPASSION CANADA

Prepared by Hari Bapuji under the supervision of Professor Glenn Rowe

Version: (A) 2006-10-13

Barry Slauenwhite, chief executive officer (CEO) of Compassion Canada, had reason to be happy when he reviewed the figures of sponsorship growth in 2002. Compassion Canada had grown from 18,684 sponsorships in 2001 to over 21,886 in 2002, a growth of 17 percent against the 11 percent projected for the year. However, Slauenwhite needed to turn his attention to the target of reaching 100,000 sponsorships by 2013. In the last 10 years, Compassion Canada had only doubled its sponsorships. Now, the goal was to achieve a five fold growth in the same amount of time. He needed a strategic plan that was based on a comprehensive analysis of the com-petitive landscape and resources and capabilities of Compassion Canada.

COMPASSION INTERNATIONAL INCORPORATED

Compassion Canada was associated with Compas-sion International Incorporated, a Christian non-profit ministry dedicated to the long-term holistic development of poor children, particularly those in developing nations. Everett Swanson, an American evangelist established the ministry in 1952 in the basement of his house in Chicago. During the early 1950s, Swanson went to South Korea to preach to soldiers. In Korea, he wit-nessed the conditions in which many orphaned and abandoned children lived. He was moved by their condition and established the Everett Swanson Evangelist Association (ESEA). He appealed to American sponsors to help the needy Korean children with their schooling, clothing, food and health care. In his words :

> Christians have a responsibility to share with those in need. Surely our homes are the finest in the world, and our children are well clothed and happy. Our tables are spread with good things, and we enjoy many luxuries. Our babies do not need to cry for food or milk. We ought to thank God for His great goodness to America. But while God is good to us, in Korea there are thousands of boys who walk the street carrying a little tin can or pail, begging for a little morsel of bread. More Americans put more in their garbage can every day than Koreans have to eat.

Soon ESEA grew and attracted a large number of supporters who were willing to spon-sor the costs of providing food, education and health care to the needy children. In 1963, ESEA changed its name to Compassion International Incorporated. It worked solely in South Korea until it expanded its operations to Indonesia and India in 1968. As of June 2002, its operations spanned over 22 countries in Africa, Asia, the Caribbean, Central America and South America, helping a total of 350,484 children in these countries with food, shelter, health care and education. ESEA consisted of eight entities:

Compassion International Incorporated, the founding entity in the Compassion International Incorporated (United States), Compassion Canada; TEAR Fund Great Britain (Compassion United Kingdom); Compassion Australia; TEAR Fund New Zealand; SEL France; Compassion Netherlands; and Compassion Italia. A brief sketch of Compassion organization is presented in Exhibit 1.

COMPASSION CANADA

Compassion Canada was established in 1963. It began its operations in the basement of a home in Blenheim, Ontario, and moved to its own office suite in London, Ontario, in 1972, shifting to a bigger office space in 1986. Compassion Canada's activities, as reflected in its mission and purpose, revolved around helping needy children in developing countries in the areas of education, food, health care and overall development.

Mission

In response to the Great Commission, Compassion Canada exists as an advocate for children, to release them from their spiritual, economic, social and physical poverty and enable them to become responsible and fulfiled Christian adults.

Purpose

Assisting children to be:

- Christian in faith and deed
- Responsible members of their family, church and community
- Self-supporting
- Able to maintain their health

In pursuit of its mission and purpose, Compassion Canada found individuals who were willing to sponsor the expenses for children, linked individual sponsors with individual children and helped them maintain that link. Compassion Canada believed that most

people cared enough to help needy children, if they could find a dependable and reliable mechanism through which to do so. Compassion Canada aimed to provide that mechanism in an efficient manner so that most of the money collected from the sponsors was spent on the children. In addition, it implemented projects aimed at child development through partnerships with local churches and community members who approached Compassion Canada and were approved through a stringent screening process.

"The child is the absolute key to whatever we do," said Slauenwhite. The activities of Compassion Canada aptly reflected that. As mentioned, it found sponsors who would support one or more children by giving Cdn$31 per child per month as a tax deductible donation. In addition, Compassion Canada found donors who would support larger projects aimed at developing the communities in which the sponsored children lived. A list of current community projects of Compassion Canada is presented in Exhibit 2.

CHILD SPONSORSHIP

An individual willing to sponsor a child was required to make a tax-deductible donation of Cdn$31 per month to Compassion Canada. Sponsors could choose the child of their choice or request Compassion Canada to randomly select one. The child so sponsored would be enrolled in the project of Compassion Canada and provided education, food and health care. When Compassion Canada enrolled a child in any of its projects, the funds were committed to help the child through to graduation from school (usually until attaining the age of about 16 or 17 years, depending on the education system of the country in which the child lived). However, it was not binding on the sponsor to continue to sponsor a child until this age. Sponsorship could be discontinued anytime.

Compassion Canada facilitated the interaction between sponsor and child. The sponsor was encouraged to write to the child regularly and was allowed to send monetary gifts two times in

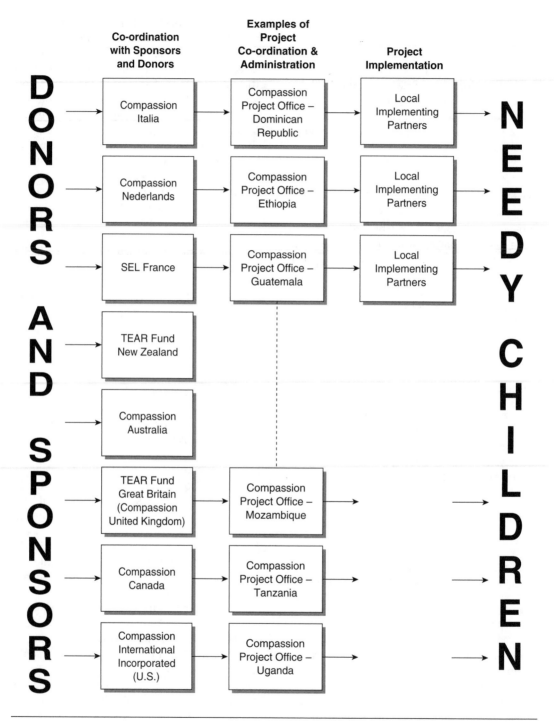

Exhibit 1   Schematic Diagram of Compassion Activities

EDUCATION

Vocational and Primary Education

These projects focus on skills development for young people. Compassion Canada's primary education efforts are presently related to programs with children that fall outside of standard child development work (e.g., street children). Vocational training involves essential life trade skills for teens in areas such as carpentry, metal-work, hairdressing, tailoring and other clothing pattern work.

Current Projects

- Bujora Children's Home Vocational Training Centre—Tanzania
- Casa de Plastilina Children's Education—Mexico
- Community Leaders Educated AIDS Response (CLEAR) Phase II—Kenya
- Kumi Staff Training—Uganda
- Meals for Children Program: Day Love Children's Project 2001-2002—Kenya
- Meals for Children Program: Mathare Street Children Rescue Centre 2001-2002—Kenya
- Mukura Technical School Expansion—Uganda
- Ukuru Community Development—Uganda

HEALTH

Primary Health Care

Compassion Canada's primary health-care partnerships focus on important preventative measures—like immunization, personal hygiene, nutrition, and health training for mothers with children under five years of age.

Current Projects

- Children's Medical Program: House of Hope—Haiti
- Children's Medical Program: Kiwoko Hospital Community Health Care—Uganda
- Community Leaders Educated AIDS Response (CLEAR) Phase II—Kenya
- Dessalines Community Health Program—Haiti
- Rubirizi Gravity Flow Water Project—Uganda
- Ukuru Community Development—Uganda

CLEAN WATER

Clean-Water Supply

Compassion Canada supports initiatives aimed at supplying clean water to families. This may take the form of gravity-fed water systems in mountainous areas, well drilling or spring capping. Often the projects also include a sanitation component, such as the building of pit latrines, as uncontaminated water and effective waste management measures need to be in harmony.

Current Projects

- Agwata Water and Sanitation—Uganda
- Rubirizi Gravity Flow Water Project—Uganda

Exhibit 2   Community Project Types   *(Continued)*

MICRO-FINANCE

Small-Business Microenterprise Development (MED)

MED helps poor people by giving them access to capital and training so they can launch and grow small businesses. It is highly effective in lifting people from the lowest ranks of poverty and does so in a way that provides dignity and a sense of self-respect. Compassion Canada supports microcredit loan projects, including programming that can involve the parents and guardians of Compassion-sponsored children.

Current Projects

- Dominican Trust Bank—Dominican Republic
- Faulu Microfinance Expansion—Uganda
- Ukuru Community Development—Uganda

AGRICULTURE

Agriculture

Compassion Canada supports community-based efforts that concentrate on objectives such as experimental crops, reforestation activities to conserve water and prevent soil erosion, vaccinations for livestock, the use of organic fertilizers and the developing of small farmers' co-operatives. The co-operatives help farmers to bring their produce to larger markets, while avoiding stiff profit charges from market middle-men.

Current Projects

- Bujora Children's Home Vocational Training Centre—Tanzania
- Casa de Plastilina Children's Education—Mexico
- Comitancillo Fruit Growers Association—Guatemala
- Ukuru Community Development—Uganda

Exhibit 2 (Continued)

Source: http://www.compassioncanada.ca/ca_communityprojects/project_types.html.

a year. Compassion Canada suggested that such gifts be in the range of $15 to $40. Implementation agencies helped the child in writing to his/her sponsor three times in a year. Compassion Canada sent the sponsor periodic updates on the progress of the child. In addition, it sent a biannual publication (Compassion Today) that featured Compassion Canada's work worldwide and a newsletter about Compassion Canada's work in the country where the child lived. If a sponsor decided to visit his/her child, Compassion Canada provided translators and gave out necessary information to the sponsor. The customer service centre of Compassion Canada handled the interaction with all sponsors.

Compassion Canada was very particular about emphasizing its belief in Christianity and its philosophy of using the Christian message to help develop each child and that child's family. It believed that church was a reliable and dependable infrastructure in most parts of the world. Therefore, it partnered only with churches and Christian agencies to support each child and to implement community projects. It focused on obtaining sponsorships from Christians, particularly the Evangelical Christians because Christians have a *"biblical obligation"* to help the poor. Of Compassion Canada's over 20,000 sponsor-base, 60 percent were Evangelical Christians while 37 percent were other Christians. The remaining three percent were non-Christians who shared the philosophy of Compassion Canada in its entirety.

It is not simply child sponsorship that we are interested in but child development in a Christian way. If we have a large number of non-Christian sponsors, it would be difficult for them as well as for us. There were occasions when we turned down offers of huge money from some donors because they did not share our philosophy. They would either ask us to work on areas that we were not interested in or ask us to be secular. In fact, we even stopped actively approaching the Canadian government for financial support because it expected agencies that received government aid to maintain a secular nature in their activities. In addition, government aid had the potential of diverting a large part of our energies towards interfacing with them.

—Barry Slauenwhite, CEO

In the past, Compassion Canada targeted all segments of the population, including young and high school-age sponsors who were more ready to lend a helping hand. However, over time, the focus has been refined to target young married couples and post high school sponsors who tended to remain sponsors for a longer time. Compassion Canada enlisted the support of sponsors largely through promotion and advertising. It adopted a multipronged approach to promotional campaigning. First, it deployed Christian speakers and artists who supported Compassion Canada and were willing to promote its cause as part of their speaking or singing engagement. These artists became the ambassadors of Compassion Canada's cause. Second, it advertised on a growing network of 15 Christian radio stations throughout Canada. Third, it requested sponsors to promote its cause, in what was termed "Awareness to Advocacy." Sponsors were encouraged to approach pastors to promote Compassion Canada one Sunday each year; the Sunday selected was the last Sunday in May. Further, sponsors were encouraged to enrol new sponsors and volunteer their own time and effort to promote the cause of Compassion Canada.

Compassion Canada acquired sponsors through many ways. It participated in Christian events such as Kingdom Bound, Creation West, Teen Mania, Missions Fest Edmonton, and YC Edmonton. It helped sponsor these events and used them to promote the concept of child sponsorship and enrol new sponsors. It received sponsorships as a result of the Compassion Sunday that was held in churches. Speakers and artists who promoted the cause of Compassion Canada often persuaded their audience members to sponsor children. Compassion Canada's own staff, volunteers, existing sponsors, Internet and the Compassion Today magazine were other sources through which new sponsors were acquired. Acquisition of sponsorships through each of these sources is presented in Exhibit 3.

Acquiring sponsors was not an easy task and required investment of resources in advertising and marketing. Compassion Canada believed that it was important to be cost-effective, not only in sponsor management but in the sponsor acquisition as well. Accordingly, the ministry strived to bring down these costs continuously each year. In 2001, Compassion Canada spent an average of $103 to acquire a sponsor, whereas in the years 1999 and 2000, the costs were $121 and $130, respectively.

Compassion Canada strived to ensure that overhead costs (cost of raising funds and administration costs) were less than 20 percent and program costs (costs towards child support, grants and services, field services, sponsor ministry and gifts in kind) were over 80 percent. A breakdown of the costs over the last five years is presented along with a pictorial representation of how sponsorship money was spent in Exhibit 4.

Compassion Canada consisted of 27 full-time employees. Besides the full-time employees, many individuals who shared its cause volunteered their services. These volunteers attended the office as per a prearranged work schedule and performed activities such as mailing, reading letters, sending letters, etc. About 40 volunteers performed the work of three full-time staff members in 2002. Availability of staff was reviewed every quarter to ensure that an appropriate number of employees were available to smoothly manage the operations. An additional employee was hired for every 1,000 new sponsorships expected. When a new employee was

Source	Number
Christian Events	766
Canadian Office (from another sponsor/donor, Web, etc.)	749
Campaigns (such as Compassion Sunday)	529
Speakers	310
Staff	302
Volunteers	213
U.S. Office (from other sponsors, Web, etc.)	116
Artists	46
Advertising (Compassion Today magazine)	31
Other	303

Exhibit 3   Sponsorships by Source (July 2000 to June 2001)

Source: Company files.

hired, besides the qualifications, their sense of commitment to Compassion Canada's cause and philosophy was evaluated. Typically, Compassion Canada employees were over-qualified for their jobs but joined because they had *"a sense of calling"* and decided to do something that was intrinsically satisfying. Each employee was trained in Compassion Canada's systems department for a period of six months before being given a formal responsibility. Compassion Canada had not laid off any employee in its 40-year history although some were asked to leave for reasons of under-performance.

When an employee had served Compassion Canada for a period of five years, that person was sent to visit one of the overseas projects to meet with sponsored children and to witness in person the real impact of their work. Major events and achievements were celebrated within Compassion Canada. For example, when Compassion Canada crossed the 20,000 sponsorships mark, Slauenwhite organized a huge dinner for the employees because crossing that mark meant that Compassion Canada had *"changed the lives of 20,000 children."*

Compassion International Incorporated, with which Compassion Canada was associated, relied heavily on planning and co-ordination. Consequently, Compassion Canada was required to send monthly projections of its growth to Compassion International Incorporated. These projections were made one year in advance and were based on sound planning. Each of the projections was supported by the campaign events planned, number of people expected to attend and the number of people likely to become sponsors. When an individual became a sponsor, their profile was prepared and added to the sponsor database. These profiles were periodically analysed to understand the characteristics so that persons with similar profiles could be targeted in the future for child sponsorships. Although the growth in Compassion Canada was high, it was controlled growth.

CHILD DEVELOPMENT STRATEGY

Compassion Canada's approach to child development was different from the approach of other

Activity	2002	2001	2000	1999	1998	1997
Raising funds	838,367	722,639	676,558	660,881	646,761	601,032
Administration	522,267	495,512	430,420	438,813	335,638	328,519
Child support	6,311,438	5,407,600	4,842,005	4,498,724	3,482,028	3,215,897
Sponsor ministry	431,236	442,808	315,630	266,564	294,198	273,411

Notes:
- *Child support* component reflects the money used to provide learning opportunities for registered and sponsored children.
- *Sponsor ministry* supports letter translation, pays cost of child photographs and other incidental expenses related to strengthening the relationship of child and sponsor

Typical distribution of sponsorship income

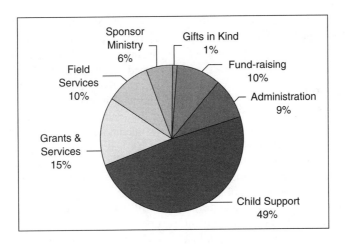

Exhibit 4   Usage of Sponsorship Income (1997 to 2002)

Source: Company files.

similar organizations. The organization believed that to develop a child, one must help the child directly by providing food, education, health care, shelter and spiritual development in a Christian way. Accordingly, Compassion Canada focused most of its energies on child sponsorship. Other agencies followed a somewhat different strategy. They focused their energies on helping the communities and families to become self-sufficient. Focus on children was, therefore, not as visible in their projects and activities, although their mission was "child development."

Most of the child sponsorship agencies followed a community-based approach to child development, while Compassion Canada employed a direct approach in which the child sponsorship money was spent exclusively on child development by linking the sponsor and the child on a one-to-one basis. Compassion Canada's other programs ran parallel to child sponsorship and supported child development in an indirect manner. The organization raised money for community projects through a separate stream, and utilized them and accounted for them under a separate heading. On the other hand, the money raised by the organizations that followed the community-based approach was pooled together and centrally allocated for various projects aimed at child development, including direct benefits to children in the form of education, food and health care. Among the child sponsorship agencies in Canada, World Vision Canada, Foster Parents Plan and Christian Children's Fund of Canada were prominent competitors for the sponsorship revenue that Compassion Canada needed to fulfil its mission. Financial and other details of these organizations and Compassion Canada are presented in Exhibit 5.

World Vision Canada

World Vision Canada (WVC) was "a Christian humanitarian organization that reached out to the World's poor." It was established in 1950 to care for orphans in Asia. WVC worked to "create a positive and permanent change in the lives of people suffering under the oppression of poverty and justice through long-term sustainable development." WVC's approach to child development was based on its community-based strategy, i.e., to initiate projects that were aimed at community development so that the community itself became self-sufficient over time and took care of its children. It developed an area development program (ADP) model to help communities achieve sustainable development. Activities included emergency relief (in cases of natural calamities such as drought, floods, earthquake, etc.), health related projects (such as tuberculosis, AIDS and nutritional health projects), and long-term development projects (such as sanitation, irrigation, vocational training and farming).

Almost 80 percent of WVC's funding came from private sources, including individuals, corporations and foundations. The remainder came

from governments and multilateral agencies. Besides the cash contributions, WVC accepted "gifts in kind," typically food commodities, medicine and clothing donated through corporations or government agencies.

Approximately half of WVC's programs were funded through child sponsorship. In 2001, more than 207,000 Canadians supported its child sponsorship program. The money so received from Canada and other countries across the world was pooled together and centrally allocated to projects that were designed to support 1.6 million children in 40 countries.

Foster Parents Plan

Foster Parents Plan (FPP) of Canada was a member of Plan International, which was founded in 1937, as "Foster Parents Plan for Children in Spain" to help children whose lives were disrupted by the Spanish Civil War. With the outbreak of the Second World War, Plan International extended its work to include displaced children within war-torn Europe in the 1940s. Gradually, its operations expanded to other countries and as of 2001, it was organized into 16 national organizations, of which Canada was one (also known as donor countries), an international headquarters and over 40 program countries.

FPP implemented projects in health, education, water, sanitation, income-generation and cross-cultural communication. Most of the funds for its community projects came from individual sponsors. FPP actively involved local communities in setting up and implementing projects, including families and children. Its motto was "sustainable development: a better world for children now and in the long-term future." FPP believed that to help a child in a lasting way, the organization must also help that child's family and the local community to become self-sufficient.

FFP identified the countries in need of development work with the help of a number of criteria, such as infant mortality rates (more than 25 deaths per 1,000 live births), per capita gross national product (less than US$1,700), and

Item	Compassion Canada	Foster Parents Plan	World Vision Canada	Christian Children's Fund of Canada
Revenue				
Child Sponsorship Income	7,065,231	36,892,048	131,082,000	9,960,794
Government Grants	185,391	2,507,319	21,292,000	317,568
Investment Income	161,160	577,698	274,000	n.a.
Other Income[1]	890,045	2,294,478	43,074,000	16,962,304
Total Income	8,301,827	42,271,543	195,722,000	27,240,666
Expenses				
Program Expenses[2]	6,690,790	33,575,328	157,002,000	22,633,973
Fundraising[3]	1,026,443	5,233,845	27,675,000	2,296,944
Administration	559,143	3,463,798	8,463,000	1,610,020
Total Expenses	8,276,376	42,272,971	193,240,000	26,540,937
Surplus	25,451	(1,428)	2,482,000	699,729
Number of Children Sponsored[4]	18,684	110,000	272,186	n.a.
Number of Sponsors	15,945	n.a.	223,995	n.a.
Sponsorship Cost in Cdn$ (per month per child)	31	31	31	29

Exhibit 5   Financial and Operational Details of Compassion Canada and Other Organizations (as of 2001)

Notes:

1. Other income includes income in the form of bequests, value of goods donated, and grants and donations for one or more specified or non-specified causes.
2. Expenses on all programs except in the case of Compassion Canada (where they pertain only to the expenses on child sponsorship).
3. Compassion Canada costs mentioned under two heads: marketing and community development
4. Foster Parents Plan figure based on the information on the Web whereas figures of other agencies are taken from their annual reports.

Source: Company files.

physical quality of life index (less than 80). As of 2001, about 111,000 children were sponsored by Canadians, and more than 1.3 million children were sponsored throughout Plan International worldwide.

After identifying the need, FPP worked in partnership with local non-government organizations and communities to effectively reach its goals. It aimed to work with them as long as was necessary to strengthen their capacity to provide their children with stability, protection and security in a sustainable way. Each community project took at least 10 to 12 years to achieve sustainable development.

In 2001, when Canadian contributions were combined with those of other supporters around the world, over $365 million went to program implementation. Of this amount, over 24 percent was spent on habitat projects, roughly 20 percent on education, over 11 percent on health, 12 percent on building relationships and six percent on livelihood.

Christian Children's Fund of Canada

Christian Children's Fund was founded in 1938 by Dr. J. Calvitt Clarke, a Virginia missionary, to care for Chinese-Japanese war orphans. He called it the China Children's Fund. It expanded into Europe during the Second World War and became Christian Children's Fund. CCF Canada (CCFC) was formed in 1960. As of 2001, more than 600,000 children were supported by CCFC and its International Co-operative of Christian Children's Fund around the world.

CCFC believed in making the communities self-sufficient so that children were taken care of by the community in the long run. The sponsorship amount received each month was spent on "providing food, clothing, shelter, medical care, education, school supplies and love to the sponsored" child. It was also spent to provide food, health care, vocational training, and agricultural expertise to the sponsored child's family and to the child's community. CCFC's projects included clean water wells, immunization programs and micro-enterprise training.

The organization derived its revenue mainly from monthly sponsorship support for children, families and communities. Other sources of support were: donated goods and contributions, general contributions and bequests from public, and restricted or specific contributions that were donated for a particular purpose or project.

COMPASSION CANADA'S TARGET OF 100,000 BY 2013

Barry Slauenwhite, the chief executive officer of Compassion Canada, believed in taking a professional approach to the management of non-profit organizations. With experience in industry and pastoral service and the sense of God's calling in his heart, he was in a perfect position to professionalize and grow the activities of Compassion Canada.

Compassion Canada had set itself a target of 100,000 child sponsorships by 2013. To achieve that target, the organization needed to reach its projected figure of 26,150 for 2003 and then grow at the rate of 15 percent per year. Projections and growth in child sponsorships over the past few years are presented in Exhibit 6. Reaching the figure of 100,000 in 2013 would be a great achievement for Compassion Canada for it would mark two milestones: 50 years of operations and 100,000 children.

Number of children sponsored	2002	2001	2000	1999	1998	1997	1996	1995
Projected	20,775	17,800	16,473	15,732	14,898	14,196	13,330	12,310
Actual	21,886	18,684	16,659	15,377	14,505	13,556	12,818	12,088

Exhibit 6   Growth in Compassion Canada—Projected Versus Actual

Source: Company files.

You're an Entrepreneur

But Do You Exercise Strategic Leadership?

Prepared by W. Glenn Rowe

If you are an entrepreneur, you are already in a leadership position. An important question you need to ask is: what type of leadership do I exercise? Answering this question may determine how your business will perform in the future. This article describes three types of leadership (Managerial Leadership, Visionary Leadership and Strategic Leadership) and the expected consequences of each on future business performance.

MANAGERIAL LEADERSHIP

Some entrepreneurs exercise managerial leadership. As managerial leaders they influence only the actions/decisions of those with whom they work and are involved in situations and contexts characteristic of day-to-day activities.

They may make decisions that are not subject to value-based constraints. This does not mean that they are not moral or ethical people, but that as entrepreneurs they may not include values in their decision-making because of certain pressures such as enhancing profitability.

These leaders are driven by bottom-line agendas that affect financial performance in the short-term. They want to maintain stability and to preserve the existing order. They are more comfortable handling the day-to-day activities, and are short-term oriented.

Managers will, at best, maintain wealth that has already been created and may even be a source for future wealth destruction as they are generally unwilling to invest in long-term investments such as, human resource training and development, promotion, marketing, capital investment, and capital renewal.

Table 1 summarizes characteristics of managerial leaders, visionary leaders and strategic leaders.

VISIONARY LEADERSHIP

Most entrepreneurs are visionary leaders who influence the opinions and attitudes of others within the organization. They are concerned with insuring the future of an organization through the development and management of people.

Their task is multi-functional, more complex and integrative. Visionaries are more likely to make value-based decisions and are more willing to invest in innovation, human capital, and creating/maintaining an effective culture to ensure an organization's long-term viability.

Not only is visionary leadership future-oriented, but it is concerned with risk-taking. Furthermore, visionary leaders are not dependent on their organizations for their sense of who they are. Under these leaders, organizational control is maintained through socialization and the sharing of, and compliance with, a commonly held set of norms, values, and beliefs.

It is imperative that entrepreneurs exercise visionary leadership to ensure the long-term viability of the organizations they lead. However, organizations that are led by visionaries without the constraining influence of managerial leaders are probably more in danger of failing in the short-term than those led by managerial leaders. Since visionary leaders are willing to risk all, they may inadvertently destroy the organization and destroy wealth.

STRATEGIC LEADERSHIP

"Strategic leadership presumes that entrepreneurs and their employees have a shared vision of what your organization is to be."

Table 1   Strategic, Visionary, or Managerial—What Kind of Leader Are You?

Strategic Leaders
• Display a synergistic combination of managerial and visionary leadership. Emphasize ethical behaviour and value-based decision making. • Oversee operating (day-to-day) and strategic (long-term) responsibilities. • Formulate and implement strategies for immediate impact and preservation of long-term goals to enhance organizational survival, growth, and long-term viability. • Have strong, positive expectations of the performance they expect from superiors, peers, subordinates, and themselves. • Believe in strategic choice, i.e., their choices make a difference in their organization and environment.

Visionary Leaders	Managerial Leaders
• Are proactive, shape ideas, change the way people think about what is desirable, possible, and necessary. • Work to develop choices, fresh approaches to long standing problems; work from high-risk positions. • Are concerned with ideas; relate to people in intuitive and empathetic ways. • Feel separate from their environment; work in, but do not belong to, their organization. • Influence the attitudes and opinions of others within the organization. • Know less than their functional area experts. • More likely to make decisions based on values. • Are more willing to invest in innovation, human capital, and creating and maintaining an effective culture to ensure long-term viability. • Believe their choices make a difference in their organizations and environment.	• Are reactive; adopt passive attitudes towards goals. Goals arise out of necessities, not desires and dreams; goals are based on past. • View work as enabling process involving some combination of ideas & people interacting to establish strategies. • Relate to people according to their roles in the decision-making process. • See themselves as conservators and regulators of existing order; sense of who they are depends on their role in the organization. • Influence actions and decisions of those with whom they work. • Are experts in their functional area. • Are less likely to make value-based decisions. • Are more likely to engage in, and support, short-term, least-cost behaviour to enhance financial performance figures. • Believe their choices are determined by their internal and external environments.

"There are three categories of people— the person who goes into the office, puts his feet up on his desk, and dreams for, 12 hours; the person who arrives at 5 a.m. and works for 16 hours, never once stopping to dream; and the person who puts his feet up, dreams for one hour, then does something about those dreams."

—Steven J. Ross, Former Chairman and co-CEO of Time-Warner

Strategic leadership is defined as the ability to influence your employees to voluntarily make decisions on a day-to-day basis that enhance the long-term viability of the organization while at the same time maintaining the short-term financial stability of the organization.

Entrepreneurs and employees make decisions every day as they interact with their firm's stakeholders, customers, suppliers, the communities in which they operate, and each other. What needs to be addressed is: are these decisions in accordance with the strategic direction of the organization? Will these decisions enhance the future viability of the organization, as well as the short-term financial stability? The answer is ABSOLUTELY.

It makes sense to suggest that if you can count on employees to voluntarily make decisions that benefit the organization, entrepreneurs will not have to expend as much effort on monitoring and controlling their employees. Further, entrepreneurs will have more capacity to examine what the organization needs to do, both in the short and long term.

On the other hand, if employees do not know the strategic direction of the organization they may inadvertently make decisions that damage it. Influencing subordinates to voluntarily make decisions that enhance the organization is the most important part of strategic leadership.

Noel Tichy argues that, "When you can't control, dictate or monitor, the only thing you can do is trust. And that means leaders have to be sure that the people they are trusting have values that are going to elicit the decisions and actions they want."

As presented above, the definition of strategic leadership presumes an ability to influence one's employees. It further presumes that the entrepreneur understands the emergent strategy process given that it has a greater impact on performance than the intended strategic planning process. This is related to understanding the importance of voluntary decision-making.

The decisions voluntarily made and the actions voluntarily taken by employees on a day-to-day basis eventually determine what strategy will emerge. Entrepreneurs who are strategic leaders understand and utilize this emergent process to ensure the future viability of their organizations.

Strategic leadership presumes that entrepreneurs and their employees have a shared vision of what the organization is to be so that day-to-day decision-making, or emergent strategy process is consistent with this vision. It presumes agreement between entrepreneurs and their employees on the opportunities that can be taken advantage of, and the threats that can be neutralized, given the resources and capabilities of their organization.

Entrepreneurs need to develop the skills and abilities that are required to exercise strategic leadership. Those few that are managerial in nature need to develop their visionary side and those who are visionary need to develop their managerial side. To demonstrate that entrepreneurs need to exercise strategic leadership two entrepreneurs who made a difference to their firms and to their industries will be discussed next.

"Without effective strategic leadership, the probability that a firm can achieve superior or even satisfactory performance when confronting the challenges of the global economy will be greatly reduced."

—R. Duane Ireland
and Michael A. Hitt

TWO ENTREPRENEURS WHO WERE STRATEGIC LEADERS

Konosuke Matsushita is the founder and former CEO of Matsushita Electric. At $49.5 billion, his revenue growth was the highest of any 20th century entrepreneur. The next closest were Soichiro Honda at $35.5 billion and Sam Walton at $35.0 billion. Matsushita was an incredible visionary who demanded revenue growth but with even more dramatic profit growth. One story describes how he told his senior managers that within five years he wanted revenue growth to quadruple and profit to more than quadruple. This goal was achieved in four years. How did he do this? Matsushita concentrated on creating products for his customers that created value in their minds that was greater than what they expected. However, he always wanted it done at a profit for his company. Matsushita's long-term vision was for the products his companies sold to create worldwide prosperity in such a way that in several hundred years there would be world peace.

The second entrepreneur is Bob Kierlin. Kierlin is the CEO of Fastenal, a company that sells nuts and bolts. His leadership style is characterized by employee empowerment, participation, wage compression (he pays himself $120,000 US per year) and promotion from within. However, he strongly encourages profitable revenue growth. This has been very beneficial for his employees, customers, and shareholders. In 1998, Fastenal's market value added was $0.077B—it was $1.609B in 1996—an increase of $1.53 billion. Kierlin started Fastenal in 1967 because he was unhappy with the bureaucracy at IBM.

These strategic leaders believed that their decisions would affect their companies' environments. They put great emphasis on achieving their visions by influencing the attitudes as well as behaviours of their employees. Moreover, they also ensured that their visions were achieved in a manner that was best for their employees, customers, and shareholders. In essence, these leaders were able to manage the paradox of investing strategically in their employees, in promotion through advertising, in research and development, and in capital equipment while still ensuring that their organizations were financially stable in the short term.

The Paradox of Leading and Managing

A recent Statistics Canada study found that the two most important reasons for the bankruptcies of small-to-medium-size firms were (1) poor overall management skills, such as lack of knowledge, lack of vision, and poor use of outside advisers, and (2) imperfect capital structures due to either institutional constraints or managerial inexperience.

The authors argue that managers in small firms need to be trained in general management and financial management skills. It is interesting that this study found a need for visionary and managerial leadership in small-to-medium-size firms just as it is needed in large firms such as General Motors and IBM.

Being a strategic leader is exciting as you create chaos, make mistakes, get occasionally rapped on the knuckles by your employees, and even occasionally have to apologize to your employees for creating too much disorder before they were ready for it. But the rewards are worth it as those with whom you work become energized and more productive—they accomplish more in less time and do not have to work dreadfully long days away from their families. Employees come to enjoy work more, as they become more creative and innovative, and more prone to taking risks because they know this enhances long-term viability.

Working through the paradox of leading and managing is an exciting challenge. One that is demanding and difficult, but one that is achievable for entrepreneurs. Entrepreneurs should start thinking of themselves as strategic leaders who have to accept and merge the visionaries and managerial leaders in their organizations. Fight against the constraining influence of financial controls and fight for the exercise of strategic and financial controls with the emphasis on strategic controls. The reward will be wealth creation and the achievement of above normal performance.

12

WOMEN AND LEADERSHIP

LAURA GUERRERO

The University of Western Ontario

Early in her career, Oprah Winfrey realized that her business success depended in large part on her personality, an appealing, down-to-earth image she carefully presented to what would become millions of adoring fans. She translated that insight into a decision to maintain complete control of all that is Oprah. She has kept her companies private and preserved majority control—even though she might have become even richer by going public.

—Pandya and Shell[1]

Academic researchers began to study gender and leadership in the 1970s. Early research asked, "Can women lead?" However, more recent research asks, "What are the differences in leadership style and effectiveness between men and women?" and "Why are women so underrepresented in executive leadership roles?" (Hoyt, 2007). This chapter looks at the differences in leadership style and effectiveness between men and women (Daft, 2005; Dubrin, 2007). It then looks at explanations for the underrepresentation of women in higher leadership positions. Finally, it discusses approaches to promoting women in leadership.

GENDER: EXAMINING LEADERSHIP STYLE AND EFFECTIVENESS

Academic researchers have not agreed on whether there are gender differences in leadership style and effectiveness. Some findings seem to indicate there are no differences, while others find small but robust differences. Eagly and Johnson (1990) found that, contrary to expectations, women were not more likely to lead in a more interpersonally oriented manner and less task-oriented manner than men. However, women were found to be more likely to lead in a participative (democratic) manner than men. Other studies have found that women are undervalued compared to men when they occupy a typically masculine leadership role and when the evaluators are men (Bartol & Butterfield, 1976). It has been suggested that women may use a more democratic leadership style to obtain more favorable evaluations (Hoyt, 2007).

Recent has research found that women's leadership style tends to be more transformational than that of men (Daft, 2005; Eagly, Johannesen-Schmidt, & van Engen, 2003). Transformational leadership includes four components: idealized influence, inspirational motivation, intellectual stimulation, and individualized consideration. All are positively related to leadership effectiveness (Lowe, Kroeck, & Sivasubramaniam, 1996). This may be one of the sources of the modern popular view that women are better leaders.

Researchers have also studied the effectiveness of female and male leaders (Yukl, 2006). A review of published research showed that men and women were equally effective overall, but women and men were more effective in leadership roles that were seen to be congruent with their gender (Eagly, Karau, & Makhijani, 1995).

THE GLASS CEILING

Women occupy nearly half of the labor force in many countries, but they are still underrepresented in top positions in business and government. Women are only 15% of managers and legislators in countries such as Iran and Iraq and as many as 46% in the United States, 39% in Russia, and 35% in Canada (*The world's women,* 2005). While these figures may suggest adequate representation in some countries, looking at top leadership positions, such as women's share of parliamentary or congressional seats, U.S. women only have 14% of the seats, Russian women 10%, and Canadian women 21%. In contrast, countries such as Cuba, Denmark, Finland, Norway, and others have more than 35% of the legislative seats filled by women (*The world's women,* 2005).

The invisible barrier that prevents women from moving into top leadership positions is called the glass ceiling (Daft, 2005; Yukl, 2006). The glass ceiling can also be a barrier to other minorities. Women who are part of a racial or ethnic minority face additional challenges in the workplace. Removing barriers to advancement for women and other minorities has several benefits. First, it offers equal opportunity and, consequently, benefits society and more individuals. Second, it benefits businesses, governments, and their stakeholders by increasing the talent pool of candidates for leadership positions, which results in the availability of more qualified leaders. Third, having a more diverse profile of leaders makes institutions more representative of society. Finally, research shows that diversity is linked to group productivity (Forsyth, 2006), and gender diversity is linked to better organizational financial performance (Catalyst, 2004).

EXPLAINING THE GLASS CEILING

Human Capital Differences

One explanation for the glass ceiling is that women have less human capital invested in education and work experience than men (Eagly & Carli, 2004). But women are obtaining undergraduate and master's degrees at a higher rate than men (Hoyt, 2007; National Center for Educational Statistics, 2003). Women are 48% of law degree graduates, but only 17% of partners are women (National Association for Law Placement, 2005).

Another explanation is that women have less work experience and employment stability because they may have had to interrupt their career to take care of their child-caring and domestic responsibilities, which are distributed unequally between genders. This explanation has some merit since it has been found that women with children are more likely to work fewer hours than women without children. In contrast, men with children are likely to work more hours than men without children (Kaufman & Uhlenberg, 2000).

Women respond to work-home challenges differentially. Some choose to attempt to excel in every role, others choose not to marry or have children, while others choose part-time employment in order to meet work and family commitments. Often, women who take time off from their career have to reenter at a lower position than the one they had when they left. This makes it more difficult to be promoted to higher leadership positions.

Another explanation for the existence of the glass ceiling is that women choose not to pursue leadership positions for cultural reasons and instead choose to focus on raising a family. However, this argument has not found support in research (Eagly & Carli, 2004). Other explanations for the lack of representation of women in the top levels of management include women having less developmental opportunities, having less responsibility in the same jobs as men, having less accessibility to mentors, and being in positions that do not lead to top leadership positions.

Gender Differences

Other attempts to explain the glass ceiling suggest that there are differences in leadership style and effectiveness between men and women. However, as mentioned earlier, research has not found evidence that women leaders are less effective or that their leadership style is a disadvantage for them. On the contrary, women are more likely to use transformational leadership, which has been positively linked to performance. Another attempt to explain the leadership gap is the alleged difference between genders in commitment and motivation to achieve leadership roles. However, research has shown that women and men show equal levels of commitment to paid employment. Both men and women view their role as workers as secondary to their roles as parents and partners (Bielby & Bielby, 1988; Thoits, 1992).

One difference that researchers have found is that women are less likely than men to promote themselves for leadership positions (Bowles & McGinn, 2005). One other difference is that women are less likely than men to ask for what they want and negotiate (Babcock & Laschever, 2003). These findings may be interpreted as reluctance on the part of women to take these roles or engage in such behavior due to the social backlash that they may face if they do promote themselves or negotiate aggressively.

Prejudice

Another explanation for the glass ceiling is gender bias resulting from stereotypes (or cognitive shortcuts) such as that of men as leaders and women as nurturers. These cognitive shortcuts suggest to people ways to characterize groups or group members, despite different characteristics among group members (Hamilton, Stroessner, & Driscoll, 1994; Hoyt, 2007). Stereotypes are not necessarily used intentionally to harm others. However, stereotypes can lead to discrimination in the selection and promotion of women to leadership positions and, therefore, can be very harmful. Women of color face prejudice not only as a result of their gender but also because of their ethnicity or race.

Another source of bias and prejudice is the tendency of people to report more positive evaluations of those who are more similar to them. This has the potential of putting women at a disadvantage when male leaders are in charge of promoting someone to a leadership position. Research has found that women respond in one of two ways to female leadership stereotypes. They either conform to the stereotype or engage in stereotype-countering behaviors. Women who are confident are more likely to engage in stereotype resistance, and those who are less confident are more likely to assimilate to the stereotype.

BREAKING THE GLASS CEILING

While there are still barriers for women in political and business leadership roles, there has been improvement in the past 20 to 30 years. Changes in organizations and in society are making it somewhat easier for women to reach top leadership positions. More organizations are starting to value flexible workers and diversity at all levels. Organizations can use career development, networking and mentoring, and work-life support programs to help ensure that women have equal opportunity to achieve top leadership roles in the workplace. There is evidence that society is also changing and that there is increasing parity in the involvement of men and women in child care and housework (Eagly & Carli, 2004). In response to the glass ceiling, some women have opted for starting their own ventures, which allow them to have leadership positions and flexibility, rather than waiting for the business organizations to change to adapt to their needs.

NOTE

1. Oprah Winfrey is chairman of Harpo, Inc.

REFERENCES

Babcock, L., & Laschever, S. (2003). *Women don't ask: Negotiation and the gender divide.* Princeton, NJ: Princeton University Press.

Bartol, K. M., & Butterfield, D. A. (1976). Sex effects in evaluating leaders. *Journal of Applied Psychology, 61,* 446–454.

Bielby, D. D., & Bielby, W. T. (1988). She works hard for the money: Household responsibilities and the allocation of work effort. *American Journal of Sociology, 93,* 1031–1059.

Bowles, H. R., & McGinn, K. L. (2005). Claiming authority: Negotiating challenges for women leaders. In D. M. Messick & R. M. Kramer (Eds.), *The psychology of leadership: New perspectives and research* (pp. 191–208). Mahwah, NJ: Lawrence Erlbaum.

Catalyst. (2004). *The bottom line: Connecting corporate performance and gender diversity.* New York: Author.

Daft, R. L. (2005). *The leadership experience* (3rd ed.). Mason, OH: Thomson, South-Western.

Dubrin, A. (2007). *Leadership: Research findings, practice, and skills.* New York: Houghton Mifflin.

Eagly, A. H., & Carli, L. L. (2004). Women and men as leaders. In J. Antonakis, R. J. Stenberg, & A. T. Cianciolo (Eds.), *The nature of leadership* (pp. 279–301). Thousand Oaks, CA: Sage.

Eagly, A. H., Johannesen-Schmidt, M. C., & van Engen, M. (2003). Transformational, transactional, and laissez-faire leadership styles: A meta-analysis comparing women and men. *Psychological Bulletin, 129,* 569–591.

Eagly, A. H., & Johnson, B. T. (1990). Gender and leadership style: A meta-analysis. *Psychological Bulletin, 108*(2), 233–256.

Eagly, A. H., Karau, S. J., & Makhijani, M. G. (1995). Gender and the effectiveness of leaders: A meta-analysis. *Psychological Bulletin, 117,* 125–145.

Forsyth, D. R. (2006). *Group dynamics* (4th ed.). Pacific Grove, CA: Brooks/Cole.

Hamilton, D. L., Stroessner, S. J., & Driscoll, D. M. (1994). Social cognition and the study of stereotyping. In P. G. Devine, D. L. Hamilton, & T. M. Ostrom (Eds.), *Social cognition: Impact on social psychology* (pp. 291–321). New York: Academic Press.

Hoyt, C. L. 2007. Women and leadership. In P. G. Northouse (Ed.), *Leadership: Theory and practice* (4th ed.). Thousand Oaks, CA: Sage.

Kaufman, G., & Uhlenberg, P. (2000). The influence of parenthood on work effort of married men and women. *Social Forces, 78*(3), 931–947.

Lowe, K. B., Kroeck, K. G., & Sivasubramaniam, N. (1996). Effectiveness correlates of transformational and transactional leadership: A meta-analytic review of the MLQ literature. *The Leadership Quarterly, 7,* 385–425.

National Association for Law Placement. (2005). Retrieved June 28, 2006, from http://www .nalp.org/press/details.php?id=57.

National Center for Educational Statistics. (2003). *Digest of education statistics, 2002–2003.* Retrieved April 12, 2006, from http://nces.ed.gov/programs/digest/d04/lt3.asp#c3a_5.

Pandya, M., & Shell, R. (2006). *Lasting leadership.* Upper Saddle River, NJ: Wharton School Publishing.

Thoits, P. A. (1992). Identity structures and psychological well-being: Gender and marital status comparisons. *Social Psychology Quarterly, 55,* 236–256.

The world's women. (2005). Progress in Statistics (ST/ESA/STAT/SER.K/17), United Nations Publication, Sales No. E.05.XVII.7. New York: United Nations.

Yukl, G. (2006). *Leadership in organizations* (6th ed.). Upper Saddle River, NJ: Pearson-Prentice Hall.

THE CASES

Anita Jairam at Metropole Services

The senior project manager at Metropole Services is getting the sense that her business relationship with her software development group is taking a turn for the worse. According to her, she was their project manager, and it seemed strange that her team members—all subordinates—were excluding her from an important client meeting. She must figure out what is wrong and take the appropriate steps to correct it immediately.

Women in Management at London Life (A)

A task force must make recommendations to increase the number of women in the management ranks in the company. Various factors help or impede this initiative, including the leadership of the CEO, the attitudes of some of the existing managers, and the attitudes of one senior female manager in the company.

THE READING

Leveraging Diversity to Maximum Advantage:
The Business Case for Appointing More Women to Boards

Women bring a different perspective to decision making. Yet where that perspective is, arguably, needed most—on boards—women are noticeably underrepresented. In this article, Ivey's Dean Carol Stephenson, who sits on several boards, makes a strong and compelling case for why there should be more women on more boards and what companies can do to identify and help more women to become board members. The case for why there are so few women on boards has become stale and easily refutable, which is why directors must read this compelling business case.

ANITA JAIRAM AT METROPOLE SERVICES

Prepared by Ken Mark under the supervision of Professor Alison Konrad

Version: (A) 2005–12–16

INTRODUCTION

"I cannot wait to see how pleased our client will be when we deliver this IT project to them one week ahead of schedule," beamed Anita Jairam, senior project manager at Metropole Services. Based in Newark, New Jersey, Metropole Services was a software development firm focusing on the U.S. health-care industry.

METROPOLE SERVICES

Metropole provided information systems integration support for the many software applications that were being adopted in healthcare. For example, after a health-care centre decided to implement patient monitoring software and hardware, Metropole would work with the centre's current IT staff to integrate the software into the centre's IT network. This involved a high degree of collaboration between client and service provider. Jairam met her counterpart at the centre at least once a week and communicated by e-mail or telephone at least once a day.

Internally, Jairam had to interpret her client's instructions and provide guidance for her team of eight software developers stationed in Newark. In addition, Jairam had scheduled weekly meetings with her supervisor, company founder Chandra Mishra, over video conference. As this was a rapidly growing start-up with 30 people in total, Mishra handled a variety of roles including business development, human resources and strategy. During the past three months, Mishra had been stationed in Hyderabad, India, where he was working to set up an offshore location for software development. While Mishra had promised meetings with Jairam every week, more often than not, they were postponed or cancelled. Jairam estimated that she may have spoken to Mishra a total of four times in the past quarter.

ANITA JAIRAM

Jairam had graduated from a prestigious East Coast business school and had finished her undergraduate studies at the Chennai campus of India's Indian Institute of Technology. She had always been in the top 25 percent in her class and was very ambitious. In her first job after her undergraduate degree, she had worked for a large consumer packaged goods manufacturer in India. There, she was part of a team of account executives whose goal was to sell new products to Indian retailers. She recalled her experience at this first job to be quite enjoyable—though she added that she had nothing to compare it to. The hours were long, nine to 10 hours per day, and everyone was preoccupied with executing sales plans. Jairam could not remember any instances of employee training other than the two-day orientation and introduction she was given at the start of her contract. Her team was a mix of male and female employees, and everyone seemed to be eager to prove to management that they were candidates for promotion. Because of her above average performance, Jairam was part of the 20 percent of account executives promoted to the account manager during the first round of promotions. (There were promotion rounds every six to 12 months.)

Promotions had been based solely on sales results. Jairam had the good fortune to be selling into a fast-growing group of retail outlets whose purchases of packaged goods grew rapidly every year. But by no means was Jairam merely fortunate that her accounts were growing. Because she was able to sell additional non-food product lines to her accounts, she beat out another male account executive on her team and was promoted six months ahead of him. Understandably, she was very proud of her work ethic and achievements.

In her new role, Jairam was in charge of six account executives selling health and beauty care products. At the start of the fiscal year, she met with all six and set sales targets for the first quarter. During the first quarter, delivery disruptions threatened the business, but Jairam was able to find an unorthodox solution by using a third-party logistics provider to deliver the goods. Working around the clock, Jairam multi-tasked between answering sales-related questions from her team and tracking shipping progress on her laptop computer. For the rest of that first year as an account manager, there always seemed to be

one external crisis or another that demanded her attention. Fortunately for Jairam, she had a motivated team of account executives working on her team who were able to conduct their business largely independently. After that first year, Jairam was identified as one of the top five candidates for promotion. But opportunity, in the form of a job offer from a start-up, came calling.

JOINING METROPOLE

When he heard about Jairam's success in problem-solving, Mishra was convinced that she was the right person to help him grow his small company. Mishra had been a medical doctor in the eastern United States for the past 20 years before he started Metropole. Concerned at the slow pace of IT adoption in the health-care sector, Mishra was convinced that someone like him, who knew the health-care system, could make a significant contribution to health care productivity and earn a decent living doing it. Relying on his network of contacts in India, Mishra had started Metropole three years ago to help health-care providers integrate IT into their workplace. But while he had no shortage of talented software developers, firm growth had been slow as Mishra lacked project management expertise.

Through his network, Mishra arranged a meeting with Jairam and was so impressed with her success that he offered her a job, including generous stock options, the same day. Jairam seized this opportunity and, within a month, had moved to Newark. She entered an organization that was operating very quickly and had limited systems in place. Managers seemed to be constantly overwhelmed with either client requests or software issues to fix, there were no set meetings or set targets for the year, and, although each person had a different business title, there seemed to be significant overlap in operating roles.

After providing a quick overview of the firm, Mishra immediately handed to Jairam her first assignment: working with a team of eight software developers to integrate a new patient monitoring system. With tight deadlines to manage and being new to the organization, Jairam believed that she had a lot to prove as she settled into the organization. Her first agenda item was to meet with all eight developers over lunch. As all eight were located in the same office building, she scheduled a meeting for Monday afternoon, a day least likely to conflict with client meetings.

She noticed that three of the eight developers showed up 10 minutes late for the luncheon. Wanting to start off on pleasant terms, Jairam said nothing to them, cheerfully greeting them at the door. As she introduced herself and explained what she intended to do for the year, she was interrupted by one of the eight, Vivek. Vivek was the team's unofficial leader, since the team had been without a project manager for the past two months. Vivek commented:

> We're very happy to meet you and we want to work with you to deliver this project. But as you know, we're already way behind schedule and, if possible, we should get back to work now and resume our introductions when the project has been delivered. I want to know if this is okay with you.

Pleased to know that her team was eager to get going with work, Jairam agreed to cut short her introductory lunch by half an hour and allow her team to return to their desks. In a converted conference room, all eight members worked alongside each other, sharing advice in an ad-hoc manner. Jairam listened enthusiastically as she met each team member in turn and asked them to explain their role to her. Every member of the team seemed to be extremely committed to the project and indicated that they were glad that she was coming on board. Jairam could not help noticing that she was the only woman in the room.

She left to go back to her office in order to attend her first client meeting. The client explained the urgency of the project, and Jairam reassured him that the team would do all in its power to get the project back on schedule. At 8 P.M. that evening, Jairam returned to the conference room to switch off the lights before leaving. She was surprised to see that her entire team was still present, still working on the project. One

member greeted her and assured her that they were staying later by choice. Jairam was very impressed by their dedication and asked whether she could help with anything. When the group said they had been about to go for take-out, Jairam offered to pick it up for them.

When she returned with food, she sat down with the entire team for a 20-minute break and talked to them about their work. She was not surprised to hear that all eight had been working with the company from the very start. They spoke enthusiastically about the future value of their stock options in the company and kept repeating that they were proud to be owner-operators and that this was a once-in-a-career opportunity. Jairam had never met such dedicated workers.

For the rest of that week, on-site meetings with the client kept Jairam out of Newark. She kept in touch with her team by e-mail and was pleased to hear that their progress was faster as a result of having her as the key client contact.

When she returned the next Monday, Jairam spoke to Mishra briefly and proudly indicated that progress had been made. On her lunch break, which she took in her office in order to read the latest news on CNN.com, Jairam was interrupted by a team member who wanted to know whether she could help them get tea from the local Dunkin' Donuts. Of course, said Jairam, she would be glad to.

Over the next two weeks, Jairam seemed to thrive in her new role. When she reported to the client that the time deficit had been eliminated (they would deliver the project on time), the client was ecstatic. He indicated that there would be a lot more work for Metropole to bid on if the project were delivered on time. To give Jairam a sense for the variety of projects available, he arranged for her to tour the facility, meeting with eight to 10 different IT managers. Jairam conservatively estimated that up to four times Metropole's entire firm revenues was available, if she could just manage the execution of the current plan and gain credibility.

When she returned to the office after an absence of a (productive) week and half, her team casually chided her about her absence and the fact that they had to send out a member to get their regular order of tea and food. Jairam apologized for her absence and eagerly recounted her client meetings and the opportunity that lay before them. Her team spontaneously erupted in applause, and they celebrated by going to a nearby restaurant for a meal.

As the deadline approached, Jairam's days in the office included a combination of client meetings and e-mail missives to her team members. At 11 A.M. and 4 P.M. each day, she promptly headed out the door to Dunkin' Donuts to bring back drinks for her team. At 6 P.M., she would take dinner orders and bring them back. This arrangement worked nicely, except for one or two instances when she mixed up an order or two. When she saw the dissatisfied look on her team members' faces, she immediately offered to return to the donut shop or restaurant to get the correct order, which she did.

Two weeks before the deadline, Jairam knew that her project was in superb shape. She anticipated delivering the project a week early and indicated to Mishra (on only their fourth telephone meeting since she started at the company), that much more work was available. Mishra's enthusiasm was evident in the tone of his voice and he congratulated Jairam on a job well done.

Returning to check on her team, Jairam asked them to take a five-minute break to discuss follow-on work. As she began talking about another upcoming project, she was interrupted by Vivek, who said that he had to get back to his coding. Jairam excused him from the meeting.

One of the remaining team members was surprised to hear about future projects. "We assumed you'd be heading back to India to get married," he laughed. "How old are you? You must be no older than our daughters, who are all happily married now."

Jairam was caught off guard. But she recovered and replied, saying that she had no intention of starting a family in the next few years. She was very excited about her prospects at Metropole, she offered, and she wished to be able to lead the company's North American

expansion. She indicated that she wanted to take on greater management responsibilities in the near future. At this point, Vivek returned to the room and conversation shifted to another topic. Jairam, wishing to leave them to their work, took their dinner orders and left to drive to the restaurant.

The next day, Jairam returned to the office to hear that there was a minor issue: a section of code written for the project was not working out as expected. As the code was written in a software language familiar to her, Jairam asked to take a look at it. Immediately, she noticed the error and informed the team member how to correct it. Her team member appeared skeptical and, in front of Jairam, turned to his colleague for advice. His colleague looked over the section of code and confirmed that Jairam was correct. Jairam, pleased that her judgment was correct, smiled and walked away.

The client was visiting Metropole's Newark site that day, and Jairam had planned a meeting and a facility tour. She assembled her entire team in a meeting room and was preparing to start her introduction when Vivek started speaking directly to the client. Vivek proudly indicated that the team was on track to deliver the project a week ahead of schedule and that everyone had contributed greatly to the effort. Not wanting to interrupt the flow, Jairam remained silent, interjecting now and then to provide missing information. At the end of the client meeting, and as they were leaving to start the tour, Vivek turned to Jairam. He said, "I hope you don't mind that I started that meeting. I was very pleased at my team's effort and wanted to congratulate them in front of the client for the work they've put in thus far."

Jairam assured him that it was no problem, that she was glad that he took the initiative. As they turned to rejoin the group, Vivek turned to her: "Would you mind going to fetch us our teas? I'll meet with the client and get us started on the next project. Remember, I like my tea extra hot."

It dawned on Jairam that her relationship with her team might not be what she had assumed it to be. She was their project leader, and it did not seem right that she would not be present for the client meeting. As he hurried back to the group, Vivek added, "And by the way, when we met yesterday night, the team and I agreed that it would be helpful for me to resume my client contact duties. Let's sit down later to see how you can refocus your efforts to target future clients." Jairam was stunned. She had been unaware that the team had met the night before to discuss this. Did they even have the authority?

It was 11:30 A.M. in the morning, a half hour since the client had left on a facility tour with the team. Jairam had been standing in the same spot in the conference room, thinking about her reaction to what she believed was a sudden shift of events in the past few days. Although it was not clear what the issue was, she knew that something was wrong and had to be corrected immediately.

WOMEN IN MANAGEMENT AT LONDON LIFE (A)

Prepared by Gavin Hood under the supervision of Jeffrey Gandz

Copyright © 1988, Ivey Management Services   Version: (A) 2001-07-24

In September 1981, a management task force was established to discuss the managerial development and promotion of women at London Life. Specifically, the task force was responsible for reviewing policies, procedures and attitudes affecting the development of women into supervisory and management positions. They had just one month to recommend to the senior management operating committee what action, if any, London Life should take to address the current under-representation of females in management positions.

LONDON LIFE INSURANCE COMPANY

London Life was founded as an insurance company in 1874 to serve a small number of London clients and, by 1981, had the fourth largest assets of all Canadian insurance companies and was one of the largest mortgage lenders in Canada. The company served Canadians at all income levels with life insurance, health coverage, pension and other financial products through more than 100 regional offices. Operating statistics are summarized in Exhibit 1. The company had a sales force of 2,089 employees, the largest

insurance sales force in the country, supported by an administrative staff of 2,535, over 1,000 of whom worked at the head office in London, Ontario.

In 1977, Brascan Ltd., a Canadian holding company, acquired a significant stake in London Life. Earl Orser was brought in from Brascan and appointed as chief operating office, and subsequently as president and chief executive officer. His evaluation of the organization led him to restructure management and focus the company strategy on marketing and investments. No layoffs occurred during the restructuring, but the previously highly paternalistic company atmosphere was transformed to a performance orientation in which employees were expected to make a productive contribution to the company's operations.

The new management philosophy was based on improving service, increasing employee productivity and reducing costs. In addition to structural reorganization, head office renovations, state-of-the-art office planning and new computer technology aimed at making the company's operations more efficient were begun in 1981. It was clear at that time that the future organization would be flatter, with fewer levels

	1977	1978	1979	1980	1981
Premium Income					
Individual	284	286	299	332	396
Group	159	172	152	299	260
Total	443	458	451	631	656
Total Assets	2926	3223	3513	3860	4318
R.O.A. %	8.23	8.56	8.92	.16	9.57
Net Income					
Total	n/a	29	35	53	46
Shareholder	n/a	10	12	23	23
R.O.E. %	n/a	9.6	11.1	18.6	16.2
Employees					
Sales	2112	2154	2071	2084	2089
Admin	2480	2490	2478	2421	2535

Exhibit 1   Operating Summary ($ Millions)

of management, and that there would be a gradual reduction in total number of staff as more and more computer technology was introduced. (Exhibit 2 outlines the projected number of management openings at head office and in the sales divisions.)

WOMEN IN MANAGEMENT AT LONDON LIFE

When Earl Orser joined London Life he raised the issue of the relatively few women in management at a strategic planning meeting. In 1981, females held 14 of 595 management and senior technical positions at London Life despite the fact that 73 percent of the head office staff were female (Exhibit 3). At the next level below this (supervisory and specialist), females represented 47 percent of the population.

In 1981, the Ontario Provincial Government was strongly urging employers to create equal working opportunities for women. There were various initiatives taken including the establishment of the Ontario Women's Directorate, the creation of a ministerial portfolio responsible for women's issues, and active consideration of various legislative initiatives including employment equity and pay equity in the public and private sectors.

At that time, many insurance companies—which were very large employers of women, primarily in administrative and clerical roles—were addressing the concerns of women. Of the "Big Eight" life insurers which dominated the industry, the Prudential, Metropolitan, ManuLife, Mutual Life, and Sun Life all had women board members. While London Life had no women on its board, London Life's female distribution and management representation were about average for the industry.

Orser's view was that London Life could be missing an opportunity to improve its performance because it was not developing the managerial potential of female employees, many of whom had extensive experience in the insurance industry and had a high level of commitment to London Life. This view was apparently shared by some other managers and executives in the company, although not many considered the

	1983	1984	1985	1986	1987
Projected employee growth	22	12	10	4	4
Projected retirements	0	2	6	4	5
Projected terminations	0	0	0	0	0
Projected openings	22	14	16	8	9
General Sales Division					
Projected employee growth	6	5	6	7	7
Projected retirements	4	4	3	4	4
Projected terminations	2	2	2	2	2
Projected openings	12	11	11	13	13
District Sales Division					
Projected employee growth	8	7	8	7	8
Projected retirements	9	9	10	10	11
Projected terminations	19	24	25	29	28
Projected openings	36	40	43	46	47
Group Sales Division					
Projected employee growth	5	4	4	5	0
Projected retirements	1	1	1	0	0
Projected openings	6	5	5	5	0
Corporate projected openings	76	70	75	72	69

Exhibit 2   Projected Management Openings—Head Office

	Male	Female
Total Corporate Management	98% (595)	2% (14)
Head Office Management	95% (231)	5% (11)
Individual Sales Division Management	99%	1% (2)
Group Sales Division Management	98%	2% (1)

Exhibit 3   Female Management Representation by Division

issue to be a high priority. He encouraged the human resources department to hire an experienced consultant, Fran Kennedy, and to develop a strategy and action plan to address this issue.

In response to Orser's expressed concerns, the human resources department held a series of three meetings, in which a total of thirty women, representing positions ranging from clerical to the management level, discussed women's opportunities, the attitudes in the company toward promoting women into managerial positions, and women's level of aspirations. Two of the generalizations drawn from these sessions were that: (a) women were not aware of the opportunities that existed in their departments or, for that matter, in other departments, and (b) women did not receive the necessary support from their spouses to pursue managerial opportunities. Most married women reported that they assumed sole responsibility for household management and were in no position to take on the longer and more irregular hours, and travel, required of management personnel. In fact, it was quite difficult to assess the attitudinal environment because most women had simply never considered the possibility of moving into management.

Following these sessions, the director of human resources recommended a program to encourage more career-oriented women inside and outside of London Life to become aware of, to get interested in, and to prepare themselves through effective career planning for managerial and higher specialist career opportunities throughout London Life. Excerpts from the memo are outlined below:

> By learning to assess their personal/career needs realistically and to acknowledge their strengths and limitations, more women should gradually qualify and be appointed to managerial and higher specialist positions over the next three years.
>
> Developing the potential of employees is good business. This program would affirm better utilization and efficiency of our human resources and payroll dollars as more women progress to higher responsibilities. Such equal career opportunities could attract more qualified, career-oriented women to the company legitimately outside the current restraints of our present job posting program, whenever necessary. Both the morale and quality of work life should be enhanced. Lastly, such action should lessen the potential attractiveness of third party pressures/intervention, whether they be from government (federal, provincial, municipal) or unions.
>
> We have very few women in higher level positions. This is a current and historical fact. With a few encouraging exceptions, the past five years have seen minimal senior appointments of women for finance, marketing (home office), investments, actuarial, group and administration, while many men have been promoted internally and appointed from outside. There are five women compared to 138 men in positions at or above manager level at home office today.
>
> There is a need to take "affirmative action" to correct past career inequities to make sure every employee has the chance to reach his or her full potential, based on performance and personal responsibilities for one's own career growth.
>
> We would like to see more women qualify and be selected for such future opportunities. Both Premier Davis and Labor Minister Elgie are also encouraging voluntary affirmative action programs for 1981. As we know, this movement is not a fad, but a major social force with growing impact on business.

Subsequent to the submission of the memo, twelve managers holding the following positions were appointed to a task force to study the situation, assisted by the external consultant, Fran Kennedy:

- Human Resources Consultant
- Program Coordinator, Employee Relations
- Vice-President, Investments
- Director, Human Resources
- Manager, Group Regional Office Services
- Manager, Individual Product Design, Marketing
- Vice-President, Group Insurance
- Operations Improvement Consultant
- Manager, Underwriting Operations
- Manager, Group Underwriting
- Manager, Administrative Services

Their mandate was to recommend to the operating committee the particular steps that should be present in a development program and to suggest changes to company policies which discriminated against women. The task force scope for making recommendations was unlimited.

HUMAN RESOURCE POLICIES AT LONDON LIFE

London Life had many policies and procedures which the task force realized had some impact on the progression and status of women within the company.

Salaries

Salaries were determined by market wages, job complexity, and individual performance. Benchmark internal salaries were compared annually with those at other local companies and large national employers by a management committee and the senior job evaluation staff. Internal job comparisons based on know-how, problem solving, accountability and working conditions, determined relative salary ranges. Immediate supervisors reviewed employee achievements and development to determine their salary within the defined range. Employees transferred for development received salaries corresponding to their performance and the salary range for the new job.

Maternity Leave

Eighteen weeks of maternity leave were available to women at London Life. During this maternity leave, Unemployment Insurance covered 60 percent of salary up to a maximum of approximately $20,000 over 15 weeks. A woman's position was not posted unless she resigned before going on leave, declared that she was not returning from the leave, or did not return to work at the end of the leave.

Flexible Hours

With management consent, employees could select start and stop times for their job within ranges which were deemed acceptable to the function of the departments in which they worked. In practice, people could elect a working day which was somewhere between the hours of 7.30 a.m. to 6.00 p.m.

Promotion

Promotion to supervisory and managerial positions depended on training and technical knowledge, attendance, ability to work with others, and self-development. Progress was reviewed annually by an employee's immediate supervisor. Positions up to first line supervision were posted at London Life. Management, senior technical positions and task force opportunities were not posted and were filled by candidates nominated by their senior managers. The job posting system is outlined in Exhibit 4.

Personal Development

London Life offered nine different life insurance courses and reimbursed 100 percent of tuition and 50 percent of textbook costs for external self-improvement courses. Funding for external courses was subject to approval by the human resources department and the employee's manager. It was extremely rare for individuals in non-managerial positions to request or take such courses.

WOMEN AT LONDON LIFE

Before the introduction of job posting and an extensive compensation review in the early 1970s, female high school graduates were essentially hired to be clerks. Because there was no maternity leave policy before 1970, pregnant women had to leave the company and reapply for their old jobs if they wanted to return.

Diane Haas, a member of the task force established to look at this issue and one of the very few women who had risen to the middle management level in the company, gave other members of the task force with less experience at London Life a brief history of what it was like for women in the company in the fifties and sixties:

> When I started working here, women earned approximately one half of what the men earned and women's raises were typically one third of what the men's were. So there was definitely pay discrimination in those days.
>
> Women tended to be longer term employees. They trained most of the males who were hired, in anticipation that within two years, those same men, better or worse, would become their bosses. I remember challenging my boss about this in the mid-1960s and basically what he said to me was: "Hey lady, you're a second salary. He has to support a family. Tough luck!"

ELIGIBILITY

All employees except for those employed on a temporary basis may apply for any posted position. You should, however, assure yourself that you have at least the minimum qualifications required for the position in which you are interested. The selection process gives consideration to education and experience, length of service, job performance, attendance and supervisor's comment on your recent performance appraisals as indicators of potential for advancement. Other factors could also play a key role, depending, of course, on the type of opening, e.g., ability to communicate verbally and/or in writing, diplomacy, telephone courtesy, ability to work with minimum supervision, etc.

POSTING PROCEDURES

Vacancies from the S02 position level up to and including division supervisor will normally be posted. Positions posted remain open for at least three days while qualified applicants are considered. Since new postings are made regularly, it's a good idea to read the job postings daily on the bulletin board in your department or the staff lounge. The information posted includes job title, department, division, position level, a brief description of the job and any special qualifications, as well as the number of vacancies that exist. If a job appeals to you, you should post for it immediately.

Jobs on which no selection is made are normally posted a second time. The word REPOSTED will be printed on the second posting description. Only applicants who did not apply on the first posting are eligible to apply for the reposted position.

A record of all past job posting descriptions for each department is maintained in Employment Services for your perusal.

If you are interested in the regional office positions, contact Employment Services for further information.

WHAT TO DO NEXT

If you see a position that appears particularly well suited to you, pick up an application either in your department, the lounge or Employment Services. Fill it out and send it to Employment Services. You should feel free to talk with your supervisor or section head about your interest in the position. However, should you wish your posting application to be kept confidential, this will be done.

Attach a resume if available. This will be kept on file by employment services and included on future applications until such time as you wish to revise it.

When you post for the first time, a member of the Employment Services staff will contact you as soon as possible to discuss your work experience, qualifications and interests and try to answer any questions you may have. An interview with the supervisor in the department where the vacancy exists will then be arranged in Employment Services. At that time, the requirements of the position will be explained and other points discussed, including an appropriate flexible hours schedule.

Should you take sick after the posting or are away because of any illness or maternity leave at the time a posting of interest arises, **it is your responsibility** to get in touch with Employment Services. Arrangements can then be made, if feasible, for an appropriate interview by the area involved either personally or by telephone.

If you should post on a job and know that you will be absent shortly thereafter, please bring your posting application directly to Employment Services. This will ensure that the appropriate interviews are conducted before you leave.

NOTIFICATION

After all candidates have been interviewed, you will be notified of the result of your application.

Exhibit 4   Excerpts From the Job Posting Guidelines   *(Continued)*

If you are successful, your transfer date will be determined after consultation with your present and prospective departments. The transfer should normally take place within two weeks from the day you are selected. If your application was not selected, you are free to consult your present supervisor and/or Employment Services concerning your career plans.

ADMINISTRATIVE GUIDELINES

If you are successful in receiving a new job posting, you would normally not be expected to apply again for a new position for at least six months.

Exceptions to the job posting principle will occur whenever:

1. personnel become available for transfer as a result of reorganization, reduction in the work load or the introduction of a systems change. In situations of this kind, the normal job posting policy may not apply, as those employees made available for transfer should receive first priority.

2. the reduction of a unit's staff complement occurs as the result of a resignation, posting, etc. and it is desirable to fill that vacancy from within the unit **without** restoring the complement to its original strength.

3. the employee is following an approved career progression within the unit and the staff complement is not to be increased, e.g., progressing from a grade 1 to a grade 2 clerk.

4. when a position is reevaluated, the person occupying it assumes the new level without the need for a posting.

5. a new job is created in the unit that can be filled by means of present staff, without requiring an increase in that unit's staff complement.

6. the employee's job has been phased out due to reorganization, redundancy or systems change and, therefore, no replacement is required.

7. temporary jobs, positions of a project nature and unique back-up training situations occur. The Company reserves the right to transfer or hire personnel throughout its operation without using the job posting system.

8. jobs require specialized qualifications and/or experience not available within the Company.

9. jobs are normally held in reserve for employees returning from maternity leave or extended illness.

Exhibit 4 (Continued)

In the early 1970s, there were some major corporate changes made with regard to measurable things, pay equity and job evaluation based on the job, not the incumbent. In 1973, London Life completely changed their salary positioning. We used to be one of the worst payers in the city. Now we are good, around the median.

The interesting thing is that I wasn't aware of the changes taking place. There was no announcement, the changes were evolutionary rather than revolutionary. What hasn't changed are the soft factors. Most men don't recognize that there are talented women around who want to get ahead.

I believe that a lot of long term female employees have said to themselves, "Hey, getting ahead here is a lost cause. I'm not going to fight the system; I'm going to come in, work my 9-5 and then go home." It was really uncomfortable to be one of the scrappers. You were fighting an uphill battle against discrimination. Most women didn't even think about promotion. It was just too frustrating.

The task force coordinator, a member of the employee relations department, added her own views:

There is a lot of subtle discrimination at London Life. Most male managers don't realize that they are preventing women from being promoted. As entry level employees, men tend to promote the fact that they are career-oriented. When they ask to take self-improvement courses, they get management approval, because the courses develop their ability to meet future responsibilities.

Women, on the other hand, are limiting their horizons to becoming supervisors. That's perceived as their ceiling, and we don't have many examples to contradict the perception. If women don't tell their managers that they aspire to a higher position, their requests for the same courses will be turned down, because the development isn't necessary for their current job. Therefore, men get the posted jobs, because they are better qualified.

The human resources manager on the task force pointed out that the recent hiring history and practices of the company made it difficult but not impossible to address the issue of moving more women into management:

From the early 1970s to the 1980s, all of our recruiting has been at entry level positions. We are hiring at the clerical level, not university graduates, male or female. I would also agree that we aren't encouraging women to excel. There is very little cross fertilization and we aren't encouraging women to take extra courses, to take a chance. I think that opportunities exist and women aren't taking advantage of them, but I also think that because they aren't considering themselves as potential candidates, they aren't coming forward.

Diane Haas, who had spent most of her career in operations as a clerk, a senior clerk, a section supervisor and then a division supervisor, related her experience of some men's attitudes to her progression into management:

Men in this company, with some exceptions, don't think they have to be concerned about women as competition. There is the odd woman like myself starting to progress, but as much as anything my progress has been based on tenure and experience. In most men's minds, I am a credible person, not necessarily a female. Men accept that there will always be the odd female who will bubble up, but there's certainly no concern on their part about having to be as good as the women.

The new director of human resources really rattled my own cage about three years ago. He told

me to get moving and start to chase opportunities that were there.

Three or four months after I moved to human resources, I was promoted to a manager. The immediate talk was, "She got the job because she was a woman." Subsequently, I got a position as a more senior manager in marketing. There were 22 applicants for that job. The manager who selected me told me that he thought I was the best candidate but an awful lot of the other 21 people indicated to him that they felt he had made the decision based on the fact that I was a woman.

A senior manager of Property and Investments talked about his views on the promotion of women:

There are issues associated with promoting women that have nothing to do with competence.

To start with, I don't think that society has accepted the concept of role reversal. If a woman is not a single career person, there is a whole set of associated problems. Not very many married women will uproot their spouse from his career. The concept still is that the male partner's career should be fostered. This is a real problem, because one of the conditions of contest in my organization is that you have to be mobile. I believe very strongly that the qualitative judgement needed to become an investments manager is only going to be achieved by working in three or four different market places. The dynamics that influence value in each area, in each region of our country are very different. Without experiencing all of them, you are not a fully seasoned mortgage lender.

It's also my observation, without a lot of experience, that women don't focus on their career in the same way as men do. There is not the expectation in most women that they will work for 40 years. The path they are setting out at the age of 23 or 24 is not a 40-year path. It's until they get married, until they have children, until a lot of things happen. That's not a universal statement, because if a man or a woman were to approach something with a single-minded purpose, I think either one is going to achieve it. Not many men approach their career in that manner, but I think fewer women do, because they have these other uncertainties as to which direction they are going.

So it's my recent experience—and I guess it's not unique to me—that women have a harder time progressing even though they understand the conditions of contest for getting ahead. They are less willing to give up friends and a social environment outside of work. It's also a very rare exception where, when there is overtime to be done, the woman will stay and the husbands are home at four o'clock to pick up the children.

Another reality is that most women have gaps in their career. Women do get pregnant, and if a woman is going to have two to three children, the gaps in her career are more than an irritant. From a philosophical point of view, it's fine, but if you have a key person who disappears for five months every two to three years, it's going to be difficult to build around. We have become a lean organization and we don't have three or four layers of competent people who can step into the gap. We plan and make sure that we have someone to pick up the pieces, but the person who has to fill in is already fully employed, so it stresses the whole organization when you do it.

The biggest danger I caution, is that you can't force increased female representation in management faster than natural growth will allow it to happen. I wouldn't like to see a United States quota program. If it was mandated that I had to hire a female manager from the outside, presumably I could, but I don't do that with men, because I believe very strongly in training our own managers for reasons of consistency of ideas and focus. Quality control is very important in investments. Loan losses can be significant if you don't know what you are doing and it's an area where there is a wide divergence of thought. I don't think equal representation objectives for management should ever transcend the fundamental objectives of the business.

Diane Haas expressed her own concerns about quotas which specified the percentage of various levels of management which had to be filled by women:

I don't agree with the classic affirmative action program, that says you must have 20 percent of women in management, for two reasons: first, from a corporate perspective, it's quite conceivable that you will get people who are not qualified in those positions because you are striving to achieve quotas; second, I think it's grossly unfair to put people in positions that they have trouble coping with. There are still days when I scare the living daylights out of myself doing what I'm doing, thinking, is this for real or am I a fake? So I can imagine what someone who is not qualified would feel in the job.

I'll be darned if I want to see women in management who are not good, who are not qualified and who cannot handle it. I think if that happens, the reflection of non-performance is on all the women in management, not just the ones who are failing. Right now, we are like giraffes in the forest. We are a very visible small minority and we are being watched. Therefore, it's crucial that we do well. I don't want to see someone, a non-performer, promoted simply because of their sex. At the same time, we have to get commitment from a predominantly male management to start encouraging women to develop.

THE TASK

As the meeting ended, the task force coordinator summed up the task:

We have only three or four meetings left to complete our recommendations, so we have to start developing our plan. Where should we start? What do we need to do to tackle this issue?

LEVERAGING DIVERSITY TO MAXIMUM ADVANTAGE

The Business Case for Appointing More Women to Boards

Prepared by Carol Stephenson

Women bring a different perspective to decision making. Yet where that perspective is, arguably, needed most, on boards, women are noticeably under-represented. In this article, Ivey's Dean, who sits on several boards, makes a strong and compelling case for why there should be more women on more boards and what companies can do to identify and help more women to become board members.

The poet Ezra Pound once said that: "When two men in business always agree, one of them is unnecessary." Many companies appear to recognize this truism and the fact that diversity fosters ideas and learning. Some have established comprehensive strategies to recruit and retain employees from different cultures and backgrounds. Others promote diversity and its benefits in their corporate vision statements. And many carefully portray diversity in their annual reports and advertising campaigns.

Unfortunately, however, few Canadian companies have boards with a range of people with different interests and backgrounds. Still fewer have plans in place to address diversity at the board level. The majority continue to be governed by all male, all white board members who share largely the same backgrounds, circles of influence and views.

William Donaldson, chairman of the U.S. Securities and Exchange Commission recently wrote: "Just as we strive for diversity in our workforce, we should strive for diversity of thought and experience on our boards. Monolithic backgrounds are destined to foster monolithic thinking." And I believe that monolithic thinking leads to missed opportunities, unresolved issues and potentially unworkable solutions.

However, as research on the impact of women on leadership teams demonstrates, diversity often eliminates this stagnation. Gender diversity, in particular, brings a number of other vital benefits to the boardroom as well. So, if a company is serious about cultivating a dynamic and diverse leadership team, then having more women on the board is a great way to begin.

This article first presents some of the compelling evidence for why companies need more women at the board level. Second, it elaborates on why women are not progressing as quickly as they should. Third, it prescribes some preliminary actions to address these issues. Essentially, this article underscores the fact that women merit a place at the board table—not simply for equity reasons, but because it makes sound business sense.

WHY MORE WOMEN SHOULD BE ON MORE BOARDS

Let's look at some of the reports and studies that substantiate the valuable contributions women make in positions of executive and board power.

In January 2004, the New York research group, Catalyst, released a study which examined the financial performance of 353 companies for four out of five years between 1996 and 2000. Catalyst found that the group of companies with the highest representation of women in their senior management teams had a 35 percent higher Return on Equity (ROE) and a 34 percent higher Total Return to Shareholders (TRS) than companies with the lowest women's representation.

This mirrors the results of a longer-term study led by Roy Adler, a marketing professor at Pepperdine University in Malibu, California and executive director of the Glass Ceiling Research Centre. This study tracked the number of women in high-ranking positions at 215 Fortune 500 companies between 1980 and 1998.

The 25 companies with the best record for promoting women to senior positions, including the board, posted returns 18 percent higher and returns on investment 69 percent higher than the Fortune 500 median of their industry.

Similarly, the Conference Board of Canada tracked the progress of Canadian corporations with two or more women on the board from 1995 to 2001. The Conference Board found that these companies "were far more likely to be industry leaders in revenues and profits six years later."

Interestingly, this 2002 Conference Board report also refutes some of the most common myths about the impact of women on corporate boards. These myths include widely held misconceptions such as: women only care about the "soft" issues; women don't have the financial or strategic acumen needed at the board level; and women will hamper board unity.

To the contrary, the Conference Board concludes that: "Far from focusing on traditionally 'soft' areas, boards with more women surpass all-male boards in their attention to audit and risk oversight and control." Specifically, its research shows that:

- 74 percent of boards with three or more women explicitly identify criteria for measuring strategy; only 45 percent of all-male boards do; and
- 94 percent of boards with three or more women explicitly monitor the implementation of corporate strategy; 66 percent of all-male boards do.

The Conference Board further concludes that the diversity that women bring enriches "the leadership palette with different perspectives" and that this "diversity enables constructive dissent that leads to board unity."

The Conference Board's research points to other critical benefits. For instance, gender diversity on the board and senior management team helps organizations to attract and retain valuable female talent. Also, "CEOs report that having women on boards contributes to positive attitudes among female employees."

In addition, the advantages that women bring in terms of ethical conduct are clearly significant:

- 94 percent of boards with three or more women ensure conflict of interest guidelines, compared with 68 percent of all-male boards, and
- 86 percent of boards with three or more women ensure a code of conduct for the organization, compared with 66 percent of all-male boards.

Women apparently broaden the focus of a board as well. When more women are on the board, the Conference Board found a major increase in the use of non-financial performance measures—such as innovation and social and community responsibility. As the Conference Board believes, "the factors that appear to be influenced by more women on boards are precisely those that have the most impact on corporate results."

Another important consideration is the fact that women have a deep and intimate knowledge of consumer markets and customers. Women, for example, control 80 percent of household spending, and using their own resources, make up 47 percent of investors. They buy more than three quarters of all products and services in North America.

The influence of women in business-to-business markets is also growing, especially here in Canada. There are more women entrepreneurs per capita in Canada than in any industrialized country. According to the Prime Minister's Task Force on Women Entrepreneurs, more than 821,000 Canadian women entrepreneurs annually contribute in excess of $18 billion to Canada's economy. Their numbers have increased more than 200 percent over the past 20 years and they represent the fastest growing demographic in our economy today.

Sadly, the progress of women in advancing to the board level is not as impressive. According to the 2003 Catalyst Census of Women Board

Directors of Canada, women hold 11.2 percent of board positions in the Financial Post 500, up from 9.8 percent in 2001. That's less than a two percent gain.

And the proportion of companies with no women directors has remained the same since 2001, 51.4 percent. What's more, women chair only three of the 243 publicly traded companies on the Financial Post 500.

WHY AREN'T MORE WOMEN ON BOARDS?

The most common reason given for why more women are not occupying positions of corporate leadership is that they do not have the operational experience required. Catalyst, for example, blames the gap on the fact that women often choose staff jobs, such as marketing and human resources, while most senior executives and board positions are filled from the ranks of line managers with critical profit-and-loss responsibility.

Recently, several business researchers and observers have also speculated that women are not advancing because they do not have the ambition and competitive drive of men. New York psychiatrist, Anna Fels, author of Necessary Dreams: Ambition in Women's Changing Lives, believes that women are conditioned to be "selflessly unambitious." From an early age, they learn that in order to be liked, they must play down their accomplishments. Consequently when they join the corporate world, they fail to push for raises and promotions.

Similarly, Linda Babcock and Sandra Laschever, co-authors of Women Don't Ask: Negotiation and the Gender Divide, say that girls are taught to be "communal," to make relationships a priority and to focus on the needs of others instead of their own needs. This makes them hesitant to negotiate for more pay or greater responsibility on the job.

A third common reason given for why women don't advance is that business—and society in general—still doesn't adequately compensate women for shouldering more family responsibilities. Consequently, women are paid less and

don't advance as quickly or as far up the corporate ladder as men do.

For example, economist Stephen J. Rose and Heidi I. Hartmann, President of the Institute for Women's Policy Research in Washington, released a report earlier this year that compares the earnings of the average woman with those of the average man in the United States. Based on Bureau of Labour Statistics, the report shows that the average American woman earns less than half—about 44 percent—of what the average man earns over the course of his career.

Why? Outright discrimination is part of the reason. Another reason is that the majority of women and men still work in largely sex-segregated occupations, leaving women stuck in lower-paying jobs. However, a third reason is that few companies have found ways to help women blend their family responsibilities with the demands of the job. Rose and Hartmann found that women are sometimes treated equally, mostly when they behave like traditional men and leave their family responsibilities at home.

On the other hand, some experts dispute the belief that women are not as ambitious as men. Catalyst, for example, polled more than 950 Fortune 1000 executives within two to three reporting levels of the CEO and conducted in-depth interviews with more than 30 female and male executives. Women and men reported "equal aspirations to reach the corner office, and women who have children living with them are just as likely to aspire to the CEO job as those who do not."

These survey results also refuted the contention that only women care about achieving a balance between their working and personal lives. For example, both women and men reported that they employ similar advancement strategies and have experienced similar barriers during their rise to the top.

Catalyst further uncovered "striking similarities between men and women regarding work/life balance management: 51 percent of women and 43 percent of men reported difficulty in achieving a balance between work and personal lives, and women and men participants equally desire a variety of informal and formal flexible work arrangements." Nevertheless, as women advanced to senior levels, Catalyst reported that they have made more trade-offs than men between work and their personal lives.

From my experience, women are just as committed as men to achieving corporate success and career excellence. I have also found that men and women often express the same desire for balance between their work and personal lives. And I know that women can and do make powerful contributions to their organization's success, even though they are less likely to brag about their accomplishments.

What's more, so what if women prefer marketing or human resources as career paths? Are these functions any less important than operations or finance to the success of a company? Should these "softer" considerations be absent from discussions of corporate direction and strategy? And in an era where corporate social responsibility, trust and caring are the hallmarks of enduring corporate success, are not the tendencies of women to be more attuned and attentive to the interests of others invaluable to companies?

WHAT SHOULD
COMPANIES AND WOMEN DO?

To benefit from the increasingly important assets that women bring to companies, I believe that corporate boards must not only recognize those assets, but also develop a plan to ensure that their boards become more gender diverse. This plan should stem from a careful analysis of the current skills and experiences of board members, thus identifying any existing gaps.

Then, boards should actively seek out potential female candidates who could address these gaps. This means expanding the scope and depth of the search for new directors. For example, board recruiters could approach women's business groups or solicit the recommendations of female executives, both within and outside the company.

Contacting universities and business schools are other excellent ways to find out about potential leadership talent. At Ivey, for example, most of our students in the regular MBA program have at least five years of management experience. Our executive MBA program attracts business leaders with established credentials in a wide variety of industries, and in both the public and private sectors.

There is also the "Women in the Lead/Femmes de Tete" Directory, co-sponsored by Ivey and HSBC Bank Canada. Developed by Doreen McKenzie-Sanders, it compiles the credentials and experience of more 568 Canadian women with impressive achievements in a range of industries.

In addition to improved recruiting, effective diversity plans should include programs to assist women to succeed in their new responsibilities, such as mentoring, corporate orientation and in-depth briefings on core business and industry issues. These programs ultimately benefit all new board members.

Overall, the board's diversity plan should be specific and measurable, with clear accountabilities. But, this is not about establishing quotas. Rather, an effective diversity initiative examines and evaluates results, not just numbers.

Nevertheless, I don't believe that boards are solely responsible for the poor representation of women on corporate boards. Women must also actively seek out potential opportunities to serve at the board level. No one can sit back and expect board appointments to come their way.

To attract board invitations, women must promote their accomplishments, build and leverage their connections, and seek opportunities to enhance their qualifications. And when they join a board, they must be willing to invest their time and talent toward learning and contributing to a healthy discussion of the issues. Once more women take charge of their own future, the fruits of their efforts will blossom, grow and spread the seeds for future opportunities.

FULLY LEVERAGING DIVERSITY

There is a powerful business case for why corporate boards should bring more women around the board table. As the research proves, companies with female board members can expect significantly higher returns and better overall financial performance.

More female representation also translates into improved risk management and audit control, increased ethical oversight and a broader, more accurate assessment of the company's success.

Equally important, with more female leadership, companies are better able to attract more female talent. They send a powerful message to the women who already work for their organizations that their contributions are valuable—that their voices are heard. They demonstrate to employees, investors and other stakeholders that diversity truly matters to their corporate success.

Indeed it does. When companies bring together a diversity of people—especially at the board level—ideas flow and innovation soars. Improved strategies emerge. Better decisions are made. A virtuous circle of continuous learning is created and sustained. In an economy where knowledge drives results, diversity is a precious asset.

13

CULTURE AND LEADERSHIP

LAURA GUERRERO

The University of Western Ontario

With so much going on in the world it's a task just to keep in touch with the changes that can make a difference to your own life. It's a grind but it is exciting as well. The successful CEOs of the future will need incredible wide-ranging and diverse sources of information.

—Warren Bennis

Although there are no formal theories of global leadership, there are several ways in which culture affects leadership. As the trend toward globalization continues, there is increased frequency of contact between people of different cultures (Daft, 2005; Dubrin, 2007; Yukl, 2006).

Adler and Bartholomew (1992) suggest that global leaders need to develop the following cross-cultural competencies. First, leaders need to understand the business, political, and cultural environments worldwide. Second, leaders should learn to understand perspectives, tastes, trends, and technologies of many other cultures. Third, they need to learn to work with people from other cultures. Fourth, they should be able to adapt to living and communicating in other cultures. Fifth, leaders need to learn to relate to people from other cultures from a position of equality rather than a position of cultural superiority.

CULTURE, DIVERSITY, ETHNOCENTRISM, AND PREJUDICE

Culture can be defined in several ways. Northouse (2007) defines *culture* as "the learned beliefs, values, rules, norms, symbols, and traditions that are common to a group of people."

Related to culture are terms such as *multicultural* and *diversity*. *Multicultural* refers to a way of seeing or doing things that takes into account more than one culture. A multicultural leader is one with the attitudes and skills to build relationships with and motivate followers who are diverse across lifestyles, social attitudes, race, ethnic background, gender, age, and education (Dubrin, 2007). *Diversity* refers to the existence of different cultures, ethnicities, socioeconomic levels, sexual orientation, or races within a group or organization (Yukl, 2006). Some people now use the term *inclusion* instead of *diversity* to highlight that organizations need to include as many diverse people as possible in organizations (Dubrin, 2007).

Related to leadership and culture are the concepts of ethnocentrism and prejudice. *Ethnocentrism* is "the tendency for individuals to place their own group (ethnic, racial, or cultural) at the center of their observations of others and the world" (Northouse, 2007). Although ethnocentrism is a natural tendency, it can act as an obstacle to effective leadership because it prevents leaders from understanding and respecting the views of others. Ethnocentrism creates challenges for minority leaders and subordinates (Daft, 2005).

Another natural tendency is that of holding prejudices. *Prejudice* can be a perjorative "attitude, belief, or emotion held by an individual about another individual or group that is based on faulty or unsubstantiated data" (Northouse, 2007). Prejudice is often held against people or groups of people based on their race, gender, age, sexual preference, or other characteristics. Like ethnocentrism, prejudice prevents the leader from understanding and appreciating other people. Successful global leaders need to be able to recognize and minimize their own ethnocentrism and prejudice toward others, as well as manage others who may be ethnocentric or prejudiced.

CULTURAL DIMENSIONS

Many studies have addressed the issue of identifying the different dimensions of culture. One of the best-known studies is Hofstede's (1980, 2001). Hofstede identified five major cultural dimensions: power distance, uncertainty avoidance, individualism-collectivism, masculinity-femininity, and long-term/short-term orientation.

A more recent and comprehensive study by House and his colleagues (2004), known as the GLOBE studies, has identified nine cultural dimensions. The word *GLOBE* stands for Global Leadership and Organizational Behavior Effectiveness. These are the cultural dimensions identified by GLOBE researchers (Northouse, 2007; Yukl 2006):

- *Uncertainty avoidance* refers to the degree to which a society depends on established social norms, rituals, rules, and procedures to avoid uncertainty.
- *Power distance* describes the extent to which members of society expect and are comfortable with power and wealth being distributed unequally.
- *Institutional collectivism* refers to the extent to which society encourages institutional or societal collective action as opposed to individual action.
- *In-group collectivism* refers to the extent to which individuals express pride, loyalty, and cohesiveness toward their organizations or families.
- *Gender egalitarianism* refers to the degree to which a society deemphasizes gender differences and supports gender equality.
- *Assertiveness* refers to the degree to which individuals in a society are assertive, confrontational, and aggressive in their interaction with others.

- *Future orientation* describes the extent to which individuals in a culture participate in future-oriented behaviors such as planning, investing, and delaying gratification.
- *Performance orientation* refers to the extent to which a society encourages and rewards individuals for superior performance.
- *Humane orientation* refers to the extent to which a society encourages and rewards individuals for being fair, philanthropic, generous, and kind to others.

The GLOBE study grouped the 62 countries into 10 clusters that share language, geography, religion, and historical connections. The regional clusters are as follows: Anglo, Latin Europe, Nordic Europe, Germanic Europe, Eastern Europe, Latin America, Middle East, Sub-Saharan Africa, Southern Asia, and Confucian Asia. The results of the study indicate that although scores *within a cluster* were correlated, they were unrelated to the scores in *different clusters*.

Leadership Behavior and Culture Clusters

The general purpose of the GLOBE study was to determine whether cultural differences were related to different leadership views (Yukl, 2006). GLOBE researchers used the implicit leadership theory (Lord & Maher, 1991), which states that people have implicit beliefs about the attributes and characteristics that distinguish leaders from nonleaders and effective leaders from ineffective ones. GLOBE researchers identified six global leadership behaviors (Northouse, 2007):

- *Charismatic/value-based leadership* is the ability to inspire, motivate, and expect superior performance from followers based on strongly held core values. This type of leadership would result in being visionary, inspirational, self-sacrificing, trustworthy, and performance oriented.
- *Team-oriented leadership* places emphasis on team building and having a common purpose among members of the team. This leadership type is collaborative, integrative, diplomatic, compassionate, and administratively competent.
- *Participative leadership* emphasizes the involvement of others in making and implementing decisions. Participative leaders are democratic.
- *Humane-oriented leadership* places emphasis on being supportive, considerate, compassionate, generous, and sensitive to other people.
- *Autonomous leadership* requires an independent and individualistic leadership style, which includes being self-directed and unique.
- *Self-protective leadership* refers to a leadership style that focuses on ensuring the safety and security of the leader and the group. This type of leadership is self-centered and interested in preserving the status of the group and the leader, even if it causes conflict with others.

The GLOBE researchers used these six global leadership behaviors to determine what leadership view each culture cluster held. Not surprisingly, it was found that different culture clusters had different leadership profiles. However, it was also found that certain leadership characteristics were valued across cultures, and some leadership attributes were found to be universally undesirable.

The universally desirable characteristics of an outstanding leader are trustworthiness, fairness, honesty, having foresight, planning ahead, being encouraging, optimism, dynamism, building confidence, being motivational, dependability, intelligence, decisiveness, being effective at bargaining, being a win-win problem solver, having communication skills, being informed, being administratively skilled, coordinating, being a team builder, and being excellence oriented (House et al., 2004).

The attributes that were found to be universally viewed as obstacles to effective leadership are were being a loner, being asocial, noncooperativeness, irritability, not being explicit, being egocentric, ruthlessness, and being dictatorial (House et al., 2004).

The importance of considering culture in leadership is growing due to globalization and our increased interdependence with people of other cultures. Being aware that cultural differences affect the way people view the world and the way they act and communicate with others helps leaders be more effective. Leaders who understand culture and its impact can adjust their leadership style to be more effective with people of different cultural backgrounds (Daft, 2005; Dubrin, 2007; Yukl, 2006).

References

Adler, N. J., & Bartholomew, S. (1992). Managing globally competent people. *Academy of Management Executive, 6,* 52–65.

Bennis, W. (2006). *Leading from the top: An interview with Warren Bennis, Des Derlove* (EMFD Thought Leadership Series). Accessed May 29, 2006, at www.efmd.org/html/

Daft, R. L. (2005). *The leadership experience* (3rd ed.). Mason, OH: Thomson, South-Western.

Dubrin, A. (2007). *Leadership: Research findings, practice, and skills.* New York: Houghton Mifflin.

Hofstede, G. (1980). *Culture's consequences: International differences in work-related values.* Beverly Hills, CA: Sage.

Hofstede, G. (2001). *Culture's consequences: Comparing values, behaviors, institutions, and organizations across nations.* Thousand Oaks, CA: Sage.

House, R. J., Hanges, P. J., Javidan, M., Dorfman, P. W., Gupta, V., & Associates. (2004). *Leadership, culture, and organizations: The GLOBE study of 62 societies.* Thousand Oaks, CA: Sage.

Lord, R., & Maher, K. J. (1991). *Leadership and information processing: Linking perceptions and performance.* Boston: Unwin-Everyman.

Northouse, P. G. (2007). *Leadership: Theory and practice* (4th ed.). Thousand Oaks, CA: Sage.

Yukl, G. (2006). *Leadership in organizations* (6th ed.). Upper Saddle River, NJ: Pearson-Prentice Hall.

The Cases

Salco (China)

Salco (China) is a global manufacturer of burners for hot water boilers and industrial furnaces and ovens. The company has recently hired a new operations manager for its plant in China, whose mandate is to improve the efficiency of the Beijing office, to eliminate Salco's Chinese distributors' poaching behavior, and to elevate Salco's brand equity in the Chinese market. After implementation, the initiative to eliminate distributors' poaching had failed, and the company's operations manager must determine why this initiative failed and prepare a report for senior management.

Intel in China

The newly appointed division head must examine organizational or communication problems within a division of a billion-dollar semiconductor manufacturer. The manager made a decision, which an employee emotionally responded to, creating the potential for conflict within the department. Cross-cultural issues come into play, given that the manager, although originally from China, was educated and gathered extensive experience in the West and was thus considered an expatriate by his employees. The manager must also examine the effect of organizational culture on an employee's behavior.

Grupo Financiero Inverlat

A small team of Canadian managers from a large financial institution is faced with the challenges of managing a recently acquired Mexican operation. Managers must cope with a language barrier and cultural differences as they try to restructure the overstaffed Mexican financial institution.

THE READING

Global Fatalities: When International Executives Derail

Developing global executives is an expensive proposition that can produce a significant return—provided that the corporation uses the knowledge and expertise it gained from earlier experiences effectively. These coauthors interviewed 101 individuals who succeeded in their international postings and concluded that poor management of three factors contributes to the failure of international executives: the individual, the cultural context, and organizational mistakes. Based on their book, *Developing Global Executives: The Lessons of International Experience,* the authors outline and discuss the steps an organization can take to ensure that executives posted abroad will be successful.

SALCO (CHINA)

Prepared by Alan Yang under the supervision of Professor Joerg Dietz

          Version: (A) 2003–08–19

On Wednesday, November 18, 1998, Dahong Wong, China operations manager of Salco, a globally operating manufacturer of burners, received a call from Don Miller, Asia Pacific area manager at Salco's headquarters in London, England:

Dahong, I just asked for change, not for a revolution. Don't take a machine gun and shoot at everybody. The situation is getting out of hand. We need to meet, when I come to Beijing next Monday.

Miller had hired Wong three and a half months earlier with the mandates of increasing brand equity in China, optimizing channel performance and improving the efficiency of Salco's Beijing office. Wong admittedly felt that he had not made much progress, but he did not understand why. What should he report to Miller in the upcoming meeting?

DAHONG WONG'S CAREER (1990–1998)

After his graduation from Beijing University with a bachelor's degree in business administration in 1990, the then-22-year old Wong started working as a project manager in the Beijing office of Watson Consulting, an international consulting firm (see Exhibit 1). The office mostly produced customized reports about China for foreign companies. Wong recalled that, after about six months, he felt overqualified, once he had brought his English up to par and had learned the basic frameworks for writing reports.

He also viewed himself more as a people person than as an analyst.

In 1992, Wong left Watson Consulting for Denver Pneumatic, a U.S.-based manufacturer, as a sales engineer. As the first staff member of the electric tool division in the company's Beijing office, his task was to sell electric tools to industrial clients and to develop the division. Peter Yu, his supervisor recounted:

Wong is a born salesman. He has a great business sense and is very convincing. He knows how to approach an issue, when to compromise and what to achieve in a deal. Customers enjoy his personal and humorous style. He also travels like a bee. He always has many leads, talks with many customers, and as a result, he brings in a lot of orders. Customers trust him. Wong also is a "parrot." When he started, he knew very little about technical stuff,

---

Dahong Wong	
Professional Experience	
Sales Manager, Denver Pneumatic, **Beijing China**	1992–1998

- Promoted from a sales engineer to senior sales engineer and to sales manager in 18 months.
- Developed and led a top-performing sales and support team of 10+ to develop new business and deliver superior value-added services, achieving the highest customer satisfaction.
- Built mutual trust and positive working relationship with customers to generate $20 million sales revenues annually, exceeding sales quota by over 30 percent in four consecutive years and achieving highest level of sales target fulfilment in the whole company.

Consultant, Watson Consulting, **Beijing China**	1990–1992

- Conducted market research and presented insightful recommendations on sales and marketing to IKEA and Tetra-Pak; these recommendations were made part of their China marketing strategies.
- Organized and conducted feasibility study that led to the successful setup of Sino-Sweden Dairy Training Center, the first foreign-invested project done in China after June 4th, 1989, and the Tiananmen Square Massacre.

Education

Beijing University, **Beijing, China**	1986-1990
Bachelor of Business Administration	

Achievements and Interests

- 1st Prize in a nationwide spontaneous speech contest on free trade — **1990**
- Chief editor of the student magazine HORIZON — **1989–1990**

Exhibit 1   Résumé

but he mimicked other colleagues and customers. Now he sounds like an expert, discussing complex technical issues with grey-haired customers.

By 1994, Wong had been promoted to senior sales engineer and then to sales manager. In 1996, Wong managed a team of six sales engineers, three technical support engineers and one secretary. Wong described the situation:

> My fast promotion to sales manager was nearly unprecedented in the company's history. People used the phrase "riding a helicopter" to describe my career at Denver Pneumatic. I know they were jealous. So what? My performance spoke for itself. I could always "fix" the tough customers, but they could not. Most importantly, Yu backed me up strongly. As a result, I enjoyed great respect from my staff for four reasons: First of all, I recruited those guys. I knew them. They were selected to suit both my personal style and the job requirements. Second, I was here first; I'm like a founder of this office. If you know more stories both about internal politics and customer demands, you have more power. Third, I trained them. They learned a lot from me. Fourth, I could nail down the "tough deals." When you are able to accomplish supposedly impossible missions, your subordinates have no choice but to bow to your legend. How would they ever dare to even imagine "climbing up over my head?"[1]

SALCO

Industry and Company Background

Burners were electromechanical appliances that were designed to regulate combustion applications. Most burners were components of hot-water boilers. They were also used in absorption chillers, industrial furnaces and ovens, ceramic kilns and car painting booths. In recent years, the traditional markets for burners in Europe and the United States had become saturated. But emerging markets in Asia, the Middle East and parts of Africa were growing rapidly.

Salco, founded in the early 1900s in England, was a leading European manufacturer in the heating ventilation and air conditioner industry in

Europe. In 1997, Salco built burners in the domestic (201,000 units), commercial (35,000 units), and industrial (1,400 units) segments. Most burners were exported. Robert Johnson, director of the commercial department, commented:

> With a 70 percent export rate, we are one of the largest burner exporters in the world. We are very strong in Europe, but we are now building a global customer portfolio to diversify our export business. China is the most important emerging market, and I believe that soon it will be the single largest burner market worldwide. Currently, I'm satisfied with our growth there.

Salco China

After entering the Chinese market in 1995, Salco established a Beijing office to support its distributors—initially only Longli Trading Company (Longli)—and, starting in 1996, Everest Company Ltd. (Everest) and Kenergy Mechanical Engineering Company (Kenergy)—with marketing-related information and technical support. Salco had exclusive contracts with these distributors, forcing them to carry only Salco burners. The distributors were expected to carry and offer the complete line of Salco burners. As a rule of thumb, the prices for domestic burners ranged between RMB2,000 to RMB5,000; for commercial burners RMB5,000 to RMB20,000 and for industrial RMB20,000 and up. The gross margin for all types was roughly between 10 percent and 15 percent.

Moreover, each distributor had an assigned territory (see Exhibit 2). Sales in other territories were not allowed. According to the contract, the distributors had three major responsibilities. First, they were responsible for the funding of purchases, minimizing the financial risks for Salco. After placing an order with Salco, they had to open a letter of credit through their banks with Salco's bank. That way, the distributors had to purchase the burners from Salco, and their opening banks needed to effect the payment once Salco had dispatched the ordered burners. Second, the distributors were responsible for arranging local transportation and for keeping a

Distributor	Province
Longli	Guangdong, Guangxi, Yunnan, Hunan, Jiangxi, Hubei, Fujian, Hongkong, Sichuan, Tibet, Hainan
Everest	Shanghai, Jiangsu, Zhejiang, Shandong, Henan, Anhui
Kenergy	Beijing, Tianjin, Liaoning, Jilin, Heilongjiang, Inner Mongolia, Shanxi, Shaanxi, Hebei

Exhibit 2   Assigned Territories in China

"sufficient inventory" at their cost. Third, the distributors had sales and service functions, which included maintenance checks and repairs.

The Distributors

Wei Lam had established Longli as a family business in Guangzhou in 1995 with the sole purpose of selling Salco burners. As Salco's first Chinese distributor, Longli covered 10 southern provinces of China and Hong Kong. Miller had chosen Longli as a distributor because of his long-standing relationship with Lam and because of Lam's deep knowledge of burners and the burner market. Although Longli sold 3,458 domestic, 568 commercial and 52 industrial burners in 1997, it had a reputation among customers for being consistently out of stock.

Everest was a large Chinese trading firm headquartered in Hong Kong. It had subsidiaries in all major cities including Beijing, Shanghai and Guangzhou. Everest had a small but rich territory—the five most developed provinces in China and Shanghai. In 1996, Miller had chosen Everest because it had strong guanxi (connections and networks) in the greater Shanghai area and a strong financial base. Everest's business with Salco burners had taken off immediately. In 1997, it sold 3,075 domestic, 433 commercial and 48 industrial burners.

Concurrently with Everest, Miller had also selected Kenergy, a subsidiary of a state-owned research institute in Beijing, as a distributor. The company had been going through the privatization process since 1996 and, therefore, its management team, which would own it after the privatization, was highly committed to growing the business. Its territory covered that vast area of eight northern provinces and Beijing. Kenergy, which previously had distributed Korean-made burners, had a large customer base and a strong technical sales team. Kenergy's customers were highly satisfied with the after-sales service and technical support, but some customers complained of Kenergy's higher prices relative to those of the other two distributors. In 1997, Kenergy sold 4,354 domestic, 876 commercial and 33 industrial burners.

Despite the territorial arrangements, some customers, mainly those for commercial and industrial burners, checked the prices with all three distributors, in part because a customer's assigned distributor had frequently run out of stock. In addition, all major players in the Chinese burner market knew each other, and Salco was, as competitors and customers acknowledged, the "black horse" among burner manufacturers.

Salco's Beijing Office

In 1998, Salco's Beijing office had three staff members: Don Miller, Jun Yuan and Lilly Pan.

Miller, who constantly travelled between the United Kingdom and China as well as other Asian countries, recruited Wong in June 1998 as Salco's China marketing manager, effective August 1, 1998. Wong's responsibilities were to increase brand equity in China, optimize channel performance and improve the efficiency of the office. He was also to be in charge of office operations.

Wong did not find it easy to leave Denver Pneumatic, but he finally chose to "wash his hand in a gold basin."[2] Wong said he sensed that it would be hard to make further career progress without a change. He also noted:

> Moving to Salco was associated with a 50 percent pay raise. I got the opportunity to learn channel management. It did not matter to me that it had little to do with direct sales. I thought that either way I would deal mostly with people. I "had seen all kinds of birds in the forest"[3]—bosses, subordinates and customers—for so many years. It would be easy for me to survive the three-month probation period.

Don Miller

As the Asia Pacific area manager, the 38-year-old Miller had offices in London, England, and Beijing. He had been in charge of building the Beijing office, and, although he was its chief representative, he was in the office only every one or two months for a few days. When he was in the office, he was typically quiet but friendly, saying that he enjoyed the distance of the Beijing office to the headquarters in London, that "place of gossip and politics." Occasionally, he complained that Salco kept him too busy to have a family and at the same time did not promote him fast enough. Wong began to feel that Miller was waiting for a promotion or an outside job offer.

Jun Yuan

The 29-year-old Yuan had a master's degree in science (with a specialization in thermo engineering) from one of China's top universities, where he had held the important position of vice-president of the student body. He had joined

Salco two years ago after quitting his job in a state-owned design institute because, as he put it, he did not want to be an engineer. He was the technical manager of the office with the responsibility of providing technical training and counselling to distributors and customers. This responsibility included decision-making authority over compensations to distributors for "epidemic burner defects": a distributor was able to get compensation anywhere from several thousand RMB to several hundred thousand, once approved by Yuan, who had a budget equivalent to two percent of the year's revenue (revenue in 1998 was US$6.3 million).

Yuan always wore a pair of thick, black-framed glasses that reduced his eyeballs to small black points; he talked at a slow pace. He frequently talked about the large market potential for burners and related products in China and marvelled about the entrepreneurial achievements of his former classmates, who already had made "millions of U.S. dollars." Yuan worked hard and was always the first one to arrive at the office each morning.

Lilly Pan

Having previously worked for three years as a secretary and receptionist in the local offices of multinational companies, the 25-year-old Pan was the first local staff member in the Beijing office. She was deeply involved in the process of setting up Salco's Beijing office under Miller's leadership. Pan felt pride in her role and Miller occasionally referred to her as "the co-founder." When Miller first introduced Pan to Wong, he also called her "his most favorite secretary," causing Pan and Miller to smile. Her responsibility was to be the liaison with headquarters. Her main task was the scheduling of deliveries from England: it was largely up to her to determine which distributor's order should be dispatched first, especially during rush seasons when burners were in high demand. She also managed the office's everyday funds.

Pan always started the work day by doing her make-up. At work, she often complained about

her lack of time "for her pet doggie Albert, daddy and mommy." She also frequently screamed at janitors, the property manager and employees in other offices.

WONG'S FIRST THREE MONTHS AT SALCO

First Week of August

Wong started working for Salco on Monday, August 3, 1998. After his first day at work, he felt disappointed about the size of his new work environment: "Only 200 square metres and two subordinates," he noted. At the same time, he found this encouraging because, as he said, "With my experience of managing about a dozen people, this office should be a small piece of cake." Wong, Pan and Yuan had lunch together on Wong's first day, which gave Wong a positive first impression of Pan and Yuan. At the end of his first week, Wong noted:

> Yuan and Pan really are great people to work with. Pan is outspoken. She is very communicative in English and Chinese. She really knows how to talk. She also seems to be an independent person who enjoys her lifestyle with her memberships at a couple of beauty salons and fitness clubs. And she is emotional about her work, showing her great commitment to the office. She described with great passion how she helped Miller set up the office, but also almost burst into tears when talking about the distributors, who were "not polite enough" to her. It seemed that she expected me "to teach these arrogant distributors a good lesson."
>
> Yuan shows great respect for me. He always addresses me as "Manager Wong" rather than "Dahong" or "Mr. Wong." I feel flattered to be treated like this by someone who was the vice-president of the student body at one of China's most prestigious universities. He always works very long hours, saying that this is the advantage of being a single man, who does not have to rush home to cook. Yuan also is so confident and mature, and he has promised to spare no effort to support me in my mandates. He also told me that my experience is strong enough to deal with the

distributors, and he dismissed my concern about a lack of knowledge about burners with a wave and smile, saying that "the manager does not need to have such small dirty skills." He would handle that stuff. Gee, what else could you expect from a good subordinate like Yuan?

Last Three Weeks in August

During in the second week of August, Pan began to arrive one or two hours late to the office each day. Wong thought that her late arrivals resulted from extended parties and dinners. One day, Pan showed up at the office at lunch time. When Wong questioned her during lunch, Pan responded angrily in a loud voice:

I don't have your good luck of sitting in the office from nine to five. If you wish, I'm willing to switch my job with yours. You go dealing with the red tape in the customs and tax offices, and I'll sit in the air-conditioned office, making phone calls. Dahong, you should pay more attention to the distributors, not me and Yuan.

Meanwhile, Yuan ate his lunch and read the day's *Beijing Youth Daily,* not reacting to Pan's outburst. Wong was confused by Yuan's behavior, but did not mention it. Moreover, within one week Wong received two faxes from the shipping department at Salco's London headquarters with complaints about: (1) the infrequent responses by the Beijing office, and (2) the large number of mistakes in the shipping information provided by the Beijing office. When Wong spoke to Pan about the faxes, she shrugged and said that "they made mistakes too."

Towards the end of August, Wong planned to visit the distributors. For one of the flights to the distributors, Yuan made about a dozen calls to help Wong find a ticket. Eventually, Wong had the one-week trip scheduled starting August 24. On August 20, when Wong asked Pan to confirm the flights and book hotels for him, she replied that she was not his secretary and that the office did not have the funds to pay for the trip. Wong was shocked. A secretary at Denver Pneumatic would have never given such a response. Wasn't

he supposed to be in charge of office operations? Now he wondered exactly what that meant. He took it for granted that it included control over the office funds, but this had never been formally defined. And didn't Pan know that he was in charge? Did she legitimately think that she had the authority over the office's account? Because Miller was on vacation until September 1, Wong could not get in touch with him. Wong felt that he had not choice but to call the distributors one by one to cancel the trip. Yuan said that he felt sorry for Wong and that it was not just that Wong did not have control over the funds. Tied to the office, Wong continued to spend most of his time reading files to better understand the situation with the distributors. Frequently, he also called the distributors to discuss issues. On the basis of Yuan's sympathy and earlier help in organizing the trip, Wong started to consider Yuan as an ally. He began to confide in Yuan when problems with the distributors, Pan or Miller came up.

First Two Weeks in September

On September 1, Wong contacted Miller, who immediately instructed Pan to release the funds for Wong's business trips. Yet, the funding issue left a bad aftertaste with Wong, who decided that he would raise his concerns in a one-on-one meeting with Miller during Miller's next visit to Beijing in mid-September. From September 8 to 12, Wong finally visited the three distributors in Beijing, Shanghai and Guangzhou.

Wong had mixed reactions to his visits with the distributors. Each distributor seemed to respect him and Salco. The distributors were always very kind to Wong, and they always stressed that they would never want to lose Salco's business. However, they also gave him conflicting information on many issues. Wong had learned from the files that each distributor had engaged in cross-territory poaching, i.e., selling burners in a district that was assigned to another distributor. In a consistent fashion, each distributor always accused the other two of violating the contract first and appeared to be a victim. Another source of confusion was that Pan and Yuan continued to describe the distributors as "rogues and villains" with very low moral standards, who needed to be ruled with an "iron-wrist," but it appeared to Wong that the distributors treated Pan and Yuan with silk gloves. Whenever Wong tried to argue with Pan and Yuan over the distributors, they raised numerous examples to prove Wong's judgment wrong. Wong occasionally was suspicious about Pan and Yuan, but he could not understand why they should try to mislead him about the distributors. On the basis of the examples that his colleagues provided, he felt that they also had a point with their negative assessments of the distributors.

Second Two Weeks in September

On September 15, Miller arrived in the office. Yuan and Pan were excited to see Miller, and Miller made faces when Pan was touching his fresh-cut hair. Yuan gave Miller Chinese herbs believed to enhance a man's potency. Miller noted that he did not need them, but still accepted the gift. Wong thought Miller looked tanned and energetic after his vacation, but also felt Miller's smile at him was a bit forced.

During his one-on-one meeting with Miller, Wong raised his problems in the office. To achieve his mandate of improving its efficiency, he needed more authority within the office, particularly access to funds and the authority to hire and fire staff. He also needed a laptop computer and a cell phone. Miller replied:

> Dahong, the issue of power is a non-issue. As the China operation manager, you have the highest salary in this office and the greatest power. Your colleagues and distributors all know that, and you have authority and access to the office funds. Note, however, that hiring and firing is not the way to run this office. To abuse power is more harmful than not to have it. See, I will not fire you because last month you arrived late in the office three times. And don't worry; I will get you a laptop and a cell phone soon.

Wong felt a chill in his bones, when he heard Miller's response and did not know how to respond. Obviously, Miller had a spy in the office.[4] Wong continued by sharing his opinion about the distributors with Miller, saying that, while they had engaged in contract breaches, overall, the distributors appeared to value Salco's business. Miller's response was that Wong should not jump to conclusions just because the distributors treated him nicely. He asked why Wong would want to be on their side and concluded by saying that clarifying the situation with the distributors was exactly the job for which he had hired him.

Month of October

One morning early in October, Wong found a laptop and a cell phone on his desk. On the same day, Pan also got a cell phone. On another morning, Wong found part of an unsent fax on the fax machine signed by Yuan. It was a synopsis of a business plan for distributing air heaters in China for a European company. When asked by Wong about the fax, Yuan immediately turned pale, explaining that he was "simply helping a friend to send a fax." He said he would not use the office fax machine for his own purposes again.

During the month of October, Wong continued to collect information on the distributors. As he had suspected earlier, cross-territory poaching was the most serious problem. When one distributor sold burners to customers in another distributor's territory, the discount for the customer typically exceeded the 25 percent limit stipulated in the distributor agreement. The harmed distributor would retaliate by offering even lower prices to "steal" customers in the territory of the infringing distributor. The cross-poaching had several negative consequences for Salco. First, it drove down the prices for Salco burners, which, as Wong thought, harmed Salco's brand equity. Second, customers who had bought their burners from the "wrong" distributor typically did not receive satisfactory after-sales maintenance services. Third, as a result, Salco began to lose its "dark horse" image in the burner market.

Wong found out that Everest accused Wei Lam and his company of "having fired the first shot." Lam, however, argued that he had been the only Chinese distributor in 1995 and that if he sold in other territories, he sold only to his old customers. Lam found that selling to old customers was entirely acceptable, whereas the poaching by Everest and Kenergy was "sheer stealing." Wong commented:

> On the surface, poaching is the result of an "it is okay to feed your cows on your neighbor's grassland" mentality. The issue, however, is more complex. Typically, the distributor who sells the burner also sells the spare parts. The margin on these spare parts is 15 percent to 20 percent higher than it is on the burners. If the distributors have a larger base of sold and installed burners, they also have more sales of spares. The problem is compounded by the lack of respect that the distributors have for the contracts. Salco forced these contracts onto the distributors, not understanding that they do not care. In addition, Salco currently uses only three distributors in a country of 1.2 billion people. Inevitably, there are coverage deficits, which customers exploit.

On top of that, you have to understand that in this new economy, most Chinese entrepreneurs are very concerned about the longevity of their endeavors. Change happens very quickly, leading people to believe that making a quick buck is the right strategy. In that sense, the behavior of the distributors is entirely understandable. On the other hand, if this behavior becomes the new code for society as a whole, then China will face serious economic problems because of a lack of trust. This lack of trust, in turn, leads to higher transaction costs. Unfortunately, as of today, the quick-buck attitude has already spread like a virus. You can hear it everywhere: "use your power as much as possible today before it expires," "planning your business can never catch up with changing your business," and "distant water won't help put out a nearby fire." The incentive systems in many organizations also reflect the short-term mentality: in all likelihood, the distributors' salespersons are paid on the basis of their monthly, quarterly or annual sales, totally disregarding the long-term consequences and indirect costs associated with achieving these sales targets. Of course, the quick-buck attitude comes along with decaying business ethics.

Wong also viewed the distributors' chronic lack of inventory as a problem:

> Inventory requires funding, but the distributors argue that they are short on working capital and cannot afford a large inventory. I believe, however, that the cause of the lack of inventory is the absence of mechanisms for forecasting demand and subsequently fine-tuning the inventory. The folks at headquarters have already repeatedly complained that the Beijing office has "too many rush orders" and "great volatility in its orders." I don't think it's a big deal for our office to build a forecasting model. We would need, however, the cooperation from the distributors. They would have to provide their monthly and seasonal forecasts to us, but they are not doing their homework. They just complain.

The distributors had raised other issues to Wong. Kenergy complained about the lack of training on Salco burners and about frequently less-than-competitive prices; Longli asked for more support in the funding of orders; and Everest found that Salco was not fair on the issue of compensating for epidemic defects.

Month of November

By early November, Wong finished a first draft of a distributor restructuring program (DRP). His analysis had made him aware of the complexity of the situation, but he felt that his mandate of improving channel performance forced him to come up with a quick solution. According to his draft, effective January 1, 1999, distributors would be punished with a one percent increase in price on their next order if they sold a burner outside their territory. Moreover, distributors would have to disclose all customer information to Salco, and they would have to provide seasonal sales forecasts, which they had to adjust on a monthly basis. A deviation of larger than 10 percent in sales volume from the forecast would be punished with a price increase on subsequent orders.

For Wong, this first draft was only a starting point. He found it almost a bit too aggressive and asked for Yuan's opinion. Yuan was very excited at the draft, but said that it was not tough enough. He suggested that Salco keep a "deposit for fines" of US$5,000 from each distributor that a distributor would lose upon violation of a rule. He also asked Wong to include a punishment for "stock-outs" (lack of inventory) in the DRP. Wong and accepted these suggestions. Wong also asked Yuan whether he should get Miller's feedback on the DRP. Yuan reminded him what Miller had said in their meeting in September, namely, that dealing with the distributors was exactly what he had been hired to do. Subsequently, Wong decided to proceed without consulting Miller, thinking that a successfully implemented initiative would be a great way to impress Miller. Moreover, his three-month probationary period had now passed, and he could not wait for the rabbit to die so that he could catch it.[5] He scheduled a meeting with the distributors for November 18, 1998, in Shanghai to announce the DRP.

On November 18, 1998, all three distributors and Wong gathered in a meeting room of the Hilton Hotel in Shanghai for a full-day meeting. Wong hoped for a positive meeting, noting that the Chinese pronunciation of the number 1118 was "must, must, must, be fortunate." In the morning, Wong and the distributors went through the sales budget for the current year and then proceeded to discuss next year's sales budget. At the beginning of the afternoon session, Wong gave a presentation of the DRP. Bin Kong, an alumnus of the very prestigious Yuan Jun University and general manager of Kenergy, said:

Mr. Wong, allow me to be direct. Your proposals are fundamentally wrong. We are not your enemy, but your friend. Why should Salco treat us this way? The iron fact is that we have worked hard for Salco and have been so successful. You make a good salary because of us. Without us, you could drink only north-west wind.[6] Get real! We are not beggars, and we can distribute burners for somebody else. I see no reason for passing on customer information to you. You are like a dog who tries to

catch mice.[7] How could you convince me that you do not use our information for your own purposes?

Wei Lam from Longli said:

Manager Wong, how old are you? Thirty years? OK. I forgive you because you are still young. I was far more naïve than you when I was your age. The Cultural Revolution is over; the era of "reporting to Chairman Mao from morning till night"[8] is over. What's the use of these hectic reports? Do you really think they work? Life is short, do something useful, OK?

Sheng Xu, sales manager for Everest, noted:

Dahong, I appreciate your effort to bring order to Salco's China business. We know that you need performance to justify your salary, but you just can't do things that way. Cross-territory poaching is a problem, but not a serious problem. Everybody has that problem. Our working capital is tight enough; why should I deposit another US$5,000? You have been with Salco for only three months. It's too short a time for you to understand the business. We distributors are much easier to deal with than some people around you. We have been able to fulfil the budget year after year. Don't be too demanding on us. We have problems, as have you. Crows everywhere are equally black after all. There is no perfect company, right?

As Wong listened, he could feel his face reddening in anger and embarrassment. He stopped the meeting and said he would schedule a second meeting soon.

WHAT NEXT?

Miller called Wong in the late afternoon in his hotel room. The phone call prompted Wong to review his performance in the past three months. He felt as if he was riding on a tiger's back—difficult to pull back. He knew he would be in for a tough meeting with Miller next week. What had gone wrong? Was his analysis flawed? Was his plan flawed? What should he have done to avoid this disaster? Whom could he trust? Wong suddenly recalled Mao's famous motto: "Who is our enemy, who is our friend; this is the most essential question for any revolution."

NOTES

1. Chinese metaphor: to outperform one's boss, take his/her position and to flourish.
2. Chinese metaphor: chose a completely new career path.
3. Chinese metaphor: had a lot of experience in dealing with different types of people.
4. Sun Tzu's "Art of War" has a chapter that highlights the use of spies as a winning strategy (Chapter 13).
5. Chinese metaphor: The chance of catching a rabbit that died is very slim. Instead of waiting, one must act to get things done.
6. Chinese metaphor: to have nothing to eat and drink.
7. Chinese metaphor: describes a person who is too inquisitive and cares about things that are none of his/her business (dogs can catch mice, but catching mice is the business of cats).
8. This was a slogan during China's "Cultural Revolution."

INTEL IN CHINA

*Prepared by Donna Everatt under the supervision of
Professors Kathleen Slaughter and Xiaojun Qian*

Version: (B) 2002–11–07

In October, 1999, Charles Tang, newly appointed manager of marketing programs of Intel China in Beijing had just emerged from an emotionally-charged meeting with Yong Li, an account manager in Tang's division. The meeting, attended by Li's direct supervisor, Qing Chen, was convened by Tang to discuss Li's feelings regarding a decision Tang had made to discontinue a project that had been assigned to Li by his previous supervisor. Despite what Tang considered to be sound business logic supporting his decision, Li's resistance left Tang wondering whether there were extenuating factors he needed to consider. Tang also wondered whether the blow-up with Li was an isolated incident, or whether it signalled deeper organizational or communication problems in his newly acquired division.

INTEL

In the mid-1960s, Intel introduced the world's first microprocessor, sparking a revolution in the technological industry. Intel was an unequivocal success story—its strategy of "driving new technology, serving global markets, and increasing customer preference for the Intel brand, while delivering excellent financial results to our stockholders" had served them well over the years. By 1996, driven by strong sales of the Pentium® processor, Intel was on its seventh consecutive year of record earnings of both sales and revenue, and had reached the US$20 billion in revenues milestone. 1997 was another year of record revenues (an increase of 20 percent) and record net income of almost US$7 billion, up 35 percent over 1996. However, 1998 brought weaker than anticipated demand for personal computer (PC) products, which led to lower first quarter revenue and earnings. Dr. Andy Grove, the founder and enigmatic leader of Intel, referred to first quarter 1998 results as "disappointing," and stated that the "PC industry seems to have gotten ahead of itself, building more product than customers wanted." First quarter 1998 revenue of US$6 billion fell seven percent;

net income and earnings per share declined 36 percent from the first quarter of 1997. The company widely expected revenue for the second quarter of 1998 to be flat, and year-to-date performance during the year had reflected this expectation.

Intel's global mission was nothing short of being the "pre-eminent building block supplier to the new computing industry worldwide." Thus, a major part of Intel's strategy was its commitment to creating microprocessors that the software of the next millennium could tap into. Concurrently, Intel followed a strategy of encouraging the developments of software engineers so they could push the envelope in software design to ensure that users would receive the benefits of the most advanced hardware Intel was developing. To help strengthen the Pentium® brand name, Intel focused on emerging markets with programs that stimulated demand for Intel products. Intel had succeeded tremendously in its branding campaign, and was considered one of the world's top 10 brands. Indeed, in 1997, over half (56 percent) of Intel's revenue was generated outside of the United States, with the Asia-Pacific region and Japan accounting for almost a third of Intel's revenue. In 1999, Intel considered China to be their single most important market.

Intel People's Republic of China (PRC)

Intel PRC Corporation established a representative office in China as early as 1985; however, it was not until 1993 that Intel felt the time was right to more fully enter the Chinese market with the establishment of two wholly-owned foreign enterprises. The first, Intel Architecture Development Co., Ltd. (IADL), was responsible for the sales, marketing and development of Intel's products and services in China. IADL's 250 employees were located in 13 offices throughout China; however, the Shanghai office with 100 employees and the Beijing office with 80 were the largest. The second, Intel (China) Technology

Co. Ltd., was the entity of Intel's assembly and testing plant operations.

IADL employed more than 80 engineers who worked with local and multinational software vendors to develop innovative consumer and business applications to PC users in China. IADL's charter was for "accelerate technology adoption in the PRC by providing technical and marketing support to local software developers." Initiatives included a developer support program, which included seminars, matchmaking events, training and conferences for Chinese software engineers and a donation of more than RMB$1.5 million of Pentium II processor-based development systems to assist leading Chinese software developers in bringing advanced software to local and international markets.

IADL's mandate was critical to Intel's growth, as senior management was aware that regardless of its research and development (R&D) expenditures, without software applications that could take advantage of the latest hardware developments, the user would not receive the advantage from that innovation. Thus, according to Tang, Intel's role in China was to act as a matchmaker, bringing all pieces of technology together to help China's PC users to understand how computing could help them in a comprehensive way. Tang explained that Intel looked at technology from a "total solution standpoint."

> By the time we start developing a new chip, we're already looking at what applications it will support and what solution it provides to the user. Thus, by the time the chip is ready to go into market, the platforms, the solutions are all ready so it is coordinated. This way, we're all moving forward and everybody wins.

By 1999, Intel had become involved in "just about every operation in the IT industry in China" and was aggressively marketing Intel-branded products throughout the country. Though still at its early stage of development, China's computer market had been growing twice as fast as the world average, and was poised to become the second largest computer market in the world by the end of the century.

With its large population and fast economic growth, China's potential was extremely attractive to multinationals. As a global leader, Intel was well-positioned to capitalize on this opportunity and Charles Tang was one of the most important players in advancing Intel's presence in China.

CHARLES TANG

Tang had not returned to China since his departure eight years prior and his home country had changed dramatically during that time. Beijing had undergone a rapid period of extensive growth and the ubiquity of shiny modern buildings and presence of so many foreign firms was a shock to Tang. However, despite the changes in Beijing that he saw, Tang had the advantage of being previously exposed to the reality of life in Beijing, which could overwhelm many expatriates—the crowded streets, the pungent aromas emanating from the street markets, traffic congestion, punishing heat, and air quality for example. Tang commented that he had known of other Chinese nationals who had returned to the mainland, and despite the fact several months had elapsed, they still did not feel comfortable being in China and never really could adjust to life there after having lived in the United States or Europe. Though he initially felt "like a tourist," after having spent just one weekend wandering through the street markets, alleyways and pathways through the heart of Beijing, he was convinced he had made the right decision and had not looked back since.

Tang was one of the first three employees who were transferred to China from other Intel sites in 1993 to more firmly establish Intel's operations in the mainland. Tang gained experience in many areas, including a two-year stint in Shanghai to help establish Intel Architecture Laboratory there. During his time there, Tang established Intel's software developer support program—an integral part of Intel's China strategy. The account managers (AMs) in Tang's department played a critical role in this support effort. Their prime mandate was to forge and nurture relationships with prestigious Chinese software developers and vendors. By 1999, Tang reported directly to the president of Intel PRC and oversaw critical areas such as government relations, as well as industry and community programs, which included donations to many of the top universities in China to support research and teaching activities, as well as donations of equipment, upgraded on an annual basis.

The scope of Tang's development projects ranged from the grassroots community level such as a program that would sponsor Chinese high school students to attend a popular international science and technology fair in the United States, to investigating strategic investment opportunities. Tang also played a leading role on Intel's corporate advisory board, a body that was comprised of some of the most prominent Chinese influencers, both from the IT industry and academia. The board's broad mandate was to "spearhead industry programs by working with trade associations and industry leaders to influence the development of programs throughout the region to promote indigenous development of the industry by transferring Intel's acquired experience and expertise locally."

YONG LI

Yong Li was one of four AMs, each of whom had individual projects in addition to their primary responsibility. According to Tang, an AM's required skill set included the ability to interact as an Intel ambassador with senior managers and owners of the software firms with whom Intel was developing relationships. This involved effectively communicating Intel's IT strategy, "not from a technical viewpoint but rather from a strategic perspective," while ensuring full customer satisfaction on a daily basis. Another critical strategic component of the AMs' responsibilities lay in their ability to consistently recognize the possibilities of advancing the mutual interests of IADL and their clients—a key part of Intel's strategy in China. An AM's ability to exceed his clients' expectations was determined by his effectiveness in mobilizing Intel's internal resources, which involved extremely strong people skills and the ability to consistently demonstrate a mature, professional and diplomatic manner.

THE ISSUE

When Tang took over Intel's Beijing division, he was eager to familiarize himself with the operation of each department, and to aid him in this, he reviewed the files of all employees to understand their roles. Using his best judgment, Tang reassigned work as he deemed necessary, to ensure that each employee was working, both individually and within a team, toward advancing the strategic goals of the department and thus Intel in China. The same rationale was behind a reassignment of various departmental managers, and in the process, Tang reassigned the AMs under Qing Chen, a Beijing native. Though she had worked for a multinational before joining Intel, this was her first managerial position.

Tang's attention was drawn to Li's project upon reviewing Li's employee file. Though Tang felt the basic concept behind the project to be sound, he felt that it had expanded to such an extent from that which was initially proposed that it was not reasonable to expect that Li could realize the project's goals without it interfering with his primary duties of servicing his account base. The scope of the project had mushroomed in part due to the perspective of Li's previous supervisor who, according to Tang, was a very ambitious person who "approached everything on a grand scale with massive goals."

Initially, the project assigned to Li was the creation of a manual providing local software vendors with tips on running their enterprise, such as marketing various software products or how to manage or set up distribution channels, for example. However, Li approached the project with such unchecked zeal that it quickly transformed from a manual to a book form, with a chapter dedicated to comprehensive business planning issues, beginning with such basics as how to incorporate a

business in China, sourcing venture capital, and the development of a comprehensive marketing plan tailored for software products.

Tang described the project as a "portable MBA-type book, covering essentially every topic a software company would need to know to do business in China." This was such an ambitious project, and Tang estimated it could take up to one year to complete, not including the two months of research Li had already conducted. Upon review of the file, Tang concluded that Li, a new and relatively young employee, without significant exposure to the business world or the software industry, did not have the background or expertise for this type of book. Tang felt that the project would be better suited to a writer who specialized in issues in the software industry. Given that there were many other projects that could be assigned to Li, which were of a more appropriate scope and focus, Tang instructed Chen to inform Li that work on the project was to be halted immediately, and that Li should be assigned a new project.

When Chen informed Li of Tang's decision to cancel the project, Li "totally rejected her," and he was not willing to even listen to the rationale behind the decision. Chen turned to Tang for assistance as she was at a loss as to how to reconcile Tang's demand with Li's desire to continue with the project and his agitated state that it had been cancelled. Tang decided that given Li's reaction, the best course of action was to bring them all together, and he scheduled a meeting as soon as he could to resolve the issue. Tang was conscious of handling the situation in such a way that did not undermine Chen's authority, as he felt that the empowerment of direct supervisors was critical. On the other hand, Chen confessed she was confounded by Li's reaction.

LI'S PERSPECTIVE

During his brief history with Intel, Li had dedicated himself to exceeding his clients' service expectations. Indeed, Tang readily acknowledged that Li had excelled at developing relationships with senior management in the companies in his assigned account base. Tang agreed that this was no small feat, as Tang's client base included some of China's most influential software firms, and in some cases had been so successful that he had created strong '*guanxi*' with senior management at those firms. *Guanxi* was the basis on which business in a Chinese context thrived. Loosely translated as 'relationships,' *guanxi* was such an integral part of doing business in China, that it was essentially impossible to do without it. Thus, when *guanxi* was established, it was protected at great cost, as it was widely considered to be the single most important factor in a successful business transaction. Its value in a Chinese business context could not be underestimated.

Li's success, therefore, in the realm of his primary duties was indisputable; however, he also applied himself equally to conducting research for his project and took ownership of it very seriously. Upon hearing that Tang had cancelled his project, he voiced his opinion immediately to Chen, saying that the two months of work he had conducted on his project were "wasted." Moreover, it was Li's strong contention that Tang altered not only one of his projects, but the essence of his responsibilities in one broad stroke, without due consideration, thereby undermining his efforts to date. Li continued:

> This is typical of expat managers—they come along and don't really care about what the workers are doing. They don't show respect and change the workplace according to their whim without providing explanation, and without warning.

Li felt that Tang had caused him to "lose face." Causing another to "lose face," could result in irreparable damage to the interpersonal relations between those two parties.

TANG'S PERSPECTIVE

Though he had heard through Chen that Li was very upset, Tang was previously unaware of the extent to which Li felt he had 'lost face.' Tang

was thus largely unsure of how his actions could have affected Li at such an emotional level, and he took a few moments to consider his perspective of the situation. Tang acknowledged that Li was successful in establishing strong relationships with his clients. However, Li won various concessions for his clients through a demanding style toward his colleagues and a single-mindedness of purpose. Another talent that Tang acknowledged Li brought to his AM position was his ability to "think big." However, Li's assertive manner was not commonly found in traditional Chinese workplaces, and some of his colleagues, both within his department and throughout other departments which Li relied upon, were uncomfortable with Li's level of zeal. Complicating the situation was Tang's assumption that Li had not been formally indoctrinated to the Intel culture.

To demonstrate the Intel culture, Tang explained that Intel's employees throughout the world were characterized by their energy and youth, and thrived in a dynamic and creative environment. Tang further explained that in order to sustain intense levels of innovation, a degree of dissension and constructive criticism was encouraged; however, policies that helped advance Intel's 64,000 employees globally in the same direction were required. Tang explained a crucial part of Intel's culture—which was in place to achieve this end—the "disagree and commit" philosophy.

> If a consensus has been established that a particular course of action or a decision is appropriate, any individual employee would not only have to commit to that decision, but if he or she were responsible in any way in implementing it, this concept would dictate that they act as if they were in 100 percent agreement with the decision. This means that once the course of action had been decided, it should not be discernible who was for, and who was against the decision before it was made. This is a condition of employment at Intel. It is the professional code on which I was brought up on at Intel.

Given Li's reaction, Tang wondered whether he had communicated to Li, and potentially his other employees, the quintessential role that this philosophy played in Intel's culture.

Tang reflected upon what other factors he should consider in analysing Li's behavior beyond his inexperience and apparent ignorance of Intel doctrine and considered potential underlying cross-cultural issues that might help to explain Li's behavior, while at the same time increase his understanding of all his employees. Although Tang had grown up in China and pursued his undergraduate degree in China, he had received a graduate degree from study in the United States as well as almost a decade of Western experience. Thus, he found himself in a precarious balance between two cultures. This created a rather unique situation for Tang— internally, he was perceived as a expatriate, yet because of his precise fluency in Mandarin and obvious comfort in Chinese culture, Tang felt he was perceived externally as a local Chinese.

TANG—AN EXPATRIATE OR A LOCAL?

When Tang first returned to China, when meeting with local government officials, he had a difficult time in persuading them that he was directly authorized to make decisions. First, at 33, he was significantly younger than most senior managers at multinationals in Beijing. Second, most often local Chinese did not hold positions of such power in multinationals.

To establish his credibility externally, Tang used a clever and effective technique. When Tang first met with the officials, he noticed that when he proffered his opinions directly, many of the local officials did not have confidence that Tang was empowered to make decisions. After trying a more direct approach, when a decision was consequently required, Tang told the officials that "I should check with my boss" but offered his decision in the interim. In subsequent meetings, it became clear to the local officials that Tang's "boss'" decision correlated precisely with Tang's personal decisions, time and time again. Thus, in time, he succeeded in establishing his credibility.

On other occasions, when he encountered a reticence among senior external managers or officials, he used another technique, equally effective. Tang would say, "I'll see if I can set up a meeting with my boss to discuss this issue, but may I have some background information to impart to him on which he can base his decision." This would allow Tang to obtain the required information on which to base his decision, which he would disclose at the following meeting. In these ways, Tang artfully managed his credibility as a local Chinese with external stakeholders. However, internally, Tang was perceived as an expatriate.

Tang was aware that being perceived as an "outsider" could undermine his ability to persuade his department that they were all part of the same team. Complicating the issue was not only Tang's expatriate status (one of few at the time), but as an expatriate, Tang received a better pay and benefit package than local (Chinese) employees. Tang saw where he had advanced in relation to his employees as "just going through a different process to get to where we are, but now we're all at the same place—part of the Intel team." According to Tang:

> Work really doesn't have anything to do whether you're an expatriate or local Chinese—it has to do with your ideas, how you understand strategy, technology and marketing—that's work. As long as you focus on that, and once your employees begin to focus on that, perceived differences really become a non-issue.

Tang dealt with the potential for conflict because of his rank or his experience in the United States by largely ignoring it, but Tang did not view this as an abdication of his responsibilities. On the contrary, Tang believed that by working hard and proving himself trustworthy, his employees would come to see that "we're all working together." According to Tang:

> How people look at you and how they feel about you has everything to do with how you make them feel about you. If you want to be seen as different, and if you want them to see you as different, they will. If you want to distance yourself from them you can. However, if you want them to see you as one of them, they will.

Tang was cognizant of some basic tenets on which the foundation of organizational behavioral differences as generally found between Chinese and Western firms were based, and acknowledged that both his Western education and experience as well as his exposure to Eastern business cultures affected his interpretation of the situation he was facing with Li. What challenged Tang also, with regard to managing Li, was how much of a departure Li's behavior was from what Tang considered to be a traditional Chinese business culture. Tang wondered whether he should question some of his beliefs about Chinese communication patterns and organizational behavior. Had things changed drastically since he had been away or was Li's behavior out of the ordinary?

ORGANIZATIONAL DIFFERENCES

Differences in Communication Patterns Between the East and the West

Generally speaking, Chinese organizational structures were more vertically layered than Western firms, resulting in dense reporting lines and bureaucratic administrative mechanisms. Moreover, Chinese organizations were most often led by a strong autocratic figure who took an active role in daily operations as well as the strategic direction of the firm. Whereas in some Western firms the organizational structure, supported by cultural influences, encouraged a degree of dissension and disagreement to advance the firm's organizational effectiveness and strategic direction, generally speaking Chinese firms operated on a principle of unquestioning adherence to the direction as dictated by senior management.

In contrast to Eastern management style, in Tang's opinion, Western organizational and communication systems promoted a more open discussion between managers and their employees. Tang's management experience suggested to him that employees in the West had a higher propensity to be more open and possessed a greater

willingness to listen to their bosses if they had established a proven track record of being reasonable and open-minded. In contrast, Tang felt there seemed to be more suspicion among employees toward their supervisors in an Asian business context, as they managed with a much more closed style.

Though Tang considered his management style to be a mixture of Eastern and Western characteristics, he felt that many Western management principles manifested themselves more strongly. For example, he considered being open with his employees an integral part of managing, and indeed had succeeded in encouraging many of his employees to treat him as a confidant. On several occasions, he had been approached by members of his team and had held closed-door, one-on-one discussions regarding various aspects of their personal and professional lives. Tang was proud of the role he was able to take in acting in this capacity for his employees. On a broader level, Tang did his best to ensure that his employees' needs and concerns were addressed. For example, Tang ensured that his employees' salaries were commensurate with their responsibilities, and competitive as compared to other multinationals for employees working in a similar capacity. Tang considered actions such as this to be critical in establishing his employees' trust in him. It was actions such as this that reinforced Tang's belief that his employees were more comfortable approaching him than they may have been with an expatriate manager from North America or Europe.

THE DECISION

In this context, Tang was confounded by Li's reactions. Why did he respond so emotionally and what could he now do about it? Li was otherwise a promising employee who had forged valuable *guanxi* with his accounts. Tang did not want to risk losing him. Moreover, on a personal level, Tang cared about the welfare of his employees and, thus, it was upsetting to him that he may have caused his employee some distress.

Tang considered whether in light of Li's emotional attachment to the project he should allow him to continue with it, as in the scheme of things it was a relatively short-term project. Or was there a way to modify the project, finding a compromise between his needs and Li's desire to continue with the project? Tang was eager to have his employees contribute in such a way that would advance the strategic direction of his department, and felt strongly that whatever decision he made should be guided by that general principle. Tang knew that perhaps the easiest means to achieve this end would be to coerce Li to follow the "disagree and commit" philosophy at Intel and redirect Li's attention altogether to a more appropriate project. However, he was concerned about Li's reaction to this move, given his emotional state.

Tang also considered the idea that perhaps this issue pointed to a larger one. Were the systems that facilitated vertical communication sufficient or should he consider implementing a more effective, more formal internal communications strategy? But Tang did not have time to consider this issue at the present moment—he glanced at his watch, jumped up and hurriedly placed his laptop in his briefcase to rush to a meeting.

GRUPO FINANCIERO INVERLAT

Prepared by Daniel D. Campbell under the supervision of Professors Kathleen Slaughter and Henry W. Lane

Version: (A) 2002–10–23

By October 1996, it had been four months since management at the Bank of Nova Scotia (BNS) increased its stake in the Mexican bank, Grupo Financiero Inverlat (Inverlat), from 8.1 percent to an equity and convertible debt package that represented 54 percent ownership of the bank. A team of Canadian managers had been sent to Mexico to assume management of the ailing financial institution immediately after the deal was struck. Jim O'Donnell, now Director General Adjunto (DGA)[1] of the retail bank at Inverlat, had been there from the beginning.

Jim was a member of the original group that performed the due diligence to analyze Inverlat's finances before negotiations could begin. Later, he and his wife Anne-Marie (also an executive with the bank) were the first Canadians to arrive in Mexico in May 1996. Since then, 14 additional Canadian managers had arrived, and restructured the four most senior levels within Inverlat. The pace of change had been overwhelming. Jim now wondered how successful his early efforts had been and what could be done to facilitate the remaining restructuring.

A BRIEF INVERLAT HISTORY

In 1982, in his last days as leader of the Mexican Republic, President Lopez Portillo announced the nationalization of Mexico's banks. They would remain government institutions for the next eight to 10 years. Managers characterized the years under government control as a period of stagnation in which the structure of the Mexican financial institutions remained constant despite substantial innovations in technology and practice in the banking industry internationally.

Many Inverlat managers claimed that their bank had generally deteriorated more than the rest of the banking sector in Mexico. Managers believed that there was no overall strategy or leadership. Lacking a strong central management structure, each of the bank's geographic regions began to function independently, resulting in a system of control one manager described as "feudal." The eight regions developed such a level of autonomy that managers commonly referred to Inverlat not as a bank, but as eight small banks. The fragmented structure made new product development almost impossible. When the central corporate offices developed a new product, they had no guarantee that it would be implemented in the regions and ultimately, the branches. The power struggle within the regions demanded such loyalty that employees often had to say: "I cannot support you (in some initiative) because my boss told me not to."

In 1990, an amendment to the Mexican constitution allowed majority private sector ownership of Mexican commercial banks. Between 1990 and 1992, 18 banks were privatized by the Mexican government, including Inverlat. BNS, looking to expand its interests in Latin America, purchased eight percent of the company in 1992 for Cdn$154 million.

Under the structure of the newly privatized bank, there were three corporate cultures: that of the original bank; that of the Casa de Bolsa, the bank's brokerage house; and that of the new chair of the bank, an executive from Banamex, Mexico's largest financial institution. Many senior Banamex executives were invited to join Inverlat; some even came out of retirement to do so. The Banamex culture soon dominated the organization, as senior management tried to create a "Little Banamex." Inverlat managers without a history in Banamex said that the strategy could never function because Inverlat did not have the clients, technology, or financial resources of Banamex.

Inverlat's leaders did recognize, however, that the years of stagnation under nationalization had created a bank that had failed to create a new generation of bankers to reflect the changing times. They realized that the bank required a rejuvenation, but the managers did not have the knowledge or the capacity to effect the change.

Nowhere was the lack of development more prominent, and ultimately more devastating, than in the credit assessment function. The banks pursued a growth strategy dependent on increased lending but, unfamiliar with the challenges of lending to the private sector, failed to collateralize their loans properly or to ensure that covenants were being maintained. In early 1995, following a severe devaluation of the Mexican peso, Mexico's credit environment collapsed; so did the bank. The Mexican government assumed responsibility for the bank, and BNS was forced to write down its original investment by almost 95 percent to Cdn$10 million.

NEGOTIATIONS WITH BNS

Management at BNS chose to view the loss in value of their investment as a further buying opportunity and, in early 1996, they began negotiations with the Mexican government. BNS contributed Cdn$50 million for 16 percent of new stock in the bank and Cdn$125 million in bonds convertible on March 31, in the year 2000 for an additional 39 percent of equity. If, in the year 2000, BNS decided not to assume ownership of the bank, it could walk away without converting the debt and retain a much smaller portion of ownership.

As the majority shareholder until the year 2000, the Mexican government contracted BNS to manage the bank. A maximum of 20 BNS managers would be paid by the Mexican government to manage Inverlat on the government's behalf. If BNS wanted more Canadian managers to work in the bank, BNS would have to pay for them. It was intended that the Canadian managers would remain at Inverlat only until the Mexican managers developed the skills to manage the bank effectively on their own.

With the exception of a handful of the most senior officers in the bank, employees at Inverlat had no direct means of receiving information about the progression of the negotiations with BNS. Instead, they were forced to rely on often inaccurate reports from the Mexican media. As the negotiation progressed, support among Inverlat employees for a deal with BNS was very strong. Inverlat employees did not want to become government bureaucrats and viewed BNS as a savior that would bring money, technology and expertise.

EMPLOYEE EXPECTATIONS

Soon after the deal was completed with BNS, however, the general euphoria was gradually replaced by the fear of actions the Canadians were likely to take as they assumed their management role. Senior managers were worried that they would be replaced by someone younger, who spoke English and had an MBA. Rumors, supported by inaccurate reports in local newspapers, ran rampant. One newspaper reported that as many as 180 senior level managers would be imported to Inverlat from BNS in Canada.

Anxiety mounted as speculation increased about the magnitude of downsizing that BNS would implement as it restructured the bank in its turnaround. Although BNS had purchased banks in other Latin American countries, few Inverlat employees, including the most senior management, had any knowledge about the strategies that BNS management had used. Inverlat managers felt that their employees viewed BNS as a "gringo" corporation, and expected them to take the same actions other U.S. companies had taken as they restructured companies they had purchased in Mexico. Most believed that if any foreign bank purchased Inverlat, most of the senior management team would be displaced and up to half of the bank staff would be let go. Similarly, very few managers knew the details of the contract that limited the number of managers that could come to the bank from Canada.

Very few of the Mexican employees had had any significant contact with Canadian managers, but the majority expected behavior similar to that of U.S. managers. Only a handful of senior level managers had been in contact during the

due diligence and the Canadians realized that they required greater insight into the Mexican culture if they were to manage effectively. As a result, the members of the senior team that were going to manage the Mexican bank arrived in Mexico one month in advance to study Spanish. The Canadian managers studied in an intensive program in Cuernavaca, a small city 80 kilometres southwest of Mexico City. During the three-week course, lectures were available on the Mexican culture. Mexican managers were extremely impressed by this attempt by the Canadians to gain a better understanding of the situation they were entering and thought the consideration was very respectful. One manager commented that:

> At the first meeting, the Canadians apologized because it would be in English, but promised that the next would be in Spanish. The fact is, some are still in English, but the approach and the attempt were very important.

Four months later, the Canadian team was still undergoing intense tutorial sessions in Spanish on a daily basis with varying levels of success.

Canadian managers said they were trying to guard against putting people into positions simply because they were bilingual. A Canadian manager, expressing his commitment to function in Spanish, commented that:

> There are 16 Canadians down here and 10,000 Mexicans. Surely to God, the 16 Canadians can learn Spanish rather than trying to teach the 10,000 Mexicans English or having people feel that they are being left out of promotions or opportunities just because they don't speak English. This is a Spanish-speaking country and the customers speak Spanish.

INVERLAT AND BNS CULTURES

In Canada, BNS was considered the bank with the most stringent financial control systems of the country's largest banks. Stringent, not only in deciding not to spend money in non-essential areas, but also in maintaining a tough system of policies and controls that ensured that managers held to their budgets.

Inverlat executives, on the other hand, were accustomed to almost complete autonomy with little or no control imposed on their spending. Very little analysis was done to allocate resources to a project, and adherence to budget was not monitored. Mexican managers believed that greater controls such as the ones used by BNS should be implemented in Inverlat, but they also felt that conflicts would arise.

An early example experienced in the bank was a new policy implemented by BNS management to control gifts received by managers from clients. BNS managers imposed a limit of 500 pesos[2] for the maximum value of a gift that could be received by an executive. Gifts of larger value could be accepted, but were then raffled off to all employees of the bank at Christmas. Some Mexican managers took offence at the imposition of an arbitrary limit. They felt that it was an indication that BNS did not trust their judgment. Managers thought that it would be better if the bank communicated the need for the use of good judgment when accepting gifts and then trusted their managers to act appropriately.

MANDATE OF BNS

Two months after the arrival of the Canadian executive team, the new bank chairman, Bill Sutton, gave an address to 175 senior executives within Inverlat. The purpose of the address was threefold: to outline management's main objectives in the short term; to unveil the new organizational structure of senior level managers; and to reassure employees that no staff reductions would be undertaken for the first year.

The primary objectives, later printed in a special companywide bulletin were the following:

1. Identify all non-performing loans of the bank.

2. Develop an organization focussed on the client.

3. Improve the productivity and efficiency of all operations and activities.

4. Improve the profitability of the 315 branches.

5. Develop a liability strategy.

6. Improve the integrity of the financial information.

These objectives were generally well received by the Mexican managers. Some criticized them as being too intangible and difficult to measure. Most, however, believed that the general nature of the objectives was more practical, given the type of changes that were being made in the first year. They did agree that the goals would need to be adjusted as planning became more focussed during the 1997 budget planning process.

The new management structure differed sharply from the existing structure of the bank. The original eight geographic regions were reduced to four. Managers were pleased to see that the head of each of these divisions was Mexican and it was generally viewed as a promotion for the managers.

The second change was the nature in which the Canadians were added to the management structure. The senior Canadian managers became "Directores Generales Adjuntos (DGAs)" or senior vice presidents of several key areas, displacing Mexican managers. The Mexican DGAs not directly replaced by Canadians would now report to one or more of the Canadian DGAs, but this was not reflected in the organization chart (see Exhibit 1). Mexican DGAs retained their titles and formally remained at the same level as their Canadian counterparts.

Mexican managers later reported mixed feelings by employees about whether or not they worked under a Canadian or Mexican DGA. Many felt that a Mexican DGA and his (there were no female DGAs working within the bank) employees were more "vulnerable" than a Canadian; however, senior managers also felt that they had an opportunity to ascend to the DGA position when it was being held by a Mexican. Many felt that Canadian managers would always hold the key positions in the bank and that certain authority would never be relinquished to a Mexican. This was not the message that BNS management wanted to convey. One of Jim O'Donnell's first comments to his employees was

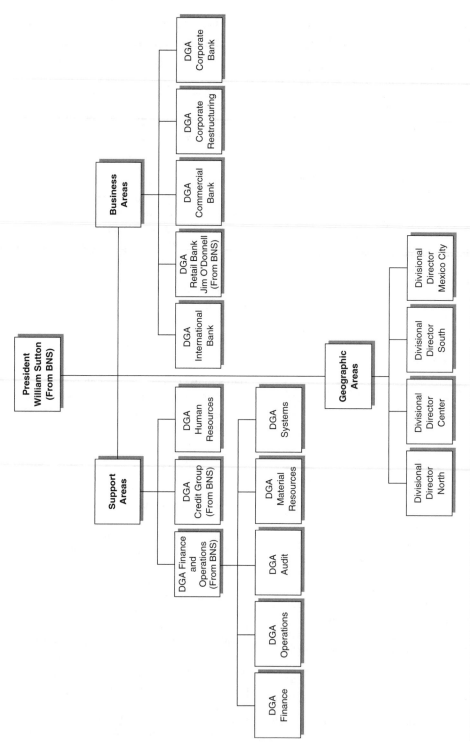

Exhibit 1   Grupo Financiero Inverlat Organizational Chart (Post Re-Organization)

that he would only be in Mexico until one of them felt confident that they could fill his shoes.

The last message was the new management's commitment not to reduce staff levels. A policy of "no hires, no fires" was put in place. Employees were able to breathe a sigh of relief. Many had expected the Canadian management team to reduce staff by 3,000 to 5,000 employees during the first several months after their arrival.

THE COMMUNICATION CHALLENGE

Canadian and Mexican managers already experienced many of the difficulties that the two different languages could present. Many of the most senior Mexican managers spoke English, but the remaining managers required translators when speaking with the Canadians. Even when managers reporting directly to them spoke English, Canadians felt frustration at not being able to speak directly to the next level below. One manager commented that "sometimes, I feel like a bloody dictator" referring to the need to communicate decisions to his department via his most senior officers.

Meetings

Even when all managers at a meeting spoke English, the risk of miscommunication was high. A Mexican manager recalled one of the early meetings in English attended by several Mexicans. Each of the Mexican managers left the meeting with little doubt about what had been decided during the meeting. It was only later, when the Mexicans spoke of the proceedings in Spanish, that they realized they each had a different interpretation about what had transpired. What they found even more alarming was that each manager had heard what he had wanted to hear, clearly demonstrating to themselves the effect of their biases on their perception of events.

This problem might have been exacerbated by the way some of the Canadians chose to conduct meetings. Mexican managers were accustomed to a flexible atmosphere in which they were free to leave the room or carry on side-conversations

as they saw fit. Canadian managers became frustrated and changed the meeting style to a more structured, controlled atmosphere similar to what they used in Canada. The Mexican managers were told that breaks would be scheduled every two hours and that only then should they get up from the table or leave the room.

Canadian managers believed that the original conduct of the Mexican managers during meetings was due to a lack of discipline and that the new conduct would lead to higher productivity. The Canadians did not recognize the negative impact that could result from the elimination of the informal interactions that had occurred in the original style.

Beyond Language

Despite the cross cultural training received in Cuernavaca, some Canadians still felt they had a lot to learn about the cultural nuances that could create major pitfalls. Jim O'Donnell recalled a meeting at which he and several Mexican managers were having difficulty with some material developed by another Mexican not present at the meeting. Jim requested that this manager join them to provide further explanation. Several minutes later, as this person entered the room, Jim said jokingly, "OK, here's the guy that screwed it all up." The manager was noticeably upset. It was not until later, after some explaining, that Jim's comment was understood to be a joke. Jim said it brought home the fact that, in the Mexican culture, it was unacceptable, even in jest, to be critical of someone in front of other people.

This was easier said than done. Often, what the Canadians considered a minor difference of opinion could appear as criticism that Mexican managers would prefer be made behind closed doors when coming from a more senior manger. One Mexican manager commented on the risks of disagreeing with an employee when others were present:

> When someone's boss is not in agreement, or critical of actions taken by an employee and says something during a meeting with other employees

present, other managers will use it as an opportunity to also say bad things about the manager. Instead, when a disagreement arises in an open meeting, the senior manager should say "see me later, and we will discuss it."

To the contrary, the Canadian managers were trying to encourage an environment in which all managers participated in meetings and positive criticism was offered and accepted.

Mexican Communication Style

On verbal communication, one of the original Inverlat managers commented:

In Mexico, interactions between individuals are extremely polite. Because Mexicans will make every effort not to offend the person they are dealing with, they are careful to "sugar-coat" almost everything they say. Requests are always accompanied by "por favor," no matter how insignificant the request.

Mexicans often speak the diminutive form. For example: *Esperame* means *Wait for me. Esperame un rato* means *Wait for me a moment.* A Mexican would more often say *Esperame un ratito.* "Ratito" is the diminutive form meaning "a very short moment." It is not as direct.

This politeness is extended into other interactions. Every time a Mexican meets a coworker or subordinate, a greeting such as "Hello, how are you?" is appropriate, even if it is the fourth or fifth time that day that they have met. If you don't do this, the other person will think you are angry with him or her or that you are poorly educated.

One Canadian manager explained that some of the Mexican managers he dealt with went to great lengths to avoid confrontation. He was frustrated when the Mexicans would "tell him what he wanted to hear." Often these managers would consent to something that they could or would not do, simply to avoid a confrontation at the time.

Other Messages: Intended or Otherwise

Due to the high level of anxiety, Mexican managers were very sensitive to messages they read into the actions taken by the Canadians. This process began before the Canadians made any significant changes.

As the Canadians began to plan the new organizational structure, they conducted a series of interviews with the senior Mexican managers. The Canadians decided who they would talk to based on areas where they believed they required more information. Unfortunately, many managers believed that if they were not spoken to, then they were not considered of importance to the Canadians and should fear for their positions. Even after the organizational structure was revealed and many Mexican managers found themselves in good positions, they still retained hard feelings, believing that they had not been considered important enough to provide input into the new structure.

Similarly, at lower levels in the bank, because of the lack of activity in the economy as a whole, many employees were left with time on their hands. Because many employees feared staff reductions at some point, they believed that those with the most work or those being offered new work were the ones that would retain their jobs.

Communications as an Ongoing Process

When Jim held his first meeting with the nine senior managers reporting to him, he began by saying that none of them would have their jobs in two months. Realizing the level of anxiety at that point, he quickly added that he meant they would all be shuffled around to other areas of the retail bank. Jim explained that this would give them an opportunity to learn about other areas of the bank and the interdependencies that needed to be considered when making decisions.

Jim stuck to his word, and within two months, all but one of the managers had been moved. Some, however, had experienced anxiety about the method by which they were moved. Typically, Jim would meet with an employee and tell him that in two or three days he would report to a new area (generally, Mexican managers gave at least a month's notice). When that day arrived, Jim would talk to them for 30 to 45 minutes about their new responsibilities and goals, and then he would send them on their way.

For many of the Mexicans, this means of communication was too abrupt. Many wondered if they had been moved from their past jobs because of poor performance. More senior Mexican managers explained that often these managers would come to them and ask why Jim had decided to move them. Most of the Mexicans felt that more communication was required about why things were happening the way they were.

Accountability

Early on, the Canadian managers identified an almost complete lack of accountability within the bank. Senior managers had rarely made decisions outside the anonymity of a committee and when resources were committed to a project, it was equally rare for someone to check back to see what results were attained. As a result, very little analysis was done before a new project was approved and undertaken.

The first initiative taken by the Canadians to improve the level of analysis, and later implementation, was the use of what they called the "business case." The case represented a cost benefit analysis that would be approved and reviewed by senior managers. Initially, it was difficult to explain to the Mexican managers how to provide the elements of analysis that the Canadians required. The Mexicans were given a framework, but they initially returned cases that adhered too rigidly to the outline. Similarly, managers would submit business cases of 140 pages for a $35,000 project.

Cases required multiple revisions to a point of frustration on both sides, but it was only when an analysis could be prepared that satisfied the Canadians and was understood by both parties, that it could be certain that they all had the same perception of what they were talking about.

Some of the Mexican managers found the business case method overly cumbersome and felt that many good ideas would be missed because of the disincentive created by the business case. One manager commented that "It is a bit discouraging. Some people around here feel like you need to do a business case to go to the bathroom."

Most agreed that a positive element of the business case was the need it created to talk with other areas of the bank. To do a complete analysis, it was often necessary to contact other branches of the bank for information because their business would be affected. This was the first time that efforts across functional areas of the bank would be coordinated. To reinforce this notion, often Canadian managers required that senior managers from several areas of the bank grant their approval before a project in a business case could move forward.

Matrix Responsibility

Changes in the organizational structure further complicated the implementation of a system of accountability. Senior management had recognized a duplication of services across the different functional areas of the bank. For example, each product group had its own marketing and systems departments. These functions were stripped away and consolidated into central groups that would service all areas of the organization.

Similarly, product groups had been responsible for the development and delivery of their products. Performance was evaluated based on the sales levels each product group could attain. Under the initial restructuring, the product groups would no longer be responsible for the sale of their products, only for their design. Instead, the branches would become a delivery network that would be responsible for almost all contact with the client. As a result, managers in product groups, who were still responsible for ensuring the sales levels, felt that they were now being measured against criteria over which they had no direct control. The Canadian management team was finding it very difficult to explain to the Mexicans that they now had to "influence" instead of "control." Product managers were being given the role of "coaches" who would help the branch delivery network to offer their product most effectively.

As adjustments were made to the structure, the Mexican managers' perception of their status also had to be considered. In the management hierarchy, the Mexican managers' relationships were with the people in the various positions that they dealt with, not with the positions themselves. When a person was moved, subordinates felt loyalty to that individual. As a result, Mexican managers moving within an organization (or even to another organization) often did so with a small entourage of employees who accompanied them.

STAFF REDUCTIONS

As services within the bank were consolidated, it was obvious that staff reductions would be required. Inverlat staff were comforted by the bank's commitment to retain all staff for the first year, particularly when considering the poor state of the economy and the banking sector; but, even at lower levels of the organization, the need for reductions was apparent. Some managers complained that the restructuring process was being slowed considerably by the need to find places for personnel who were clearly no longer required.

Motivations for retaining staffing levels were twofold. First, BNS did not want to tarnish the image of its foreign investment in Mexico with massive reductions at the outset. When the Spanish bank, Banco Bilbao Viscaya (BBV), purchased Banca Cremi the previous year, they began the restructuring process with a staff reduction of over 2,000 employees. BNS executives thought that this action had not been well received by the Mexican government or marketplace.

The second reason BNS management felt compelled to wait for staff reductions was that they wanted adequate time to identify which employees were productive and fit into the new organizational culture, and which employees would not add significant value. The problem was, quality employees were not sure if they would have a job in a year, and many managers thought that employees would begin to look for secure positions in other organizations. One Canadian manager commented that even some employees who were performing well in their current positions would ultimately lose their jobs. Many thought action needed to be taken sooner than later. A senior Mexican manager explained the situation:

> Take the worst case scenario, blind guessing. At least then, you will be correct 50 percent of the time and retain some good people. If you wait, people within the organization will begin to look for other jobs and the market will choose who it wants. But as the market hires away your people, it will be correct at 90 percent of the time and you will be left with the rest.

Until that point, not many managers had been hired away from the bank. Many felt that this was due to the poor condition of the banking sector. As the economy improved, however, many believed that the talented managers would begin to leave the bank if job security could not be improved.

Jim felt that something was needed to communicate a sense of security to the talented managers they could already identify, but he was not certain how to proceed.

CONCLUSION

Jim felt that the Canadian team had been relatively successful in the early months. Many managers referred to the period as the "Honeymoon Stage." It was generally felt that the situation would intensify as managers looked for results from the restructured organization and as staff reductions became a reality. Jim then wondered how he could best prepare for the months ahead.

Much of the communication with employees to date had been on an ad hoc basis. Jim did not feel they could take the risk of starting reductions without laying out a plan. The negative rumors would cause the bank to lose many of its most valued Mexican managers.

NOTES

1. Director General Adjunto is the Mexican equivalent of an Executive Vice President.
2. In late 1996, one Mexican Peso was valued at approximately US$0.0128.

GLOBAL FATALITIES

When International Executives Derail

Prepared by Morgan W. McCall, Jr. and George P. Hollenbeck

Take a quick look at why global executives fail and you'll likely see personality flaws. However, the reasons for failure are deeper and more complex.

Developing global executives is an expensive proposition, especially when expatriate assignments are involved. But the investment can produce a significant return—provided that the corporation uses the knowledge and expertise gained from the experience effectively. When things go wrong, the investment is lost, and usually, so too is a person who was judged to be quite talented. Can these losses be prevented? Maybe, but the answer to that question depends on what causes such derailments. If the complexity and ambiguity of international work make selection errors unavoidable, then the derailment of executives is just another cost of doing business. However, if derailments occur because of something that can be corrected or prevented, then a significant payoff is possible.

To shed some light on the dynamics underlying the derailment of global executives, we interviewed 101 individuals who were successful in their international postings. With an average of nine years experience abroad, they were in a unique position to observe other global executives come and go. The 121 tales they told are the basis for the conclusions we have developed about the underlying causes of international executive failures.

Three factors contribute to the failure of international executives:

The individual

The cultural context

Organizational mistakes

1. THE INDIVIDUAL

Executives contributed to their failure in two ways. Some personal attributes and types of behaviours just don't play in international settings. However, more often, it wasn't simply a personal flaw that prevented an individual from succeeding. Rather, it was the complex interaction of a person's strengths or weaknesses with a change in the situation. We will consider both causes.

Fatal Flaws

The successful executives we interviewed described over 300 flaws in the behaviour and management skills of the executives they had observed. A few of these flaws were factors regardless of the situation or context.

Foremost among them was a failure to adapt to change. What needed to be adapted to varied considerably—bosses, business strategy, leadership philosophy, changes in markets and technology. For many of those ill-fated executives, their inability or unwillingness to change was rooted in a career spent in a silo, or in a single function, which gave them a narrow perspective and made them unable to see the big picture. Unwilling to appreciate another point of view, some executives either refused to accept change or would not put energy into their effort to change.

Another flaw or set of flaws in the "clearly lethal" category resulted in bungled relationships with key people—customers, partners, senior management or peers. The bungling was especially toxic when it occurred in conjunction with a decline in performance or some significant mistake. In a global environment, quality relationships are crucial in certain countries and business situations (such as sensitive negotiations, joint ventures and cross-cultural alliances). Although a lack of people skills is annoying in any environment, the consequences are particularly severe in an international setting.

Other flaws led some executives to hesitate when action was needed, to default on promises made to senior management, and, when things subsequently went wrong, not to ask for (or accept) outside help. Powerful and successful executives in trouble may try to deal with matters on their own, viewing offers of assistance or advice as interference from the outside. This can be a fatal mistake, made all the more likely whenever, as an expatriate, the executive has lost contact with the rest of the company.

Complex Interaction

But just having flaws is too simplistic an explanation for the derailments that were described to us. As we have all observed, there are people who have glaring flaws who don't derail, while some with overpowering strengths actually do. Still others with no apparent flaws early in their careers seem to develop them later on. And for still others, there is no apparent cause for the flameout. Moreover, the international executives in this derailed group were unusually talented to begin with. They were often described as having multiple strengths, rarely found together, such as brilliant and interpersonally skilled, technically skilled and shrewd about people, or people- and results-oriented. How could such gifted and successful people derail?

The paradoxes can be resolved if derailment is considered as a dynamic process rather than the inevitable result of some personality flaw. Indeed, if one assumes that there are no unqualified strengths and few universally fatal flaws, the data begin to make sense. We identified four patterns that describe the dynamics of many of the derailment scenarios.

1. Early strengths that led to success became weaknesses later on. Most often, this took the form of exceptional technical, functional or market expertise that resulted in early successes and promotions, but later on blinded the executive to the bigger picture or the need for different skills essential to a higher-level job.

2. Long-standing flaws that became salient when something changed in an executive's situation. Some leaders, for example, had always been abrasive and arrogant, but because they got great business results, they were never damaged by their flaws. Their sins were forgiven in light of their bottom-line performance. When the results weren't as good as expected or when the situation changed so that relationships (and not single-handed bravado) were critical to meeting the bottom line, the flaws "suddenly" emerged and the executive derailed.

3. An executive's constant success. Some executives began to believe that they were as good as they seemed and, like the Greek tragic heroes, their hubris led to their demise.

4. Some executives appeared to be just unlucky, ending up in the wrong place at the wrong time or running afoul of the wrong person. What happened, at least on the surface, was not the person's fault. But while ill fortune appeared to cause these derailments, other factors usually contributed to the fall. It was frequently suggested that the same events might not have derailed someone else—that there was something about the way the executive handled the situation, or about bridges burned in the past, that contributed to the outcome. In short, one of the other dynamics—not bad luck—may have been the real culprit.

While some flaws were uniformly problematic (e.g., failing to adapt to changed situations or an "appalling lack of people skills"), and others emerged when an executive's immediate situation changed, the vast majority of international derailments were anchored in the cultural context itself.

2. THE CULTURAL CONTEXT

It was rarely sufficient to say that an executive's traits or flaws "caused" him or her to derail—most of these executives were extraordinarily talented individuals—unless one could place that trait or action in a larger context. For global executives, that context was almost always cultural.

Working abroad increases stress through its isolation, family pressures, and the broader job responsibilities it often entails. International executives may find themselves dealing with political issues, government corruption, bribery and a variety of contextual issues without the help that would be available in the home country. Contributing to the stress, but demanding in their own right, are the difficulties of understanding and being understood in one or more foreign languages, and the often subtle differences in values, norms, beliefs, religions, economic systems, and group and community identities.

The natural reluctance of people in organizations to be candid with each other can be magnified by cultural norms, as well as by the inability of outsiders to read the subtle cues. One executive, quite successful in a series of functional assignments, was promoted to a general manager's job outside of his own country. He did well initially, probably because of his functional expertise, but when things started to go wrong, he did not realize it. When he realized it, he didn't have the ability or business knowledge to diagnose the problem and figure out what was wrong. One can't help but wonder if he could have drawn on the expertise of others had this happened in his home country.

Different economic, religious, government and social systems in some countries have direct effects on how business is carried out. Here, complexity again takes several forms, including the potentially lethal—or at least convoluted— web of relationships and the presence of different business models and practices. As we interviewed executives, we saw how the web of relationships can grow more and more complex: from subordinates from a different culture who don't speak the executive's first language, to subordinates from multiple cultures speaking multiple languages in one region, to subordinates from multiple cultures speaking multiple languages and physically dispersed around the globe. To thicken the mix, add a boss from a different country who speaks a different language or multiple bosses from different countries in a matrix structure, and so on, through suppliers, customers, partners, shareholders, peers, consultants and others. As if that weren't complicated enough, different countries may have different business models, different definitions of ethical behaviour and different business approaches and systems.

All these complexities and others too numerous to recount, create a fertile context for derailment. The more relationships an executive has to cultivate, and the more varied they are, the greater the chances that some of them will go wrong. The greater the differences in how business operates in the countries involved, the greater the likelihood that an executive will make erroneous assumptions or commit errors without even knowing that anything is amiss. The more diverse and culturally different the countries, the greater the likelihood that seemingly extraneous factors—or what would be extraneous factors in the home country—will affect business results, the outcomes of deals and negotiations, and other activities for which the executive is accountable. In other words, not only are the executive's actions more likely to be ineffective or even counterproductive, but more circumstances will be beyond the executive's control and more likely to affect outcomes, regardless of the executive's actions. And for all the reasons we pointed out above, the executive may not get timely feedback or pick up the clues that anything is wrong in time to do anything about it.

Although cultural and business differences create a complex and sometimes treacherous context for executive action, international assignments also come with particular seductions that can lure executives onto the path to derailment. Being on their own, often far from direct supervision and with tremendous authority over local operations, global executives can come to believe that they are all-powerful, even above the law. Feeding self-aggrandizement were the perks of foreign duty, which might include servants, cars and drivers, luxurious homes, impressive expense accounts, invitations to galas and state affairs, and other special treatment that, over time, some executives began to view as entitlements.

Even if an executive completes an expatriate assignment successfully, he or she still faces a final risk that may cause derailment—repatriation. Though it is tempting to view coming home as an easy transition, it turns out to be anything but. Executives may return to find that they have lost their business networks and their friends, that their home country is not the same as it was when they left, and—perhaps the unkindest cut of all—that no one cares. Their living conditions may actually be worse, with no servants, drivers, luxurious homes, access to exciting events, or relationships with top business and government leaders. They may come back to less important jobs and reduced responsibility, they may find themselves outside the mainstream, and they may feel that their organization does not take advantage of or appreciate what they have learned. In such circumstances, the skids are greased for derailment.

3. ORGANIZATIONAL MISTAKES

Neither individual attributes and behaviour, nor the cultural context, were sufficient to explain all of the derailments. The organizations for which the derailed executives worked made numerous mistakes that contributed to, or in some cases directly caused, their derailment. The fall of one executive provides an example: "The company contributed [to the derailment] when they led him to believe they would back him up no matter what. But they didn't. They backed him when things went right, but they deserted him when things went wrong." Absence of honest feedback was pervasive, as were mixed messages or unclear expectations from "back home." Companies picked people who were obviously wrong for the assignment, promoted people too fast (they were "untested"), or kept them out too long. Frequently, expatriate executives did not have access to the kinds of technical or other support that domestic executives could call upon.

International assignments also come with particular seductions that can lure executives onto the path of derailment.

The complexity of the global context increases the odds that the organization will make various mistakes that contribute to derailments, most of which are avoidable: giving little or no feedback, little monitoring, tolerating existing flaws and lack of support. Because organizations can influence these and similar factors, we fault them for being lazy, or worse, negligent. Although we don't absolve executives from being responsible for their actions, the organizations' lapses increase the probability that flaws and inappropriate or ineffective behaviour will go unnoticed and uncorrected until it is too late.

Some cases of global derailment resulted from poor selection decisions, usually made for technical or political reasons without considering the potential consequences. Organizations chose people who obviously would not fit in the environment, failed to prepare them properly for the challenges ahead, and/or failed to communicate their expectations or changes in expectations. In still other cases, organizations made decisions that directly affected the executive's operation without considering the situation "on the ground." At times, an organization made strategy or design changes without consulting, or even informing, the local executive.

Derailment risk is high for foreign nationals coming to headquarters and for other executives returning home. Organizations seem to botch their part in both events consistently, contributing to an already difficult situation for the executive.

Finally, we were told of derailments in which an executive's career was exploited for short-term gain. In these circumstances, the organization, purposely or not, knew that the situation was not viable—the executive was assigned an impossible job, or one that would almost certainly create an aftermath so intolerable that the executive could not survive.

> *Organizations made decisions that diirectly affected the executive's operation without considering the situation "on the ground."*

Preventing Derailments

A single intervention or a smattering of human resource programs for international executives will not prevent events as complex as those leading to global derailments. Like global executive development itself, preventing derailment requires an integrated approach that connects strategic intent with the systems and practices that affect the selection, development and movement of global executives.

To begin with, solutions must address all three culprits in derailment: the executives' strengths and weaknesses, the global context in which the executives are placed, and the organizational practices that surround the whole process. All three depend on the fundamental strategic issues facing a global business. Only the strategy can determine how many and what kinds of global executive jobs are required, and how many and what kinds of executives are needed to fill them. Only the strategy can determine how many truly global executives are needed (if any), how many foreign nationals are necessary, how the international jobs will be structured and positioned, the extent and nature of alliances, how business will be done internationally, and so on.

There are important differences in the development of local nationals, host-country nationals and third-country nationals, and for this reason lockstep or undifferentiated development programs are likely to be ineffective for many in the international pool.

Further, global executive jobs, whatever the home country of the executive, are fraught with dangers, not the least of which is the increased probability of derailment associated with poorly designed and poorly managed assignments. Much can be done to improve the ways these jobs are structured, the processes by which performance is monitored, and the feedback processes associated with them.

To emphasize the strategic and structural aspects of developing international executive talent is not to say that individual development should be ignored. There is no question that many of the essential skills needed in global careers can be learned, and that very few individuals are so naturally gifted that they need no further development. While there are limits to what an organization can do to make someone grow, there is a lot they can do to help people who want to grow. These include providing opportunities, early in a career, to work with people from other countries and to be part of activities that cross borders, to work under competent bosses with international experience and perspective, and to live and work as an expatriate. These kinds of experiences, combined with effective assessment and feedback, seem to be essential ingredients in developing global talent.

14

ETHICAL LEADERSHIP

Hong Kong's traditional business environment encouraged you to stay focused on one thing only: business. But this is no longer applicable. Businesses now need to think about the community and the effects their actions may have on the community at large. My involvement in community activities has an added benefit: it allows me to gain a much wider perspective for my own business activities. Wearing more than one hat, I am not only responsible to my shareholders, but also to the communities that I live and work in—and to the people around me. Companies nowadays need to be much more well-rounded in order to become good corporate citizens.

—Bernard Chan[1]

This chapter presents a guide to ethical decision-making in situations that will confront you as a leader and discusses several ethical perspectives that should help you make ethical decisions. There is constant debate as to where a chapter on ethics should appear in any book (e.g., textbooks, casebooks). In this book, I decided to place it last. I do this for one very specific reason. I want ethics and its intersection with leadership to be the last thing you read and consider as you finish your course on leadership. In my own teaching and research, I am struck by the number of times that what seem to be innocuous decisions can turn into very "dicey" ethical situations. In my previous life as a naval officer in the Canadian Navy, I was often presented with situations that required me to think through several ethical dimensions before making a decision. Consequently, I hope and expect that this chapter will be one you return to many times as you develop as a leader in the organization you join after you finish your current degree.

Concern regarding leaders and their ethics has been central to everyday life throughout our history. Unfortunately, it is also a very messy topic on which to do research. Consequently, research regarding leaders and their ethics is very sparse (Yukl, 2006). Recent research (Ciulla, 1998; Phillips, 2006) has begun to delve into these issues. Ciulla (1998) discusses how leadership theory and practices may lead to a more just and caring society. Phillips (2006) defines CEO moral capital and presents a more formal definition of moral capital.

CEO moral capital is the belief that the CEO justly balances the disparate interests of individual and group stakeholders to achieve positive returns that benefit the firm, its stakeholders, and the CEO.

Moral capital is the belief that an individual, organization, or cause justly balances the disparate interests of stakeholders to achieve positive returns that benefit their collective and individual purposes.

These definitions describe how CEOs and other individuals are viewed by their followers, peers, and superiors and, as Phillips (2006) argues, are based on their perception of the CEO's (or an individual's) character and behavior.

A DEFINITION OF ETHICS

In the Western world, the definition of ethics dates back to Plato and Aristotle. Ethics comes from *ethos,* a Greek word meaning character, conduct, and/or customs. It is about what morals and values are found appropriate by members of society and individuals, themselves. Ethics helps us decide what is "right and good" or "wrong and bad" in any given situation. With respect to leadership, ethics is about who leaders are—their character and what they do, their actions and behaviors.

ETHICAL THEORIES

As suggested above, ethical theories fall into two broad categories: those theories related to leaders' conduct, actions and/or behavior, and those related to leaders' character. For those theories related to conduct, there are two types: those that relate to leaders' conduct and their consequences and those that relate to the rules or duty that prescribe leaders' conduct. Those theories related to consequences are called teleological theories (*telos* being a Greek word for purposes or ends). These theories emphasize whether a leader's actions, behavior, and/or conduct have positive outcomes. This means that the outcomes related to a person's behavior establish whether the behavior was ethical or unethical. Those theories related to duty or rules are called deontological theories (*deos* being a Greek word for duty). These theories focus on the actions that lead to consequences and whether the actions are good or bad. Those theories related to character are described as virtue-based approaches.

Teleological Approaches

There are three approaches to assessing outcomes and whether they are viewed as ethical. First, *ethical egoism* describes the actions of a leader designed to obtain the greatest good for the leader. Second, *utilitarianism* is about the actions of leaders that obtain the greatest good for the largest number of people. Third, *altruism* is a perspective that argues that a leader's conduct is ethical if he or she demonstrates concern for others' interests, even if these interests are contrary to the leader's self-interests.

Deontological Approach

This approach is derived from *deos,* a Greek word meaning duty. It argues that whether or not an action is ethical depends not only on its outcome but also on whether the action, behavior, or conduct is itself inherently good. Examples of actions and behaviors that are intrinsically good, irrespective of the outcomes, are "telling the truth, keeping promises, being fair, and respecting others" (Northouse, 2007). This approach emphasizes the actions of leaders *and* their ethical responsibility to do what is right.

Virtue-Based Approach

Virtue-based theories are related to leaders and who they are and are grounded in the leader's heart and the leader's character. In addition, these virtues can be learned and retained through experience and practice. This learning occurs in an individual's family and the various communities with which an individual interacts throughout his or her lifetime. This perspective can be traced back to Plato and Aristotle. Aristotle believed that individuals could be helped to become more virtuous and that more attention should be given to telling individuals what to be as opposed to telling them what to do (Velasquez, 1992). Aristotle suggested the following virtues as exemplars of an ethical person: generosity, courage, temperance, sociability, self-control, honesty, fairness, modesty, and justice (Velasquez, 1992). Velasquez (1992) argued that organizational managers should learn and retain virtues "such as perseverance, public-spiritedness, integrity, truthfulness, fidelity, benevolence, and humility" (Northouse, 2007).

THE CENTRALITY OF ETHICS TO LEADERSHIP

Ethics is central to leadership because of the nature of the relationship between leaders and followers. Leaders influence followers—this means they affect followers' lives either negatively or positively (Yukl, 2006). The nature of the influence depends on the leaders' character and behavior (particularly the nature and outcome of behaviors). Leaders have more power—interpersonal and/or formal hierarchical power—and therefore have a greater responsibility with respect to their impact on their followers. Leaders influence followers in the pursuit and achievement of common goals. It is in these situations that leaders need to respect their followers and treat them with dignity—in other words, as individuals with distinctive identities. Finally, leaders are instrumental in developing and establishing organizational values. Their own personal values determine what kind of ethical climate will develop in their organizations.

ETHICAL LEADERSHIP: THE PERSPECTIVES OF SEVERAL LEADERSHIP SCHOLARS

In this section, I review the perspectives of three prominent leadership scholars as these perspectives relate to leadership and ethics. I focus on Heifetz (1994), Burns (1978), and Greenleaf (1970, 1977).

Heifetz and Ethical Leadership

Heifetz (1994) emphasized conflict and the responsibility of leaders to assist followers in dealing with conflict and effecting changes that come from conflict. He focused on the values of followers, the values of the organizations in which they work, and the values of the communities in which they live. For Heifetz (1994), the paramount responsibility of leaders is to create a work atmosphere characterized by empathy, trust, and nurturance and to help followers to change and grow when faced with difficult situations (Northouse, 2007; Yukl, 2006).

Burns and Ethical Leadership

Like Heifetz (1994), Burns (1978) argued that leadership (especially transformational leadership, as described in Chapter 9) is about helping followers achieve higher ethical standards when differing values conflict—especially when conflict is confronted during difficult situations. He argued that the interaction of leaders and followers should raise the ethical behavior and character of both. Leaders would do this by assisting followers to emphasize values such as equality, justice, and liberty (Burns, 1978; Ciulla, 1998).

Greenleaf and Ethical Leadership

Greenleaf (1970, 1977) espoused servant leadership. This perspective comes closest to altruism described earlier. The underlying tenants of servant leadership are as follows: Leaders need to be aware of followers' concerns and needs, leaders need to attend to followers' needs and concerns, leaders need to empathize with followers, leaders need to nurture and support followers, and leaders need to look after followers. Servant leaders make others better by their presence. Through serving their followers, servant leaders encourage followers to gain more knowledge, freedom, and autonomy and to develop as servant leaders themselves. In addition, Greenleaf believed that servant leaders have a broader responsibility to society to accept the "have-nots" and to set right inequalities and social injustices (Graham, 1991; Northouse, 2007; Yukl, 2006).

All three perspectives emphasize the relationship between leaders and followers and argue that this relationship is at the heart of ethical leadership. The ideas presented by these three scholars are similar to and in agreement with Gilligan's (1982) ethic of caring. This has become a central principle in ethical leadership research and is considered of paramount importance to organizations as it is of critical importance in developing collaboration and trust among leaders and followers (Brady, 1999).

ETHICAL LEADERSHIP PRINCIPLES

In this section, I present five principles that are believed to lead to the development of ethical leadership. These are respect for others, service to others, justice for others, honesty toward others, and building community with others (Dubrin, 2007; Northouse, 2007).

Respect for Others

Ethical leaders treat others with dignity and respect. This means that we treat people as ends in themselves rather than as means to our own ends. This form of respect recognizes that followers have goals and ambitions and confirms followers as human beings who have worth and value to the organization. In addition, it leads to empathy, active listening, and tolerance for conflicting viewpoints.

Service to Others

Ethical leaders serve others. They behave in an altruistic fashion as opposed to behaving in a way that is based on ethical egoism. These leaders put followers first—their prime reason for being is to support and nurture subordinates. Service to others is exemplified through behaviors such as mentoring, building teams, and empowering (Kanungo & Mendonca, 1996).

Justice for Others

Ethical leaders ensure that justice and fairness are a central part of their decision making. This means treating all subordinates in very similar ways, except when there is a very clear need for differential treatment and there is transparency as to why this need exists. In addition to being transparent, the logic for differential treatment should be morally sound and reasonable.

Honesty Toward Others

Ethical leadership requires honesty. Dishonesty destroys trust—a critical characteristic of any leader-follower relationship. On the other hand, honesty increases trust and builds the leader-follower relationship. Honesty means openness with others, in that we express our thinking and our reality as fully as we can. This means balancing openness with disclosing only what is appropriate in a given scenario. Dalla Costa (1998) says that honesty for leaders means the following:

> Do not promise what you can't deliver, do not misrepresent, do not hide behind spin-doctored evasions, do not suppress obligations, do not evade accountability, do not accept that the "survival of the fittest" pressures of business release any of us from the responsibility to respect another's dignity and humanity. (p. 164)

I would argue that leaders need to ensure that *what they believe, what they think, what they say,* and *what they do* are internally consistent. This internal consistency, along with openness, will build trust among followers toward the leader.

Building Community With Others

Ethical leaders build community with others. This is crucial because leadership is about influencing others to achieve a communal goal. This means that leaders develop organizational or team goals that are appropriate for the leader and his or her followers. These goals need to excite as many people as possible, and ethical leaders achieve this by taking into account the goals of everyone in the team or organization.

HOW DOES ETHICAL LEADERSHIP WORK?

I am hoping that this chapter will enable you to better understand yourself as you develop your leadership skills, knowledge, and abilities. Use the thinking on ethical leadership in this chapter as guidelines in making your decisions. Remember that the relationship between you and your followers is at the heart of ethical leadership and requires that you show sensitivity to others' needs, treat others in a just manner, and have a caring attitude toward others. Being an ethical leader will be easier if you entrench the following questions into your thinking (Northouse, 2007):

- Is this the right and fair thing to do?
- Is this what a "good" person would do?
- Am I respectful to others?
- Do I treat others generously?
- Am I honest toward others?
- Am I serving the community?

As Chan's (2006) quote at the beginning of the chapter illustrates, leaders must be concerned with more than running their businesses. They must be concerned with their employees, their customers, their suppliers, their communities, their shareholders, and themselves. Leadership is influencing people to achieve communal goals—ethical leadership is achieving those goals in a way that is fair and just to your employees, your customers, your suppliers, your communities, your shareholders, and yourselves (Daft, 2005; Phillips, 2006).

Note

1. Bernard Chan is President of the Asia Financial Group and Asia Insurance Co. Ltd., Director of Asia Commercial Bank Ltd., and adviser to Bangkok Bank Public Co. Ltd. He has served on the Executive and Legislative Councils as well as many other private and public organizations in Hong Kong.

References

Brady, F. N. (1999). A systematic approach to teaching ethics in business. *Journal of Business Ethics, 19*(3), 309–319.

Burns, J. M. (1978). *Leadership.* New York: Harper & Row.

Chan, B. (2006, April 11). Wearing many hats (Part 6 of 8, Ivey Leadership Series). *South China Morning Post,* Business Section.

Ciulla, J. B. (1998). *Ethics, the heart of leadership.* Westport, CT: Greenwood.

Daft, R. L. (2005). *The leadership experience* (3rd ed.). Mason, OH: Thomson, South-Western.

Dalla Costa, J. (1998). *The ethical imperative: Why moral leadership is good business.* Reading, MA: Addison-Wesley.

Dubrin, A. (2007). *Leadership: Research findings, practice, and skills.* New York: Houghton Mifflin.

Gilligan, C. (1982). *In a different voice: Psychological theory and women's development.* Cambridge, MA: Harvard University Press.

Graham, J. W. (1991). Servant-leadership in organizations: Inspirational and moral. *The Leadership Quarterly, 2*(2), 105–119.

Greenleaf, R. K. (1970). *The servant as leader.* Newton Centre, MA: Robert K. Greenleaf Center.

Greenleaf, R. K. (1977). *Servant leadership: A journey into the nature of legitimate power and greatness.* New York: Paulist.

Heifetz, R. A. (1994). *Leadership without easy answers.* Cambridge, MA: Harvard University Press.

Kanungo, R. N., & Mendonca, M. (1996). *Ethical dimensions of leadership.* Thousands Oaks, CA: Sage.

Northouse, P. G. (2007). *Leadership: Theory and practice* (4th ed.). Thousand Oaks, CA: Sage.

Phillips, J. R. (2006). *CEO moral capital*. Unpublished doctoral manuscript, University of Western Ontario.

Velasquez, M. G. (1992). *Business ethics: Concepts and cases* (3rd ed.). Englewood Cliffs, NJ: Prentice Hall.

Yukl, G. (2006). *Leadership in organizations* (6th ed.). Upper Saddle River, NJ: Pearson-Prentice Hall.

THE CASES

Laurel Upholstery

A senior manager at Laurel Upholstery learns from an unexpected meeting with a former senior manager at the firm's Montreal factory that only managers of a certain origin—regardless of seniority or performance—were being promoted into top management positions. Although the former manager alleged he had no interest in pursuing the matter, he was frustrated enough to leave the firm and indicated that the matter seemed serious enough to warrant further investigation.

Price of Speaking Out Against the Betrayal of Public Trust: Joanna Gualtieri (A)

A real estate analyst has been hired as a government employee to manage Canada's overseas property holdings, including its embassies and diplomatic residences. Despite strict government regulations regarding the procurement of overseas accommodations and policies relating to fiscal accountability, the analyst has witnessed the luxurious accommodations enjoyed by diplomatic staff posted abroad. She documents the abuses and reports the finding to her supervisor, who does nothing. The analyst must decide whether to take her finding further.

Pembina Pipeline Corporation

Pembina Pipeline Corporation transports light crude oil and natural gas liquids in Western Western Canada. The president of the company is abruptly awakened one night by a phone call from his operations manager. He is informed that one of Pembina's pipelines has burst and is spilling thousands of barrels of crude oil into a nearby river. Emergency crews have responded to the disaster, but more help is needed. The president has to decide the best way to handle this situation with the media and plan a strategy for the company in containing the spill.

THE READING

Ethics or Excellence? Conscience as a Check on the Unbalanced Pursuit of Organizational Goals

That the terrain of decision making is mined with moral hazards has never been much in doubt. But the real question for executives is this: Just how can you make your conscience your guide? This author has suggestions and strong advice that, when taken, can help restore public confidence in business leaders.

LAUREL UPHOLSTERY

Prepared by Ken Mark under the supervision of Professor Michael Sider

Version: (A) 2006-01-30

INTRODUCTION

On May 5, 2005, Joe McKinley, senior manager at Laurel Upholstery, was in the midst of an unexpected meeting at his firm's Montreal factory with James Shedd, a former senior manager. Shedd was a senior manager who had recently left Laurel to enjoy an early retirement. "That's the official, politically correct version," confided Shedd to McKinley. "The real reason why I left was because I didn't see a future for me in the company."

"They're only promoting Italians," Shedd warned McKinley, who was of Irish descent. "Your best bet is to start shopping your résumé around like I did." Although Shedd alleged that he had no interest in pursuing the matter in court (he was frustrated enough to leave the firm), he indicated that the matter seemed serious enough to warrant McKinley's attention. McKinley was in charge of sales for Laurel's Northeastern region (eastern United States and Canada), and was considered to be one of the executives in line for the chief executive officer's (CEO's) job.

McKinley listened intently. Shedd's comments seemed to echo the sentiment of the managers passed over for the promotions, a few of whom McKinley had visited last week.

LAUREL UPHOLSTERY

Laurel Upholstery (Laurel) was a well-established supplier of industrial fabrics for the aerospace and military market. It had been founded in the 1960s by three Italian immigrants and was headquartered in Montreal, with sales offices in Washington, D.C., and Seattle, Washington.

Lorenzo Real, the largest shareholder of the three founders, had come from a long line of textile manufacturers in Sicily, Italy. During the early part of the 1900s, the Real family had expanded its one-factory operation to a company that employed 2,000 persons and focused on the high-end furniture segment in southern Italy. After the Second World War, Real had come to Canada, bringing along with him his immediate family. Although he had intended to take a job in the booming postwar economy, Real, to his disappointment, found that few firms were willing to hire employees who were not fluent in French. (Real, who spoke passable English, as well as his native Italian, had only rudimentary knowledge of French.) Undeterred, Real teamed up with two other Italian immigrants, and leveraged their combined capital (at that time, only $4,000) to start a high-end textile manufacturing firm to service industrial markets. In an attempt to fit in with their new country, the founders named their firm "Laurel Upholstery," after the Laurentian mountain range.

When interest in customized, high-performance fabrics grew, Laurel refocused its efforts to serve the aerospace and military markets, which were growing rapidly at that time. By the 1990s, control of the company had passed on to the founders' children, who chose to sell the majority of the firm to a consortium of investors: A Quebec-based pension fund owned 20 percent, a group of Toronto-based angel investors collectively owned 50 percent and Laurel's management team owned 10 percent (Frank Matteo, CEO, owned five percent, and each of the five senior managers owned one percent). The Real family continued to own 20 percent of the firm. Most were passive investors, meeting with management once or twice a year.

There were approximately 200 employees in the Montreal factory (30 percent of British descent, 30 percent French-Canadian, 30 percent Italian-Canadian, and 10 percent Asian-Canadian) and 31 people in the management team. Of the 31, six were considered to be senior management. Of the six, five were of Italian origin (see Exhibit 1).

McKinley had joined Laurel as senior manager of Northeastern Sales in April 2005, after spending 20 years in the U.S. furniture industry. He had been hired by Laurel's CEO to expand the firm's sales into new markets, specifically the automotive and home textile industries. Although he had only been with the company for a month, McKinley had already begun setting up meetings with prospective customers. In trying to develop these new markets, McKinley had been spending approximately 80 percent of his time traveling to Toronto and Detroit.

At Laurel's management level, 15 assistant managers reported to 10 managers, who in turn reported to five senior managers. These five senior managers reported to the CEO. In terms of cultural diversity at the management level, there were 10 French-Canadians and 21 English-Canadians (eight of British origin, nine of Italian origin, three of German origin and one of Spanish origin). Roughly half of management was Canadian-born. At the manager level, five had university degrees (two were MBAs). The other three, Bram Aachen, Raymond Moreau and Annie Gauthier, had high school diplomas. At the manager level, the average age was 39, and all had spent their entire career at Laurel.

As McKinley walked with Shedd to the exit doors, he recalled that Laurel's CEO, Frank Matteo (himself of Italian origin), had ushered Laurel's four senior managers into early retirement in April 2005, awarding them generous retirement packages in recognition of their hard work in tripling sales in three years. All four were of British descent.

Instead of promoting the direct reports of these senior managers (who were of French, British and Spanish descent) into the vacant spots, Matteo had chosen instead to promote five new assistant managers—all of Italian origin—into the senior management "inner circle." These five had been hired in February 2005 and were assigned to various sales and operational roles. All five had graduated from MBA programs in Quebec in April 2004 and had worked for competitor firms for the past 10 months. Each of the five was between 29 and 32 years old. This management shuffle had been completed two days ago, and it suddenly occurred to McKinley that he was the only person in the senior management team who was from a different cultural background. McKinley had talked to some managers who were passed over for the senior management positions. Their comments are listed in Exhibit 2.

As McKinley walked into the company parking lot with Shedd, he wondered if there were any additional questions he should ask.

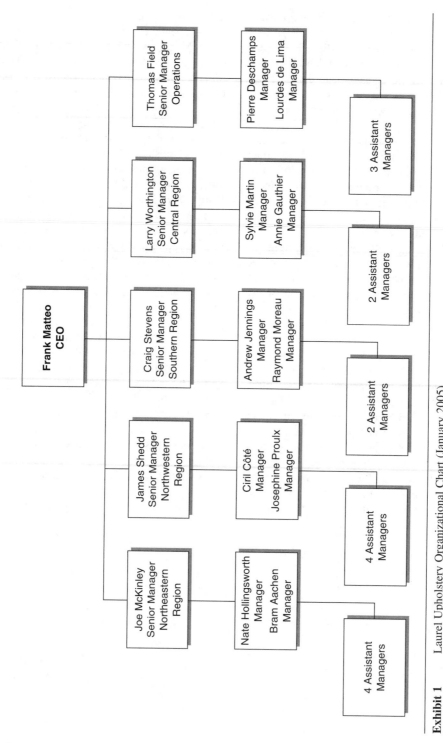

Exhibit 1   Laurel Upholstery Organizational Chart (January 2005)

Nate Hollingsworth—There certainly is a sense of frustration and I'm eager to hear why we were all passed over for the senior management positions by our reports. A few of us have talked about it and while I'm not going to name any names, some feel like they've invested their entire careers just to be stepped on. One person seemed desperate because that person had a family that counted on a salary from Laurel as their only source of income. Another person felt sick that he would be reporting to a new MBA, a former report, as his boss. We all feel humiliated and wonder what we did wrong. Now, I'm sure there were reasons why we were passed over but management is not saying so. We've delivered great results in the past three years and we know that the last quarter was a bit tough but that was not a strong reason to dismiss us. We've all lost motivation, really.

Bram Aachen—How should I respond to a request for comment? Maybe I should be wishing them the best in their new jobs. I wonder why we were never given a real reason for being left behind. We're afraid to say anything—after all, we've got decent jobs with decent pay (higher than industry average) and the benefits are spectacular. I really like the group of people here at Laurel and we've pushed through several innovative projects that were on the brink of failure. I feel like I've been part of the building of the current state of the company—we're more than three times the size we were just three years ago, a phenomenal result considering our home industry is challenged and the Northwest isn't doing too well either.

Ciril Côté—It's got to be a coincidence that all four are Italian, right? Maybe it's the fact that they're MBAs and the cream of the crop, highly motivated. Maybe the management needs fresh perspectives. But haven't we taken the company to this point with our current team? The senior managers who left trained us well and we feel that we're more than capable to shoulder the responsibilities of taking the company to the next step. I thought my competition (friendly competition) would be my fellow managers, with maybe one or two outside hires. I guess I was wrong. You never know these days. It's hard to get motivated now. And worst, when I walk through the front of the factory, our colleagues who are in the factory keep asking me why I wasn't promoted. That's got to be the worst part, feeling inadequate. Sure there's an anger but I think that we should do our best and look on the bright side of things. For me, though, I don't know if I can stay and be part of this decision. I was blindsided. I'm a fool for not seeing this coming.

Raymond Moreau—I feel like I've been hit by a train. Last week, I thought I was dreaming when the new senior managers were announced. I think the whole room was silent, with many people's eyes wide open in disbelief. No one said anything when management asked for comment—who dared? We thought it was a late April Fool's joke—seriously—until the meeting was done. Then we realized that it wasn't. I think I had to go home early that day, I don't remember. I just felt like throwing up. I lost my appetite, for sure. When I went home that night, my wife asked me if something had gone wrong at the office. I was too sad to say anything that night but I told her two days later. I just couldn't believe it. And the reaction from the assistant managers who were promoted just made it worse: It seemed like they knew it was coming, that they were the "chosen ones" and couldn't even look us in the eyes after the announcement. I know that I don't have my MBA but this couldn't be the way one treats members of a family. That's it, that's all.

Others—No Comment

Exhibit 2   Comments From Managers (Disguised)

The Price of Speaking Out Against the Betrayal of Public Trust

Joanna Gualtieri (A)

Prepared by Ken Mark under the supervision of
Professor Gerard Seijts

Version: (A) 2004–10–07

Introduction

It was late May 1995, and Joanna Gualtieri had been with the Department of Foreign Affairs and International Trade (DFAIT) in Ottawa, Canada, for about three years. Gualtieri was one of the department's portfolio managers, tasked with managing Canada's multibillion-dollar overseas real estate holdings, including embassies, ambassadorial residences and diplomatic housing.

Gualtieri's office, the Bureau of Physical Resources, had a charter, which called for overseas diplomats and staff to receive accommodation in a cost-effective, economical and efficient manner.[1] In addition, Treasury Board regulations and governing policies laid out specific rules regarding the housing of Canadian diplomats and reiterated the requirement to do so in an accountable, cost-effective way. After all, it was hardworking Canadians' tax dollars that were footing the bill. Instead, what Gualtieri found was that "you were just catering to the predilections of diplomats."

At the time she started at the DFAIT, the government was confronting many social ills, including an eroding health-care system and an education system that was losing resources. Gualtieri had believed that the change in government in 1993 would prompt her superiors to change their attitudes toward government waste and misspending. The new Liberal government had been elected based on promises of fiscal accountability and a strong emphasis on ethics in public life.[2]

During the first two years of her employment, Gualtieri had come to the conclusion that nothing would change unless she spoke up about the mismanagement of real estate assets abroad that, among other things, allowed diplomatic staff to have grandiose and luxurious accommodations and lifestyles at the taxpayers' expense. Having decided that she wanted to do something about the massive waste costing ordinary Canadians millions of dollars annually, Gualtieri contemplated whether she should continue raising the alarm with her immediate supervisor or elevate the matter to higher-ups.

The Department of Foreign Affairs

As part of the federal government's commitment to strengthen Canada's influence in the world, the DFAIT represents Canada around the world through its network of embassies and offices. It was estimated that there were 4,000 pieces of property—consulates, agency buildings and diplomat housing—managed by the department, with an estimated total value of Cdn$2 billion to Cdn$3 billion.[3]

The DFAIT had strict regulations governing the procurement and management of this vast property portfolio. Treasury Board rules also directed that stewardship and fiscal prudence had to be exercised in the expenditure of public funds. To use an example, a diplomat of a certain rank and family size (e.g., single, as opposed to married with children) would, pursuant to the Treasury Board Guidelines, be required to live in an approximately 1,000 square foot apartment or house.

Prior to the 1970s, these regulations were loosely drafted and regularly ignored by the department's managers. In response to complaints about lavish spending of taxpayers' dollars, a bureau in the DFAIT was set up with the mandate to enforce and further implement the real estate regulations. By the 1990s, it was clear that the diplomats and managers had found a way around this internal checkpoint—they simply ignored it.

JOANNA E. GUALTIERI

Gualtieri had been an Ontario lawyer since 1988. She was also an experienced renovator and real estate owner, having owned property since she was 20. Her father, a professor of religion and ethics and a United Church of Canada minister, wrote his doctoral dissertation while his family lived in Italy.[4] In the years following, Gualtieri had lived in the United States and India, and had traveled extensively throughout Europe, Africa and Asia. When she initially applied for the job of real estate analyst in February 1992, Gualtieri was extremely excited about the prospect of working on important assignments in exotic locales. Her extensive knowledge of construction and real estate, coupled with her international travels, made her a perfect fit for the job.

On her first trip abroad, Gualtieri attended a function at the Canadian embassy in Tokyo. She had just discovered that the main diplomatic site in Tokyo had been valued as high as Cdn$2.5 billion. Under governing regulations, such a drastic appreciation in property value would have earmarked it for serious consideration for sale, or severance and partial sale, with another more modest property being purchased to replace it. What was more astounding, however, was the fact that significant portions of the property were underutilized or sitting vacant so the Ambassador could enjoy a bigger garden while millions of dollars were spent annually to lease other accommodations.

Gualtieri could find no evidence that anybody had taken steps to investigate the option of disposing of part of the property or at least developing more housing on the site so that expensive leases could be terminated. Gualtieri went on to discover that homes ranging in value from Cdn$20 million to Cdn$40 million were housing single families and multimillion-dollar, government-owned condominiums were sitting vacant while the Canadian diplomats demanded that other larger and more luxurious accommodations be rented at huge costs to the Canadian taxpayer. Living lavishly in Tokyo, which had the highest land costs in the world, was the departmental way.

During the function, a high-ranking embassy official (who had heard Gualtieri was in Tokyo to pursue a full feasibility study of the diplomatic accommodations) warned her not to interfere with "how things were done."[5] This directive left Gualtieri confused, as her job was to curb out-of-control spending.

She traveled to other places, such as Kingston (Jamaica), Guatemala, Mexico, Sao Paulo and Brasilia (Brazil) and Copenhagen (Denmark). Gualtieri began to see a pattern, noticing that diplomats, in particular, were living in extravagant, "palatial" residences, often more than 3,000 square feet in size and costing Cdn$100,000 per annum in rent and fees. It appeared to Gualtieri that expensive residences were the norm.

On one occasion, Gualtieri, in a report to her supervisor, described a diplomat's residence as "lavish." Her supervisor immediately crossed out the word "lavish" and warned her not to use such language again.[6] Her initial excitement about the analyst position faded, and was replaced by disillusionment.

Gualtieri documented assiduously what she was witnessing. She reported the abuses of real estate regulations to her supervisor, and expressed concerns that the department was ignoring its responsibility as stewards of massive sums of public monies, but he did not act on the information that he received. She also had concerns regarding the bureau's failure to maintain proper records of its business dealings and its practice of studying issues to death, creating an illusion that things were be done, while in reality the status quo was maintained.

Gualtieri estimated that the mismanagement of overseas properties had cost the taxpayers about Cdn$2 billion between 1986 and 1998. She was ostracized for her allegations of wrong-doing at the DFAIT. She observed that:[7]

After raising my concerns, I was banned from going on trips because management didn't want me making cost-effective changes to living arrangements for diplomats.

In fact, the more I started to identify problems at the places I went, the more my bosses tried to prevent me from doing my job. They even told me whom I could talk to.

By September 1994, she had compiled a filing cabinet full of documents. For example, in another display of waste and lack of accountability, a Canadian trade diplomat in Mexico demanded to live in the former residence of the ambassador of New Zealand who had decided to relocate to less expensive accommodations. In fact, Gualtieri identified significant overhousing in Mexico and wondered why the majority of Canada's diplomatic leases were each about US$45,000 per annum, while the Americans paid only US$23,000 for many of its leases. Gualtieri learned that there was a saying in diplomatic circles that the Canadians always had the nicest, most expensive accommodations. Also in Mexico, Gualtieri saw $7 million in Canadian government allocation for North American Free Trade Agreement (NAFTA) initiatives, including a permanent trade centre, squandered because of poor management. The centre was closed soon after it opened.

In Brazil, she saw Canadian government-owned condominium apartments sold at losses because, although luxurious, the occupants complained that other Canadian diplomats were living in homes with private swimming pools and beautiful gardens. Gualtieri documented many other examples of waste of taxpayer money. In Guatemala, Gualtieri had been dispatched with only days notice to "rubber stamp" the purchase of three condominium apartments. Finding them to be located in the newest, most luxurious condo development with privately keyed elevators, three swimming pools and sprawling grounds, Gualtieri opposed the purchase as there were other suitable and more cost-effective options. In Tokyo, Gualtieri witnessed a Cdn$20 million house sit vacant for three years while the diplomat who was intended to occupy it spent more than Cdn$300,000 per annum of public monies to rent something more to his liking.

A lot had changed since Gualtieri had first raised the abuses of real estate regulations and the absence of stewardship with her supervisor. During the difficult times at work, a typical day at her office involved her sitting at her desk with little to do. During one of her frequent bad days, she might be yelled at and ridiculed and humiliated by one of her bosses in front of other employees, interrupted or ignored at meetings and completely bypassed during work sessions that directly involved her job.

Nevertheless Gualtieri decided that something had to be done about "a regime that preaches accountability while acting so contrary to the public interest."[8]

Her first instinct was to go straight to the deputy minister, three levels above her supervisor, to report her findings. But upon reflection, Gualtieri knew that the DFAIT—indeed, the public service as a whole—valued and respected the hierarchy. Approaching superiors above her own supervisor would not be tolerated. Gualtieri wondered how she should, once again, discuss her concerns with her bosses. Or, alternatively, should she go public with allegations of mismanagement and waste of millions of dollars of taxpayers' money? The latter approach didn't seem all that unreasonable given the significance of her findings and the fact that her efforts to curb misspending of taxpayers' dollars had already been met with stiff resistance and fierce opposition. How confident should she be that people higher up in the hierarchy would be more open toward her accusations?

NOTES

1. Lynne Cohen," Whistling in the Wind," Canadian Lawyer, November-December, 2003, pp. 35-41.

2. Ibid.

3. Ibid.

4. Ibid.

5. Ibid; Molly K. Amoli Shinhat, "Bill C-25 Leaves Civil Servants Open to Harassment: Gualtieri," The Hill Times, October 27, 2003, p. 13; Aaron Freeman, "A Conversation With a Government Whistleblower," The Hill Times, August 26, 2002.

6. Lynne Cohen, "Whistling in the Wind," Canadian Lawyer, November-December, 2003, pp. 35-41.

7. Ibid; Molly K. Amoli Shinhat, "Bill C-25 Leaves Civil Servants Open to Harassment: Gualtieri," The Hill Times, October 27, 2003, p. 13.

8. Aaron Freeman, "A Conversation With a Government Whistleblower," The Hill Times, August 26, 2002.

PEMBINA PIPELINE CORPORATION

Prepared by Ken Mark under the supervision of Professor Alexandra Hurst

Copyright © 2001, Ivey Management Services   Version: (A) 2001–07–06

INTRODUCTION[1]

Patrick Walsh, president of Pembina Pipeline Corporation, was abruptly awakened by a telephone call from Jim Thomas, his operations manager. It was 4:30 a.m. on August 2, 2000, in downtown Calgary, Alberta, and Thomas had no time for pleasantries:

> Walsh, I just heard from one of our pipeline operators that our new Taylor-Prince George pipeline burst open this morning! Get up! We're leaking thousands of barrels of crude into a pristine salmon river. Our emergency response crews have started containment efforts but we're going to need much more help. What are we going to do next?

A wave of panic shook Walsh awake. Grabbing his car keys and the cellular phone, he scrambled into his Ford Explorer and began driving to Pembina's Calgary head office. Negotiating corners with one hand on the steering wheel, Walsh kept Thomas on the line:

> I want to know all the details of the spill now! Our first concern will be to contain the oil! I'll join you in a few minutes at the office and we'd better come up

with something. Damn it, Thomas, we don't even have media relations people, much less a PR agency!

PEMBINA PIPELINE CORPORATION

Involved in the transportation of light crude oil, condensate and natural gas liquids in western Canada, Pembina Pipeline Corporation owned the Pembina Pipeline Income Fund (the Fund), a publicly traded Canadian income fund. This fund was established in 1997 to give the investing public the opportunity to participate in a stable, well-managed pipeline transportation entity that had provided high quality, reliable service to the Canadian oil and gas industry since the mid-1950s. The Fund was intended to provide unitholders with attractive long-term returns through its investment in Pembina, which had a mandate to efficiently operate its pipeline systems and actively seek expansion opportunities. The Fund paid cash distributions to unitholders on a monthly basis. The trust units traded on the Toronto Stock Exchange under the symbol PIF.UN.

Pembina's pipeline systems served a large geographic area with 7,500 kilometres of pipeline and related pumping and storage facilities. The systems were well positioned in the heart of western Canada's oil and natural gas production areas. There were four systems in total:

- Peace Pipeline System—Central Northwest Alberta
- Pembina Pipeline System—Central Southwest Alberta
- Bonnie Glen Pipeline System—Central South Alberta
- Wabasca Pipeline System—Northern Alberta

Collectively, Pembina's pipeline systems transported over 40 percent of conventional light crude oil production in Western Canada.

OPERATIONS

Pembina's pipeline systems were maintained and operated by a dedicated group of field employees located in 10 field offices. Pembina's corporate head office was located in Calgary, Alberta, where technical and administrative staff supported the pipeline operations. Through its pipeline, Pembina transported light crude oil, condensate and natural gas liquids. Virtually no heavy oil was transported on any of the Pembina systems, nor was Pembina a natural gas carrier. The company did not own the product it transported but, similar to a trucking company, it took custody of the product from when it entered the pipeline until it was delivered to the owners.

Pipelines and the materials used in them were designed, built and tested to high standards. When pipelines were properly maintained failures due to pipe breakdown were rare. Pembina had several maintenance programs in place to ensure line integrity. These were:

Internal Inspection Program

Internal inspection tools were designed to allow pipeline operators to measure the wall thickness along the pipe so that areas of metal loss could be located and repaired. These tools had been incorporated into Pembina's monitoring program, and pipeline systems were inspected on a rotating seven-to-eight-year cycle. Pembina's pipeline

systems, with the exception of the recently purchased Federated system, were last checked in 1998.

Hydrostatic Testing

Government regulations required new pipelines be filled with water and pressure tested to 125 percent of their licensed maximum operating pressure before the lines could be put into service. The hydrotest was designed to reveal any structural weakness in the pipe or welds. Although not a regulatory requirement, all of the major pipelines in the Peace and Pembina System (built prior to 1970) had been hydrostatically retested. The first two phases of hydrostatic testing of the 16-inch mainline had been completed and confirmed the strength and quality of the pipe tested.

Bacterial Monitoring and Treatment

Pembina's pipeline systems employed programs of regular product sampling and testing for bacteria. Producers with excessive bacteria were required to treat their tanks with a biocide to kill the bacteria. Similarly, biocide was periodically shipped through pipelines to control and kill bacteria.

Cathodic Protection

Cathodic protection systems were used on steel pipelines to impress a small voltage on the pipe to help protect it from external corrosion. Every month, readings were taken on Pembina's pipelines to ensure that these systems were operating at effective levels. A complete cathodic protection survey was done annually in compliance with regulatory requirements and any necessary repairs or adjustments to the systems were made. Evaluation of the survey results provided important information on the condition of the pipeline coatings.

EXPANSION

Pembina intended to continue to expand its service through new battery and facilities connections, tie-ins to third-party pipelines, and expansion of Pembina's existing systems to service new oil- and gas-producing areas. Ongoing exploration and development activity by the producer community was expected to continue to fuel demand for pipeline service in the regions served by Pembina's pipeline systems, particularly on the Continental System operating in northwestern Oregon and northeastern Washington.

The most significant increase in throughputs on the Pembina System could potentially come from technology developments to improve the recovery of crude oil in the oil fields. It was estimated that only 21 percent of initial crude oil in place was recoverable using present technology.

Pembina's management was actively reviewing potential acquisitions and believed that Pembina was very well positioned to take advantage of any favorable opportunities to acquire or otherwise expand Pembina's business.

INCIDENT CONTROL MECHANISMS

While environmental incidents had never occurred on Pembina's pipeline systems, Pembina maintained insurance to provide coverage in relation to the ownership and operation of its pipeline assets. Property insurance coverage provided coverage on the property and equipment that was above-ground or that facilitated river crossings, with recovery based upon replacement costs. Business interruption insurance covered loss of income arising from specific property damage. The comprehensive general liability coverage provided coverage in actions by third parties. The latter coverage included Pembina's sudden and accidental pollution coverage, which specifically insured against certain claims for damage from pipeline leaks or spills.

THE PIPELINE BREAK

Thomas continued to feed more information to Walsh:

> At about 1:20 this morning, the pipeline break and subsequent spill of crude oil occurred at mile post 102.5 of the Federated Western Pipeline—the same pipeline company that we bought 12 hours ago.[2] The break released crude oil into the Pine River just upstream of Chetwynd, B.C.

Our emergency response field team set up a control site half a mile downstream from the spill. A second control site was set further downstream at the creek's entry into the Pine as a precautionary measure, and a third control site beyond the town of Chetwynd is to be set up today.

When he heard that the spill had occurred near a small town and could threaten its water supply, Walsh knew that there was no stopping immediate media coverage. He let Thomas continue uninterrupted.

> We've set up vacuum facilities at each control site which are being manned right now, removing oil from the river. My guys are telling me that we'll lose as much as 6,300 barrels.[3] In the next hour, I'm going to set up a mobile lab to continuously test the water upstream from Chetwynd. I'll also contact district officials to inform residents along the Pine River of the situation and to put in guidelines to restrict their water usage.

AT PEMBINA'S HEAD OFFICE

Walsh parked his car and ran up two flights of stairs to the office. Thomas and the crew of pipeline monitors were hovering over a computer screen detailing Pembina's network of pipelines. Walsh knew that he would need help in dealing with the media. Even if he were able to contact and retain a media relations firm, he realized that the initial press release would be his responsibility. Thomas exclaimed:

> We still do not know what caused the pipeline break, but I can tell you that we have between 70 to 80 people already onsite, beginning clean-up activities. They're using oil booms to stop the flow of oil and sponges to soak up what they can.

A map of the area was laid out on the table. Walsh could now clearly see the proximity of the town of Chetwynd to the spill. He knew that the health of the town and surrounding area would have to be his first priority. First, Pembina had to contain the oil spill.

It was 5 a.m. and daylight would break within the next two hours.

Notes

1. This case was written with public sources and the permission of Pembina Pipeline Corporation. Some facts have been altered.

2. The deal to purchase Federated was completed on July 31, 2000 (see Exhibit 1).

3. This amount (6,300 barrels) was equivalent to one million cubic metres of oil.

NEWS RELEASE

Attention Business Editors:

Pembina Pipeline Corporation Completes Purchase of Federated Pipe Lines Ltd.

Not for distribution to United States Newswire Services or dissemination in the United States.

CALGARY, July 31 /CNW/ - Pembina Pipeline Income Fund (TSE-PIF.UN) announced today that its wholly-owned subsidiary Pembina Pipeline Corporation has successfully completed its purchase of 100% of the shares of Federated Pipe Lines Ltd. from Anderson Exploration Ltd.'s subsidiary, Home Oil Company Limited, and Imperial Oil Limited. In a related transaction, Pembina closed the purchase of the Cynthia Pipeline from Imperial on the same date.

Following the completion of this transaction, Pembina's combined pipeline network comprises roughly 7,000 kilometres of pipeline and related pumping and storage facilities and in 1999 transported 548,400 barrels per day of crude oil, condensate and natural gas liquids. The Federated acquisition entrenches Pembina's position as Canada's leading feeder pipeline transportation business. Total consideration paid by Pembina for the Federated shares was $340 million, including the assumption of Federated debt. A further $9 million was paid for the Cynthia pipeline. The transactions were financed utilizing a new $420 million syndicated credit facility arranged with a Canadian chartered bank.

Pembina is working toward the timely and orderly integration of the Pembina and Federated pipeline networks, and expects a seamless transition during the consolidation process. The combination of these considerable pipeline operations is expected to produce significant synergies and operating efficiencies which will provide substantial value for Pembina's customers and Unitholders of the Fund. Incremental cash flow generated by the acquired assets is expected to be sufficient to service the acquisition debt as well as fund an increase in the distribution payments to Unitholders of the Fund once the pipelines have been successfully integrated.

Pembina's purchase of the pipeline assets of the Western Facilities Fund for $40.3 million is scheduled to close in late August 2000 following approval by the Unitholders of Western.

The Pembina Pipeline Income Fund is a Canadian income fund engaged, through its wholly-owned subsidiary Pembina Pipeline Corporation, in the transportation of crude oil, condensate and natural gas liquids in Western Canada. Trust Units of the Fund trade on the Toronto Stock Exchange under the symbol PIF.UN.

This news release contains forward-looking statements that involve risks and uncertainties. Such information, although considered reasonable by Pembina at the time of preparation, may prove to be incorrect and actual results may differ materially from those anticipated in the statements made. For this purpose, any statements that are contained herein that are not statements of historical fact may be deemed to be forward-looking statements.

Such risks and uncertainties include, but are not limited to risks associated with operations, such as loss of market, regulatory matters, environmental risks, industry competition, and ability to access sufficient capital from internal and external sources.

This news release shall not constitute an offer to sell or the solicitation of an offer to buy securities in any jurisdiction. No securities of Pembina Pipeline Income Fund have been registered under the United States Securities Act of 1933, as amended, and such securities may not be offered or sold in the United States absent registration, or an applicable exemption from the registration requirements of such Act.

Exhibit 1   The Purchase of Federated Western Pipelines

Source: www.pembina.com December 29, 2000.

ETHICS OR EXCELLENCE?

Conscience as a Check on the Unbalanced Pursuit of Organizational Goals

Kenneth E. Goodpaster

That the terrain of decision making is mined with moral hazards has never been much in doubt. But the real question for executives is this: Just how can you make your conscience your guide? This author has suggestions and strong advice that, when taken, can help restore public confidence in business leaders.

—Kenneth E. Goodpaster

If the contemporary business with its foundation of human assets is to survive, it will have to find better ways to protect people from the demands of the jobs it gives them. Neglecting the environment may drive away customers, but neglecting people's lives may drive away key members of the workforce.

—Charles Handy

Excellence and competitiveness in a global economy are aspirations that we renounce at our peril. At the same time, there is a hazard associated with these aspirations that can threaten the ability of both individuals and organizations to achieve them ethically. Is this the choice: excellence or ethics, competitiveness or conscience? The answer to this question has never been more important for business decision making.

In this article, I describe the hazard and offer some suggestions for a preventative ethical response. I begin with two illustrations that represent the tragic side of decision making, but I am not suggesting that these cases are the *norm* in business. Still, in a July 2003 Zogby Poll of college seniors, 56 percent of respondents agreed (41 percent disagreed) with the proposition that "the only real difference between executives at Enron and those at most other big companies, is that those at Enron got caught."

TWO TRAGIC EVENTS IN 2003: AN INDIVIDUAL . . . AND AN ORGANIZATION

The Individual

The story of Andrew Fastow, ex-financial officer of Enron, is an intriguing one. Fastow was a corporate climber who saw in Enron CEO Jeffrey Skilling a "mentor" who could help him realize his dreams of achieving power and influence. In a *New York Times* article, David Barboza says that when Fastow was in high school he quarrelled with teachers about his grades, and that former Enron colleagues called him prickly and a bully. "Those who know Andrew S. Fastow, the man at the centre of the Enron scandal, say they often got the sense that he had something to prove," writes Barboza (*New York Times*, October 3, 2002). No one has alleged "evil intent" on Fastow's part, but a "distortion of judgment" would seem to be an understatement in characterizing his behaviour.

The Organization

On Feb. 1, 2003, the space shuttle *Columbia* disintegrated on re-entry after completing its mission, killing all seven astronauts aboard—an uncanny reminder of the 1986 NASA *Challenger* disaster. In its report into the disaster, the Columbia Accident Investigation Board (CAIB) observed that "there were echoes of *Challenger* in *Columbia*."

And in the *New York Times*, David Sanger wrote:

> The same keep-it-flying culture found to have disregarded ample evidence of a fatal flaw in the O-rings in the *Challenger* case failed again to heed warning signs that foam debris could cause deadly damage to the aging, fragile *Columbia*. (NYT, August 27, 2003)

The CAIB was very pointed in attributing the *Columbia* disaster to a persistent cultural malaise at NASA:

> In the board's view, NASA's organizational culture and structure had as much to do with this accident as the external tank foam. Organizational culture refers to the values, norms, beliefs and practices that govern how an institution functions. At the most basic level, organizational culture defines the assumptions that employees make as they carry out their work. It is a powerful force that can persist through reorganizations and the reassignment of key personnel. (*NYT*)

NASA's culture was obsessed with launching a critical section of the space station by Feb. 19, 2003. According to CAIB's report, the date seemed "etched in stone," and NASA employees had a sense of being "under the gun." The intent was certainly not evil, and yet this is another tragic example of "distortion of judgment."

There was a common pattern at work in the conduct of both Andrew Fastow and NASA that may have been legal, but nevertheless had catastrophic results. The idea that there is a parallel between the decision-making dynamics of individuals and organizations is at least as old as Plato, and yet is rich in significance for modern business life.

THREE SYMPTOMS OF THE HAZARD: FIXATION, RATIONALIZATION AND DETACHMENT

The cases of Andrew Fastow and NASA typify the hazard associated with the pursuit of

excellence and competitiveness: Most executives and managers have to confront the three important symptoms of the hazard: fixation, rationalization and detachment.

Fixation. Bowen H. McCoy described this symptom in his essay "The Parable of the Sadhu," in the *Harvard Business Review*, in which a group of mountain climbers in the Himalayas, intent on reaching the summit, faced a painful decision. At 18,000 feet, they came upon an Indian holy man, a sadhu, who was lost and in serious danger of dying from exposure. The group had to decide whether to take the sadhu to safety or to continue toward the summit (*HBR*, September/October, 1983; re-published as an *HBR* classic, May 1997).

McCoy described his passion and rationalization under stress, and the group's decision to continue toward the summit. He pointed to his main "excuses," but he knew they were not adequate:

> I felt and continue to feel guilt about the sadhu. I had literally walked through a classic moral dilemma without fully thinking through the consequences. My excuses for my actions included a high adrenaline flow, a superordinate goal and a once-in-a-lifetime opportunity—factors in the usual corporate situation, especially when one is under stress.

McCoy applied his parable to individual managers and their pursuit of goals, and to the leadership of groups. In his mountain-climbing experience, he saw a symptom of the ethical challenges in business life:

> Had we mountaineers been free of physical and mental stress caused by the effort and the high altitude, we might have treated the sadhu differently. Yet isn't stress the real test of personal and corporate values? The instant decisions executives make under pressure reveal the most about personal and corporate character.

Like McCoy and his party, Andrew Fastow seems to have fixated on "superordinate goals" and lost his balance. Under stress, the decision makers at NASA also seem to have ignored values like honesty and concern for safety in favour of lesser values like security and efficiency. Their superordinate goals took on lives of their own, trumping other considerations. (The CAIB report specifically refers to "the intense pressure the program was under to stay on schedule, driven largely by the self-imposed requirement to complete the international space station.")

Rationalization. Professors David Messick and Max Bazerman have explored another symptom of the hazard: rationalization. They point out that behaviour is easily *rationalized* by subtle distortions of judgment stemming from our views of *ourselves*, *others* and the *world* around us.

There is a tendency to reduce the number of possible consequences or outcomes to make the decision manageable. In extreme cases, all but one aspect of a decision will be suppressed, and the choice will be made solely on the basis of one "privileged feature." Loyalty is often one of the privileged features of a decision-making situation. Some kinds of loyalty—like the loyalty of Andrew Fastow to Jeff Skilling, or the decision makers at NASA to cost controls and scheduling— cause people to lose their balance. Loyalty can be an excuse for selective perception and narrowed judgment. As Holman W. Jenkins Jr. noted in *The Wall Street Journal* (August 28, 2002):

> As CEO, Jeff Skilling had set a goal of ridding Enron's balance sheet of poorly performing or volatile assets. Did he decide at some point (well before his congressional testimony) that it would be better not to know exactly how Mr. Fastow, his protégé, was achieving his desired goal?

The CAIB investigation of NASA reviewed the history of foam strikes on the Orbiter so as to determine how managers "rationalized" the danger of repeated strikes on the space shuttle's thermal protection system. The board concluded:

> [Space Shuttle Program] management techniques unknowingly imposed barriers that kept at bay both engineering concerns and dissenting views, and ultimately helped create "blind spots" that prevented them from seeing the danger the foam strike posed.

Detachment. Several decades ago, psychoanalyst and author Michael Maccoby described a third symptom of the hazard in his insightful but disturbing book *The Gamesman*. He said "careerism" was an emotionally self-destructive affliction suffered by many successful executives, and offered his take on what lay beneath this condition:

> Obsessed with winning, the gamesman views all of his actions in terms of whether they will help him succeed in his career. The individual's sense of identity, integrity and self-determination is lost as he treats himself as an object whose worth is determined by its fluctuating market value. Careerism demands (emotional) detachment.

Maccoby believed that emotional detachment corroded integrity, and that it led to the disintegration of character because it did not allow for a proper balance among the traits of the "head" (e.g., initiative, co-operativeness, flexibility, coolness under stress) and traits of the "heart" (e.g., honesty, friendliness, compassion, generosity, idealism). In his view, managers needed to integrate qualities of the heart with qualities of the head, but the imperatives of running modern corporations often prevented this kind of wholeness.

Maccoby had identified a central risk of business life, namely, that it is not only the mental health of business professionals that is at risk but their moral integrity as well. Integrity is a kind of wholeness or balance that prevents individuals from bypassing the qualities of the heart or anesthetizing their humanity in the face of strong temptations to do so. Maccoby saw integrity as demanding balance and participation by the whole person in decisions and actions.

Fastow appears to have suffered from Maccoby's sense of detachment, projecting a dual persona. Reported David Barboza:

> [Enron colleagues] say that during angry bouts, he was known to leave profanity-laced messages on the voice mail of colleagues. He could also be charming and generous, former colleagues said. He would reward employees with vacation travel when they met goals, for example, and defended them in Enron's competitive culture.

Apparently, Fastow viewed his business behaviour as a kind of "game" whose logic was very different from "real life," a game with characters out of the movies:

> Mr. Fastow became adept at creating complex partnerships to finance new projects. He worked on a series of partnerships—including one called Joint Energy Development Investment Inc., known by its acronym, Jedi, and one of several partnerships named for *Star Wars* characters.

As for NASA, the CAIB report described decision making during the flight of the *Columbia* as both "separated"—walled-off from concerned engineers—and "detached":

> A tile expert told managers during frequent consultations that strike damage was only a maintenance-level concern and that on-orbit imaging of potential wing damage was not necessary. Mission management welcomed this opinion and sought no others. This constant reinforcement of managers' pre-existing beliefs added another block to the wall between decision makers and concerned engineers. Another factor that enabled mission management's detachment from the concerns of their own engineers is rooted in the culture of NASA itself. . . . When asked by investigators why they were not more vocal about their concerns, debris-assessment team members opined that by raising contrary points of view about shuttle mission safety, they would be singled out for possible ridicule by their peers and managers.

This commentary represents a cultural analogue to detachment in personal decision making. Writing in the *New York Times*, John Schwartz and Matthew Wald said, "[T]here was rising pressure to play down risk and to place success—measured in terms of things like on-time launching of components for the space station—over safety."

CONVERGENCE OF THE THREE SYMPTOMS

These three symptoms—fixation or singleness of purpose under stress, rationalization and detachment—form a pattern. Each is discernible in the stories of Andrew Fastow and the NASA disasters. Fastow was driven by a singleness of purpose: namely, personal ambition and personal stress.

In many ways, Fastow possessed the traits that Ron Daniel, former managing director of McKinsey & Co., seemed to think were important to his organization. "The real competition out there isn't for clients, it's for people. . . . And we look to hire people who are first, very smart; second, insecure and thus driven by their insecurity; and third, competitive. Put together 3,000 of these egocentric, task-oriented, achievement-oriented people, and it produces an atmosphere of something less than humility. Yes, it's elitist. But don't you think there has to be room somewhere in this politically correct world for something like this?" (*Fortune*, November 1, 1993).

Fastow also had a mentor who reinforced his drive; he rationalized his behaviour, engaging in selective perception about context and consequences; and he possessed detachment, allowing him to repeat his activities over a considerable period of time.

NASA's singleness of purpose surrounding scheduling was equally clear, creating stresses that led to rationalizations. Once described as "an enlightened alliance between science and democratic tradition," NASA appears to have switched to selective perception in the face of safety warnings. (David E. Sanger wrote: "To those who remember the *Challenger* investigation, it was an echo of the suppressed memorandums that the commission uncovered, when engineers sent out urgent warnings that it was too cold to launch the *Challenger*, and were ignored. 'It's the same damn thing,' said Gen. Donald Kutyna of the Air Force, retired, a gadfly on the *Challenger* panel along with the physicist Richard Feynman. 'They didn't learn a thing. We had nine O-rings fail, and they flew. These guys had seven pieces of foam hit, and it still flew.'")

As to detachment, one NASA observer remarked that the organization's "conflicting goals, roles and expectations produced an almost schizoid character." The CAIB report spoke of the "cultural fence" that "impairs open communications

Each participant is asked to reflect on a grid as it applies in his or her own situation. Then small groups (six to eight persons each) are asked to discuss and identify for the large group the most significant examples of gaps between aspirational values and values-in-action. I make it clear that this is not an exercise in corporate "gossip" and that the purpose is to learn a certain kind of discernment that all effective leaders must develop.

Executives are "given permission" to find hypocrisy gaps as well as bridges for those gaps. This exercise is usually carried out in the presence of a senior leader who might be able to explain certain apparent anomalies or to address them in a practical way once they have been identified.

In his recent book *Authentic Leadership*, former Medtronic CEO Bill George comments that identifying this kind of information is critical: "Values begin with telling the truth, internally and externally," he writes. "Integrity must run deep in the fabric of an organization's culture. It guides the everyday actions of employees and is central to its business conduct. Transparency is an integral part of integrity. The truth, both successes and failures, must be shared openly with the outside world. . . . When the company's leaders become role models for its values, the impact on the entire organization is tremendous. The trust of the leadership is earned through practising the company's values every day, not just by espousing them. But when leaders preach one thing and practice another, commitment is quickly lost and employees become doubly cynical" (*Authentic Leadership*, Bill George, Jossey-Bass, San Francisco, 2003).

Such messages from a CEO to the leaders and managers in an organization can have enormously salutary effects. Messages to the contrary, of course, can have pathological effects. In writing about former Enron CEO Kenneth Lay, Warren Bennis wrote that

> Mr. Lay's failing is not simply his myopia or cupidity or incompetence. It is his inability to create a company culture open to reality, one that does not discourage managers from delivering bad news. No organization can be honest with the public if it is not honest with itself. (*New York Times*, February 17, 2002)

From detachment to engagement. Avoiding what we have called detachment amounts to keeping the head and heart in healthy communication with one another. This can be achieved in two important ways.

- First, by emphasizing the mission of the company in human terms—offering reasons of the heart, not just the head, for what the company contributes in the larger scheme of things.

Charles Handy seems to be gesturing toward this idea in a recent article: We need to eat to live; food is a necessary condition of life. But if we lived mainly to eat, making food a sufficient or sole purpose of life, we would become gross. The purpose of a business, in other words, is not to make a profit, full stop. It is to make a profit so that the business can do something more or better. That "something" becomes the real justification for the business. Owners know this. Investors needn't care ("What's a Business For?" Charles Handy, *Harvard Business Review*, December 2002).

- Second, by encouraging effective service to the community as a whole—in particular, service to the less advantaged. This service needs to come from the corporation itself, its senior leaders, and from rank and file employees. It is difficult to remain indifferent in the regular presence of human needs. It is not difficult to become indifferent if we distance ourselves from those needs.

In his analysis of the "knowledge worker" and the specialization that the knowledge organization brings with it, Peter Drucker asks a powerful rhetorical question: "In a society of organizations, each of the new institutions is concerned only with its own purpose and mission. It does not claim *power* over anything else. But it also does not assume *responsibility* for anything else. Who, then, is concerned with the common good?" (*The Atlantic Monthly*, November, 1994).

Drucker's implication is that social awareness is not optional for private sector professionals—it is essential, and more needed in today's knowledge economy than ever before. Jeffrey Garten, dean of the Yale School of Organization and Management, suggested in a recent book that the imperative of service is more intense for business leaders since 9/11 and Enron than ever before:

> In the future, the most effective global CEOs will give more attention to the relationships between their companies and the societies in which they operate. These executives will think about corporate citizenship and social responsibility, not just as philanthropy and good public relations, but as an integral part of their business strategy. They should be careful not to overpromise, but they should also not shy away from using their considerable energies and talents to invest in the full development of the society around them. (*The Politics of Fortune: A New Agenda for Business Leaders*, Harvard Business School Press, Boston, 2002)

Finally, let us return to Charles Handy, who makes a complementary point—that the needs of the balanced professional are as much a factor in this context as the needs of the community:

> In the knowledge economy, sustainability must extend to the *human* as well as the *environmental* level. Many people have seen their ability to balance work with the rest of their lives deteriorate steadily as they fall victim to the stresses of the long-hours culture. An executive life, some worry, is becoming unsustainable in social terms.

The development of the heart is as much an obligation of corporations and universities as the development of the mind.

A Challenge for Cultures and Curricula

Our reflections on Andrew Fastow and NASA revealed that a hazardous pattern was at play. This pattern manifests itself not only in the lives of individuals but also—and not coincidentally—in the cultures of organizations. We have identified its symptoms and we have given it a name, teleopathy.

The Enron catastrophe and the NASA *Columbia* disaster would not have happened in the absence of teleopathy. Unless executive development programs and business schools embrace a new agenda, we can expect more tragic scandals and further erosion of society's confidence in the business system.

By their very nature, the demands of professional life foster intensity in the individual and the collective achievement of goals and objectives. Without countervailing cultural influences, such intensity can become insanity. Fixation, rationalization and detachment must be met, respectively, by *perspective*, *frankness* and *engagement*, both in the lives of executives and in the lives of corporations. These are the elements of conscience, and conscience is our primary check on the unbalanced pursuit of goals and purposes.

About the Editor

W. Glenn Rowe served in the Canadian Navy for 22 years. While still in the navy, he completed his Master of Business Administration degree at Memorial University of Newfoundland part-time (1983–1986) and taught on a part-time basis for 2 years (1986–1988) in Memorial's Faculty of Business Administration. In 1990, he retired from the navy and became a full-time lecturer in the Faculty of Business Administration at Memorial. In 1992, he began studying leadership within the context of strategic management at Texas A&M University, where he completed his PhD in 1996. He rejoined the Faculty of Business Administration at Memorial in September 1995, where he taught strategic management and strategic leadership to undergraduates, students in the MBA and EMBA programs, and participants in the Executive Development Program. Professor Rowe joined the Richard Ivey School of Business as a faculty member on July 1, 2001. He is the faculty adviser for the PhD program in general management/strategy and teaches strategy and strategic leadership to undergraduate business students, MBAs, EMBAs, and doctoral students. He serves as a reviewer for several academic journals and is active in the community. He has served as the Vice-Chair of the Board of Directors of The International Alliance for Missions and as a member of the Board of Directors of the Newfoundland and Labrador Employers' Council. He is an active consultant and has facilitated strategic-thinking sessions for several organizations such as the Alliance for the Control of Tobacco (Newfoundland and Labrador), the Newfoundland and Labrador Medical Association, Fishery Products International, Gros Morne National Park, and Sir Wilfred Grenfell College. He is the coauthor of a strategic management textbook and its associated casebook, both of which are in their second edition.